THE ARNOLD HISTORY OF EUROPE

The Arnold History of Europe

This new series explores European history, from the last years of the Roman Empire to the end of the twentieth century. Each volume tackles a broad sweep of history, not invariably sticking to conventional periodizations, and asks bold questions of its material. The series aims to make sense of periods and eras, across countries and cultures, but without trying to homogenize everything.

Volumes covering the following periods are in preparation:

1789–2000
by James F. McMillan

1600–1800
by Anthony F. Upton

300–1000
by Guy Halsall

THE TRANSFORMATION
OF EUROPE
1300–1600

DAVID NICHOLAS

Professor of History, Clemson University, USA

A member of the Hodder Headline Group
LONDON • SYDNEY • AUCKLAND

Co-published in the United States of America by
Oxford University Press Inc., New York

First published in Great Britain in 1999 by
Arnold, a member of the Hodder Headline Group,
338 Euston Road, London NW1 3BH

http://www.arnoldpublishers.com

Co-published in the United States of America by
Oxford University Press Inc.,
198 Madison Avenue, New York, NY 10016

British Library Cataloguing in Publication Data
A catalogue record for this book is available from the British Library

Library of Congress Cataloging-in-Publication Data
Nicholas, David, 1939–
The transformation of Europe 1300–1600/David Nicholas.
    p.   cm. — (The Arnold history of Europe)
Includes bibliographical references and index.
ISBN 0-340-66207-7 (hb) — ISBN 0-340-66208-5 (pb)
    1. Europe—History—476–1492. 2. Europe—History—1492–1648.
I. Title. II. Series.
D202.8.N53 1999
940.1—dc21   98–51966
                                                                            CIP

Production Editor: Wendy Rooke
Production Controller: Priya Gohil
Cover Design: Terry Griffiths

ISBN 0 340 66207 7 (hb)
ISBN 0 340 66208 5 (pb)

1 2 3 4 5 6 7 8 9 10

Typeset by Phoenix Photosetting, Chatham, Kent
Printed and bound in Great Britain by
MPG Books, Bodmin, Cornwall

What do you think about this book? Or any other Arnold title?
Please send your comments to feedback.arnold@hodder.co.uk

Contents

List of Maps	vi
Introduction	1

Part I. Birth and Rebirth, 1300–1450 — 13

1. Europe in the Era of the Hundred Years War — 15
2. Of Nations and States: The Institutions of Government — 53
3. Economic Integration and Social Change in Late Medieval Europe — 85
4. Late Nominalism and Early Humanism: The Cultural Life of the Late Middle Ages — 123

Part II. The Modern State and the Ancient State of Mind, 1450–1600 — 167

5. From the Politics of Religion to the Religion of Politics — 169
6. The 'Renaissance State'? — 217
7. The Besieged as Besieger: West European Expansion in Asia, Africa, the Americas and Slavic Europe — 259
8. The 'Long Sixteenth Century' in the Economic and Social Development of Europe — 290
9. The Later Renaissance: From Classical Humanism to Vernacular Classicism — 343
10. Antiquity and Modernity: The Religious Division of Europe in the Sixteenth Century — 378

Conclusion: Retrospective, Prospective and Perspective — 427

Endnotes — 441
The Rulers of Europe — 453
Suggestions for Further Reading — 457
Index — 469

List of Maps

1.1   England and France in the Era of the Hundred Years War   20
1.2   The Burgundian State   31
1.3   The Swiss Confederation in the Early Fifteenth Century   42
3.1   The Spread of the Great Plague   92
3.2   The Major Cities of Europe, 1300–1600   101
4.1   The Universities of Europe   136
4.2   Renaissance Italy   147
5.1   The Iberian Peninsula   169
5.2   Habsburg and Valois   178
5.3   The Netherlands during the Wars with Spain   201
6.1   The Territorial Unification of France, 1300–1600   238
6.2   Germany and Adjacent Areas in the Early Sixteenth Century   254
7.1   The Expansion of Europe in the Fifteenth and Sixteenth
      Centuries   260
7.2   Eastern Europe and the Ottoman Empire   278
7.3   Trade Routes, 1300–1600   284
8.1   Industrial Production and Raw Materials in Europe,
      1300–1600   312
10.1 The Religious Divisions of Europe, 1550–1600   404

Introduction

This book is the work of a man who, although he has been considered a 'medievalist' throughout his professional life, sees important changes towards 'modernity' occurring at the onset of the fourteenth century, the period in which most of his original research has been concentrated. It adopts a somewhat unconventional but not radical chronology, including periods variously distinguished as the 'late Middle Ages', the Renaissance, the Reformation and/or the early modern era.* The division of the seamless web of history into periods is always arbitrary, for barring a cataclysm, impossible from a technological perspective until quite recently, development proceeds gradually. What in retrospect appear to be critical turning-points in some places or for some broad developments are less applicable to others.

The three centuries covered here mark numerous important transitions. Only in religious history does there appear to be some justification for retaining the traditional notion that the 'modern age' began around 1500, and even here the institutional break of the Protestants with Rome cannot conceal fundamental continuity of expression and attitude. Whether one thinks of the late Middle Ages or the Renaissance appears to depend mainly on whether the focus is northern Europe or Italy, but we shall see also that the 'humanist' movement in Italy began as a radical, if atavistic, break with the more evolutionary cultural approach of medieval intellectuals, and in its turn it had become a conservative educational establishment throughout Europe by the seventeenth century.

In political terms, the period opens with the Hundred Years War between England and France. In 1300 England was the only monarchy of Europe that had both a strong territorial base and an institutional structure through which most of those territories were controlled on behalf of the crown. The

---

* Part of the work on this book was done during a sabbatical leave from Clemson University in the spring semester, 1997.

French-speaking kings of England only became 'English' during the four-teenth and fifteenth centuries during the conflict with the French monarchs. Until their rule in Gascony was ended, a development that meant that their alliance was less valuable in civil wars within France, their main policy objectives were to use resources from England to add to or consolidate their hold on territory in France. The Hundred Years War (actually, wars) had a more immediately devastating impact on France, where virtually all the fighting was done, than on England. But by removing the English, the Hundred Years War simplified the French kings' task. France became a nation between 1337 and 1559, when the last of the great territories held in fief from the French crown by nobles would fall to the monarchy.

Nation-states were mainly created not by sentiment or even military conquest, but by dynastic accident, most often the marriage of a king to a woman whose male relatives had died. The marriage of a future king and a ruling queen, as happened with Ferdinand of Aragon and Isabella of Castile in 1469, created a personal union, but might not (and did not in their case) lead to the immediate institutional unification of the kingdoms. The corroborating example of Scotland and England comes immediately to mind: they had the same king from 1603 onwards, but were the same kingdom only from 1707.

In 1300, however, England was a national monarchy ruled by Frenchmen, as it had been since the Duke William of Normandy seized the English throne in 1066. The French kings were the most powerful princes of France, and thus appeared well-positioned eventually to rule most, if not all, French-speaking people. Spain had some of the characteristics of a federal – if not exactly national – monarchy. But this level of consolidation did not occur in Germany, or in Italy, the heartland of the medieval Roman Empire. The power of territorial princes and cities in Germany and of city-states in Italy, together with the fact that the imperial title remained elective, had eroded whatever possibility might have existed for transforming the powers the emperors enjoyed in theory into a real state authority. The religious division of Germany in the sixteenth century simply gave an excuse for what had already happened at the territorial level. From 1300 to around 1450 the various princes of Spain were rivals, while the English and French monarchs were concerned with fighting each other and their own rebellious subjects. But the Aragonese kings had long had territorial interests in Italy, and beginning in 1494 the French fought them in a series of devastating conflicts that shattered the Italian city-state 'system' and seriously compromised the territorial independence of the popes. By 1600 the Spanish monarchy was weak, if less federal and more national than earlier, those of France and England much stronger, and that of Germany, which was associated with the imperial title, was effective mainly in southern Germany, in the household lands of the Habsburg dukes of Austria, who were always elected emperors after 1438 and who had managed to make the title hereditary in fact by the late sixteenth century.

Government through the use of institutions and office-holders who continue to function through changes in princely regimes had developed in England before 1200, but the bureaucratic state developed at the national level in France and, to a lesser extent, in Iberia only during the three centuries after 1300. Some territorial principalities, which were much smaller, also developed institutions, although their sophistication varied considerably. In several provinces that were eventually included in France local customs persisted enough to hinder the efficiency of royal government, which did not replace its predecessor but rather was superimposed upon it. In the German and Slavic East, the monarchies were weak, and accordingly most functions of institutional government remained concentrated at the local level, usually in the hands of the territorial nobles.

The kings had always had the authority to legislate, but governments in the early Middle Ages incurred such minimal expenses that the prince was expected to finance his operations without taxation, by using his income from the royal domain. If he needed more than this and occasional feudal payments from the great nobles, he was expected to get the formal consent of those from whom he sought the money. The extended and expensive wars of the late Middle Ages, however, forced the kings to tax frequently and to make the non-feudal social groups subject to taxation. In England this resulted in the development of the Parliament, an institution that developed into a form recognizably similar to its modern descendant between 1275 and 1350. Parliament began as an enlarged session of the royal council and was accordingly judicial in character, but it was involved in making statutes by 1300. When a king began using these same meetings to gain approval of extraordinary taxes, England had a partly representative assembly that could impose severe restrictions on him.

In France, by contrast, the *parlement* that in England evolved into a legislative and taxation assembly remained a court, while taxation was taken over by the Estates-General, assemblies convened by legally defined social classes (clergy, nobility and bourgeoisie). Yet the Estates-General could not bind the nation, for they lacked proctorial power; they could only recommend a tax or policy to local provincial Estates. Hindered to a great extent by the great size of France, they were unable to use the military emergencies and personal incompetence of some kings to gain a measure of power comparable to that of the English Parliament.They even established a tax-collecting bureaucracy that they then turned over to the king, whereas the financial capacity of the English Parliament extended only as far as national taxation and did not include the royal domain. Thus when the English kings reconstituted their domain after 1461, they were able to finance most domestic operations of government without involving Parliament. But the French kings taxed virtually at will.

As their financial resources increased, the princes of Europe generated bureaucracies to administer the money. In England Parliament generally kept control of the taxes that it voted, for that money went into the royal

Exchequer. But when the king could dispense with Parliamentary taxation, he was free to manage his money through departments in the royal household. The French kings had no such problems. The distinction between household and court was less important there than in England except in the matter of justice, where the *parlements* handled an increasing variety of types of litigation.

The burgeoning bureaucracies of the late medieval state intruded not only into the traditional areas of justice and finance, but also into local government. In France a royal bureaucracy in the major cities in effect replicated the local councils that had controlled local policy since the granting of town charters during the central Middle Ages. There is an element of this in Castile as well, but there and in England the kings were generally content with having the right to approve or reject nominations to local offices that were made locally, according to traditional procedures. The increased weight of royal administration was more noticeable in the rural areas, except in England, where the kings allowed local Justices of the Peace a relatively free hand as long as disorder was kept to a minimum. In France and Spain, however, stifling bureaucracies took form, creating a situation where offices, which brought incomes to their holders and in many cases carried a presumption of noble status, were bought and sold without regard to the professional credentials of the holder.

The nature of law was changing fundamentally in the centuries after 1300. Although the traditional distinction between areas of written Roman law and oral or customary Germanic law has been overdrawn, those parts of Germanic Europe whose customs had not been committed to writing before 1300 were affected by the spread of the principle that written law is superior to unwritten. Even where older customs had been written, doubtful points were increasingly adjudicated on the basis of Roman law, which provided a reasonably consistent and certainly a unitary procedural guide. Roman law no more permitted the violation of individual property rights than did Germanic, and in some areas, notably law of agency, was less sophisticated. But it was state law: while Germanic practice emphasized private responsibility and arbitration, Roman law gave more arbitrary discretion to the head of the state.

Europe underwent a profound demographic recession after 1300, especially after 1348. During the central Middle Ages populations had expanded beyond the capacity of the farm economy to support them, but what began as an ecological problem was deepened by a series of plagues that diminished populations to far below optimum levels. The crisis was accompanied by chronic overproduction of food, for the farmers, ill understanding market mechanisms, produced more than was needed to feed the population that was so much reduced, particularly in the cities. The cities correspondingly benefited by low food prices, so attracting immigration that compensated to a great degree for the loss of population during the plagues. Although the cities lost a higher percentage of their inhabitants in the plagues than did the rural areas, urban immigration was sufficiently intense that the urban sector gained relative to the agrarian in the long term.

As the pressure on resources eased, however, per capita productivity increased, and the demographic recession and realignment was accompanied by a rise in the standard of living. Farmers compensated for low grain prices by changing to other crops, whose value rose, and by increasing the extent of animal husbandry. Manufacturing became less solely utilitarian and luxury-oriented than previously, as a wide range of medium-priced consumer items entered the market. Thus recovery from the recession was accompanied and, to a great extent, caused by the spread of a commercial capitalism that integrated the diverse economic regions of Europe into a coherent entity. The two great weaknesses of the late medieval European economic system were a dearth of coin and an over-dependence on imports, each of which was being redressed even before the overseas discoveries of the late fifteenth century.

The church continued to be an important force in politics and intellectual life. Although there was some sympathy for the local clergy, the institutional abuses of the church such as pluralism, nepotism and intransigence where the financial claims of the church were concerned dominated public perceptions. Most persons simply practised their own devotions and dissociated themselves from the institutional church except at the great liturgical festivals. The German emperors and kings of Aragon had seen the popes as essentially political rather than spiritual leaders for centuries, and this perception had spread even before 1300 to the French and English kings.

Discontent was soon vented in the form of doctrinal heresy. The ideas of John Wycliffe in England and Jan Hus in Bohemia initially received support from powerful political interests, and each eventually led to civil conflict, which in the Bohemian case resulted in a partial victory for the heretics. The notion that the pope was the superior of kings in the divine order dominated most political theory before 1300, but it was forcefully combated in the late Middle Ages, in part through a revived political Aristotelianism in the case of Marsiglio of Padua. Finally, the nominalist thought of William of Ockham and his followers created a philosophical basis not only for scepticism, but also for the divorce of faith from reason, which had been linked in the theology of St Thomas Aquinas in the thirteenth century. The impotence of man, and consequently his need to rely on God's grace, was a foundation of Martin Luther's thought.

Accompanying the disenchantment with the church was the increased estrangement of the church and theology from major currents of secular intellectual life. A buoyant literature had developed before 1300 in the various French and German vernacular languages, and they were joined in the fourteenth century by English and Italian. In northern Europe works of art were becoming more realistic and, with more patronage from secular rulers whose wealth had been increased by the institutional changes of the late Middle Ages, were increasingly at the service of the state.

The late fourteenth and early fifteenth centuries are associated also with important changes in intellectual life in Italy that would subsequently be adapted by north Europeans. The 'Renaissance' was a rebirth of interest in the philological and rhetorical aspects of Greek and particularly Roman culture. While during the Middle Ages classical models had been used and analysed in the context of contemporary legal problems and also of theology, a new appreciation developed in Italy of the achievements of the past in their own terms. Often, however, this appreciation was uncritical. The 'humanists' were essentially philologists who considered the Latin language to be barbaric in the form in which it had evolved since antiquity. Not realizing that Latin itself had changed during the Roman centuries, they insisted that the elementary curriculum in the schools include classical grammar rather than that based on the fourth-century scholar Donatus and his later commentators. Logic was de-emphasized in favour of rhetoric.

The humanists' insistence on using archaic classical Latin doomed what had been an international language of scholarship, for the vocabulary of the ancients was simply inadequate to express thoughts springing from a different cultural context. Classical studies thus became the mark of the wealthy, educated man, who had enough leisure to be unconcerned with the skills of making a living and preferred to devote himself, in a model suggested by Cicero's orations, to the civic life. Education was for life at court. Before 1450 the educational notions of the Italians had little impact on northern Europe, but thereafter their insistence on establishment of the correct text, together with the political context of 'civic' humanism, would lead to a culture that essentially used the content of the classics rather than their form, and expressed itself in the vernacular languages.

During the 'long sixteenth century' the federated kingdoms of Castile and Aragon moved towards, although they did not reach, a national monarchy. The Swiss Confederation became independent of the Holy Roman Empire in 1495, and the United Provinces (the northern Netherlands) separated from Spain and became, in fact, a separate state, although one which was only recognized formally in 1648. The century is justly and unfortunately renowned for a high level of internal and foreign warfare, much of which was ostensibly for religious reasons, as the secular state became the enforcement agent of religious orthodoxy. Yet the doctrines of Martin Luther, the first great 'Protestant' reformer, gained substantial adherence and princely support only in the Empire and Scandinavia in the first half of the sixteenth century, and thereafter were placed on the defensive; while Ulrich Zwingli's movement did not spread outside Switzerland. Elsewhere, theological Protestantism remained moribund (Henry VIII's break with Rome was institutional, not doctrinal) until the late 1540s in England and the 1550s in France and the Netherlands with the rise of Calvinism.

Overarching the religious divisions of Europe were dynastic rivalries.

When Charles V of Habsburg, who already ruled the Low Country states as his paternal inheritance, became king of Castile and Aragon in 1516 and Emperor in 1519, succeeding his maternal and paternal grandfathers respectively, the Valois kings of France saw a threat of encirclement that led them at various times in the first half of the century to ally with the Turks against the Habsburgs, who in theory ruled most of the rest of the continent. Religious and dynastic concerns became intermingled in the second half of the century. The Habsburg domains were divided, but Philip II of Spain made his business the religion of France and England, where he had no dynastic cause to intervene, and of the Netherlands, where his intransigence led to the loss of the seven provinces of the north, although Spain retained lordship over the southern Low Countries.

The nearly constant warfare, combined with the need to keep domestic peace in the tinderbox atmosphere emotionally charged by religious sentiment, strained the resources of government. Tragically, the princes of Europe simply added bureaucracy and tax to bureaucracy and tax, without streamlining, systematizing or equalizing the burdens. By 1600 a state apparatus was in place which was financially and, in some contexts, intellectually oppressive and inefficient, amounting to a larger and coarser version of the institutions of government that had developed during the period of the Hundred Years War.

The Portuguese and Castilians had been exploring and colonizing the major island groups off the Atlantic coast of Europe since the fourteenth century. These efforts intensified after 1415, when the Portuguese seizure of Ceuta gave them a base for further exploration down the western coast of Africa. The initial goal was African spices and particularly gold, but ultimately the Portuguese hoped to round the tip of Africa and proceed to Asia, which they did in 1498. The result was considerable wealth for Portugal and a great increase in the volume and quality of spices available on European markets.

In 1492, after the Portuguese had rounded the Cape of Good Hope but before they completed a sea voyage to Asia, Christopher Columbus convinced Queen Isabella of Castile to finance a voyage westward to search for a more direct route to Asia. Instead of Asia, he found the Americas. His further explorations and those of others brought the Spaniards control over the West Indies, Mexico, Peru and eventually other areas that could be explored and settled using the first conquests as bases. Exploitation of the newly discovered continents produced agricultural raw materials, cotton and particularly supplies of gold and silver that would replenish the money supply of Europe, a supply that was constantly being depleted to pay for naval stores and other raw materials from the Baltic and Slavic East as well as for Asian and African spices.

The English did not undertake significant explorations until the mid-sixteenth century, while it took the French until the early seventeenth. The English concentrated on finding a sea passage through the Eurasian land mass to the spices of Asia, but this brought them instead an expansion of their Baltic trade, and control of most of the trade of the expanding Russian state with western Europe. The growing power of the states of Poland–Lithuania and Russia in effect replaced the declining empires of the Teutonic Knights and the Livonian Brothers of the Sword. However, except for the assumption of the Polish crown in 1572 by Henry of Anjou, who became King Henry III of France in 1574, western monarchs were too caught up in their internal rivalries and concerns over American and Asian markets to demonstrate great concern with what was happening on the eastern and northern peripheries of Europe. Even the threat from the Turks, which was of a religious as well as political nature, affected mainly Hungary and the Balkans and the eastern Mediterranean trade. By the century's end the Turks were trading actively with the westerners, although they continued trying to expand overland in the east.

The sixteenth century was the longest period of sustained economic growth that Europe had experienced since the late thirteenth century, but it came with a price. New supplies of silver from within Europe were alleviating the bullion shortage even before the Castilian conquests in the Americas. American metal largely paid for the Spanish military machine, and the greater availability of money made it possible for Europeans to continue to import heavily from the German–Slavic East and Asia. It contributed to an inflation that was not great by twentieth-century standards but was still marked enough for contemporaries to be aware of it; prices quadrupled in Spain and doubled elsewhere, with the steepest increases coming on food. Thus the fundamental cause of the price rise of the sixteenth century was that population was again outstripping the food supply, as it had before 1300. Real wages declined, most sharply in the cities, where prices of manufactured goods rose in the wake of increased demand. Yet the peasants were not able to capitalize on the demand for food and were often undersold, especially by the cheap grain imported from eastern Europe.

Europe was a much more urbanized place in 1600 than in 1300, but much of the growth came in the capital cities, which mushroomed, and port towns that could benefit from the colonial trade. As in the late Middle Ages, most large cities were dominated by a commercial élite, and they had little major industry. Urban manufacturing entrepreneurs frequently hired rural workers, particularly for less skilled jobs in textiles and construction. Although this contributed to high unemployment in the cities, it gave opportunities to rural workers to escape the 'shear' of low grain prices combined with high costs of manufactured items. Thus, by 1600 the lines of demarcation between the urban and rural economies were more blurred than they had been in the late Middle Ages. All cities experienced severe problems of structural poverty, and most of them undertook centralized measures of poor relief. In England and France the national governments often mandated such policies while leaving the details up to local magistracies. The infrastructure of trade, particularly of finance, continued to be dominated by the Italians through most of the sixteenth century, using essentially the same techniques as in the late Middle Ages; but as economic power shifted toward the Atlantic, Dutch and English vessels began entering the Mediterranean late in the century, and economic hegemony would pass definitively to the northern powers by the 1630s, when Italy was to suffer a serious depression from which it would not recover quickly.

The growing power of the commercial economy was felt also on the social group that purported to disdain moneymaking and value only the respectability of leisure and living on land rents: that is, the nobility. But while the older noble lineages continued to dominate command positions in the armies, the proletarianizing of warfare caused by gunpowder meant that they were swamped in the armies of the sixteenth century, even more than in those of the late Middle Ages, by mercenaries and citizens from the lower social orders. While the titled nobles continued to be a mainly land-based group, the lesser nobles saw an infusion of new blood both from the wealthier peasants and especially from wealthy upper-middle-class families who were in a position to buy land, titles of nobility, offices or all three. In England money only bought land, which did not in itself convey nobility, and only in the seventeenth century did the crown make titles available for sale. But in France and Spain offices were being sold in the sixteenth century, contributing to bloated and ineffective bureaucracies and also diminishing the tax base, since nobles there were exempt from direct taxation. Money, at all events, was the route of access into the nobility, provided that it was spent appropriately and that, once ennobled, the newcomer ceased small-scale trade and investment and 'lived nobly'. As the culture of Italy spread to the north, the nobles were trained in a common humanist classical culture that valued public service – particularly at court – and landholding, and which disdained the process of accumulating wealth while valuing extremely the consumer goods that wealth could buy.

The 'later Renaissance' witnessed a drift away from the pure Latinate classicism upon which most Italian humanists of the fifteenth century had insisted. Greek studies had a brief vogue, but the language seems to have been beyond the ken of most western scholars. In creative work, writers of literature and history broke away from classical models. Although they sometimes used themes from ancient history or mythology, more often they were concerned with events and situations closer to their own time. Part of this was the growing impact of religious concerns in the sixteenth century. The zeal of the Italian humanists to establish completely accurate texts was extended by the north Europeans, such as Erasmus, into an effort to establish correct and original texts not only of the Latin classics, which most of them appreciated but did not venerate, but also of the Bible and other Christian holy writings in particular.

The Italian humanists and their northern imitators revolutionized educational curricula not by introducing the classics, which had always been there, but by insisting that the only Latin appropriate for study by gentle-men was that of Cicero and the Caesars. The problems with this notion had been less serious when it was confined to a small group of intellectuals, but became more obvious as the cult of classical Latin became the foundation of educational curricula throughout Europe. The changes that had developed in Latin during the Middle Ages ('medieval Latin') had kept the language alive. Now it became a cultural affectation of those who were being educated for high positions in the church, education (where the curriculum in effect became self-perpetuating) and government, where courtiers were getting a humanist culture that, with local variations, marked gentlemen everywhere in Europe. Yet, after their school days, even the gentlemen read and usually wrote in their local vernacular languages, reserving Latin for conspicuous display through quotation in their vernacular works and among themselves.

Accordingly, particularly after 1550, the original culture of Europe broke away not only from the Latin language but increasingly from Roman models of style and theme. Shakespeare, who is usually considered a figure of the late Renaissance, used classical themes only in some of his histories; for most of them, and for all his non-historical work, he was concerned with more modern stories, even using more recent Italy for the setting of *Romeo and Juliet* and other works. The classical curriculum remained a pedagogical atavism from which most original work was divorced, but it was important as the common intellectual property of the governing élites of church and state.

In the last analysis, the two most important intellectual developments during the 'long sixteenth century' – the insertion of archaic classicism into the educational curriculum and the religious division – were made possible by the most important technological change: the development of printing with movable type, which spawned a veritable 'information revolution'. Most of the early printers were scholars, and all had to make money by selling books, broadsheets and pamphlets. Printing made information available much more cheaply than had been possible when manuscripts were the only means of dissemination. Depending on the reader and his or her tastes, it fostered depth of understanding or superficial recitation of catchphrases. Some printing establishments, such as the Aldine Press of Venice, specialized in scholarly works in Latin, but most interspersed these in their inventories with recent original works of literature, practical manuals on everything from cooking to clothing and religious broadsheets. The secular and ecclesiastical princes of Europe relied on the printers for rapid diffusion of laws and information. Some favoured printers got government contracts for printing officially permit-ted Bibles and other religious literature. Since illustrations and technical diagrams could be duplicated by printing, comparison of anatomical drawings became as easy by using printed editions as comparison of variant versions of scriptural passages. Regrettably, printing also made it easier for Protestants to visualize the pope as a devil and for Catholics to see Martin Luther as a donkey.

The break that historians have traditionally made between 'medieval' and 'modern' is predicated upon the religious division of Europe in the sixteenth century. Yet all major departures of the Protestant theologians from Roman Catholicism had antecedents in the work of such late medieval thinkers as William of Ockham, John Wycliffe and Jan Hus. The decrees of the council of Trent, which in 1563 fixed the parameters of modern Roman Catholicism, contain no dogma that would have surprised those who attended the council of Constance in 1414. Furthermore, if 'modern' is characterized by a secular outlook, the absurdity of such a periodization becomes apparent. If the kings of the fourteenth century had largely begun the process not of separation of church from state – which occurred nowhere until the late seventeenth century and then only exceptionally – but of placing the church under state control, the process was finished by Luther and Calvin.

More laypeople were aware of religious issues in 1600 than in 1500 and felt deeply about them, but Alexander Pope's line 'A little learning is a dangerous thing' is never more applicable than here. Most people who converted to Protestantism were prompted by anticlericalism or concern over church abuses. Although more people were reading devotional material than ever before, with the capacities of printing, few were reading theology, and still fewer had deep understanding of the complexities of Lutheran or Calvinist belief. Instead, they recited memorized catechisms that told what they believed and gave them the certainty that those whose catechisms were different were less worthy than they. What most believers knew of other creeds was confined to what their rulers permitted to be said about them in print, which was usually distinctly unflattering. The Protestant emphasis on reading the scriptures personally and making informed decisions was honoured more in theory than in practice, for while rates of literacy were unquestionably rising in the sixteenth century, particularly in the cities, most people were not reading theology, but rather material that was of practical value in the world or had entertainment value. Regarding the next world, they were content to believe what the secular authorities and their churches told them. The cause of religious sophistication was not advanced thereby, nor by the the practice of criminalizing religious belief as sedition, as happened in both Protestant and Roman Catholic Europe, or stigmatizing 'peculiar' or unpopular persons as witches. If 1300 marks the end of an age of faith, 1600 is the midpoint of the age of hysteria.

BIRTH AND REBIRTH, 1300–1450

1

Europe in the Era of the Hundred Years War

In the last quarter of the thirteenth century Europe was plunged into a profound economic, social, political and institutional crisis. By 1330 a basic state structure had emerged that would not be fundamentally modified, although some details would be changed, before 1450. The one exception would be the Burgundian state which grew up on the eastern and northern frontiers of France that almost became a separate polity in the early 1470s.

France and England at the Turn of the Fourteenth Century

The fortunes of the English and French crowns had been intertwined since the conquest of the English crown by the duke of Normandy in 1066. When the daughter of Henry I of England and Normandy married Geoffrey of Anjou, and their son and heir Henry II married Eleanor of Aquitaine in 1152, an empire was created that dwarfed the French royal domain, which was centred on a Paris–Orléans axis. French became the language of the English court; Henry III (1216–72) was the first Angevin king who even read English, and Edward III (1327–77) was the first who spoke it well. All of the continental territories of the French princes who were kings in England were held in fief of the king of France, who in fact held less land than they in the twelfth century. In 1204–5 the French king, Philip II 'Augustus' (1180–1223), used a quarrel over feudal jurisdiction with King John (1199–1216) of England as an excuse to seize Normandy. Before his death in 1223 he had gained all English-held territory north of the Loire river, and his successors gradually extended their sway into the south-west. In 1259 the Peace of Paris left the English in possession of Gascony, the part of Aquitaine centred on Bordeaux and the Garonne river valley with their lucrative wine trade. In return the English king rendered liege homage to the French for this territory, acknowledging thereby that the loyalty that he owed for Gascony took priority over all other engagements.

Much of the political and military history of western Europe between 1300 and 1450 is the story of how the fortunes of the English and French crowns became extricated from each other. The peace of 1259 was short-lived. Although Henry III of England was duke, not king, in Aquitaine, there was a problem in one king becoming the liegeman of another. King Philip IV 'the Fair' (1285–1314) of France was an enigmatic figure who relied strongly on civil lawyers trained at the universities to justify his claims to intervene actively in the internal affairs of the great vassal states of the crown. Philip's ultimate goal may have been extending the borders of royal France north to the Scheldt and east to the Rhine, and his marriage to the heiress of Champagne would lead in 1361 to the incorporation of that commercial, wealthy and urbanized county into the royal domain. In Gascony, Edward I (1272–1307) of England held a second great fief, where by the 1270s the French crown was encouraging appeals from local courts directly to Paris, bypassing the English justices. Appeals to Westminster and Paris were particularly common from turbulent Bordeaux.

England had a long tradition of economic and political bonds to a third great fief, Flanders, the leading principality of the Low Countries, whose enormous cities of Ghent, Bruges and Ypres imported the highest-grade wools from England and manufactured it into luxury textiles for export. In turn, Flemish merchants handled much of England's export trade, including but not limited to wool, through much of the thirteenth century. A 4-year embargo of English wool exports to Flanders between 1270 and 1274 cost Flanders its monopoly of the English export product and led to competition with the cities of the central Low Countries, particularly Brabant. This episode begins the English habit of using economic pressure to assure a Flemish alliance, which was necessary to provide friendly territory for an English landing for an invasion of France from the north.

French pressure on Gascony led to war with England in 1294. The English were joined by Flanders in 1297, when Count Guy of Dampierre (1280–1305) renounced his fealty to the French, and England tried to invade France through Flanders. The effort was unsuccessful, and the truce late in the year left the Flemings, among whom strong pro-English and pro-French parties had developed, at the mercy of the French. Flanders was occupied by a French army in 1300–1, but ejected the French in the famous 'Matins of Bruges' uprising in 1302. Count Robert of Béthune (1305–22) in 1305 accepted a punitive peace agreement that provided a substantial indemnity for the French. This arrangement was changed in 1312, when in the Peace of Pontoise the French agreed to return half the payment to the count in return for the cession to the French crown of the Flemish castellanies of Lille, Douai and Orchies, whose inhabitants spoke French. From then on until these territories were returned to Flanders in 1369, Flanders was a purely Flemish-speaking principality for the only time during the Middle Ages. The county was divided, however, between its Francophile counts and the English-leaning cities. Although Flanders remained, despite its turbulence, the leading political and economic power in the Low Countries, it continued to lose ground to Brabant, and increasingly, Holland.

English involvement with Flanders, on France's northern frontier, was answered by French interference with English designs in Scotland. Edward I essentially was attempting to make Britain into a single kingdom in the same way that Philip IV hoped to recover the French crown fiefs. The English kings had fought in Wales with uncertain results for centuries before Edward subjugated the Welsh and joined Wales to England by the Statute of Rhuddlan of 1284. The Welsh occasionally rose thereafter, but the English problems there were nothing in comparison to Scotland. In contrast to Wales, which was ruled by a network of lords who had no clear bonds of subordination among themselves, Scotland had kings who recognized the English monarchs as feudal overlords. Relations were generally correct until 1286, when the death of King Alexander III of Scotland left the crown to his granddaughter Margaret, daughter of King Eric III of Norway and Alexander's daughter. Edward I, seeing an opportunity to accomplish a union by dynastic means, tried to force the Scots to marry her to the future Edward II of England; but she died on the way to Britain from Norway.

With the extinction of the royal dynasty, the Scots somewhat surprisingly agreed to accept Edward I's arbitration between rival candidates for the crown. Edward chose John Balliol over Robert Bruce in 1292, but expected Balliol to act as an English puppet, to the extent of allowing English garrisons in Scotland and permitting appeals from Scottish courts to Westminster. When in 1294 Edward demanded Scottish troops for his invasion of France, the Scottish magnates forced Balliol to defy Edward. Balliol allied with France at this time against the English, paralleling the English alliance with Flanders on the northern frontier of France.

Edward deposed Balliol and tried to rule Scotland by commissioners. There were serious problems apart from the fact that the two had separate monarchies: Scotland was ruled by Roman law, England by common law; and the Scots spoke Gaelic, the English French or English. In 1297, as his campaign in Flanders was failing, Edward was catastrophically beaten at Stirling Bridge by a new Scottish leader, William Wallace, and had to make a hasty peace on the continent and return to Britain. He defeated Wallace at Falkirk in 1298 – the first battle in which the English used the longbow – but Scottish resistance continued, and he spent most of his last decade campaigning fruitlessly against the Scots. Wallace was captured and executed in 1305 as a traitor, although he was a foreign national; and in 1306 Robert Bruce, grandson of the claimant of 1290, declared himself king.

Prologue to the Hundred Years War

The conflict of the 1290s foreshadowed the Hundred Years War, with the same issues and systems of alliances. The truce of 1297 between France and England was only finalized in 1303, with the stipulation that Isabella, Philip IV's daughter, would marry Edward I's heir. Their nuptials occurred in 1308, after he had succeeded his father as King Edward II (1307–27). Her dowry was Ponthieu, the first property in northern France that the French had given the English since the capture of Normandy in 1205.

Despite the treaties, mutual annoyances such as piracy and reprisals against merchants continued to trouble the interrelations of Flanders, Scotland, England and France throughout the 1320s. Edward II tried to ignore the Scots, but Bruce's depradations on the frontier had become so serious by 1311 that the English invaded. At Bannockburn in 1314 an English army of 20,000 was slaughtered by a Scottish force half its size. Scottish raids into English territory continued until 1323, when Edward II agreed to recognize Bruce as king if he would stop the raids. By the treaty of Northampton of 1328 the English recognized Scottish independence and Robert Bruce as king. By the time Bruce died in 1329, he had created a nation. The bond with France was to be a linchpin of Scottish foreign policy until 1603: rarely did the English get into military engagements in France that were not accompanied by a Scottish invasion of northern England.

The war between England and France re-erupted in 1324 when the French retook Ponthieu in retaliation for English seizure of a stronghold that the French had built in a demilitarized part of Gascony. An uneasy peace arranged in 1325 quickly broke down, but further hostilities were deferred temporarily by domestic concerns in both monarchies. In 1327 Edward II was overthrown and soon executed by a baronial conspiracy led by his French wife and her Welsh lover Mortimer. The new king, Edward III (1327–77), was not yet 15.

King Charles IV (1322–8) of France, the last male of the Capetian dynasty, died in early 1328. Although succession in the female line was permitted in default of males in all French territorial principalities, an assembly dominated by the greatest titled nobles, the 'peers of France', chose instead to give the crown to Charles IV's cousin in the male line, Philip count of Valois (King Philip VI, 1328–50); for adherence to the normal rules would have made the young Edward III of England, whose mother had been a daughter of Philip IV, king also of France. Later the Valois' lawyers 'discovered' that the Salic Law (the sixth-century code of the Salian Franks) required that kingship be inherited strictly in the male line, while other types of property could be inherited and transmitted by females. Since Edward III's regents felt that they had to accommodate the new regime, he did simple homage to Philip VI for Aquitaine in June 1329. Philip persisted in his demand for supreme or liege homage, and Edward III agreed in 1331 in principle to do so, but he never in fact rendered it. In claiming the crown later, Edward would renounce his acts of homage, blaming the fiasco on his youth and bad advice.

Aggravations continued on both sides. In 1332 Edward Balliol, John's son, invaded Scotland against Bruce's young son David II (1329–71). When Balliol defeated the Scots at Dupplin Moor and accepted English suzerainty, Edward III renounced the treaty of 1328 as having been done while he was a minor. The Scots expelled Balliol in December 1332, and Edward invaded to restore him. Although initially unsuccessful, the coalition defeated David II's forces at Halidon Hill in 1334, and Balliol assumed the crown. But Scottish resentment at the Balliols was strong, and by 1341 David II's allies had recovered most of Scotland, permitting the king's return from exile in France. David raided England frequently in the next years, generally coinciding with English campaigns in France.

The Hundred Years War: The First Phase (1337–1369)

The conflict between England and France that began in 1337 is usually called the 'Hundred Years War'. Actually it was a series of wars in distinct phases, punctuated by long periods of comparative peace. It was 'national' between England and France only to a limited degree, for while tenancy of the French throne was a question between England and France, the status of Gascony gave it the overtones of a civil war within France, a motive that is especially clear after 1113.

When the English gave sanctuary to the pretender to the county of Artois, which the French crown claimed, Philip VI declared Gascony forfeit. Edward III in turn used French aid to the Scots as a pretext for war. At a Parliament in early 1337 reference was made to 'Philip who calls himself king of France'. Edward III renounced his homage for Gascony and claimed that it was held in full sovereignty, free from feudal obligations.

Realizing that war with France was coming, the English in 1336 had imposed an embargo on the sale of wool to Flanders. Counter-measures by Philip VI to hold the allegiance of Flanders proved ineffective. In 1338 a revolutionary regime came to power in Flanders, led by Jacob van Artevelde, chief captain of Ghent, the largest and most turbulent city of Flanders. By late 1339 the Flemings had expelled their Francophile count Louis of Nevers (1323–46), and van Artevelde got the embargo lifted by taking Flanders into an English alliance. Flanders became the linchpin of a Low Country coalition that included Brabant and Hainault. The alliance system also included German princes, notably Lewis, duke of Bavaria and Roman emperor (1314–47). On 26 January 1340 Edward III entered Ghent and was acclaimed king of France there.

In June 1340 the English and Flemings won an important naval victory over the French off the Flemish coast at Sluis, the outport of Bruges; but the

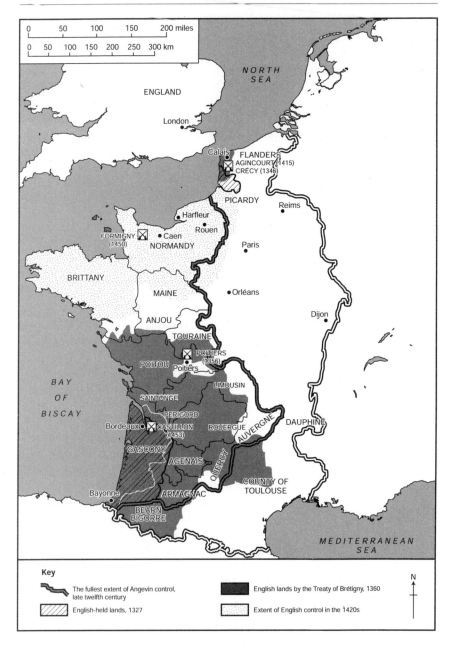

Map 1.1 England and France in the Era of the Hundred Years War

attempt to move south into France miscarried. Control of Tournai, on the border, was the key; and the French, aided by dissension between the leaders of Flanders and Brabant, managed to withstand a siege of the city in the autumn of 1340. The truce of Esplechin, arranged in September, was prolonged several times into 1345. The English Low Country coalition broke apart. England could generally count on the alliance of a substantial party within Flanders, although not the count himself; but this time the other principalities observed neutrality or supported the French. Lewis of Bavaria, who had supported the English, defected in 1341, and his successors generally favoured the French, particularly after a Bavarian dynasty gained control of Holland, Hainault and Zeeland in 1345.

Although direct military action between the French and English was ended temporarily, the two parties continued jockeying for position. When Duke John III of Brittany died in 1341, the English supported the claim to the succession of his half-brother, John of Montfort. Charles of Blois, the husband of John III's niece, had French support. The French and English both needed to control the Breton coast, and the French also hoped to incorporate Brittany into the royal domain. The war dragged on until 1365, when King Charles V of France recognized John IV of Montfort as duke, on condition of his acknowledgement of vassalage; but thereafter Montfort moved away from his English alliance and could never be trusted fully by either side.

When formal hostilities between the English and French resumed, the badly outnumbered English tried to avoid battles, preferring to turn their unengaged troops loose on the civilian populations. Near Crécy in Ponthieu the French trapped an English force that was entrenched on a hilltop but pinned against the sea; but the battle of Crécy (26 August 1346) was a disaster for the French. Philip VI's knights attacked in individual contingents, rather than *en masse*, and were decimated by the English longbowmen. Count Louis of Nevers of Flanders, king John of Bohemia and other prominent nobles perished, and Philip VI had to flee. The novelty of the battle was that knights dismounted and fought, mainly with longbows and pikes, as well as the fact that Edward III commanded his army in person; and the outcome gained him immense prestige. In 1347 Edward seized the city of Calais, which in 1363 would become the location of the English wool staple. Yet the English lacked resources to exploit their victory to the fullest.

The Scottish theatre also was active. In October 1346 David II was captured at Neville's Cross, during a raid that he had launched to try to diminish the impact of the French disaster at Crécy. Peace talks dragged on until 1357, when in the Treaty of Berwick Edward accepted a ransom for David II and abandoned Balliol's claims. Although the truce persisted until 1384, the Scots continued to raid. English preoccupation with France prevented the kings from exercising real overlordship in Scotland: English magnates in the northern marches defended the area against the Scots, but their resulting great power created problems for the monarchy in the fifteenth century.

As the French tried to regroup after Crécy, the great plague (see Chapter 3) paralysed Europe, and there was a lull in the fighting until 1355. Hostilities were then reopened in the southern theatre of the war, which had been relatively quiet in the 1340s. Edward III's son and heir, Edward the 'Black Prince' (1330–76), successfully raided along the south French coast and reached the borders of Navarre. In 1356 the French and English met in a major engagement at Poitiers. The French outnumbered the English; but, as at Crécy 10 years earlier, the French knights made cavalry charges against an entrenched English position and were picked off by longbows. Just as Crécy made Edward III's reputation as a military genius, so Poitiers did for the Black Prince. King John II (1350–64) of France was captured and held for an enormous ransom, while English raids from Normandy continued, and Paris was seriously threatened in 1358.

The Treaty of Brétigny and Its Aftermath

The two sides agreed in 1360 to the treaty of Brétigny, whose terms would become a benchmark. John II was released in return for a first payment on his ransom, now fixed at 3 million *écus*; he voluntarily returned to England when his government defaulted on the rest, dying in captivity in 1364. Edward III agreed to renounce his claim to the French throne, while the French were to give the English full sovereignty over a much-enlarged territory that included Gascony, Poitou, Ponthieu, Guines and Calais, not all of which was in Edward III's possession in 1360. In return, he renounced Normandy, Anjou and Maine. Although these terms were never implemented, English negotiators frequently returned to them as a policy goal, which has caused some to argue that Edward III's claim to the French throne may have been a tactical manoeuvre to force the French to surrender Gascony to him without the bothersome bond of vassalage.

The 1360s were quiet, as both sides tried to achieve by diplomacy what they could not do by military engagement. By this time it was clear that Louis of Male, count of Flanders (1346–84), would be succeeded by his only legitimate child, his daughter Margaret, whose hand thus became the most prized in Europe. Edward III hoped to gain her for his fourth son Edmund; but Pope Urban V, after disallowing this match on grounds of consanguinity, permitted Margaret to be affianced to Philip, duke of Burgundy, the younger brother of King Charles V of France (1364–80), to whom she was related in the same degree. The marriage took place in 1369 and brought the Walloon castellanies back to Flanders. When Margaret's father died in 1384 Flanders moved into a French political orbit, despite considerable opposition to this in its cities. Although traditionally independent, Flanders gave the Burgundians considerable trouble through 1453 and became the second major component of a Burgundian empire controlled by a French duke.

The English and French also became involved in the 1360s in a civil war in Castile. When Edward III allied with Peter I 'the Cruel' of Castile in 1362, he gained the assistance of Castile's navy against the French. But Henry of Trastamara, Peter's half-brother, gained the ear of Bertrand Duguesclin, a Breton who was making his military reputation and would become commander of the French forces when the war against the English formally resumed in 1369. Duguesclin invaded Castile in 1365 and deposed Peter, who fled to the court of Edward the Black Prince, by now prince of Aquitaine. Edward invaded in 1367 and at the battle of Nájera defeated Henry and made Duguesclin his prisoner. But fortunes were reversed in 1369, when Henry defeated and killed Peter in battle. The house of Trastamara would rule Castile into the modern period. The claims of Peter's dynasty passed to his eventual son-in-law, John of Gaunt (1340–99), the Black Prince's younger brother, who married Peter's daughter Constance in 1371 but would be unable to campaign in Castile until 1386. In 1388 John of Gaunt gave up his claim to the throne when his daughter married Henry of Trastamara's son, the future Henry III of Castile (1390–1406); Gaunt's older daughter married John I (1385–1433), the first of the Avis dynasty of Portuguese kings.

The Hundred Years War: The Second Phase (1369–1375)

The terms of the treaty of Brétigny were never implemented, and Aquitaine remained a fief of France. Charles V was thus able to use resentment there over the hearth tax that the Black Prince had imposed to pay for the Castilian campaign to stir up trouble. In early 1369 the French invaded both Aquitaine and Ponthieu and declared the Black Prince a contumacious vassal. Edward III in turn formally resumed his claim to the French crown. Despite the conflicts in Castile, the English appear to have been caught unprepared by the resumption of hostilities. The Black Prince's administration in Aquitaine was resented, and after he compounded his reputation for brutality by sacking Limoges in 1370, because the city's bishop had negotiated with the French, he surrendered administration of Aquitaine to his father in 1371. The Prince had become incurably ill during the Castilian campaigns and went into a premature decline, dying in 1376.

The French had prepared their ground well. Both sides avoided battle in this stage of the war. The English made sorties into Normandy, while the French raided into undefended parts of Gascony. The Scots were still a danger on England's northern frontier and forced the English to commit forces there that could have been used in France. John IV of Brittany provided some help for the English with a formal alliance in 1372, but he was again with the French by 1382. The alliance with the Trastamaras gave the French a navy that they used against English shipping, and pirates threatened the English coast. The truce of Sint-Baafs-Vijve (1375) left the English only with a much-diminished Gascony; their other conquests were gone.

The Hundred Years War: Forty Years of Irritation (1375–1415)

The diminished pace of hostilities after 1375 was connected to domestic concerns on both sides. Edward III of England was sinking into senility, dominated by his mistress Alice Perrers and John of Gaunt, his unpopular third son. The revolution that had brought Edward III to the throne had left him free to elevate earls and dukes upon whom he could rely. This group of titled aristocrats served him well, but he lived so long that by the 1360s they were dying and being replaced by persons whose loyalty was considerably more problematical. In 1376 the Black Prince briefly gained control of a Parliament (the 'Good Parliament') that banished Gaunt and Perrers, but they returned later in the year after the prince's death, an event that also made John of Gaunt the king's oldest surviving son. Although Gaunt was rumoured to be plotting a coup, Edward was succeeded when he died in 1377 by Richard II, the Black Prince's 10-year-old son.

The reign of Richard II (1377–99) was turbulent. The regency was dominated by Gaunt, who was resented by Gloucester, the king's other surviving uncle. Taxation had been based on the 'lay subsidy' of a percentage of income from movable property and land, but the new regime experimented with a head tax, of a fixed amount per person above the age of 14. Nearly annual taxation had been unheard of before the wars, and liability to a tax on the person as opposed to property was considered a mark of serfdom. Thus the 'poll tax' was unpopular and led to the the the 'Peasants' Revolt' of 1381, which shook the foundations of the monarchy (see Chapter 3). The young king's boldness saved the situation but did not improve his position for long. Although Richard distrusted Gaunt, the latter's departure for Castile in 1386 gave the signal to the 'Lords Appellant', five nobles whose leaders were Gloucester and Henry of Derby, Gaunt's eldest legitimate son. In 1386 the 'Wonderful' parliament impeached the royal chancellor, Michael de la Pole, appointed a committee to govern England for a year, and informed the king that parliament could depose a king who governed against the law and the advice of the peers. In 1387 Richard restored de la Pole and raised an army, and judges declared the decrees of 1386 illegal. After the Lords Appellant in turn raised their own army, Richard had to call the 'Merciless Parliament' of 1388. This parliament executed the king's chief officers and prominent Londoners who had supported him. Gaunt's return, followed by the king's declaration in 1389 that his minority was ended, ended the domestic crisis until 1397.

Charles V (1364–80) of France had been served as his father's regent after 1356. As king he had been responsible for the military build-up that had reversed the fortunes of the war. A noted bibliophile, he quickly became known as 'Charles the Wise'. But he died prematurely, leaving the throne to his older but less competent son, Charles VI (1380–1422). The first three years of the new regime saw civil conflict; for Charles V, convinced as most of his contemporaries were that taxation was sinful, had abolished the *taille* (hearth tax) on his deathbed, and this left his son's regents with no choice other than bankruptcy or restoring the tax. When they opted for the latter, revolts broke out in the major cities of northern France that were only quelled in 1383 in settlements that ended most of the liberties, however minimal, that the French cities had. The revolts in France were inspired in part by events in Flanders, where the cities had been in rebellion since 1379 against the count. Leadership of the Flemish rising was assumed, as usual, by Ghent, whose leader by early 1382 was Philip van Artevelde, son of the captain of the 1340s. French forces aided the duke of Burgundy in 1382 in putting down the worst of this rebellion, but a final peace was only reached in 1385, by which time Burgundy was ruling Flanders through his wife. Philip was noted for his distaste for the English, and the inheritance had given him control of the substantial Flemish navy. England was in serious danger of invasion in the late 1380s, and piracy was rampant in the English channel. Even after a three-year truce was reached in 1389, the sea lanes continued to be dangerous.

Charles V had continued his predecessors' habit of granting *apanages* to the great princes of the royal blood. Louis VIII (1223–6) had granted territories to each of his sons to rule on behalf of the king. Given the rapid expansion of the royal domain under Louis IX (1226–70), it was possible for him to keep inherited property in the domain and limit the *apanages* to acquisitions. Louis and his immediate successors had treated the *apanages* as gifts for the lifetime of the individual, to revert to the crown when the beneficiary died. But they became hereditary in the late fourteenth century, with the provisions that John II (1350–64) and Charles V (1364–80) made for their younger sons. The *apanagists* maintained expensive households and competed for patronage at an inefficient and bloated court at Paris.

The Great Schism

Another of Charles the Wise's dubious achievements was creating a division in the papacy that would vex Europe for nearly half a century. Most thirteenth-century popes had been from Roman noble families who regarded the pontificate as a source of family patronage. Naturally, they had rivals, and the residence of the popes at Avignon and the fact that they and most of the cardinals were French (see Chapter 4) had created a power vacuum in central Italy into which local lords moved. From 1353 Pope Innocent VI (1352–62) began a systematic attempt to reoccupy the papal state (the Romagna), a goal that meant conflict with other Italian powers. The pacification of the Romagna was close enough to being accomplished by 1367 that Pope Urban V (1362–70) was able to come to Rome for three years. When Gregory XI (1370–78) removed permanently to Rome and was succeeded by an Italian in 1378, Charles V's agents provoked the divided election that returned one pope to Avignon.

The ensuing 'Great Schism' of the papacy became a political issue between England and France. England and most of Germany and Italy supported the line of popes that stayed at Rome, while France and her allies, Scotland and Castile, and Naples and Milan, where the ruling dynasties had French ties, supported the Avignon popes. Richard II of England seems to have been genuinely interested in a peace with the French that would include a withdrawal of obedience by the English and French from their respective popes. In 1396 a twenty-eight-year truce was made that was accompanied by the marriage of the widowed Richard II to the 8-year-old Isabelle, daughter of Charles V. The boundaries actually changed little between English- and French-held territory after the treaty of 1375, which had left the French holding more territory than they had in 1327; and neither party fulfilled its pledge to withdraw obedience from its pope, evidently fearing to act first.

Frailty and Faction in France

Charles VI's mental balance was never strong, and in 1392 he went insane. The king's madness was not permanent, but his periods of lucidity became ever briefer during the remaining thirty years of his life and reign. When Charles was sane and at least in nominal control of the government, he tended to rely on his younger brother, Louis, duke of Orléans, who was married to Valentina Visconti, daughter of Giangaleazzo Visconti, duke of Milan. The idea of a potential king marrying into a city family would have been unthinkable a century earlier, but not in the late fourteenth century, for the attractions of Milanese money were plain.

When the king was mad, however, the regency was dominated by his uncles, all of whom held extensive *apanages*: the dukes of Anjou and Berry, but the major power at court was Philip 'the Bold', duke of Burgundy (1369–1404). A third centre of power was queen Isabelle, nicknamed Isabeau, niece of duke Albert of Bavaria, whose Wittelsbach dynasty also ruled Holland, Hainault and Zeeland. Burgundy and Orléans thus vied for influence in Italy and the Empire. Burgundy was generally allied with Florence and the Wittelsbachs of Bavaria against Orléans, who was allied with the imperial house of Luxembourg and the Visconti. In 1380 Queen

Joanna of Naples, who had no children, adopted Louis of Anjou, the oldest brother of King Charles V of France, as her heir, and Louis' son in turn allied with Louis of Orléans. This created the basis of the Angevin claim on Naples, which passed to the French crown a century later. The Avignonese Pope Clement VII (1378–94) had tried to secure French help in Italy by offering Louis of Orléans an Adriatic kingdom centering on Genoa. Orléans was able to establish himself in Genoa, and the French ruled the city until 1409. The Orléans position was also strengthened within France, when Louis bought the estates of the great general Enguerrand de Coucy from his heiress.

The growth of Burgundian power is one of the most important aspects of this period, which is truly revolutionary in building the political map of modern Europe. In 1404–5 Philip 'the Bold' and his wife Margaret of Flanders were succeeded in the duchy and county of Burgundy, Flanders, Artois and the County of Rethel by their son John 'the Fearless' (1404–19). At least through John, who got his nickname through his conduct on the 'Nicopolis Crusade' of 1396 (see below), the Burgundian dukes used their non-French territories to help them play power politics in Paris, particularly by taxing wealthy Flanders mercilessly. They also used French money and diplomatic influence to consolidate their power in their own territories. While French money and influence were used in the Low Countries on behalf of the Burgundians, these resources and also troops were deployed for Orléans in Italy, where Duke Charles was campaigning in the 1390s on behalf of his father-in-law, and in Liguria to validate his own claims on Genoa.

The English Revolution of 1399

Richard II had taken personal control of his government in 1389. He lived eight years in superficial agreement with his opponents, the Lords Appellant, while building up his retainership, who wore the badge of the White Hart. In 1397, however, he arrested three of the five Lords Appellant at a friendship banquet, and soon had them executed. In 1398 he banished the other two, including Henry Derby, son of John of Gaunt, initially for ten years in Derby's case. When John of Gaunt died in early 1399, he extended this to life exile and confiscated the earldom of Lancaster. Ostensibly to protect his rightful inheritance, Derby invaded from France while Richard was campaigning in Ireland. The king's support evaporated when he returned, and he was taken prisoner. In a stage-managed scene recorded in the Parliament roll of 1399, Richard abdicated; then a bill of particulars detailing his crimes was read in Parliament, concluding with the statement that these deeds warranted deposition. The throne was declared vacant, and Henry, now earl of Lancaster, claimed the crown by right of descent from Edward III and was acclaimed by Parliament. The scene thus had elements both of abdication and of deposition and revolution. Richard II died the next year, allegedly by starving himself.

Richard II had left no children. His rightful heir was the earl of March, the grandson of Lionel of Clarence, second son of Edward III, but his claim was passed over. King Henry IV (1399–1413) was the oldest legitimate son of John of Gaunt, Edward III's third son. The Lancastrians' title would not be challenged until 1460, in the person of Richard, duke of York, descended on his mother's side from Lionel of Clarence and on his father's from the duke of York, Edward III's fourth son. But the claims of Parliament, which had clearly had some role in bringing them to the throne, weakened Henry's ability to act independently, and his support was firm only in south-eastern England. Henry IV was also faced with a rebellion by Lollards (see Chapter 4) led by Sir John Oldcastle, a Mortimer–March rebellion in Wales that received Scottish help, piracy in the English channel, and troubles with the powerful north English nobles, the latter in league with his son and eventual heir Henry.

Civil War in France

Conditions also deteriorated at the French court. John the Fearless lacked his father's finesse. In 1407, when his agents assassinated Louis of Orléans, John took public responsibility for the deed, but insisted that the devil had made him do it, a proposition that has a certain verisimilitude. He had to flee Paris hastily; but by 1408 he was back, and through his spokesman, the university theologian Jean Petit, he defended his action before the royal Council on grounds of the subject's duty to slay a tyrant. The new duke of Orléans, Charles, was only 13 and lacked the warrior's temperament. In 1406 he had married no less a figure than Charles VI's daughter Isabelle, the unconsummated widow of Richard II of England. This marriage and Orléans' descent from Charles V, while the Burgundians were descended from Charles V's younger brother, made Orléans a potential heir to the throne if all Charles VI's sons should predecease their father, which was distinctly possible. The Orléans house had prestige, but it sadly lacked resources: their lands were in the provinces and could not rival Burgundy's power in the north. Once restored to the court, Burgundy dominated it and in addition consolidated his faction's control of the city of Paris.

After Isabelle's death in childbirth, in 1410 Charles of Orléans married Bonne, daughter of Count Bernard VII of Armagnac, which brought him two advantages: an enormous dowry, since the Armagnacs were eager to have the prestige of an alliance with the house of Orléans, and a father-in-law who was a better soldier than he was. After 1416, when Armagnac became Constable of France, the Orléans faction would generally be called the Armagnacs.

Both sides in France were negotiating with the English by 1411, generally offering territorial concessions. With the Armagnac army controlling the suburbs of Paris, the Burgundians and their powerful and violent allies, the butchers of Paris, gained control of the capital in April 1413 and conducted a reign of terror for several months. Conditions were so dangerous that the royal court, which generally leaned toward Orléans, had to leave the city. The two sides distributed badges to their supporters; at a critical moment, the Burgundians purged all who did not wear their insignia. But the Orléanistes regained control of the city in September and ousted the Burgundians.The fact that the Orléanistes controlled the government gave the Burgundians the excuse to claim that they were the reform party, desiring only to purge the corrupt royal court.

The Hundred Years War: The Climactic Phase (1413–1435)

In the year of the Burgundian terror Henry V (1413–22) succeeded his father in England and moved toward war with France. While his predecessors may have thought of the claim to the French crown as a negotiating position, with absolute sovereignty over Gascony being the real goal, Henry V felt that he was divinely called to be king of France, and the chaos in France afforded credibility to his claim. As early as 1414 his war demands on the Orléans government included his eventual marriage with Catherine, Charles VI's daughter; the French agreed in principle, which explains why Henry and Catherine remained unmarried until rather advanced ages. Henry also demanded conditions that were unacceptable: her dowry should include the restoration in full sovereignty of all territory promised by the Treaty of Brétigny, together with Normandy, Touraine, Maine and Anjou on the same terms, and the money still owed on John II's ransom. The English also wanted the homage of Brittany and Flanders changed to these terms, since the young duke of Brittany was controlled at this time by John the Fearless of Burgundy. But the French government refused this, fearing that it would drive Burgundy into an English alliance.

Thus in 1415 Henry V invaded a France that was controlled from Paris by the Orléans faction. In September he took Harfleur, and on 25 October he met a substantially larger French force at Agincourt in Artois. The French again charged with their cavalry; the English centre withdrew, then reformed to attack the French from the flanks. The field was muddy, enmiring the horses. The casualties included most of the older generation of princes who had opposed Burgundy. There were numerous prisoners, including Charles, duke of Orléans, who would remain in England until 1440. As the highest-ranking French prisoner, his presence gave the English diplomatic leverage, particularly since after 1417 Charles VI had only a single son left; had he died, Orléans could have inherited the French crown. Agincourt was the most complete English victory of the Hundred Years War.

Yet the French refused to negotiate. The English fought in Normandy but were unable to take Paris, without which there was no hope of a successful conclusion of the war. In 1416 the Holy Roman Emperor Sigismund offered to mediate, but the plan came to nothing. Queen Isabeau had been exiled by Armagnac and Charles, the 15-year-old Dauphin (the title of the heir to the French throne since 1349, as the English crown prince has been the Prince of Wales since 1301). She escaped and set up a rival court with the duke of Burgundy at Chartres in November 1417. The next year the Burgundians retook Paris and reinstalled Charles VI, with considerable slaughter, while the Dauphin escaped to southern France.

The deadlock was broken in the English favour in the autumn of 1419. On 10 September the Armagnac leaders and the Dauphin enticed John the Fearless of Burgundy into an ambush at Montereau and murdered him in retaliation for the 1407 death of Louis of Orléans, with the Dauphin, Charles, being implicated in the plot. The new duke of Burgundy, Philip 'the Good' (1419–67), openly allied with the English in December. Burgundian-controlled Paris thus fell without a struggle to the English.

The Treaty of Troyes (21 May 1420) was intended to be a permanent settlement of the war. Henry V and Catherine of Valois were to be married, and Henry dropped his demand for a dowry. Charles VI was to continue on the throne, but at his death Henry would become king in France, followed there and in England by his issue by Catherine. The excuse given for disinheriting the Dauphin was his involvement in the Burgundian assassination of 1419. This arrangement looked extremely promising on paper, given that Charles VI was 52 and debilitated in 1420 and Henry V was a vigorous 33. But both men died in 1422, leaving Henry, the 9-month old son of Henry V and Catherine of Valois, as heir to both kingdoms. A regency was established, led by the uncles of young Henry VI (1422–61/71): the duke of Bedford was in charge of operations in France, while the duke of Gloucester was to manage affairs in England.

The Dauphin naturally did not accept this arrangement and took the name Charles VII (1422–61), establishing a capital at Bourges and later moving to Tours. His troops did garrison the major towns on the south bank of the Loire river, but until 1429 his regime was noted chiefly for its torpor. The English had a firm base in Gascony, and in most of northern France English rule was accepted in the 1420s as the only way to get peace. The English administered Normandy well, generally using Frenchmen in the bureaucracy except at Paris and in garrisons, which were exclusively English.

Matters changed abruptly, however, when Joan of Arc, a peasant girl who experienced visions telling her that God was calling her to save France from its oppressors, got an audience with Charles VII and convinced him to give her command of military operations along the Loire. She led the defence of Orléans against an English attempt to seize it, which would have opened southern France to English penetration, and forced them to

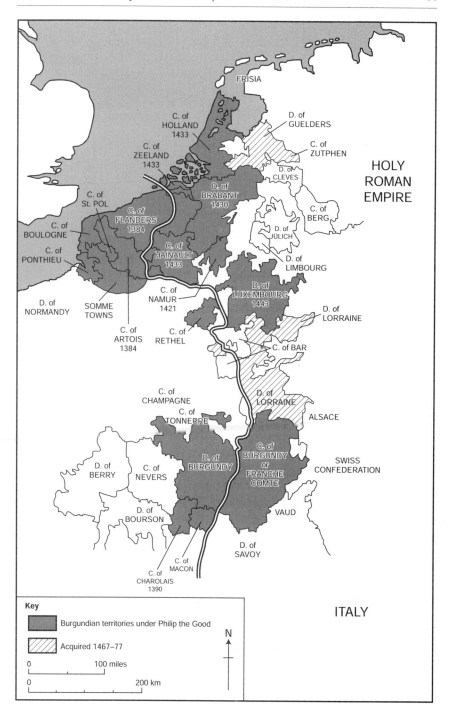

Map 1.2 The Burgundian State

withdraw. This made it possible for the Dauphin to be crowned at Reims on 17 July 1429. The symbolic value of this act was enormous, for coronation at Reims, with its elaborately symbolic ceremonial, had been necessary for the French kings for centuries. Jeanne continued the campaigns until the Burgundians captured her in 1430 and handed over to the English, who tried and burned her as a witch. To try to hold the north the English arranged a coronation of Henry VI in Paris, but this lacked the symbolic value of Charles VII's unction at Reims.

The Duke of Bedford tried to keep the Burgundians pacified, but his younger brother and rival, Humphrey duke of Gloucester, made his position difficult. Philip 'the Good' of Burgundy hoped to extend his rule over Brabant by marrying his nephew, Duke John IV of Brabant, to Jacqueline of Bavaria, the heiress of Hainault, Holland and Zeeland. In 1422, however, Jacqueline petitioned the pope for an annulment of this marriage, then married Gloucester without waiting for the pontiff's decision. By 1425 the Burgundians were at war with Jacqueline and Humphrey, and in 1428 Jacqueline had to recognize Philip the Good as her heir. As English military fortunes declined after 1429, the Burgundians became unreliable allies. In 1435, the year of Bedford's death, the peace of Arras settled Burgundy's feud with Charles VII, and the English were left with no powerful allies on the Continent. Philip immediately tried to seize Calais from the English with a Flemish army; although the plan miscarried, English resources were committed in the Low Countries until 1439.

Henry VI declared his minority ended in 1437, but his incompetence quickly became apparent. Disorders mounted in England, and the king came under the domination of the duke of Suffolk. By 1444 the English had been weakened to the point where they were willing to give up Henry's claim to the French throne in exchange for Normandy in full sovereignty. The Truce of Tours of 1444 provided for the marriage of Henry VI to Margaret of Anjou, Charles VII's niece by marriage, without addressing the question of sovereignty. This was supposed to stifle French ambitions; yet Henry undermined the war effort in 1445 by promising secretly to surrender Maine to the French. Faced with English resistance, the French required until 1448 to take Maine, then turned to Normandy in late 1449 and took it in less than a year. Most of Gascony fell in 1451, although the English were able to retake Bordeaux until 1453. Of the once enormous English possessions on the continent, only Calais was left (until 1558).

The rapid collapse of the English position on the Continent exacerbated rivalries at court. Civil conflicts racked England from 1450. Suffolk was murdered, and Jack Cade's rebellion in 1450 highlighted the problem of an incompetent king who was receiving bad advice. In August 1453 Henry VI went insane, only recovering his lucidity at Christmas 1454. In 1455 military engagements began between the court faction, now led by Queen Margaret and the earl of Somerset, and Richard Duke of York, a descendant of Edward III's second eldest son who would claim the throne in 1460 shortly before his death in battle on New Year's Eve. By the spring of 1461, however, this phase of the 'Wars of the Roses' (so called after the white rose of York and the red rose of the house of Tudor, which through its descent from the Beauforts, the originally illegitimate children of John of Gaunt, carried the banner of the Lancastrians after 1471) ended with the ascent to the English throne of his son, Edward (King Edward IV, 1461–83).

The Consequences of the Hundred Years War

The Hundred Years War was most obviously a conflict between England and France. The exclusion of the English kings from western France was a major step toward the unification of the modern French nation. But it was also a French civil war, not only because the English kings were also French princes, but also because other French princes took the English side at times. The portions of France that were included in the royal domain had greatly expanded and had received some of the institutions of a centralized monarchy through the achievements of the Capetian kings. Yet the geographical extent of the domain had become so large, and the incursions of the kings outside their own lands so blatant by the early fourteenth century, as to cause resentment. Beginning with the charter movements of 1315 (see Chapter 2), the older unity began to fracture, and local particularism and institutions, fostered by the practice of granting *apanages* to the younger sons of the king, caused France to resemble a confederation of principalities more than a national monarchy by 1380. This situation continued through the period of the Hundred Years War, but the removal of the duke of Gascony as the most powerful territorial prince facilitated the centralizing efforts of the kings in the following century.

The Late Medieval Military Revolution

The Hundred Years War period saw important changes in military tactics and strategy. Gunpowder was developed in China, but was rarely used in military engagements in Europe until the 1330s. By 1400, however, all armies were using cannon to demolish fortifications. This remained the major use of gunpowder until the second half of the fifteenth century, when the hand-held, single-shot arquebus came into general use. Particularly from the fifteenth century, armies often travelled with their cannon broken down to ease the burden of carriage over muddy roads, then resmelted them before the action began. The inconvenience of transporting ammunition thus led to some standardization of calibration of guns among armament manufacturers. Cities, whose fortifications were more extensive and difficult to breach than castle walls, replaced castles as key strategic points, their gates often used as arsenals for storing artillery during peacetime, firepower being used by defenders as well as besiegers. From 1367 Charles V of France often allowed one-quarter of the taxes raised in a locality to remain there to pay for maintaining the fortifications. Until the 1430s the cannon generally fired stone missiles, but then there was a shift to cast iron, which was more expensive but did not shatter on impact and could be made to a uniform size and in greater quantity. In response to this change, city walls were lowered and made thicker. The growing importance of sieges in the last stages of the Hundred Years War diminished the importance of cavalry and elevated that of the archers, but the fact that fighting on horseback was such an essential part of the ethos of the nobles meant that cavalry continued to have an importance that was disproportionate to its military effectiveness.

Yet, although military technology did improve and tactics change, this in itself was not a major element in the growing expense of warfare to governments. Armies generally remained small. Granted that cannon were expensive, the crossbow, longbow and pike were not. At the very time when rulers were creating a broad tax liability under law through assemblies, and were accustoming their subjects to frequent taxation, the armies were destroying the economic tax base by striking civilian populations and were making the levies even more burdensome than would otherwise have been the case.

The major expenses of war to the kings continued to be for wages and provisions for the troops, for the hired armies were being kept in the field longer than before and thus were being paid much more than even the mercenary forces of the thirteenth century. By 1300 the feudal host, consisting of persons who owed uncompensated military service on horseback as a result of holding fiefs directly of the king, was rarely summoned. It was called for the last time in England in 1327. Even during Edward I's campaigns in Wales in the 1270s and 1280s most troops received wages, and by the 1340s virtually all did so, including the noble commanders.

Troops were raised in several ways. Since 1285 Englishmen had been required to arm themselves with weapons befitting their wealth and social rank. Although this was intended initially to provide a local militia for defence, it meant that the English were much more used to war than most Frenchmen were. The local militias had to be kept in readiness for police work as well as military duty and this, together with the need to maintain large garrisons in Wales and on the Scottish frontier, meant that the English had a relatively larger body of semi-trained troops upon whom they could call than did the French. Edward III in 1363 required regular archery training for civilians, from whom he would recruit troops for the next campaign, complaining that this salutary aspect of male education had fallen into desuetude. Most soldiers hired by the English were volunteers with at least some training in arms.

The Hundred Years War saw the triumph of the professional mercenary soldier over the knight who owed military service as a result of his land tenure and/or social rank. Even in the early stages of the war the English were using mainly mercenary troops, hired by contracts of indenture made with their captains. The commanders, who were often landed gentry, received sums from the crown, then paid their own troops. The French had always used some mercenaries, but only did so in large numbers mainly from about 1400 until the end of the war. The kings on both sides also paid many of their soldiers directly, using household departments as war offices. By 1450 the armies were made up almost exclusively of mercenaries. But the troops were frequently unpaid, and during the long intervals of peace their commanders lost control of them and they turned to pillage. To make matters worse, the English capitalized on this situation by sending *chevauchées*, raids by mounted troops whose intention was to devastate cities and destroy property and crops. Since virtually all military engagements of the war were fought in France, the English made war on civilian populations, which made them particularly odious to the French. The increased size of the armies and their brutality against non-combatants evoked for the first time complaints against war itself. Even the chronicler Jean Froissart, who tended to dote on glorious deeds of battle, cast opprobrium on the brutality of the Black Prince's sacking of Limoges in 1370. The most famous was the French courtier and man of letters Philippe de Mézières, who in 1395 addressed an open letter on the blessings of peace to Richard II, complaining particularly that as warfare was now becoming the business not of aristocrats, for whom it was a matter of social ethos, but of people who made their living from it, it was becoming more a case of stealing and pillaging than of honourable combat.

These measures were obviously *ad hoc*. Charles VII of France in the 1440s created the basis for a standing army, but one that was so dispersed that it was difficult to use on short notice. In the basic ordinance of 1445 the crown named captains and provided money to pay them. In 1448 *francs-archiers* were established as a permanent force drawn, in theory, from all communities. The changes of the 1440s generally kept middle-level nobles in the most important command posts, but the emphasis changed to service that was paid directly by the state rather than by indentured captains on an *ad hoc* basis if troops were needed. From 1445 the leaders were appointed by royal commission rather than strictly by birthright. Yet this democratizing tendency cannot be carried too far, for the nobles were trained for war, if most often for the – by now anachronistic – horseback warfare, and thus they had some understanding of battlefield tactics. All armies, even city militias, tended to reserve the higher commands for nobles, while the lower posts went to commoners. With the final victory of gunpowder after 1450, the armies became much larger, with command positions held by the aristocrats, while commoners were literally and figuratively the cannon fodder.

Warfare on the seas became important for the first time, although the only major naval battle of the Hundred Years War was at Sluis in 1340. The

English had a decent merchant marine but not a navy, and the French were even less prepared. Both sides used the Castilian navy, which was organized under an admiral, often a Genoese, until 1405. Pirates wreaked considerable havoc on 'unfriendly' shipping in the Channel, often with the tacit permission of their home governments. Since princes considered trading with their enemies a violation of neutrality, there was open season on ships from smaller principalities with fluctuating allegiances, such as Brittany and Flanders before 1384. Of the minor parties in the war, the Flemings probably had the best navy, which the dukes of Burgundy were able to use to threaten the English coast in the late 1380s. The English used mainly English mercenaries, doing little on-site recruiting in France, but they seem never to have had serious problems getting troops to and from the Continent.

The Iberian Peninsula

Spain at the beginning of our period consisted of several distinct states, whose eventual union appeared no more inevitable than did that of the French principalities. Their institutions probably varied more among themselves than the French (see Chapter 2). Yet, as had been true in France, there was a sense of Spanish identity in addition to loyalty to the individual kingdoms. The word *Hispania* was in common use throughout the Middle Ages to designate the entire Iberian peninsula.

Although the history of the Iberian peninsula is commonly seen in the light of the Christian conquest from the Muslims, who had held all but the extreme north as late as the early eleventh century, that undertaking consumed attention and resources mainly before 1250 and in the half-century after 1450. After 1248 the Muslims held only the small state of Granada in the extreme south. Portugal, which had broken away from Castile in the twelfth century, had roughly its present borders. Blocked on the east by Castile, Portugal turned toward Atlantic expansion in the fourteenth and particularly the fifteenth century. The small kingdom of Navarre, including the modern Basque country in the western Pyrenees, was ruled by a French dynasty.

The largest and most powerful kingdoms were Castile and Aragon. Aragon proper was poor and landlocked, but the state also included Catalonia. The dynasty was Catalan, and Catalans dominated the state and economy. Catalan adventurers in the fourteenth century won, but then lost, the Duchy of Athens, and Sicily and Sardinia were incorporated into the Aragonese crown in 1409. The kings of Aragon also had claims in southern Italy, the result of the marriage of the daughter of Peter of Aragon to Manfred, bastard of the emperor Frederick II (1212–50), and warfare in Italy against the French house of Anjou in the late thirteenth century. In Italy as on their northern frontier, the Aragonese assumed a militantly anti-

French posture into the fifteenth century. The major city was Barcelona, in Catalonia, the most important port of the western Mediterranean until its decline after 1430 due to trade imbalances and the virtual collapse of the city's textile industry. The Aragonese state also included Valencia, which had been largely Muslim until the Aragonese took it in 1238. The city of Valencia took over some of the trade of Barcelona after 1450.

Castile consisted of central Spain, an area mainly of mountains and thin soil with a small coast on both the Atlantic and the Mediterranean. It had borne the brunt of the fight against the Muslims, a development that had produced a powerful nobility and a network of fortified towns that had been established along the frontiers as they were pushed south. The Castilians had brutally expelled the largely rural Muslims from Andalusia after conquering the region in the thirteenth century. The land was given to soldiers who quickly sold it to nobles and to the military orders of Calatrava and Alcantara. While Andalusia had enjoyed prosperity and a diversified agricultural regime under the Muslims, it now became a land of large farms given over largely to grain and animal husbandry. Andalusia also had a large Jewish population, somewhat richer and considerably more urbanized than the Muslims, but they were not molested until the late fourteenth century.

Civil conflict after 1282, broken only by Alfonso XI's reign (1311–50), prevented further Castilian action against Granada. Alfonso's son was Peter 'the Cruel' (1350–69), whose rule was challenged for the next two decades by his illegitimate half-brother Henry of Trastamara, who disliked Peter for personal excesses and also for his toleration of the influential Jewish community in Castile. Henry took the dangerous step of allying with the French against his brother, and the resultant civil war, as we have seen, only ended in 1388.

The family link between Castile and Portugal through marriage of their kings to daughters of John of Gaunt was paralleled when the native dynasty in Aragon died out with Martin I in 1410; in 1412 the Compromise of Caspe gave the throne to Ferdinand of Trastamara, an uncle of John II of Castile (1406-54). The Aragonese branch of the Trastamara continued to own considerable property in Castile, which helped to bridge the antagonism between the two countries. Aragon had a largely absentee monarchy after Alfonso V 'the Magnanimous' (1435-58) moved his court to Naples, and after 1443 he governed Aragon through viceroys. His successor in Aragon was his younger brother, John II (1458-79), father of Ferdinand.

Jews and Muslims in Late Medieval Spain

Ethno-religious relations became a poisonous political issue in Spain in the fourteenth century, involving the large Muslim and Jewish populations. The Castilian Christians had expropriated large numbers of Muslim peasants after the conquests in the thirteenth century. Still, the Mudejars (Muslims) were allowed to have their own judges and courts until this privilege was withdrawn in 1412. In Castile Christians were entitled to trial by Christian judges and could only be convicted on the testimony of Christian witnesses, but Mudejars could be convicted on Christian testimony by the fifteenth century.

The Jews were badly treated everywhere in western Europe. They were expelled from England in 1290 and from the French royal domain in 1307, and were then readmitted at various points during the fourteenth century, but under such stifling restrictions that few came. Many of them moved to eastern Europe, where various princes, needing Jewish capital to finance economic expansion, gave them formal privileges, such as security of debt and person and freedom to practise their religion. The wholesale expulsions of Jews only became widespread east of the Rhine from the 1420s onwards.

Yet Spain is a case apart. Until the early fifteenth century the Jews of Spain were the strongest in western Europe, both in terms of numbers and of integration into the majority Christian society, and because of the wide range of social and economic roles and status that they enjoyed. In contrast to the rest of Europe too, the Jews were also not the only large ethnic or religious minority in Spain. They did not play much political role except in an advisory capacity unless they converted to Christianity, which explains why so many of them converted while retaining much of their ancestral custom and heritage.

Even the Trastamara dynasty found it impossible to do without Jewish financiers. The famous pogroms of 1391 are clearly a watershed, starting in Seville and then spreading to the other large cities. Although the number of deaths has been exaggerated, there was considerable loss of property. Agitation then died down until the Dominican preacher St Vincente Ferrer stirred up mobs again in 1411. Curiously, there is at least as much evidence of public hostility towards the former Jews who converted and their descendants, lumped together as *conversos*, as to the unbaptized Jews. Especially from 1449, *conversos* were increasingly distinguished in Castile from Old Christians. Preachers taught that they could never be true Christians, for their blood was tainted. The Spanish Inquisition as initially established in 1478 was thus directed not against Muslims or Jews, but rather against *conversos*, who were suspected of remaining Jews in all but name and of having converted solely for material advantage.

Germany

The often-noted territorial fragmentation of late medieval Germany is most true for the extreme west. Conditions there had deteriorated since 1231, when the emperor Frederick II's Statute in Favour of the Princes permitted all German lords to exercise regalian right (whatever the king could do himself) on their domains. This made all of them, not just the imperial princes, independent in law, and in the next years the greater principalities disintegrated internally just as the Empire had done earlier. Yet central and eastern Germany had several large and reasonably coherent states: the duchies of Bavaria (ruled by the Wittelsbachs) and Austria (ruled by the Habsburgs), and the states of the Teutonic Order in Prussia and the mark (march or frontier) of Brandenburg.

The king of Germany was considered to be Holy Roman Emperor-elect, and was expected to be crowned in Rome by the pope. The imperial title gave him nominal overlordship over the eastern Low Countries, most of Germany, parts of southeastern Europe including the kingdom of Bohemia, and Italy as far south as Rome. In fact, the emperors had little impact in Italy after 1273, when Frederick II's last legitimate grandson was executed. In Germany their influence was felt mainly in their family territories, where they held the same rights that other princes did, but with most emperors these were substantial lands. The emperor had the right to grant and regrant imperial fiefs, a power that some used very effectively for patronage, and some broader distinctions, such as the right to bestow a royal title on a lesser prince.

The Habsburg dukes of Austria consolidated their power in the south and east and held the imperial title for much of the fourteenth century, but the title was not hereditary, but rather resulted from the choice of seven electoral princes designated by the emperor Charles IV's 'Golden Bull' of 1356. Only from 1438 were the emperors always Habsburgs, and it took a century after that before the Habsburg heir could assume that he would be chosen emperor. Rudolf of Habsburg (1273–91) had been the first emperor chosen after the demise of the Hohenstaufen dynasty in 1254. From a power base which had originally been in what is now Switzerland, he extended his family's domains in 1282 into the East Mark (Austria), which thereafter became the centre of his family's power. The rivals of the Habsburgs prevented them from establishing a continuously ruling dynasty on the imperial throne, although Habsburg control of Austria was never questioned.

The house of Luxembourg was the Habsburgs' main rival for most of the period between 1346 and 1437, although, interestingly, Habsburg power in 1438 was accomplished by a marriage between the two rival houses. Charles VII of Luxembourg (who was emperor from 1308 to 1313) was a minor prince, but he established the future of his house by marrying the heiress of Bohemia, although their son King John 'the Blind' of Bohemia, who died at the battle of Crécy in 1346, was passed over for the imperial crown because of his youth in 1314. Instead the Luxembourgs supported the Wittelsbach duke Lewis IV of Bavaria, but Frederick of Habsburg contested the election until 1322. Lewis was not a Luxembourg puppet; although the Luxembourgs had claims on the margraviate of Brandenburg, he granted it to his own son. Lewis also extended his family's interests in the

Low Countries by giving Holland and Zeeland to his Luxembourg wife, who already ruled Hainault, when her brother Count William IV died in 1345. Lewis' reign is most noted for his battles with Pope John XXII (1316–34), who refused to recognize his title and declined to crown him emperor during his Italian expedition of 1327–30. The emperor in turn gave sanctuary to the pope's political and ideological opponents.

Tensions eased somewhat after John's death in 1334. In 1338 the Declaration of Rense meant that whoever was chosen by a majority of the electors automatically became emperor, regardless of whether the pope followed it with a coronation. The early 1340s, however, saw problems between Lewis and the other princes. The year before he died in 1347, a bare majority of electors (the three archbishops and the candidate's father) elected Charles of Luxembourg, who agreed with the pope to repeal the Declaration of Rense. Lewis' death simply sealed the deed. Under the Francophile Charles IV (1346–78) and most of his immediate successors, priority was given to the household and dynastic interests of the emperor, while the power of the imperial office continued its decline.

An informal electoral college had been choosing new emperors since the thirteenth century. In 1356 Charles issued the 'Golden Bull', which formalized the seven-member electoral college that had become customary. It consisted of the archbishops of Mainz, Trier and Cologne, and four lay princes: the Count Palatine of the Rhine, the Duke of Saxony, the Margrave of Brandenburg and the King of Bohemia. This group became fixed until the seventeenth century. It excluded the two most powerful lay princes of Germany, the Habsburg dukes of Austria and the Wittelsbach dukes of Bavaria. And it established primogeniture as the basis for succession in the families of the imperial princes, the top level of the hierarchy in Germany, and gave them but not the lesser princes regalian rights, such as control of the mints, mines and the Jews, who were considered imperial serfs. Thus the Golden Bull made possible stronger local government in Germany, below the level of the emperor. Yet this point should not be overemphasized, for numerous knights still held tiny territories in full sovereignty, mainly in the south-west, and the territorial princes were also weakened by the expansion of some city governments into territories beyond their walls.

Charles IV's hopes of extending his family's influence in the west were dashed, but through an eventual tie with the Habsburgs they played a glorious role in central and eastern Europe. He arranged the election of his son Wenceslas (Wenzel) (1378–1400/19) as emperor, but Wenceslas was a drunken incompetent who reversed his father's pro-French policy by marrying his sister Anne to Richard II of England. His Wittelsbach enemies in Bavaria, in turn, saw one of their own become Queen of France. The German electors in 1400 deposed Wenceslas as emperor in favour of the Wittelsbach Rupert, elector of the Palatinate; but he remained king of Bohemia.

The fortunes of the Luxembourg family were preserved by Wenceslas' younger brother Sigismund, whose election as King of Hungary Wenceslas had arranged in 1387 by marrying him to the daughter of King Louis the Great. When Rupert died in 1410, Sigismund was chosen his successor, and he also assumed the crown of Bohemia when Wenceslas died in 1419. Sigismund was in many ways an enlightened ruler. Realizing that the Empire was really a federation, he worked with regional interests to institutionalize the imperial peace. But he became entangled in the Bohemian civil war (see Chapter 4) after 1419. In 1438 Sigismund was succeeded as emperor by his son-in-law, Albert of Habsburg, who in turn was soon succeeded by his son Frederick III (1440–93). The Luxembourg family inheritance thus passed through the female line to the already-powerful Habsburgs.

Frederick III was not highly regarded by contemporaries, but he established his family's fortune by gradually reuniting his family's properties (the Habsburg domains had been split between different branches in 1365). Native dynasts cut short the Habsburgs' hopes of ruling Bohemia and Hungary, but the family was to regain Hungary in the sixteenth century. Most importantly, Frederick III married his son and eventual successor as emperor Maximilian to Mary, daughter and eventual heiress of the last independent duke of Burgundy, Charles the Rash. The descendants of Maximilian and Mary would rule Spain, Hungary and the Low Countries as well as Germany in the sixteenth century.

Switzerland

The mountain cantons of Switzerland had been the original seat of the Habsburgs' power, but the rulers concentrated on Austria after they became its dukes, losing interest and control in Switzerland, although it contained the critical mountain passes to Italy. The later Swiss Confederation takes its name from Schwyz, one of the original three 'forest cantons' that formed an alliance in 1291 and subsequently defeated the Habsburgs at Morgarten in 1315. Three major cities (Lucerne, Zürich and Bern) and two more rural areas had joined by 1353. The cantonal alliance became independent in fact after the Swiss defeated the Habsburgs again at Sempach in 1386, and in law by a concession from the Emperor Maximilian in 1499. Another five cantons had joined by 1513. Although unique among medieval polities as a successful federated state, lacking a strong central authority even in theory, Switzerland was too incoherent a political unit to be a threat to foreign powers. Each community kept its own government, with the Confederation coordinating only foreign and military policy. The confederates fought among themselves, often with urban interests opposing rural ones. The Swiss were the most feared and highly paid mercenary soldiers of Europe in the fifteenth and early

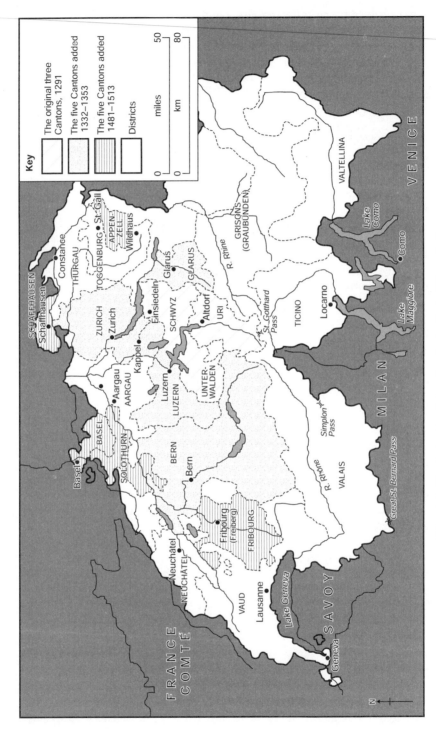

Map 1.3 The Swiss Confederation in the Early Fifteenth Century

sixteenth centuries, with the crossbow and particularly the pike being their weapons of choice. Military changes in Germany made them unnecessary thereafter, and Switzerland's importance became mainly in religion, as the home of Zwingli and the haven of Calvin.

The Hanse

The Hanse of northern cities is the most famous German urban league, but it is atypical in being concerned with economic policy. It had a central Diet (Assembly) that passed resolutions, generally concerning commercial policy and sometimes the military measures needed to enforce them; but these were not binding on the members. Other 'urban' leagues were political creations. They sometimes included knights and princes who were interested in preserving and enforcing the 'public peace' that the emperors proclaimed periodically. They occasionally intervened to stop or prevent disorder in member cities, but they were essentially *ad hoc* alliances for the particular purposes of independent cities.The Saxon League, which also included rural lords, was formally established in 1382 and was periodically renewed. Its members paid their contributions to the league to the three largest cities (Magdeburg, Brunswick and Göttingen), who thus converted their primacy in the League to political advantage. Despite the fact that the emperors disliked the leagues, in 1415 Sigismund tried to link the various urban leagues and lords in a peace association. However, he could not get the leagues to cooperate among themselves, and dissidents in the cities disliked the emperors' reliance on the urban patricians.

Italy

The emperors had possessed little power in Italy since the late thirteenth century, although 'Ghibelline' and 'Guelf' factions that were nominally pro- and anti-imperial respectively disrupted the peace in many north Italian cities. Lombardy and Tuscany were evolving into territorial principalities based on their largest cities, particularly in the case of Lombardy under the Visconti dukes. Small states such as Urbino and Ferrara dotted the central Italian landscape, but the papal state was the dominant power there. In the south the kingdom of Naples, which included Sicily, had risen on the ruins of the empire of Charles of Anjou by 1300. His great-grandson was Louis I the Great, King of Hungary, while another branch of the Angevin house ruled in Naples. For most of the fourteenth and early fifteenth century this structure did not alter fundamentally, save that the absence of the popes in France between 1305 and 1377 created a power vacuum in central Italy.

Naples, the largest city of southern Italy, was an important part of the power struggle between the French and Aragonese. Ladislas of Naples

(1386–1414) tried to re-establish his family's claim to Hungary, which was in Luxembourg hands after 1387. Their control of Naples weakened after his death, and in 1442 Alfonso I 'the Magnanimous' of Aragon, who had ruled Sicily since 1416, took Naples and made it his capital. The Neapolitan crown reverted to Ferdinand of Aragon in 1503. But the Hungarian branch of the Angevins had produced Marie, who married Charles VII of France (1422–61) and became the mother of King Louis XI and grandmother of King Charles VIII, who thus claimed the title of king of Naples in 1494.

Northern Italy was dominated by the great city-states. Each of them continued to consolidate power over its *contado* (the rural environs that had been subordinated legally and economically to the city), but each was also feeling pressure from foreign powers. The chronic disorder of the north Italian cities was yielding to despotisms in the fourteenth and fifteenth centuries, generally a dynasty that had originated in the city itself. The process began with the smaller places, most of which were still closely tied to the rural nobility, as in the early Middle Ages. The Della Scala family of Verona and the Este of Ferrara had begun as city officials in the thirteenth century, then had gradually subverted republican institutions while keeping the form of the choking network of councils and bureaucracy that had characterized Italian urban government during the central Middle Ages.

Milan was the earliest of the large north Italian cities in which a despot took power and transmitted it to descendants. Giangaleazzo's Visconti [Viscounts] family had been archbishops of the city in the thirteenth century and thereafter were recognized as vicars of Milan by the emperors. The Visconti established separate capitals at Pavia and Milan in 1359. Giangaleazzo Visconti of Pavia in 1382 captured his kinsmen and ruled thenceforth from Milan. He quickly expanded Milanese territory, and was threatening Venice and Florence when he died unexpectedly in 1402. The power vacuum was only ended when Filippo Maria Visconti took power in 1412.

The Milanese example illustrates a theme of late medieval politics that is sometimes overlooked: although the Holy Roman Emperor had little real power, he still had immense prestige and could confer titles that might legitimize a usurpation after the fact. Obviously the emperors could appoint imperial vicars; but since dukes were also under them in dignity in a status- and symbol-conscious age, Borso d'Este, whose family had been ruling Ferrara for years, was recognized as duke of Modena and Reggio by Frederick III in 1452. In marrying his daughter to Maximilian, son of the emperor Frederick III, Charles the Bold of Burgundy hoped to curry favour with the emperor that would lead him to recognize Charles as a king rather than simply as duke.

The other Italian powers had acted in concert against Giangaleazzo Visconti, and did so again when Ladislas seemed about to impose a Neapolitan hegemony over the rest of Italy before he died prematurely in 1414. In response first to Giangaleazzo and then to Ladislas, Venice for the first time established power over a mainland *contado* by taking Padua,Vicenza and Verona in 1405. Florence, after controlling most of Tuscany in fact for several centuries, finished the job by annexing Pisa, Siena and Pistoia formally. Foreign threats continued: the French ruled Genoa, which alone of the great north Italian cities lacked a large *contado*, between 1396 and 1409. Genoa, whose internecine quarrels were notorious even for Italy, then fell to Milan in 1421, was ruled again by the French between 1458 and 1464, then finally again by Milan.

Venice managed to preserve its republican institutions. The doge (duke) of Venice was a figurehead, although one who directed considerable patronage to his family and presided over the all-important city ceremonies. Real control in the city was exercised by an oligarchy of families in the Great Council whose names were inscribed in a 'Golden Book', which was closed in 1297 except for the addition of 30 families after 1381; they were being rewarded for their service in Venice's long war with its commercial and overseas political rival, Genoa, that ended successfully in that year. A Senate of noble families and the Ten, a committee of public safety, handled most ordinary policy. The Venetian oligarchy was less restricted than has been thought, however, for the title of 'noble' extended to all families in the Golden Book as supplemented, and the reduction of population after 1348 had actually created a situation in which a relatively broad oligarchy ruled the town. Not all the Venetian nobles had financial resources that matched the social pretensions that their distinguished ancestry imposed on them, and some actually depended on the profits of state office to support themselves. But after a conspiracy was quashed in 1355 there was no threat to the independence of Venice's republic or republican institutions.

Florence was ruled by a tumultuous oligarchy but, except in 1343 when the duke of Athens Walter of Brienne briefly became war captain, the city avoided one-man rule until the fifteenth century. Florence was ruled by a complicated system by which persons of sufficient wealth and appropriate political affiliation and lineage were eligible to be chosen by lot to one of the numerous city councils. In practice prominent families used their private wealth and, when possible, the resources of the Florentine state to build up clienteles as they jockeyed for power. The strain of intermittent warfare with Milan, the other major land-based power of northern Italy, was exacerbated by the lack of a satisfactory tax base until 1427, when the regime agreed to a direct tax, the famous *Catasto*. In 1434, however, Cosimo de' Medici managed to get control of the councils of the city and banish his major rivals. Although Cosimo did not hold major offices himself, he operated skilfully behind the scenes and controlled elections, using his family's financial resources to extend its political influence, as was customary for princes of this time. He ruled much less obtrusively than some of his contemporaries. His short-lived son, Piero, managed only to hand power on to his own son Lorenzo 'the Magnificent' (who ruled from 1469 to 1492); he played the prince and, concerned with patronizing the intellectuals who have immortalized his name, neglected both Florence's diplomatic position and his own family's banking interests.

The rise of despots was thus tied to various considerations, including internal faction, threats from outside and the inability of local governments to resist foreign armies. The shift from the feudal levy in the north and the volunteer force or – in the case of the cities of both Italy and the north – the citizen militia, to the use of professional soldiers by all parties was as revolutionary in Italy as in the northern monarchies. Citizen militias were no longer trained and armed to the point where they could fight effectively against professional soldiers. The Italian cities began supplementing their militias with mercenaries in the thirteenth century. The most notorious were the English and French mercenary soldiers of the popes and their opponents, who, unemployed after the peace of Brétigny, devastated central Italy in the 1360s and 1370s. But thereafter the cities and princes generally used native Italian *condottieri*, military captains who contracted with a government to provide and generally lead troops. The most successful was Francesco Sforza, who abandoned his family name, Attendolo, in favour of the nickname Sforza, meaning 'Force'. He made himself indispensable to duke Filippo Maria Visconti of Milan, married his daughter and heiress, and in 1450 simply assumed the title of duke of Milan himself.

The Italian City-State System

During the great age of the *condottieri*, the late fourteenth and early fifteenth centuries, the five great powers of Italy were consolidating and enlarging their states at the expense of the smaller ones. Cosimo de' Medici's diplomacy created the basis for a kind of Italian state system with the peace of Lodi of 1454. Cosimo made peace with Francesco Sforza of Milan, ending Florence's long hostility with the Milanese, and convinced the Venetians to accept the legitimacy of Sforza's regime. From this time the northern Italian powers tended to be allied uneasily against those in the south: Naples, and a papal state that had become powerful again after 1417. Until the French invaded Italy in 1494, the peninsula would enjoy a period of peace broken only by Florence's war with Pope Sixtus VI in 1478 and a war of Venice against Milan and Naples over Ferrara in the 1480s.

Western Europe Under Siege: Turks, Mongols and Slavs

While except for Italy, Switzerland and the Netherlands, national monarchies – or units that would eventually turn into them – characterized western Europe, the German and Slavic East knew the enormous but loosely structured monarchies of Poland–Lithuania, the heir in a certain sense of the state that the Teutonic Order had established in the thirteenth century, and Bohemia. Farther east, the Russian state was evolving out of the grand duchy of Moscow, while on the south-eastern frontier of Europe a resurgent Byzantine Empire yielded, in the fifteenth century, to the inexorable advance of the Ottoman Turks. The relations of Europeans with the cultures on their peripheries is obviously critical to our understanding of the expansion of European interests and culture in the Atlantic that becomes so obvious after 1390 and especially 1420.

Westerners had colonized Slavic Europe since the early Middle Ages, intermarrying with the local aristocracies and becoming the dominant element in many town patriciates. Developments in the east were intruding increasingly into westerners' calculations after 1300. Part of this was a concern with religion and security: Hungary was the frontier against the Turkish threat in the south and east, while Poland was the buttress against the northward expansion of Lithuania, and against the Mongols who occupied most of Russia. Somewhat later Lithuania, now Christianized, became a frontier against Russian expansion into Estonia and Livonia. Economic ties quickened as the west became increasingly dependent on imported raw materials from eastern Europe. The Baltic trade dominated by the German Hanse was complemented by an increasingly active trade westward from Poland and the south-east. Royal dynasties that originated in western Europe also ruled much of eastern Europe in the late Middle Ages: members of the French house of Anjou and the imperial house of Luxembourg and their successors, the Habsburgs, occupied the strategically important throne of Hungary.

The Byzantine Empire

The eastern or Greek Orthodox church had been separated from the Roman church of western Europe since 1054. Although eastern and western Christendom cooperated on occasion against the Muslims, relations between them were uneasy, and Constantinople was seized and sacked by the knights of the Fourth Crusade in 1204. A Latin Kingdom was established there, but it faced both frontier problems and internal resistance from the Greeks. In 1261 the Paleologus dynasty assumed the imperial throne as leaders of a coalition of Greek princes, but the power of the emperors was never restored securely. The revived empire was much smaller than its predecessor, consisting of north-western Asia Minor, parts of Thrace and Macedonia and scattered islands and territories in mainland Greece. While the empire before 1204 had had provincial governors who reported to the emperor, members of the imperial family were now granted 'despotates' that were similar to the *apanages* of the western princes, whose rivalries made it difficult for the empire to function internally.

Charles of Anjou, the younger brother of King Louis IX (1226–70) of France, had established a state based on southern Italy and Sicily that was in serious disarray from native resistance by the time of his death in 1285. Although Charles encouraged a crusade against the resurgent Greek and accordingly, in western eyes, heretical Empire in Constantinople, the emperor Michael VIII warded off the danger by capitalizing on hostility in the west toward the Angevins and dangling the prospect of unification of the churches before the pope's eyes. The Angevin claims ultimately passed to Naples, which lacked the strength to realize them; and interest in a crusade shifted from the Greeks toward the Turks, who were now perceived as the far greater threat.

The Ottoman Turks

Various groups of Turks had disrupted the security of the Byzantine Empire for centuries. The Ottoman Turks took their name from Osman, who ruled an emirate in Asia Minor in the early fourteenth century. They had ejected the Byzantines from Asia Minor by 1326, and court quarrels at Constantinople after 1341 weakened the Greeks still further. The Turks still did not attack the eastern Mediterranean aggressively, perhaps to avoid striking directly at the commercial and territorial interests of Italian city governments and individual families on mainland Greece and the islands.

Thus the Turks traded with the Italians, who were considerably better navigators than they were until the fifteenth century, and fought the Byzantines in the Balkans. Osman's troops in 1345 crossed into Thrace, the first penetration of Europe by the Turks. By 1356 Constantinople was virtually isolated from the west. Murad I (1362–89), the first of his line to assume the title of Sultan, took Adrianople in Thrace in 1369. He was killed at Kosovo in 1389, but the Turks won the battle when his son Bayezid I (1389–1405) took command. Bayezid imposed direct rule over the Balkans, as Murad had not done, and laid siege to Constantinople.

Hungary, allied by marriage with the Luxembourg dynasty of Bohemia from 1387, was now the chief bulwark in Europe against the Turks. The efforts of King Sigismund of Hungary (1387–1437) to get help from the west for a crusade materialized in an enormous French and Burgundian force that was crushed at Nicopolis in 1396. Many prominent persons were killed, while others were held for enormous ransoms, like John of Nevers, heir to the duchy of Burgundy.

The failure of the Turks to capitalize on Nicopolis to penetrate further into Europe was due to a threat from the east. The Mongol Timur 'the Lame' (Tamerlane) had reconstituted the empire of Genghis Khan. He defeated the Turks at Ankara in 1402 and held Bayezid I captive until his death. The westerners seem to have thought that the Mongols could be

Christianized, and actually tried to interest them in a crusade against the Muslims. Turkish Muslims and Latin Christians alike were saved when Timur returned east. His empire disintegrated after his death in 1405.

Bayezid's realm was divided among his three sons, but was reunited under Sultan Mehmed I (1413–21), who campaigned mainly in Anatolia and the Balkans. Murad II (1421–51) consolidated his predecessors' conquests. The Turkish threat to the Balkans became worse after Sigismund's death in 1437, but the governor of Transylvania, John Hunyadi, defeated the Turks in 1442 by using firearms; then the Turks started using them. This success led to a revival of interest in the crusade to help Constantinople and the Hungarians. John V (1341–91) had been the first Byzantine emperor who tried to get military help from western Europe by promising reunion of the eastern and western churches. Manuel II (1391–1425) made more serious overtures, and his successor John VIII (1425–48) agreed in 1439 to a reunification of the Latin and Greek churches. But the Patriarch of Constantinople denounced this heresy, and the late emperors thus faced a rearguard action at home that undercut the only diplomatic effort abroad that might have saved them. The military situation continued to deteriorate. The Hungarians and a papal force were defeated at Varna in 1444; thereafter, with the further defeat of Hunyadi at Kosovo in 1448, the Ottomans occupied Wallachia and the entire area south of the Danube. The only successful resistance in the area was from George Scanderbeg in Albania.

Sultan Mehmed II (1451–81) was generally underestimated at first in the west. In 1453 the Turks took Constantinople, an event that shocked the west and led to new efforts to call a crusade. By 1460 Mehmed had occupied the Morea, and the Greek Empire of Trebizond on the Black Sea, the last Greek outpost in the east, was lost in 1461. Mehmed II made Constantinople his capital; but although Islamic law required him to allow his troops to sack the city for a day, he tried to repopulate it with Greeks and generally respected their religious traditions. Even so, Constantinople's population was predominantly Muslim by 1477. The Byzantine empire had become effectively Turkish. Although the Danube frontier was stabilizing, the Turks had new successes elsewhere. It was only Mehmed II's premature death in 1481 that gave the western powers a brief respite.

The Germans and the Slavic East

In eastern Europe the period from 1300 to 1450 saw the decline in power of the Teutonic Knights, together with the rise of Poland as a recognizable and western-leaning political entity. From the 1230s the Teutonic Knights, the third of the great crusading orders, had disengaged from the Mediterranean and Palestine and crusaded against the Slavs in eastern Europe. Before 1300 the Knights had established a state in Prussia that was nominally a vassal state of Poland, and from this base they fought the Russians and helped Livonia against Lithuania. That the Lithuanians were pagan gave a crusading rationale for the activity of the Teutonic Order in this 'other Hundred Years War'. The Lithuanians invaded Poland 16 times between 1250 and 1325, but Prussia and Livonia blocked their expansion to the Baltic. The forested terrain made campaigning difficult and prolonged the conflict. The Order had too few brethren, at most 1,500, to fight the Lithuanians alone; it could not count on help from its nominal overlord, Poland, which was just as hostile to the Order as to the Lithuanians. Thus the Order recruited soldiers in Germany and to a lesser extent France and England.

Poland was a more serious threat to the Teutonic Order than Lithuania was. In 1308 the Order seized eastern Pomerelia from Poland. By mid-century the Poles were directing their attention eastward, forcing Lithuania to cede most of Ruthenia in 1366. Poland emerged as a great power during the reign of Casimir III 'the Great' (1333–70), but with his death the succession was clouded, passing initially to his nephew, King Louis of Hungary. When Louis died in 1382, his daughter Mary (Jadwiga/Hedwig) succeeded to both thrones. The Polish nobles were willing to recognize her only if she ruled in Poland alone. The marriage of Jadwiga of Poland and Jagiełło of Lithuania in 1386 in theory created an enormous state that was a threat to the Teutonic Order, not only by linking resources, but also because the baptism of Jagiełło as Władysław and his promise to convert his subjects brought to an end whatever crusading rationale the Order's battle with Lithuania had had. Władysław remained king in Poland after Jadwiga died in 1399. Although he remained Grand Duke in Lithuania, he yielded real power there to his cousin Witold. Relations with the Teutonic Knights remained unsettled, but by 1408 it was clear that Władysław would support Witold against the Order in Lithuania.

In 1410 the Poles and Lithuanians defeated the Teutonic Order disastrously at Tannenberg. Thereafter the Knights' position declined sharply. Faced with rural depression and depopulation in Prussia, the Order became even more oppressive and increased labour services on peasants. The cities of Prussia also declined; this was especially serious, since the Order had gained much of its money from the sale of grain to the west. The Order, as a monastic group, had not struck firm roots, and both the towns and nobles were complaining, by the fifteenth century, about the Knights' unwillingness to fight personally and about high taxes and constant warfare. A Union of Prussian nobles was founded in 1440 which became involved in war with the Order in 1454, encouraged by Poland. The Union offered the lordship of Prussia to Casimir IV of Poland, who in turn made extensive concessions to the Prussian Estates and held out the prospect that Poland's now-booming export trade would go through the Prussian cities. The Knights' fortress headquarters, the Marienburg, was lost in 1457, and they moved their capital to Königsberg in East Prussia. In 1466 the

Peace of Thorn returned Pomerelia to Poland; the Order kept Königsberg and East Prussia. In 1525 the last Grand Master of the Teutonic Order, Albert of Brandenburg, a member of the Hohenzollern family, became a Lutheran and was invested as Duke of Prussia by King Sigismund I of Poland.

Russia

Poles, Lithuanians, Teutonic Knights and Swedes all at various times fought the Mongols who still controlled most of Russia, and for most of the fourteenth century they, rather than the grand dukes of Moscow, seemed to be carrying most of the burden. Alliances were not invariably along ethnic, let alone religious lines; the Lithuanians took most of the Ukraine from the Mongols in 1362, but then joined the Mongols against the Muscovites. The sharp decline of Mongol power in Russia in the late fourteenth century gave the grand dukes their opportunity, but they also had to fight the Lithuanians in the north and west. Grand dukes Basil I (1389–1425) and Basil II (1425–62), despite problems during the latter's minority, cemented an alliance with the eastern orthodox church, the Russian princes and the gentry. Until the late fifteenth century most contact between Russia and western Europe had been economic, through the trade of the Hanse outpost at Novgorod. The first of the grand dukes of Moscow who had significant diplomatic relations with the west, Ivan III 'the Great' (1462–1505), seized Novgorod and stopped paying tribute to the Mongols. By marrying the niece of the last Byzantine emperor, he implicitly claimed that he was the heir of the defunct eastern Roman empire. Court intellectuals began writing of Moscow as the 'third Rome', succeeding the original and Constantinople. His grandson Ivan IV ('the Terrible') assumed the title of tsar (Caesar – emperor) in 1547.

*   *   *

The fourteenth century witnessed virtually constant discord in western Europe. As armies became professionalized and paid, the need of states for more revenue from their subjects increased dramatically. This is less true of the east, where armies were smaller and campaigning more intermittent due to the climate. England had a strong monarchy by 1200, even if the dynasty was hardly English, but its basis was the legislative and judicial authority of a king who was generally able to pay his expenses from revenues of his family domains and the incomes that he enjoyed as regalian right, such as the profits of mines, tolls and fees owed when he authorized an individual or group to do something that was technically at his own disposal. The strain on the king's financial resources even in England was becoming evident during the thirteenth century, however, and it became insupportable during the fourteenth. The French monarchy ruled a less coherent territory than the English and was supported by a less unitary institutional structure for generating revenue, even on the king's domains. The Spanish kingdoms were occupied with expansion southward against the Muslims in the thirteenth century, and it is thus no coincidence that assemblies with revenue-granting functions developed earlier in Iberia than in the northern kingdoms. The rising expenses, occasioned by the wars of the late Middle Ages, and the institutional measures taken to meet them, were the catalyst for the development of the modern bureaucratic state.

2

Of Nations and States: The Institutions of Government

The Beginnings of the Secular Institutional State

Government as we understand the term today developed during the three centuries after 1300 in western Europe. The best examples of precocious institutionalization are England, where the process was well under way before 1200, France and, to a lesser degree, the Iberian kingdoms. Several territorial principalities also developed strong governing institutions before 1450, particularly in the Low Countries, and the process spread to some German states in the sixteenth century. In several of the provinces that eventually made up France, local customs gave rise to legal and, to some extent, judicial and financial particularism, but rarely did this process become as thorough as with the monarchies. In the German and Slavic East most functions of government devolved to the local level, and in places without strong cities this meant the rural nobility. Princely government there became significantly institutional only in the modern period.

The progressive nationalization of kingship in the late Middle Ages was accompanied by the institutionalizing of monarchy. The Germanic law codes of the early Middle Ages made the king the law-finder, responsible for ascertaining the time-honoured oral customs of the folk and, from the sixth century on, committing them to writing. Even as early as the seventh century, however, King Wihtred of Kent noted that he was in fact a lawmaker, taking those of his predecessors' laws that pleased him, omitting those that did not, and adding some of his own. European law thus had a substantial customary element that weakened in the late Middle Ages but was never obliterated. Nowhere could a custom become a statute unless the king had indicated his approval of it by issuing it, usually in at least perfunctory consultation with his council of advisors. Until the composition of the council was formalized as the 'tenants-in-chief' (those who held fiefs directly from the king rather than indirectly of him from another lord), until they ceased accompanying the king on his travels and until their right to participate in issuing legislation was made statutory as opposed merely to being desirable, law was in principle the king's responsibility.

Legislation is obviously tied to the judicial function of the state. If the king can use a network of courts to punish violations of the laws that he issues, his position is strengthened immeasurably. But while lawgiving is a function of kingship, holding courts is not. From this perspective the English kings had powers by 1300 that were much more extensive than those of continental rulers. The English kings had distinguished 'pleas of the crown' by the early Norman period as matters over which royal courts had original jurisdiction, which amounted to most criminal actions in the modern sense. The extension of pleas of the crown was accompanied in the twelfth century by the establishment of circuit courts responsible to the king. But even pleas of the crown required a complaint to get them into the royal court, for there was no *ex officio* prosecution. All lords, including the kings, exercised civil jurisdiction over dependents on their domains. Unfree persons, not a large group by 1300 except in England and the German and Slavic East, were automatically judged in their lords' courts. In addition, King Henry II (1154–89) made available 'assizes' and writs for litigants to purchase that, in effect, required the franchisal court to do as the initiator of the action wanted, or have his reason for refusing to do so heard in the royal court. By 1200 the English royal courts normally handled, in the modern sense, all criminal and land cases.

But even as late as 1300, only in England did the king exercise justice in large parts of his realm outside the royal domain, the areas that he owned personally. The French kings claimed the right by Louis VII's time (1137–80) to legislate for all of France, but they lacked an enforcement mechanism to give effect to their statutes outside their domains. The French royal domain was very small as late as 1180, but was dramatically increased in size with the annexation of English-held territory in the thirteenth century. The French king ruled his domain through a network of provosts (purely domain officials) and bailiffs and seneschals (who, like the English sheriffs, combined financial functions in the domain with holding public courts). Each of the great crown fiefs had its separate financial institutions as well as courts that escaped the monarchy's control. There was no mechanism comparable to the English assizes that transferred civil actions from seigniorial courts to the royal court.

The fourteenth century was the defining moment in the development of the bureaucratic state. In England the creation of permanent institutions that allowed government functions to continue even when the king was absent or incompetent tended to limit the power of the monarchy in favour of groups of subjects. In France and Spain, by contrast, the institutionalization of royal government had taken the contrary course even before 1450, giving the rulers a tool that could preserve autocracy beyond the lifetime of the individual ruler.

The very nature of monarchical power was changing in the late Middle Ages. While in earlier times the king had gained and held power from land-holding and the use of land for patronage and income, royal authority depended in the fourteenth century on the extent to which he could still make laws without involving other persons or groups, whether he had to get consent for taxes that he levied outside his own domain, and, to a much lesser degree, the extent to which he could divert the local emoluments of the increasingly sophisticated trading and financial networks into his coffers.

Well into the thirteenth century the kings were generally able to live off their domain incomes, mainly rents and judicial fines, supplemented by payments owed by their tenants-in-chief but not by other subjects. These sources were generally sufficient to run the limited institutions of royal government in peacetime, but they were inadequate to pay for wars. Louis IX (1226–70) had to borrow immense sums from Italian bankers and exact extraordinary aids from his subjects to pay for his fruitless crusades. By the last quarter of the thirteenth century, the growing hostilities between England and France and the English activities in Wales and Scotland forced kings to seek more effective ways both to collect extraordinary aids from their vassals and to get money from other subjects who were not their direct vassals: the clergy, the lesser nobles and the townspeople.

One approach to the cash-flow problem was to try to equate subject and vassal in law. While only vassals were obliged to render mounted military services for their lords, all subjects were bound to take arms to defend the homeland. Thus Philip IV of France tried in the 1290s to collect an aid from all his subjects in lieu of requiring them to fight personally against the English. English legists of the thirteenth century, notably Henry Bracton, argued that all franchises were ultimately derived from the king: thus from 1278 holders of private courts were required to prove 'by what warrant' they held them. From this the conclusion was logical that if all franchises are ultimately royal, all land was fief held of the king, and thus transfers of land should occur in the royal court, and the king was owed the various feudal incidents (such as relief – that is, inheritance duty – a fee for permission to alienate the fief or wardship over minor heirs) whenever such an action took place. In 1290 Edward ended subinfeudation by statute, which over time meant that lords between the king and the actual possessors of land simply dropped out of the hierarchy. By the time of Henry VII (1485–1509), the king was in effect the lord of most land in England. Yet even in England some private courts remained until 1536.

The Development of Representative Institutions

The Evolution of the English Parliament

Magna Carta (1215) had required the king to obtain the assent of his council of tenants-in-chief before he collected any 'extraordinary' aid (that is, aid beyond the feudal payments). The term 'Parliament' was first used for a parley or meeting of the king's great council in 1239 by the chronicler Matthew Paris. Parliaments were common enough by 1258 for the Provisions of Oxford to require King Henry III to summon three a year, a demand never enforced. The earliest Parliaments were thus sessions of the king's council, but sometimes they were supplemented by persons not on the council who presented petitions to it. In 1254 for the first time Henry III summoned the knights of the shire, landholders who were not his tenants-in-chief, to a Parliament, and in 1265 representatives of the boroughs. Although they were sometimes called thereafter, their presence remained somewhat exceptional until the 1320s. All parliaments heard petitions from persons who were not on the council, and as late as the fifteenth century parliament records kept the distinction between petitioners (the Commons) and respondents (the Lords).

Most Parliaments in the late thirteenth century did not vote financial aid to the king. Yet the wars of the English against France and Scotland so strained the resources of the monarchy that Parliament, which until then had been essentially a judicial assembly, had to develop some financial functions. The change becomes clear in the 1290s, when foreign complications intensified the domestic problems of both France and England. Edward I had to call many more Parliaments than his father, and for the first time began using them not only to hear petitions, but also to gain approval of money grants. Between 1275 and 1290 extraordinary aids were approved in three Parliaments, but the king thereafter took several without gaining consent.

Resentment over direct taxation, combined with the unhappiness of lords whose ancestral rights were limited by Edward I's statutes, boiled over, and in 1297 Edward I had to concede the 'Confirmation of the Charters', in which he agreed that for extraordinary taxation he had to get the consent of the 'greater part of the community' of the kingdom. Furthermore, an extra-ordinary aid from feudal vassals is not the same thing as a national tax. At this time royal taxation for some purpose other than national emergency, most often war, was so unusual that in 1297 the nobles who forced the Confirmation of the Charters on the king said that they feared that Edward's taxation might 'be turned into a servile obligation for them and their heirs because these [payments] may at a future time be found in the rolls', for liability to a payment over which one had no control was the mark of a serf. Thus the king conceded the principle that such taxes were not given in perpetuity and had to be reapproved by the appropriate body each time they were to be collected. In the context this apparently meant the Parliament. Thereafter many, although not most, Parliaments handled financial matters; all continued to handle petitions. A petition, once approved by the Council and the King, was law. Although Parliament did not attach conditions that the king redress stated grievances to money grants until the reign of Edward III, the king's right to issue statutes unilaterally was ended by 1300. Lawmaking required the consent of Parliament.

Corporatism and Representation

Royal and princely governments before 1200 consisted of the king and individual persons whom he employed or consulted, either out of inclination or necessity. More persons were becoming involved in government after 1250, although to see the evolution of the state in the late Middle Ages in terms of a democratizing process is a gross distortion even for England. The change includes some expansion of the numbers of persons who participated directly in government, but it consisted even more of numbers of people who participated through representatives. The development of corporations, which is one result of the revival of Roman law in medieval Europe, is fundamental to the birth of the modern institutional state. A corporation is a group of persons who can function as a unit before the law just as individuals can, bringing and answering suits, holding property and participating in public life. When the king was essentially the chief feudal overlord, he operated the government by acting directly with individuals, his vassals, and through them with their vassals and other dependents. The feudal relationship still dominated government in northern Europe in 1200, but it was seriously weakened by 1300. Monarchs still dealt with the great nobles as individuals, but they interacted with towns, villages, the lesser nobility and, in some contexts, entire social groups as corporations. The spread of the Roman legal notion of procuration, by which a group designates a proctor to act on its behalf and is bound by that person's actions, was a precondition to the participation of corporations in national government. Curiously, this develops in England earlier than on the Continent; thus, in 1295, Edward I summoned representatives 'with full and sufficient authority on behalf of themselves and the community' that sent them.

Just as the English Parliament was unusual in combining a right to legislate and a right to vote taxes, so its social composition has no parallel on the Continent. Knights and burgesses attended only 4 of 30 parliaments held between 1272 and 1297, but they attended 3 of the 7 called between 1307 and 1310 and all but 2 between 1310 and 1327. Most meetings of Parliament had a bicameral structure by 1327. The great lords, who were summoned individually, were almost entirely laymen by this time. They met separately from the Commons, although the name 'House of Lords' was not used until the sixteenth century. The two representative elements, two knights from each shire and two burgesses from each place designated as a 'borough', generally met together by 1327, although they occasionally still had separate assemblies. Their presence was thus normal, although not absolutely essential, to the Parliament by 1327. The knights and burgesses were presenting petitions jointly in Edward II's period, and they met together in the 1330s to debate royal requests for taxes.

The fact that the knights, the lesser aristocracy, met with the townsmen is a feature of the English Parliament that distinguishes it sharply from most continental assemblies. The two houses did not have equal power: the Lords heard petitions presented by the Commons, and many members of the Commons were clients of the great nobles who sat in the Lords by hereditary right. In 1429 the right to vote in county elections was limited to freeholders whose land was worth 40s. per year, thus disenfranchising most lesser landholders from participating in the choice of knights of the shire. There was nothing comparable for the boroughs, but their representatives were chosen by increasingly oligarchic city councils, with the result that Parliament remained quite aristocratic. Realizing that knights had more real influence than themselves, town governments often sent knights to Parliament; and since the gentry whom they favoured were often retainers of the lords, the great lords dominated the Commons *de facto* as they did the Lords *de jure*. Although they sat with the burgesses, the knights frequently conferred with their patron lords during meetings of Parliament.

The English Parliament is also exceptional in not being based on the principle of 'Estates' in the sense of legally defined social classes, although some parliamentary records do refer to Estates. After the 1290s the great prelates, who were the first Estate in most Continental assemblies, dropped out of the English parliament and voted taxes for the king in a separate assembly called Convocation. The lower clergy, too, no longer attended Parliament after 1332, and did not become involved in secular legislation. While on the Continent the greater and lesser nobility were merged into a single group, the second estate, in England the greater nobility was defined as the 'parliamentary peerage' who enjoyed the right to individual summonses to Parliament. The lesser nobility, really an aristocracy, sat not as individuals but as representatives of shires.

Parliament was growing stronger during Edward II's reign. An extraordinarily restrictive coronation oath imposed on him in 1308 required him to abide by laws determined by the community of the realm. The Ordinances of 1311 placed the king under the supervision of a baronial committee and required that two Parliaments be called yearly. Yet it does not seem to have occurred to the embattled king that he could dispense with Parliament, which by now was an integral part of his government. In 1322, when Edward had defeated his opponents and was at the height of his power, he issued the Statute of York, which required that the great affairs of the realm 'be considered, granted and established by our lord the king and with the consent of the prelates, earls, and barons, and of the community of the kingdom'.[1] A statute of 1330 ordered annual parliaments; and while this remained a dead letter, they were summoned frequently in the early stages of the Hundred Years War, because of the need for taxes. Most meetings were short, lasting two to three weeks.

The Incidence and Nature of Royal Taxation

Although the English and French had known that a war was coming, the events leading up to 1340 caused crises for which both governments were unprepared. The war meant virtually annual taxation in England, and changed Parliament into an institution that was at least as important for money as for petitions. The financial leverage of Parliament was used in the early stages of the Hundred Years War to strengthen its role in statute-making. In 1341–2 Edward III, faced with a threat that it would refuse to vote a war aid, agreed to stop annulling by administrative ordinances statutes previously passed by Parliament and assented to by the king. Parliament had its own speaker by 1376, and by the late 1390s was claiming the right of free speech for its members; it impeached some of Richard II's councillors, and was strong enough to participate in deposing him in 1399.

Most parliamentary taxation from Edward II's time onwards was the 'lay subsidy', most often one-tenth of the movable property of burgesses and one-fifteenth of that of free residents of the shires. A quota system was superimposed on this in 1334: all parliamentary taxes were supposed to return £37,429/18/1/2d. If more was needed, an additional subsidy was voted; and when the population fell after 1349, per capita taxation thus rose.[2] The wealthy obviously paid more under this arrangement than the poor. The poll or head tax, involving a set amount per person, favoured the wealthy and also had servile connotations under the law that taxes based on property did not. Thus Richard II's government aroused a storm of opposition by levying three poll taxes in the four years after 1377, the agitation culminating in the Peasants' Rebellion of 1381. Parliament went back to percentage taxes on movable property thereafter, and from that point only the percentage varied, not the principle.

No annual budget was possible until the distinction beween 'ordinary' (domain) and 'extraordinary' (parliamentary or 'lay' subsidies) income receded into insignificance in the late sixteenth century. Parliament and the king sparred over whether he could levy indirect taxes, the most lucrative of which were the customs on imports and exports, without the consent of Parliament. Technically the amount of the wool subsidy was in Parliament's hands after 1356, but in fact Edward III levied it unilaterally until 1362, when he accepted the principle that they required parliamentary consent. From the period of Richard II, however, Parliament sometimes voted customs to the king for life at the beginning of his reign.

In principle taxes were supposed to be used to meet emergencies, while the ordinary expenses of government were to be defrayed from the resources of the royal domain. Accordingly, peacetime taxation caused adverse comment. But, particularly after 1350, central and local governments alike invested considerable money in conspicuous consumption. They bought increasingly exotic and luxurious goods, and staged public festivals of a highly symbolic nature, as these were considered an important aspect of building loyalty to regimes. The best examples are the cult of the monarchy in France, which received new impetus from the veneration of Charlemagne that was fostered even more by the Valois than by the Capetians, and particularly the 'theatre state' of the Burgundian dukes in the Low Countries in the fifteenth century. The fact that taxation was still nearly annual during the largely peaceful reign of Richard II, combined with the luxurious lives of such potentates as John of Gaunt, doubtless explains much of the public discontent during his reign.

Parliament reached the apogee of its power before the seventeenth century in the reign of Henry IV (1399–1413). Plagued both by an uncertain royal title and less 'ordinary' (not granted by Parliament) revenue than Richard II had enjoyed, Henry agreed in 1406 to nominate his councillors in Parliament and govern with their advice. This was later withdrawn, but in 1407 Henry made a concession that did last: money bills had to originate in the House of Commons. During the minority of Henry VI (1422–61) the Commons began introducing petitions that were framed in the exact language of the statutes that they became when the king had assented.

Yet Parliament had a potentially fatal weakness: it could not meet unless the king summoned it. If he needed neither money nor the approval of statutes, he had no reason to call Parliament. It met 151 times during the fourteenth century, obviously sometimes several times a year, but there were entire years when no Parliament met. There were only 92 Parliaments, however, between 1390 and 1530, and all but 20 of them met before 1461. While Richard II's 22-year reign (1377–99) saw 25 Parliaments, Edward IV's 22-year reign (1461–83) saw six. Parliament thus was meeting less frequently after the military and financial emergency of the Hundred Years War.[3] Thus, while its powers in lawmaking were no longer questioned, its financial importance declined in the late fifteenth century. Kings issued ordinances when Parliament was not in session, sometimes obtaining its ratification of them as statutes later, when they had to call Parliament into session. But the kings only summoned Parliament when they needed money; and as non-parliamentary resources became more available to the kings after Edward IV and Henry VII (1485–1509) in effect reconstituted the royal domain, the crown did not need to levy annual taxation except during

Henry VIII's wars in the sixteenth century and, more regularly, under Elizabeth. Thus the distinction between ordinary (domain and regalian-right) and extraordinary (taxation) income remained important in England long after it had receded into insignificance in France.

The Estates-General in France

In France, as in England, the basis of the king's authority was initially dual: in a material sense through his domain, and in a legal and moral sense as legislator. The king was the only lay prince who received the anointing that gave divine sanction to his rule and made disobedience to him sacrilege. This ideology went much farther in France than in England, particularly from the fourteenth century onwards. The 'thaumaturgical king' could cure scrofula, and particularly from the period of King Charles V (1364–80) the king as embodiment of the nation and descendant of ancestors real and mythical was consciously cultivated.

While in England the legislative power of the king became circumscribed by Parliament, this did not happen in France, where royal ordinances and 'establishments' had the force of law throughout the entire realm including the *apanages*, and not only on the royal domain. The English distinction between ordinance as an administrative use and statute as a binding law did not exist in France. Both the English Parliament and the French *parlement* began as courts, but the French institution remained purely judicial except that the *parlement* of Paris, the chief court of the royal domain, could refuse to record a royal act that it considered contrary to custom; and by 1450 the king could circumvent even this limited power.

Like the English kings, the French monarchs had to devise new sources of 'extraordinary' income in the late thirteenth century to supplement the 'ordinary' income from their domain; but unlike their English relatives, by 1450 they had escaped virtually all taxpayer constraints on the invention, collection and disbursement of taxes. Philip IV (1285–1314) levied repeated tithes on the French clergy, often using the income for war expenses after 1284. Pope Boniface VIII in 1296 issued a bull forbidding payment of clerical taxes to secular rulers without the pope's permission, but it was quickly withdrawn. While the English coin remained stable, the French kings severely debased theirs, giving them the opportunity to repay the face value of debts in money that had less intrinsic value than the money in which the debt was contracted. Like the English rulers, they borrowed heavily from Italian financiers. French dependence on Italian loans continued in the fourteenth century, while the English kings preferred native sources of credit, particularly the merchants who controlled the export of English wool.

Philip IV also required rear vassals, as well as those who held fiefs directly from him, to pay a feudal aid when he married his eldest daughter and knighted his eldest son. Although towns were not collective vassals of the king, they also paid these aids. Philip tallaged the Jews repeatedly, and finally expelled them from the royal domain in 1306. He also used sales taxes, began levying import and export duties and established a customs service. All these impositions were based on the principle that the king could tax for the defence of the realm by declaring a state of emergency even if he did not summon an army. Philip's measures aroused such intense opposition, however, that in 1303 he changed the basis of taxation from the feudal bond to the general levy: while the king's vassals owed annual military aid for whatever purpose he chose to use it, all male citizens had a duty to serve in the militia to defend the homeland (the general levy or *arrière ban*). Instead of requiring several million adult males to report for duty, the king required nobles to pay one-fifth of their annual income, and subjected all others to a hearth tax in lieu of serving in person.

Although the outcome in France was very different from what happened in England, the two seemed to be evolving in parallel directions from the 1290s until into the early fourteenth century. In each case the crown's financial needs led to increased taxation and, initially, the growing power of consultative assemblies. The war on the Flemish frontier, which demanded an army in most years between 1297 and 1320, had the same impact on French finances that problems with the Scots had on England. Kings and other princes had met occasionally with assemblies, which in France were organised on the basis of Estates in the sense of legally defined social classes: representatives of the clergy as the first Estate, the nobility (everything from titled lords to humble knights, since, unlike in England, the rank of knight conveyed nobility) as the second and the bourgeoisie (residents of chartered communities called 'bourgs', not bourgeoisie in the modern sense) as the third. Philip IV convened the first Estates-General (Estates of the entire realm) in 1302 to approve an aid to deal with the emergency caused by the Flemish defeat of a French army at Courtrai. As was true of the English Parliament, the Estates-General was also consulted on aspects of policy that lacked a financial dimension, in this case to gain support for Philip's actions against the pope. Another Estates-General was called in 1308 to associate the nation with the king in his controversial proceedings to dissolve the Knights Templar, heretofore bankers to the crown. Meetings of the Estates-General were frequent in the early fourteenth century, always for the purpose of voting taxes; but they became unusual after 1360.

Some French provinces had their own Estates. Most of them were in the north, in the provinces annexed earliest to the royal domain. There was a separate Estates-General, for example, for Languedoc. While the English parliament could vote taxes binding on the entire realm after it developed a financial competence in the early fourteenth century, the Estates-General could only recommend measures to regional Estates, which sometimes, as happened with the 1314 subsidy, refused to comply. Each Estate had one collective vote, which naturally meant a more complete domination of the powerful, particularly in the first two Estates, than happened under the English parliamentary structure. Over time the clergy established the principle that they were exempt from direct taxes because they prayed for the king's success, and the nobles were exempt because they fought. Since an Estates-General contained only three votes, these two managed to shift direct taxation to the Third Estate, the bourgeoisie, in the course of the fourteenth and fifteenth centuries.

Yet even in the early fourteenth century taxation was still extraordinary. It was considered so iniquitous to use taxes for ordinary expenses or for purposes not stated when the tax was levied that in 1314 Philip IV on his deathbed ordered repayment to the taxpayers of a tax that he had taken for a campaign in Flanders that had to be cancelled. In late 1314 leagues of notables were formed to resist further taxation in several provinces outside the royal domain, notably those such as Burgundy, that had their own Estates. The movement spread throughout the kingdom in 1315, but was strongest in Normandy. Charters were extracted from the crown by noble leagues in individual provinces in 1315; and both in being couched in terms of confirmation of nobles' privileges, and in pledging the crown to end arbitrary exactions, they have similarities to the English Magna Carta of 1215. Unlike Magna Carta, however, they applied only to provinces, not the whole nation, and they were very general, simply confirming old liberties without specifying what they were. Ominously for the future, only the charter of the Normans showed an understanding of the fact that some taxation was necessary and tried to regulate it; the others were concerned only with preserving the privileges of particular groups, particularly the nobles.

The disparity of interests among and within the provinces, particularly the discord between nobles and townspeople, also hurt efforts to develop national institutions that might resist the king. The chaos at the court of Charles VI shows that what would be France by 1559 was still a federation of crown princes in the early fifteenth century. There was no more reason at that time to think that France would become unified as a nation than Germany; the difference was that the princes in Germany were able to consolidate their independent authority in the sixteenth century, in part as a consequence of the religious situation, while those of France were not. There was little 'French' national sentiment until the concluding phases of the Hundred Years War, and the Gascons actually seems to have preferred the English to the French.

After the charter movement petered out, the kings negotiated frequently with local assemblies, but they avoided national assemblies until forced by an emergency to deal with them. The Estates-General called in 1320 and 1321 would not vote a tax in peacetime, and they did not meet again until 1343, when the military situation required aid. The emergency caused by the disaster at Crécy forced Philip VI to call Estates-General in 1346 and 1347, and the Estates of Languedoil met in 1351 and 1355–6.

Until this time the Estates-General met less frequently than the English Parliament, which is hardly surprising in view of the much larger size of France and its political fragmentation; but its tax-voting function was comparable to that of Parliament. The Estates-General did not, however, have the legislative or consultative capacity that enabled Parliament to transfer the threat of denying taxes into leverage over other aspects of royal policy. The crisis of French royal finance began in 1356. Even before the king was captured at Poitiers, the Estates-General, actually meeting in separate assemblies for the north (*pays d'oui*) and the south (Languedoc), voted new war taxes: a sales tax (*maltote*) of 3.3 per cent in the north and 2.5 per cent in the south, and a *gabelle* on salt, which was essential for meat preservation. The *gabelle*, which in other contexts in the late Middle Ages usually means an indirect tax, began in France as the royal monopoly on salt production, evolving into a requirement that households buy a quota of salt, and finally into a tax on salt. The northern Estates then decided that they preferred a direct tax to the indirect *maltote*.

When the king was captured at Poitiers later in 1356, his ransom was added to the burden of taxation. In 1357 the Estates-General forced the Dauphin as regent to issue the 'Grand Ordinance' as their condition for voting the ransom. The Ordinance required regular meetings of the Estates, and allowed them to choose the members of the royal council. Addressing a major problem, given the difficulty in a national assembly for all of France, it set up a committee of 15 to control finances, coinage and foreign policy when the Estates were not in session. But this was the last time the Estates-General tried seriously to link tax-voting and legislation. The Estates-General at Paris was compromised irretrievably by its involvement in the Jacquerie of 1358 (see Chapter 3). The regent annulled the Grand Ordinance, and the Estates could do nothing in 1360 when the government simply raised the ransom by imposing *aides* (the old *maltote*, sales taxes generally and a wine tax) and the *gabelle*. An Estates-General in 1363 approved all of these, and added new direct taxes: a *fouage* (a hearth tax on every house containing a nuclear family) in the north and the *taille* (a tax per unit of land) in the south. A first payment of two million *écus* obtained the king's release in 1360. The government did not have the money to pay the rest, and the chivalrous monarch voluntarily returned to captivity in England in 1363 (the French were still making payments to the English on John II's ransom as late as 1400). In the early 1370s the victorious campaigns against the English had to be paid for, and the continued burden of the ransom helped to accustom the French to regular taxation.

To handle the income from the new national taxes that did not come from the domain, the Estates-General in 1356 established six 'General Superintendants' (*Généraux*) whose work could be audited by the royal Chamber of Accounts. The *Généralités* were subdivided into *élections* under at least two *élus* with their own courts and bureaucracies. The borders of the *élection* often corresponded to the bishopric, although this did not mean that it was a compact territory. In the early 1360s the Estates-General surrendered control over these taxes and the mechanism for collecting them to the crown. The king then used regional rather than national assemblies to get the money that he needed beyond this. Although traditionally a distinction has been made between *pays d'Élection*, where royal officials collected taxes with little challenge, and *pays d'États*, where local Estates imposed limitations, some parts of France that had Estates also had *élus*. The *aides* were generally leased to local tax farmers, who leased taxes from the government for a lump sum of money, and then collected the tax in question. They functioned in single communities in the fourteenth century, but in the fifteenth they often farmed the taxes for several places, even an entire bailliage or an *élection*. The tax farmers were called 'financiers' in the sixteenth century.

The crown continued to collect the new taxes until Charles V abolished the *fouage* on his deathbed in 1380. The *aides* were abolished the next year by his successor's regents, but looming bankruptcy forced them to reimpose the *taille* in early 1382, whereupon disappointment that the tax burden was not really ending resulted in riots in the major cities. Once the revolts had been suppressed in 1383, however, royal finances reverted to the older pattern. The next years saw colossal waste at a bloated and venal royal court, and when military activity resumed in 1413 the French were unprepared for it. Between 1369 and 1421 the Estates-General met only in 1380–1 and 1413, but they frequently met annually between 1421 and 1448, voting money to fight the English and demanding administrative reforms, in return, which Charles VII implemented. The king levied numerous *fouages* with the consent of the Estates, but most were on individual provinces, not the realm. This was not a conscious policy – he began it when, as Dauphin, he only controlled certain provinces and could tax only them – but it established the principles that the prince controlled taxation and that it need not be equitable nor general even within the domain. In 1435 the Estates of *Longuedoil* re-established the *aides* and *gabelles* of 1360 for 4 years, and after this grant was reapproved in 1436 these taxes were levied without further consultation until 1789. In 1439 the same body approved a general *taille*, by now a direct tax that combined features of the earlier *taille* and *fouage*. The taxes were voted for one year to support a standing army; but since the army remained in existence, so did the taxes. Long before 1450 the French crown was getting most of its income from taxation. The distinction between ordinary and extraordinary income was thus much less important in France by 1450 than in England. The extent of the royal domain mattered less to the Valois kings than to the English rulers, who were able to finance most of their domestic operations without taxation. The French kings taxed without the Estates-General for domestic administration and warfare alike, while the English only needed to tax during warfare, but could not do so without involving Parliament.

This cooperation between Estates and monarchy ended after the English were expelled in 1453, but the Estates-General never recovered the ground that they had lost. The size of France was a problem: in 1468, called by Louis XI (1461–83) for consultation in a matter not involving taxes, the Estates-General asked the king to use his own judgement in the future and not involve them, 'for the Estates cannot be assembled easily'.[4] As a national assembly they never had the status under law that provincial Estates possessed, including the power to bind a constituency. Yet except in Languedoc, which averaged two meetings per year between 1418 and 1444, most provincial Estates did not meet even annually. The Estates of Languedoc followed the Catalonian practice of appointing syndics or proctors to act during periods when the full body was not meeting. Local populations preferred their own assemblies, and the kings found them less dangerous than a national assembly. Yet they were dominated by the tax-exempt groups, clergy and nobles, who of course lacked the incentive that the English knights had, as well as the great lords, all of whom were subject to direct taxes, for limiting the arbitrary power of the king to legislate and tax. The Estate structure itself meant that the assemblies, national and provincial, saw themselves more as defenders of the privileges of their groups than as national representatives.[5]

Representative Institutions in the Iberian Peninsula

Castile and Aragon also had representative assemblies, which, like the French, were structured on the Estate principle. The *Cortes* of Aragon is older than the English Parliament, and it retained considerable power into the seventeenth century. It had a *brazo* [Estate] *popular* for representatives of 22 towns and three rural communities, and was thus much smaller than the English House of Commons, to which 37 shires and usually about 75 boroughs sent two delegates each. The clergy met as a separate estate, and there were two Estates of nobles, *ricoshombres* and *hidalgos*, corresponding to the English distinction between great nobles and knights or lesser nobles.

The Aragonese *Cortes* was the only assembly of Latin Europe that still had a legislative function, as well as tax approval, as late as 1500. By the sixteenth century it was actually better able than the English Parliament to prevent excessive royal taxation, although its statute-approving powers were weaker than those of Parliament. The *Corts* of Catalonia under the crown of Aragon had a single chamber for nobles, many of whom were active in commerce, in contrast to nobles in England and France. As early as 1289 the *Corts* tried to influence royal policy while it was not in session by appointing a standing commission, but these deputations came to identify more with the rulers than with the assemblies, and tried to block the full assemblies from meeting. These assemblies had to vote direct taxes and thus were more powerful at a national level than the French Estates-General;

given the size of the states involved, a more appropriate comparison would be with the Estates of one of the French provinces.

Royal government was stronger in Castile than elsewhere in Spain, while the Aragonese *Cortes* was stronger than the Castilian. The Castilian *Cortes* also had a three-estate structure, as well as the power in principle to vote taxes; but, as happened in France, the Castilian kings in the fourteenth century began to bypass the tax-voting assemblies by devising new levies that did not come within the purview of the *Cortes*. Alfonso XI (1312–49) levied high export taxes on wool, as Edward III of England did, and raised the rate of the sales tax, the *alcabala*, the equivalent of the French *aides*. During the crisis beginning in 1385 the *Cortes* met frequently, but never annually. Throughout the fourteenth century the kings normally submitted legislation to the *Cortes* for approval; but as the monarchy regained control in the fifteenth century the influence of the assembly waned, in part because of the weakness of the Castilian towns. Many of their leading citizens were *hidalgos*, and thus identified more with rural interests, while individual estates negotiated with the ruler. In the late fifteenth century the nobles and clergy lost interest and simply stopped attending, and the result was that the *Cortes* became virtually a single-house assembly, not meeting at all between 1480 and 1498. A total of 39 towns, each with two representatives, were the only curb on royal absolutism by the early sixteenth century.

Germany

Most German principalities had Diets (*Landtage*) in the late Middle Ages, and there was also an imperial *Reichstag*. Most Diets were organized by an Estate principle, although the bourgeoisie were usually the last to gain the right to attend: their real power depended on how financially dependent on them their princes were. The *Reichstag* was advisory, lacking authority either to legislate or approve taxes. It was attended by whoever the emperor summoned, usually some 30 imperial princes, the bishops and other leading clergy and a varying contingent of lesser lords. The imperial cities gained the right to attend the *Reichstag* in the fifteenth century, but the emperor also invited other towns. The Diet considered measures proposed by the emperor through his chancellor, who presided at the meetings; but it had no right of enforcement, and regional interests were so discordant that little of substance was ever approved.

The Dynamics of Representative Institutions

Virtually all assemblies suffered an important limitation: they met only when the prince, as the supreme lawgiver, called them, and only until he dismissed them. In stable rural societies, where power was exercised by great lords, representative assemblies met infrequently, briefly and with a limited agenda. This is true of the provincial estates in southern Italy, and most of Germany, central Europe and France. When the lesser nobility was numerous and powerful enough to dispute power with the great nobles, the result could be an assembly with considerable power, as happened in Poland and Lithuania. In rural areas with some cities and a specialized labour force, and which participated in interregional and international markets, assemblies were more numerous and at least tried to influence policy beyond simply approving taxes. Some of them tried to overcome the disadvantages of periodic meetings by appointing standing commissions and officials. Some assemblies in this category were based on functional social differentiations, as in England, while others were based on a version of the Estate structure, as with the French Estates-General and the Aragonese and Castilian *Cortes*.

In densely urban areas that were subject to a central administration under a prince, but in which the cities had extensive privileges, economic policy was critically important, particularly since it was usually necessary to import food and industrial raw materials. Here assemblies met more frequently and were often dominated by towns, and their decisions were then ratified by the princes. Rural jurisdictions were also represented, but tended to play a subordinate role to the urban. A small number of representatives was sent from each of many jurisdictions, with rapid rotation of personnel and short meetings. Flanders, Brabant, Holland, Bohemia in the early fifteenth century, and Friuli are examples of this type of jurisdiction. The situation in Flanders is especially interesting. During the fourteenth century Ghent, Bruges and Ypres had a recognized corporate existence as the 'Three Cities', their delegates usually meeting with the count of Flanders between 20 and 30 times per year. From 1395 they were joined by the semi-rural castellany of Bruges and became the 'Four Members' of Flanders. This group met with the Burgundian count even more frequently through 1411. The number of meetings then declined for the rest of the century, but the duration of individual meetings lengthened. The Members exercised some limited judicial functions, legislated, particularly on economic policy, but also on defence and military questions, and combined this with the right to approve taxes requested by the count. Other Low Country assemblies, although hardly representative – delegates to the Members were usually aldermen accompanied by the city attorney and town clerk – had similar rights, a fact that helps to explain the continuation in the sixteenth century of the medieval tradition of independence in this part of Europe.

In areas that had cities but a less dense concentration of them than in the Low Countries, and without a powerful central authority, cities and territories sometimes had their own assemblies, not invariably meeting together. When they did meet together, it was usually under the Estate structure. This is confined largely to Germany, particularly the areas with urban leagues. Finally, northern Italy is a case unto itself. The cities were extremely large and had to support themselves by overseas trade. There was no cooperation between the rural areas, which were dominated by the cities, and the *contadi* had no separate representation or assemblies. Such representation as existed occurred within the framework of city government.[6]

The Royal Household and the Courts

England

All rulers of Europe relied on a council of advisors and a household that handled daily business. In the feudalized parts of Europe the council initially consisted of the direct vassals of the king. They functioned as the highest court in cases where vassals were involved, and as the royal domain expanded, so did their judicial functions. The nature of the original Norman royal council was preserved less in the Council than in the House of Lords after Parliament developed. The Lords had original jurisdiction over peers, and could try other cases in which the king had a direct interest, as well as those that had originated as petitions in the House of Commons. The English central courts originated in this court of the tenants-in-chief, which then became professionalized as law became more complex: the Court of Common Pleas, for legal actions in which the king had no personal interest, originated in the twelfth century, the King's Bench in the thirteenth, for cases that he would hear personally or where his interests were directly involved. In practice, cases came without discrimination to these courts, either of which could be appealed only to the king and his council.

Circuit judges originated in the twelfth century, gradually supplanting the declining courts of the county sheriffs, but their commissions were so general and their appearance so infrequent that in the 1290s the royal government began appointing Keepers of the Peace as subordinates of the sheriffs. In 1330 the Keepers were given the power to indict as well as apprehend criminals. In 1361 they became Justices of the Peace, and were given the right to try both trespassers and felons. The circuit justices were abolished. In 1362 quarter sessions, courts under the Justices of the Peace, were established, and they had virtually superseded the shire courts by 1400. By 1380 they could try all criminal cases except treason. The Justices of the Peace developed a general supervision of the counties, including the militia. Originally two justices were appointed per county, but by the sixteenth century the average number was 40 per county. The justices were unpaid; they recovered their costs of administration through court fines.

There was no equivalent of the Justices of the Peace in France, where local police and judges received wages. The justices undoubtedly quieted much disorder in the counties, but reliance on unpaid officials who combined police work and justice makes overly optimistic assumptions about human nature. The Justices of the Peace or their clients were often parties to the cases that they judged. The Justices sometimes cooperated with lawbreakers, and their patronage networks sometimes hindered the course of justice. Furthermore, so many exemptions were allowed under the common law, in contrast to Roman law, that the fact that a case was in principle royal did not always mean swift justice. The common law had intricate procedural safeguards for the accused, and jurors were reluctant to convict when the punishment for felony was death or mutilation. Even when a conviction had been obtained, most kings issued wholesale pardons for a price or in return for the accused entering the army: the depradations of retainers (see Chapter 1) were serious in the fifteenth century. All of these considerations meant that England was notorious for disorder even on the war-torn Continent in the late Middle Ages.

The organs of the modern state were born in the division of the previously undifferentiated royal court (*curia*) into councils, autonomous departments of admistration and courts that did not follow the king about, but rather had permanent bureaux in one place. This process was well under way in England by 1200, on the Continent by 1300. It was an accomplished fact by 1600, by which time the kings travelled much less, residing in a national capital. The household consisted of the officials who served the king in a domestic capacity, ranging from cooks to the marshals who kept the horses ready. But some offices in the household had more skilled functions. For example, the head of the royal chamber, the chamberlain, disbursed funds to other offices in the household; and even after the kings established treasuries and accounting offices outside the court, like the English Exchequer, the chamberlain still handled some money. As the business of some departments became complex and they developed large staffs, they left the household and established separate offices, a process known as 'going out of court' in England. When this happened the king lost some control over the offices; and when they became departments of state the nobles gained more influence over them. Other departments in the household replaced the departed, and the kings relied on them, since they were easier to control.

The distinction between household and council was blurred by 1300. 'Council' was no longer an enormous group of tenants-in-chief, but rather those persons who were in constant attendance on the king and whose advice he trusted. The royal Council of the thirteenth century would become the Privy Council by the fifteenth. It could handle financial and judicial matters, and generally advised the king. Although as late as 1307 it was firmly in the king's control, as he maintained his right to choose his own advisors, the lords controlled the Council by 1377. Its core was the chancellor and the treasurer, both of whom were in the household, and some 20 sworn councillors.

Modern students of government tend to think of offices as having distinct tasks that, in principle, will not be duplicated by others; but medieval government was not this tidy. The English kings, who were much more threatened by Parliament than the French were by the Estates-General (except briefly after 1356), devised a myriad of methods to keep government branches from knowing what the others were doing and to keep administrative departments that had gone out of court – and were thus overseen by the barons who controlled Parliament – from encroaching on the departments of the royal household, which remained under the monarch's personal control. The most famous example is the Wardrobe, which began as the branch of the Chamber where the king's jewels were kept. The Chancery was the secretariat which, although it had gone out of court in France, remained in the household in England during the fourteenth century. Chancery controlled the Great Seal, which was used to attest state documents. But during the thirteenth century the kings developed the practice, which the barons tried to end by the Provisions of Oxford of 1258 and in the Ordinances of 1311, of issuing writs under the Privy Seal, which was kept in the Wardrobe, to divert money into the household departments that normally would have been paid into the Exchequer. By the late thirteenth century the king had built the Wardrobe into a war office through which his funds were being funnelled. As the Privy Seal came under closer scrutiny – its keeper was normally a baron and a member of the royal council by 1400 – Edward III began using the Signet Seal, which became a separate office under Richard II. The Exchequer, whose procedures had changed little since the mid-twelfth century, was thus frequently bypassed in the early fourteenth century; but its importance revived from the 1340s, when parliamentary taxation, which was paid directly into the Exchequer, became a major part of the king's income. With the revival of the Exchequer the Wardrobe declined.

Chancery itself shows differentiation and duplication of function as both secretariat and court. Although in principle the head of the royal writing office, the chancellor was the most important household advisor of the king. Chancery also had a court that was already functioning at times as a court of equity, handling cases where the antiquated procedural rules of the common law perpetrated injustice, although this became a major part of its business only from the late fifteenth century.

France

Justice and finance remained domanial longer in France than in England, since although the king could issue laws, he could not enforce them outside the royal domain. The domain was divided into bailiwicks in the north and seneschalsies in the south. The bailiffs and seneschals were similar to the English sheriff in their domain functions, and, like the sheriff, declined in importance in the late Middle Ages. They had subordinates and councils who had administrative, judicial, military and financial duties, and collected the ordinary revenues of the domain, notably rents and profits of justice, while the *élections,* whose area often was the same as a bailiwick or seneschalsy, handled extraordinary incomes in the same territories. The financial officers of the bailiwicks and seneschalsies reported to the Treasurer of France and thus to the six *Généraux* of Finances by the late fourteenth century.

Household

The effacing of the distinction between household and court that we have noted in England existed in France, but the nature of the French household had become very different by the late Middle Ages. French government departments did not go out of court: the kings were able to keep the growing royal administration centred in the household. While crown and baronage in England vied to centre government in departments that were responsible to each of them, the bloated French royal household became a source of graft and patronage without parallel in late medieval Europe.

The royal household (*Hôtel*) had three divisions, with its functions limited to the royal domain. The financial arm consisted of the *Chambre-aux-Deniers* whose English equivalent was the Chamber. A branch of the *Chambre-aux-Deniers* was called the *Argenterie* (money office); its English equivalent was the Wardrobe. The *Chambre-aux-Deniers* accounted in principle to the Chamber of Accounts, which was the financial arm of the royal Council. Finally, the household had its own court, the Pleas of the Household, which was a relic of the earlier practice of the king dispensing justice as he moved about. It handled cases of personal interest to the king, but it was not the same as the English Court of King's Bench, which was a judicial session of the council rather than the household; and it was not restricted to cases from the royal domain. The Pleas of the Household was more similar to the English Court of Chancery than to King's Bench.

The Court and Justice

The French royal court in one sense was the entire royal establishment, the *Cour.* In an official capacity, it was called the *Conseil.* As with the English 'Council', the *Conseil* often meant a 'Privy Council' of advisors, while the court in a broader sense could sit on either judicial or financial business. When it did, 'courtiers' and specialists also attended. The chancellor had been part of the household initially, although by this time he was really part of the court. When the French royal court met on judicial business, it was called *parlement.* As late as 1300 the same masters sometimes sat on both the *parlement* and the Chamber of Accounts, due to the relative simplicity of the business being transacted; but these two were separated in practice during the fourteenth century into distinct branches of the court as the administrative state became more professionalized.

This term *parlement* came gradually into use in the late thirteenth century for the royal court at Paris, paralleling the contemporary use of 'parliament' in England, although the use of the word was only invariable from 1360. Most councillors were great nobles and masters in the thirteenth century, but they yielded in the fourteenth to 'masters' with legal training. After 1366 the *parlement* enjoyed the right to choose its own president, and from the late fourteenth century it recruited all its own members.

The *parlement* of Paris was the supreme court of the royal domain, a territory that encompassed less than one third of present-day France in the mid-fifteenth century, but which grew rapidly thereafter. It was a court of original instance for all cases concerning the king or his estate, and was a court of peers for the nobility. Until after 1450 the only other *parlement* was that of Languedoc, which, like Paris, originated in the thirteenth century, but which was only fixed at Toulouse in 1443. Bordeaux, which was under English rule until 1453, received a *parlement* in 1463. Normandy had a *parlement* called the Norman Exchequer in the twelfth century, but it was lost in the fifteenth century and was only reconstituted in 1499. The *parlement* of Burgundy was fixed at Dijon in 1493, and three others were added in the sixteenth century. Appeals could be pursued from other parlements to the *Conseil*, but not to the *parlement* of Paris. Paris did, however, hear appeals for other regions that had no *parlements*.

Parlement consisted of three distinct tribunals. The *Grande-Chambre* (Great Chamber) was a supreme court, hearing only reserved cases, the equivalent of the English pleas of the crown, and appeals. There was no appeal from its verdicts except to the king and the *Conseil*. An ordinance of 1345 fixed its structure with three presidents and 30 masters. In 1345 15 of them were clergy, a higher percentage than was true of the English parliament and the common-law courts, and the other two branches of *parlement* had a predominance of clergy. Church courts were much more powerful on the Continent than in England. Most canon lawyers also studied the civil law, and their expertise was valued. Only after 1450 did laymen become the majority element on the French *parlement*, although they increased rapidly thereafter. The *Chambre-aux-Enquêtes* (Inquests) heard cases sent there from the *Grande-Chambre*. It included specialists for northern and southern France, whose legal regimes were quite different in the early fourteenth century but which became more uniform through this period, as Roman law came increasingly to be preferred to older customary practice in the north. The *Chambre-aux-Enquêtes* had 57 masters by 1336 and clearly handled the core of the *parlement*'s business. Finally, the *Chambre des Requêtes* (Pleas), with five justices in 1336, was responsible mainly for cases that were exempt from the jurisdiction of the other tribunals. It had original jurisdiction over cases involving the royal prerogative and regalian right;

the domain; privileged urban communities; and all persons with letters of protection from the king, as well as appellate jurisdiction over all cases within the royal domain, such as those originating in the courts of the bailiffs and seneschals.

The Court and Finances

The Court as a financial institution had been dividing from the judicial and, like it, becoming professionalized in the late thirteenth century. It was formally established as the *Chambre des Comptes* by royal ordinance in 1320. The Chamber of Accounts was an audit department, with a personnel of 16 in the early fourteenth century, but it grew steadily. Its English equivalent was the Exchequer, which had existed by 1107, and it also handled extraordinary revenue until 1356, auditing the accounts of household officers, the mintmasters, foresters and separate war treasuries. The Treasury originally administered ordinary revenue through four regional treasurers, releasing money on mandates from the Chamber of Accounts. In 1390 a Court of the Treasury was initiated, but it was never important, since by 1390 most of the king's income came from taxation and not from the domain. This court went out of existence in the sixteenth century. In 1390 a Court of the Aids (*Cour des Aides*) was established to handle extraordinary income, produced by national taxation. This was the most important fiscal arm of the monarchy in the fifteenth century.[7]

The Burgundian State

While England since the twelfth century had been the closest thing to a centralized administrative state that Europe knew, and the French kings were trying to centralize and standardize even as they ejected the English from France, the Burgundian state was deliberately kept decentralized until after 1467. The term 'Burgundian' is misleading, for the Netherlands produced much more revenue than the duchy and county of Burgundy, and after 1420 the rulers spent most of their time in Brabant or Flanders. The Flemish count had established a Chamber of Accounts on the French model in 1382, which Philip the Bold moved to Lille in 1386, when he established a similar Chamber for Burgundy at Dijon. The component principalities of the Burgundian state kept their specific institutions. Consultation was constant with the prince or, under the Burgundians, his local representatives. With the annexation of Brabant a third Chamber of Accounts was established at Brussels, which gradually replaced Bruges in Flanders as the favourite residence of the long-lived Duke Philip the Good (1419–67). There was a central Council of State, but only after 1440 were the councils of the component principalities subordinated to it. The Estates of individual provinces sometimes met together in the fifteenth century: that of 1464 is usually considered the first Estates-General. But the dukes remained largely itinerant, and in constant touch with the great officials of court. A civil service of several hundred persons developed, often underpaid but rewarded through patronage.

The Iberian Peninsula

The central offices of justice and finance in the Iberian kingdoms were similar to those of France. The major offices of the household, such as chancellor, constable (an office that revived in importance in both France and Castile during the Hundred Years War), and chamberlain were common throughout Europe. The chancellor was particularly important in Aragon, where he presided over the final court of appeal (as the chancellor could preside over the French *Grande-Chambre*) and over the royal council. Aragon, which was a federated kingdom, used viceroys or lieutenants-general in its overseas territories of Sardinia, Sicily and Majorca in the fourteenth century, and the absence of King Alfonso V in Naples in the fifteenth century caused this system to spread to Catalonia and finally to Aragon itself. Another important office in Catalonia, particularly in the fifteenth century, was the *Generalitat*, a standing committee that functioned while the *Cortes* was not in session, with judicial powers of interpreting the laws and the right to collect and audit extraordinary funds authorized by the *Cortes*. It developed a large bureaucracy and acted *de facto* as the treasury, issuing bonds that became a primitive form of a public debt. While in Castile the crown assumed these powers, in Catalonia the rulers had to respect the *Generalitat*.

Castile had a *contaduría de cuentas* that paralleled the French *chambre des comptes*. The kings realized considerable income from levies on the church, which was under stricter royal control in Spain than in France, and from taxes on Jews and Moors that did not apply in the north. The sales tax, the *alcabala*, was granted to Alfonso XI in 1342 by the Castilian towns, which evidently had already been levying such a tax with the king's consent. Later the *Cortes* voted the *alcabala*, but by the early fifteenth century the kings were simply levying it without involving the assembly. The rate was 5 per cent during the fourteenth century and 10 per cent in the fifteenth, by which time over half the income of the monarchy came from the *alcabala*. The *Cortes* was generally rather generous in voting subsidies during warfare, and the popes authorized crusading aids levied on the church for the campaigns against the Muslims.

Financial administration also was similar to the French example. Household finance was under the *mayordomo mayor*, the equivalent of the French and English chamberlain, but the Trastamara monarchs appointed *contadores mayores*. By the 1390s they were grouped into two sections: the *contadores mayores de hacienda* for tax collection, and the *contadores mayores de cuentas* for accounting. A single *maestre racional* directed financial administration in Aragon. As happened in France but not in England, tax farmers leased most indirect taxes on varying bases, from a single tax for a single year in a single community to comprehensive farming of taxes in larger areas and for some years at a time. Taxes voted by the *Cortes* were generally not farmed, as was true of the *taille* in France. Judicial administration in Spain was also similar to that in France. The Castilian kings were still itinerant to a greater degree than the French or the English, and thus central judicial institutions came later to Castile. The *cortes* of 1371 established the *audiencia* as a central court, located from 1390 at Segovia and from 1442 at Valladolid.[8]

The Bureaucracy

The involvement of subjects in princely government through meetings of Estates, principally for finance and statute-making, is one side of the growth of the modern state. Bureaucracy is the other. Paradoxically, in both England and France aspects of local government remained or became decentralized as the claims of the crown exceeded its capacity to enforce them. Philip Augustus (1180–1223) had increased the royal domain tremendously at the turn of the thirteenth century, and Languedoc had been added before 1300. But the practice of granting *apanages* (see Chapter 1) retarded this development, and the only significant additions to the French royal domain in the fourteenth century were Dauphiné in 1349 and Champagne in 1361. Thus local governments were firmly in place in most areas long before they were absorbed by the crown. The most rapid period of growth of the royal domain after 1223 was the century after the end of the Hundred Years War, beginning with previously English-held Gascony in 1453.

Except in cities that had the right by charter to choose their own officials, a nominally royal bureaucracy was installed. In both the Spanish kingdoms and France in the fourteenth and fifteenth centuries, some government offices were given to financiers, who were then expected to advance sums to the royal government. Tax farming was widespread. The reliance of these states on their own officeholders for short-term credit meant that there were limits beyond which they could not go in limiting those office-holders' privileges. Although there were complaints about non-residence, arguments that office-holders could only be removed for malfeasance, giving them *de facto* life tenure, were becoming common.

It is a short step from this to actual sale of offices. While in England most local office-holders were unpaid and thus relatively independent of the crown until the sixteenth century, in France they were paid. But some offices were being sold in France by 1300, and the practice was common by

1450. Traffic in offices began in Castile under the Trastamara kings after 1369, which amounted to turning offices into private property. The Castilian *Cortes* complained repeatedly, but that fact alone shows that the ruler was able to disregard it. The 'Cabochien Ordinance' issued by the royal government under the threat of the rebels who held Paris in 1413 also forbade the holding of more than one office by the same person, sale of offices, non-residence and appointment of deputies by an absentee office-holder; but it was never implemented.

Thus the civil service developed in France and – to a much lesser extent (until later) Castile – as a virtual caste, with most positions filled by patronage. University education became important, although not always essential; the most important criterion was the money that one paid for the office. The practice of selling offices often began when the previous holder resigned in favour of a third person, took a fee from the new holder and then recommended him to the king. Although wages for office-holders were low, the profits of patronage were high, and there was a tendency for offices to run in families even before the French were selling large numbers of them. Granted that sons tended to succeed fathers as Justices of the Peace, the rate of turnover in offices was much higher in England than in France. Furthermore, the rank equivalents of the 'gentry' who controlled local offices in England (see Chapter 4) were considered nobles in France, a status that conveyed exemption from direct taxes and gave the French lesser nobility considerably more reverence toward the state than their English counterparts displayed. While offices conveyed honour in both, only in France and Spain did they convey nobility and thus offer financial advantages.[9]

The Crown and the Cities

The burgeoning of royal government in France, Castile and England in the late Middle Ages restricted even the limited degree of local autonomy that the cities there had possessed. In the Low Countries, Italy and Germany, however, cities were much more independent in fact, although rarely in law. Urban governments in these areas had more sophisticated institutional structures and provided a wider range of services than did the kings: in even the most tightly administered national state the prince was lucky if he could monopolize lawgiving and law enforcement, preserve domestic peace, conduct defence and collect and borrow or otherwise extort the money that he needed for these functions.

The cities did all of this, and in addition maintained schools, handled poor relief (an area into which princely government only began extending in the mid-fifteenth century), and through the occupational guilds managed commercial policy and supervised industrial regulations. The Flemish and German cities experimented with annuity rents, where the purchaser pays a lump sum in return for an annual payment for a term of years or life: and in the fourteenth century this grew into what amounted to funded debts. The Italian cities were even more precocious, if somewhat less systematic, in this regard, consolidating the various loans that they had made from their citizens into a *monte* or debt that paid interest on shares. Virtually all Netherlandish and German (although not Italian) cities had one or more central accounting offices that collected taxes and accounted for expenditures.

Apart from the fact that cities were governed by councils drawn by various criteria from the local notables, often with some participation by the prince, we know little of how they managed their internal affairs before 1300. Most thirteenth-century cities were ruled by élites with a strong base in landholding, whose organ of control was a council of *Schöffen* (*échevins* in France). A separate council of *jurés*, who were representatives of the sworn association of town inhabitants, was found in some cities, usually dominated by merchants who had become rich in inter-regional trade. There were thus two levels of the municipal élites: the older landholding element ('magnates' in Italy), and the upper merchants, who constituted the élite of most nominally 'craft' guilds. In England the 'freedom of the borough' involved membership in the guild merchant, without which one could not sell on the city market. By the late thirteenth century the Italian cities had a complex mechanism that allowed factions, most of which were based on the clienteles of extended families, to share the posts on the several town councils. These rotated frequently: every two months in the case of Florence. The northern cities more often changed the council annually. Eligibility to serve on the major councils depended on a combination of political affiliation (the Ghibelline party in Milan and the Guelf party in Florence, for example), social rank (magnates were excluded in some cities), and membership in a politically recognized guild.

In the late thirteenth century some artisans began entering city governments in northern Europe, but they served as individuals rather than as representatives of their guilds; and almost without exception they were merchants who were the élite members of guilds that were nominally artisan. During the fourteenth century many northern cities gave specific guilds the right to seats on the councils, and others the right to a certain number of seats as a group; for example, the various construction trades might have one or two members of the council. A variant on this was combining several guilds into a political but not occupational unit so that the wealthier would have disproportionate influence.

Virtually all city councillors came from prominent and wealthy families and held office for essentially social reasons. But city government became increasingly complex during the fourteenth and fifteenth centuries, and this required the service of professionals and the development of such services as writing offices. Little information generated by municipal chanceries before 1300 survives except from Italy, but the volume of local documentation becomes overwhelming in the fourteenth century, just as it does from royal governments. City governments maintained their buildings, bridges, streets, waterways and sometimes sanitation. Although it was expensive, most cities were able to fund such items with minimal taxation. There is little evidence of significant municipal debt before 1300, but except in Italy most cities incurred severe debts during the late Middle Ages because they owed increasingly onerous subventions to their princes.

The accounting procedures of the Italian cities were more sophisticated but less centralized than in northern Europe, but records there were being kept in writing by the mid-twelfth century. Our knowledge of city finance outside Italy becomes stronger in the fourteenth century. While municipal financial institutions in France and Iberia were not patterned on the royal ones, the cities began developing more rational accounting and keeping more accurate records during the period of the Hundred Years War, as the financial demands of the kings required them to raise and keep track of larger sums of money. The great impulse to record-keeping in the Flemish cities was an outcry over municipal indebtedness from the 1280s, but this in turn was caused to a great degree by the fact that the cities had to borrow to pay the increased demands of the Flemish counts. In France the crown made such inordinate demands on the cities that virtually all went over to written accounts during the early stages of the Hundred Years War; and most German cities were keeping financial records and proceedings of the councils in writing in the thirteenth century. In each of these cases a close parallel exists between the need for more information and accordingly better records, to support more sophisticated local governing institutions at the turn of the fourteenth century.

Most cities preferred to use indirect taxation, but some used direct taxes based on either self-declaration of assets or, in some cases, the estimation of a city assessor. The most famous urban direct tax is the *catasto*, levied at Florence in 1427 and occasionally thereafter. Governments were also requiring written evidence for cases to be handled in court – canon law had recognized the priority of written over customary law as early as 1140 – and this was being extended to commercial engagements. As fiscal machinery was developed to handle the king's needs, it stayed in place, sometimes with the taxes themselves, during peacetime, and became the basis of municipal budgets.

The cities also used tax farmers. Although tax farmers had an unsavoury reputation, from the standpoint of the employing government they had one great advantage: since they were used mainly for indirect levies, whose incomes varied greatly, the annual auction of the excises gave the city governments a decent idea at the beginning of the year of what receipts would be, and they could plan accordingly. Ghent, which was probably typical, realized between 80 and 90 per cent of its ordinary income in the 1360s and 1370s from farmed taxes. This gave a certain security to local finances that royal governments completely lacked, and may explain their turning to tax farming in the late fourteenth century, long after the largest cities began doing it. Since only the kings' domain revenues were stable, and their importance in the total income of the crown was diminishing sharply in the fourteenth century and most of the fifteenth except in England, national taxation levels might be crushing one year and insignificant the next, depending on the military circumstances.

Municipal governments in England were weaker than in France or even Castile, although the towns were guaranteed representatives in assemblies in each of the monarchies and thus gained some coherence as a social 'class' in national policy. The French kings abolished some communes, but except at Paris, which they controlled directly, they generally left local city councils in place, although they encouraged appeals to the royal courts from them. The expansion of the judicial and particularly the financial arm of the monarchy meant duplication of function. Throughout Europe central governments began encroaching on areas of economic regulation and social policy, such as education, that earlier had been left to the cities. When town governments dealt as collectivities with the central regime, it was usually to ask for tax relief. Even as the English kings relied more on local élites and less on officials of the royal court for governance in the shires, the central government was issuing regulations that eroded even the limited autonomy that English local communities had possessed. The Ordinance and Statute of Labourers of 1349 were the first royal laws that dealt with economic matters involving mainly the lower classes, who had been left to their own lords and/or to local governments before now. The change also involved some civil remedies not present in the common law, such as complaints about inferior workmanship and liability in civil actions. These actions, which are assumed today, were not present in royal law before the mid-fourteenth century. Thus policy was increasingly formulated at the national level, but enforcement became more localized than before.[10]

In France, which alone of the western national monarchies had no work-able national representative assembly by the late fifteenth century, the cities more often simply lobbied the central government, maintaining agents at the *Conseil* or *parlement* for the purpose, and thus showed no coherence of interest that transcended the interests of particular communities. The extent to which the French government had imposed its own officers in the towns, particularly the *élus*, had weakened the city governments without putting a strong royal network in place; the kings often sent the same directive to the royal officials and the town *échevins* to make certain of compliance. By the fifteenth century the *élus* had become a *de facto* council supplanting the *échevins* in many cities. The closest thing to a privileged estate of towns that France had was the *bonnes villes*, the walled towns which from the time of Charles VII had a special status, including exemption of their citizens from the *taille* and from the obligation to quarter soldiers, and in some cases even from the general levy.[11]

Changes in the Law

The growing power of national governments, and the elaboration of bureaucracies and institutions there and at the local level in the late Middle Ages, naturally had an impact on the evolution of law. Europe had a bewildering diversity of legal regimes in the late Middle Ages. Even in England the common law was supplemented to some extent by local and village customs, which the central courts generally respected in civil actions. The common law was written royal law, overriding ancient custom, and it was essentially procedural. Since it included diverse remedies that could benefit both plaintiff and defendant, depending on the context, the result was to transfer cases from the franchisal courts of the great barons to the overloaded royal courts without guaranteeing either fairness or speed. The use of chancery as a court of equity, in effect bypassing the common law, contributed to this diversity. Even after franchisal courts were ended in 1536, local custom ruled in cases that were not appealed to the king's justice; and the church courts also continued to be important in civil actions concerning tenants on their estates and persons in holy orders.

While the common law gave a national and written basis to the English court system, the customs of the Germanic tribes that had settled in northern France, particularly the Franks, had evolved into complex regional codes by the late Middle Ages. The customary law of Languedoc was Roman, derived from the vulgarized Roman law that the Burgundian and Visigothic rulers of the area had used for their Gallo-Roman subjects in the early Middle Ages. Roman law was revived as an academic discipline in the eleventh century when the *Body of the Civil Law*, the code compiled on the orders of the Byzantine emperor Justinian in the early sixth century, became more widely known in the west. From this point the customary law of Mediterranean Europe was quickly absorbed into written Roman practice.

It has thus been customary to distinguish southern France, Iberia and Italy as 'lands of written [Roman] law', while the north was a 'land of customary law'. This distinction has been much overdrawn even for the period before 1300, for the customs of the north were frequently put into writing before then. Roman law recognized the validity of custom as a source of law while preferring written, and canon law recognized the superiority of written law over oral tradition. Laws were not the only social arrangements that were committed by preference to writing: the period after 1300 witnessed a flood of statutes, commercial records, testaments, private correspondence and municipal records. Contemporaries noted and court records bear out a great increase in litigiousness after the plagues of the fourteenth century. People were demonstrably more violent than before, and the elimination of entire families in the plagues meant disputes over inheritances among distant relatives. By 1300 it was assumed by courts virtually everywhere that a transaction had to be in writing, at least in a private document if not recorded by a magistrate, to be uncontestably valid. The right of the state to issue laws was expanding into a right to confirm and/or to record private agreements and turn them into binding contracts.

While during the central Middle Ages the rights of the individual or group generally took precedence in law – if not always in practice – over the imperatives of the state, and the prince was thought to have reciprocal obligations toward his subjects or vassals, from 1300 to 1600, admittedly more after 1450 than before, there was a movement away from this in the direction of state absolutism. Roman law was incontestably state law, without much of a role for the corporate privileges so important in medieval custom, or for the rights of categories of subjects. The *Body of the Civil Law* contains some maxims that can be used to favour wide public participation, notably 'What concerns all must be approved by all'; but its overwhelming thrust, and the opinion of most of its medieval commentators, favoured the discretion of the prince, particularly as lawmaker, believing that 'what pleases the prince has the force of law'. As the lawmaking powers of princes became divorced from the need to consult assemblies except in England, Catalonia–Aragon and the Netherlands and some small principalities elsewhere, by 1450 Roman law was becoming a tool of centralization and absolutism under the prince, beginning in Latin Europe, where the Roman tradition was older and stronger, and then spreading to Germany in the late fifteenth and particularly the sixteenth century. The princes of Continental Europe were taking the powers that Roman law gave to the emperor to apply to themselves and thus provide a justification for the tremendous growth of the institutions of state power that had taken place under the impulse of the heightened demand for money, soldiers and officials.

This line of reasoning, although essentially correct in its broad outline, cannot be applied rigidly. The various legal regimes of Europe had much in common. All European legal traditions make the ruler God's representative on earth. Customary, Roman and common law defined social and political relations in terms of the material rather than a transcendent world. The ruler who did not rule his people as God decreed could be restricted. All the legal traditions, too, respected the property right of the free citizen that could not be infringed by the state, although Roman law allowed reason of state to seize property and violate rights under more circumstances than did the other two. This power was most often used to subordinate corporate privileges, notably those of village and urban communities, to the state, but nowhere did it become the justification for seizing the property of the individual citizen. As Brian Downing says, 'Late medieval Europe is distinguishable from other parts of the world by binding legal codes setting procedural and substantive boundaries for many aspects of social, economic, and political life.'[12]

Provinces and town governments codified their laws, which usually consisted of an original charter supplemented by statutes and the rulings of magistrates. Villages regulated agricultural practice and social relations with bylaws. As even these old customs became written law, they could be changed by the ruler, who had the power to modify custom. As early as the period of Louis IX (1226–70) the French royal government was empanelling local juries to provide the details of local custom, which were then put into writing; but there remained a considerable sphere for oral custom through testimony in court cases. In 1454, with the Ordinance of Montils-les-Tours, the royal government ordered that all customs be put into writing, systematizing what had begun in the thirteenth century. This was an important stage of standardizing between the earlier, written law regimes of the south and the customary laws of the north. Whenever a custom had no firm answer to a legal question, it was decided according to Roman law. In most parts of Continental Europe magistrates who were versed in local custom but had no university training in law dominated city councils into the fifteenth century, but by 1450 they were yielding to those who had studied Roman law.

Accompanying the more formal structuring of legal procedure and of the relation of law to the state was the growth of a legal profession. In 1250 few litigants found it necessary to employ lawyers; by 1450 most did. Persons skilled in the Roman law, most of them trained at the University of Montpellier, had been important tools for the French kings against the great feudatories from the late thirteenth century. Philip IV's use of Guillaume de Nogaret and Pierre Flote is especially well-known; both were from lesser noble families who used the study of law as a means of restoring their and their families' fortunes, as the king rewarded their services with lands and titles. Litigants needed skilful pleaders in the increasingly complex civil cases that resulted from the proliferation of inheritance actions after the plagues and from the growing complexity of procedures as they were committed to writing; and as lawyers became more important in society, they became subjects of criticism by moralists and of ridicule by satirists. On the Continent Roman law was a university discipline, and university faculties were consulted on doubtful points of interpretation. In England the common law was largely case law, as fixed by royal enactments, and older customary law. Thus lawyers were trained at the common-law courts. The Inns of Court began as lodging-houses that catered to students attending the court sessions at Westminster, but they expanded in the late Middle Ages into formal schools administered by practising lawyers.

In addition to becoming written and, on the Continent, Roman, law was becoming more rational and state-enforced after 1300. These two developments, however, were not the same. Some supernatural elements are present in procedures favoured by Germanic customary law, notably the ordeal, which was rare after 1215 and virtually gone by 1300, replaced by Roman practices of evidence and proof, notably the inquest. The Roman view of the prince as lawgiver took longer to become accepted, and criminal as well as civil procedure changed. Before 1300 most criminal actions required a formal complaint. Since the statutes provided corporal punishments for felony convictions, most preferred to arbitrate and settle even homicides by an out-of-court payment of damages to the deceased's family, as in the early Germanic period. But particularly after 1350, in western Europe although not on the peripheries, the state began to assume *ex officio* the right to ascertain and punish crime. City governments were more precocious in this regard than the national monarchies, increasingly requiring litigants to agree formally to keep the peace; and since this agreement was done before a magistrate, violation of the peace became a violation of the peace of the town, punishable by police power. In rural areas dominated by the aristocracy, however, out-of-court arbitration and compensation were still considered the most appropriate way to settle disputes regarding honour between social equals. When the dispute was between persons who were of unequal status, most often in the case of property offences, the letter of the law was more often observed.[13]

* * *

The necessity of increased state responsibility and expenses was not the mother of invention of the state apparatus of late medieval Europe, but it certainly catalysed it. National and regional governments obtruded on the discretion of individual citizens and even more of local governments by 1450 to a far greater extent than in 1300. Despite the violence and disorder of the period, most of the formal institutional changes were accomplished legally. They left England with a monarchy that was weaker institutionally than in 1300, given the need to bargain with Parliament for money, but which was still very powerful. France and Castile had been less precocious than England in developing a bureaucratic state responsible to the crown, but in the century and a half after 1300 they quickly developed a far more oppressive and expensive domestic state apparatus than that of England. Evidently more by accident than by design, and certainly not through the competence of the individual kings, the French crown by 1450 was constrained by no significant institutional power other than the inertia of its own bureaucracy. This statement would become true of the Castilian monarchy, but not until the next century.

The economic changes that accompanied the growth of state power in late medieval Europe are often associated with the population regression that began in the late thirteenth century and intensified after 1348. But this is only part of the story. Europe had also become a single interrelated commercial nexus that linked the various economic regions with a much more sophisticated infrastructure than before. Europeans had always traded with one another and with outsiders for luxuries and for items that were not available at home, but now they became much more dependent on one another for basic goods and services. The justly famous expansion of European interests in Asia, Africa and the Americas in the late fifteenth century was preceded by economic consolidation and integration in the period between 1300 and 1450.

|3|

Economic Integration and Social Change in Late Medieval Europe

Antecedents of a Crisis: The Overheated Economy of the Late Thirteenth Century

While the central medieval centuries were a time of economic and demographic growth, contraction began around 1270 in Mediterranean Europe and had affected all of the north by 1310. The depression deepened with the plagues of the mid-fourteenth century. Relative stability in the early fifteenth century was succeeded by a long period of economic growth that began around 1470, was broken briefly by a crisis in the 1550s, then recovered until a new subsistence crisis in the 1590s. In some areas the indices of economic growth persist until the 1620s.

The expansion of crop production and rural population in the twelfth and early thirteenth centuries had resulted from extending arable land, mainly by reclamation from the sea and by bringing swamps and forested areas under cultivation, rather than from technological improvements that would have improved per capita yields. Qualitative improvements in agricultural technique, although documented earlier, only came into general use in the late thirteenth century, just as the problem of soil exhaustion from overcropping was becoming serious. Finally, medieval agriculture much more than industry was labour-intensive rather than technologically proficient, at least until after the plagues of the fourteenth century. Much of the problem was lack of peasant capital and the constriction of the common agricultural routines of northern Europe, which did not permit farmers to do absolutely what they wanted even with land that they owned.

The Origins of Commercial Capitalism in the Middle Ages

The three centuries after 1300 see the triumph of commercial capitalism, but only at the end of the period is there much evidence of industrial capitalism. Capitalism is difficult to define, but in capitalistic economies few if any persons produce all their necessities, and they are thus dependent on a market mechanism either for food, for the tools to produce it or for the services to market it. Capitalism assumes private ownership of the means of production which, as we have seen, was guaranteed by all legal regimes of Europe, and the more or less free capacity to increase wealth through competition.

The essence of capitalism is investing money that is not needed to buy present necessities to make more money that can be used in the future; but investment carries the possibility of loss as well as profit. Europe has supplies of silver but had to trade for gold. A great increase in the supply of money had facilitated the commercial growth of the central Middle Ages. By 1250 princes had to buy large quantities of food to supplement the rents in kind provided by their estates, and enormous cities had developed that had to obtain grain to feed their populations. Thus market relations involving money were the way in which most services were compensated and most manufactured goods were bought. Farmers who grew a surplus sold it for money to townspeople, and to other farmers whose lands did not support them and who had to survive by taking other jobs. Many and perhaps most Europeans were using money to buy food by 1300.

By 1300, however, a dearth of bullion had become apparent that reached its nadir between 1390 and 1420. The output of the mines declined, but an important component of the problem was also a negative balance of trade. Europe developed a trade imbalance with the Levant in the late thirteenth century. Thus silver, the normal medium of exchange in Europe, moved eastward and was not compensated by the gold that easterners used to pay for western goods, mainly manufactures. This problem was only ameliorated with the opening of new mines in central Europe in the fifteenth century. Thus, just as government expenses were multiplying in the 1290s, princes lacked sufficient coin to pay for their enterprises. The French kings responded by debasing their coins. Prices rose, but the rulers were able to pay the face value of their debts without correction for inflation. Paradoxically this also contributed to severe inflation in England, which kept a stable coin, since the stability caused silver to migrate there and thus lose its intrinsic value.

A network of inter-regional exchanges had been created before 1300 that continued to expand thereafter, albeit in the absence of one controlling assumption upon which commercial capitalism was predicated: an abundant supply of capital. Wages were still paid in coin, and for most market transactions even the severely debased 'black money' sufficed. Yet supplies of coin were inadequate for large-scale transactions, which thus required the use of fiduciary money and credit mechanisms. Credit facilities, however, were primitive throughout this period, even in the Italian cities. Obviously there is more evidence of capitalism in the cities than in the rural areas, but this is not to say that capitalism was absent from rural Europe. In areas with large numbers of peasant proprietors some speculated on the land market, buying plots from their less fortunate neighbours, and lords and townspeople, of course, had more opportunity to do this.

Another aspect of capitalism is that labour is usually rewarded by a wage unless one is working for oneself. Lords in the central Middle Ages had retained substantial portions of their estates, called 'demesnes', that were cultivated for their use, usually accompanying this with cash and kind rents. Wherever demesne farming persisted after 1200, labour was needed only in the peak seasons of planting and harvest. By 1300 virtually all villages had a number of persons who did not hold enough land to permit them to support a household and were thus willing to work for a wage. Thus virtually all urban labourers, including many apprentices, and many rural workers received a money wage from their masters throughout the period covered by this book. Many lords had found it more efficient to hire labourers for wages even in the thirteenth century, and by 1349 most demesnes were farmed largely in this way, with some help from the labour rents of unfree tenants. Overpopulation by 1300 and the resulting competition for jobs, combined with the dearth of coin, meant that real wages (the nominal wage adjusted for changes in the cost of living) began dropping in the late thirteenth century. Yet lords did not always benefit from this situation. Although rents and interest rose, the overall rate of inflation was just over 2 per cent annually on rents and 1 per cent on grain, rates comparable to those of the misnamed 'price revolution' of the sixteenth century.[1]

Most persons who owed substantial labour services as rent were their lord's serfs, called villeins in England, bound to his court and to various payments in money and kind. Even in places where there was no longer serfdom, free villagers paid money rents but were still bound to do 'boon services' during the peak seasons of harvest and planting for their lords as part of their rent. The services exacted of prosperous villeins (those with a virgate of land or more) often included working on the lord's demesne with a labourer hired by the villein, a fact that shows how large and fluid the labour market was. Yet the obligations of villeinage were normally incumbent only on the head of household; thus a villein might owe labour as rent for his tenement, or a free farmer might owe boon services, but his wife and children did not and were quite capable of managing the family homestead, at least if the children were old enough to work and too young to have established their own households.

Money rents dominated everywhere, and the cash rents owed by villeins were frequently lower than what lords charged free tenants on the same estates; for the villein's tenure was 'customary', which included a rent that remained fixed when his heirs took over the tenement. Lords had more discretion with free tenants and could more easily rent to them for a term of years, then raise the rent when the term expired if the land market was tight. Yet the total value in coin of the labour services, mortuary duties and various 'rents of recognition' that were owed only by serfs was generally more onerous than the obligations of free tenants. None the less, serfdom had a crucial protection for the villein: as long as the rents were paid and the labour performed he could not be ejected from his tenement. Free tenants were less protected by manorial custom than the villeins were, although they had some protection from the royal courts that villeins lacked. Free tenant farmers who rented rather than owned their land were the major victims of the tendency of lords to raise rents to take advantage of the land hunger resulting from overpopulation in the early fourteenth century.

By 1300 most farmers were producing for market, not simply for their own consumption. Both farm and industrial prices were quite high for most years between 1290 and 1330, and this situation generally benefited the producer and hurt the consumer. Since overpopulation was worse in the cities than in the rural areas, the farmer who had enough surplus to make it profitable to market could charge high prices to the city folk who were dependent on his grain. Only if he needed industrial goods produced in the cities would this balance be redressed to some extent. Few farmers needed the luxury textiles that were the stock-in-trade of the urban economies, and most villagers bought their tools from local smiths. Only after the plagues did high industrial prices have much impact on the farmers.

Great lords, who had large amounts of land which were often scattered in many places that could be potential markets, access to labour for their estates and many rents in kind, were the major beneficiaries of the high prices on food. But smaller farmers could also benefit, and from this perspective the development of an improved network of overland transport, the use of carts for carrying goods to market and the development of horse-rather than ox-hauling in the thirteenth century were critically important. Even a small surplus could be marketed profitably when transport costs were low, because the market was close to the site of production. Thus even small farmers could do well in areas of incipient capitalism, where there would be a dense population that was occupationally differentiated and had some rural industry, good access to markets, a generally free peasantry and good soil.

Early capitalism also had an impact on rural industrial production. The population growth of the central Middle Ages had created enormous cities that depended for food on a rural economy that was no longer able to feed the farmers adequately, let alone provision the urban markets. A specialized and highly differentiated workforce existed in the cities by 1300, which became tightly regulated by occupational guilds as population and demand for unspecialized goods declined in the fourteenth century. Yet even in the thirteenth century there was a large amount of rural industry, most obviously in such areas as mining and ironworking, and the pull of an urban market injected a wage-earning, capitalist element into the rural economy through the various construction trades. Many – in the less skilled building crafts, most – of the labourers came from the rural environs of the city and returned to their farms at night. Some rural labour was admittedly the result of need: women, particularly widows, did considerable amounts of baking and brewing.

Rural work was also important in exportable industries such as textiles. Woollen clothmaking was highly specialized, with different people spinning and combing the yarn and fulling the cloth, stretching it on frames, weaving, dyeing and performing a myriad of finishing operations. Thus the textile merchants of the cities bought the raw wool and 'put it out' to the various craftsmen, to whom they paid wages. When the textile was finished, the merchant as the owner of the raw materials in it was able to sell it. The merchants often used rural workers for the less skilled tasks, such as spinning and fulling. This practice was bitterly resented by the urban workers, who could not work as cheaply as farmers, to whom industrial jobs were second occupations, often done by the housewife while her husband concentrated on field labour. 'Putting out' became even more common in the late Middle Ages than before, but with the difference that by this time some villages were developing their own clothmaking independent of, and sometimes in imitation of, that of nearby cities.

The State and the Economy: The Beginnings of National Economic Policy

The state, although becoming more intrusive in the late Middle Ages, owned few assets, and for all the inroads of national government on local autonomy, most industrial regulation remained at the local level. Yet the heavy hand of government was not unfelt on the economy. Most rulers into the thirteenth century tried to live off their 'ordinary' revenues, domain rents, regalian right and feudal payments. They realized that tolls on trade, which only a king could grant, could increase their revenue, and accordingly promoted it with charters. But as their need for money increased in the thirteenth century, they began to develop new ways to tap the wealth that trade had generated. This meant new forms of economic regulation and also monopoly: for since states had small bureaucracies before 1300, it was easier to collect large sums from a few payers than small sums from a broadly based tax-paying population. Thus governments gave 'staple' or monopoly privileges to cities, requiring that certain goods be unloaded at the favoured site, or gave them the sole right within their domains to manufacture a particular textile, then exacted high fees or taxes from the places that were thus made artificially prosperous.

It was even easier to grant export privileges to foreign merchants, often including tax advantages that were not enjoyed by native merchants. Given that a small number of persons was involved, the mechanics of this were simple: the foreigners paid dearly for their charters, and they were expected to make substantial loans to the prince who had granted them. The foreigners were unpopular, and this also made them easier to control. Most of the long-distance carrying trade of Europe was thus handled until well into the fifteenth century by Italians and Germans. But in the fourteenth century rulers also began using native merchants as sources of loans, and this meant that something had to be done to make them more competitive with the aliens. The English kings, making an exception for the export licences given to Italians and Hansards, gave a monopoly on other wool exports to fluctuating syndicates of native merchants, usually London-dominated, who were expected to advance the king large sums of money in return.

Some state regulation was thus done more for political than economic reasons. Philip IV of France embargoed the export of coin to Italy to force Boniface VIII to yield in their quarrel over clerical taxation (see Chapter 4). In 1270, as a result of a quarrel with the countess of Flanders, the English prohibited wool exports to Flanders, which needed it for the textile industries that employed as many as half the households of its cities.The wool trade became involved in financing the early stages of the Hundred Years War. In 1336 the king imposed another wool embargo on Flanders to force the regime there into an English alliance. He simultaneously gave selected English merchants a monopoly on the export of wool in return for a substantial loan. This was a dangerous business for them, for Edward's financial and personal credit were not good. As smuggling rose, the king seized substantial quantities of wool and sold it to the merchants in return for bonds that were never redeemed. Although the merchants became more cautious after this fiasco, the wool trade, with the product now taxed at 40*s*. per sack, about one-quarter of the value of the highest grades of English wool, remained critical to royal finances. From 1363 a wool 'staple' was fixed permanently at Calais, managed by a 'Company of the Staple'. This did not, as was once thought, mean that all who wanted to buy English wool either had to get export licences from England (in return for a fee, Italian merchants were permitted to export directly from Southampton) or come personally to Calais, for the wool could be bought through Italian and Flemish bankers at Bruges in return for credits.

The economic regulations of princes could have unforeseen consequences. By unilaterally sextupling the customs on wool exports between 1275 and 1297, Edward I of England raised the purchase price of the wool so astronomically that some Continental buyers looked elsewhere for their supplies of all but the best wool. Others who continued to buy the English product were being priced out of the market. The royal policy meant such high overseas prices on the wool that increasing amounts of it stayed in

England, whose textile manufactures for export grew in the late Middle Ages. Although English broadcloths were not as fine as the Flemish export textiles, they were able to compete successfully with them in all but the most aristocratic of markets because they were substantially cheaper: English clothiers did not have to factor high overseas transport costs and export taxes into their product, and the English clothmaking guilds, which were considerably weaker politically than the Flemish, were not able to get wages as high as were often paid on the Continent. Most English cloth in the late fourteenth and fifteenth centuries was exported to the Netherlands, where it could be sold legally except in Flanders, and to eastern Europe, generally through the offices of the merchants of the German Hanse (see below) in London.

By the late fifteenth century the value of cloth exports exceeded that of wool, a result hardly foreseen by a king who only wanted more customs revenue. As more English wool remained at home, some of the demand for high-quality wool on the Continent was filled from the late fourteenth century by Castilian wool, although it was less good than the English product. In 1273 Alfonso X of Castile permitted the Mesta, an association of sheep growers who specialized in the Merino, to take their sheep on a specified grazing circuit through Castile. This gave Castile its first major exportable commodity and a source of tax revenue to the kings; unfortunately, it also ruined the farmland through which the sheep moved.

The Late Medieval Agrarian Crisis

The rate of population growth slowed in the late thirteenth century, although the continued expansion of city markets concealed the structural problems in the rural economy and provided some outlet for farmers whose lands had been reduced by sale or subdivision into plots that were too small to sustain a household. Most harvests were good until the 1290s, but the problems of continued population growth were exacerbated by a worsening climate that began in that decade and reached its nadir in the 'little ice age' of the seventeenth century. The Scheldt river in Flanders was frozen over for 17 days in February, 1387, and this was no isolated example. Heavy rainfall caused flooding; considerable land that had been reclaimed from the North Sea was inundated in 1404 and not recovered again until the modern period.

Europe could not feed its population adequately. Its unoccupied land was unsuitable for agriculture. In Italy there was a severe problem of peasant debt to lords in the late thirteenth century, for the farmers fell into default on rents during bad years and had to use precious seed corn as food. Lords did not generally foreclose on them, since they were more likely to collect the debts from resident tenants than from persons who had been forced away, presumably into a city. But economic bondage in areas such as Italy,

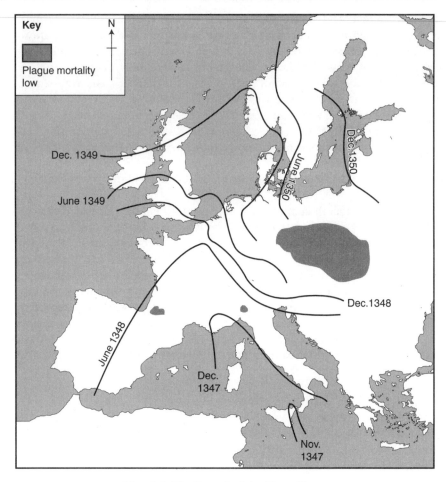

Map 3.1 The Spread of the Great Plague

whose farmers were legally free, was becoming a serious problem by 1300 and would intensify.

The first major crisis of the new century began in 1310 with a series of bad harvests caused by torrential rainfall. The harvest in north-western Europe failed almost completely in 1315, with food prices in the cities reaching several times the normal, a fact that shows clearly that the natural disasters began only after the infrastructure of a commercial, capitalistic market economy was already in place. A 'plague', probably typhus, visited the malnourished population in 1316, and the combined famine and epidemic produced a mortality rate of between 5 and 10 per cent even in places that had good access to grain, and a higher one in isolated places and the largest cities. Separate epidemics affecting animals, mainly sheep, commenced in 1316, and this drove prices of meat and wool upward. Some relief was obtained with grain imports from the Mediterranean, now possible with the development of a regular connection (see below) over Gibraltar. The crisis of 1315–16 accelerated a population decline that had already begun in most areas before 1315, but after 1322 the drop again became gradual. Growing disorder and the onset of war were already depressing population and productivity still further when another famine struck in 1340, affecting the Mediterranean areas as well as the north.

Europe had thus experienced population decline for roughly half a century before the famous 'Black Death' struck in 1348–50. The term 'Black Death' was first used in Swedish and Danish works of the sixteenth century to indicate the awfulness and unknown, not the medical aspects of the disease.[2] The expression was slower to spread to Germany and England – mainly from the nineteenth century in both – and it is still rarely used in Italy. The 'bubonic' plague, so called because of the black pustules (buboes) that formed in the extremities, has given a collective name to three plagues that raged throughout Europe. The bacillus was brought by fleas that lived on the backs of brown rats. It began in China and was brought west on Genoese ships at the end of 1347. It had spread throughout central France by the summer of 1348, to southern England by the winter of 1348, then to the rest of Britain and the Low Countries in 1349. Then it moved eastward into Germany and Scandinavia, and finally into the German–Slavic East. Recovery from bubonic plague is possible if the pustules do not break, but a pneumonic plague, which was carried in the lungs and spread by human contact, and septicaemia also raged in these years and were invariably fatal. Contemporary sources can only describe symptoms, and some of those noted in the years of the Black Death are similar to anthrax. Ergotism, which results from consumption of a fungus that develops on rye, was also widespread. Other illnesses that today are more readily identifiable and controlled, such as influenza and typhoid, seem to have been called 'plague' without discrimination by late medieval writers.

Europe as a whole probably lost one-third to two-fifths of its population in the two years after 1348, and some large cities lost half their inhabitants. Yet the long-range impact of the disaster was quite diverse depending on individual circumstances. The human tragedy is unimaginable; yet even after the famines and plagues of the early fourteenth century, population levels were still so high in 1348 that the massive depopulations had an initial economic impact that was not entirely baneful. Critical to our under- standing of the long-range structural changes is the fact that the plagues did not stop in 1350. Totally apart from localized epidemics, there were pandemics in 1358, one in 1361 that became known as the 'plague of the children', another in 1368–9 that was more severe in the Low Countries than that of 1349, and one in 1374–5 that was particularly bad in England. The cycle of plagues then slowed somewhat: the next one that affected all Europe came in 1400. Another gap of a generation followed until a pandemic in 1438, but except in the Low Countries there were frequent epidemics until the 1480s, with the 1430s and 1470s particularly severe in England. Population thus declined or at least did not recover significantly until after 1450.

Predictably, the plagues were especially virulent among the the biologically weakest, the elderly and the very young. Although birth rates rose after each plague, as parents tried to replace lost children, the frequency of the plagues in the generation after 1350 meant that many of these children did not live to maturity and have children of their own. Thus replacement rates remained low, and populations continued to drop even more than can be accounted for by plague mortality alone. Despite this, there is little evidence until after 1375 of jobs being unfilled, or rural land falling vacant; for the population was so high that whoever was lost could be replaced. In parts of England the labour shortage only became permanent after the 1390s. The crisis is associated with low farm prices, but the worst of the grain-price drop likewise occurred after 1375 in northern Europe and 1395 in Italy, not 1348.

It thus appears that, for at least a generation after 1348, the horrifying epidemics were simply bringing population down to a level that could be fed with the existing agricultural technology. Population decline, worsening climate and even, in some areas, worsening yields on grain do not necessarily mean a lower standard of living unless there is severe over-population, which remained the case until around 1375. This, of course, takes long-term trends, which homogenize extremes into averages. Prices suggest that there were some bad harvest years in every decade between 1290 and 1370, but the problem was especially severe before 1330. The last quarter of the fourteenth century was better; then 1400–40 was bad, but this period opened and closed with pandemics. The worst years for famines apart from plagues were 1437–40. Except in England, 1440–70 generally saw both high wages and high prices, a fact that doubtless contributes to the image of a 'golden age' at that time in the Burgundian Netherlands.[3]

Yet while long-term worsening climate and population decline did not necessarily mean lower living standards, short-term fluctuations usually did. The plagues generally struck during the warm months, when crops were planted or harvested. Thus food was scarce after each plague, and prices rose. Whether to take advantage of the high prices or to forestall an expected scarcity, or both, lords paid extremely high wages to farm labourers, upon whom they now relied instead of serfs for the bulk of their workforce, to get lands back into cultivation. This did not hurt only the great lords, for many middling farmers also had to hire labourers in the peak seasons since they had too much land for them to work personally or with their families. Thus the English Parliament issued the Statute of Labourers in 1349, which fixed wages at the levels of 1346. Similar statutes were issued by the French kings and some German princes. Yet although the courts tried to enforce the Statute of Labourers, the law was behind practice; wages paid to farm labourers in England were twice as high in real terms in 1400 as in 1300.

But high wages were not the only problem affecting the farmers, for from an economic perspective the labourers were not really needed. Much farm production was geared toward the high prices of the urban market, but mortality from the epidemics was higher in the cities than in the rural areas. The result was long-term overproduction that drove grain prices down after the momentary high prices of the years just after each plague. Two other practices also contributed to low grain prices. First, city governments, faced with potential revolution when bread prices were high, began stockpiling grain when prices were low and selling it below market value when they rose again, usually during and just after the plagues. Second, and more important, a substantial long-distance trade in grain was developing in northern Europe. The Italian and Iberian cities had long been dependent on grain imported from Sicily, the Black Sea area and northern Africa. By the mid-fourteenth century the cities of the German Hanse were building much larger boats than before and using them to bring shiploads of grain and other raw materials from eastern Europe, which was much less densely populated than the west and had an exportable farm surplus. It was often easier and safer, particularly in theatres of war, to obtain large quantities of food from distant areas than to patronize local farmers. As demand markets became centred in the cities and as large-scale seaborne transportation over great distances became possible, low transport costs often caused local farmers to be undersold.

The farmers were caught between high wages paid to labourers and low grain prices. Many abandoned their farms to move into the cities, where, given higher mortality than in the countryside, they stood a statistically greater chance of being cut down by the next plague. For although the population of most cities declined sharply during the plagues, they recovered more rapidly due to immigration than did the rural areas. Europe thus became a more urban place in the late Middle Ages than before; for although population only reached its 1300 levels again toward 1600, more of the population by the later date was in the cities, particularly the growing national capitals.

The depression on grain prices was long-term, lasting into the late fifteenth century in most areas. But there were options for farmers who did not move into the cities. Low grain prices induced farmers, when village agricultural customs such as collective ploughing of the fields did not prevent individuals from doing this, to supplement grain with cultivation of vegetables, for which prices remained high. While most places had rotated two or three fields in the central Middle Ages, as many as six fields under cultivation were not uncommon by 1450. Industrial raw materials, notably dyes, were also being grown. As lack and expense of labour and low demand caused grain acreage to fall out of cultivation, many farmers shifted to stock rearing, which is much less labour-intensive and thus more cost-effective than crops. Prices of animal products such as meat, butter and cheese remained high. Sheep had an obvious importance for their wool, which was always highly lucrative: the profitability of wool would lead to increased enclosures of individual strips of land and of village commons, although mainly after 1470. Cattle were important for meat – inventories of distributions at hospitals and almshouses show much more meat and vegetables in the diet even of those receiving poor relief than before – and for industrial by-products such as leather, which was produced in much greater quantity in the late Middle Ages than before. Raising more animals also produced more manure, the major fertilizer used, which had been in short supply in the late thirteenth century as human and animal populations pressed on the same resources. Some chemical fertilizers were also supplementing manure. With more diversified agricultural regimes, Europeans were eating a more balanced diet after the plagues than before.

Social Changes in Rural Europe

Except in England and regions of the Continent where the commercial economy was less pervasive, notably Castile and parts of south-eastern France, legal serfdom was unusual by 1300. Lords got most of their income from rents, sales of grain and judicial fines; thus cash rather than services or other obligations based on personal status were important to the lords. Freedom cannot be equated with economic prosperity, for the problems of the peasantry affected the market relations of producers, regardless of their legal standing, and in the case of the French peasantry the warfare, civil at times and international at others, led to widespread expropriation and depopulation. After 1300 the power of kings in central Europe was diminishing, and thus, in contrast to the monarchs of western Europe, they were in no position to protect the peasantry against the growing power of the territorial lords. The landed aristocrats, most of them descendants of German settlers who had colonized the area, thus turned the peasants into serfs. The market for grain in still densely populated north-western Europe, and the obvious suitability of the underpopulated, fertile and flat north German plain, encouraged the lords to impose labour services and hinder the mobility of their dependents. Serfdom also revived in parts of south-western Germany after 1400. Using Roman law, lords consolidated their authority as the sole powers within the state, a very effective device against the mainly oral customary law on which peasant liberties were based.

   The fates of the peasantry in England and on the Continent started to diverge in the late fourteenth century. An uprising of peasants and small townspeople in south-eastern England in 1381 began as a revolt against the imposition of the third poll tax in four years, and at twice the rate in 1381 as in 1377. Discontinent was fanned by the fact that many lords in the immediate aftermath of the plagues tried to impose labour services on farmers whose ancestors had owed them. The disorders rapidly escalated into a general protest against the social order. Led by Wat Tyler, the 'peasants' broke through the gates of London, killed the archbishop of Canterbury and the royal chancellor and controlled the city for several days before they were routed by royal troops. Inspired by preachers who inveighed against distinctions of rank when God had created all equal, the rebel leaders presented a coherent, issue-driven programme to the authorities, demanding the abolition of serfdom and the commutation of labour services into a fixed money rent of 4 pence per acre of land. Given the immense variation in local conditions of tenure, the latter imperative ignored supply, demand and the market. Richard II, then aged 14, none the less acceded to these demands, only to withdraw them after the peasants were no longer a threat.

Yet, despite brutal punishment of the rebels, the incidence of serfdom in England did gradually decline. As the governments of kings and local princes expanded and became institutionalized they encouraged peasant emancipation, which placed farmers under the jurisdiction of royal rather than princely courts. When conflicts erupted in Catalonia between landlords and the *remenças* (serfs), who wanted freedom to leave their tenures, given the opportunities that depopulation provided, King Alfonso V freed the *remenças* in 1455 by ending the customs that bound them to the land; but only after 1486 was it clear that noble resistance through the Catalan *Generalitat* would not reverse the decree. The *remenças*, although technically bondsmen, were generally prosperous and objected less to seigniorial rents than to restrictions on their mobility.

While rents on farmland had been high in the early fourteenth century due to population pressure and the resultant land hunger, they now stagnated, as lords were in effect competing for tenants in the late fourteenth and fifteenth centuries. At the same time royal incursions were making the lords' franchisal courts less lucrative. Given high wages and diversifying agricultural regimes, it became increasingly common for bondsmen simply to pay a fee to their lords for permission to stay off the manor and seek employment elsewhere, which in turn was loosening the real bonds of serfdom. The customary tenure of the thirteenth century was evolving in England into copyhold tenure, in which the obligations were copied into the manor court roll in what amounted to a title deed.

The land market became more fluid in the fifteenth century. Many displaced farmers moved to the cities. Often lacking marketable skills and a family tie that would give entry into a guild, many of them contributed to the growing problem there of urban poverty and unemployment. Despite the volatile land market, however, peasants rarely moved from one village to another. Those with an adequate amount of land had no reason to move; and those who had too little could not save enough to buy land elsewhere. Mortgages in the modern sense were available only to persons who started with large amounts of capital, and thus buyers of real estate in both cities and the rural areas needed to have most of the purchase price in cash on hand.

Thus the volatility of the land market is only explicable through village *coqs*, called franklins in England, buying up land as their less fortunate neighbours had to sell, often after a bad harvest. The sellers then, lacking money to buy other land, had to become mainly wage-earners, sometimes keeping enough land to farm a small garden. Many lords also were leasing their demesnes to prosperous free villagers, who accumulated additional land by leasing copyholds. In areas of partible inheritance, plots that were too small for a single family farm might be combined by a real-estate entre-preneur. As personal subjection declined in the fifteenth century, and population decline made larger amounts of land available for purchase, consolidating small properties into viable farms became easier. Although the greatest lords were being hurt by low rents and the expenses of conspicuous consumption, middle-level gentry, such as the famous Paston family in England, were able to accumulate many different tenancies, with different juridical status, into reasonably coherent holdings and thus work their way into the lowest level of the aristocracy.

The Urban Crisis

Except for the national capitals that developed in the modern period, the urban map of Europe was virtually complete by 1300. The population expansion had created some enormous cities: Paris was the largest, with some 200,000 souls, while Granada, Venice, Genoa and Milan had between 100,000 and 150,000, Florence, Seville and Ghent between 75,000 and 95,000, and Cologne, Naples, Barcelona, Palermo and Siena between 50,000 and 60,000. The cities absorbed populations from their rural environs, and thus had a supply of labour that gave rise to occupational differentiation and the production of manufactured goods.

With their inhabitants in dense contact with one another, cities invariably experience higher death rates than in the rural areas, and household sizes tend to be smaller. The cities naturally experienced much greater short-term losses from the plagues than did the rural areas. The agricultural depression was so severe after the plagues, and the market for urban manufactures and the opportunities for jobs in the service sector so sufficient, that while few cities regained their pre-plague populations before 1500, their losses in the long term were relatively less severe than those of the rural areas.

As was true of the countryside, urban populations generally stabilized after the shock of the plagues until about 1375. The exceptions are cases such as Ghent, where the causes of high mortality and insufficient compen-satory immigration were as much political as bacteriological. But by 1400 immigration was no longer sufficient to keep the cities as buoyant as before. Birth and replacement rates seem to have dropped after 1400 after a rise since 1348. Particularly in England, some cities underwent severe decline after about 1420. York is a prime example of a city that experienced an expanding market for industrial goods after 1350, in this case cloth, providing jobs that attracted immigrants. But when demand dropped, and weaving in Yorkshire began competing with the city's product, the result was inevitable decline. Of the cities noted above, with populations over 50,000 in 1300, only Paris grew in the fourteenth century, and political turmoil may have dropped its population to as low as 30,000 by the 1430s. The others declined sharply: in the Italian examples to perhaps one-third of their 1300 levels by 1450, in the north European cases to roughly half. Bruges and London, which had no more than 35,000 persons in the early fourteenth century, are the sole examples of modest growth among the larger cities.

Immigration, however, led to significant problems in the cities. Most of the immigrants were unskilled and thus flooded the market for low-level jobs. In reaction, most occupational guilds in the cities, particularly those that were guaranteed seats on the city councils, made mastership more difficult to obtain than before as they tried to secure what was seen, not in every case correctly, as a shrinking market for their sons. Some made mastership hereditary, but most simply set higher entry fees or required more training from children of persons who were not masters in the guild than from those with prior family contact. Most industrial production was still conducted in the home, and fathers trained one or more of their sons or occasionally daughters in the family trade; but since not all children could be accommodated by the guild, this was sometimes restricted to the eldest son, or to sons who were born after the father had become a master. Formal apprenticeship was needed for persons who had not been trained in the father's craft or were not following his trade. Craftsmen who had been trained but could pay the entry fees or meet other requirements of the guilds worked for a wage as journeymen; for many this was as high as they could go, as mastership became more difficult for outsiders to attain. Journeymen associations thus are found in many parts of Europe, particularly in France and the German Rhineland, although the authorities considered them potentially revolutionary and frowned upon them.

The urban occupational guilds thus became increasingly aristocratic in the late Middle Ages. Virtually all of them developed an élite of merchants who bought raw materials and sold them to others in the guild. In some cases the guild élites specialized in goods that had nothing to do with the occupation that gave the guild its name. The export of wool from York was handled by the mercers, while the grocers did so from London; many of the merchants of the Company of the Staple that controlled the English wool export at Calais were London grocers, who imported spices and exported wool.

Limiting mastership did not mean that persons who were not masters could not work; rather, they could not become masters, a distinction that gave them political rights – for the guilds had a political dimension through their control of seats on the city councils – and allowed them to own their shops and train apprentices, and thus become work-givers rather than employees. In cases where one master took work from another, in the case of the construction trades, for example, masters were paid at a higher rate than journeymen, often double. Masters could work as long as jobs were available, but others could only work when masters needed them. The independent master, as opposed to one who took work from another because he could not or did not wish to keep his own shop, usually continued to practise his profession, but he was also a work-giver who paid wages, a clear change from the period before the late thirteenth century. Then as now, persons who employed others did not have a salary in the modern sense of a guaranteed compensation for given work performed, but rather took whatever profits remained after expenses, including employees' wages, were deducted, reinvested some of it if they chose in the business or some other source, and lived on the rest. The degree of conspicuous consumption varied with the amount or percentage that was reinvested in the business and its assets, which often included the family home or part of it.

Yet the officially recognized guilds do not even begin to account for the number of trades that were practised in the labour market. Some guilds were actually composites, grouping people in different occupations for the sake of a corporate place on the magistracy. Most guild regimes were established in the fourteenth century, and specialities that were not covered by their privileges, some of which were very narrowly written, had more open rules of employment. The smaller the city, the less likely it was to have a rigid corporate structure. In 1368 Augsburg, a substantial but hardly dominant city of southern Germany, gave two representatives on the city council to each of nine guilds that were 'great and honourable' (including the weavers), or that had a long history in the city, and one each to the other trades. The year before this change Jacob Fugger had come to Augsburg from a nearby village and had taken work as a weaver. From here he expanded into the wool trade, cloth merchandising and trade in other materials, such as dyes used in clothmaking. He and his sons invested their profits in mines and eventually in overseas exploration. By the late fifteenth century the Fuggers were the major financiers of the Holy Roman Emperors, and Augsburg was the greatest city of its region.

Textiles continued to be the urban industry *par excellence*, but here too there were changes. We have seen that cloth was being made in the rural areas and reaching a wider market through the cities. Most cities produced different grades of cloth. Some continued to concentrate on luxury woollens, in effect abandoning the market for the lighter and cheaper grades to small towns and the rural areas, but the market in heavy cloth was never large enough to support large-scale production. Cities such as Ghent and Florence, that concentrated on luxury cloths, were thus exceptional. Heavy woollens thus no longer dominated clothmaking to the extent that

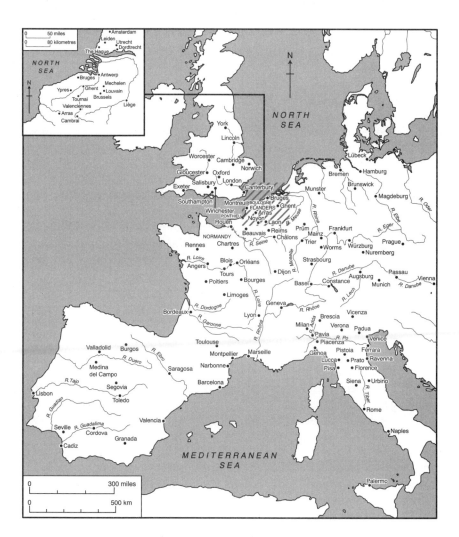

Map 3.2 The Major Cities of Europe, 1300–1600

they had earlier. While fine English wools continued to dominate luxury manufacture, which was almost exclusively urban, inter-regional trade revived in linens, most of which were made in the rural areas. Mixed fabrics such as fustians (cotton and linen) also entered the market in large quantities. The importance in the medieval textile industry of cotton, a vegetable fabric like linen and thus cheaper to raise than wool, and lighter and open to more uses, has often been under-estimated. The climate meant that it could be grown only in the east, and Venice became the major centre for re-export to the north.

Totally apart from guild restrictions, all cities had to import food and industrial raw materials. The larger and more diversified the labour force, and the more luxurious or exotic the goods that it manufactured, the more dependent the city was on the arrival of cargoes of wool, dyes or other necessities from distant regions. The Italian convoys generally made no more than a half-dozen voyages annually to Bruges, and then the goods had to be conveyed under often dangerous conditions to the home market. The problem was particularly acute in the more skilled occupations, which were also the most restrictive. By contrast, unskilled jobs such as porters, dock-workers and domestic servants, which might require some general skills but rarely a specific trade competence, were available in profusion, particularly in the service sector. Except for domestic service, however, they too were intermittent, with work contracts sometimes made by the day and rarely for longer than a week. Illness was a complication for persons who were not continuously employed. If you got sick, you stopped working until you got well or died. For the self-employed, such as a master artisan, this might simply mean that his wife or children took over until he recovered. The problem was more acute for journeymen, for whom a serious illness or injury could mean a family sinking into destitution.

Some cities expanded into inter-regional trading, but exportable industry remained secondary in virtually all cases until the fourteenth century and, in most, considerably later. In the late Middle Ages, however, the extent of industrial operations within the cities increased; and except in the few cases where politically powerful guilds were able to impose industrial protectionism on the local market, urban merchants also bought wholesale the industrial goods being produced in the rural areas and brought them into international markets. These products were generally not of as high quality as the best urban manufacture, but they were good enough to reach a wide market, not only in western Europe but increasingly in the German–Slavic East, which developed a major demand for north-west European textiles, as the north-west in turn was fed by German grain. Concentration of trade in the cities thus promoted industrialization, and brought a greater diversity of goods into international trade. Most cities also imported large quantities of cloth from other cities as well as selling their own. The drapers' guild of London, for example, imported Flemish cloth and only in the fifteenth century began trying to sell locally made cloth.

The cities had originated as markets for the raw materials of their rural environs, and all continued to be that, simply to feed their populations. Grain policy was always a major concern of the cities and a means of capital formation for their élites. The cities benefited from the low food prices after 1348, but they were seriously threatened by interruptions of supply, particularly during wartime or following a bad harvest. Some cities, as we have seen, stockpiled grain when prices were low, and fed their populations at or near cost during scarcity. Cities that were able to get control of substantial areas outside their walls, as had been the case for centuries in Italy and as developed in the late Middle Ages in parts of the Low Countries and Germany, required their dependent farmers to bring their crops to the city market; and virtually all insisted that grain remain in the city for an interval before being re-exported, to give all potential purchasers a chance to buy. Only in Italy, and there exceptionally, did this go to the extent of trying to turn the rural areas into industry-free zones that could feed the city. Places that were too large to be fed by their immediate environs financed convoys, made contracts with merchants to guarantee supplies, and in some cases established municipal grain offices. Grain merchants were always among the richest people of the city. When account is taken in addition of the service sector, such as shippers who brought grain to the city and the porters who carried it from the docks to market, and the numerous persons in the food and beverage trades, food-related occupations were the largest population group in most cities that were not dominated by an export industry. The business of most city people was feeding and clothing other urbanites.[4]

Urban poverty

Most immigrants to the cities obviously did not enjoy the good fortune of Jacob Fugger. As the cities lost population in absolute numbers, but gained in proportion to the rural areas, indigence became a serious problem. The incidence of poverty is hard to measure before 1300, for the sources generally use 'poor' to mean 'weak' rather than 'not having enough income or land'. The church defined the poor in the scriptural sense as those who could not support themselves without assistance, notably widows, orphans and the physically incapacitated. Poverty in an economic sense only became a serious enough problem for governments to pay much attention to it around 1300 and particularly after 1350, when it was exacerbated in the rural areas by the depression of grain prices and in the cities by the large number of immigrants and, in many cases, war refugees. The high death rates, always worse in the cities than in rural Europe, sharpened the problem of widows who had no professional skills. The cities thus had large numbers of persons who were physically capable of work but who could not find jobs, first in the overpopulated conditions of the early fourteenth century and then in the economic uncertainties after 1348.

While before 1300 poverty concerned the non-working poor, and was handled mainly by the churches and individual acts of charity, the problem now became the working poor. Although overall standards of living were rising in the late Middle Ages, such calculations are based on the fact that more and better manufactured goods were available than before, that food supplies were more abundant in respect to the diminished population, and that they were better balanced among the food groups. This higher standard of living was available for purchase by persons who had enough land to support a family or who had reasonably steady employment. An important problem both for contemporaries and for us in measuring their reactions to conditions was that the supply–demand mechanism was ill-understood; this explains the push to produce more grain even when prices were low, a problem that large numbers of lords, more than individual peasants, only began to understand in the late fifteenth and particularly in the sixteenth century. Averages thus are meaningless: although the long-term trend was for lower grain prices, they fluctuated wildly from year to year and even season to season. An income that was adequate in a year when grain prices were low was a starvation wage when they were high.

Poverty was obviously widespread, but efforts to quantify its extent can raise more problems than they solve. The chronicler Giovanni Villani, writing around 1338, shortly before the great plague, reported that more than 17,000 persons received money that a wealthy Florentine bequeathed to all beggars of the city, and this did not include the more than 4,000 'shamefaced poor and those in hospital and prisons and the religious mendicants'. Villani considered this a high figure, and thought that it must have included foreigners in the city; but the statistic would be driven the other way by the fact that the needy who did not beg were not included. Given the population of Florence at the time, it suggests a poverty rate of about 20 per cent,[5] which is consistent with figures from other Italian cities before the plagues.

For the north European cities our problems are complicated by a high incidence of fiscal or tax poverty that is not the same as indigence. City governments in England were complaining of high royal taxes at the very times when they were building new town halls. For obvious reasons, most persons dislike paying taxes and will take all legal and sometimes illegal measures to keep their tax burdens low. Thus some areas where taxes were high, such as the Low Countries, have an incidence of between 20 and 40 per cent of tax poverty, but never define what 'poor' means in terms of minimum income. Some persons whose wealth was small enough to exempt them from direct taxes were still able to rent or even own houses. Dijon in 1397 exempted 83 per cent of its households from tax; but by 1434, after the city began distinguishing 'miserable' persons (the working poor) from beggars, the figure became 58 per cent miserable, 27 per cent mendicant. When comparison over a long term is possible, as at Lübeck in 1380 and 1460, it suggests a slow long-term rise in the number of indigent persons;

but as with grain prices, short-term fluctuations in time of plague and civil turmoil are absorbed in this.[6]

The tax policies of the cities had elements that both favoured and hurt the poor. Virtually all cities exempted persons below a given but fluctuating income level from direct taxes on property, and most taxed upper-income groups at a higher percentage than the poorer citizens. Balancing this is that cities relied heavily on indirect taxes that were levied at the city gates and on the markets, and these applied to food and drink. Comparison of wage levels with food prices suggest that a continuously employed master artisan could do rather well; but despite the low grain prices, a journeyman, who usually earned half as much as a master for the same work, would have to work almost continuously to feed a family of four, and most journeymen were only intermittently employed. Unskilled labourers were even worse off, and family incomes were supplemented by charity, second jobs or the employment of wives.

Facilities existed in most cities to care for the poor, but access to most of them was restricted. 'Hospitals' at this time were often lodging houses rather than medical centres. Most large cities had several even before 1300, including some in the suburbs to accommodate transients. They ranged from a few hostels (mainly in ports or other major centres with a large transient population) that could house several hundred persons – the 30 hospitals of Florence could accommodate 1,000 poor in 1339 – to the vast majority that supported a handful of poor. Virtually all foundations before 1300, and most thereafter, were founded by private donors, but they were supplemented in the late Middle Ages by almshouses established by guilds for indigent masters and, often, journeymen, and for their widows and orphans, and by lay charity at the parish level. City governments provided some financial assistance to these foundations, and some oversaw their accounts, but most of them were operated by churches, lay parish organizations such as the Poor Tables of the Low Country cities, or the descendants of the founders. Charitable confraternities also developed in most churches; their purpose was to cultivate the devotion of the patron saint or the Virgin Mary, but some also dispensed charity.

City governments became concerned with revolutionary tendencies on the part of the able-bodied poor. The cities were disorderly, with a high level of violence, although most of it seems to have been instigated by the more prosperous citizens in the course of litigation and vendettas rather than the indigent. They disliked the public display of poverty, and by 1400 some cities were expelling poor persons who congregated around churches loudly begging for alms. They made a natural and often accurate association of vagrancy with poverty and crime, and as early as the 1350s some cities, including Paris, were forcing able-bodied beggars to labour on the expensive public works that were the pride of the city fathers. Some cities that were quite generous to private relief foundations in the fourteenth century reduced the amount of their contribution in the fifteenth. After

1450 princely and even national governments began to intervene in policy toward vagrancy, where this had generally been left earlier to local discretion.[7]

The Urban Rebellions of the Late Middle Ages

The late medieval cities were extremely disorderly. Yet the various problems that we have documented – widening gaps between rich and poor, a higher standard of living that was not shared by many and perhaps most, unemployment, restrictions on the labour market and on political participation – do not seem to have been involved conspicuously in any of them, except the famous Ciompi uprising at Florence in 1378.

We must distinguish between the generally violent tenor of life and armed insurrections. City governments forbade large weapons, and some required that they be left at the gates by newcomers, but statute was easier than enforcement. Most persons carried at least a small knife; butchers, whose livelihoods depended on large knives, were among the most disorderly elements of all late medieval cities. Taverns, brothels, public baths that were often fronts for prostitution, and gaming establishments abounded. Excise figures suggest per capita consumption of beer and wine that would stagger modern sensibilities. Family solidarity was very strong in the cities, particularly among the older and wealthier lineages, and vendettas disturbed the public peace: insults in word and gesture that infringed honour account for many of the disturbances. Although most deeds of violence were settled by arbitration in the fourteenth century, this was yielding to *ex officio* prosecution by the city courts in the fifteenth; and although most city regimes did not have the right to impose punishments that included shedding blood, sentences of death or mutilation handed down in princes' courts were generally carried out in grotesque public spectacles in a city or a special place of execution in the suburbs. Urbanites were inured to violence and suffering.

But most 'revolutionary' activity of the late Middle Ages was political rather than economic, and the most common cause of urban rebellions was taxation or other political grievance against the prince. The famous 'Jacquerie' of the Paris region in 1358 began as a rural uprising against the high taxes demanded to pay the ransom of the king and other nobles captured by the English at Poitiers. The involvement of Paris in it was tied to the activity of the Estates-General; the leader of the Paris insurgents, Étienne Marcel, held the office of provost of the merchants and was one of the wealthiest men of the city. We have seen that the disturbances in the French cities between 1380 and 1383 concerned the tax policy of the crown. The first great Flemish rebellion, between 1338 and 1349, concerned the need to secure English wool for the textile industries of the Flemish cities. The second, between 1379 and 1385, erupted because the count of Flanders favoured Bruges over Ghent in a sphere-of-influence question. The famous rebellions of London in the 1380s involved fissures between two groups within the merchant élite, all of whom lent money to the crown but who had different interests in overseas trade. The fact that the grocers and fishmongers were on one side and the drapers on the other has caused some misunderstanding that the issue was one of the artisanry trying to keep food prices down; in fact the drapers were not artisans, but rather importers of foreign cloth, and while the fishmongers did sell fish many of them also invested in overseas trade, while the political élite among the grocers consisted of spice and wool merchants.

Only the Ciompi rising at Florence has an economic element. The oligarchy of Florence was quite narrow, but family factions fostered chaos in Florentine political life. When Florence got into a war with the pope in 1378, supplies of wool and grain could not reach the city. The Ciompi (wool carders) were not formally recognized as a guild, but they and their allies rebelled in the summer of 1378, demanding production quotas on woollen cloth, cheap grain, the ending of arrest for debt and a political agenda that included opening seats on the main city council, the *Signoria*, to three new guilds in addition to the 21 older ones: the Ciompi themselves, the dyers and the doublet-makers. But the disorder was ended by autumn; the Ciompi were expelled from the regime immediately, the other two lesser guilds were expelled in 1382, and the network of family oligarchs that had ruled Florence became even tighter until the advent of the Medici in 1433. As stated in the *Later Medieval City*, 'Although this was the most intellectually radical and agenda-driven urban revolt of the fourteenth century, most of the rebels were not ordinary labourers, but were small shopkeepers, some with investments in the public debt, and were led by aristocrats.'[8]

The Commercial Revolution of the Late Middle Ages

While populations and total production of food dropped sharply in the late Middle Ages, standards of living rose because a rise in per capita productivity accompanied the population decline, and producers learned to escape low prices on traditional farm products and industrial goods by growing or manufacturing different items for which demand was increasing. The qualitative amelioration was linked to a considerable degree with improvements in the techniques of trade that made it possible to move and sell profitably greater quantities not only of luxuries but also of basic consumer goods. The chief beneficiaries of this change, however, were the moneyed groups of court and city. The agricultural depression deepened with low grain prices, and the cities began to have a serious problem of poverty as unskilled workers streamed in to escape the farm depression and the devastation of warfare.

The European market economy had developed in the central Middle Ages on the bipolar axis of Italy and a northern region that included northern France, the Low Countries and England. The linchpin was the fairs of Champagne, where merchants of the Mediterranean and the north traded with those of Germany and south-western France. The fairs were linked by a staggered calendar to regional fairs where the goods obtained from the Italians could be sold. This commercial structure matured in the late Middle Ages with the addition of the German and Slavic East as a third element in long-distance trading. Before the 1390s virtually all contact with non-Europeans had been in the African interior and with the east through Italian merchants, but exploration of the Atlantic in the fifteenth century gave Europeans new routes into sub-Saharan Africa and, eventually, Asia. The culmination of this process came with the inclusion of the Americas into a European economic system in the sixteenth century.

The market network of the late Middle Ages was centred on the cities, which in the long term were affected less by the depression than the rural areas. The well-documented rise in the standard of living was a consequence of a more diversified and bounteous diet becoming available to a smaller population, but much of this was channelled through urban markets and did not benefit the farmer, whose surplus was working against him economically. The political might of the urban militias had created city-states in Italy long before 1300, and *de facto* and, in a few cases, *de jure* it did so in the north in the late Middle Ages. In virtually all areas the cities exercised pressure on their rural environs, and in many instances forced farmers to bring their goods to the urban market, where the citizens had first rights to buy, then often re-exported the rest to more distant locales, raising the price of the food to compensate them for their service.

Of equal importance, the most conspicuous aspect of the rise in the standard of living was the development of pride in luxurious consumer goods that were either imported through the cities and distributed within their environs, or in some cases, were produced by the growing industrial capacity of the city itself. It was not only princes who took pride in display and ostentation. Courts continued to be important markets for luxuries, but by the fifteenth century there was substantial demand among the urban élites for fine textiles, jewels, works of art, animals and exotica from the east. But demand for imports was also generalizing. Edible spices, and such foods as dried fruits and rice, that had once been luxuries, were now cheaper – and would become still cheaper in the late fifteenth century – and thus achieved a demand market outside the aristocracy.

Late medieval Europe consisted of economic regions that cannot be defined rigidly, but as a point of interaction of inter-regional and local trade the notion of regions is helpful. One, or sometimes several major cities were the nucleus of the region. Most urban networks were linked by the great rivers and their tributaries. The network produced and transmitted goods and to some extent services, and it tended as a whole to interact with foci that became increasingly distant but also limited in the late Middle Ages, as both domestic and inter-regional trade became concentrated on the large cities. But the region tended to be dominated socially, economically and sometimes politically by its major city or cities. The direction of money and population flows, and how wealth was recycled within the region, were both important, thus positing an intense interaction of the cities and the rural areas. More broadly based regional economies developed between 1300 and 1600 than before; but while in the seventeenth century, with the hegemony of Amsterdam, the interaction of these regions was based on banking and credit, it was mainly based on the exchange of goods during the hegemony of Bruges and, later, Antwerp between 1300 and 1560.[9]

During the early and central Middle Ages in Italy, and to a lesser extent in urbanized northern Europe, rural aristocrats spent time in the cities and were the major part of their élites. As the cities grew, their dense populations became increasingly dependent on their environs for food, which in turn enriched the urban élites, who in Italy sold food in the city, and in the north more often controlled the mechanisms by which food was imported. But a major change began in the late thirteenth century which was more or less completed by the early seventeenth century: urban money was going to the countryside less exclusively than before to pay for farm products, which could now be imported more cheaply from regions far from the immediate environs of the city, and more in the form of investment by city people in rural land. With investment in land comes the urban penetration of the territorial nobility that is such a mark of the nobility of the robe in France.

Most long-distance merchants diversified their operations, rarely sinking a substantial portion of their capital into a single venture or commodity in view of the dangers of piracy, shipwreck and ambush of overland cargoes. It has been argued that the disruptions of warfare and excises, and the cost and risk of ships, produced such a rise in transaction costs that long-distance trade, while increasing in volume, was profitable only for luxury goods. Yet while this reservation may work for Italian trade, it ignores the parallel expansion of the grain and forest product trade of the German Hanse, the league of north German cities that maintained joint resident offices in London and the eastern English ports, and on the Continent at Bergen, Novgorod and, most importantly, at Bruges. While the Russian and Scandinavian as well as Flemish markets had been penetrated by Germans in various loose unions in the thirteenth century, it was only in the last quarter of the thirteenth century that a 'German Hanse' was formed. The Hanse soon dominated the North and Baltic-Sea-carrying trades and controlled the export of the raw materials of the East, which were critically important for the densely urbanized north-west European Continent in the fourteenth and fifteenth centuries, even with the population decline there. Baltic grain came in such bulk that it could often undersell native merchants, who had to worry about cartage to market over dangerous roads, and it accordingly contributed to the perpetuation of the low grain prices that plagued farmers in western Europe. Hanse merchants also carried the manufactures of the north-west to the markets in the German east, that were expanding as the Italians, who had bought considerable Flemish cloth in the thirteenth century, now manufactured more of their own. The Hanse was strong enough to mount a successful naval blockade of Flanders over a commercial issue between 1358 and 1360 and to fight a successful war against the king of Denmark between 1368 and 1370.

The European economy thus became much more tightly integrated after 1300 than before. In 1277 the first galleys went from Genoa through the Strait of Gibraltar and on to northern Europe, initiating what has been called the 'commercial revolution of the late Middle Ages'. This trade quickened after 1310. Larger boats were built, and in 1316 grain from Italy for the first time was brought in large amounts to the famine-stricken north. Italians dominated the international market in goods and financial services in the fourteenth and fifteenth centuries. Merchants of the various Italian city-states, officially acting independently of each other but sometimes cooperating, established merchant colonies in the northern ports, as they had long done in the Near East, selling their goods to local importers by acting through native brokers.

The Italians brought wealth and commercial contacts wherever they went. Regular galley voyages from the Mediterranean to the North Sea ports bypassed the Champagne fairs, which could only be reached by over-land routes. Most of the fairs' international trade was picked up by Bruges in the fourteenth century, which became the 'marketplace of the medieval world'. The Italians and Hansards both established offices there (and dealt with each other scarcely at all, and then through brokers of Bruges). The papal capital of Avignon, Paris, London and Barcelona all had a substantial resident Italian population of traders and financiers. Since the Italians' customers either bought on credit or exchanged goods directly with them, as in the exchange of English wool for Italian foods and spices, the Italian presence meant the development of banking and an increased sophistication of credit mechanisms.

The Italians dominated the trade of the Mediterranean, sharing it to some extent with Barcelona and the Catalans, and the contacts of the Mediterranean with the North Sea. They were not concerned with the Baltic, which was controlled by the Hanse, but Venetian capital was involved in much of the German expansion in the east in the fourteenth and fifteenth centuries, particularly the expansion of mines there. Much of the internal trade of southern Germany went over Nuremberg, which became the most important city of medieval Europe to have trade based on control of land routes rather than waterways. As was true of many inland cities, Nuremberg got a 'staple' or monopoly on traffic on the roads that inter-sected on its territory, and the city built this into a more general control of its environs. By 1400 Nuremberg merchants, with some competition from Cologne, controlled the trade of south Germany with Venice across the Brenner Pass. Nuremberg alone was the depot through which the metals and raw materials of Hungary and Bohemia reached western markets, while western manufactures, in turn, reached these areas through Nuremberg. From 1360 Nurembergers had trading privileges in Poland, and from 1373 had access to the Baltic by arrangement with Lübeck, the most powerful of the Hanse cities. The Nurembergers were active at the fairs that were established at Frankfurt for the Rhineland trade, and those at Antwerp and Bergen-op-Zoom that would eventually rival and finally supplant the international trade of Bruges. Naturally, they expanded into finance and established partnerships with Flemings at Bruges.

Commercial Techniques

Given the difficulty in paying for goods with coin that had to be transported as bullion, commercial instruments had developed long before 1300 at the fairs. But by the late thirteenth century the more serious problem was too little bullion and debasements of existing money. The debasements started a cycle of unstable exchange rates that were catastrophic for the large banking firms that had extended credit to princes and to businesses. A series of bank failures occurred at the century's end, beginning with the Buonsignori firm of Siena in 1298. Florentine banks picked up some business from the Sienese, but they in turn suffered when Edward III defaulted on his war loans from the Bardi, Peruzzi and Acciaiuoli in the 1340s.

The variable exchange rates, however, provided a means of extending credit. Church law prohibited usury, which was defined as any guaranteed interest on a loan, but repayment of an amount larger than what was advanced was permissible if the labour of the recipient was involved or if the lender incurred risk. The Italians developed the bill of exchange in the thirteenth century, and with the expansion of their operations in the north after 1300 this became the chief means of transferring funds between different coinages. Loans could be contracted by using one coinage to buy a bill that would be repaid in another in a foreign port. Thus, since the exchange rate would fluctuate, the purchaser could gain or lose, although there was usually margin to guarantee profit for a creditor and loss for a debtor. Thus debasement was accompanied by the development of other instruments of exchange that intensified inflationary pressures but also facilitated the extension of credit.

This system also required persons who used the bills either to go to the foreign port where they could be cashed – most unusual in this period of increasingly sedentary businessmen – or have a partner or correspondent in the foreign port who could buy a new bill payable in the original taker's currency and in his home city. The bill of exchange could thus be used to contract loans, pay for goods or speculate on the vagaries of the exchange rate. No coin changed hands except at the beginning and end of the operation, and if goods were involved, not necessarily even then. This would have been inconceivable before the changes after 1277, with more frequent contact between ports, colonies of Italians residing in north European ports and the existence of a money market.

The Italians also pioneered other techniques that were strikingly under-utilized by northerners until the sixteenth century. They were using cheques for domestic transactions by 1300, and by 1400 these, together with bills of exchange, could be transferred between parties by endorsement. Maritime insurance was developed at Genoa in the late thirteenth century. Standardized forms were being used for insurance contracts by the fifteenth century; only the name of the captain and the ship, amount, premium, and other variables had to be filled in. Double-entry bookkeeping, which records liabilities and assets of the firm simultaneously, was invented at Florence in the late thirteenth century, although it was not widely used until later. The Italians and their customers maintained accounts in the northern and eastern ports with local moneychangers, who could make payments by book transfers without coin changing hands. The fact that most merchants dealt in a plethora of goods facilitated this; an English grocer, for example, who sold wool to the Italians at Bruges that he had bought in northern England would be paid in spices, and over time the accounts would synchronize. In this way a considerably expanded international trade in luxuries developed in the late Middle Ages, despite the dearth of bullion. Given the constantly changing bullion content of most coin except the English, and accordingly of exchange rates, the moneychangers had to have considerable technical expertise. They also functioned as bankers, taking money on deposit and investing it. They were not limited to foreign opera-tions; large numbers of local merchants had accounts at the exchanges, some of which were maintained by city governments, particularly in the fifteenth century, and transferred money among themselves by ledger alterations just as the international operators did.

The economies of the French and English states were cripplingly dependent on supplies of spices and minerals from Italy and of food and forest products from the German and Slavic east. Even during the thirteenth century there was a monetary drain toward the Mediterranean, for the Italians bought mainly English wool and Flemish cloth at the fairs in exchange for dyes and minerals and more luxurious oriental fabrics. The most important Italian monopoly was alum, a mordant for fixing dyes, of which Genoese-controlled Phocaea was the only known source until it was discovered in the papal states in 1459. The galleys returned to Italy with ballast, for the Italians had little to import from the north except English wool, and they did that by special export licenses granted by the crown. The Italian firms' dangerous practice of lending money to French and English rulers is explained in part by the fact that they could not safely bring bullion back to Italy, particularly given its scarcity, yet had enormous book credits in the north. The accumulation of wealth in Italy in the fifteenth century that helps to explain the cultural flowering there is due in large part to the overwhelmingly favourable balance of trade that the Italians enjoyed with northern Europe. Given that north-western Europe was exporting manufactured items to the German and Slavic east in return for raw materials, the balance of payments in that direction was probably negative, although perhaps less catastrophically so.

The Pre-Printing Information Revolution of the Late Middle Ages

Even local commercial transactions had normally been conducted in writing in Mediterranean Europe during the thirteenth century by using notarial instruments, but there are few commercial records in the north this early. In the fourteenth century, however, writing became basic to the success of virtually all enterprises. Merchants, whose profits might depend on momentary fluctuations of supply of and demand for critical goods in distant parts of Europe, had to keep abreast of a myriad of situations. Prices fluctuated less seasonally on luxuries than on bulk consumer goods, but even in the latter case an interruption of critical supplies could be catastrophic; for consumer demands were so sophisticated by 1300 that no city or region could satisfy from internal sources the demand even for necessities as defined by that time, let alone luxuries. The money market was based on daily quotations that were only possible in the climate of resident colonies in all major ports overseas, and partnerships in which a firm that did not maintain its own office in a given city could count on an ally to represent its interests there. Thus a network of informants developed whose information conditioned military, diplomatic and economic calculations. Rumour was endemic, and information gained in a merchant house could be picked up by government authorities. Francesco Datini, a merchant of Florence and Prato who was active between 1364 and 1410, handled his business by correspondence rather than in person. He exchanged a voluminous correspondence, at times involving as much as 10,000 pieces per year, with his factors (agents) in Barcelona, Valencia, Avignon, Genoa and Pisa.[10]

Status and Class in Late Medieval Europe

One consequence of the economic and political changes of the late Middle Ages was to make it much easier for townspeople to enter the nobility. Their incentives to do so were social everywhere, since nobles were considered to have qualities of spirit that distinguished them from lesser mortals, but they included very real economic advantages on the Continent. Except in eastern Europe, where the landed nobility ruled a servile and generally docile peasantry, the old noble lineages lost much of their political and certainly their economic power. Noble families whose incomes came mainly from fixed rents on land had to find other sources of money or face ruin. Often royal patronage provided the additional revenue; other noble families intermarried with wealthy urban families with aspirations to gentility. The wealth that the urban élites were accumulating was generally invested in conspicuous consumption. Luxury goods are one obvious such commodity, as with the rural aristocracy. But the merchants also wanted the social respectability that came with investment in land. Landholding was a route into the nobility, which conveyed political privileges in local Estates and, in some areas, exemption from direct taxes. Most land remained in the hands of the older lineages, which were based in the countryside. In Italy the rural and urban aristocracies had been hard to distinguish for centuries, but in the fourteenth century increasing numbers of wealthy townsmen in the north also were investing in rural land.

Possession of land was often accompanied by the right to hold a court; and even though private courts in western Europe were generally limited to petty civil cases by the fifteenth century, the right to hold one was a social distinction. With continued rural landownership over two or three generations, movement into the nobility was possible, particularly after rulers began selling patents of nobility in the fourteenth and, particularly, the fifteenth century. With massive urban investment in rural land in the fourteenth century, an age of rapidly rising taxes, the question naturally arose of the tax status of rural land owned by townspeople. In Flanders and Italy the cities were generally powerful enough to keep their tax assessments low in relation to the concentration of wealth in the cities. Florence had abolished the *estimo* (direct tax) in the city in 1315, but kept it in its dependent countryside (*contado*); however, so much land was being held by city people who were not subject to the *estimo* that the value of the tax declined sharply. Tax exemption in France for city-based nobles of the robe on their rural properties in the sixteenth century would have the same result.[11]

The increased power of the state in fixing social relationships fundamentally changed the nature of the nobility. In the early Middle Ages the power of command over persons exercised independently of the state had been the basis of determining noble standing. In the late Middle Ages the issue was the enjoyment of privileges within and guaranteed by the state, such as tax exemption and the right to sit as individuals in Parliament rather than be represented there by others: thus in the late Middle Ages high office within the state rather than freedom from it became the key. By 1450 the nobility in most of western Europe – Italy is a conspicuous exception – was a legally defined group, but it was not homogeneous. It contained an upper group: the *caballeros* of Castile, the nobility of the sword in France, the parliamentary peerage in England. The lesser nobles, the nobility of the robe in France, the *hidalgos* in Spain, and to a lesser extent the gentry in England, were a partly urban group who enjoyed the social prestige of nobility and, on the Continent, its political and financial advantages, but they were not considered social peers of the older, titled, landed lines.

It is a truism that early modern Europe was a status-based society, rather than class-based in the modern economic sense. Social status was a question of esteem and honour that came from functions that were based essentially on services that were particularly valued, rather than on the production of goods. The profession of arms conveyed more elevated status in the late Middle Ages than in the early modern period, with the widespread use of gunpowder and mass armies; but the officer corps, positions involving command just as the nobility did, still conferred honour. In practice status was based largely on ancestry and landholding, which gave access to offices, including military commands, that conveyed honour. Ancestry and land-holding were variables that could be determined to some extent by choice, but in the case of ancestry was determined in advance. One could not change one's ancestors, but by a good marriage choice one could affect the standing of one's descendants, and the purchase of land by someone who did not inherit it was a conscious choice that could have an immediate impact, although it more often required a generation or two. Status thus usually changed slowly, but it was not unchanging. It was less mobile than now, when the acquisition of wealth alone can convey legitimacy unless the money is acquired by socially unacceptable means.

Although we tend to think of the early modern state as incipiently absolutist, at least in theory, the process of institutionalizing it after 1300 gave persons outside the nobility access to some political recognition and, in some cases, actual power. In 1300 the nobles were the main force who had some power, if not the authority, to limit the king, and this was done through the royal council. Even the English Parliament and the Aragonese *Cortes,* eventually the most powerful of the representative assemblies of western Europe, were in their infancy, and were most regularly attended by nobles, always greater and sometimes lesser.

By 1450 several important changes were evident that had become still firmer by 1600. First, persons outside the ancient bloodlines, particularly townspeople, entered the nobility everywhere. But in England a sharp distinction was maintained between the parliamentary peerage, which was a genuine nobility, and the gentry. Entry into the parliamentary-titled peerage was initially at the discretion of the king, but was becoming hereditary from the late fourteenth century; despite the civil discords, there were no new entrants to the parliamentary peerage between 1388 and 1424.

Neither the English nobles nor the county gentry had the privileges of the nobles on the Continent, where distinctions of prestige remained between nobilities of sword and robe in France, and between *caballeros* and *hidalgos* in Spain, although legally the two were the same in most respects, including that of exemption from direct taxes. In each case movement into the nobility was possible with enough money, patronage and investment in rural land. Landownership was the main avenue through which the city élites entered the nobility. The rate of merchant entry into the aristocracy quickened after 1350, with land values down and much land available to buy. Conversely, gentry also held some urban property, especially if they were lords of boroughs.

In addition to ancestry and landholding, nobles had to live in a manner befitting their status. Those who had purchased noble rank had proof of their standing, but others required the intangible asset of recognition by their peers. In France nobles lost their rank if they engaged in trade or manual labour, both of which were not honourable and entailed 'derogation' of status. Although in fact some did get into trade, particularly in food, this was a product of landownership and thus did not affect their status adversely. The weakness of the Roman law of agency meant that as Roman law spread, it became easier for nobles to employ persons to do the trading for them, and this subterfuge preserved the noble's rank. They were also expected to live primarily if not exclusively on rents, rather than wages or other payments coming from the performance of services or the sale of goods, and were expected to consume conspicuously on items that had no discernible economic return: buildings, jewels, fine art, exotica from the east, whatever could display the grandeur of the buyer. The patronage of royal courts became increasingly important in the fortunes of nobles in the national monarchies. Great lineages maintained houses at London and Paris in addition to their country residences in the fourteenth and especially in the fifteenth centuries.

A critical and very difficult question is the relationship between knighthood and nobility. The burdens of knighthood in warfare and in local government were sufficiently onerous that many who could have become nobles by lineage simply did not have themselves dubbed. While in the period of Henry III (1216–72) persons who held the substantial income of £20 were required to be dubbed knights or pay a fine, the dividing line was £100 by the early period of Edward III. Although there was some reluctance in England to make knights of people in trade, the distinction was not as great as in France. Even as early as Edward I's reign, most judges at the great central courts were knights. The London élite also contained many knights. There are not many examples – the de la Poles of Hull are a conspicuous exception – of townspeople entering the parliamentary peerage in England until the fifteenth century.

Part of the problem is that the words from the Continental languages usually rendered as 'knight' in England do not convey the social distinction of English knighthood. The knights in England had originally been a diverse group, not always associated with mounted military service, and they certainly were not nobles. The French *chevaliers*, by contrast, were mounted warriors and were noble. The German *Ritter*, which is translated 'knight' in English, is actually closer in meaning by 1350 to French *chevalier*, but initially it had been closer to the English knight; many of the lesser German nobles had originated in serf lineages that had ennobled themselves by doing honourable service for their lords. All sons in France inherited knightly rank; not so, however, in England, where only the eldest son did so. Thus *chevaliers* and *écuyers* were noble, but knights and esquires were not. Yet the distinction between esquires and knights becomes blurred after 1363, when the esquires were given the right to have coats of arms and had the same status-clothing privileges as knights of that level of income. Esquires included younger branches of knightly families and sons of knights who had not yet been dubbed. By the mid-fifteenth century 'gentlemen' had also become armigerous, as the lowest rank with a coat of arms. As the highest rank among the armigerous, knights became less numerous and more socially exclusive in the fifteenth century than they had been earlier.

Given that nobility had an uncertain relation with knighthood and that, except in England, it was available for purchase and conferred tax exemption, the percentage of nobles in the population was quite high, reaching about 10 per cent in Castile. This includes the titled lines and the *hidalgos*, who were the rough equivalent of the nobility of the robe in France. In France it was much lower in the fourteenth century, perhaps 1 per cent, but rose considerably in the next two centuries, as more townspeople purchased status. A tax on incomes from land in 1436 in England suggests a figure of 1,000 (including families) in the parliamentary peerage, 5,000 knights and their families, and 22,000 gentry, for about 1.7 per cent of the population. The English nobility was thus the most select in western Europe, and it lacked the most important economic perquisite of nobility on the Continent: exemption from direct taxes.[12]

Women in Late Medieval Europe

The situation of individual women obviously varied with circumstances. In the late Middle Ages, as now, most persons married. For a valid marriage the church required only that the couple be of age, consent freely and consummate the marriage. The presence of a priest, although desirable, was not absolutely necessary, even though marriage was considered a sacrament. Women were considered the wards of their fathers and then their husbands in all the legal regimes of western Europe. In most places males were given priority in inheritances, although women were rarely totally excluded. A woman's dowry, which was separated from her parents' property during their lives and given to her when she married, was her property, although her husband could manage it. The medieval church did not permit divorce except for very specific causes, notably impotence in the male or consanguinity, but the dowry was normally returned when it did occur. The church and often the secular authorities arranged property divisions when the couple simply agreed to live apart.

In contrast to the modern norm, when spouses are likely to will all property to the survivor, and only at the second death do children or other heirs become involved, married persons were legally linked to their natal families in the late Middle Ages. Thus a widow with children had to divide her husband's estate with them. In some areas of northern Europe widows got a share of the common property of the marriage in outright ownership. Almost everywhere they also received life use of a share of their late husbands' estates, often taking the property into subsequent marriages before it could be recovered by the first husband's biological heirs.

Noblewomen are a case apart. Given the amount of property involved in a noble marriage, including the size of the dowry, parents usually oversaw their daughters' social contacts with care, prevented elopements and arranged their marriages. The family's wealth meant that noblewomen did not have to worry about life's necessities. Many noblewomen managed their family estates, particularly the domestic side and record-keeping, while their husbands dealt with their more public aspects. Most had some education, often more than their husbands, and some had independent cultural interests. Some were able to accumulate considerable properties through successive marriages; rarely, however, did a noblewoman try to function independent of her family's lands and other property.

Girls of the middle and lower social orders, by contrast, had to make a living if they did not marry, and often even if they did, and had more freedom than noblewomen to choose their husbands. Many women worked with their husbands, particularly in such domestically related occupations as food and drink preparation and selling, but some wives of businessmen with inter-regional contacts were also their husbands' *de facto* business partners, becoming actively involved in the firm's operations. Others, however, did not; and since women were much less likely than their brothers to receive professional training from their fathers, the death of the spouse could mean impoverishment, particularly when the dowry or the marital assets had been small. Although some guilds permitted a widow to maintain her late husband's shop as long as she did not remarry or until a son grew old enough to take over the business, this was not an invariable rule, and there was usually a time limit on it. Not surprisingly, a disproportionate number of recipients of public assistance in the late Middle Ages were orphans and widows.

Many women doubtless influenced public affairs by giving counsel to their politically active husbands, but only in a handful of cases did they ever occupy a guild magistracy, and women never sat on city councils. In the twelfth and thirteenth centuries, before occupational guilds had rigid professional standards and in most cities before they were guaranteed seats on the city council and thus controlled municipal policy, women were found in a wide variety of occupations. After 1300, however, their professional involvement diminished. Although a few continued to work independently, most were either domestic servants or practised a trade that could be conducted in the home. Some women operated stalls on marketplaces and controlled booths in the cloth hall in some cities. Particularly in the rural areas, but to some extent also in the cities, they brewed and sold ale, but rarely beer, which required the use of imported hops and a more complex process. Occupations that were well-paid, highly skilled or required much physical strength had only a handful of women. Women generally received a much lower wage than men, often half, for the same work. The legal and economic situation of women was thus declining in the late Middle Ages as the goods that they could make without the involvement of a husband were restricted, the market value of what they could make declined, and in the service sector they were restricted to low-status jobs.[13]

European Expansion: The First Phase

Much has been written about the impact of overseas exploration on the economic evolution of Europe during these centuries. Although the major developments would only come after 1450, significant beginnings were made in the previous century. Yet while the long-range importance of the expansion was incalculable, the direct impact on western Europe before 1600 is perceptible only in limited areas. This is first, because these were voyages of exploration. Until the 1490s there was no colonization except on the Atlantic islands, and large-scale settlement of the sort that had accompanied the German expansion into the Slavic East in the twelfth and thirteenth centuries, or the Christian advance against the Muslims in Spain, simply did not occur until even later. Second, although converting the natives to Christianity was often stated as a motive, all explorers and their sponsors were seeking mainly raw materials and other riches, preferably slaves from Africa and spices from Asia, and later gold and silver from the Americas. The focus was thus more on exploitation than on reciprocal trade.

There is little evidence that their navigational techniques had anything to do with the westerners' successes. Most of the naval technology that they used to dominate the Asian trade was of Asian origin, and was already known, if not widely used, before 1400. The compass, invented in China in the late eleventh century, spread in the west in the thirteenth. Portolan charts were developed in the fifteenth century, as were trigonometric tables. The astrolabe was invented in the twelfth century but was rarely used by sailors before the fifteenth. The Mediterranean galley was low-slung and powered by oars, and it was unsuitable for cargo. For more distant voyages the Europeans had to use sails, which were first used on northern ships. The development of the stern rudder with a lever principle for steering, and of the use of multiple sails, were important in increasing the ships' mobility. The Portuguese caravels used the lateen (triangular) sail, which had been developed by Arab sailors, in combination with the traditional square rigging. But a 100-ton caravel could only carry a trading cargo of about

5 tons, given the need to carry provisions for the crew. The caravels were also large enough to permit them to carry guns and eventually cannon, which is how the Portuguese eventually managed to defeat Arab ships in the Indian Ocean.[14]

Africa was a critical focus, for it was the major source of gold for western Europe and a point of access for Asian trade. Asia was divided into spheres of influence by warring native potentates for most of the fifteenth century, just as the spice trade with Europe was quickening. As the caravan routes across Asia became more dangerous, maritime trade in the Indian Ocean, linking them with the Red Sea and mainly in Muslim hands, became more important. Thus Italian traders frequented the ports of Syria and Egypt to buy Asian goods from the Muslims. The land route through Asia declined until after the Turkish conquest, making the eastern Mediterranean trade even more dependent than before on Venice, whose colonies of Cyprus and Crete gave bases in the east that could secure the trade routes. Thus, far from hindering Italian trade with Asia, the Turkish conquest of the residual Byzantine empire between 1453 and 1461 may actually have furthered it. Castilian and Portuguese efforts to penetrate Africa, then eventually to reach Asia by going around it, were part of a western Atlantic effort to circumvent the trade of Venice, in large part by using the capital of Genoese merchants living in Castile.

The early phase of the Atlantic expansion was part of a broader shift of commercial pre-eminence from the eastern Mediterranean in the central Middle Ages to the western Mediterranean after the 'commercial revolution' of the half-century after 1277. The galley voyages of the Italians to Bruges were comparable in difficulty and significance to the efforts of the Portuguese in the late fifteenth century to move into the south Atlantic.[15] The early explorations originated from the Iberian peninsula, which has both a Mediterranean and an Atlantic coast. The Aragonese secured the Atlantic islands in the fourteenth century, beginning with the annexation of Majorca in 1343. There was substantial colonization by Catalans, and foreign communities under their own law – first the Jews and, soon afterwards, the Genoese – were quickly established in the Majorcan towns. From Minorca the Aragonese subsequently began conquests off the African coast.

Castile and Portugal were Aragon's dynastic rivals for domination in Iberia. The conquest of Andalusia in the thirteenth century was of critical importance in providing an Atlantic coastline for Castile. The initial conquests there, like the later Atlantic colonial enterprises, depopulated the natives and resettled the area with colonists. Genoese merchants and other foreigners were given resident colonies in newly founded Cadiz and in Seville, which became the major outpost of Genoese African trade in the fifteenth century. Genoese capital became critical for Castile's overseas expansion. Until the fifteenth century most Genoese were transients, staying a few years but then returning to Genoa, but many were settling permanently by that time and intermarrying into the native Sevillian aristocracy.

The Atlantic islands are the major exceptions to the rule that early exploration produced only minimal resettlement. Exploration of the Canaries began in 1339 by Italians based in Castile and particularly Majorca, and was continued after 1343 by the Aragonese. The extent of navigation to the Canaries makes it likely that the Azores were known in the fourteenth century, but after the 1340s only missionary work was undertaken until an expedition by Portugal in 1370. Both the Canaries and the Azores required a voyage of several weeks and meant that sailors were accustomed not to following the coastline, but rather to sailing towards a point in the ocean. Colonization began with the Canaries, most importantly with a French expedition supported by Genoese financing in 1402. The leaders did homage to the Castilian crown in 1403, and by the mid-fifteenth century the language and institutions were Castilian. Colonization was slow, amounting to an upper class of landowners from the mainland, for a large native population on the Canaries sufficed for labour, and only in the 1490s was the conquest complete. The prevailing wind systems linked the Canaries to the new world, but would have stopped the Portuguese from exploring west from the Azores even had they been interested in this rather than Africa.

Iberian expansion in Africa is associated with Prince Henry of Portugal (1394–1460), known as Henry the Navigator. The younger son of the Portuguese king, John I, and with no prospects for the throne, Henry was steeped in chivalric literature and conceived of grand crusades, with little thought to the practicalities. Checked in the Canaries, where he tried for a time to reverse the Castilian gains, Henry turned his attention to the colonization of Madeira and the Azores, considerably north-west of the Canaries. The Azores served as a port of call for ships returning from Africa. Mali, the remotest known point on the gold road, had been the major source of gold for Europe, but this had been obtained through middlemen in the Maghreb. The Maghreb also exported grain, which was in chronically short supply in Portugal, and imported fine cloth from Europe while exporting coarse fabrics to black Africa. A prime motive in the European exploration of Africa was thus to get the gold at its source, farther south, and bypass the Maghreb. The gold trade, not African spices, was the principal attraction of the Atlantic, stimulating the discoveries of the fourteenth and fifteenth centuries.

The Portuguese seized Ceuta in 1415, which they hoped would give them access to the Sahara routes, but the Muslim positions could not be dislodged. Thus they in effect decided to outflank the Muslims by using the Atlantic. Using his position as Grand Master of the Order of Christ (the Portuguese heirs of the Knights Templar) as a source of money, Henry financed numerous voyages of exploration. Significant amounts of gold reached Portugal from the mid-1440s. Cape Bojador was rounded in 1434, followed by gradual penetration farther south; Cape Verde was rounded in 1444. In 1460, the year of Henry's death, the Portuguese were trading for gold and slaves north of Cape Palmas.[16]

* * *

Despite the demographic recession that was begun by ecological crisis and deepened by the plagues, western Europe in the late Middle Ages had developed an integrated commercial economy that was strong enough to provide an economic underpinning for the institutional expansion of the states and, to some extent, to finance their rulers' political and military ambitions. This phase of the development of commercial capitalism, paradoxically, was accomplished in the face of a serious scarcity of coin. The various sectors of the European economy were interdependent but imbalanced, for there was a serious balance of payment problem between north-western Europe and Italy, and a somewhat less significant one toward the German and Slavic East. Although the end of the Byzantine Empire in 1461 removed a barrier to Turkish expansion in Europe, it had little economic impact, and the effort of principally Iberian explorers to find new routes to obtain Asian spices and African gold had other causes, notably the great power of Venice in the eastern Mediterranean. Although the end of the Hundred Years War was followed by localized conflict in the Low Countries and France, with the dissolution of the Burgundian Empire and the more famous Castilian campaign against Muslim Granada, Italy, England and most of France and Germany began to recover. When new silver supplies were discovered in the late fifteenth century, just as the demographic recession was ending, Europe was poised for a period of political and economic growth.

4

Late Nominalism and Early Humanism: The Cultural Life of the Late Middle Ages

The late Middle Ages is usually associated with a growing secularization of thought and expression. While essentially accurate, however, this view must be qualified. People were not becoming less religious but, facing different problems and considerably better informed than their ancestors, they were more inclined to form their own conclusions on religious questions. They were certainly not becoming more rational. Most who thought about it believed that this world and the next formed a single cosmos. God and the devil were real and acted directly on human affairs. Everybody who could afford them wore amulets. Omens and celestial portents were universally believed. Belief in astrology was almost universal. Horoscopes were devised for royal newborns, and their erroneous predictions never caused the practitioners to question the validity of the belief. All feared the artifices of sorcerers, and the royal astrologers had their own room in the palace at Paris. When Charles VI of France went insane, Duke Philip the Bold of Burgundy planted the suspicion that Valentina Visconti, the Italian-born duchess of Orléans, had bewitched him; she was ultimately banished from court for this reason.

There was a gnawing sense that the church was not fulfilling its mission. The papacy had little real political influence after 1378, but local churches remained extremely wealthy, and the great bishops still held important secular offices. Benefit of clergy, which permitted trial in church courts of clergy accused of misdeeds, was a continuing problem that was only limited in the northern monarchies from the late fifteenth century. The aspect of 'papal monarchy' that touched most believers directly was the financial rather than the political, and the spectacle of institutional greed and the lavish lives and accumulation of church livings of popes and cardinals caused adverse comment. Many people thus withdrew emotionally from organized religion, attending mass once or twice a year and concentrating on private devotions.

Problems of a top-heavy central bureaucracy and inadequate staffing at the local level plagued the church. Bishops and archbishops were generally natives of the area to which they were assigned, or of neighbouring regions; but their jurisdiction could be overridden by papal legates, who could act as though the pope were present. Virtually all legates were Italian or natives who were papal creatures. Some parts of Europe were 'underchurched'. Populous Flanders did not have a native bishopric, but rather answered to four: Utrecht, and three in France. The sense of alienation from a foreign church was also deep in Germany, where the monarchy was too weak to halt the pope's fiscal exactions. The pope 'provided' (appointed) to many middle- and lower-level church offices, but also to a few bishoprics. Since most great bishops and abbots combined several church incomes ('pluralism') to accumulate a large total income, although this was forbidden at various times by the popes, some local benefices had no resident tenant, and the practice of giving vacant benefices as a kind of stipend to university scholars contributed to absenteeism. In these cases the Latin liturgy was often memorized by vicars who simply recited it without understanding what they were saying. Most evidence of anticlericalism in literature concerns the upper clergy; there was considerable sympathy for the overworked parish priest.

The Separation of Church and State

In the area of church–state relations, as in so many others, an important caesura is reached in the late thirteenth century. The development of the institutional–territorial state rendered null the church's claims of theoretical supremacy over the state, which had been really effective only in the two centuries after the Investiture Contest and then only for the Empire. The number of clergy in secular bureaucracies was declining severely in the thirteenth century, even in secretariats, as literacy among laypeople became more common. But the change was not sudden or total. The first royal council in England that was composed entirely of laymen was that of Elizabeth I in the sixteenth century, and clergy remained on the royal councils even longer in France and Spain. Before 1300 most judges were clergy, but in England the court of King's Bench was lay by 1341. The first lay chancellor of England, the head of the royal secretariat and traditionally the stronghold of the clergy in the royal government, was Robert Bourchier, who assumed office in 1340.

The church itself was becoming more bureaucratized and judicial, with the elaboration of a code of canon law and network of church courts. As there was less of a need for clergy in secular bureaucracies than there had been earlier, aspiring clerical politicians turned to the papal government for preferment. The church still had considerable judicial power, but. it was exercised mainly over the clergy. Few laypeople were being tried in church courts by 1300 except for dependents on church estates, and those who were free could always appeal to a secular court. While Rome and the greatest bishoprics and archbishoprics continued to exert considerable informal influence, the lesser bishoprics and smaller local churches were generally poor, politically impotent, and got little respect from the laity. The church's efforts in the secular sphere were hindered by the superior physical power of national and regional states. Immunities (territories outside the purview of the public authorities) held by local churches held out better against royal encroachment than did lay immunities, since church property was inviolable under canon law. But as charitable donations of land to the churches were diminishing, and the churches were increasingly converting their lands to liquid capital, their assets were much more conveniently used for the purposes of secular governments.

The popes had successfully fought the German emperors in central and northern Italy, but had also raised up a menace in the house of Anjou that would be even more powerful in the long run. As had been true for centuries, the papacy became involved in the labyrinthine fights of the noble families of the city of Rome. Pope Boniface VIII (1294–1303) used the patronage available to the holy see to further his own Gaetani family and hurt their arch-enemies, the Colonna. More fatefully, he quarrelled with Edward I of England and Philip IV of France, who were preparing to go to war with each other, and who insisted on the right to tax their clergy if those clergy consented. Boniface maintained that local clergy could not consent to an aid that would diminish the church's resources without papal approval. When in 1302 Philip IV put a French bishop on trial in a secular court for treason, violating the principle of trial of clergy in church courts, matters escalated into a propaganda campaign, including bulls allegedly issued by the pope that had in fact been forged by the French. The culmination was Boniface's famous bull, *Unam Sanctam* (One Holy Church) of 1302, in which he claimed that all human creatures had to be subject to Rome to attain salvation. Philip IV in response sent agents to Italy to kidnap Boniface, bring him back to France and try him for heresy. They were ejected from Italy after seizing the pope briefly, but he died soon afterwards.

An interregnum in the papacy was followed by the election of the archbishop of Bordeaux as Pope Clement V (1305–14). Since Bordeaux was an English-held city, his election was seen as a compromise between the English and French sides. As Clement moved across southern France toward Rome, his progress was interrupted by royal agents and he never got outside France. The next seven popes were French. From the time of John XXII (1316–34) they resided at Avignon, a papal territory in what is now southern France where they built an enormous and highly decorated palace. John XXII's military campaigns against the emperor Lewis of Bavaria cost one-third of the ordinary budget of the papacy. Before Pope Gregory XI returned to Rome in 1377, the college of cardinals and most of the upper bureaucracy of the church had become French, guaranteeing majority sentiment in the college in favour of continuing the French line of popes. Although the extent to which the church became a tool of the French crown has perhaps been exaggerated, only the French liked this arrangement: the English and Germans viewed the Avignon popes with some justification as pawns of the French kings, while the Italians wanted the pope as bishop of Rome to return to his see. The humanist Petrarch referred to the popes' residence at Avignon, which paradoxically was the city where Petrarch grew up, as the 'Babylonian captivity', a term that has lasted to the present day.

Most political theory throughout the thirteenth century had exalted the supremacy of the church, and viewed the secular state and its regulations as the necessary consequence of man's fall from grace: civil society thus supposedly existed only in order to prepare man for the hereafter. But the crisis between the popes and the English and French kings between 1297 and 1305 virtually ended whatever strength these ideas had held even in theory. In response to the conflict between Philip IV and Boniface VIII, thinkers such as Giles of Rome argued, from an Augustinian perspective, that the essential functions of the state, justice and the exercise of *dominium* were only possible in a state informed by the church. James of Viterbo used a more Aristotelian argument in favour of the pope's supremacy that the church is the most perfect *regnum* (realm), which in turn is the highest form of human society. But such arguments were unusual by this time. John of Paris wrote around 1316 that the church as a spiritual institution held temporal possessions by gift of the secular authority, and that *regnum* did not need sanctification by the church to be legitimate. Dante Alighieri's *On Monarchy*, written to justify the claims of the emperors to supremacy in Italy, separated *regnum* and *sacerdotium* (episcopacy) completely. The heavenly and temporal ends were both of divine origin; man's earthly destiny was thus an end in itself. The ramifications of the 1302 episode were deepened in the 1330s, when Pope John XXII's fiscality and relentless persecution of the 'Spiritual Franciscans' (see below) caused even greater disquiet with the spiritual head of Christendom.

John XXII's conflict with Lewis of Bavaria caused the emperor to make his court a haven for secularist political thinkers who were fleeing the pope. William of Ockham, and particularly Marsiglio of Padua, evolved a fully developed theory of state supremacy. Roman law and the political thought of Aristotle were at least as influential as literary humanism in developing a modern theory of the state. Marsiglio used Aristotle's view of political society to argue that the secular state is not imposed from the top, let alone as the result of sin, but rather is the result of an agreement by the citizens to delegate powers to governing authorities. Jurists such as Cino of Pistoia reached the same conclusion by using Roman law. Cino's pupil Bartolus of Sassoferrato went further to develop the idea of representation, which is weak in Roman law, to have the people choosing organs of state that can make their wishes felt. By 1350 only the pope's most ardent defenders argued that the pope was supreme in the material world. Man's end was in civil society.

Thomas Aquinas had derived *natio* [nation] from *nasci*, 'be born'; thus 'natural birth' meant birth into a nation. The future lay not with the city-states of the Ciceronian civic humanists, but with the state as political society generally, and with the nation-state, which could and after 1494 did marshal resources that compromised the integrity of the Italian city-states. Aristotle's idea that the state was a natural forum of human society refuted religious ideas that it is necessary only because of man's fall from grace, and his victory as consummated in the work of Marsiglio of Padua was basic to the supremacy that the state and civil society enjoyed over the church – in fact by 1300, and in virtually all political theory by 1450. The nation-state had personal, territorial and cultural elements, while the king was a judge, enforcing the rule of a secular law that was becoming increasingly unitary with the spread of the Roman law at the expense of custom.[1]

The Theory of Conciliarism

The popes were also threatened seriously by the growing strength of the idea that supremacy within the church, even in doctrinal matters, belonged not to the pope, but rather to the entire body of Christians as represented through a council of bishops. Even in the late thirteenth century canon lawyers had addressed the question of whether there could ever be recourse against a heretical pope. John of Paris argued that the pope derived his authority from the whole body of the faithful as represented by their proctors, the cardinals. Later conciliarists were more radical. The fact that there was no authority within the church that could limit the pope helps to explain why some clergy such as Wycliffe, who wanted reform of an increasingly secularized church, turned to the secular arm, which would have a material interest in divesting the church of its property and political influence, developments that in the eyes of many reformers would force the church to confine itself to its properly spiritual mission. Marsiglio of Padua and William of Ockham also argued that a church council was supreme over the pope, on grounds that the power of the keys (the power to bind and loose in heaven and earth) had been given not to the pope as an individual but rather to the entire community of the faithful as represented in the council. Marsiglio attributed the power to summon the council to the secular ruler, since religious discord was a matter of vital concern to civic authorities. He further argued in his great work *Defender of the Peace* that it was the citizenry or the 'weightier part therof', and not God, which had given power to a 'human legislator' who thus acted on behalf of the body politic. Authority in the state must be unitary, and the aim of the ruler was concord among the citizenry. Marsiglio identified the temporal claims of the popes as the major source of discord, and accordingly gave the secular rulers the power to end them if they found them inconvenient.

The Great Schism and the Practice of Conciliarism

After Pope Gregory XI (1370–8) returned from Avignon to Rome and died there, the overwhelmingly French cardinals wanted to return to Avignon; but the threat of violence from the Roman mob, which insisted on a Roman or at least an Italian as pope, forced them to choose the Archbishop of Bari as Pope Urban VI (1378–89); he was to be the last pope who was not a cardinal at the time of his election. Urban was a difficult personality, and when he ordered the cardinals to confine themselves to a single church living, the majority of them concluded that he was a heretic. With material support from the court of King Charles V of France, they withdrew to Avignon and chose as the new pope Clement VII (Robert of Geneva, 1378–94), whose major claim to fame had been as a general during the reconquest of the Romagna.

The popes were thus already under as severe pressures from within the church as secular rulers were from their assemblies when the divided election of 1378 eroded their position still further. Secular rulers provoked the establishment and perpetuation of the Avignon papacy, then took the lead in promoting the church council that repaired the 'Great Schism'. With English, French and imperial support, a council was called at Pisa in 1409 to end the division, choosing a third pope without getting the other two to abdicate. Thus another council met at Constance in 1414 under the patronage of the emperor Sigismund (1410–38), who was already king of Hungary and would succeed his brother Wenceslas as king of Bohemia in 1419. The council got the Roman pope to abdicate; those of Avignon and Pisa continued to exercise their functions, but were declared deposed by the council.

The council discussed general questions of church institutional reform, mainly fiscal rather than doctrinal, but the major problem concerned the role of future councils. The majority simply wanted to choose a new pope and carry on as before. Oddo Colonna was thus chosen in 1417 as Pope Martin V (1417–31), and other issues of institutional reform were deferred. The final decree of the Council of Constance, *Frequens*, specified a timetable for future meetings of councils and instructed the pope to act with the council to remedy the most frequently cited abuses: the credentials of the cardinals as spiritual leaders, provision to benefices and pluralism and various financial concerns. The council still disputed the popes' claims to 'plenitude of power', which had been taken over from the language of Roman civil law and interpreted by the popes as giving them the power to dispense with canon and civil law. But subsequent popes were able to divide later councils, the most important of which met at Basel in 1431 and at

Florence in 1439. The pope's prestige against the council was enhanced when Pope Eugenius IV left Florence and called his own council at Ferrara in 1437, which gained the submission of the Greek orthodox church and a promise of reunification with Rome; and in 1460 Pope Pius II, the noted humanist Aeneas Sylvius Piccolomini, condemned as heretical the opinion that a council could limit the power of the pope.[2]

Although the pope defeated the councils, secular control over the national churches in a form that severely limited the pope's control over them was made more secure in the late Middle Ages. Shock over the crudity of Philip IV's treatment of Pope Boniface VIII cannot conceal the fact that after 1300 few lay rulers even pretended to treat the pope with reverence or deference. The French tilt of papal politics in the fourteenth century fanned anticlerical sentiment, as did the Avignon popes' invention of new clerical taxes and extension of papal control over appointments. The practice of reserving a growing number of benefices to the pope's appointment had the salutary impact of breaking local patronage networks and may have provided a better trained clergy, but it was much resented for installing foreigners in church livings, usually Italians and in some cases the pontiff's own kin. In England, for example, the number of foreigners provided (appointed) during Edward III's reign was one-fifth the number of Englishmen, and a disproportionate number of the foreigners were in conspicuously high positions, particularly livings in cathedral chapters. The popes also provided to university positions. In 1351 the Statute of Provisors gave the English king authority to expel from the country anyone appointed to a church living by the pope, while the Statute of Praemunire of 1353 forbade suits in the pope's or other foreign court without the king's permission.[3]

In a Concordat of 1418, evidently the condition for English support of Martin V against the Council of Constance, the pope formally conceded to the English king the authority over the church in his realm that his predecessors had enjoyed in actuality since 1351. The English rulers thereafter nominated bishops and many of the holders of livings in cathedral chapters themselves, and the king commonly taxed the church after this without consulting the pope, as well as diverting church revenues to the state's needs. Under similar circumstances in 1438 Pope Eugenius IV, needing French support against the Council of Basel, agreed to the Pragmatic Sanction of Bourges, which vested most rights that the pope had previously enjoyed over incomes and major church appointments in France in the crown. The king was unable to enforce this until in 1516 a new agreement, the Concordat of Bologna, guaranteed the pope specific incomes from the French church but left the king free to take other revenues and generally to manage personnel questions in the church. The Gallican church from this time was clearly a supreme and national church. In 1439 the diet of Mainz reached a similar agreement with the pope for the empire, but the emperors were too weak for this to have much impact.

Heresy

The political thought of anti-papal theorists naturally evoked pontifical anathema, but the late Middle Ages also saw heresy in the areas of theology and religious ritual. There are important differences, however, between this and the unorthodox beliefs that the church had faced before 1300.

Long before 1300 the church had a serious problem of diminishing recruitment into the older orders. The Benedictine, Cluniac and other monastic orders from the early Middle Ages had been extremely aristocratic for centuries, and the nunneries even more so. Most monks came from families that were prominent enough to afford the high entry fees that most abbeys charged, and were generally cloistered in or near their home areas. Families that wanted to preserve their property intact for one son would pay handsomely to cloister another, usually the younger one, so making him ineligible to participate in the eventual parental inheritance. Nunneries were even more expensive, charging the girl's dowry as the condition of admission. The monasteries were much resented; they provided easy lives for the monks, for the estates provided far more food and other goods than were needed for bare support, and the requirement of manual labour contained in the rule of St Benedict had long since diverged from actual practice for most monastic orders. Although the political and legal privileges of the churches – particularly the monasteries – were eroding in the late Middle Ages, this does not mean that the monks were having a hard time.

The earlier heresies had been defused to some extent by the mendicant or 'begging' orders, the largest of which were the Franciscans and Dominicans, both founded at the turn of the thirteenth century. The early mendicants had filled a real spiritual need. The popes always preferred the Dominicans to the Franciscans, who were less amenable than the Dominicans to direction from above. The Franciscans had also been embarrassed by a split in the generation after St Francis's death into rival branches, the Conventual Franciscans favouring relaxing St Francis' strict vow of poverty and the Spiritual Franciscans, who included such persons as William of Ockham, insisting that poverty was essential to the order's mission. Earlier popes had made a distinction between ownership and use that had permitted the Franciscans to hold property through third parties; but in 1323 John XXII declared that distinction invalid and ruled it a heresy to believe that Jesus and his disciples had not owned property. He spent considerable energy persecuting the Spiritual Franciscans, whose Italian branch, the Fraticelli, went underground and developed considerably more radical ideas than those concerning property.

In the late Middle Ages the 'mainstream' mendicants became agents of suppression of aberrant belief. The papal Inquisition, which had begun in the early thirteenth century but had died down for lack of cooperation from secular authorities, was revived in the 1320s. Many of its leaders were

Dominicans. Both the great mendicant orders, particularly the Franciscans, preached incendiary sermons against the Jews. The fact that the mendicants continued to beg for alms when property held for them was supporting them handsomely led to considerable adverse comment, such as Geoffrey Chaucer's classic portrait of the venal friar. The newer orders had thus become just as doctrinally rigid and as wealthy as their forebears.

The popes, fearing heresy, stifled spontaneous religious expression and insisted that groups that wanted to practise a more mystical or severe piety than that offered in the traditional orders form a new order under strict rules. They also came down hard on the Rhineland mystics. The Dominican friar Meister Eckhart (*c.*1260–1328), scion of a knightly family in Thuringia who received his mastership in arts at Paris in 1302, lectured there intermittently and at the Dominican school in Cologne. In 1329 Pope John XXII condemned 28 of his opinions as heretical. Eckhart was in the Thomist tradition that was standard for his order, but he added an element of Neoplatonic mysticism. He wrote in both Latin and German. The thrust of both his widely read *Klosterpredigten* [abbey sermons] and of his scholarly work was that the soul is encompassed by a conscious act in the God who permeates all creation. Eckhart's disciple Johannes Tauler (1300–61) complemented his metaphysical emphasis with a practical focus on the ethical rebirth that results from the soul's perception of God.

The Beguines were pious laywomen, mainly in the Low Countries and the Rhineland, who led lives of quiet piety and dispensed charity. Most of the Netherlanders lived in cloisters, but the Rhenish Beguines did not do so until they were required to in 1312. Some uncloistered Beguines, who were less strictly supervised, fell into heresy, and the entire movement came under suspicion. John XXII forced the Beguine houses to affiliate with one of the mendicant orders. Yet suspicion did not always extend to individual holy persons. St Catherine of Siena (1347–80) was a Dominican tertiary, which gave her orthodoxy in the popes' estimation. She practised extreme asceticism, which with her mystical *Dialogue* gained her a large following in the Italian cities. Crowds accompanied her wherever she went. Like Petrarch, she urged the pope to return from Avignon to Rome and actually negotiated between the papacy and Florence when the 'War of the Eight Saints' erupted between the two in 1378.

Late medieval heresy developed in large part because some clergy had become disenchanted with what they regarded as a secular church. John Wycliffe (*c.*1330–84) was an Oxford intellectual who accumulated several absentee livings, a practice that he deplored in his writings. He was a follower of William of Ockham, arguing that only through God's grace was salvation possible, not through works or the sacraments. God's will was paramount. Wycliffe inveighed against canon law and the papacy, and urged that the scriptures were the only authoritative version of the word of God, arguing that the lawful exercise of lordship over humans depends on whether the person exercising it is in a state of grace. Even more radically, he declared that the secular authority had the right to decide whether a clergyman who was exercising dominion had fallen from grace. Wycliffe's early protector, John of Gaunt, deserted him when he described the church as a community of believers and questioned transubstantiation, the doctrine that the bread and wine in the mass become the actual body and blood of Jesus. Wycliffe also translated portions of the Bible into English, and by 1395 his followers, known disparagingly to the authorities as Lollards ('mumblers'), had rendered the entire Vulgate into the vernacular; while his works, in effect urging disestablishment of the church and surrendering of church property, gave slogans to the peasants in the uprising of 1381. Although his works were declared heretical in 1380 and 1382, he was not molested and died peacefully in 1384, his writings anticipating all later Protestant doctrines except justification by faith alone. Despite anti-Lollard legislation from 1401 and the repression of a Lollard rebellion led by Sir John Oldcastle after 1405, Lollardy survived underground along the Thames valley and in the Coventry and Bristol areas.

The Bohemian reformer Jan Hus was exposed to Wycliffe's ideas when Czech students began studying at Oxford in the wake of Richard II's marriage to Anne of Bohemia in 1382. Supported by King Wenceslas, Hus began preaching in 1402 and became rector of the University of Prague in 1410. He came to the Council of Constance in 1414 under safe-conduct of the emperor Sigismund to present his views, but he was imprisoned and burned the next year as a heretic. Outrage over his execution led to rebellion in Bohemia. Although Hus had not followed Wycliffe in arguing that the bread and wine in the Eucharist did not become the actual body and blood of Christ, his followers went farther than he and also began teaching that scripture was the only source of authority. The 'Utraquist' movement thus began with a demand that the laity be given communion in both kinds. In the 1420s the 'Taborites' (who took their name from a mountain in southern Bohemia, which they named after the Biblical Tabor), led by the nobleman Jan Zizka, taught that the second coming was imminent and that rituals not mentioned in the Bible should be abolished, and they sustained a rebellion until 1434. The peace, essentially based on the status quo, allowed the rebels a separate church that gave communion in both kinds on condition that they accept other doctrines of the church; thus the web of Christendom was no longer seamless, for there were two Bohemian churches, the Catholic and the Utraquist. Long before Martin Luther, the churches of northern Europe had thus achieved far-reaching independence from Rome, but under local secular protection.

There was thus no institutional response by the church to heresy except papal anathemas. The earlier heresies had reached the masses, particularly in the towns, but no royal prince had fostered them. There was a political dimension to the late medieval heresies that was potentially very dangerous to the church: Wycliffe's heresy received initial support from John of Gaunt, and Hus's doctrines provoked a nationalist revolution in Bohemia.

Philosophy and the Decline of the High Medieval Synthesis

Wycliffe and Hus disputed orthodox views of the transcendent significance of ritual, church–state relations, and what they perceived as secular abuses by a nominally spiritual entity. But the church also faced a threat from philosophical doctrines that struck at the epistemological basis of religious revelation, with the late medieval schools becoming a battleground between followers of the Greek philosophers Plato and Aristotle. Most early medieval thought had been essentially Platonic as transmitted through the Neoplatonism of St Augustine (353–430), who believed that we gain knowledge through illumination that is imparted through God's grace, and that sensory perception was the lowest and least reliable way to gain knowledge.

As with Plato, Aristotle too was first known in the west mostly through commentators, but in his case they were Muslims. Some translations were being made directly from Greek into Latin by the late twelfth century, and this led rapidly to a revival of Aristotelian studies. Although initially controversial, Aristotle's logical works in 1255 became the basis for the curriculum in the trivium, the first three subjects (grammar, rhetoric and logic) of the liberal arts course. His scientific works, which caused less disquiet for Christians than his ethical and metaphysical treatises, were used in the quadrivium (arithmetic, geometry, astronomy and music); and after 1366 licentiates in Arts at Paris were required to know his complete works.

The conflict between the Neoplatonic and Aristotelian epistemologies produced a philosophical division. 'Realists' argued that the only reality was the general idea, such as goodness, and that individual 'good' entities or persons were simply material reflections of that abstraction. This is an essentially theological view, for God is ultimate truth and goodness. 'Nominalists' held that general ideas are mere intellectual conveniences or names (Latin *nomina*) and that only individual entities are real. Until the thirteenth century, nominalism was generally associated with Aristotle's work. St Thomas Aquinas (1225–74) and other synthesisers, however, reconciled Aristotle to their own satisfaction with an essentially realist position: God is the ultimate idea, pure actuality without potentiality, but knowledge that is derived entirely from sensory perception can impart an understanding of the world of matter, then extrapolate from that to prove that a world exists beyond the material. Divine illumination is then needed to gain insight into the nature of the non material cosmos.

But the Thomist synthesis of faith and reason encountered strong opposition. Nominalism and realism were still lively issues in university circles at the turn of the fourteenth century. The extreme realist position was associated with Duns Scotus (John Duns the Scot, c.1270–1307). Scotus argued that the unique character of all beings was expressed in a specific form, the *haeccitas* (thisness). God was ultimate form, and all creation occurs through a conscious dictate of God's will, which at times, Scotus suggests, can move God as a separate force, is omnipotent and can overturn the physical and moral order of the universe.

The nominalist position was associated with the English Spiritual Franciscan William of Ockham, who was also a noted conciliarist and, through his religious affiliation, an enemy of Pope John XXII. Ockham considered reason an imperfect tool, given that it often deceives its users; thus Aquinas' effort to use reason to buttress faith fails. Ockham argued that when faced with two arguments, one should choose the simpler ('Ockham's razor'); but certain knowledge about even individual entities, let alone general concepts (which are mere conveniences to link objects or ideas that appear similar to our reason) cannot be obtained through reason. Some of Ockham's followers were religious sceptics, but most followed Ockham himself in believing that only God's grace and our faith in it could provide order in this chaos. Ockham also distinguished between God's absolute power and his covenanted power; although, as Scotus said, God *could* change his mind and act contrary to his previous positions, he *will* not do so because divine revelation is his covenant with humankind, in which he establishes the rules by which he will govern the universe. Ockham and Scotus diverged over the reality of forms: for Scotus they were ultimate reality, while Ockham followed Aristotle in denying that they existed apart from matter. Yet in practice the conclusions of Ockham and Scotus were quite close in divorcing reason from religious faith. None the less, some university faculties divided into stridently hostile Scotist and Ockhamist factions.

The Institutions of Education

The universities of Europe had diverse origins and institutional structures. A 'university' in the modern sense was called a 'general studium' in the Middle Ages because it attracted students from all parts of Europe; founding one required confirmation by the pope or the emperor. Licences granted by a general studium were recognized as valid everywhere, while the credentials of graduates of a cathedral or municipal school might not be transferable. The word *universitas* means the guild or guilds of persons who set curriculum and other policy for the entire studium. In northern Europe this was usually the masters who taught in the arts faculty, often while studying toward a doctorate in one of the 'higher' faculties (canon law, civil law, medicine or theology). In the south, where some universities did not have arts faculties until the fourteenth century, the ruling guild was usually of students in the subject of the higher faculty. They were thus of the same age and educational level as the masters of the northern universities.

Particularly in England and France, the late medieval 'university' was a network of independent colleges. Initially founded as hostels for poor students, they began offering instruction when masters took their lodgings in the colleges, and had developed into places for residential instruction by the fourteenth century. Although there were only two English universities, Oxford and Cambridge, they had many more colleges than did the continental universities. Law, which was a university discipline on the Continent, was taught in England at the Inns of Court, colleges that developed near the common-law courts at Westminster where the students heard cases. By 1350 the university at Paris had at least 20 colleges, the most important of which were the Sorbonne, founded in 1258, and the College of the Eighteen. Most of the others were small lodging-houses. In Italy colleges always remained charitable foundations and did not become educational institutions.

There were about 20 universities by 1300. Most had some distinction and were known for a speciality. The Italian universities are an exception to this rule to some extent, for the strong municipal schools and schools operated by religious orders, particularly the mendicants, partially obviated the need for an arts faculty. Florence had a university after 1321, but lack of interest led to its demise. Refounded in 1348, it only became a distinguished centre after 1396, when it attracted the Greek scholar Chrysoloras, who was fleeing Byzantium. The University of Naples was also founded twice, in 1224 and 1266, while the university at Rome resulted from the unification of two universities founded by different popes. In France Toulouse, which had benefited from the unwillingness of the authorities at Paris to allow the teaching of Aristotle, became, with Orléans, the leading French universities for legal studies, while Montpellier rivalled Salerno for medicine. Each of the Spanish kingdoms also had universities by 1300.

Except in England the universities multiplied after 1300: between 1350 and 1500 some 50 were founded. Much of this was the result of national considerations, for warfare made students reluctant to venture into hostile territory. Aix was founded in 1413 by the count of Provence, Poitiers in 1431 by King Charles VII, who was then at Bourges, to rival Paris. Caen in 1437 and Bordeaux in 1441 were founded by the English, who occupied those cities at the time. The first university in eastern Europe was Kraków in 1364, followed by Buda in 1389. The first – and for long the only – one in the Low Countries was Louvain, founded in 1426. The first university in the Empire was founded at Prague in 1347 by the emperor Charles IV, the second by his rival, Duke Rudolf IV of Habsburg, at Vienna in 1365. Heidelberg, Cologne and Erfurt existed before 1400. Germany had another 13 universities by 1500, most of them political creations, giving Germany the largest concentration of educational institutions in Europe; but most of them were small, and they were certainly the most provincial. They were 'complete', with arts and the four higher faculties, on the Paris model. But while most universities in Italy, Spain, and France were known for the excellence of their higher faculties, the less-developed German universities concentrated on the arts.

Map 4.1 The Universities of Europe

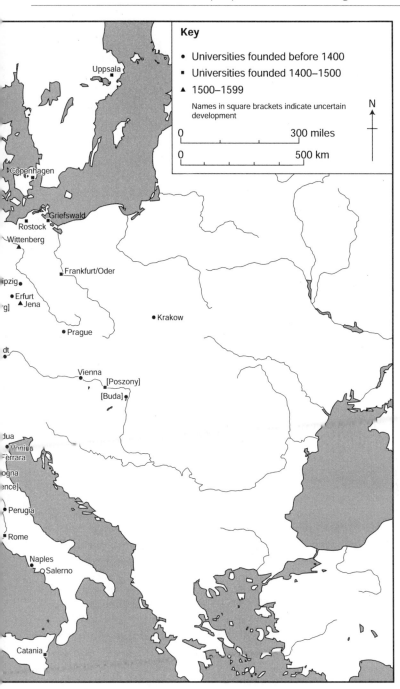

Key

- Universities founded before 1400
- Universities founded 1400–1500
▲ 1500–1599

Names in square brackets indicate uncertain development

0   300 miles

0   500 km

N

Uppsala

Copenhagen

Griefswald
Rostock
Wittenberg

Frankfurt/Oder
ipzig
Erfurt
g]   Jena

Krakow

Prague

dt

Vienna
[Poszony]
[Buda]

dua
Venice
Ferrara
ogna
nce]

Perugia

Rome

Naples
Salerno

Catania

Even before 1450, university or other professional education was desirable for advancement in all skilled occupations that lacked a manual component, notably law and the church. Edward III's reign in England witnessed a major shift toward university graduates among English bishops, and toward canon law rather than theology as the preferred discipline. While bishops had always been in high positions in secular administration, they were now becoming more professionalized and trained administrators than before 1300.

The number of local schools also multiplied, particularly in England, where numerous grammar schools were established in the late Middle Ages. In 1382 William of Wykeham founded the school at Winchester, which attracted the sons of many nobles. In 1440 King Henry VI established Eton, and there were perhaps 400 grammar schools in England by 1500. Although England was not noted for the vitality of its creative life in the fifteenth century, levels of literacy, promoted by the large number of grammar schools, were probably higher there than in most areas of the Continent except Italy.

On the Continent, most cities maintained schools and paid the salaries of the masters. The churches had initially controlled all education, but by 1300 new lay schools had been established in most parishes. They were usually confined to the elementary subjects in the beginning, while the cathedral school, under the supervision of the bishop, still handled the more advanced subjects that impinged on theology. The vernacular language was used for instruction, but the curriculum included translations of Latin works. Children, both boys and girls, were expected to attend school in Cologne in the fourteenth century, although most attended only long enough to reach basic literacy before becoming apprentices for practical training. Thus by 1300 in northern Europe as well as Italy most merchants were literate in the vernacular, but not in Latin: and levels of literacy were lower in rural areas.

The Spread of a Vernacular Culture in Northern Europe

Princely courts dispensed an immense amount of patronage in the late Middle Ages. Kings and queens did not sponsor much creative work in the sense of providing stipends to support writers and artists until later. They received dedications of works by authors who hoped for commissions or gratuities, accumulating books and manuscripts and hiring the best artists and sculptors to adorn their palaces and tombs. Charles V of France amassed a library of about 1000 books in the Louvre palace, most of them in French, with a preponderance of chivalric romances.

The growing splendour of the courts of the younger brothers and uncles of kings sets the tone for much of the literary and artistic endeavour of northern Europe in the late Middle Ages. The opulence of John of Gaunt's palace, the Savoy, caused so much resentment that the rebels of 1381 destroyed it. The French royal princes dispensed considerably more largesse. The duke of Berry, the younger brother of Philip the Bold of Burgundy, was an ineffectual politician, but he was incomparably the greatest royal patron of the arts of his day. He is associated particularly with the *Très Riches Heures*, a calendar illuminated by the Limbourg brothers and Jean Colombe, and collected some 300 manuscripts illuminated by the finest artists of the time. His library contained many chivalric romances and histories, but these were outnumbered by his religious works. The great tragedy of his life was the burning of his library during the civil wars.

Except for the warrior John the Fearless, the dukes of Burgundy were also important patrons of culture. Philip the Bold, like his brother Berry, was a collector who consumed conspicuously, but he also sponsored artists. He and his duchess had a collection of about 200 books. Except for missals and some devotional works, none of them were in Latin, a language that he evidently did not know; and he owned considerable religious material in French, favouring also chivalric romances, crusading histories and lyric poetry. He commissioned Christine de Pisan (below), the finest poet of her day and a scholar of note, to write a life of his brother Charles V. As John of Gaunt had supported Wycliffe, so Philip of Burgundy patronized the Paris theologian Jean Gerson. The most famous monument to his largesse is the Charterhouse of Champmol at Dijon, the capital of ducal Burgundy and the site of his tomb with his sculpted effigy by Claus Sluter of Haarlem. Philip generally favoured Netherlandish painters, notably Melchior Broederlam of Ypres, from whom he commissioned the masterly shutters of the altarpieces of the Charterhouse.

The cultural patronage of the Burgundian dukes is associated especially with Duke Philip 'the Good'. While his father and grandfather had been politically active at the French royal court, Philip's interest was in securing the independence of Burgundy. Thus he spent most of his time in Flanders and Brabant, particularly at his favourite residences in Bruges and Brussels. He patronized Flemish painters, commissioning numerous works from Hugo van der Goes, Jan van Eyck and others. Flemish book illumination also became renowned under his patronage, although most of the artists remain anonymous. Wealthy burgesses of the Netherlandish cities followed his example in commissioning paintings: the most famous example is the Adoration of the Lamb triptych, commissioned by Joos Vijt of Ghent for St Bavo's cathedral in his native city.

Philip the Good turned public display into an instrument of policy to inculcate reverence for his regime. In his time, theatre became statecraft. He shared his ancestors' fascination with history and romance, and parades with tableaux were held in the major cities, particularly after the end of the Flemish rebellion in 1453, replete with symbolism from the Bible and ancient mythology, that lauded the wisdom and beneficence of the prince. Festivals sponsored by the city governments had generally had a long history in the Netherlands, and they became more numerous in the fifteenth century, although generally displaying much less elegance than Philip's promenades. Philip also cultivated the nobility through lavish perquisites at court. Imitating the English royal Order of the Garter (1348) and the French Order of the Star (1351), he founded the Order of the Golden Fleece in 1430 to honour knighthood and its mystique. The first members were from all parts of the Burgundian domains, but Philip was soon offering positions in the Order to foreign allies whom he wished to cultivate; and when his descendants ruled Spain and the Empire in the next century, the Order became truly international. Much of the artwork sponsored by the Burgundians and their wealthy subjects during this time features elements of the Golden Fleece legend.[4]

The period of the Hundred Years War fostered a search for national history in France and England that produced less critical consciousness of history than the creation of national myths. Although France was not unified territorially for a century after 1453, the English, who by then could not be considered French princes by any stretch of the imagination, were the most obvious foreign presence there. Both sides used propaganda to manipulate public opinion, although treatises were often in Latin and amounted to preaching to the converted. The French kings were seen as heirs of Clovis, and the cult of Charlemagne was fostered, particularly by his namesake Charles V. Royal entries, processions into their major cities, became laden with symbolism, particularly at coronation rituals. Paris was the son of Priam, king of Troy; Brutus the Trojan allegedly founded London. While France as a place came from Troy, its rulers descended from the Romans. The inconsistency of these legends seems to have bothered no-one.

Yet during the late Middle Ages a significant number of voices was being raised against the expense of war and its horrors for non-combatants. Sir Jean Froissart usually described war from the attacker's perspective, but he also recognized its destructiveness. His description of the insensate pillage of Limoges by the Black Prince's troops in 1370 is extremely moving. The French chronicler Jean de Venette took a civilian's view of the devastation of the French countryside after the battle of Poitiers. Although the war's destructiveness did not affect England directly, several English writers addressed the issue. Wycliffe regarded war as evil, and John Gower, who wrote an English poem *In Praise of Peace*, saw it as the result of greed. Chaucer too expressed doubts about it; he alone of the three had seen military service. On the French side, the courtier Philippe de Mezières, whose main fame derives from his open letter promoting peace to Richard II and Charles VI in 1395, criticized the use of tax revenue for the purposes of war as early as 1340 in a treatise called *Against the King's Taxes*. The most important critique, although perhaps not the most influential at the time, was the *Tree of Battles* of Honoré de Bouvat, written in the 1380s and concentrating on the rights of non-combatants, such as merchants whose goods were seized in military reprisals.[5]

English Literature of the Late Middle Ages

Late medieval culture is often seen in the light of the Italian Renaissance, particularly in its early and almost purely classical phase. While this is unjust, it is true that the greatest authors in northern Europe were English, who, interestingly, are clustered in the last quarter of the fourteenth century. A substantial vernacular literature had been written in French and German before 1200 and in Netherlandish during the thirteenth century. The period from 1300 witnesses some waning of original inspiration there, but also the development of English and Italian, in the latter case basically Tuscan, into literary languages.

Although French was still the language of the ruling Plantagenet dynasty in England, it was no longer spoken exclusively by all with social or cultural pretensions even during the thirteenth century. English as a symbol of a growing national consciousness against France was used increasingly under Edward III. It became the language of the law courts in 1362, but only around 1430 did it become the language of Parliament and Chancery. The record of Parliament's deposition of Richard II in 1399 contains material in English, French and Latin. In the fifteenth century, however, English became a truly national language. As was true of the other vernacular tongues, it encompassed numerous local dialects; and it was the east Midland dialect, used by Geoffrey Chaucer and spoken in London and at both universities, which eventually became the standard version.

English was also the vehicle of patriotic expression. The victory at Agincourt in 1415 gave birth to one of its most famous patriotic songs, the 'Agincourt Carol', whose stanzas extolling the mighty deeds of Henry V are in English, while the refrain is the Latin *Deo gratias*. Political ballads abound during the conflicts of the fifteenth century. The *Gest of Robin Hood* was written about 1400 as a collection of previously composed tales. The hero had already entered folk myth; William Langland's peasant epic *The Vision of Piers the Ploughman* refers to rhymes about Robin Hood.

The English drama also took form during this time, with miracle and morality plays. The miracle plays were usually near-literal versions of Biblical stories, while the morality plays were drawn from life and described contemporary situations. While the miracle plays were initially staged in churches, by the fourteenth century dramas of various sorts were also being performed by wandering bands of players. The English ties to the Netherlands gave birth to the *Everyman* cycle in the late fifteenth century, which developed in imitation of the Dutch *Elckerlyck* and the literary conventions associated with him. Many of the merchants who led the mercers' guild of York, which staged the plays during city festivals, had lived in Bruges and were familiar with Flemish cultural life.[6]

Three of the great figures of English literature flourished in the last quarter of the fourteenth century. They were followed by a notable decline; not until Shakespeare does one encounter a figure of significance comparable to Geoffrey Chaucer. As Latin became the language of the universities and of religion, except in Italy, and French, although known by most educated Englishmen, was increasingly avoided, English became the normal language of expression. John Gower, who died around 1408, was the last important English writer who wrote with equal facility in all three languages. His *Mirour de l'omme* (*Mirror of Man*) was a social critique, specifying the vices peculiar to each social group, a technique that William Langland employed through a peasant voice. The *Vox Clamantis* (*Voice of the Accuser*) was similar in subject, but arranged its criticism by social estate, distinguishing the vices of clergy, nobles and laity and including a denunciation of the Peasants' Revolt of 1381. Gower's *Confessio Amantis* (*Lover's Confession*) was a collection of love stories illustrating the seven deadly sins. It was written in English, despite its Latin title.

William Langland is known for a single work, *The Vision of Piers the Ploughman*, an alliterative poem written in several versions between 1360 and the early 1380s. Langland referred to himself in the work as 'Will'; he seems to have been a deacon from the London area. It is written in the first person as the dream visions of Piers (Peter), who falls asleep and sees 'a fair field full of folk' going about their occupations. There is social commentary, with the vices of each group highlighted, and political satire, including a description of the 'Good Parliament' of 1376 as an assembly of rats who were being duped by a cat, John of Gaunt. The poem is didactic, with severe criticism directed at the church and particularly the friars. *Piers the Ploughman* was the first completely successful effort to portray the common person sympathetically in literature. It was immensely popular; more manuscripts survive of it from the fifteenth century than of any other single work, including Chaucer's. Langland was an indigenous genius, limiting his work to the English scene and without a trace of French or Italian influence. The wide readership of the poem and Langland's sophistication are a very flattering commentary on the education available to commoners at this time. We do not know how much formal education Langland had; two centuries later, William Shakespeare went no further than grammar school.

Langland was most unusual in being a successful man of letters who received no court patronage and held no offices. Geoffrey Chaucer (*c.*1342–1400), however, had a public career, married a woman whose court connections enhanced his own, and held several royal offices while he wrote his immortal masterworks. Typically, he was well educated in the classical tradition but knew no Greek. He knew enough Latin to translate from it, but in contrast to his Italian contemporaries and Gower he never wrote Latin works. His Italian was excellent, and he also read the classics in French translations.

Chaucer got his start as a *valettus* in the household of Lionel of Clarence, second son of Edward III. His wife was the sister of the mistress and eventual third wife of John of Gaunt. Thus it was only natural that Chaucer entered Gaunt's service when Clarence died, and went on to become an esquire of the king's household in 1372. Many of his works, particularly the early ones, are courtly poems in the French tradition, and the court patronage that he received was doubtless due to these works, which could be read publicly.

But Chaucer's enduring fame is from his English work, which was based on Italian models. Between 1368 and 1378 he undertook three diplomatic missions to Italy and became familiar with the major works of Petrarch and Dante Alighieri; but his most important debt was to Giovanni Boccaccio. He must have owned copies of Boccaccio's major works, and he took many of his story ideas from them, though adapting them to the tastes of the English court. Chaucer's *Troilus and Criseyde* is a longer, more philosophical and courtly and less sexual adaptation of Boccaccio's *Filostrato*; it is generally acknowledged as the masterpiece among his finished work, a narrative love poem addressed to a courtly audience, as *Filostrato* was not. His *Legend of Good Women* also has stories similar to those in Boccaccio's *De claris mulieribus*. And most obviously, his unfinished masterpiece, *The Canterbury Tales*, which he wrote between 1386 and his death, is an adaptation of Boccaccio's *Decameron*.

Chaucer may not have understood the extent of his own debt to Boccaccio, whose influence on his work is a century earlier than any other significant evidence of Italian and/or humanist influence on English writers. Boccaccio's interest in Greek qualifies him as a humanist, but it was Boccaccio the storyteller rather than Boccaccio the philologist and scholar of literature who appealed to Chaucer.

Chaucer was Controller of the Wool Custom in London between 1374 and 1386. In the course of his work he undoubtedly acquired considerable knowledge of foreigners and heard stories from them. Yet his literary work has no obvious debt to his own or his acquaintances' experiences; for example, while both Gower and Langland refer to the events of 1381 in London, Chaucer never does. His early diplomatic missions exposed him to cultural currents in France and Italy, but in the form of books that he took back to England.

The plan of the *Canterbury Tales* is familiar and needs no elaboration here. It is the only major work of Chaucer that was not directed to a court audience. The Prologue seems to embody some 'Estate satire', in a conventional three-Estate scheme, while the tales show his familiarity with all traditional topoi of medieval literature: courtly romance, the beast fable, moral tales, and his skill at satire and parody, although his critiques are always detached. The last of the tales are more meditative, and in some cases cynically despairing; the Manciple's Tale is probably the last one that he finished.

French Literature in the Fourteenth and Fifteenth Centuries

Considerable literature was written in France in the courtly tradition in the late Middle Ages, but most of it did not reach the standard set by earlier work. The leading fourteenth-century poets were Guillaume de Machaut (1300–77), Eustache Deschamps (*c*.1345–*c*.1405) and Sir Jean Froissart (*c*.1337–after 1404), whose *Chronicles* are an invaluable, if not always accurate, portrayal of events during the Hundred Years War. Machaut and Deschamps were essentially courtly lyric poets. They wrote some allegorical poems, and they standardized the stanza, rhythm and rhyme scheme of the *ballade* and *rondeau*. Froissart's poetry, however, is generally more original than this. In *L'Épinette Amoureuse* (*The Thorn of Love*) he tells of episodes during his youth, some of them perhaps apocryphal. He also wrote an auto-biographical *Dit du Florin* (*Florin's Story*). While the English nobles did not do much writing, some French courtiers also wrote lyrics, and several of them collaborated on the *Cent Ballades* (*A Hundred Ballads*) (1386–92).

The greatest French poets of the fifteenth century were the very different Charles d'Orléans and François Villon. Charles (1394–1465) was the son of Louis d'Orléans and thus the leader of their faction against the Burgundians in the civil conflicts of the early fifteenth century. He was captured at Agincourt in 1415 and remained in England until 1440, hostage to his refusal to acknowledge Henry VI of England as king of France. Even before his captivity he wrote some *ballades* and *rondeaux*, but most of his literary output, miniatures that are exquisite in form and delicate in feeling, was composed during his imprisonment, although he continued to write occasionally after his release.

François Villon (*c*.1431–63) existed on and wrote about the social margins of Paris. A master of arts at the university, he was exiled twice for homicide and robbery and spent time in prison. His first poem, *Les Lais* (*The Lays*) (1456), good-humouredly says farewell to his friends and leaves them imaginary bequests, while his *Testament* (1461) describes his suffer-ings in prison. His poetry describes in more graphic terms than any other in the Middle Ages the physical suffering and privation of poverty and illness, his later poems showing a sense of ageing and anticipation of death in a man just past 30. Villon's most famous poem is the macabre 'Ballade of the Hanged', written in 1463 when he had just escaped the gallows. His fate thereafter is unknown.

Excellent historical writing was also produced in France. The official court work, the *Grandes Chroniques de France* (*True Chronicles of France*), was kept at the abbey of Saint-Denis from 1285 onwards. Two contributors to it during our period are especially notable: Jean Juvenel des Ursins, the archbishop of Reims (1384–1402), the son of Jean Jouvenal, provost of the merchants of Paris and a royal councillor; and Jean Chartier, a monk of Saint-Denis, who carried it from 1422 to 1461. The chronicle is thus contemporary with what it describes, although its point of view is always that of the Valois court. Jean le Bel (*c.*1290–1369), from a patrician family of Liege, wrote his *Vrayes Chroniques* (*True Chronicles*) of events in France and the Low Countries between 1329 and 1361. Froissart, whose *Chronicles* are longer and better known, borrowed much of his early material from Jean le Bel, acknowledging his debt to his predecessor. His colourful descriptions and his fascination with chivalric ideals and with nobles and battles have tended to obscure the fact that he was a serious, analytical historian who went beyond simple recitation of events, providing some of our best narratives of such events as the English peasant rebellion of 1381 and the second van Artevelde rebellion in Flanders. He spent time in both the English and French courts, but passed most of his maturity in his native Hainault, where he received reports from informants. He is naturally more accurate on the northern events with which he was familiar, and less successful on the wars in Brittany and Castile than on those in the Low Countries and England. When his poetic output is added to his history, Froissart emerges as the most prolific and in many respects the best literary stylist of fourteenth-century France.

Froissart's chronicle was continued to 1454 by Enguerrand de Monstrelet. Georges Chastellain (*c.*1405–75), considered the finest historian of his day, began a chronicle in 1455, much of which is now lost. But the finest historical work of the fifteenth century is the *Memoirs* of Philippe de Commines (*c.*1447–1511). Commines began in the service of Charles the Bold of Burgundy, then switched in 1472 to Louis XI of France; and his work is less a history than an analysis of the different policies and motives of the two princes. He was aware of the limitations of both the men whom he served, and he analyses their motives and the success and failure of their public policies.

France also produced significant works of scholarship and other didactic literature in the fourteenth and fifteenth century. An elderly and anonymous 'Goodman' of Paris (now thought actually to have been from the lesser nobility) wrote an entertaining manual of instruction for his teenage bride full of information about household management, recipes, remedies, and patriarchal counsel that she should learn well from him, so that she would be a credit to him when she survived him, as he anticipated, into a second marriage. Christine de Pisan (1365–1430) was the most profound writer of the late Middle Ages, and it is all the more remarkable that a woman should take this position in a period when females rarely had the opportunity to write as a career; indeed, she complained that she was deprived of formal education because she was a woman. She was born at Venice, moving to the French royal court when her father became Charles V's physician. It must have been in the royal library there that she read mythology, philosophy and history. She was married at 15, then widowed at 25 with two children. With a family to provide for, she was able to support herself with her writing, a feat unusual for either gender at this period. She wrote conventional courtly lyrics, including 300 *ballades*, 70 *rondeaux* and 20 *virelays* between 1393 and 1402. Beginning with the *Book of the Duke of True Lovers*, she adopted an epistolary form in some of her writings, in this case from a male perspective. She was a literary critic, lashing out at the misogyny of the popular *Romance of the Rose*. Her masterpiece is probably the *Book of the City of Ladies* (1404–5), a set of biographies of women in history and mythology, with moral lessons drawn to reinforce women's good reputation and refute their critics. A separate work, the *Treasury of Ladies*, described the domestic duties of the noblewoman, adding that she should know law and estate management to conduct affairs during her husband's absence. Toward the end of her life she wrote the autobiographical *Book of the Road of Long Study*. Her most popular work was *The Book of Feats of Arms and of Chivalry*, which she says was to help noblewomen pursue the military profession; it contains considerable practical advice on tactics, strategy and logistics. Her interest in this exceptional topic is found in what is probably her last work, a *Ditié* of 1429 in which she compared Joan of Arc to Esther, Deborah and Judith, who had saved their people, and predicted that Joan would lead the Christians against the Saracens.

German Literature in the Late Middle Ages

Most notable literature from late medieval Germany is on religious themes, particularly that of mysticism. The older courtly lyric, the *Minnesang*, and the epic had declined. Although Germany produced no Froissart or Chastellain, most large cities sponsored their own chronicles, which were kept across several generations by the city clerks. Some of these, notably the Cologne and Augsburg chronicles, were quite sophisticated and give us our best narratives of the factional conflicts that stirred the cities. Miracle and morality plays were also produced in the German cities, as in the English, and some lyric poetry was written in burgher circles by both laity and monks. The amount of secular literature in Germany increases in quality and quantity after 1400, including a considerable amount of moral satire.

The Italian Renaissance

The cultural developments associated with the Italian 'Renaissance' and the manner in which they were imitated in northern Europe are a leitmotiv of the history of this period. Much has been claimed for them. For a balanced

Map 4.2 Renaissance Italy

assessment, we must move away from clichés such as 'modernity' and 'rebirth', and examine precisely what those changes were and how the changes themselves were adapted. We find that the Renaissance was really a backward-looking movement, rather than a progressive one, and that as the educational ideals of the Italian humanists came to dominate outside purely literary and artistic circles, they had a retardant impact in some areas, notably that of science. A conscious desire for 'rebirth' only occurs in the fields of art and literature, where there was an effort to emulate the distant past and denigrate the immediate past. Francesco Petrarca (Petrarch) (1304–74) thought that a millennium of barbarism separated the Romans from his own achievement in recreating and carrying on with their civilization, but the dubious honour of coining the term 'Middle Age' for the intervening centuries belongs to Flavio Biondo (1392–1463).[7]

Part of the problem in evaluating the Renaissance is the lack of a workable definition of what it involved. The term is commonly used to mean the fourteenth, fifteenth and early sixteenth centuries in Italy, the fifteenth and most of the sixteenth in the north. Yet any period of that length will obviously witness important changes. The real question is the extent to which those changes were merely time-conditioned and evolutionary, or truly revolutionary from a structural perspective.

Through most of the thirteenth century pre-eminence in creative activity had rested with the north Europeans, particularly the French and to a lesser degree the Germans. The achievements of the scholastic philosophers, the spread of literacy through the universities, the glories of the Gothic architectural style, the development of a cultural tradition in the vernacular languages, all surpassed the Italians and even more so the English and the Iberians. Lay literacy was probably more widespread in Italy than anywhere else in Europe, but before 1300 it was expressed mainly in business writing and administrative documents, and much even of this material was in Latin. Although some humanists lumped law together with the natural sciences, as disciplines that focused on the narrowly particular and had no connection with virtue, the precocious development of a legal profession in Italy conditioned an appreciation of statecraft as an integral aspect of the Roman heritage. Even before 1300 Italy thus had an unusual extent of Latin literacy among the laity, as reflected in the notarial registers and documents of municipal administration and the stylistic convention of quoting extensively from the ancients. By the time of Petrarch and the other early humanists there was thus a social and legal groundwork for a more strictly cultural revival of antiquity.

Yet in the three centuries covered by this book an internally paradoxical development occurred. The Italians developed a distinctive culture based on an admiration of classical antiquity, particularly that of Rome, although from the late fourteenth century there was also a substantial admixture of Greek; and in the beginning it was slavishly uncritical. This culture of classical 'humanism' developed synchronously with a flowering of a native culture that was expressed in various vernacular dialects, particularly Tuscan, which the popularity of the works of Dante Alighieri helped to make the standard Italian language.

Dante Alighieri

Dante Alighieri (1265–1321) is often considered the greatest literary figure of the Middle Ages. Exiled by factional conflict from his native city in 1302, he always refused repatriation, even when his literary fame caused the Florentine government to ask him to return. Dante's earliest work, *The New Life* (c.1292), is a collection of lyric poetry and prose in the courtly tradition, focused on his platonic love for 'Beatrice'. His next work, *The Banquet* (c.1304), is an uneven allegory praising a feast of love and knowledge, but it shows considerably more learning than *The New Life*. His greatest work, the *Comedy* (the adjective *Divine* was added to it by editors in the sixteenth century) was written during his long exile and left unfinished. The title refers to the classical division of drama into comedy and tragedy; although this is a very serious work, it ends happily with beatitude. Its 100 cantos are divided equally (after an introduction) into sections on Hell, Purgatory and Paradise. The poet falls asleep on Good Friday and has a dream vision in which God gradually reveals himself. The poet Virgil, the symbol of pre-Christian human reason, guides Dante through Hell and Purgatory, but leaves him, as reason must, at the gates of Paradise. Beatrice, now symbolizing revelation and divine love, and St Bernard of Clairvaux, representing theological contemplation, take the poet into Paradise on Easter Sunday. The poet meets figures from history and literature on his journey; Dante's political opponents are consigned to various circles of the Inferno.

The accomplishment of Dante Alighieri illustrates the sort of education available to Florentine laymen, though with the caveat that he seems to have been mainly self-taught. He combined an encyclopaedic knowledge of ancient science, contemporary theology and the French courtly poetic traditions, and his classical training was excellent. Dante is a transitional figure: a layman with firm scholastic training, yet one who was more concerned with practical, moral and political questions than with theology and the other abstract disciplines. He knew Latin well enough to compose his *On Monarchy* in it, to reach an international audience; but his only other Latin work was *Concerning the Eloquence of the Vernacular Language*, which he wrote to justify to scholars his use of the Tuscan language for serious work. Such defensiveness would have been unnecessary in a north European scholar this late. Yet Coluccio Salutati, the influential humanist chancellor of Florence, was upset enough by the popularity of Dante's Italian work to call him 'a poet for shopkeepers'.

The classical tradition had long been at the base of the formal education of Italian merchants. The curriculum of the elementary schools that were maintained by most cities began with literacy in the local vernacular and included some reading of commercial documents and elementary calculation. Pupils then progressed to the Latin classics in translation and also to the best Italian work, including Dante Alighieri and Giovanni Boccaccio's *Decameron*. Only boys who were destined for the church or high government office went to Latin grammar schools. Latin was thus taught only to an élite who had some practical use for it. Businessmen not only read widely in Italian; they also wrote original works, including bawdy stories in imitation of some of Boccaccio's, and *ricordanze* (family chronicles) in which they described their family lives and marriage alliances and strategies, as well as giving an indication of their broader cultural interests in some cases. More Italian than northern merchants read works of literature for enjoyment. Vernacular law, history and medical books and the *Divine Comedy* were found in many private libraries, and some had French works, such as courtly romances and the *Cent Nouvelles Nouvelles,* a prose collection of stories in French similar in subject to (if usually more refined in tone than) the *fabliaux* of the thirteenth century. The Latin works of Petrarch and other humanists were found in only the biggest libraries and in those of the great merchant princes who were their patrons.

The Cult of Antiquity

The self-conscious idea of a cultural revival based on antiquity, specifically classical literature, and associating this with a repudiation of medieval civilization, came with Petrarch, a Florentine who spend most of his life outside his city, the son of an exile from Florence who had taken employment with the papal court in Avignon. Petrarch had an immense reputation as a scholar. He considered the Latin that had evolved in the millennium since Cicero had written to be debased, and felt that educated persons should imitate the language of the ancients, setting out his principles of style and education in his voluminous *Letters*. Petrarch's influence in establishing humanist educational ideals as a programme is undeniable; yet his uncritical admiration of the ancient Latin authors, particularly Cicero, caused him to borrow their phraseology out of context and imitate them rather than build on them. He lacked critical sense: his *Letters* are still read for their pedagogical importance, but his personal favourite of his compositions was *Africa*, an epic poem in Virgilian style and metre. It is a great irony that Petrarch's most widely read works are his sonnets – he invented the form – written in the vernacular that he disdained for serious work, to his platonic lady, Laura.

A critical role in the spread of Petrarch's ideas comes with Giovanni Boccaccio (1313–75). Before meeting Petrarch, Boccaccio wrote mainly in Italian. His masterpiece is the *Decameron*, a collection of folk tales told on

10 days by 10 young people (hence the title) who had fled Florence to escape the plague. Boccaccio adapted some stories from a previous oral tradition, but he invented others. This work has continued to delight scholars and amateurs alike. Geoffrey Chaucer, as we have seen, borrowed substantially from the *Decameron* and also from *Il Filostrato* (c.1338), Boccaccio's poetic rendering of the Troilus and Cressida story. Boccaccio met Petrarch in 1350 and became the leading promoter of his ideals of proper classical studies in Florence, and most of his work thereafter was in Latin and adopted classical style and themes, although one exception is a biography of Dante Alighieri in Tuscan, written around 1354. While Petrarch's Greek was halting at best, Boccaccio was important in reintroducing Greek studies to western Europe.

The intellectuals of the Renaissance are often credited with developing a new appreciation and sense of history, but this is true only in a limited sense. Scholars of the Middle Ages revered the past, especially the ill-understood Roman Empire, which had seen the birth and coming to power of the Christian church and its political role, still very real in the late Middle Ages. Intellectually they concentrated on the Roman Empire. Medieval scholars thought of the literary classics of antiquity as part of an eternal present that should be interpreted allegorically to grasp their transcendent significance. Renaissance scholars interpreted them as written for a different audience in a different time and place, thus displaying a historical consciousness, although they romanticized the different time and place. Depending on the circumstances of patronage, scholars of the Renaissance venerated either the Republic or the early, pre-Christian Empire. Reverence for the past was a constant; the Italians of the Renaissance revered different pasts from those that had been fashionable in the late Middle Ages.

As specific times in the past became idealized as centres of virtue, the Italian humanists developed a new sense of history as moral philosophy. Renaissance education assigned a high position to poetry and history, neither of which had been studied as such in the Middle Ages, and de-emphasized mathematics and the scientific side of philosophy. The best writers of history of the Renaissance, such as Leonardo Bruni and, later, Niccolò Machiavelli, used original sources where they knew them, and analysed and suggested cause and effect rather than simply citing political and military facts. Bruni's scheme of history interpreted five specific civilizations of the past in terms of the rise and decline of liberty. This cyclical view is in sharp contrast to the linear sense of history prevalent in the Middle Ages, when history was perceived as the story of God's revelation and man's march toward the end of days. Bruni was also the first Christian historian who disputed the the notion of medieval thinkers that the Roman Empire had been a high point of human development, since Christianity was born during that period. Rather, he saw the emperors as destroyers of the liberty that had developed in the city republics of Athens and Rome, based on free discussion and citizen involvement. He thus associated republican institutions with the freedom necessary for the exchange of ideas.[8]

Most medieval writers of history, even the later ones such as Froissart, were really chroniclers rather than historians. Although much more sophisticated than early medieval writers, the historians of the period of the Hundred Years War are valuable only for what they said about their own times, events that they had witnessed, heard about from witnesses or occasionally read about. Even Froissart, although he goes beyond the bare facts in some cases, did not try to analyse the past for its moral lessons or provide broad interpretations. In so far as this was being done outside Italy in the fourteenth century, the explanations were religious. Both the Italian writers of the Renaissance and most northern authors dealt with purely secular topics, but the Italians analysed written documents to carry their story back into antiquity, and subjected their material to causal analysis that generally lacked more than a perfunctory nod toward divine providence. Machiavelli in particular preferred *Fortuna* (Fortune personified) to *Deus* (God) as a cause of events for which he could find no rational explanation.

Historians and philologists of the Renaissance developed the notion that the past should be understood in terms of its own context, but this was never without regard to the moral lessons that it taught. Ancient authors had been interpreted in the Middle Ages in the light of their commentators' present in an effort to grasp their allegorical or transcendent significance, but no effort was made to place them in their own historical contexts until the Renaissance. In contrast to the scholastic thinkers, the humanists emphasized the original meaning of words, not their interpretation or transcendent significance. Philology was thus the key to understanding, and history became the subject from which moral lessons could be gleaned. Yet this has the danger that history became a particular form or adjunct of literature. Leonardo Bruni simply lifted large sections of the great Roman historians Livy and Tacitus to suit his purposes in writing about Florence, confident that his sources would be known to his readers and that their phraseology was better than his.

The Educational Revolution of the Early Renaissance

By 1600 a firm grounding in Latin and some knowledge of Greek were necessary for a person to be considered educated. 'Medieval' Latin was an international language of education and diplomacy in 1300; by 1600 it was generally dismissed as barbaric, but classical Latin was inadequate to express the original thoughts of educated persons, who learned about the achievements of the Greeks and Romans in their own languages but commented on them in the modern vernaculars. The full text of Quintilian's *Institutes of Oratory* was discovered in 1416, followed by Cicero's

Concerning the Orator in 1421. Cicero was relatively uncontroversial, but much of the academic infighting of the late fifteenth and early sixteenth centuries, particularly in the northern universities, concerned replacing the text of Donatus, the mid-fourth century grammarian who had emphasized writing and the mechanics of language, with Quintilian, whose subject was public speaking. Pier Paolo Vergerio (*c.*1368–1444) argued in *On Noble Customs* that the basic goal of education, and the most suitable for princes, was the inculcation of moral character, which was best done through the liberal arts. Gasparino Barzizza (1360–1430) and particularly Guarino Guarini da Verona (1374–1460) at Ferrara and Vittorino da Feltre (*c.*1379–1446) at Mantua established schools whose methods and curricula became influential in northern Europe as well as Italy. Leon Battista Alberti's treatise *On the Family* also became influential among the aristocrats of Florence for its emphasis on teaching children reading, classics and *abbaco*, a complex system of practical commercial mathematics that was based on Leonardo Fibonacci's thirteenth-century *Book of the Abacus*. Alberti argued that fathers should not decide children's vocation at birth, but later, after they had observed them develop. He emphasized good manners and refinement, foreshadowing the weakening of the urban aristocracies by the growing power of the urban-princely courts.

The Renaissance educational revolution involved making classical Latin grammar and rhetoric the key disciplines of the liberal arts curriculum, displacing logic. By 1500 the medieval curriculum in basic Latin literacy had largely been replaced by Cicero and Quintilian. Disputation, the essential element of logic, was de-emphasized in favour of rhetoric, declamation and recitation; accordingly, logical argument was often displaced by repeating the phraseology of classical authors. But while in Italy this educational revolution occurred in the Latin grammar schools, it came later to the north and centred there on the universities, which were very different institutions from those in Italy. Italian universities were essentially schools of law and medicine that took only older students, while northern boys entered the universities younger, usually around the age of 14, and got their liberal arts training there. Much of the apparent cultural difference between Italy and the north is explained by this simple difference in the structure of educational institutions: to train boys in the classics at the same age as in Italy, the northerners had to change the curriculum in the universities, while the Italians did not.[9]

Schools everywhere also emphasized the ethical content of classical works and the importance of literature and philosophy over the 'vile mechanical arts'. The Renaissance humanists had an optimistic view of human nature. In modern terms, they thought that it was not genes but environment, which can be controlled, which determined character, generally rejecting the Christian notion of limited determinism based on original sin and preferring the Roman idea of the nature of the newborn child as a blank slate which is then formed by good and bad experiences.

Educating the child was therefore a serious matter, and Renaissance educators emphasized training the whole person, the body as well as the mind. The most famous educational treatise of this period is a late work, Baldassare Castiglione's *Book of the Courtier* (1528), but it simply puts a more court-oriented and social-climbing cast on an educational change that had become fixed by the time he wrote.[10]

Greek

Knowledge of Greek authors never died out in the Middle Ages, but few could read them in the original languages. The translations into Latin were not very good, consisting mainly of philosophical treatises that could be adapted to theological systems. The Renaissance saw a great increase of interest in Greek literature and philosophy, for its contribution to Roman culture was recognized. Interest in Greek studies was fanned by the presence of increasing numbers of Greeks in the west as the troubles of Constantinople mounted. Coluccio Salutati, the first chancellor of the Florentine Republic and the owner of an impressive library, was instrumental in the refoundation of the University of Florence in 1385. His influence led to the establishment of the first chair of Greek in Europe at the university for the Greek émigré Manuel Chrysoloras in 1396, and the chair remained after Chrysoloras left in 1399. Salutati was the main force behind making Florence the leader in Petrarchan humanist studies. His official position, combined with his scholarship and his understanding of the importance of the Greeks in the evolution of Roman thought, spread the new learning in governmental and business circles that provided patronage. Interest grew as more Greeks came west, particularly the large numbers who attended the Council of Florence/Ferrara in 1438–9. Yet, although Chrysoloras later lectured elsewhere in Italy and at Paris, his teaching had a significant impact only at Florence.

Particularly in the early phase of the Renaissance, books, which were hand-copied and sometimes illuminated, were regarded as works of art, and collecting them sometimes became an end in itself. The Florentine businessman Niccolò Niccoli is the most famous of the collectors: as was true of other Florentine art connoisseurs, his interest was aroused by the Greek lectures of Manuel Chrysoloras, and he collected over 146 Greek and many Latin manuscripts. Niccoli was no scholar; he could scarcely read the Greek manuscripts that he collected. In his will, however, he provided for a library to house his collection. Three of his executors were members of the Florentine ruling family, the Medici; and most of the rest were scholars. In 1441, four years after Niccoli's death, Cosimo dei Medici transferred his library to the Dominican friary of San Marco, and as other books were donated to the place, it became the first public library of Florence. Cosimo also had his own library, now called the Laurentian after his famous grandson. Other libraries followed. The personal collection of Pope Nicholas V became the nucleus of the Vatican Library, and when Cardinal Bessarion gave his books to Venice in 1468 the donation became the foundation of the Biblioteca Marciana.

Although the early humanists insisted on rigorous use of classical models, their concern for purity of the original language did not extend to Greek, which as a group they never read easily. Critical study of the original Greek texts came later and is associated with the theological concerns of the northern humanists. The Italians made new translations, many of them at the court of Pope Nicholas V (1447–55), and by the end of the Renaissance virtually all that we now know of the corpus of ancient Latin and Greek authors was complete, with the Greeks available in Latin translation.

Latin thus remained the language of scholarship in the Renaissance, as it had been in the Middle Ages; but it was a different, more classically Ciceronian and rhetorical Latin. The early humanists hoped to make it a language of modern literature, but this part of their programme was still-born in the north and eventually failed in Italy too. The medieval context explains much of this. Latin had remained a language of literature longer in Italy than in the north: while French and German have early literary works of high quality, Italian and English do not, for they developed later. Returning to Latin as a literary language was much less an atavism in Italy than in the north, and may explain why the northerners, except for such people as Erasmus, never used it much, preferring instead to write on classical themes in the vernacular.[11] Even in Italy the problem of Greek and the difficulty of accommodating all modern vocabulary to the classical showed that the uncompromising attitude of the early humanists toward medieval Latin and the vernaculars was unrealistic. The later humanists were much more willing to accommodate, although before 1450 Leon Battista Alberti was the only major figure in the Florentine Renaissance who wrote in Italian (in his treatises on the family and on painting) as well as in Latin. But a sign of the times is that while the major authors of the early Renaissance wrote in Latin for scholarly audiences, they permitted translations of their works into Italian.[12]

Philosophy During the Early Renaissance

The Italian Renaissance is associated with the growing veneration of Plato and of philosophical and literary studies at the expense of Aristotle and the scientific tradition that had dominated the medieval universities. In fairness, much of the problem with Aristotle was that his work was used differently in north and south. Until the fourteenth century, after he had become the core of the curriculum in the arts and theological faculties of the northern universities, the Italian universities did not teach theology or philosophy at all. These subjects were taught in the mendicant schools, while the universities were schools of rhetoric, law and medicine. In the universities Aristotle's writings were used as an adjunct of medical study in a way similar to that in which the northerners used them for philosophy and theology. Thus, while northern Aristotelianism was religious and ethical, Italian Aristotelianism was secular.

This, combined with the poor translations from Aristotle's Greek into Latin used before the fourteenth century, may explain Petrarch's reaction against Aristotle's work, since Petrarch, like Erasmus later, claimed that he wanted to use literature in search of purer texts and simpler religion. Most of the early humanists, including Petrarch and Salutati, were deeply religious. Much of Petrarch's attack was on features peculiar to Italian Aristotelianism; and the anti-Aristotelianism that developed later in the north was really directed more against Aristotle's scholastic commentators and the rigid methodology that they developed than against the philosopher himself.[13] Yet the fact remains that the Italian critique of Aristotle was a revolt of the arts and literature against the domination of the schools by science and medicine, and this deprives it of much of its claim to originality. The self-conscious enthusiasm and a sense of novelty that Italian Renaissance painters and writers displayed were naively uninformed: Aristotle, whose works had been common currency among educated persons in the west since the thirteenth century, has had far more impact on modern thought than any other ancient author.

Humanism

The use of 'humanism' as an umbrella term of convenience for the intellectual innovations of the Renaissance has posed more problems than it has answered. 'Humanists' in fifteenth-century usage were students of what today are called the 'humanities' – literature and languages, poetry, history and ethics – but in their case this must be restricted to the works of classical antiquity. The applied and performing arts were not subjects of academic study, and accordingly the great artists were not humanists. The term 'humanism' came into use much later and suggests that the humanists had a coherent programme or central doctrine. This was simply not the case.

There was no philosophy of humanism; most of the scholars who are now called humanists were philologists, not philosophers, whose overriding concern was with using correct classical Latin. Certainly the humanists of the Renaissance did not exalt human or mundane concerns at the expense of religion: virtually all of them were at least conventionally religious, and some went beyond that. Medievalists have understandably seen much less that is original in Italian humanism than do persons who approach the past from the present and have little idea of the pre-1300 antecedents of the intellectual currents of the Renaissance. Both the scholastics and

Renaissance humanists revered and imitated the classics; the difference is that more classical texts were known by 1450, Cicero and Plato were better-known, and classical studies in the fifteenth century emphasized declamation and rhetoric rather than the logical application of secular classical texts to theological or scientific questions. The humanists' main concern was with using correct classical Latin. Yet their Latin works, atavisms in an evolving intellectual climate, have not stood the test of time. The only Latin works of the Renaissance that are still read for their intrinsic interest as opposed to intellectual or antiquarian curiosity are later: Pico della Mirandola's *Oration on the Dignity of Man* (1486), and works by northerners, including several by the Dutchman Desiderius Erasmus and the *Utopia* of the Englishman Thomas More.

Humanism was associated with the cities, both in Italy and as transposed to the north, although in some contexts it was grafted onto the chivalric-literary topoi that had dominated French literature since the central Middle Ages. Lauro Martines has rightly called humanism a 'program for ruling classes',[14] for it emphasized reverence for a distant past that was of little practical use to most persons. In its most esoteric form, Renaissance humanism and the cult of the classics simply became a way of distinguishing persons who were being educated, specifically for a public career in what was regarded as an imitation of the Roman civic tradition, from those who were not.

Cicero and Civic Humanism: Philosophy, Rhetoric and the Early Renaissance State

Plato and Cicero were the great classical recoveries of the Renaissance, and they led to different traditions. Little of Plato's work was known directly before the fourteenth century, although the version of his thought taken over by St Augustine from the Neoplatonists had a considerable impact on Christian theology. But in the 1440s more of his dialogues were recovered, and they sparked immense interest. Plato was concerned with a realm of transcendent ideas. Although his ideal Republic would be ruled by philosophers – a position from which, later in life, he retreated in favour of a more conservative approach based on veneration of the traditional gods – he was essentially a contemplator. Plato's great vogue came mainly in the half-century after 1450 and was largely confined to Florence.

By contrast, Cicero's influence was a constant in the fifteenth and sixteenth centuries and was one of the novel features of Renaissance scholarship, for his career was not widely known nor his works much read before the fourteenth century. He had been active in the politics of the late Roman Republic: his orations in defence of republican liberties in the wake of Julius Caesar's rise to power in the first century BC, notable for their rhetorical style as well as their substance, made him seem an ideal to the wealthy, land-based aristocrats who ruled Florence. Although Cicero valued the contemplative life, he saw it useful to humankind only if translated into action in a public career. Both as man of letters and political figure, and specifically as an orator, Cicero was of cardinal importance for the study of rhetoric and in the development of the tradition of what is now called 'civic humanism', a term referring generally to the use of classical examples to justify a particular regime or point of view. Initially it was really 'city humanism', the patriotism that Rome – republic or empire – could inspire for one's own city; but the ideal of public involvement by an educated élite that it fostered had broader applications. Italian intellectuals, lacking a national monarchy and bothered by civic tumult, yearned for the golden and supposedly orderly past of Rome.

Hans Baron suggested that when republican Florence was threatened by the tyrant Giangaleazzo Visconti of Milan at the turn of the fifteenth century, Coluccio Salutati, the chancellor of Florence, and other opponents of Milan used Cicero's ideas to justify the independence of the city and the virtues of republican government. Later outbursts of literary republicanism accompanied the threat from Ladislas of Naples a decade later. Baron's argument has been criticized on grounds that he misdated the composition of certain works, but subsequent scholarship has generally validated him in this area. He is more open to criticism, however, in his assumption that the 'civic humanists' were idealists and purely republican. Coluccio Salutati himself, whose work provided much of Baron's inspiration, addressed adulatory work couched in classical rhetoric to Giangaleazzo Visconti before Florence employed him.[15]

Thus the very aristocratic rulers of Florence patronized humanists who lauded the Roman republic, which was dominated by urban-based landholders such as themselves, but which had lacked a lasting executive in a formal sense; while those of Milan, who styled themselves dukes much earlier than their Florentine counterparts, preferred authors of the Roman Empire. While it was hard to use Cicero in anything other than a republican context, Plato could be adapted to specific forms of patronage more easily. Bruni, who was firmly republican, used Plato, but others, notably Uberto Decembrio and his followers, saw the philosopher-king of Plato's *Republic* as a prototype for the ducal monarchs of Milan.

Some humanists were simply literary hacks, available for hire by patrons. Leonardo Bruni's *Laudatio* of 1403–4 combines a praise of Florence's liberty and equality with a justification of imperialism, a notion that is even clearer in his later *History of the Florentine People*. Around 1474 the humanist Bartolomeo Platina wrote two dialogues in Platonic form, dedicating the one entitled *On the Best Citizen* to Lorenzo de' Medici and that entitled *On the Prince* to Lodovico Gonzaga, Marquis of Mantua. The two are distinguished only by inconsequential phraseology. Thus there was little difference in practice between the republics and the despotisms; it was and remains a question of propaganda. Later chancellors of Florence urged that reasons of state called for increasing its power at the cost of individual liberty.[16]

Although civic humanism thus can be identified with no coherent political agenda, the study of the classics in itself had a profound impact on political discourse. The civic humanists argued that the virtuous person should be involved in civic life. Cicero became the ideal of a committed citizen. Although some Platonists preferred solitary contemplation to public involvements, Marsiglio Ficino considered asceticism a violation of basic human nature, while Leonardo Bruni emphasized discourse and community over solitude and study. Furthermore, no educated political man could do without a classical education that would provide him with references to quote in defence of a course of action. The humanists were as insistent on quoting the literary masters of antiquity as the scholastics had been on quoting Aristotle.[17]

Although Petrarch had been involved in politics, at least for exhortation, in his literary work he exalted the contemplative, disliking the study of law as too logical. But Roman law had been the foundation of the Roman state, and thus the patronage of classically inspired intellectuals, the 'civic humanists', by rulers who sought ancient prototypes in literature and philosophy to justify their behaviour, parallels the growing strength of Roman law, in a sense legitimizing it to the literary humanists. Salutati taught that law and jurisprudence, the sciences that bring concord to human beings and produce a rationally ordered state, are superior to natural science. Law, for Salutati, was based on universal justice and is eternal. But Leonardo Bruni did not share his mentor's love of the law. Carrying Salutati's reasoning a step further, Bruni argued that law focuses on coercion of evil people and is thus inferior to literature, which highlights the good: good men need no laws, and Bruni glorified the violence of great men, who are not bound by ordinary law. But although this line of thought had some descent through Machiavelli, most civic humanists rejected it.[18]

Painting, Sculpture and Architecture

The Middle Ages has left a richer heritage in sculpture than in painting, which decays more rapidly. Although the interiors of churches had rather stylized sculptures of Christ and the saints, cathedral façades in northern Europe were adorned with figures, some realistic, some fantastic, but usually in motion and lifelike. Here again the more static tradition of sculpture that had predominated in Italy as a consequence of its Byzantine heritage conditioned the Italians to see what they were doing as more revolutionary than it would have been in a northern context. Little painting survived from antiquity, but considerable sculpture did. The Florentine Donatello (1386–1466) in his long career made innovations based on the study of ancient models. Figures became more realistic and less invariably tied to religious motifs. Even within the religious tradition, there was innovation, such as Michelangelo Buonarotti's *David* (1501), which caused a storm by depicting not a Biblical patriarch but a nude youth with a saucy demeanour.

There were no structural innovations in architecture that corresponded to the changes in painting and, to a lesser extent, sculpture. The main change was in adding a larger number of rooms, with separate quarters for each family member to ensure privacy. Roman styles dominated in Italy, and Leon Battista Alberti's *On the Art of Building* is considered the first modern treatment of building principles. Alberti tried to derive general principles of construction from the ruins of the venerated Greek and Roman past still visible in his time. Although he quoted classical authors out of context and included subjects hardly of interest to modern builders, such as circuses, Alberti in a sense created architecture as a profession by emphasizing its geometrical base and the need to adapt buildings to their physical environments.[19]

The most important Renaissance changes in artistic technique occurred in painting, but as with those in scholarship and creative work, they had an antiquarian cast. Roman art, following Greek, had concentrated on the human form; landscapes were distinctly secondary. There was a growing realism in painting, even though the subject matter of most works remained religious. And that distinction was not always absolute; although medieval painting had tended to be allegorical, allegory did not disappear in the Renaissance, and some medieval artists were quite realistic. Enough classical art survived to provide models, and in the mind even of such a late connoisseur as Giorgio Vasari (1511–74), ability to imitate the antique rather than originality was the mark of excellence. Although Italian painters rejected the artistic styles of the immediate past, it is important to be precise about what 'past' they meant. The Gothic style of northern Europe was scarcely used in Italy except at Siena and the extremely late cathedral of Milan. Rather, Vasari meant to avoid the stilted and linear Byzantine style, which was much more common in Italy and had still been evident in the work of Italian painters through the thirteenth century.

There were also perceptible differences in approach to subject-matter. In medieval art warriors of antiquity were portrayed as knights, intellectuals as clerks. But Biblical figures were less typecast, and they tended to be patterned (as the portraits of classical figures were not) on the remains of classical art. The different historical consciousness that developed in the fourteenth century affected painting as well as literature. Dante shows Virgil as believable in terms of his time, a Roman with sentiments that he might actually have held. Perhaps the most important distinction is the growing independence of the individual from the story, even in religious themes: while medieval art had subordinated individuals to the religious themes, giving the personalities little independent value, the Italian artists imitating the Greeks and Romans gave a more human cast even to religious painting.[20]

The artistic revolution was fostered by two technical innovations. The north was actually more precocious in painting than Italy. Oil painting was invented in the Netherlands. The Italians picked it up through Netherlanders who visited Italy, and even more from the business contacts in Bruges of patrons of art. The 'Adoration Altarpiece' that Hugo van der Goes did for Tommaso Portinari, the factor of the Medici bank at Bruges, caused a sensation when Portinari sent it to Italy around 1478.[21] Italian painting became considerably more sophisticated when they began using oils, which made features and emotions deeper. When the Italians combined the use of oil paints with the science of drawing in mathematical perspective, which was invented by Filippo Brunelleschi around 1420, it gave them an incontestable technical advantage. Masaccio's painting of the Trinity in S. Maria Novella in Florence was one of the first to apply perspective systematically in practice; Alberti's *On Painting* was the first to describe it in writing. The mixing of mathematics with art was consummated by Luca Pacioli, who in 1484 wrote a *Summa arithmetica geometria proportioni et proportionalita*, which included a book on double-entry book-keeping as well as his ideas on lettering and artistry. Perspective did not spread to the north until Netherlandish painters saw examples of Italian painting in Bruges and were inspired to learn the technique. Despite the advantages of perspective, the Italians learned more from the Netherlanders than they taught them until the early sixteenth century, when Raphael and Leonardo developed a distinctly Italian style, in which the techniques that the Netherlanders had applied to religious themes were used for classical topoi.[22]

Cultural Patronage and Public Display

Although the notion that economic gain was not reprehensible began with the medieval scholastics rather than the humanists, city people exhibited much less reluctance during the Renaissance than before to display wealth just as kings and nobles had always done. The fact that the humanist plant only flowered with liberal doses of liquid capital in the form of patronage by wealthy rulers and citizens meant that their works departed completely from any lingering notion from medieval thinkers that riches were debasing. Cicero had disdained petty commerce, but he considered trade on a grand scale ennobling, for it created the wealth that could lead to leisure, an income based on rent rather than manual labour, and time for civic involvement, which at that time was unsalaried. In this early period of commercial capitalism, Leonardo Bruni and other humanists saw the desire for money as natural: Bruni thought that money meant to a city what blood meant to an individual. In addition to giving to the poor, which was often done perfunctorily and as part of one's will, the better to ensure the efficacy of this last good work after one's death, the urban aristocracy patronized writers and artists and built and lavishly adorned palaces, both private residences and civic buildings such as halls and churches.

Jakob Burckhardt's classic *The Civilisation of the Renaissance in Italy* has conditioned subsequent interpretations of this aspect of late medieval civilization. The Renaissance state was a work of law, not, as Burckhardt thought, a 'work of art'. He also saw the artist emerging from medieval anonymity to develop into a person whose genius was recognized as worthy of independence and respect. There are serious problems with this notion, among them the fact that few artists were geniuses: the word *artista* did not exist during the Renaissance. Vasari, writing at the end of the period, in a work whose purpose was not only to give anecdotes but also to provide a rationale for the 'artist' as a particular type of worker and scholar with specific skills, called them *artefici del disegno*, 'artisans of drawing'.

Artists as a group were known for loose living. Their confraternities (*sodalitates*) became notorious for licentious entertainments, particularly plays. The social position of the artist depended among other things on his family origins and how he comported himself, particularly in dress. Sculptors, who did dirtier work than painters and were often covered in dust, tended to have a lower status than painters. Although modern culture tends to see writers and artists as kindred spirits, the artists were really closer to the craftsmen, since they worked with their hands, while the humanists were in the milieu of the clerics, whose creativity was mental and thus, in their own view, of a higher order. The intellectuals disliked the idea of handworkers obtaining 'glory', which in their view could not be obtained legitimately except through letters: artists made things with their hands, painters were also shopkeepers, and neither of these lines of work ennobled them in the minds of the Cicero-absorbed humanists. Artists belonged to guilds, and in the Florentine structure of composite guilds the affiliation could be a considerable distance from what we think of as art.[23]

Artists and writers did not create masterpieces in spontaneous outbursts of genius. They had to live, and they depended on the patronage of the wealthy for support. Accordingly, they tailored their work to meet the demands of the market, particularly in cases where they were appointed to a court position or were working on commission. The nudes of Titian (*c.*1490–1576) were produced for a market for erotic portraits on bedroom walls. The economic changes of the late Middle Ages, in transferring considerable capital from northern Europe to Italy, made a vast amount of money available for conspicuous consumption, including but not limited to patronage art. Wealth was becoming more concentrated on the courts of princes, who were interested in cultural patronage that would enhance their images, and in cities, whose élites provided goods to the princely courts and consciously imitated them.

At least in the fifteenth century, patrons, not artists, determined the subject matter and medium of art works. Patronage at Florence, Venice, Rome and the princely courts at the smaller centres produced very different results; but in each case artistic quality was a distant second in the minds of the patrons to cost or perceived cost, which gave prestige to the patron. While we now tend to rate painting highest on the creative scale, followed by sculpture, then architecture, the order was reversed in the fifteenth century. What counted was cost, external more than internal display, and permanence. Bronze statuary and tapestries were expensive, while marble and especially fresco were much cheaper and thus counted for less. The notion that artists freely explored their ideas and created their masterpieces for enlightened patrons who were eager to acquire these works of genius is a myth. While modern art historians are interested in changing artistic styles, this counted for nothing to patrons, and contemporaries regarded the patron, not the artist, as the creator. This only changed somewhat in the sixteenth century, when art came to be appreciated for its own sake, and courts hired artists and architects for their reputations and gave them more – but not total – discretion in what they did.

Dante Alighieri and Petrarch were expatriate Florentines, and Boccaccio was also a native of the city. Educational opportunities were unusually great there, and after 1396 Florence was the main focus of the revived interest in Greek studies as well as the leading banking centre of northern Italy: and its industrial capacity was also strong, although Milan, with its development of armaments, probably had the most highly developed industry of Italy. Yet the extent of artistic patronage probably had more to do with making Florence the leading centre of the early Renaissance than any other single consideration. Wealth there was concentrated, and city offices and networks of patronage and clientage contributed to its accumulation. The great families were able to combine personal wealth with the incomes from numerous city offices to which they engineered their clients' election to build up impressive networks of influence. With limited potential for industrial investment, faction leaders paid the debts and helped with the dowries of their allies in exchange for their assistance or acquiescence in matters of state.

Florence underwent an evolution from mainly guild and corporate to individual and princely patronage of art in the fifteenth century, paralleling the decline of its civic institutions. The guilds helped to make the city a centre of cultural patronage, for they were responsible for the maintenance and decoration of the major churches. The cloth merchants' guild commissioned the famous Baptistery doors, sponsoring the competition in which Lorenzo Ghiberti's design was chosen over Filippo Brunelleschi's. Brunelleschi did not suffer: he got the contract from the Wool Merchants' Guild in 1418 to design the new Cathedral.

The number of Florentine bankers who built and adorned churches is quite striking. Some contemporaries thought that Cosimo de' Medici did so to expiate his sense of guilt for taking usury, and some of his contemporaries stated this as their motive for endowing chapels with art work. The Medici building programmes seem actually, however, to have sprung more from a desire to enhance their family's renown through association with the revival of antiquity. Cosimo saw artistic patronage as one way to solidify his image. He spent immense sums buying patronage rights to local churches and having them beautified as public monuments to his liberality: his family palace with its chapel were his only major private projects. As Medici control over the city tightened in the second half of the fifteenth century, corporate patronage declined and was replaced by private patronage, mainly by Medici clients. The Florentine élite undertook an orgy of display: some one hundred palaces were built or remodelled, and many more received interior adornment. Both north European and Italian paintings, even those with religious themes, show a concern with elaborate and often imported fabrics, furnishings and carvings. Patrons of art wanted paintings that would memorialize and celebrate what they owned.

Although patrons were more honoured by contemporaries than the artists to whom they gave commissions, painters and sculptors were very sought after. The interiors of residences were generally sparsely adorned, if at all, before 1400. After 1450 there was much more market for paintings among the non-royal lay élite. There can be no doubt that artists achieved a new dignity in the Renaissance through heightened demand for their works in secular society as well as in churches; while in their turn they directed entire workshops of journeymen who did the actual work under the master's supervision, just as in a weaver's establishment. Gentile Bellini in 1474 was given a long-term commission to paint the 22 frescoes in the Great Council Chamber of the Doge's Palace in Venice, requiring many years to complete. His chief assistant was his brother Giovanni, but by 1495 the project was occupying nine painters who were Bellini's employees, including two apprentices. Giovanni in turn took over supervision for a year while Gentile was painting for the Turks. The Venetians had made a treaty with Sultan Mehmet II in 1479 that included the loan of a Venetian painter to the Ottoman court. During his year in Istanbul, Bellini painted the sultan, naturally in an Ottoman rather than an Italian style.[24]

Natural Science in the Renaissance

The major achievements of the Renaissance were in literature and philology, the plastic arts and what we would now call the social sciences, including statecraft. By no stretch of the imagination can it be construed as a period of great advance in the natural or applied sciences or technology. Petrarch considered nature so complex that an attempt to understand it bordered on sacrilege, inveighing 'against a certain doctor' that rhetoric was the mistress, medicine the servant; for doctors cared only for bodies, philosophers and orators for minds and souls, a notion that sounds suspiciously similar to the attitude of medieval theologians toward physicians, although exalting literature instead of God.[25]

Except for the perfection of navigational devices known since the thirteenth century, the major technological advances of the early Renaissance were made in northern Europe, notably gunpowder and printing with movable type, both of which originated in China. Minor changes were made in textile technology, but all were refinements on the basic machines that had been developed in the Middle Ages. Machines were still powered exclusively by wind, wood and particularly water; coal was increasingly used as heating fuel, but its carbon content prohibited its use in ironworking, the major industrial operation that required intense heat. The same was true of agriculture: technological changes, including crop rotation and the introduction of new crops, came before 1300 or after 1700. The physical layout of the villages did not change except for diminishing the common fields and village commons by enclosures, and this occurred mainly in England. Transportation still used draught animals and carts, and the time required to get from place to place under ordinary circumstances did not diminish much, becoming only minimally if at all cheaper. Technical and technological progress during the early Renaissance was thus limited and did not involve basic principles.

*   *   *

The term 'universal man' or 'Renaissance man' is sometimes used even now to mean someone who has some knowledge of many topics and skills, and who is usually articulate enough to convey the impression that his knowledge extends to understanding. Knowledge in the Renaissance had increased to the point where no one could master everything of significance, as Aquinas and the other masters of medieval synthesis thought they had done. In the later Renaissance the attempt to find universal keys to knowledge would take on a scientific and increasingly magical rather than theological cast. Such a figure as Leonardo da Vinci, who first became a scientist and mathematician in order to become an artist, links the liberal and the 'mechanical' arts. Leonardo, however, was a lonely figure who left no disciples and who was considered a magician by his contemporaries. Most thinkers of the early Renaissance revelled in style and considered it substance.

PART

II

THE MODERN STATE AND THE ANCIENT STATE OF MIND, 1450–1600

|5|

From the Politics of Religion to the Religion of Politics

The political map and dynastic alignments of Europe changed fundamentally in the sixteenth century. The end of the Hundred Years War severed the English tie with French affairs, and the French crown established the modern boundaries of the country in the century after 1453. France's great antagonist by 1520 was no longer England, but Spain. Although technically still distinct, Aragon and Castile came under the same ruler in 1516, and the

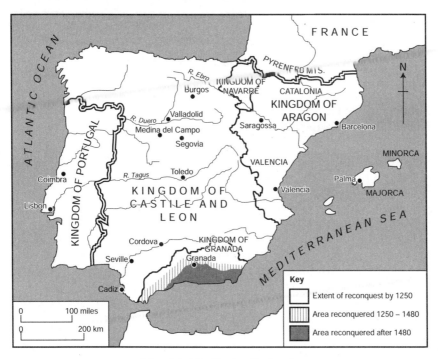

Map 5.1 The Iberian Peninsula

additional strength in Europe of the federated Spanish monarchy was supplemented by the profits of an overseas empire from which only Spain and Portugal derived substantial benefits before the seventeenth century. The Burgundian empire disintegrated after 1477, and the dynastic realignments brought the hereditary Castilian monarchy and the elective imperial title into the hands of a French-speaking Burgundian Habsburg prince who also ruled the Netherlands. The Italian cities continued to dominate financial markets and much of the trade in eastern luxuries, but Venice was the only one that was able to translate this into continued political influence. The other Italian cities became pawns, as Italy was invaded first by the French and later by Spaniards. At mid-century the bond of Empire and Spain was broken formally, but the two tended to coordinate policy, and later in the century the northern Netherlands broke off from Spain and formed a federated state that was independent in fact, although its status was only confirmed in 1648. The Dutch Republic was thus the successor state to the Burgundian empire, but it was centred on Holland rather than on Flanders and Brabant.

The Unification of Spain

The long and generally tranquil reign of John II of Castile (1406–54) was followed by a period of turbulence. His son and successor, Henry IV (1454–74), was known as 'the Impotent' even after the birth of his daughter Juana in 1462. Isabella was born in 1452 to John II and his second wife, Juana of Portugal. Henry subsequently renewed the offensive against Granada, the only remaining Muslim beachhead in the Iberian peninsula, but he was an indifferent campaigner who bestowed rewards on the 'wrong' persons according to the noble conventions of the day and took tribute from Muslim towns rather than laying them waste. Dissidents also criticized him for tolerating Jews. When civil war erupted in 1464, the rebels crowned Isabella's brother Alfonso as king. The two sides were reconciled in 1468 after Alfonso died and Henry began treating Isabella as his heir, in effect disinheriting Juana, who was called 'la Beltraneja' after the nobleman who was rumoured to be her father.

Aragon also experienced discord. King Alfonso V 'the Magnanimous' (1416–58), who had lived in Italy after 1435, was succeeded in Aragon by his brother, John II (1458–79), while Naples went to his illegitimate son Ferrante (1458–94). John II was able, but was already 60 when he became king. A civil war was fought over the succession between 1462 and 1472 between partisans of the heirs of John II's sons by successive marriages, and Louis XI of France used the confusion to annex Cerdagne and Roussillon in 1463.

In 1469 Isabella, heiress presumptive in Castile, married Ferdinand of Aragon, her second cousin, who had been made king of Sicily by his father.

The marriage was opposed by Henry IV, who wanted a French marriage, and Isabella's tutor Carrillo, the powerful Archbishop of Toledo, who preferred a Portuguese match. Ferdinand was handsome and dashing, and at age 17 already the father of two bastards. He got rights of survivorship in Castile, and Isabella in Aragon, but the two kingdoms were to revert to the heirs at the second death. Since wives were normally the wards of their husbands, who could thus act for them, Ferdinand had to make concessions. He was given the title of king in Castile, but he agreed to respect Castilian law, use Castilians in the bureaucracy, and that all enactments would require their joint signatures.

The joint regime began with domestic conflict and continued with the final campaign against Granada. A civil war was necessary to end the claims of Juana la Beltraneja, but Isabella was recognized as queen when Henry IV died in 1474. Afonso of Portugal, who hoped to marry Juana la Beltraneja and assume her claim to the throne, invaded Castile, supported by Louis XI's money. Local brotherhoods (*hermandades*) existed throughout Castile, amounting to vigilante organizations supported by tax revenue that kept the peace and dispensed summary justice. In 1476 an inter-regional 'holy brotherhood' (*Santa Hermandad*) was founded; it was disbanded in 1498 and replaced by a standing army directly responsible to the crown. The last pockets of resistance were subdued in 1477. The capture of Seville in July secured control of Andalusia, and through it gained access to Africa and its gold mines. Isabella quickly began licensing explorations, with the crown to take one-fifth of the proceeds. Andalusian magnates had navigated without constraint off the Iberian coast and Africa, and the move meant new competition with Portugal.

Religious Policy in Spain

Isabella was extremely devout. A harbinger of the future was given in 1476, when the *Cortes* decreed imprisonment for Jews and Muslims who owed money to Christians. The Jewish communities, which heretofore had chosen their own officials, were to be given Christian *alcaldes*. But Isabella was even more hostile to *conversos* than to professed Jews, seeing ethnic diversity as a pollution and a threat to stability. Some *conversos* of Andalusia had flirted with the Portuguese as the less oppressive authority, and those of Seville had opposed the *Santa Hermandad*. Although Isabella had initially appointed some *conversos* to the hereditary municipal councils, she turned against them from 1478, and factions formed between Old and New Christians. Increasingly the term *converso* was used broadly to refer to Jews who had converted in or since 1391, when riots had erupted against them and many accepted baptism to save their lives.

Pope Sixtus IV authorized a Spanish inquisition in 1478, expecting a tribunal under the bishops, but Isabella in founding it in 1480 declared it a royal court. Its purpose was to distinguish real from false converts to Christianity. Burnings of *conversos* for heresy began at Seville. They were excluded from churches by 1500, and in 1501 service on the royal council was forbidden to children of relapsed *conversos* up to two generations. Exceptions were sometimes made, but the threat of detection by the Inquisition was always a powerful weapon. The Spanish Inquisition lacked the procedural safeguards that the papal inquisition of the Middle Ages had used, including confiscation of the goods of the condemned by the inquisitors and secret denunciations. Ferdinand extended the Inquisition to Aragon in 1481; it was thus the first institution common to Castile and Aragon. Sixtus approved naming Torquemada as inquisitor general in Aragon in 1481, and by 1484 a single code of procedure for all of Spain had been approved.

From the *conversos* the Inquisition turned to the still-numerous Jews in Spain. The fall of Granada in January 1492 was followed quickly by an order requiring them to leave Spain by the end of July without taking gold, silver, money, arms or horses. Their confiscated property went to the monarchy; Isabella even charged them an embarkation fee to board ship. But the sudden exodus left gaps in finance and the professions that were filled not by native Castilians but by foreigners, especially the Genoese, Flemings and Germans who had financed so much of Castile's exploration and colonization of the Atlantic islands. Although many of the 100,000 to 200,000 Jews who left in 1492 went to North Africa, some went to Portugal, whose king, Manuel I, gave them 20 years' exemption from inquiry into their religious beliefs. Although some atrocities occurred, the overall impact was much less severe than in Spain. Portugal also still had a large 'new Christian' (*converso*) population in the sixteenth century.

Granada

The second great matter of policy for Ferdinand and Isabella was the conquest of Granada, which they began in 1480 and completed in 1492. In contrast to their harshness toward the Jews, Ferdinand and Isabella made a relatively generous settlement with the Moors in 1492, for they were in no position yet to do much that would upset the natives. In practice the crown only got the patrimony of the Muslim Nasrid dynasty, while Castilian nobles acquired properties from confiscated estates. Although some 6000 Moors were permitted to emigrate in 1493, the aristocrats who remained were given posts in the royal administration. The new Archbishop of Granada was Hernando de Talavera, who took a scholarly interest in Arabic studies and opposed forced conversion. But after Archbishop Cisneros of Toledo gained the royal ear in 1499, mass conversions began. A brief revolt was crushed easily, followed by another forced conversion, and an edict of 1502 ordered the expulsion of all Moors who had not converted.

Spain was thus purged of Jews and Muslims. In 1496 the Borgia Pope Alexander VI, himself a Spaniard, gave Ferdinand and Isabella the title 'Catholic Kings' for their services for Christianity against the Moors, Turks and Jews, and for Aragonese help in the papal states and that of Naples against the French. The crown's hostility to non-Christians, however, was heightened into paranoia after the split within the Christian community began in 1517.

The End of Independent Burgundy and the Beginning of Dynastic Confusion

Burgundy had reached the height of its power under Duke Philip 'the Good' (1419–67), but structural weaknesses were apparent. His control had slackened in his last years, and he fought bitterly with his heir and less openly with his overlords, Kings Charles VII (1422–61) and Louis XI (1461–83) of France. The new duke, Charles 'the Bold' or 'the Rash' (1467–77), opened his reign by needlessly provoking a rebellion at Ghent. As his father had done, he resisted French claims that the *parlement* of Paris should hear appeals from Burgundian courts, and he established an army on the borders of France to repel attack. His anti-French stance was enhanced when he married the sister of Edward IV of England, and he continued his father's negotiations with the emperor Frederick III, who alone had the right to elevate his duchy into a kingdom. Charles' reign saw important domestic initiatives. Philip the Good had preferred not to press legislative or judicial unity in his various domains; they kept their separate institutions until 1473, when a *parlement* and chamber of accounts were established at Mechelen in Brabant for the Netherlands, and a States-General[1] to vote taxes, although they had no competence in the duchy or county of Burgundy.

Charles' most formidable opponent was the French king, Louis XI. After 1469 Charles was trying to seize territory in Lorraine that would give him an unbroken frontier on France's eastern border, but this brought him into conflict with the great cities of Strasbourg, Basel and Bern, and Bern was in the Swiss Confederation. Charles' enemies formed a grand alliance against him in 1474. He was occupied thereafter almost entirely by revolts in Alsace and Lorraine until his death in battle at Nancy at the beginning of 1477. The Burgundian state broke up after the death of its duke. Charles's sole heir, his daughter Mary, married Maximilian of Habsburg, son of the emperor. After her death in 1482 Maximilian spent a decade in military and diplomatic efforts in the Netherlands to secure the interests of their son, Philip. As he matured, Philip 'the Handsome' gravitated towards his French Netherlandish advisers and opposed his father's hopes to extend imperial influence in the region. In 1496 Philip and his sister Margaret married siblings: John, the only son of Ferdinand and Isabella of Spain, who died later that year, and his sister Joanna.

An England Destabilized, 1450–1497

The rapid English collapse in Gascony after 1447 shocked the competing factions at the English court. Compounding the military debacle, the Exchequer was in debt to roughly five times the annual ordinary income of the crown by 1450: although King Henry VI was incompetent, no mechanism existed to control him. After the death in 1450 of the royal favourite the earl of Suffolk, a power struggle intensified between the factions of York and Beaufort/Somerset, the latter descended from the originally illegitimate children of John of Gaunt. A rebellion led by Jack Cade presented grievances against corruption and called for the king's advisers to give him proper advice and to rule according to law. When the king suffered a mental collapse between August 1453 and Christmas 1454 the Somerset faction was in control, and Richard, duke of York, seems to have feared for his safety. The 'Wars of the Roses' are so called from the white and red roses on the coats of arms of the houses of York and Tudor respectively. Hostilities began in 1455 with the first battle of St Albans, where Edmund Beaufort, earl of Somerset, perished. He was succeeded by his brother John, whose daughter was the wife of Edmund Tudor and mother of the eventual King Henry VII. York became Protector of the king, but the queen was able to rally the Lancastrian forces. In 1460 Richard of York claimed the throne by rightful descent from the duke of Clarence, second son of Edward III. Battles raged for most of that year, and at Wakefield on 31 December York lost his life. In 1461, however, his son Edward defeated the Lancastrians at Towton Moor and assumed the throne as Edward IV (1461–83). Henry VI was imprisoned in the Tower of London, and Queen Margaret of Anjou and her son Edward fled to France.

The support of the earl of Warwick, son of the brother of Edward IV's mother, Cecily Neville, was critical, and he expected to play a major role with the other northern barons in the new government. Warwick married his daughter Anne to Richard, earl of Gloucester and the king's youngest brother, and wanted Edward IV to marry a French princess and begin to mend relations with the ancestral enemy. Edward, however, alienated Warwick by his marriage to Elizabeth Woodville, a widow with two sons who brought a number of patronage-hungry relatives to the court, and who, as the king's subject, could bring him no diplomatic advantage. In 1470 Warwick made contact with Margaret of Anjou and Louis XI of France. Edward IV was caught by surprise, and he had to flee to the Netherlands for a few months in 1470–1. He quickly returned, and Warwick was killed at the battle of Barnet in 1471, Prince Edward dying later that year at Tewkesbury. Edward's next younger brother, the earl of Clarence, had helped Warwick in 1470, only changing sides at the last moment. He continued to plot against Edward during the 1470s, and Edward in exasperation finally had him executed in 1478. He relied thereafter on his always-loyal youngest brother, Richard earl of Gloucester. Gloucester built up his affinity in the north, which became the stronghold of the Yorkist regime, and there was no further serious challenge to Edward's rule.

Edward IV died unexpectedly in April 1483. His two sons were still minors, and his provisions for a regency were inconsistent. Evidently fearing for his life in a Woodville-dominated regency, Richard of Gloucester used the pretext that Edward's marriage to Elizabeth Woodville had been uncanonical, and his sons' births thus illegitimate, as his excuse to seize the throne from the older boy, Edward V, and have himself crowned as Richard III (1483–5). Edward and his younger brother Richard disappeared into the Tower of London and were not seen alive after the summer of 1483. By year's end Richard had disposed of the nobles who through their retainers were most able to give him trouble. Disaffection mounted, and in August 1485 a small force led by Henry Tudor, earl of Richmond, son of Margaret Beaufort and thus Lancastrian, defeated and killed Richard at Bosworth.

The reign of Henry VII (1485–1509), the first of the Tudor dynasty (1485–1603), appears more a turning-point in retrospect than it did at the time, for the new king's throne was unstable, his genealogical claim weaker than that of any previous English king since 1066. He married Edward IV's daughter Elizabeth, producing two sons (Arthur, born 1487, and Henry, born 1491) and several daughters; but the Yorkists had male relatives still alive. More threatening, however, were two pretenders: Lambert Simnel, the son of a joiner from Oxford who had such a strong resemblance to the son of the late duke of Clarence that even Elizabeth Woodville was fooled; and Perkin Warbeck, the son of a boatman of Tournai who claimed to be Richard, younger brother of Edward V. Simnel's hopes were dashed at the battle of East Stoke in 1487. Warbeck invaded in 1495 with token help from the governments of Charles VIII of France and the emperor Maximilian and a serious ally in James IV of Scotland. The military threat was over by late 1497, when James negotiated a peace that was finalized in 1502 by his own marriage to Henry VII's daughter, Margaret. This marriage provided the link with the English monarchy that in 1603 would result in the king of Scotland becoming King James I of England.

France under Louis XI and Charles VIII (1461–1498)

Louis XI (1461–83), 'the Spider King', appears to be a more effective king now than he did during his life. In 1465 he faced a 'War of the Public Weal', in which most of the great feudatories participated, that nearly cost him his crown and forced him to make concessions, including surrendering the towns along the Somme to Burgundy. Hostilities and negotiations continued intermittently, most seriously in 1475 when a coalition that included Burgundy, Edward IV of England and the constable, the commander of the royal armies, threatened an invasion. The conspiracy disintegrated. Edward IV was bought off for a pension (the treaty of Picquigny). Only after Charles the Bold's death in 1477 was Louis completely secure, and even here he mishandled the situation by invading the Burgundian domains, bringing down on his head the wrath of Maximilian, the contracted husband of Mary of Burgundy. The treaty of Arras (1482) did, however, award the duchy of Burgundy to France, along with Franche Comté (the county of Burgundy) and Artois.

Charles VIII (1483–98) became king at the age of 13. Louis of Orléans, son of Charles duke of Orléans (see Part 1) and heir to the throne unless the boy-king had children, claimed the throne and was supported by the still-independent duke of Burgundy, Ferdinand and Isabella (who were upset because of Louis XI's seizure of Roussillon in 1463) and the Habsburgs (who were unhappy about the intervention in Burgundy). Orléans' claim was disputed by Anne of Beaujeu, the king's sister and wife of the future duke of Bourbon. Orléans called a meeting of the Estates-General in 1484, but it supported Beaujeu, and civil war ensued between the Orléans and Burgundian factions. When the duke of Brittany died in 1489 his widow, Anne, tried to forestall a French annexation with help from England, the Empire and Spain; but when that did not materialize she married the young Charles VIII in 1491. Eventually she went on also to marry his successor, Louis XII, and continued to rule an independent Brittany until her death in 1514; only in 1536 did the duchy pass from her heirs to the crown.

Charles VIII, by now occupied with dreams of empire in Italy, made peace with his opponents in France. By the Treaty of Senlis (1493) Charles abandoned Artois and Franche-Comté to Maximilian, buying off Henry VII with a pension and surrendering Cerdagne and Roussillon to Aragon. The French monarchy's interests in Italy were of long standing. As heirs of the house of Anjou the Valois kings had disputed Naples with the Aragonese king Ferrante, although not with Ferdinand. Orléans' family had claims to the duchy of Milan, so Charles became reconciled with him in order to gain his cooperation.

The peace in Italy established by Cosimo de' Medici at Lodi in 1454 was coming apart. Florence was ruled by his grandson, Lorenzo, a patron of the arts but a much less astute banker and politician than Cosimo, and from 1492 it was ruled by Lorenzo's incompetent son, Piero. The duke of Milan was a child, Giangaleazzo Sforza, but the power behind him was his uncle Ludovico, 'the Moor', which offended Giangaleazzo's wife, the daughter of the king of Naples.

By the time the French invaded, Florence and Naples were allies against the alliance of the French with Milan, who had invited the French into Italy with the thought that they would strike Naples. The opening Italian campaign was easy. The Medici regime was deposed early in the fighting by a reaction led by the Dominican friar, Girolamo Savonarola, and in March 1495 Charles VIII entered Naples. This success led, however, to the intervention of Aragon, with Ferdinand forging the League of Venice, which included the pope, Maximilian, Milan and Venice: in short, everybody who had something to gain by a French defeat. Charles had to retreat, and when he died childless in 1498 he was succeeded by Louis of Orléans as Louis XII (1498–1515).

The interests of the new king were more in Milan than Naples through his grandmother, Valentina Visconti. He secured the city in 1499–1500 (Ludovico the Moor was imprisoned in France until his death in 1508). In 1503 the French lost Naples to a Spanish force, but they consolidated their control over Genoa in 1507. Although Pope Alexander VI (1494–1503) was a French ally, Julius II (1503–13) opposed the French. He also had a grudge against Venice, which had seized papal lands in the Romagna after 1503, and in 1508 he arranged the League of Cambrai of France, Maximilian and Naples against Venice, which had to surrender its conquests the next year. But Julius' attention was turned now toward the French. He revived Ferdinand's alliance system of 1495 by negotiating a 'Holy League' in 1511 with Venice, Spain, Maximilian, the Swiss and England. Except for the rupture between England and Spain in the 1530s, the Holy League remained the cornerstone of the European alliance system throughout the sixteenth century, defeating Louis XII at Novara in 1513. Louis's successor was Francis I (1515–47), who was both his cousin and son-in-law. In 1515 Francis' troops crushed the League's Swiss mercenaries at Marignano, near Milan, and re-established French control in Lombardy. Seeing no alternative, Pope Leo X (1513–21) agreed in 1516 to the Concordat of Bologna with the French, and Spain made peace in 1517.

The Burgundian Inheritance and the Western Alliance System

But it was a very changed Spain by 1517. Isabella's and Ferdinand's only son, John, died shortly after his marriage in 1496. Isabella, their eldest daughter, the wife of King Manoel of Portugal, was now heiress apparent in Castile (Aragonese law prohibited a woman monarch). Had she succeeded to the Castilian throne, the Spanish kingdom would have linked Castile with Portugal rather than Aragon; but she died in 1498. Given the anti-French direction of Spanish policy, both the Empire and its Burgundian linkages and England were allies to be cultivated. Thus Ferdinand and Isabella's third daughter, Catherine, became the wife and then the widow of the English prince Arthur in 1501. To the outrage of Catherine's parents, Henry VII kept her in England with her dowry and betrothed her to his younger son Henry, a marriage that was solemnized shortly after the old king's death in 1509.

Isabella died in late 1504, leaving as heiress in Castile her second daughter, Joanna, wife of Archduke Philip 'the Handsome', the heir to the

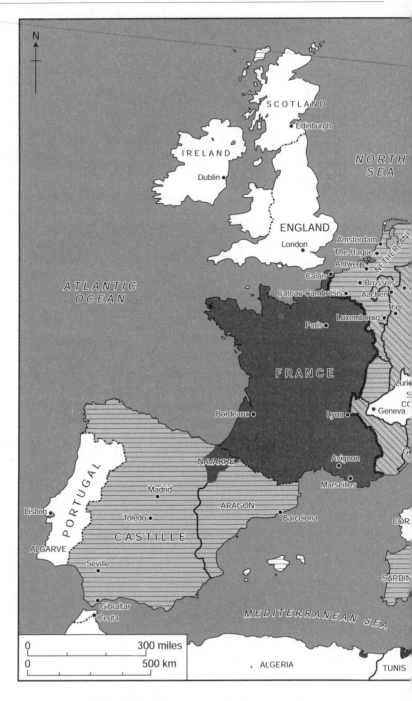

Map 5.2 Habsburg and Valois

Burgundian Netherlands and son of Maximilian of Habsburg who had been emperor since 1493. Philip spent most of his time in the Netherlands. After he died in 1506 Joanna tried to govern Castile, but her mental incapacity quickly degenerated into insanity. Meanwhile Ferdinand's royal title in Castile had lapsed with Isabella's death. As noble factions threatened to plunge Castile into chaos, Isabella's confessor, Archbishop Cisneros, persuaded Ferdinand to return. Joanna retired to Tordesillas, where she lived until 1555, and Ferdinand ruled as regent in Castile in the name of Charles, Joanna's son by Philip the Handsome. When Ferdinand died in 1516, the inheritance of the Catholic kings passed to a teenaged boy who knew no Spanish, had never been to Spain and was in no hurry to get there: Cisneros governed as regent for nearly a year until Charles arrived in Spain in 1517.

Youth Takes the Stage, 1509–1526

The first half of the sixteenth century is dominated by three notable rulers: Henry VIII of England (1509–47), Francis I of France (1515–47) and Charles V, king of Spain (1516–56) and Holy Roman Emperor (1519–56). Each ruled generally within the established laws of his kingdom while using emergencies and selective precedent to dissolve constitutional fetters on his power. The Lutheran rebellion in Germany, the most serious religious division since the Hussite rebellion in Bohemia (see Chapter 4), caused problems for Charles V in Germany and Italy, but did not disturb his relations with either France or England until the 1530s.

Each lived to an overripe maturity, but Francis I, at 21, was the oldest at his accession to the crown. Francis and Henry VIII illustrate the volatility and recklessness often associated with youth, while Charles V, the youngest of the three, was insecure and cautious. England was the weakest of the three powers and the least useful as an ally, for it had only one small possession on the Continent (Calais, the site of its wool staple), no standing army, and its navy was only established by Henry VIII himself. The accession as king in Spain in 1516 of Charles V, who already ruled the Netherlands, posed a serious threat to the territorial integrity of France. Francis I made a serious effort to have himself elected Emperor when Maximilian died in 1519, but the predisposition to follow the hereditary line, especially when it was backed by the money of the Fugger bank of Augsburg (see Chapter 8) was too strong to be overcome. It is likely that Charles V would have been a more serious enemy to France had he not been distracted by the deteriorating situation in Germany. Alone of the three young kings, Charles had an overpowering sense of his moral responsibility as ruler. He thus felt obliged to preserve true religion in Germany, but the institutional position of the emperor was too weak to provide him with the means to succeed. Until Francis I allied with the Lutheran Schmalkaldic League in the late 1530s, the chief battleground between him and Charles V was not in Germany but in Italy, where Charles had interests as king of Aragon as well as balance-of-power motives for ejecting the French from Milan.

More than the other princes, Charles V thought very largely in ethical and dynastic terms, and his policies were determined by the need to provide for his numerous relatives and hold his polyglot realms together. The success of the Habsburgs and the fear that they inspired in their neighbours can only be understood in the light of their astonishing success, like those of their Burgundian ancestors, in making marriages that could eventually lead to territorial acquisition. However different the institutions of the various states under Charles V's rule might be, they were linked by being ruled by blood relatives of the emperor or their husbands. Various Habsburgs enjoyed at least nominal rule in Austria, the Empire, Hungary, Spain and the Netherlands. Charles V's sister Elizabeth was married to King Christian II of Denmark, and in the 1530s he extended his network to Italy by marrying her daughter, Christina, to the duke of Milan, and his own natural daughter Mary to Cosimo, the new duke of Florence. The marriage of Francis I's then second eldest son, the future Henry II, to Catherine de' Medici, the niece of Pope Clement VII, was an effort to foil imperial designs in Italy; and at the end of his reign Charles tried to bring England into his sphere by marrying his heir Philip to Queen Mary.

Henry VII was never a popular king, but he was cautious and prudent and left the monarchy strong. Henry VIII (1509–47), by contrast, was a revolutionary behemoth who avoided serious challenge by making his subjects fear his volcanic inconstancy. Had religion not given Henry an excuse to restore the treasury by confiscating the assets of the ungodly, his thirst for personal military glory would have plunged England into insolvency.

Henry was generally underestimated at the beginning of his reign. He cemented relations with Spain, however, by marrying Catherine of Aragon in 1509. He dreamed of military adventure, which at the time could only mean an anti-French policy. His more responsible advisers discouraged this, but the royal almoner, Thomas Wolsey, kept his opinions to himself and thus became the king's most trusted adviser. After Henry joined the Holy League against the French, Wolsey managed a costly campaign that took Tournai and Thérouanne; but maintaining them was so expensive that Henry had to restore Tournai to the French in 1518 in return for an indemnity. The feckless English campaigns of the sixteenth century are in striking contrast to their victories during the Hundred Years War. The king had no standing army and had to use the retainers of the great nobles. English military technology was also outmoded. Their longbow was obsolete against the handgun, and they did not develop a strong artillery. Henry VIII's alliances and occasional armed forays to the Continent were military disasters, and even worse financial ones. The only successes of the English were either in naval engagements or acting as support troops, as they did after 1585 in the Low Countries.

By 1514 Wolsey was in control of most of the agencies of finance and administration – although not the courts – that operated from the royal palace. This included a network of informants set up mainly by Henry VII, who were paid out of the privy purse to report on utterances that the crown might find seditious or merely distasteful. The English monarchy, perhaps because its territory was so small, was better informed about domestic conditions than any of its Continental rivals. By 1518 Wolsey had become successively Bishop of Lincoln, Archbishop of York, Lord Chancellor, cardinal and papal legate.

The settlement of 1518 included a mutual aid treaty between Henry and Francis I which led to the famous ceremony of the Field of the Cloth of Gold in 1520. But the peace between old enemies lasted only until 1521, when Henry and the Emperor Charles V agreed to invade France, a caper into which Henry was led by his hope of marrying his daughter and sole heir, Mary, to the Emperor. Thus until 1525 Henry fought another expensive and inconclusive war with France, and it cost him six times his ordinary annual income. By 1522 he was in serious financial straits and had to levy a forced loan. This was followed by lay subsidies in 1523 and 1524 and culminated in the 'amicable grant' of 1525, which he took without consulting Parliament to support a campaign to invade and partition France in alliance with Charles V. Resistance to the 'amicable grant' was so strong that Henry abandoned it, pleading that he had been misled by his advisers, meaning Wolsey; and when Parliament refused to vote money for Mary's dowry, Charles V married Isabella of Portugal.

Charles V and Francis I: The First Phase

When Charles V arrived in Spain in 1517, he was young, did not understand Spanish and was under the domination of French-speaking Burgundian advisers who were thought to be fleecing the kingdom; in fairness, some Spaniards occupied essentially honorific posts in Flanders by 1515. This together with his physical appearance (his sloping 'Habsburg jaw' and usually open mouth were only ameliorated after 1530, when he grew the beard that most portraits show him wearing), combined with his mother's insanity, caused rumours that he was mentally defective. It took years to dispel the impression in Castile that he simply did what his advisers told him. Even in his maturity he was chronically indecisive: his personal motto was *nondum* (not yet). The Castilian *Cortes* had granted an aid on the new king's accession, but his government made the mistake of trying to get a second one before the first had expired, to help pay for his election as Emperor.

The revolt of the *comuneros* began in Castile when Charles V went to Germany in 1520 to assume the imperial crown. The leaders were local aristocrats; many were of *converso* ancestry, which gave the regime the chance to paint the uprising as a Jewish conspiracy. The agitation was confined initially to the cities of Castile, but when the royalists burned Medina del Campo, the site of international fairs that constituted the banking centre of Castile, the revolt spread to the south and outside the towns as some nobles who had been neutral joined.

The revolt was political rather than social in character. Although the rebel governments were hardly democratic, the old governing bodies were made subject to popular assemblies, and the royal *corregidores* were replaced by elected deputies who took an oath to the community. The *comuneros* were an inter-city league, whose participants were in regular communication, and a Junta of town representatives dealt directly with the king, whom it recognized as king but not as emperor. In October 1520 it sent Charles V a manifesto of demands, included having the *Cortes* meet at least every three years, even if the king did not summon it. No royal *corregidor* was to be appointed unless the local community so requested, and even then he should be a native of the city concerned. Thus the rebels hoped to reverse the centralizing efforts of Ferdinand and Isabella, although there was an element of resentment at Charles as a foreigner and absentee. The Junta asked that foreigners be removed from office, the royal household reformed, taxes lowered, and the sale of offices forbidden.

But the *comuneros* agitation began to wane when some of the Flemings returned home, and the absent king's advisers began appointing Spaniards to the regency that was dominated by Adrian of Utrecht, the king's boyhood tutor and the future pope Adrian IV (1522–3). Meanwhile, when a more radical urban movement, the *Germanía*, erupted in Valencia, the *comuneros* became more extreme, and by 1521 it was turned against the nobility, thus alienating the one group that might have mounted a successful lasting operation against Charles. The rebellion ended in a one-sided battle at Villalar in April 1521. Peace had been restored by the time Charles returned, with 4000 German troops, in July 1522, and for the next years the emperor concentrated on Italian affairs.

The Medici Pope Leo X had tilted toward France after Marignano, and favoured the election of Francis I as emperor, but he was quickly reconciled with Charles, as he needed his cooperation against Luther. In May 1521 the pope concluded an alliance with the Empire against Francis I, who hoped to consolidate his hold in Lombardy and expand against Naples. Pope Adrian IV initially hoped to bring both Spain and France into a league against the Turks, but Francis saw this as an opportunity to press Charles for concessions in Italy. But when Cardinal Soderini, the leader of the pro-French party in the college of cardinals, was found with documents urging Francis to re-invade northern Italy, Francis issued a pamphlet threatening the pope with the fate of Boniface VIII at the hands of Philip IV. Thus shortly before his death, Adrian entered what amounted to a new Holy League against France, to which the French responded by taking advantage of the *comuneros* agitation in Spain to invade Navarre and creating disturbances on their border with the Netherlands.

Francis I simultaneously used methods of questionable legality to bring the remaining great principalities in France under royal control. His effort to seize the Bourbonnais in 1523 provoked his own constable, Charles de Bourbon, to join Charles V. Bourbon was one of Charles' commanders at the battle of Pavia (25 February 1525), where the imperial forces crushed the French and captured Francis I. By the Treaty of Madrid Francis promised a huge ransom and agreed to renounce his claims to Burgundy and marry Charles' sister, Eleanore; but as soon as he was again in France, he repudiated the agreement on grounds that it was done under duress.

Meanwhile, the inconclusive military situation in Italy deteriorated. Pope Clement VII (1523–34), fearing imperial control in Italy with France defeated, formed the League of Cognac in May 1526, which included all Charles' potential opponents, England not excepted. He also absolved Francis from the obligation to adhere to the treaty of Madrid. Thus an out-of-control (because unpaid) imperial army invaded the papal states and stormed Rome 6 May 1527, beginning a sack of the city that lasted for several months while Charles V tried to decide what to do. The Peace of Cambrai (also called the Peace of the Ladies, because it was negotiated by Charles' aunt Margaret, his regent in the Netherlands, and the French queen mother and regent, Louise of Savoy) was reached on 3 August 1529. In it, the French abandoned their claims to Milan, Genoa, Naples, Artois and Flanders, but in return they got Burgundy. With outstanding issues evidently resolved in his favour, Charles V was finally formally crowned emperor at Bologna on 24 February 1530, his thirtieth birthday.

When Charles became king in Aragon and Castile in 1516, his younger brother Ferdinand left Spain so that no faction could centre around him. In 1522 he married Anne of Hungary and his sister Mary married Louis, son of the king of Hungary, fulfilling a betrothal arranged some years earlier by Maximilian. Louis was killed by the Turks in August 1526 at Mohàcs, opening the Balkans to Turkish attack and requiring Ferdinand's presence to make good his claim to the Hungarian throne. Although the details of the treaty were kept secret for 6 years, Charles remained Emperor while renouncing the Habsburg inheritance in Austria and adjacent lands to Ferdinand, whose own claims to the crowns of Bohemia and Hungary prevailed. In return, Ferdinand renounced all claim to Spain and Burgundy. Although there had been some earlier tensions between them, the two brothers remained firm allies thereafter.

Charles V and the Empire

The imperial title in Germany was an honour without much institutional backing. It was elective, although the emperor chosen since 1438 had always been the Habsburg duke of Austria. While the power of the emperors could under different circumstances have been converted into a German national monarchy, as it had been during the central Middle Ages, the real power of the Habsburgs themselves was derived from their position in Austria and the adjacent territories that their family had acquired since 1273. Charles' grandfather Maximilian had often been an impractical ruler, but the marriages that he arranged for his children and grandchildren created the basis for the Habsburgs' immense power outside the Empire.

Although in Germany Charles V had little power outside the Habsburg ancestral lands, Maximilian had tried to expand in the south-west through a complex alliance system. The Swiss confederation had been formed at the expense of the Habsburgs when it formally left the Empire in 1495, and there was a considerable danger that other units of south Germany might either join the Swiss Confederation or form their own. The cities of the south-west, faced with the overweening power of princes and rural federations in their environs, were not averse to imperial intervention until this came to be associated with a religious point of view after 1521. The Habsburgs thus sponsored two great alliances directed against the rival Wittelsbach dynasty, who ruled at Munich and Heidelberg – the Swabian League (1488–1534) and the Lower Union (established 1474 and reformed in 1493). These leagues also supported Maximilian's war in 1499 with the Swiss Confederation, which was called the Upper Union.

The term 'imperial cities' was being used by the late fifteenth century indiscriminately for both the true imperial cities, whose charters came from the emperors, and the free cities, which had them from bishops or other lords. Many of them, particularly those in the south, had substantial territories outside the city, although rarely anything as comprehensive as the *contadi* of the Italian cities. There were nearly 70 'imperial cities', by the broad definition, in 1500, roughly four-fifths of them in southern or upper Germany.

Maximilian thus had powerful motives for cultivating the cities. Austria was commercially and financially underdeveloped just as it was becoming a real player in international politics through the Habsburg involvements in the Netherlands, Spain and Italy. So much of the royal domain in Austria was mortgaged, particularly the mines, that most of its income went to creditors rather than to the crown. Most of Maximilian's loans were raised in Austria, but he also borrowed substantially from urban governments of south-western Germany and from private creditors, particularly the Fuggers and Paumgartners of Augsburg.

Charles V always tended to see Germany through a Netherlandish perspective. He knew the financial strength of the south German cities, both from the Fugger involvement in his election in 1519 and also because Nurembergers and other investors were moving into Iberia and getting into the colonial trade. Charles lacked his grandfather's German background, and he never relied on one city to the extent that Maximilian had relied on

Augsburg; but he also tended to see the south Germans as financiers without familiarizing himself with the politics of the cities and how they could affect his power base. He was diverted by Francis I in his early years, and thus he did not concentrate on German affairs. By 1524, when Charles insisted on the complete enforcement of the Edict of Worms, which had outlawed Lutheranism, the cities already had large evangelical parties. Thus when religion became the major item of domestic policy in the Empire for Charles V, the cities, whose governments under the influence of the Swiss reformer Ulrich Zwingli considered themselves and their traditions instruments of God, became a strongly anti-Habsburg power. Zwingli had hoped to form the Swiss and Swabian cities into a union, but after his death in 1531 it became obvious that a league led by Protestant princes was the way to combat the Habsburgs. The German princes formed the Schmalkaldic League that year, and several south German cities joined them. Religious division thus prevented Charles V from capitalizing on Maximilian's alliances in Upper Germany.[2]

The Reforming of Alliances in the 1530s

German Protestants and Catholics thus sparred with each other in the 1520s, with the Lutherans generally gaining territory. The emperor was too busy in Italy to implement the intransigent attitude that he displayed at the Diet of Worms in 1521 (see Chapter 10). Both sides hoped for reconciliation, particularly after Luther, the princes and the emperor were all frightened by the Peasants' War of 1524–5 (see Chapter 8). The fact that the emperor was known to agree that institutional abuses had driven the Lutherans into doctrinal error, and thus opposed the pope in favouring a church council to reform them, caused some Protestants to hope that he could be converted.

The Turks had defeated and killed King Louis II of Hungary in August 1526 at Mohàcs, opening the Balkans to Turkish attack. During the 1530s Charles V was occupied in Spain and the Mediterranean, while his brother Ferdinand ruled the Habsburg household lands and was regent over the rest of the Empire. Since Ferdinand had to cope with Germany and the Protestants essentially unaided, he incurred odium that more properly should have been directed at Charles. International powers tacitly aided the Protestants to weaken the Habsburgs. Francis I saw the naval war in the Mediterranean as a better way of tying Charles V down against the Turks than a war in the Balkans, which had the danger that the German Protestants would help Charles; and indeed they generally did vote money in the imperial Diet when Ferdinand asked for help against the Turks. Thus in 1533 Francis I openly allied with the Turks and prepared another invasion of Italy. The Genoese Andrea Doria recaptured Tunis for the emperor in 1535, and in 1537 the French helped the Turks besiege Corfu. In 1538 a naval league of Venice, the pope and Charles V lost a battle at Previsa off the Greek coast. Venice had to make peace in 1540, losing its last fortresses in Greece and paying an indemnity; while Charles' siege of Algiers in 1541 failed ignominiously.

England and the King's 'Great Matter'

England was increasingly isolated in the 1530s and more a threat to itself than to either of the great continental monarchies. France remained the national enemy of choice, and the only one against whom the English might muster troops, but relations with Spain had soured after the failure of the marriage negotiations in 1526. The major issue between the two, however, was Henry VIII's 'great matter'. The only child of Henry VIII and his queen, Catherine of Aragon, was a daughter, Mary, and the thought of a woman ruler was extremely disturbing. After 1526, by which time Catherine was past the childbearing years, Henry began to push the pope to annul his marriage on grounds that the papal dispensation that had permitted him to marry his brother Arthur's widow, in violation of the Mosaic law, was invalid. Henry seems to have convinced himself that his failure to sire sons by Catherine proved divine displeasure.

Dispensing with a dispensation was highly unusual, but not unheard-of. Pope Clement VII (1523–34), realizing Henry's theological orthodoxy, might have granted his request had the troops of Charles V, the nephew of Catherine of Aragon, not been holding Rome when the case was heard in 1529. The pope's verdict against Henry had moved England firmly into the Protestant camp by 1533 (see Chapter 10), when Henry VIII married Anne Boleyn, with whom he had been enamoured for some years. Five months after their marriage she presented him with another daughter, Elizabeth. The inevitable estrangement with Spain forced Henry to seek an unlikely ally in France.

England's break with Rome was institutional rather than theological in the beginning, concerning as it did the annulment of his marriage; but it was the first national monarchy to make such a break, and there was a danger that others might follow. Given Henry's mercurial character and the likelihood of changes during the reign of one of his children, each side was inclined to be flexible. Before being frightened by the affair of the placards in 1534 (see Chapter 10), Francis I had given every sign of being more theologically unorthodox and less morally principled than even Henry VIII, and his negotiations with the Turks and the German Protestant princes convinced Clement VII that it would not take much to make him break with the church.

The death of Catherine of Aragon in 1536, followed by the birth of a son to Henry VIII and his third wife, Jane Seymour, eased Spanish relations with England and made Henry open to blandishments about ending his alliance with France. Francis I invaded Savoy in 1536, took Turin and demanded Milan. With encouragement from the pope, Charles retaliated with an invasion of Provence. Both sides withdrew from their conquests, and the Truce of Nice (1538) guaranteed the status quo for 10 years. In 1538 Charles V and Francis I concluded a 10-year truce, and in 1539 they agreed not to make a separate peace with England. Henry VIII was thus isolated.

The Empire in the Late 1530s

Imperial relations with the German princes deteriorated in 1537. Charles sent his vice-chancellor, an intransigent Roman Catholic, to negotiate with them, but he presented them with an ultimatum instead and went on to form a Catholic League without informing the Emperor until the deed was done. This scheme accomplished nothing but to irritate the Protestants. Meanwhile divisions arose within the Schmalkaldic League, for the towns were unhappy at the princes' willingness to listen to French blandishments. But to get Protestant help against the Turks, Charles promised not to use force against adherents of the Augsburg Confession, which had been adopted by the Lutherans in 1530 (see Chapter 10).

The Emperor's designs were compromised by conditions in the Netherlands. His regent there since 1531 had been his sister Mary, the widowed queen of Hungary. When Mary tried to force recalcitrant Ghent in Flanders to contribute aid for her war in Artois against the French, the city, torn by internecine vendettas, rebelled openly and appealed to Charles. The revolt spread to most of the rest of Flanders by the autumn of 1538, and the military result was a foregone conclusion. Charles entered Ghent in early 1540 without incident, punished the rebels by show trials and withdrew all the city's privileges. The Caroline Concession of 1540 ended Ghent's independence by giving the prince the right to appoint the city councillors directly and withdrawing the councillors' right to legislate and appoint police. The guilds, which had shared political power through the councils, were reduced to having a purely industrial function.

The Early 1540s

The peace of 1538 between France and Spain was of predictably short duration. Francis I reopened contacts with the German Lutherans in 1540, while Henry VIII too sought allies in Germany. His principal secretary, Thomas Cromwell, nudged him into a disastrous marriage by proxy with Anne of Cleves, the younger daughter of one of the leading Protestant princes of the Empire, whom Henry repudiated when he set eyes on her.

English relations with Scotland also deteriorated. In 1542 Henry's nephew, James V of Scotland, died soon after losing to the English at Solway Moss. His heiress, Mary, was a week old. Henry VIII tried to arrange a marriage for her to his five-year-old son, Edward, but the Scots began military action, and the queen mother, Marie of Guise, escaped to her native France. French support for Scottish independence became a major concern for Henry VIII.

Thus when war broke out in 1542, England joined Charles V of Spain, hoping to coordinate a campaign in the west with Charles' activity in Champagne. The English managed to take Boulogne, but the rest of the campaign was brief. The Peace of Crépy in August 1543 restored the status quo of 1538, and France agreed to join Charles against the Turks. Henry VIII only made terms in 1546, when a peace gave him Boulogne, but France was able to buy it back after 8 years. The war cost Henry VIII over £2 million, roughly one-third of it coming from the sale of lands that he had seized from the monasteries, with the rest paid for by loans on the Antwerp money market and a debasement of the coin. From a diplomatic standpoint, it was a diversion that prevented Francis I from doing much damage to the imperial cause, leaving Charles free to concentrate on Germany.

Charles gained an unexpected advantage in Germany in 1540 when Philip of Hesse, the Protestant leader, contracted a bigamous marriage, causing even more than normal discord in the Schmalkaldic League. Since this weakened him in the Protestant community, Philip was prepared to negotiate with the Catholics. A 23 clause *Book of Regensburg* was compiled after meetings of the leadership in that city, but the pope, Luther and both the Catholic and Protestant parties in Germany rejected it and, with it, the emperor's hopes of reconciliation. With the Turks poised for an invasion of Hungary, Charles closed the conference quickly with a new declaration that gave protection to adherents of the Augsburg confession, including those living in the lands of Catholic princes.

Paroxysm and Denouement

As their elders passed from the scene, a new generation of German princes emerged. Albert Alcibiades, the margrave of Brandenburg-Kulmbach, was openly Protestant but none the less served the emperor. The ruling family of Saxony was divided. Duke Maurice, the son-in-law of Philip of Hesse, hoped that Charles would take the title of Elector of Saxony from his estranged and Protestant kinsman and give it to him. The Schmalkaldic League was hopelessly divided, with the members hoping to take one another's territories. In 1543 Charles V campaigned successfully in Germany, and in 1546 he invaded again from the Netherlands, controlling southern Germany by year's end. In 1547 he struck Electoral Saxony, coordinating efforts with Maurice and Albert Alcibiades. The battle of Mühlberg (24 April 1547), with Charles commanding his own troops, was a complete imperial victory. The Elector was captured, and Maurice got the Electorate and the accompanying lands. Luring Philip of Hesse into a conference with hopes of terms, Charles took him prisoner. The only serious resistance remaining was provided by the north German cities, particularly Magdeburg and Lübeck. Instead of pressing his advantage, the conciliatory emperor in June 1548 issued the Augsburg Interim, which reiterated that Roman Catholicism was the only legal religion of the Empire. But the Interim also contained vague language that could be construed as allowing belief in Luther's central doctrine of justification by faith alone, and it referred action on the marriage of priests and on communion in both kinds to the church council that had been meeting since 1545 (see Chapter 10).

1547 also saw the deaths of Henry VIII (in January) and Francis I (in March). Edward VI (1547–53), the only legitimate son of Henry VIII, succeeded at the age of nine and was placed under a regency led by Edward Seymour, his maternal uncle, who was made earl of Somerset and took the title of Lord Protector. The death of the old king made it possible for theological Protestantism to come into the open in England; but the Earl of Somerset, who had Lutheran sympathies, moved too quickly (see Chapter 10). He also had the bad judgement to enrich himself during his period of hegemony; his brother and rival, Thomas, married Henry VIII's widow, Catherine Parr, but before her death in childbirth seems to have tried to seduce the teenaged Princess Elizabeth. Somerset was thus on shaky ground when in 1549 he faced two rebellions: a conservative uprising in the south-west, whose goal was restoring Henry VIII's Six Articles of 1539, and Jack Ket's revolt in Norfolk, which was caused by anxiety over high prices and the enclosures of village common lands. After quiet was restored, Somerset was arrested and replaced as head of the regency by John Dudley, the earl of Warwick, who in 1551 became duke of Northumberland.

The reign of Henry II (1547–59) in France witnessed nearly constant war against Spain and England, although France recovered Boulogne from the English in return for an indemnity in 1549. The constable Anne de Montmorency, who had fallen out of favour with Francis I for favouring peace with Charles V, returned to power, and his nephew Gaspard de Coligny became admiral. The Lorraine-based dukes of Guise were slightly less in the royal favour but gained prestige by the presence after 1548 of the six year old Mary Stuart, the Scottish queen. Henry II married her to his oldest son and eventual heir Francis in 1558. Henry also continued his father's tacit alliance with the Turks, though more subtly.

Thus Charles V had been unable to consolidate his victory of 1547, and opposition was building up. The Augsburg Interim satisfied no one. Pope Paul III had deserted the imperial cause before Mühlberg; he now negotiated with the new French government for a League that would restore his son, Pier Luigi Farnese, to his lordship of Piacenza, where he had been ousted by a conspiracy, and liberate Italy from the Spaniards. Contrary to expectations, Paul's successor Julius III (1550–5) favoured the Emperor, even reopening the Council of Trent in 1551.

The German Settlement

Maurice of Saxony and Albert Alcibiades started negotiating with the Protestants again and with the French for the release of Philip of Hesse. Henry II allied more openly than Francis had with the German Lutherans, promising them enormous subsidies in a treaty with the Schmalkaldic League in 1551. During campaigns in 1552 Henry took Lorraine but was unsuccessful in Alsace, which had a larger German-speaking population. After a conspiracy in which Henry nearly captured the emperor, Charles V's court had to retreat into Styria. In the ensuing negotiations, Maurice of Saxony, after insisting initially on the political and religious liberty of the princes, deserted his allies again and agreed to the Peace of Passau (1552), which referred all religious questions to a Diet – Charles V wanted a church Council to handle them – and pledged the princes to renounce their French alliance. Charles then put a supreme effort into retaking Metz, which the French had taken in 1552, but he had to break off the siege in December.

In ill health for years and emotionally exhausted, Charles left Germany for Brussels in 1553, after which Ferdinand handled all German affairs. After long negotiations the Peace of Augsburg (26 September 1555) was issued by the imperial Diet, and the Lutherans and Roman Catholics acknowledged tacitly that they could not exterminate one another, and agreed to stop warfare. Each prince would determine the religion of his subjects; those who were not willing to accept the prince's religion had to leave if he forced the issue. Neither side would tolerate Anabaptists, who by now were a spent force, or Calvinists, who were just beginning to spread in Germany. The result of these agreements was considerable religious migration during the following years. Seizures of church property by Protestant princes before the Peace of Passau were allowed to stand, but those which had been made since were to be reversed. The Peace of Augsburg was a notable compromise that would be the political basis of the religious division of Germany until the next century. Yet its glaring weakness became apparent very quickly: in 1563 the Count Palatine became the first electoral prince of Germany to embrace Calvinism.

Charles V's great rivals were gone, but the chaos of the Empire had kept the cautious prince from capitalizing on the weaknesses of the new regimes in England and France. Realizing that his hope of religious unity in conjunction with church reform had failed, Charles abdicated rule over his various domains in a series of enactments in late 1555 and 1556. His realms were divided. His son, Philip II (1556–98), ruled Spain and the Netherlands. Charles' abdication of the Empire to his brother, Ferdinand of Hungary, was of dubious legality, since the imperial title was not hereditary; but the

Electors accepted Ferdinand in February 1558. Charles retired to the monastery of San Jeronomo de Yuste, in southern Spain, and died there in 1558.

England

England had been too involved in domestic travail to play an active role in the climactic events in Germany and France. The duke of Northumberland was a more radical Protestant than the earl of Somerset. A second and more radical Book of Common Prayer and a new Act of Uniformity were issued in 1552, followed by the Forty-Two Articles. Although the Lutheran Martin Bucer played an important role in writing the Prayer Book, these documents were essentially Calvinist in their view of predestination and justification by faith alone. But while they had a strongly Protestant theology, the ritual prescribed for religious services was neo-Catholic. The Forty-Two Articles would be the model for Elizabeth's Thirty-Nine Articles of 1563.

It became obvious in 1552 that Edward VI was not going to live long. To prevent the succession of Mary, the firmly Catholic daughter of Henry VIII and Catherine of Aragon, Northumberland married his son, Guilford Dudley, to Lady Jane Grey, Henry VIII's grand-niece, and then persuaded the young king to will the throne to Lady Jane without having the action confirmed by Parliament. The ploy did not work. Lady Jane ruled for nine days before the army, which remained loyal to Mary, overturned her regime.

The accession of Queen Mary (1553–8), 'Bloody Mary' to Protestant historiography in England, inaugurates a period of nearly 60 years of female rule in England. No woman had ever been a ruling queen in England, and by its very nature the event precipitated foreign involvement. Scotland's queen was Mary, daughter of King James V of Scotland and great-grand-daughter of Henry VII of England, now aged 11 and in France. Mary was strongly Roman Catholic, but in the late 1550s her Scottish subjects were being evangelized by disciples of John Calvin. Had her marriage to Francis II (1559–60) of France produced children, the Scottish and French crowns would have been united.

But had Mary Tudor's marriage yielded an heir, England and the Netherlands would have shared a ruler with Spain. When she proposed to marry Prince Philip, who would become King Philip II of Spain when his father abdicated in 1556, she provoked the rebellion in January 1554 of Sir Thomas Wyatt, whose troops nearly took London before they were dispersed. Mary married Philip despite the opposition, and Britain in the 1550s thus became a prize for both major contenders in the Habsburg–Valois conflict.

Queen Mary immediately led Parliament to repeal the religious legislation of Edward VI, including the Act of Supremacy, restore the heresy laws and petition for reunion with Rome, although she did keep the title, 'Supreme Head of the Church of England'. The cardinal and papal legate, Reginald Pole, a humanist descendant of the Yorkist kings of England who had gone into exile in the 1530s, became archbishop of Canterbury after the execution of Thomas Cranmer.

The burnings of Protestant heretics began in January, 1555 and were discontinued as counterproductive in the summer. Fewer than 300 were executed, and the only rebellion against Mary was over the Spanish marriage rather than her religious policy. Thus some have argued that Roman Catholic sentiment was still strong in England and might have prevailed peacefully had Mary lived longer. But the Protestants controlled the print media, and horror stories of heroic martyrs had considerable impact. Mary's health was already failing by late 1555, and for the remaining three years of her reign the accession of her half-sister Elizabeth, the daughter of the Protestant Anne Boleyn, was a foregone conclusion. The Parliament that met in November 1555 was less docile than its predecessor, not even bringing up Mary's request that Philip be crowned as consort. In 1557, at Philip's instigation, she dragged England into Spain's war against France and the Pope, a folly that lost Calais, England's last possession on the Continent. Mary died on 17 November 1558.

The old diplomatic system was nearing its end. Aided by an open alliance with Pope Paul IV (1554–9), Henry II campaigned both in Italy and on the Flemish frontier in 1557, but the French were routed at Saint-Quentin. In April 1559 he had to agree to the treaty of Cateau-Cambrésis, by which France formally gained Lorraine, which it had held since 1552, but surrendered all lands in Italy, ending claims that went back to the thirteenth century. The frontier of 1557 became the border with Spanish-held Flanders; and with Henry II's death in a tournament accident later in 1559, France lost its last strong king until 1589.

The Changing Focus of 'Religious' Warfare, 1559–1603

The political history of the second half of the sixteenth century was dominated by two great struggles: the French wars of religion, and the revolt of the Netherlands against Spain. Italy and the Empire, where most military action of the previous half century had occurred, remained quiet, and Spain experienced internal strife. England, meanwhile, was drawn peripherally into the struggles, particularly after 1585.

Medieval wars had invariably been dynastic: issues of policy were involved only in internal struggles. The dynastic element of foreign affairs remained strong in the sixteenth century, but particularly after 1555 a religious side to conflicts also became apparent. Religious warfare within the Christian commonwealth intensified in the sixteenth century, when national rivalries assumed a religious cast, but even this has been over-drawn. There was no international component to the religious struggles of the first half of the sixteenth century unless one considers Charles V to be a Spaniard who was trying to keep the Empire in the Roman Catholic camp. Protestant England and Roman Catholic France had been rivals for centuries, and the Catholic French were willing to use Turks and Lutherans against Charles V, likewise a Roman Catholic. After 1555 Spain intervened on behalf of Roman Catholicism in the Netherlands (where Spain had dynastic interests) and in France (where it did not), while England, as the only Protestant kingdom of Europe outside Scandinavia, was drawn into wars in the Low Countries, where it had trading, albeit not dynastic, interests, and in Germany, where it had only religious bonds – Elizabeth, who ruled a Calvinist monarchy, did not make the distinction between Lutheran and Calvinist in Germany that the Germans themselves made.

More to the point, the Spaniards aided the French crown, during its periods of orthodoxy, against the Huguenots, and the English made overtures to the Huguenots and openly aided Protestants in the Netherlands against the Spaniards. In each case there were policy concerns apart from religion that might well have caused warfare except perhaps, in the Low Countries. There was some religious conflict within Germany, both between Roman Catholics and Protestants and between Lutherans and Calvinists, but no foreign interest was involved there until the Thirty Years War erupted in 1618. And even after the Reformation, the divisions within Christianity were probably no more fundamental than divisions had long been within Islam. In the seventeenth century the religious tensions re-emerged, but more often they acted as a cloak for other causes. Most of the 'religious' wars of the second half of the sixteenth century, however, make sense only if one concedes that religion was a major concern, if not in each case the only one.

The French Wars of Religion[3]

The French monarchy reached its nadir in the three decades after 1559. Its kings were young, and personally unfit for their responsibilities. During the brief reign of Francis II (1559–60) Protestantism began making significant inroads in hitherto firmly Catholic France. The disciples of John Calvin, who called themselves the 'Reformed', were largely confined to the Swiss Confederation until the 1550s, but then they dispatched missions that were particularly successful in Scotland, the Netherlands and France, also gaining a hold in England by influencing English exiles who had fled to the Continent to escape Mary's persecutions. They were strong enough in France by 1559 to hold a national synod, and by the early 1560s they may have numbered between 10 and 15 per cent of the population of France. They were especially strong in the cities and among the nobles, both of which had influence out of proportion to their numbers because of their level of education and their understanding of how to use printing for propaganda. Their Swiss origin gave them the nickname in France of Huguenot, a corruption of the German *Eidgenoss* (Confederate).

The Reformed movement was concentrated in a belt of territory across central and southern France and in the cities, being weaker in the north and the rural areas. The appeal of Protestantism was linked to local concerns, although other forces such as language, literacy and proximity to Calvin's Geneva were also involved. The geography of the cities, often discrete nuclei persisting from the Middle Ages with their own settlement characteristics and neighbourhood associations and even governments, led to a situation where some entire quarters were dominated by the Protestants, such as the university quarter of Toulouse and the left bank at Paris.

Just as cities were divided along religious lines, so a growing breach developed also among the great princes of the realm. In a period of young kings, cliques formed around the queen mother, Catherine de' Medici, and leading nobles. Antoine de Bourbon, king of Navarre and the most inclined of the great nobles to the Reformed position, was the natural leader of the royal council in 1559, but Francis II preferred the militantly Catholic duke of Guise. The Montmorency also resented the boy king's reliance on his Guise kinsmen. Their common exclusion from court created an alliance between Bourbon and particularly his brother, Louis, prince of Condé, and Montmorency and his nephew, Coligny. With the Guises associated with radical anti-Protestantism, the Bourbons and Coligny leaned toward the Huguenots, and Guise control of the lucrative central offices was widely resented.

Francis II's death at 16 brought his 10-year-old brother, Charles IX (1560–74), to the throne, while Catherine de' Medici became regent. She had had little political influence during her husband's lifetime, but she was the power behind the thrones of her three sons who ruled France between 1559 and her death in 1589. For the first time in the history of Europe, women were wearing two crowns and dominating a third. Historical opinion has not treated Catherine gently, but in fairness she faced problems that would have overwhelmed a lesser figure. Although impeccably Catholic herself, she sought allies among the opponents of the Guises, including Bourbon and Condé.

Religion was the main, although not the only, point of contention in the French wars; but it was religion as church rather than as belief, and failure to conform to the usages of the church was a pollution of the body social that had to be removed. As the Roman Catholics began to fear that the king was the captive of the Protestants Bourbon and Condé, Guise, constable Montmorency and the sieur de Saint-André in late 1561 sought the aid of Philip II of Spain, who coincidentally disputed Bourbon's rule in Navarre. Open warfare began on 1 March 1562, when troops of the duke of Guise massacred a Huguenot congregation at Vassy whose noise had offended the great noble. The Huguenots, who had been expecting an incident, quickly seized much of the Loire valley and several cities. Condé and the Protestant nobles seized Orléans, which gave them a base on the Loire, and then went on to take Rouen on the Seine and Lyon at the confluence of the Saone and the Rhone. In the first three months of the war many other major towns, particularly in the Midi, fell to the Huguenots.

Although Montmorency's nephews led the Huguenots, he stayed with Guise and became an adviser of Catherine de' Medici, who was more inclined than the Guise faction to compromise with the Protestants. The Bourbons were also divided, and personal feuds became involved. Montmorency and Condé were both captured by the other side in mid-1562, and the duke of Guise was assassinated in 1563 by a Huguenot who implicated Coligny when under torture. Although he retracted this allegation on the scaffold, the Guises believed the confession and sought an opportunity to avenge themselves on Coligny.

The queen mother then mediated a compromise peace settlement in March 1563, in which the Protestants were restricted to the suburbs of one town in each *bailliage* or *senechaussée*, and Protestant nobles were permitted to practise their religion on their estates. The nobles thus received privileges that the majority of the Huguenots, who were in the towns, did not. Catherine's policy of moderation worked until 1567, when the Huguenots took advantage of the confusion when the duke of Alva moved troops to the Netherlands, on the 'Spanish road' on France's eastern frontier, to counterattack. In September a plot by Coligny and Condé to seize the king at Meaux was barely foiled, but the Huguenots did take several towns.

The second war ended in March 1568, but a new conflict erupted later that year. Charles of Guise, cardinal of Lorraine, persuaded the church to pay a huge subsidy to the crown on condition that the previous edicts of toleration would be revoked, thus forcing the Huguenots who had not yet taken arms against the crown to do so. When in 1570 Coligny outmanoeuvred the royal army and got his forces to Burgundy, where the Protestants were strong, Catherine de' Medici agreed to the Edict of Saint-Germain, which allowed public Protestant worship inside 24 towns where previously they had been restricted to the suburbs.

The queen mother was trying to end the struggles by arranging the marriage of her daughter Marguerite to Henry of Navarre, the leading Protestant prince of France and the heir to the throne unless one of Catherine's sons had a son. When the great personages of France were in Paris to attend the wedding, an attempt was made on the life of Coligny, followed on 24 August 1572 by the infamous St Bartholomew's Day massacre by royal troops and civilian mobs of several thousand Protestants in Paris. Who gave the order is unclear, but Catherine de' Medici, who feared Coligny's influence over Charles, and the king's younger brother, the duke of Anjou, are prime suspects. In retaliation for the death of Francis, duke of Guise, in 1563, his son Henry murdered Coligny as he recovered from his wounds. Some 3000 Huguenots were killed in Paris alone, and the violence spread to other cities. Henry of Navarre and his cousin, Henry of Condé, had to abjure Protestantism to escape; Navarre was held in custody until 1576, but he resumed leadership of the Huguenots when he was released.

The St Bartholomew's Day massacre broke the Protestant movement in France. The most likely estimate of casualties is 3000 dead in Paris and 8000 elsewhere. The Protestants were affected virtually everywhere except in the few areas where they controlled the government so totally that they could outlaw Roman Catholicism. The massacre cost the Huguenots many of their leaders and encouraged the Roman Catholics to retake places that the Protestants had seized; the noble element among the Reformed declined sharply, and the Protestant movement became associated mainly with the cities and with the Midi.

The efforts of the government to accommodate the Huguenots simply enraged the vast Roman Catholic majority. The Reformed had hurt their own cause by using the same tactics in France that had cost the Calvinists public support in the Netherlands: they destroyed images and churches, and mistreated the Catholics in the interest of purging the land of idolatry, thereby alienating much of their potential base of support. As an example, disproportionate numbers of printers became Protestants, but at Lyon the 'Griffarians', the brotherhood of journeyman printers, were upset by the efforts of the new Consistory that the Protestant rulers of the city set up in 1562 to enforce high moral standards of behaviour, such as dragging people into court on charges of drunkenness. Tensions heightened when the Consistory started denying the sacraments to striking workers. The Consistory also forbade the Griffarians' coarse initiation rite, part of which could be considered a parody of the Lord's Supper. The goddess Minerva, the Mother of Printing, presided over their celebrations. The Roman Catholics were much more tolerant of such things than the Calvinists. Thus the journeymen, who had initially leaned toward the Reformed faith, began returning to Roman Catholicism.[4]

Political Thought

The majority group of Roman Catholics naturally retaliated against the Protestants when they recovered power. The remaining Huguenots now saw the crown as their enemy, which had not been true in the first three wars. Protestant political thinkers started calling for popular sovereignty, in the first significant body of thought to argue, from a theoretical perspective, that the king could be limited. Huguenots, beginning with François Hotman, whose *Le Tigre de France* (1560) was written during the short reign of Francis II, argued that the real problem was the evil advisers of the young king, who kept him from a godly path; but the odium eventually spread to the king himself. Hotman's later *Francogallia* (1573) argued that the Franks and the Gauls had had an elective monarchy and had loved liberty, but had been corrupted toward tyranny by the Italians. Anti-Italian sentiment was common, much of it directed at the queen mother, Catherine de' Medici, and Machiavelli was often raised as the inspiration for her and King Henry III. Hotman argued that the Franco-Gauls had had a council, which he identified with the Estates-General, that could depose the king. The most radical and influential work of Huguenot political theory was the anonymous *Vindiciae contra Tyrannos* (1579), probably the work of Philippe Duplessis de Mornay, a nobleman who was adviser to Henry of Navarre, which argued that the people created the monarchy and the Estates-General elected the king, while resistance to bad law and/or over-taxation was justified as a recovery of the sovereignty of the people. Protestantism thus became associated with treason to the crown.

When Charles IX died in 1574, aged 24, he was succeeded by the duke of Anjou as Henry III (1574–89). The Huguenots now were allying with the moderate Roman Catholics, including Montmorency and the king's remaining brother, the duke of Alençon, who became duke of Anjou when Henry III vacated the title to become king. Alençon/Anjou hoped to marry Elizabeth I of England and become prince of the Netherlands, an ambition that required accommodation with the French Protestants.

During the religious wars a group of thinkers arose called *politiques* by their detractors because they placed a greater priority on civic order than on religious orthodoxy. Most of them were Roman Catholics, but they disliked the exaltation of religion over state by the Catholic League, and particularly its acceptance of Spanish help against King Henry IV. The most prominent *politique* was Jean Bodin, a lawyer who served in several Estates-General as a deputy of the Third Estate, while Anjou was the most influential public figure associated with them. Bodin's *Six Books of the Republic* were first published in 1576 in French and in 1586 in Latin. It is a confusing and internally contradictory work, as Bodin tried to keep both factions pacified. The *politiques* did not want religious toleration *per se*, but preferred it to civil discord. His question was how to provide peace; and his answer was to give supreme power to the monarch. Sovereignty was indivisible and dependent on no one, but true sovereignty must conform to divine and natural law; while the king should guarantee the civil rights of all, including the right to practise one's own religion in private.[5]

The Lull of 1576–1584

Anjou negotiated the 'Peace of Monsieur' in 1576, which gave the Reformed the most extensive rights that they would ever enjoy in France by requiring the government allow public worship for Huguenots everywhere except Paris. To prevent anti-Protestant discrimination in the courts, the *parlements* were to have both Reformed and Catholic sections. Huguenots were made eligible to hold royal offices, and they were given eight fortified towns. In reaction a Catholic League was formed, with Henry of Guise as its leader. Henry III called an Estates-General at Blois in December 1576, but the meeting was controlled by the rapidly growing League. The nobles and the Third Estate refused money, and the Estates also got the king to declare that the heir to the throne had to be Catholic. This excluded Henry of Navarre, who was second in line behind Anjou.

The seven years after 1577 were relatively quiet, although desultory local hostilities generally favoured the Catholic cause. The monarch's bizarre behaviour led to new problems in 1584, compounded when Anjou's death made the Protestant Henry of Navarre the heir to the throne. This danger revived the Catholic League and forced the Catholics into the previously Protestant position of opposition to the crown on grounds that the king had pledged in his coronation oath to eradicate heresy but was now in fact its ally. The Guises signed a treaty with Spain: Philip II pledged a subsidy for the war against the Protestants in France, while the Guises agreed to work to return Cambrai, on the Flemish border, to Philip II (Anjou had occupied it during his time in the Netherlands).The Guises also promised to publish and implement the Decrees of the Council of Trent (see Chapter 10), which the French church had resisted as a threat to Gallican liberties. Guise raised an army and in 1585 seized much of eastern France. Meanwhile Henry III withdrew all prior concessions to the Reformed, and made their religion illegal, but he was insufficiently radical for the Leaguers. The result was the 'War of the Three Henries' (Guise, Navarre and the king), the last and most deadly of the French wars of religion, between 1584 and 1593.

Henry III lost control of Paris in 1588 when Guise and the Leaguers trapped his Swiss mercenaries in the city by blockading the streets. The king escaped and in the summer made a show of peace with the League. In December Henry lured Guise into an assassination, but the League still controlled Paris, and a radical Committee of Sixteen ruled the city by terror. After Catherine de' Medici died in January 1589 the king was alone, with the radical Leaguers advocating his deposition and even tyrannicide. Jean Boucher's *The Just Deposition of Henry III as King of the French* (1589) borrows notions of resistance and popular sovereignty from Huguenot political thought, but in calling for the displacement of the king the Leaguers went far beyond what the Huguenots had said in the 1570s. Henry III thus had to make an alliance with Navarre. Their joint forces were besieging Paris when a Dominican assassinated the king, a deed that made Henry of Navarre-Bourbon king (Henry IV, 1589–1610).

For the next several years Henry IV tried to conciliate the Roman Catholics, who were now a large and growing majority, without losing his base among the Reformed. In 1593, finding himself unable to take Paris and unwilling to subject the country to further bloodshed, he made a peace with the League that included forgiving millions of *livres*-worth of debts owed by

Leaguers to the monarchy. As he had done to save his life in 1572, Henry reconverted to Roman Catholicism in what was clearly an act of political realism (whether he ever uttered the line 'Paris is worth a mass' is uncertain). Some Catholic leaders and cities received the right to exclude Protestant worship from their areas, while some radical Leaguers persisted in open alliance with Spain against a king whom most Frenchmen accepted; an assassination plot against Henry IV was a virtually annual event, and one was to succeed in 1610. Peasant disorders (the Croquants) racked the south-west and Burgundy in 1593–4, but the protests concerned taxes and seigniorial duties, together with resentment against administrative excesses and military depradations, not religion. Cardinal Charles of Guise was sceptical of the king's sincerity, but made peace in 1595; and shortly before Philip II died in 1598 Spain and France concluded the peace of Vervins, which stabilized their relations for some years. There was mutual restoration of all places held by one side in 1559 but seized since that time by the other.

Henry temporarily pacified his domestic situation by issuing the Edict of Nantes in 1598, which was to remain the governing instrument for religious relations in France until Louis XIV revoked it in 1685. The Edict was not a decree of toleration. It recognized complete freedom of conscience, and freedom of public worship everywhere for Catholics, including areas controlled by Protestants; but public services for Protestants were limited to designated places, including the residences of nobles. The Edict thus says little about belief and much about practice. While religion had been a burning intellectual question for Henry VIII and Charles V, if not for Francis I, it was a social and political matter for all their royal descendants except Philip II of Spain. The Huguenots retained the right to hold office and to attend and maintain schools. Bipartisan chambers in the courts, introduced in the Peace of Monsieur in 1576, were kept, although not every *parlement* had them and the Protestants would eventually be reduced to one judge in the *parlement* of Paris. A famous provision also allowed the Huguenots to have garrisons in 49 towns, mostly in the south-west, at royal expense. This concession was contained in a royal *brevet*, valid for 8 years, which did not have to be registered by *parlement* and accordingly could be kept secret. The last of the garrisons was gone by 1629.[6]

The Revolt of the Netherlands (to 1584)[7]

The Spanish monarchy ruled the Netherlands in the sixteenth century as the heir of the Burgundian state, which had united the seventeen provinces in the late fourteenth and fifteenth centuries. It had been a purely dynastic union. The Burgundians were based in the south, particularly in Brabant. Philip the Good established the States General, which always met in Brussels or another southern city, but the individual principalities kept their own Estates, which were unusually powerful in the late Middle Ages.

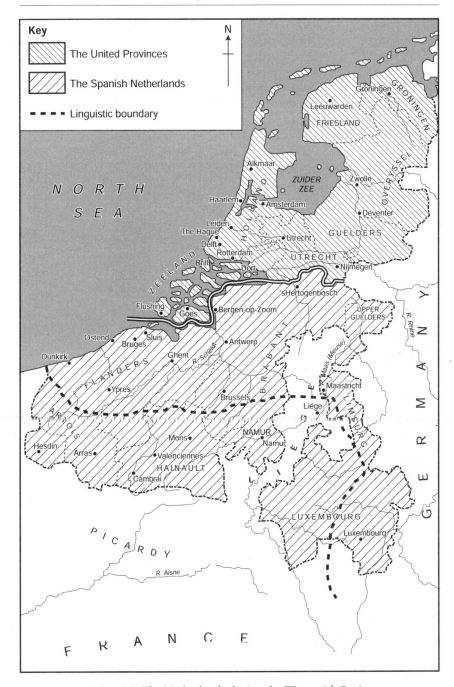

Key

The United Provinces

The Spanish Netherlands

- - - - Linguistic boundary

N

NORTH SEA

GRONINGEN

Groningen

Leeuwarden

FRIESLAND

OVERYSSEL

Alkmaar

ZUIDER ZEE

Zwolle

Haarlem

Amsterdam

Deventer

HOLLAND

Leiden

The Hague

Utrecht

GUELDERS

Delft

Rotterdam

UTRECHT

Brill

Dort

Nijmegen

ZEELAND

'sHertogenbosch

Flushing

Goes

Bergen-op-Zoom

UPPER GUELDERS

R. Rhine

Ostend

Sluis

Antwerp

BRABANT

Maas (Meuse)

Maastricht

Bruges

Dunkirk

Ghent

R. Scheldt

Ypres

FLANDERS

Brussels

Liége

LIMBURG

GERMANY

ARTOIS

Hesdin

Mons

NAMUR

Namur

Arras

Valenciennes

HAINAULT

Cambrai

LUXEMBOURG

Luxembourg

PICARDY

R. Aisne

FRANCE

Map 5.3 The Netherlands during the Wars with Spain

The rise of the Swiss Confederation and the Dutch Republic were the two most important political and institutional developments of the period from 1300 to 1600. The Swiss Confederation had originated in an anti-Habsburg rural–urban league in the late thirteenth century, and was a formed polity by 1513; the Netherlands was born from the religious warfare of the sixteenth and early seventeenth centuries. Interestingly, although we associate the 'modern' world with the national state, both these were confederations involving both rural and urban elements, but led by the most powerful cities. Just as the rural cantons were strong enough to keep Switzerland from becoming Zwinglian or Calvinist, the power of the 'stadholder' (regent) and the rural areas of the northern and eastern Netherlands was a counterweight to the power of Amsterdam and Holland. The modern Dutch state also involved the separation of the northern Low Countries from the south, which had previously dominated the region economically and had been much more populous and politically sophisticated. Its core was the coastal county of Holland, which had become the most urbanized and densely populated of the seven states of the northern Netherlands by the early sixteenth century.

The descendants of the Burgundian dukes were largely absentee, and after 1516 the prince was usually in Spain or Germany. After Philip the Handsome died in 1506, his sister Margaret of Austria served as regent in the Netherlands for him, and later for his son, until her death in 1530. She was authoritarian, relying on foreign advisers and bypassing the provincial States, and was succeeded as regent by Charles' sister, Mary of Hungary (1531–40), who ruled with a reorganized Council of Finance, a Secret Council and, most importantly, a Council of State. Although the Habsburgs tried to rule from Brussels, the States General had little power, for they met infrequently and were a purely advisery body. Binding decisions required the assent of of the provincial States.

The Burgundians had been appointing 'stadholders' (regents) since 1430. Their functions were identical to those of the French provincial governors. In the sixteenth century stadholders were often appointed for groups of provinces: from 1528 Holland, Zeeland and Utrecht had the same one, as did Flanders, Walloon Flanders and Artois. René de Chalon, the short-lived son of Henry of Nassau, stadholder of Holland, inherited his father's possessions in the Netherlands in 1538 and the principality of Orange in southern France, and was the first of his line to be styled Prince of Orange. But the stadholders were often absent, and real administration was under the permanent councils of the individual provinces.

The Habsburgs generally kept the Netherlands quiet until the 1540s, when the new war with France meant higher taxation. Until then the Habsburg–Valois rivalry had focused on Italy, but now, with the French effectively excluded from Italy, it shifted to France, which bordered the Netherlands. Francis I built new Italian-style fortresses near the Flemish border, and Charles V had to follow suit. The economic prosperity of the region, particularly the Antwerp capital market (see Chapter 8), tempted the rulers to rely increasingly on the Netherlands. To meet the new demands, direct taxes and excises were levied at the provincial level. Since the Hollanders objected to paying to defend Flanders from the French, discontent mounted in the north during the French war of 1552–9, and regional States met more frequently to cope with the financial pressures. Philip II asked the States General to approve an enormous aid in 1556, which was not voted until 1558, irritating everybody. This was the last States General in which the king and States even had the appearance of cooperation.

The Netherlands and Scotland were the only parts of Europe where a successful religious Reformation resulted from public agitation in defiance of a hostile regime, rather than being imposed by the prince. Roman Catholicism had already been weak in the Netherlands before Calvinism became important in the late 1550s. The entire Burgundian Netherlands had only five bishoprics, and all but Utrecht were in the French-speaking part. To the usual problems of worldly clergy and general inattention to duties was added an antiquated parish organization, which had been established before the thirteenth-century reclamations and thus was inadequate for urban Holland.

Thus Luther's views initially had a great impact in the Netherlands, while Charles V's power diminished the farther north and east one went. Thus, although Charles set up an Inquisition in the Netherlands in 1522, the civil authorities sometimes defied him: the Inquisition was rather active in Flanders, but it was less tolerated in the north, targeting readers and public officials, effectively enough to hinder but not stop Protestantism from spreading. Nicodemism (outward conformity while concealing one's true opinions) became widespread. The only major theological controversy within the Protestant community that had much public impact before the late sixteenth century was between mainstream Protestants and Anabaptists, who were numerous in several Dutch cities.

The situation in the Netherlands changed abruptly when Charles V abdicated. Charles had wanted to rule a Christian empire while respecting local customs and institutions; he had no desire to play the autocrat. In part through his own diffidence, but more because of limited resources and the fact that his great strength 'on paper' aroused fears, he had been unable to accomplish his designs, which were to restore the political status quo of 1516 while adding institutional but not doctrinal reform in religion.

Philip II (1556–98) was very different. A man of limited vision, a quintessential bureaucrat, he had numerous personal and family problems. Philip insisted on controlling policy from Spain, leaving little to the discretion of his regent in the Netherlands, his half-sister Margaret of Parma; and she in turn was hampered by Antoine Perrenot de Granvelle, president of the Council of State, who became despised on religious grounds by the Protestants and by all for his disregard of the law. While Charles had been a strong Roman Catholic, Philip II was fanatical, determined to help Catholics everywhere against Protestants everywhere, whatever the local circumstances. Although his rule extended 'only' over Spain, Italy and the Netherlands, Philip became as embroiled against the Calvinists in the Low Countries as his father had been against the German Lutherans. Moreover, he felt a divine mission to liberate England from its Protestant ruler and ensure that the Protestant heir to the French throne never succeeded to it. With initially greater resources, particularly from the Americas, and more restricted needs than his father, Philip none the less managed to leave the Spanish monarchy much weakened when he died in 1598.

Although it was once thought that Calvinism entered the Netherlands from the Walloon south, in fact most Protestant leaders of the 1560s had been exiled from the Netherlands to Germany early in Philip's reign and had returned. Calvin's followers became dominant in the refugee communities. Antwerp was their main centre, but congregations existed throughout the Low Countries. The Netherlands Confession of Faith (*Confessio Belgica*), written by Guy de Brès at Valenciennes in 1561 for the French Reformed, and printed in Dutch in 1562, was the basic creed.

Calvinism came into the open at Antwerp in the 'Wonderyear', 1566–7. A petition to the authorities on 5 April 1566 demanded public preaching, abolition of the Inquisition and suspension of the monarchs' edicts against heresy. Iconoclasm (the smashing of religious paintings, sculpture and other decoration) began in Flanders, then spread to Antwerp, where riots in the autumn forced William of Orange, stadholder of Holland and to that point a loyal servant of the crown, to grant Calvinists and Lutherans the standing of legal religions. Iconoclastic riots quickly erupted in other cities.

But the Antwerp riots caused Philip II to conclude that heresy was so widespread in the Low Countries that it warranted a campaign of extirpation. A petition was presented to the regent Margaret of Parma later in the year; when one of her councillors contemptuously dismissed the petitioners as 'these beggars', they took the name as a point of pride. The defeat of the Beggar army in March 1567 ended the 'Wonderyear', and royal authority was quickly restored. The regent wanted an amnesty, but Philip II would not agree, and the leaders of the rebellion who had not fled were punished severely. The duke of Alva, sent from Spain with an army, occupied Antwerp in August 1567. In September Margaret resigned and Alva became governor general.

Alva immediately set up a special court at Brussels, which quickly became known as the 'Council of Troubles' and which set about obliterating Protestantism. Between 1565 and 1577 some 800 Protestants and other rebels were convicted of heresy, most of them Calvinists and Anabaptists. The repression was most severe in the south, but some clandestine Protestant worship survived everywhere. Most Protestant leaders who could escape went into exile, where a split developed between the more rigid Calvinists, who were mainly from the south, and the latitudinarians.

At the synod of Emden in 1571 the radical position was upheld: consistories, not the civic authorities, were to appoint future ministers of the Dutch Reformed Church, and William of Orange, with his foreign ties and much greater resources than the others, was the acknowledged political leader of the exiles. By 1569 he was using his great wealth to charter pirates to prey on Spanish shipping, and mounted a propaganda campaign against the Spanish excesses from his exile at Nassau. Orange's writings emphasized the violation of liberty and the need to end tyranny, for he was not yet a Calvinist. But the synod of Emden did not express sympathy for Orange's movement, probably because his propaganda was so secular in tone, directed against Alva's tyranny and lacking a call to establish true religion.

Alva might have extirpated Calvinism had he not combined religious repression with distasteful taxation. In 1569 he tried to extract three new permanent taxes from the States General, including one per cent on assessed wealth, a permanent sales tax of 5 per cent and the 'tenth penny' as a surcharge above the sales tax.[8] The States General agreed, but the local States refused to implement them. They did vote temporary subsidies, in exchange for which Alva dropped the 5 per cent and tenth penny; but when the subsidies expired in 1571, he simply imposed the two taxes, fining local magistrates who refused to appoint tax collectors. The city governments were caught between Alva and the likelihood of rebellion by their subjects if the taxes were actually collected.

The Netherlanders then undertook what amounted to naval guerrilla warfare. The 'Sea Beggars' seized Brill and Flushing in April 1572, and by the end of April all of Walcheren island except Middelburg was in rebellion. A land army occupied Mons, and by July the rebels controlled all of North Holland except Amsterdam. Later in the summer the south Holland towns joined in, starting with Leiden and Dordrecht, the Holland towns which in 1566 had been the most loyal to the Habsburgs. In each case the Catholic churches were stripped of images and turned over to Protestant worship.

Rival meetings of States of Holland were held in the summer of 1572. The rebel assembly, at Dordrecht, acknowledged the authority of William 'the Silent' (so-called because he often kept his true opinions to himself) as stadholder. The States pledged military and financial help for the war against Spain, and Orange pledged not to govern without the consent of the States or at least a majority of them. The States thus were not only rebelling agaisnt the Spaniards; they were also becoming an embryonic government, expanding into areas of finance and justice and administration that normally had not been theirs before. Orange quickly appealed to the southern Netherlands for help, but Alva recaptured Mons and Mechelen in the autumn. A massacre of the civilians at Mechelen, Catholic and Calvinist alike, who had not tried to resist Alva when the rebels withdrew, seems to have broken resistance. Alva then invaded Gelderland and the northeast. Hoping that another bloodbath would end the revolt in the north and force the submission of Holland and Zeeland, the only areas still in rebellion, Alva exterminated the entire population of Naarden on 2 December 1572.

The sacking of Naarden was a miscalculation, for it became the highlight of an immense propaganda campaign for the Protestants. Better leadership in the north, some spontaneous local risings in addition to the Sea Beggars and more thorough Protestantization than in the south caused the leaders of the northern revolt to feel that they could only survive by continuing the revolt. Haarlem held out against Alva until July 1573, giving the rebels elsewhere time to regroup. Orange's cut the dikes along the Maas and this, and heavy rains, forced the Spaniards to withdraw in September 1574.

Luis de Requesens, who succeeded Alva as governor-general in late 1573, was more conciliatory, but Philip II was unwilling to concede Orange's two demands: toleration of Protestants, and limitation of the monarchy through the States General and the provincial States. After Requesens' death in 1576, unpaid army mutineers pillaged Zierikzee and Aalst, then sacked Antwerp in November, the 'Spanish Fury' in which 18,000 are alleged to have perished. This deed handed Orange more propaganda. The Pacification of Ghent was signed a few days after the destruction of Antwerp: the southern provinces were to join with Utrecht, Holland and Zeeland and Orange in expelling the Spaniards, and would set up a single States General for the Netherlands, to meet in Brussels. For the interim, Protestant public worship would be allowed only in Holland and Zeeland; the rest would be Roman Catholic. But all laws against heresy and suspect books were suspended; thus private but not public Protestantism was allowed in the south. The States General also agreed to recognize Orange as stadholder in the areas he then controlled.

Thus, while the south had joined the north in rebellion, the fact that it was still Catholic gave a chance for reconciliation. The States General recognized the new governor-general, Don John of Austria, when he agreed to the Pacification of Ghent and sent the Spanish troops away. But the Hollanders and Orange refused this, for it gave no guarantees for Protestants. Orange tried to radicalize the southern revolt by allying with the city militias and guilds against the city patricians and nobles, who had generally stayed Roman Catholic. In July Don John withdrew to Namur and recalled the Spanish troops. From this point the northern and southern Netherlands diverged increasingly on the issue of religion, although neither liked the Spanish presence. The goals of the revolt in Holland included ending public Catholic worship, but this was unacceptable in Flanders and Brabant, where Catholicism generally prevailed. Orange could only maintain his position in the south, where he was now also stadholder of Brabant, by promising not to undermine the position of the Catholic church and city patriciates there.

Spanish power revived later in 1578. Castile had been able only with difficulty to pay for the expensive Netherlands enterprise, but supplies of American silver suddenly increased from the mid-1570s and continued high until the end of Philip II's reign. The persistence of the Spanish offensive against the Netherlands and England, even in the face of losses, and the intervention in France were made possible only by this influx of money. The short-term benefits in the Low Countries were apparent. Orange had to move his headquarters from Brussels to Antwerp, which became the centre for the southern and increasingly Brabantine revolt. He wanted toleration for both Roman Catholics and Protestants, but his position was undercut by the fact that, just as Don John's men took southern Brabant, militias from Ghent, where Calvinism had been installed by the artisans and guilds-men in 1577, marched on various smaller communities of East Flanders and replaced the Catholic magistrates with Calvinist 'Committees', stripped the images from the churches and expelled the Catholic clergy.

The Union of Utrecht of 23 January 1579, now regarded as the blueprint for the eventual Dutch Republic, was intended from the beginning to be purely northern, excluding the areas controlled by the States General at Antwerp. Orange initially held out for a more general form of union, but growing Spanish and Roman Catholic influence in the south led him to sign the Union in May. The States of the south in their turn agreed, in the Union of Arras (6 January 1579), on reconciliation with Philip II and collabora-tion with Alexander Farnese, the duke of Parma, Requesens' successor and by far the most talented of Philip II's commanders in the Netherlands. Roman Catholicism was made the legal religion.

England in the Age of Elizabeth: The First Phase (1558–1580)

Elizabeth I (1558–1603) became queen at the death of her half-sister Mary. The new queen was not well-known; she had survived the rapid changes of regime since 1547 by keeping her opinions to herself, although her ancestry meant that she had to be Protestant. Her reign was remarkable for its length, which ensured the permanence of much of her achievement. Elizabeth's early years were marred by overseas misadventures and by a series of non-marital adventures that afford some comparison with Mary Stuart. After 1563, however, she was prudent and notoriously economical, and at least until the 1580s she was able to keep England out of most foreign involvements. Particularly early on in her reign she suffered by the very fact that she was a woman. Virtually everyone, including Elizabeth herself in public statements, postulated the natural inferiority of women. Her most influential adviser was William Cecil, a Machiavellian figure whose anti-Spanish sentiments moved the queen into a fundamental foreign policy departure in the 1570s.

Elizabeth's accession meant that a Protestant church would be estab-lished in England, but the long-term prognosis for English Protestantism, indeed for England's survival as a nation, was not good. Elizabeth was single, and she had to marry to preserve the dynasty and, it was thought, the country's independence. In response to a remonstrance from parliamentary leaders in 1559 that she should marry, Elizabeth said that her present inclination was not to do so, but few took her seriously for some years. Yet a foreign marriage had obvious risks of entanglements that would include loss of the Protestant heritage, given the dearth of Protestant princes of standing to marry a queen. The Treaty of Cateau-Cambrésis of 1559 had settled the war between France and Spain, but it was a peace of exhaustion that left the two powers still wary of each other. Given that Scotland was clearly in the French sphere of influence, Philip II, Mary's widower, initially tried to ingratiate himself with Elizabeth. He even offered to marry her or, failing that, to affiance his cousin, Archduke Charles of Austria (Ferdinand's son) to her. Other suggested husbands in Elizabeth's first decade on the throne even included King Charles IX of France.

Marriage to one of the queen's own subjects was just as problematic, among other reasons because English common law subordinated the wife to her husband. Her only serious domestic marital possibility was with Robert Dudley. After his wife died in a suspicious accident, rumours flew that Dudley and the queen were cohabiting, and by late 1561 she realized that a potentially revolutionary situation was building up. She gave up Dudley, who became earl of Leicester in 1564 and a trusted member of her council.

The Scottish Complication

The possibility that the youthful Elizabeth would marry a man suspected of murdering his wife has a certain similarity to the situation of Mary Stuart of Scotland. She returned to Scotland in 1561 as the childless widow of Francis II of France, and promptly tangled with the Lords of the Congregation, Calvinists who had been fighting over religion with her regent, her mother Mary of Guise. Mary quickly became the Roman Catholic alternative to Elizabeth. In 1565 she made a love match with Henry Stuart, Lord Darnley, who, like Mary, was a great-grandchild of Henry VII of England, Elizabeth's grandfather. However, Darnley's weakness and brutality soon alienated her. After he murdered David Rizzio, Mary's Italian secretary, in a fit of jealousy, he was killed in an explosion in February 1567, and letters that the English may have forged implicated Mary directly. The earl of Bothwell was generally thought to have done the deed; he was acquitted in court, but Mary then married him. The Scottish nobles revolted, expelled Bothwell, captured Mary, and forced her to abdicate in favour of James, her infant son by Darnley.

Mary escaped to England in May, 1568, where a courteous reception awaited her; but her presence under guard became a colossal embarrassment. The anti-Cecil group at court, including Leicester, hoped to marry

Mary – 9 years younger than Elizabeth, and probably the next queen – to the duke of Norfolk. Ridolfi, the Florentine banker of the pope in England, represented the affair to the English Catholic leaders, the earls of Northumberland and Westmoreland, as a plot to replace Elizabeth with Mary, bringing the Spaniards into it by promising a Catholic restoration in England. Leicester, by now alarmed, betrayed the plot to Elizabeth. At what was supposed to be the critical moment, the amateurish 'revolt of the earls' in the north began in late 1569, but Northumberland and Westmoreland simply walked into a trap. The issue was already lost when the pope, in a bull of March 1570, deposed Elizabeth and released her Catholic subjects from their oath of obedience to her. This simply caused her to begin persecuting Roman Catholics, who had been generally tolerated until then. However, the plotting continued and became more dangerous. In 1571 Ridolfi promised papal funds if Mary's English friends would help a Spanish invasion of England. Mary agreed and, on her urging, Norfolk joined and agreed to a Catholic restoration. The government learned of the plot, so easily that Ridolfi, who escaped to the Continent, may have been a double agent. Norfolk was executed and his title extinguished for the rest of the century. Mary was confined in a country house. Parliament pressed for her execution, but Elizabeth resisted.

England had generally tilted toward the Habsburgs against the French, but this changed in the 1570s. Elizabeth had been giving tacit support to English pirates against Spanish shipping by 1568, and Spanish support for Mary Stuart poisoned relations between England and Spain. The English also feared that the Spanish army in Flanders could be used for an invasion of England. Annoyances on the high seas worsened, and Elizabeth sent some aid to the Huguenots, while also dangling the prospect of marriage before the duke of Alençon/Anjou. After the St Bartholomew's day massacre, Elizabeth dealt with both Anjou and Henry of Navarre as religious moderates.

In the next years Elizabeth gave the Netherlandish Protestants access to English ports and allowed them to recruit soldiers there, while maintaining technically correct relations with Spain; but after 1576 English involvement in the Low Countries became more open. The events of 1579 meant that the southern Low Countries, including England's trading partner, Flanders, would remain as Spanish possessions, while the disunity of the States General hindered a coherent English policy toward the north. The Duke of Anjou also hoped that the States General would appoint him governor in the Netherlands, and in 1580 there were new marriage negotiations with Elizabeth. But by the end of the year Elizabeth had backed away. The insurgents in the Low Countries still wanted to make Anjou governor-general, but his campaign against Parma in 1582 miscarried, and he left the area permanently in 1583. Parma had reduced the major Flemish Calvinist cities by the autumn of 1584, and William 'the Silent' had to move his headquarters from Brabant to Holland.

The Revolt of the Netherlands (1584–1609)

Thus Elizabeth's foreign policy was already in a shambles when the assassination of William of Orange by a Roman Catholic fanatic in July 1584 left no leader in the northern Netherlands who still hoped to recover the south from Spain. In desperation, the States General in February 1585 offered sovereignty over the Netherlands to Henry III of France, who declined, and then in May to Elizabeth of England. By the Treaty of Nonsuch (20 August 1585) Elizabeth was given seats on the Council of State and gained the right to name a governor-general, and she accordingly sent Leicester with an expeditionary force: her first foreign commitment of English soldiers since a campaign in Scotland in the early 1560s. England would not extricate itself from war with Spain in the Low Countries and at sea for the rest of Elizabeth's reign.

Elizabeth interpreted the treaty of Nonsuch to mean that stadholders would be appointed in consultation with her; but several had already received their commissions from the States General, and in Holland and Zeeland the provincial States had appointed Maurice of Nassau, William the Silent's eldest Protestant son, as their stadholder. Elizabeth was understandably confused about the nature of the Dutch leadership; for under the terms of the Union of 1579, the States General could act only if there was unanimous consent among the seven provinces. In fact, they interpreted their mandate more broadly, and the States of Holland, by far the most powerful of the seven, pursued their own policy. Leicester tried to neutralize Holland by including Flanders and Brabant in the States General, although they were now completely lost; and he declared an embargo on trade with the enemy, including the southern Netherlands, which hurt Holland's shipping. The English troops were also undisciplined, just at the time Holland was being inundated with refugees from the south. In late 1587 Leicester returned to England.

The ancestral enemies, England and France, were forced into an uneasy alliance against Philip II, the only European prince of the time who made religion his sole criterion of foreign policy. The others had to consider issues of national sovereignty. The League party in France that preferred Catholicism as imposed by Spain even to toleration for Huguenots, let alone rule by them, was a vocal minority with no equivalent in England, even among the most adamant Puritans who were trying to push Elizabeth into a more comprehensive religious reform (see Chapter 10). In the late 1580s Cecil and other English councillors wrote increasingly of the 'queen and the state'. Corresponding to the notions of the French *politiques*, the concept was growing of the nation as a whole, transcending the purely dynastic issues that had dominated earlier foreign policy. England was the smallest European monarchy, the most diplomatically isolated, and the one most likely to be affected by a succession catastrophe: Elizabeth was clearly going to be childless, and her heir was the Catholic and pro-Spanish Mary Stuart until 1587, and thereafter Mary's son James (who was taking a pension from Elizabeth by 1586). France was in the same quandary, with a Protestant becoming heir to the French throne with the death of Anjou in 1584. The traditional Anglo–French enmity over Gascony and, to a lesser extent, Low–Country policy thus yielded to the threat that both perceived from Philip II.

Philip II did appear to be in a position in the late 1580s to end the annoyance from England, whose queen he now considered to be the reincarnation of the Biblical Jezebel. He planned to build a great invasion fleet, the Armada, to dethrone Elizabeth and initially to replace her with Mary Stuart. The evidence of Mary's negotiations with the Spaniards became so overwhelming, however, that the royal Council, without informing Elizabeth, had her executed on 8 February 1587. A first Spanish force was nearly ready to sail when in 1587 Sir Francis Drake's fleet burned it in the harbour of Cadiz. A second fleet of about 130 ships was ready by early 1588. The boats were to sail into the English channel, then take on troops from Parma's army in the Low Countries and land in England.

England had had a strong navy since Henry VIII. In 1577 the experienced navigator John Hawkins became Treasurer of the Navy and changed it from a mainly defensive force to one for attack, armed with heavy artillery but light enough to be manoeuvrable. The Spaniards did not reckon either on the shallow water of the coast of Flanders; the English, with smaller boats, were able to prevent the Spanish troops from getting to the ships. Then, over the course of several weeks, the English attacked individual and small groups of Spanish ships. The Armada was eventually caught in the tides and blown around the northern coast of Scotland, then southward through the turbulent Irish Sea, and only half the Spanish ships got back to Spain. The victory over the Armada has remained a part of English national legend to this day.

The defeat of the Spanish Armada secured Protestantism in England, but Spain remained a threat, and the English and Spaniards remained engaged on the high seas and in the Netherlands for the rest of Elizabeth's reign. The queen sent aid to Henry IV of France after 1589 until his conversion to Roman Catholicism in 1593, which was followed by his invasion of the Low Countries. Elizabeth's last 15 years thus saw enormous expenses on military matters and a corresponding sharpening of her relations with Parliament which, since it was being asked for more money, was insisting that it had the right to debate and advise the monarch on religious and foreign policy, both of which topics Elizabeth considered her prerogative.

Despite the French action, the military situation turned decisively in favour of the Protestants in the northern Netherlands in the 1590s. Philip II had decided to concentrate on France, to prevent Henry IV from consolidating power. Although the other states still resented Holland, Johan van

Oldenbarnevelt (1547–1619), the pensionary of Rotterdam who had risen in the entourage of William the Silent, emerged as the main Dutch leader. In 1586 he was made Advocate of the States of Holland, amounting to their spokesman in the States General. The States General in theory, but the States of Holland in fact, replaced the Habsburg Council of State as the chief power in the Dutch state. In the 1590s the armies of the new stadholder, Maurice of Nassau, took substantial territories on the south and east, including nearly half what the United Provinces eventually contained outside Holland. Many of them, as frontier posts, had strong fortifications. This offensive moved the border beween the Netherlands and Spanish Netherlands (the eventual Belgium) slightly south of the Scheldt, and the campaigns gave Maurice renown as a military genius, although in fact he was quite cautious and involved the States in virtually all military decisions.

The peace between Spain and France in 1598 posed a potential threat from France, but Philip II's death helped the Dutch. His will gave the Spanish Netherlands to his daughter Isabella and her husband, Archduke Albert of Habsburg, who were to reside in Brussels. Spain continued to maintain an army in the Low Countries, but the Dutch resisted compromise on religion, and the Spaniards were anxious to extricate themselves from a war they could not win and its associated expenses. In 1600 Maurice occupied north-western Flanders. The Spanish commander, Ambrosio Spinola, got behind the Dutch force in brilliant manoeuvres and actually invaded the north in 1606 before withdrawing along the line of the IJssel river. There were no further border changes after that year, and a 12-year truce with Spain was signed in 1609. Although Spain only recognized the independence of the Netherlands officially in 1648, the United Provinces were an independent state in fact.

Even before the struggle with Spain was ended the Reformed church in the Netherlands was torn by internal conflict. The north Netherlanders were more anti-Catholic than pro-Reformed in the late sixteenth century, but the Reformers gained disproportionate influence because they were more zealous and had increasing state support after the death of William the Silent, while Catholics had the stigma of being associated with Spain. Synods met annually in the individual provinces. The consistory, consisting of local church councils dominated by lay elders and deacons but also including preachers, controlled religious doctrine and practice. Many consistory leaders were city regents, and they agreed that there should be a single state church, but they resisted the preachers' demand that they end religious dissent by force. The preachers' influence increased over time, helped by the strong Calvinism of the numerous refugees from the southern Netherlands, and the dispute became extreme in the seventeenth century, involving national synods and the States-General.

Gloriana in Twilight

The English presence in the Netherlands became anachronistic as the Dutch took over their own defence. Elizabeth was 65 in 1598, having outlived her own generation of advisers. The Dutch by now wanted complete independence; Elizabeth wanted not an independent Netherlands, but toleration for Protestants and no Spanish troops in the region. When the English were left out of the peace negotiations that ended the Franco-Spanish war at Vervins in 1598, Elizabeth withdrew from the Low Countries, and in return the Dutch agreed to retire their war debt to England. The Spanish theatre shifted to Ireland, where Spanish troops helped the rebellion that broke out in 1594; England remained technically at war with Spain until 1604.

Elizabeth was not particularly popular at the beginning of her reign, but she learned to manipulate public opinion masterfully. She often showed herself publicly on 'progresses', and appeared personally at the Inns of Court. Although her councillors found her vacillating and quixotic, the public at large did not see this side of her. From about 1570 many local communities, evidently not at her instigation, began holding celebrations on 17 November, the day of her accession. Although she was notoriously parsimonious and did not give much financial patronage to writers and artists – her successors were more generous than the titulary of the 'Elizabethan' age – she was honoured by writers such as Spenser. She enjoyed the theatre, and had plays performed frequently at court. Her favourite court musician was the composer William Byrd, perhaps with poetic justice a known Roman Catholic, and the beneficiary in 1575, with Thomas Tallis, of a royal monopoly for printing and selling music. Although the Spanish and Irish wars compelled Elizabeth to ask more money from Parliament after 1585 than before, she generally got what she wanted without demur, despite the efforts of some Puritans in Parliament to disturb the religious settlement of 1563. For all the troubles of her last years, Elizabeth died a genuinely popular queen.

Spain in the Age of Philip II

Much of the internal history of Spain under Philip II is dominated, like his foreign policy, by his religious convictions and his need to find a way to pay for implementing them. He rarely left Castile after returning there from the Netherlands in 1559: his presence, and the development of a stifling bureaucracy (see Chapter 6), were enough to ensure that the changes that he fought elsewhere did not develop in his homeland. In 1558 the Inquisition discovered small Protestant groups in Seville and Valladolid that were connected to a network throughout Spain. Between 1559 and 1562 a series of public burnings that turned into spectacles was held in the two cities;

and Spanish Protestantism from this time on became an exile movement.

Only in Spain was there a significant non-Christian element in the population, even after the expulsion of the Jews and Muslims. Religious hostility was directed against them as well as the Lutherans, who were feared as a name even though it is unclear that many Inquisitors actually understood their doctrines. In 1556 Philip II confirmed earlier church legislation denying persons with Muslim, Jewish or *converso* ancestry the right to hold office in the church or government. The impetus for this policy came from the lower social orders, for much of the aristocracy came from a *converso* or Jewish background. Thus the Inquisition, which was an agency of the Spanish monarchy rather than of the papacy, could use the race issue against politically suspect nobles even when there was no serious question of religious heterodoxy.

Just as Calvinism, a more doctrinaire form of Protestantism than Luther and Zwingli had taught, became the cutting edge of Protestantism in northern Europe, so the tolerant humanism of the first half of the sixteenth century gave way to the Counter-Reformation in Spain and the south. Predictably, foreigners fell under suspicion. In 1558 Philip II's government forbade the importing of foreign books into Spain, and required that all books printed within Spain be licensed by the royal Council. In 1559 Spaniards were forbidden to study abroad. An Index issued by the Inquisition in 1551 and considerably augmented in 1559 was even more comprehensive than the Roman Index of 1559, which had no validity in Spain, and the Inquisition ordered the bishops to make searches of libraries. Although prohibition on foreign travel and contacts was never enforced completely, particularly where Italy and Flanders were concerned, Spanish cultural life definitely became the most isolated of Europe in the second half of the sixteenth century.

Perhaps no single episode illustrates the paranoia of religious officials in Spain as well as the strange affair of Bartolomé de Carranza. He came from a poor *hidalgo* family and was theologically orthodox, having served Philip in Flanders and England. Philip II appointed him archbishop of Toledo, but in 1559 the Inquisition arrested him, only releasing him a few months before his death in 1576 – the Inquisition was so powerful that even the protests of the pope could not obtain the prelate's release. Philip II could have stopped it, but the king tacitly permitted it, collecting Carranza's income while he was imprisoned. The reason for his confinement has never been explained, but may have been connected to aristocratic factional in-fighting and resentment at his humble origins. The fact that he had served in Flanders may have made him too cosmopolitan for the Spanish Inquisition.

There were also some religious conflicts outside Castile. Catalonia had a substantial Huguenot element in the 1560s, and bandit gangs crossed there from France with impunity. In 1569 a rebellion erupted when new laws against Aragonese subjects studying abroad were succeeded by royal insistence that the Catalans pay the *excusado*, a tax just authorized by the pope, and Philip had to send in the Inquisition and have the leaders arrested. Granada also had problems. The government had generally left the Muslims alone until the 1550s, but when the archbishop of Granada forbade the use of Arabic and ordered Moriscos (persons of Muslim ancestry who had converted to Christianity) to wear Castilian clothing, a serious uprising broke out in 1568 in the densely populated mountains of Alpujarras, one which took longer to crush than would have been necessary had not Castile been denuded of troops by the Netherlands rising. When the rebellion was ended in 1570, Philip ordered the Moriscos to be dispersed throughout Castile, which created a serious refugeee problem.

Portugal was the major gap in what had become an Iberian monarchy. In 1578 the childless King Sebastian of Portugal was killed fighting in Africa, leaving the throne to an aged uncle, Cardinal Henry. When Philip II was unable to get a clear mandate to assume the crown when Henry died in 1580, he simply seized it. Philip adopted a federal solution in Portugal, which kept its own language and coinage and was ruled by a separate Council of Portugal, just as Aragon's link to Castile under Ferdinand remained purely personal through the crown. Although the Portuguese empire was not well administered by this time and looked more powerful than it was, the annexation greatly increased the size of Spain's fleet and colonial empire.

The 1590s were a crisis period in Spain as elsewhere. A rebellion erupted in 1591 in Aragon over a combination of peasant discontent against the landlords, hostilities against the large Morisco population and dislike of the Castilians, who dominated the monarchy. The rebellion was ended quickly, but signs of trouble were everywhere. The Armada sent against England had cost Philip 10 million ducats, and in the mid-1590s he was spending 12 million per year. Supplies of American silver were about to peak, and even that only gave him a quarter of what he needed: the rest came from loans and ruinously high taxes on Castile. Perhaps symbolically, the century closed with a plague in 1599–1600. Philip II had failed in what he considered his divine mission to restore the Roman Catholicism of his grandfather's generation, which had been considerably less seamless, in fact, than it appeared from Philip's perspective. Convinced that this was God's punishment for his sins, the king sank into brooding introspection, busying himself with bureaucratic minutiae, and died in 1598. He was succeeded by Philip III (1598–1621), his only son from four marriages. Although Spain continued to play some role in European power politics in the early seventeenth century, its weakness was apparent by the 1620s. Charles V and particularly Philip II could not have done what they came close to accomplishing had they had only the resources of an improvident Castile and an unwilling Aragon. Their successors, drawing much less profit from Spain's overseas empire, and constricted by the Castilian bureaucracy and insupportable taxation, could only preside over inevitable decline.[9]

*   *   *

The major dynastic rivalry of the fourteenth century had been Plantagenet against Valois. The great sixteenth-century conflict was Habsburg against Valois, a conflict that arose from the labyrinthine marriage alliances of the Habsburg emperors, which brought them a nominal rule in the Empire, the kingship of Castile and Aragon, absentee lordship in the Netherlands and claims in Italy and Burgundy. Charles V ruled a territory larger than any prince since Charlemagne, but he lacked the means actually to govern it. The eastern and western portions of his domains were separated when he abdicated in 1556, and the Habsburgs surrendered their claims to Burgundy; but the Valois kings of France continued to see a threat from Habsburg control of Spain, much of Italy and the Netherlands, on the southern and northern frontiers of France respectively.

Reaction to the religious division of Europe became an important element of state policy in the sixteenth century, but except in the case of Philip II of Spain it never pre-empted other concerns. Charles V had problems in Italy and Spain, but they had nothing to do with religion; yet his troubles in Germany were almost entirely religious and not dynastic in nature. After the Peace of Augsburg of 1555, religious conflict receded in Germany and until the end of the century became a question of local concern that rarely involved the emperors. Religion, or, more precisely, church affiliation also led to domestic strife in England, France and the Low Countries. Philip II of Spain, by financing Roman Catholic efforts to end Elizabeth's regime in England and to forestall the danger that a Huguenot might succeed to the French crown, turned adherence to a particular church into a question of patriotism in England and France. His problems in the Netherlands, which eventuated in Spain's loss of the United Provinces while retaining the southern part of the region, were due largely, but not entirely, to his zeal to exterminate Protestantism. In fairness to him, he over-reacted to the iconoclastic riots and destruction of the property of Catholic churches and citizens, but some reaction in the interest of public order was necessary.

The nearly constant warfare and the domestic police efforts of the sixteenth-century regimes, variously undertaken in the interest of political orthodoxy, national security, religious purity and/or ethnic cleansing, strained the institutions of government to breaking point. Yet, although important changes were made in the nature of government, they were essentially refinements of developments that had been clear by 1450. Governments needed to broaden and rationalize their tax bases and streamline their civil services, but none did. Instead, they adopted short-term solutions to structural problems that by 1600 had created oppressive bureaucracies and inequitable distribution of public burdens in Spain and France, while England, in contrast, may have been relatively under-governed. The *ad hoc* had become the fixture. The nature and failure of these expedients will be examined in Chapter 6.

6

The 'Renaissance State'?

The features of the bureaucratic institutional state whose evolution was traced in Part I were developed further, but not modified fundamentally, after 1450. The desire of princes to control their subjects' private opinions stemmed from their sense of obligation, as God's anointed on earth, to quash every hint of religious heresy; and the ability of governments to ascertain deviations from the ruler's norm and enforce such control, in many cases maintaining domestic spy networks for the purpose, was considerably enhanced from the late fifteenth century. This, of course, required the expansion of bureaucracies everywhere: in Spain and France offices of state became necessary accoutrements of noble status. But this incorporated a paradox.

There, although not in England, noble standing conferred exemption from direct taxes. The great tax increases of the late Middle Ages were mainly the result of nearly constant warfare; while government offices grew, most office-holders had some discernible function, for few posts were purely honorific. This changed dramatically in the sixteenth century. Even more than in the late Middle Ages, office-holding and patronage rather than governmental function were the real bases of the expanding state, an important difference from more recent notions, at least in theory.

The religious changes in northern Europe and Spanish expansion overseas gave new financial resources to the monarchs and permitted most of them to bypass or at least manipulate institutions that had developed in the late Middle Ages to check the princes' financial greed. Yet constant warfare and bureaucratic growth caused an insatiable demand for money. Princes borrowed, but clumsily, and the sixteenth century was punctuated by financial crises that were largely triggered by government bankruptcy. Royal insolvency was most serious in France, which had no workable national tax-voting assembly and where the monarchy did not realize much by confiscating the property of heretics. All kings were seriously in debt by 1600; no amount of borrowing, counter-productive sale of offices that diminished the tax base, or American gold and silver could cover their staggering expenses. The strategies of the western monarchies were ultimately defeated by the inadequate means of implementation at their disposal. What was left by 1600 in France and Spain, although not in England, the federated states – the United Provinces and the Swiss Confederation – or the weaker monarchies of northern and central Europe, was a bloated bureaucracy which had never served a useful governmental function and now was an archaic residue.

Towards a General Cohesion

Capitals

The French kings were still itinerant until Louis XIV (1643–1715) built Versailles in the suburbs of Paris: Catherine de' Medici promenaded the realm for 3 years after 1564 simply to educate her sons about it. The English kings had numerous residences, mainly in the south, but the centre of administration and the normal meeting place of Parliament was at Westminster, which was then a fortified suburb of London. The Castilian court usually stayed at Toledo, but Spain only began to develop a permanent capital under Philip II, who built the Escorial palace near the geographical centre of Spain and then moved the court from Toledo to nearby Madrid, which from tiny beginnings quickly became a large city. Naples continued to be the administrative centre of Spanish Italy, and elsewhere the larger Italian cities evolved into a network of states that essentially replicated their medieval *contadi*, but with a decline of municipal institutions in favour of local *signori*. Vienna, which had been the favourite residence of the Austrian Habsburgs since the late thirteenth century, became a capital briefly in the sixteenth century, only to decline in favour of Prague under Emperor Rudolf II (1576–1612). Amsterdam was the economic capital of the Dutch Republic, but The Hague was preferred by the stadholders, and the two did not become administrative centres until later. As the government became sedentary, its bureaucracy expanded and enlarged the capital city. The capitals were essentially consumer cities, with the partial exception of London, which handled the bulk of England's export trade in the sixteenth century. Their bureaucratic and judicial element, together with the enormous expenditure of even the most impecunious monarchs on personal luxuries, caused the capitals to become sites of specialized trades and exotic merchandise.

Embassies and Ambassadors

The development of permanent capitals contributed to an important innovation of the period after 1450: a professional diplomatic corps headed by a resident ambassador in the foreign capital. The Italian cities pioneered the practice, maintaining agents in the other major cities by 1450, although generally as messengers and informants who lacked plenipotentiary power to negotiate and bind the home government. They were expected to file regular reports and await instructions before taking action, but during the religious quarrels some ambassadors intervened covertly in local affairs to further their masters' interests. Ferdinand of Aragon established five embassies, at Rome, Venice, London, Brussels and the Habsburg court, while Francis I appointed 72 resident ambassadors in addition to numerous *ad hoc* envoys. By the 1520s some courtiers were specializing in diplomacy, not only representing their home governments, but using their bureaux as espionage centres through which they could obtain key information from domestic servants and tradespeople who could move about unsuspected and whose information could be bought for a pittance. A maid of Henry VIII's unfortunate queen Anne Boleyn was an agent of the Spanish ambassador in London, whose government was mortally offended at the treatment of Anne's predecessor, Catherine of Aragon. The Spanish embassy in London fed Philip II with dispatches that probably exaggerated if not the numbers of Roman Catholics in England, then at least their political influence, and then outraged the court by intriguing with Mary Stuart. By this time most foreign emissaries were permitted to celebrate their own religious rituals in the countries to which they were assigned, except for Protestant ambassadors to Spain. The religious wars and the involvement of Spain in most of them meant curtailing permanent liaisons in foreign parts, but these were resumed in the seventeenth century.[1]

The principle of territorial immunity for foreign nationals is not new, although their formal connection with government goes beyond medieval practice. Much of Europe's long-distance trade in the late Middle Ages was conducted through colonies of foreign merchants in the major ports (Chapter 3). The Italian city governments ruled their overseas enclaved colonies directly from home. In their case, and also that of the Hanse merchants in Bruges, London and Novgorod, privileges granted by the local régime included possession of properties that were safe havens for the foreigners. Barcelona established consulates for its citizens living abroad. The consuls, who were considered agents of the home city, or other officials had jurisdiction over both criminal and civil cases involving their own nationals if no native person was involved. They handled the diplomacy of their home governments with the relevant overseas powers, and naturally this included some spying, which along with their economic privileges caused resentment. A persistent problem in Hanse relations with Flanders was the Germans' claims that their rights had been violated by an overly zealous Flemish official. The privileges were both personal/national and territorial for at least their commercial halls within the overseas community. It is not a major legal step from this to the embassy as an immune territory.[2]

The victory of the classical curriculum as the standard of education (see Chapter 9) meant that rulers and their diplomats had a common frame of reference, although, perhaps surprisingly, it was not of language. Latin had declined in favour of French as a language of diplomacy in the fourteenth century, and the classical Latin upon which humanists insisted was not suited for the subtleties of contemporary exchanges. Most rulers were at least bilingual in speech, but they did not speak Latin, although all read it. Latin was still used when the parties could not speak each other's vernacular, but by mid-century, although the greatest diplomats and resident ambassadors were all skilled Latinists, their subordinates merely read it.

The extent to which the states of early modern Europe (excluding England) were 'national' is problematical. France was only unified territorially from 1559. The 'Spanish' monarchy was really federal, and Germany and Italy remained fragmented. All the vernacular languages had so many dialects that communication between extremes could be difficult, and Latin was a palliative only among the most highly educated. While in 1500 only Spain and Bohemia had significant religious or ethnic divisions, all except Spain and Italy were bitterly divided along confessional lines by 1600, and in some places emigration for religious reasons, particularly after 1555, led to ethnic problems, although the high level of skill displayed by most refugees promoted their assimilation.

Forms of State

Monarchy was the most common form of government, but it was far from being the only one. In the Netherlands the Spaniards ruled as dukes and counts of individual principalities rather than as kings. After the Dutch Republic split from the Habsburg south after 1579, the stadholderate only became hereditary in the late seventeenth century, and was converted into a monarchy only in 1830. Maximilian I was the last Roman Emperor of the German nation who exercised even a minimum of power in Italy. His Aragonese descendants, who were not emperors after Charles V, ruled the kingdom of Naples, the only monarchy in Italy. In central Italy the popes ruled nominally, balancing the Spaniards against the French. The north Italian cities remained powerful economically throughout the early seventeenth century, and particularly in the case of Venice this was translated into international influence. But after 1450 control over the republics, city and *contado* alike, passed to *signori*, and remained with *signori* in places that had long had them, such as the Este of Ferrara. In no case did a republic replace a duchy or other quasi-monarchical principality. The most famous evolution of this sort occurred at Florence, where Cosimo de' Medici, great-great-grandson of the brother of the Cosimo who had made the family's political fortunes after 1433, became duke of Florence in 1537 and Grand Duke of Tuscany in 1569.[3]

The modern state is associated with the exaltation of reason of state over questions of public or private morality. Yet the public shock with which Niccolò Machiavelli's views on this subject were received (see Chapter 9) is a delusion: leaders have behaved in a 'Machiavellian' fashion since the beginning of human history. The very rulers who could have been the models of a non-Italian Machiavelli, notably Henry VIII of England, expressed public outrage at Machiavelli's views and had his books banned. Edward I of England may have had personal moral standards that were higher than those of Henry VIII, but he was no more sparing of his subjects' pocketbooks or deceitful and violent in his foreign policy than his descendant.

Scholars have used various criteria to classify the states of the late Middle Ages and early modern Europe. The most obvious point of differentiation among monarchies (federated states such as the Netherlands and the Swiss Confederation are a case apart) is the constitutional or parliamentary state, such as England, where legislative and financial powers are shared between the crown and an assembly representing the citizenry, and the absolutist state, in which the ruler has both executive and legislative power. Assemblies that were at least partly representative – even when based on the principle of social classes or 'estates', rather than developing a bicameral form that crossed estate lines, basing representation mostly on locality rather than social rank – tended to restrain the growth of the bureaucracy that became the instrument *par excellence* of rulers who had absolutist pretensions. As early as the Provisions of Oxford of 1258, when Parliament was in its infancy, the English barons were trying to force the king to stop channelling funds into his household bureaucracy that should have gone directly to administrative departments with permanent offices 'out of court'. Later, there was some growth in patrimonial office-holding in England when Parliament was weak in practice, such as during the Tudor period, but after 1660 Parliament regained the initiative and made offices dependent upon itself. The opposite happened in Poland and Hungary, where strong parliaments took power from the monarchy and turned it over to the local nobility, rather than to a royal bureaucracy, which they effectively prevented from forming. Thus the central parliament became an agent of decentralization, while in France and Castile, where assemblies were weak, the kings ruled a central administration through a civil service.

The size and character of the bureaucracy are thus very important. Places that already had coherent local governments when national governments were formed, rather than having local institutions superimposed by kings, were generally better able to limit royal absolutism than those where local government followed national. England relied largely on unpaid local officials who served as Justices of the Peace and in other capacities for prestige, a sense of duty and the patronage that accrued to such positions; its royal civil service was quite small. In France and Spain, royal absolutism was consolidated by an oppressive and in many cases redundant bureaucracy. Even in places where the bureaucracy was strong, previously existing local traditions restrained royal absolutism. The strength of provincialism in France and the considerable extent of local autonomy before 1450, particularly in the north, helped to defeat in practice the claims that the monarchy made to sole jurisdiction; and the federal structure in Spain, with Castile and Aragon/Catalonia linked only through the monarchy, had a similar impact.[4]

Military Changes and Public Finance

Another important variable is the extent and timing of the state's involvement in expensive warfare and international conflict. States that avoided warfare, which was even more ghastly for its victims and more ruinously destructive and expensive for its perpetrators than before, could generally avoid bypassing traditional means of raising money. Thus, even when the ruler was absolute in theory, if his needs were moderate in practice, unrest among his subjects that might have led to a greater degree of public participation remained minimal. Except for the posturing of Henry VIII in his early years and again after 1542, the English monarchs generally stayed out of war until Elizabeth's problems with Spain. Thus the crown did not have to call Parliament often for money, and governed unchallenged until it required either funds or statutes. In France and Spain, the great military powers, the crown needed so much money for warfare that the kings either acted independently, in the case where there had been no institutional constraints on their fiscal discretion in the late Middle Ages (France), or found ways to subvert their assemblies (Spain in the case of Castile, but not Aragon). An *ad hoc* expedient to meet a military emergency tended to remain in place after the problem had passed.

The most expensive of the military technological changes were fortifications, notably the *trace italienne*, which used larger, angled bastions and more elaborate outworks that were more effective against gunpowder than earlier fortification styles. The French observed this style during their Italian campaigns in the 1490s, and it had been adopted generally in northern Europe by 1600. Armies had become largely infantry by the fourteenth century, although nobles continued to dominate the cavalry and command posts. In the late Middle Ages English and Welsh infantrymen had used longbows, while pikes were preferred on the Continent, during the sixteenth century both cavalry and infantrymen used firearms, the pistol for the cavalryman, the arquebus and musket for the infantry. This change made weapons more expensive and required more training, and this in turn meant that the armies were less frequently than earlier demobilized once hostilities ceased. With the increased importance of infantry, which was generally recruited from the lower social orders, came increased importance of numbers. Armies grew to enormous size. Spain had 20,000 soldiers under arms in the 1470s, and 200,000 in the 1590s.

The French army grew less spectacularly, from 25,000 in the 1470s to 80,000 in the 1590s, nearly doubling by the 1630s. Sweden and Russia were much smaller but growing proportionally; and the size of armies everywhere grew tremendously during the seventeenth century. But while the modern state permits no legitimate military force other than its own, this was not true in the 'new' monarchies of the sixteenth century. In both France and England, clientage continued to be very important. Great nobles were clients of the king, lesser nobles of the great, and the clienteles overlapped. Much of the royal army under Francis I was made up of client-armies of great nobles; the nobles used them as independent forces after 1562. The domestic military preparedness and the large private forces that were deployed during the wars of religion cannot be explained without reference to this situation.[5]

The Notion of Nation

The modern sense of 'nation' really only takes form on the continent in the seventeenth century. Regional peculiarities continued to be profoundly felt everywhere, and in France they were hardened in religious divisions. In Spain the crowns of Castile and Aragon remained technically distinct even though they were held by the same persons after 1516, and several states were ruled by foreigners. Charles V came to prefer Spain over his other domains, but he was born in Flanders. His son, Philip II, never left Spain after returning from the Netherlands in 1559, but he was resented in Aragon as a Castilian. For most of the century Italy and the Netherlands were ruled from Spain. The German monarchy in its identification with the Holy Roman Empire was effective only in the Habsburg family lands, and Norway and Denmark had the same king from 1450, while the Balkan states were ruled variously by the Germans and French, and Poland by Swedes and Frenchmen.

Despite the large number of non-native rulers, the evolution of nations was a largely internal development. National boundaries were changed little by the warfare of the sixteenth century. Spain annexed Granada from the Moors; the Swiss Confederation *de facto* became independent of the Empire. Spain also annexed Milan and Naples, but Naples had been held for long by a branch of the Aragonese royal house. Elsewhere in Italy the local regimes changed, but there was no more development of a nation than in Germany, where the decline of the Teutonic Order was paralleled by the growth of Brandenburg and Bavaria; while, at least before 1555, the Habsburgs were probably weakened rather than strengthened by their attentions to Empire. The one major state creation, technically occurring in the seventeenth century rather than the sixteenth, was the United Netherlands, a residuum of the late medieval Burgundian state as filtered through Spanish occupation and separation from the southern Low Countries.

Changes in the Law

Most rulers of sixteenth century Europe were able to find ways to keep their subjects from limiting their exercise of power, even if they had to violate the law to do it. In England the manipulation of Parliament by the early Tudors did not destroy its effectiveness as an institution, while the Castilian kings eviscerated the Cortes, and the French Estates-General was already systemically too weak by 1500 to have had much chance of revival even when the kings were weak after 1559.

First, the kings issued increasing numbers of statutes. In England as on the Continent, the zeal to regulate and codify became a hallmark of the state. Henry VIII's eight-year 'Reformation Parliament' produced 333 new statutes. Princes used the new print medium to promulgate their regulations; as early as 1476 the Spanish kings were publicizing their statutes and administrative ordinances by having them printed in multiple copies and sent throughout their kingdoms. The French kings had their edicts printed and circulated, usually prefacing them with high-sounding clichés about freedom and nationhood. Ignorance of the law was no conceivable excuse for violating it in the sixteenth century.[6]

Second, even in Roman Catholic areas the state exercised much greater powers over the churches and their courts by 1600 than in 1400, and the Protestant states, including the petty despotisms of Germany, simply began judging actions that previously had been handled by the ecclesiastical arm. Thus the religious changes of the sixteenth century led to increased power for the state. Society's lay rulers wanted a more punitive system, but so did the church, although for different offences: the Calvinists wanted to criminalize such things as blasphemy, swearing and Sabbath-breaking, and they had considerable success in the early Dutch Republic and in Scotland. In England 'bawdy courts' continued to try morals cases involving laypeople in which no royal statute was involved, although they did not protect criminal clergy from the secular arm, as their medieval ancestors had done.[7]

The secular states exercised considerable control over their churches even before 1450, but two important changes occur in the sixteenth century. First, the pope recedes into insignificance as a factor in international relations after 1559. Whether such popes as Paul III and Paul IV fought the emperors or the French depended on which great power they thought more threatening to the papacy's and particularly their own natal families' material interests in Italy. Thereafter neither side paid much attention to them. Second, rulers had always assumed that their control over the institutions and particularly the finances of their churches gave them the right to determine doctrine, but conflicts about doctrine became much more serious after 1517, and thereafter the king regarded adherence to the state church, which included a doctrinal position, as a recognition of his sovereignty. The notion that someone could be a loyal citizen while diverging from the ruler's religious beliefs only begins to be voiced seriously in the late sixteenth century. The pope's role as the arbiter of doctrine throughout western Christendom as a whole was assumed by lay rulers, most of whom had some humanist and theological training. They legislated on religious matters for their subjects, and were ready to pounce on any suspicious utterance as a sign of heresy.

Although rulers insisted on religious uniformity among their subjects, this concern did not often extend to foreign policy. Charles V and Philip II fought the French almost continuously, although both were Catholic powers, and the French allied with the Turks against the emperor. Charles V had insisted on doctrinal uniformity among his German subjects by 1521, but he only went to war with the Protestant princes to enforce his convictions in the 1540s. After 1555 there is little confessional warfare in Germany for half a century. Elsewhere, the wars of the second half of the century were more religious in character than those of the first half. France was preoccupied with internal religious warfare, and Spain's efforts to maintain Roman Catholicism in the Low Countries, preserve it against the Huguenots in France and if possible to reimpose it in England took the form of religious crusades. By the seventeenth century a Roman Catholic-*versus*-Protestant context of the wars is possible only in Germany and in France, as the monarchy whittled away at the guarantees given to the Huguenots in 1598. Elsewhere the divisions were within either the Protestant or Roman Catholic communities.

The kings and their administrations extended their power also by claiming that if their courts did not have original jurisdiction in all cases, any matter could be appealed to them. Court records support the complaints of contemporary moralists that there was a marked increase in litigiousness after the plagues of the fourteenth century. People were demonstrably more violent than before, and the elimination of entire families made actions over inheritances among distant relatives problematical. In early modern England the number of criminal cases rose but merely kept pace with the rising population, suggesting that the rate of criminality was not increasing. Civil actions, however, rose precipitously: the number of cases handled at King's Bench and Common Pleas rose from 2100 per year in 1490 to 13,000 in 1580 and 29,162 in 1640.

Appeals, however, were encouraged selectively. Many cases continued to be handled by arbitration, as in the Middle Ages, without ever reaching formal trial. Even in England, where public prosecution *ex officio* of crime was much more common than on the Continent, the state had no interest in further punishment as long as the parties could come to an agreement on the liability of the accused before a court reached a verdict. Some cases, such as close-breaking and trespass, could be handled either by a criminal or civil prosecution in England. Criminal prosecutions brought no compensation to plaintiff, but civil prosecutions did. Thus most plaintiffs preferred civil to criminal actions, and out-of-court settlements to those in court. Arbitration was encouraged by the fact that fines were extremely high and were rising, and in both civil and criminal prosecutions they went always to the state.[8]

Thus the authorities often encouraged litigants to settle in civil actions in which the prince had no controlling interest. The Castilian *Cortes* in 1532 asked the king to refuse to hear criminal actions between relatives. Some guilds prohibited their members from bringing criminal actions against one another, and local community courts often brought cases to trial, only to find that no one was willing to testify, since testimony could expose the witness to hostility from the defendant and his friends. For all these reasons, the gaps in the court structure show both higher rates of criminality than the formal records reveal, and that for all the talk about absolutism in the early modern state, the central governments themselves had no desire to bring all legal actions under their purview, even those involving violence.

Yet there can be no doubt that conflicts were intensifying, even if many of them did not reach the courts, and the authorities felt a need for fixed rules. Roman law continued to be incorporated into the state policies of France, and it also spread elsewhere, especially in Germany and the Low Countries. The legal profession grew enormously. Critiques of lawyers are found in late medieval moralistic literature and were taken over by theologians of all persuasions in the sixteenth century, arguing that they subverted God's law for human. The regime of customary, unwritten law was thought to give the lawyers too much leeway for interpretation and corruption, and use of written codes and law books was recommended, which furthered the reception of Roman law, granted that local customs had been put into written form since the central Middle Ages. But the codes simply made everything more complicated, as people tried to get around them.

In Germany, where Roman law had the greatest impact in the sixteenth century, the change was mainly in civil law, while criminal practice was left to princely discretion. Charles V issued a common criminal code for the Empire in 1532, the *Carolina*, based on the principles of Germanic customary law, but in the absence of an imperial bureaucracy this simply established parameters within which the princes could operate. The Roman civil law that had an impact on the west was late imperial law, and by the time it had developed and been codified it contained sophisticated ideas concerning property, proof and evidence, and relied on the prince for enforcement.

The size of Germany and the institutional weakness of the emperor meant that the most successful application of Roman law and notions of juridical uniformity occurred at the local level, when the authorities were relatively unconstrained by a central authority. The late date of composition of the *Body of the Civil Law* (AD 529–535) meant that it was associated with the emperors and thus with authority, although not entirely accurately. From the emperor, lawmaking authority passed in Germany to the princes, who were as locally absolutist as circumstances permitted, collecting data, keeping people under surveillance and interrogating everyone from high councillors to obscure peasants. Given the endemic turmoil, the desire to keep track of everything was understandable. People were expected to inform on their neighbours in such matters as blasphemy, absence from church services and violations of industrial regulations. Bavarian records from the late sixteenth century show that notice was taken about absences from the annual oath-taking ceremony, who had impregnated whom, and similar concerns. Not all states of early modern Germany were strong enough to make this change good, but the authorities in Bavaria, electoral Saxony, Tyrol, Brandenburg, Austria and the archbishoprics and some bishoprics created virtual police states.[9]

Roman law also continued to have a great impact in France. Since it made the prince the lawgiver, the main source of law in France came to consist of what the king decreed by ordinances or edicts. By the sixteenth century the kings were 'reforming' local customs, claiming that the 1453 ordinance (see Chapter 2) had given the royal government the authority not only to publish ancient customs, but also to revise them, abolish old ones and create new ones. Clearly wishing eventually to have a single law of France, Francis I in 1517 appointed a commission to publish a corpus of royal sources of French law. The task was interrupted, then resumed by an ordinance of 1579. Since it was a matter of variation of detail, the codification simplified the differences and concentrated on common points. Regional customs thus became firmer, and those with the largest original area were borrowed and used as references. Popular consent remained a legal fiction, although some claimed that the local Estates had to proclaim the revised customs in order for them to have legal validity. Thus by the early seventeenth century custom had become royal law, although not a unitary royal law for the entire realm.

Limited Monarchy in England: The 'Tudor Evolution in Government'

Geoffrey Elton's classic thesis of a fundamental change in English government during the sixteenth century[10] remains the starting point of debate, but it was clearly overdrawn. Elton was thinking of the period of Henry VIII, particularly the time of Thomas Cromwell's ascendancy in the 1530s. Yet the rise of Cromwell was personal rather than being tied to an office. Virtually all monarchs relied on one or two chief ministers, but the office or offices occupied by this person might change with the death of the master or the death or disgrace of the servant. The chancellor was usually the most powerful civilian official, and Henry VIII's first chief ministers were his chancellors, Thomas Wolsey and Thomas More. Cromwell, the next royal amanuensis, controlled the court from 1534 through the position of Chief

Secretary. After his fall in 1540 the choices were less structured, particularly during Edward VI's minority regime. Elizabeth revived the position of First Secretary for William Cecil, but by the 1570s she actually relied on three major advisors, while Cecil, although still the most influential, moved to the Treasury.

Like 'Renaissance', 'Tudor' is a broad notion. Important changes in government inevitably occurred during the rule of a dynasty lasting 118 years. Significant policy developments under Edward IV, the Yorkist whom the Tudors considered a usurper, foreshadowed ones that became clearer with Henry VII. Edward made important strides in recovering and reorganizing the royal domain. Although the French monarchy by this time was sufficiently unconstrained by assemblies to be able to tax at need and regularly, the English kings had to have a large income-generating royal demesne if they were to hope to dispense with the need to ask Parliament for subsidies, which were usually voted only with conditions attached. Henry VI had granted out immense amounts of land to favourites, with the result that the deficit was at least five times the normal annual income of the crown by 1450. By a combination of confiscation of lands of his opponents, seizure of the lands of the house of Lancaster, bills of attainder and resumptions through escheat and wardship and repurchase, Edward IV began a process of reconstituting the royal domain that was continued by Henry VII, only to be reversed with the profligate expenditure of Henry VIII. Edward and Henry VII also profited by an upsurge in revenue from the customs due to an increase in cloth sales overseas. Since both kings persuaded Parliament to vote them the revenue from the customs for life, a practice considerably more controversial when Richard II had done it earlier, they had a substantial income independent of the lay subsidies voted by Parliament.

Edward IV also streamlined the central administration in ways that anticipated the Tudors. The king by now ruled most of England as domain territory. The domain was controlled by officials of the royal household, which Edward expanded. Edward's household had some holdovers from his father's and thus had a large component of York family retainers, who wore their livery and were maintained by them as a party. As it would later under the Tudors, the household controlled access to the king for ordinary business, and the first secretary, who used the signet seal, became a major figure. He was part of the royal household, and under Edward IV was also called Master of Requests, handling petitions that were directed toward the king.

Henry VII's domestic policies continued those of Edward IV and would have provided the basis for a stronger monarchy had they been pursued by Henry VIII. At the very least Henry VII doubled the royal income, and he may have nearly trebled it. In addition to the mixture of confiscations, resumptions of land to the royal domain and customs developed by Edward IV, Henry also benefited by developing his legal standing as feudal overlord of all free persons, a development that had begun by Edward I's reign in the late thirteenth century. Wardships were a particularly profitable feudal incident; when an heir was under age, the crown could sell or otherwise dispose of the rights of wardship to relatives of the young person, or to others who wanted only to exploit the ward's property. A court of wards was established, and would remain a major source of irritation until it was abolished by Parliament in 1646. The king also ordered post-mortem inquisitions when landholders died; this had the potential for disturbing so many land rights that Parliament in 1504 voted the king a subsidy and gave him an aid for knighting his eldest son (already three years dead) on condition that he cancel the inquisitions. Administrative efficiency and an unpretentious court also spared expenditure: direct taxation through Parliament was asked only twice in Henry VII's last 12 years, in 1497 and 1504.

Henry VII's council had a membership of about 40, drawn in roughly equal numbers from the lay and ecclesiastical peers and knights, lawyers and professional civil servants from the household. Its size diminished rather than increased during the sixteenth century, as it became a 'privy council'. As in France, 'council' and 'court' overlapped. While before 1450 most governments had used a single central Council, although often with sections having different functions, separate councils now became the norm. In 1484 Richard III established a separate Council of the North, which met four times per year. A Council also functioned for Wales, but the crown saw the Councils as a threat, and their competence had been limited even before Parliament abolished them and all other franchises in 1536, after which the king's writ 'ran everywhere'. By that time the council was divided for practical purposes into two functions: the Privy Council advised the king and handled administration, while the same people acting in Star Chamber were a court. Henry VIII ruled through a Privy Council of about 20 members. Elizabeth's was somewhat smaller, declining from about 20 in 1558 to 13 by the end of the reign, and under Elizabeth the clergy disappeared from the Council for the first time.

In England as elsewhere, the royal 'court' by the fifteenth century meant something besides the council: it centred on the royal household. Although the size of England made it more amenable to the royal will than was true of the continental monarchies, there is still considerable truth to David Starkey's observation that 'governments are like the dinosaur: they have difficulty in communicating between their head and their extremities'.[11] It has been argued that the personal role of the monarch in government was greater under the Tudors than before, but this is clearly inconsistent. Edward III's dynastic ambitions involved England in even more serious foreign complications than Henry VIII's; they were just more successful and less expensive. In 1600 as in 1300, the ruler's personal whims determined foreign policy, which was almost invariably moved by dynastic or religious imperatives. On the other hand, the bureaux of government handled an increasing amount of business: probably no late medieval king spent as much time on administrative matters as Henry VII or Elizabeth.

Thus it is clear that the ruler's personality was a more constant determinant of policy than the formal institutions through which he worked, at least at the central level. Henry VII, Elizabeth and Charles I were distant personalities, relying on their own counsel and a few trusted advisers, and using the staffs of the Privy Chamber to keep courtiers away from them, while Henry VIII and, later, James I interacted more with their staffs. But the size of the group in the royal palace continued to grow through patronage: and all understood that the royal will was the fount of patronage for them and their families.

Thus something as innocuous as a rebuilding of a royal palace could have an important impact on the way the business of government was conducted. When Henry VII in 1495 physically separated the Privy Chamber where he resided and worked from the rest of the Chamber, and gave it its own staff, it meant that access to him could only be gained through the Privy Chamber, and greater prestige was thereafter attached to service in the Privy Chamber and to its chief, the Groom of the Stool, who controlled access to the royal person. The rest of the Chamber developed more bureaucratic functions within the household. After the old palace at Westminster was damaged by fire in 1512, Henry VIII abandoned it to civil servants and the Parliament, and after Wolsey's fall in 1529 the cardinal's palace of Whitehall became the king's new palace, housing the Privy Council and the Privy Chamber.

Thus in the early sixteenth century the old division of administration into Household (the service areas) and Chamber (the government offices), which had held through the period of Edward IV, became tripartite, with the Privy Chamber taking on more functions of government. Similar changes occurred in France and Spain at this time, giving all of them a structure closer to those of the Italian princes than to the traditional bipolar structures of France and Burgundy. The change made it possible for the king to be separated when he chose from the importunings of his subjects, and even from members of the aristocracy who were not favoured by Privy Chamber positions, and created a narrowly based courtier regime. The Privy Chamber had its own funds, bypassing the Chamber just as the Chamber had earlier bypassed the Exchequer. Getting even routine business to the king required that the suitors outside, including such luminaries as the principal secretary Thomas Cromwell, should have their agents in the Privy Chamber: thus a network of patronage and intrigue, always implicit in the palace routine, became even more obvious.

Control of local patronage was also important. Much of the success of Cromwell's regime was due to his maintaining a network of informers in the counties who provided him with such titbits as people wishing a pox on the king, which could bring about a treason trial. The loyalty of the Justices of the Peace, about 40 per shire in Elizabeth's period, who controlled quarter sessions courts was critical. Particularly after the franchises were abolished in 1536, royal government invaded spheres previously reserved to the local, for example in regulating poor relief (see Chapter 8).

Although governments were largely bureaucratized and stationary, monarchs still moved about, followed by their courts and courtiers. The literary example of Baldassare Castiglione's courtier (see Chapter 9) increasingly corresponded to reality, and the courtier became a kind of performer. Several of the most famous English poets of the Renaissance were noblemen whose skills were honed at court: Wyatt and Surrey in the period of Henry VIII, and Sidney and Ralegh under Elizabeth. They were not just writers in the study, but also musicians who chanted their poetry, and in some cases fighters – Sidney died in Elizabeth's army in the Netherlands.

The court was a slippery slope. Sir Walter Ralegh became a favourite of Elizabeth's after a military career in Ireland, and she bestowed favours: a wine monopoly in 1583, a knighthood in 1585, estates in Ireland, warden of the stanneries (tin mines of Devon and Cornwall) in 1585, and captain of the queen's guard 1587, which required constant attendance on her. All of this got Ralegh numerous enemies, and he left court in 1589, yielding to Elizabeth's new young favourite, Essex. When Essex fell from favour in 1592, Ralegh was recalled to court, but his secret marriage to one of the queen's maids of honour got him exiled again. He became associated with the Christopher Marlowe circle, accused of atheism and dabbling in the occult. His final downfall began when he and his ally against Essex, William Cecil, began drifting apart. Ralegh's enemies convinced James I that Ralegh was opposed to James' succession, and he spent 12 years in the Tower of London during the next reign.

By Henry VII's time the English common-law courts were unwieldy and bogged down by technicalities and the corruptibility of some judges. Since the early fourteenth century Chancery had in effect functioned as a court of equity for persons denied redress under the common law, such as women who desired to sue their husbands. Cases could be appealed from the common-law courts to Chancery, which now began to take on civil cases that had previously been heard by the royal Council. The Court of Requests, which had originated in Edward IV's household, was formalized in 1516 under Henry VIII as an equity court in the royal household to give quick and inexpensive redress to poor litigants. The court of Star Chamber originated in the 1520s, consisting of the entire Council sitting in a judicial capacity. It amounted to a petty claims court at this time, permitting neither juries nor counsel for the defence. The royal government rarely initiated petitions in Star Chamber, and the court was a popular way of obtaining quick justice until Charles I's archbishop of Canterbury, William Laud, began using it to try religious offences in the 1630s.

Much has been made of the Tudors' frequent neglect and invariable manipulation of Parliament. The theory of 'king in Parliament' to the contrary, Parliament depended on the king for its existence, for he could call and dissolve it; and he needed it for only two purposes. Only Parliament could approve statutes, but the monarch could make do with the useful device of proclamations while it was not in session, and they remained in effect unless it repealed them. Edward VI's government averaged 20 proclamations per year, Mary's 11 and Elizabeth's eight. Many of Elizabeth's regulations of wages, prices and coinage, and her controversial grants of monopolies (see Chapter 8), were introduced through proclamations.[12]

The assent of Parliament was also required for direct taxation. The kings had had to call Parliament often to vote taxes during the Hundred Years War, but with the reconstitution of the royal demesne by Edward IV and Henry VII, Parliament was in session less frequently in the sixteenth century, and Henry VIII got away with blatantly illegal money-raising. His windfall confiscations of Roman Catholic property ran through the royal treasuries quickly, but they did permit him to do without Parliament for considerable periods. Yet Henry VIII used Parliament as a public relations device to debate and build public support on controversial issues, particularly his religious settlement. He got a parliament in 1529 that favoured his break with the pope and was willing to make him statutorily the supreme head of the church in England. By keeping it in session for seven years through the technique of proroguing rather than dissolving it, Henry avoided listening both to Roman Catholic sentiment and those who wanted a move toward theological Protestantism.

Elizabeth called 13 parliaments in a reign of nearly 45 years. They averaged two months in length, with a tendency to become longer and more obstreperous in her last years. Her parliaments were thus much longer than most medieval parliaments had been, but none even approached the length of her father's 'Reformation Parliament'. While earlier parliaments were mainly legislative, voting taxation only to meet emergencies, the balance between these functions began to shift under Elizabeth. Only one of her parliaments, that of 1572, did not vote an aid. The 'ordinary' income of the crown, from customs and lands, was declining in the second half of the sixteenth century: Elizabeth had an annual 'ordinary' income in her early years of about £200,000, which was increased by parliamentary grant to some £265,000. This sufficed for ordinary expenses, but the fruitless wars against the Scots and French throughout 1563 cost so much that Elizabeth tried to avoid foreign entanglements at almost all costs. In contrast to her predecessors, she conscientiously if not entirely successfully tried to live within her means and retire the huge debts of previous monarchs. Her notorious changes of policy, which were the bane of her commanders in the field in the Netherlands in the 1580s, were sometimes caused simply by the money for a campaign running out, refusing as she did to commit herself without financial backing.

Thus in the last years of her reign Elizabeth became more dependent on parliamentary subsidy. She had a surplus in the treasury of about £300,000 in 1585, which was gone by 1588. Military expenses were enormous. Between 1585 and 1603 she maintained a force in the Netherlands at a cost of £2 million, and the Irish rebellion after 1594 cost nearly £4 million. Against this, Parliament rarely voted more than £150,000 in any year. By the 1590s the ordinary income of the crown was about £300,000 yearly, raised by £135,000 in parliamentary subsidies and lesser amounts from the sale of crown lands and prizes taken at sea. Elizabeth none the less had to borrow for defence, and she died nearly £400,000 in debt, a figure that must be taken in conjunction with the fact that prices nearly doubled during her reign (see Chapter 8).[13]

From an institutional perspective, Elizabeth's late parliaments were returning England to the situation not seen since Richard II's time, of near-annual taxation. The medieval distinction between ordinary and extraordinary income had persisted longer in real terms in England than in France, where the royal domain was small but annual national taxation had become the rule by 1400. Henry VIII had had a golden opportunity to increase the royal domain through his confiscations of the lands of the monasteries after 1539, but instead of keeping it he sold most of it, generally at the rate of 20 times the anticipated annual yield of the land, to pay for his foreign ventures in the 1540s. Elizabeth sold most of what was left. The distinction between ordinary and extraordinary taxation was thus being effaced, as the defence needs of Elizabeth's last years, involving the prevention of war as well as fighting it, meant that the government could not function without more than the royal domain. Thus it is not surprising that her last parliaments raised serious issues of policy with her such as religion (1585–7) and monopolies (1601), and sometimes withheld money grants until she had agreed to other bills. Since Parliament's role was to vote direct taxes and pass statutes, and occasionally to act as a court, it followed in Elizabeth's view that it played no role in foreign policy, save that it could deny funds that she wanted to implement a particular foreign policy; and its role in domestic matters was limited to areas in which she wanted reinforcement of her actions by statute. Similarly, once Parliament by statute had made the ruler supreme head of the church, its role in religion was over: after 1563 Elizabeth never used it to build a religious consensus, and when the Puritans in Parliament tried to extend the Elizabethan settlement in the direction of a more extreme Calvinism, she felt that they were overstepping their bounds. Parliament had the freedom to vote up or down a proposal by the monarch, but it did not have the right to express opinions during debate that the ruler found uncongenial; Elizabeth imprisoned some members of the House of Commons for seditious speech.

The consensus that the early Tudors had built with the gentry was breaking down in Elizabeth's last years. Since there were two representatives per borough and two knights from each shire, town representatives outnumbered those of the counties in the House of Commons. But while the towns generally returned townsmen to Parliament in the fifteenth century, they were more often represented by gentry, some of whom maintained town houses, in the late sixteenth, and thus the lesser landowners dominated the Commons.[14] The number of lawyers, or at least of people with some legal training, was also rising in Elizabeth's last parliaments: combined with matriculants at one of the universities they accounted for almost half the membership of some of them.

Until Elizabeth began appointing Lords Lieutenant in the counties, a practice that was generalized under the Stuart kings, most local government was left to the Justices of the Peace, who combined justice with administration. 'Quarter sessions', rotated among the four principal towns of each county, were supposed to be attended by all Justices of the Peace, but in practice most of them attended only two or three sessions, and two justices constituted a quorum to hear cases. In practice they tried what in the modern sense would be called misdemeanours, while royal assize courts handled criminal actions, and quarter sessions handled violations of economic regulations, vagrancy, poaching, trespass, rioting and such actions.

On the Continent royal governments expanded in the sixteenth and early seventeenth century by increasing the number of locally based officials paid by the central regime. Their functions often overlapped those of local governments, and many of these offices were sold and became *de facto* hereditary. In England, however, the number of persons on the payroll of the central government remained small, for most royal government in the shires was handled by unpaid officials such as the Justices of the Peace. In the early sixteenth century the entire central government in England employed perhaps 500 men, including ordinary clerks. This number may have grown to 600 by 1550, but this figure must be supplemented to include the employees of royal officials, who were paid by those officers and not directly by the crown. The bureaucracy was top-heavy: the royal councillors and their households, the households of the king and/or queen, and the courtiers, most of them noble, account for a total of some 4000 persons actually living in the Palace of Westminster in Elizabeth's period.[15] Many officials who eventually moved into direct royal service got their start in the households of the great courtiers. Even thus increased, England had no more than one paid government officer per 3000 inhabitants, against 1 per 400 in France, which had a paid bureaucracy of some 40,000 by this time.[16]

The French State and the State of France in the Sixteenth Century[17]

The Council

As in England, the royal court in France became more clearly divided between judicial and advisory functions in the sixteenth century. The *conseil du roi* in France included a vast number of persons – provincial courtiers and office-holders as well as those of the central court – who when summoned to the council lobbied the court on behalf of their provinces or constituencies, and the major cities maintained a procurator at the royal court. The *Grand conseil de justice* dealt with 'privileged cases' that had been appealed from *parlement*, but occasionally a litigant simply took an action there because the legal case was too weak to have much chance in *parlement*. In 1497–8 a series of ordinances gave the *Grand conseil* a fixed form, with 20 councillors (32 by 1544), presided over by the chancellor until 1526. It remained in the household until the reign of Henry III (1574–89), following the still itinerant king about and thus holding sessions in the important cities of the realm.

From 1484 the term *Conseil Étroit* (Narrow Council) was used to distinguish the king's intimate advisers and princes of the blood from the *Grand conseil*, which was really a court. Procedures and membership were fluid, for the king could choose whomsoever he wished. Under Louis XI nobles constituted about 40 per cent of most councils whose membership can be ascertained, commoners one-third, and the rest were princes of the royal blood. The nobles evidently gained ground at the expense of the commoners in Francis I's period, as happened in England under Henry VIII before it was reversed by Elizabeth. The council thus consisted of an inner group that was more or less constantly in attendance, supplemented by others as needed, including specialists from various government bureaux. From the 1520s a *conseil privé* (privy council) that dealt with administration and finance was being distinguished from the advisers, the inner council. By the 1550s the inner council for diplomacy and policy questions, with which the king normally held a morning session behind closed doors, was known as the *conseil des affaires* or *conseil du matin*.

The Administrative Officers: The Intersection of Court and Household

Of the great offices of state, the most important in theory was the constable of France, the leader of the royal armies; but in fact the chancellor usually had more direct influence. This was a role originally filled by a clergyman, but from the reign of Philip IV in France and from the 1340s in England the office was generally alternated between clergy and laymen. Francis I's first chancellor, Antoine Duprat, has similarities to Henry VIII's chancellor Wolsey, who rose from a humble background to become the king's chief adviser informally, and finally his chancellor. Duprat was the son of a merchant who had university training in law, then passed through a *cursus honorum* starting with lieutenant of the *bailliage* of Montferrand. After his wife died in 1507, Duprat took holy orders and became an archbishop in 1525 and papal legate in 1530. Although after Wolsey the English kings generally relied on the First Secretary, in France the chancellor continued to lead the administration and often to preside over the royal court in the king's absence. The most remarkable of the later chancellors was Michel de l'Hôpital, who studied law at Pavia and after holding other offices became first president of the Chambre des Comptes in 1554, followed by chancellor in 1560. He was able to move between the religious parties and is known for his belief in religious toleration. His wife, the daughter of a judge who had persecuted heretics, and his only daughter were openly Protestant, which eventually caused his fall in 1568.[18]

The notion of *cour* as royal entourage, essentially meaning the royal household, was still new in the sixteenth century. In the central Middle Ages it had meant the crown vassals, then after the professionalization of the court into financial and judicial arms in the fourteenth century had become the administration. Royal courts were centres of government and patronage. The 'royal' court included the separate households *(hôtels)* of the king, queen, royal children, and occasionally a queen mother and/or brothers; England under Elizabeth spared vast sums simply because she was unmarried. Separate *chambres aux deniers* that had nothing to do with that of the royal household managed the finances of the separate *hôtels*. The *argenterie*, a purely financial office in the late Middle Ages, had become a separate arm that handled provisioning by the late fifteenth century, and had undergone an evolution similar to that of the English Wardrobe in the thirteenth and fourteenth centuries. Each of these departments had over-staffed branches that became colossal pockets of waste and patronage.

Even in the first half of the sixteenth century the French kings were building a court of great nobles who served in largely honorific posts at court, getting small salaries and considerable prestige. The greatest aristo-crats had important titles, such as the first duke of Guise, who was *Grand Veneur de France* (Grand Huntsman of France). But the most important household official even by the early fifteenth century was the *Grand Maître de l'Hôtel* or *de France* (Grand Master of the Court *or* of France), who oversaw the entire court. Francis I made this bureau the nerve-centre of household administration, and from 1526 possession of this office became the real source of power of Anne de Montmorency, who in addition to being Constable was also *premier gentilhomme de la chambre* (first gentle-man of the Chamber), a position analogous to the English Groom of the Stool. This gave him *de facto* control over patronage in the household.

Francis I organized the *gentilshommes de la chambre* into a group with specific functions, who advised the king and were also in charge of impor-tant functions. To some extent it was a renaming with more honourable title the older *valets de chambre*, making the office seem less a comedown for the nobles. Most of their jobs were *ad hoc*, often ambassadorial. Orders of precedence were revised to reflect their increased prestige and the fact that they now came from the higher nobility: in 1528 they followed only ambassadors and masters of the *parlement* in processions. *Bailliages*, *sénéchausées*, provincial governorships and ambassadorships usually went to Gentlemen of the Chamber, while important posts in the army were also gained by patronage through the household.

But advancement also came by attachment not only to the royal household but to influential persons who were close to the king. The courtiers tried to increase their influence at court by gaining positions there for their creatures, in a similar way to what happened at the English court under Elizabeth with the rivalry of Cecil and Leicester. For all the ceremonial and offices, the court was relatively open. The king was accessible to many people, and the architecture of the palaces until Henry III's period facilitated this; his work routine included audiences with citizens. Accordingly, despite royal efforts to police the palace, the French royal household tended to be disorderly, while the Tudor kings of England, whose own apartments were separate from the public, were much more private.

The early modern state generated an enormous amount of documentation. Rulers gave jobs as secretaries to people with humanist, and specifically rhetorical training. France had a 'company' of *notaires et secrétaires du roi* [notaries and secretaries of the king] whose privileges were fixed by an ordinance of 1482. By 1500 such posts were investments, and could be bought and sold. But, as happened with the councils, there was an inner group of secretaries who served the king directly. There were several principal secretaries in Francis I's time, each of whom handled correspondence concerning different functions, such as finance and war. None of the French secretaries seems to have had the policy-making power of a Thomas Cromwell in England or Francisco de los Cobos in Spain (below), but by Henry II's time France had four districts, with a royal secretary responsible for each. Other secretaries served the *Conseil du Matin*.

Provincial and Local Government

From a practical perspective little could be done to restrict the French king in the central court, but his ability to carry out his wishes was limited by the chaotic state of the bureaux of administration, which often prevented the monarch from exercising in practice powers that were his in theory. The approximately 80 great fiefs that still existed in 1480 had been reduced by half by 1530. Most of the territory taken from the English in the south-west went directly into the royal domain, but the duchy of Orléans was only incorporated in 1515 with the death of King Louis XII, who had been duke of Orléans. Auvergne was added in 1547, and other territory that had been part of the Burgundian domain only in 1559. Collateral heirs often made the process difficult: although Anne of Brittany was married to Charles VIII in 1491, the duchy was only absorbed into the royal domain in 1536. By the mid-sixteenth century the Bourbon lands were the main *apanage*, combined with the titular kingship of Navarre, held by Jeanne d'Albret, wife of

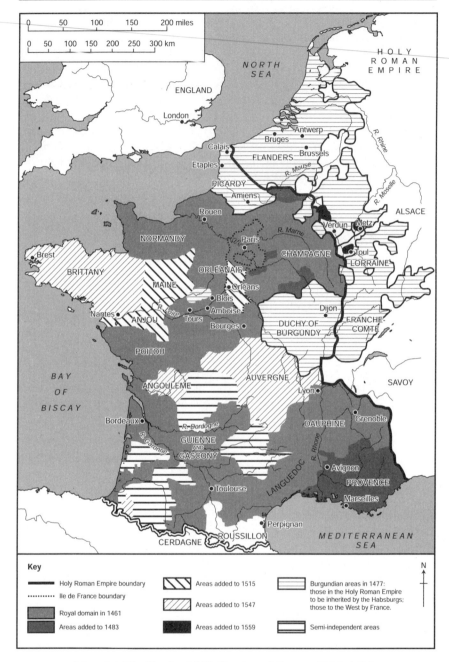

Map 6.1 The Territorial Unification of France, 1300–1600

Antoine de Bourbon. Although the crown tried to absorb the *apanages* near Paris into a central administration, those on the peripheries were governed from the royal court, though with little change in the way things were done locally. In virtually all cases, local estates and *parlements* continued to function after the province came to the crown. The *pays d'États* (Brittany, Normandy, Provence, Languedoc and Burgundy) had a strong local sense of identity that came with lengthy independence before French rule. Significant parts of southern France still acknowledged the theoretical suzerainty of the king, but were in fact independent for internal affairs.

Although a few provincial governors had appeared *de facto* in the fourteenth century, they become common only after 1450. Often called lieutenant-general, the governor was the king's personal representative, with precedence over the traditional royal officials. Although some governors turned the office into a sinecure, others were quite effective and disputed authority with the local *parlements*, which tended to safeguard local traditions at the expense of the centralizing monarchy.

Local administration remained based on the *bailliages*, which in turn consisted of local jurisdictions variously called castellanies, *prévôtés* or *vicomtés*. The number of *bailliages* nearly doubled in the sixteenth century. The *prévôté* of Paris had about 800 officers around 1450 and 900 in 1515, but it had grown to 1600 by 1559. Its *prévôté* and *vicomté*, inside and out-side the city walls, had 364 courts with high justice (hearing cases in which blood justice or banishment could be imposed). The provinces show the same trend: even Angers had 19 courts with criminal jurisdiction. This level of office-holding was a first step up the official ladder, but did not provide direct access to nobility.

In addition to areas controlled by the king directly, France had numerous seigniories controlled by local nobles. While the kings had generally brought those that were north of the Loire under their control by 1600, they were less successful in the south, where Protestant squires still controlled large areas. Most lords had only low and middle justice, so that their verdicts could be appealed to the royal courts in criminal actions; but they had almost total control of civil litigation, of which rights over lands, including income from rents and sales, were especially important. Yet too much should not be made of an opposition between royal and seigniorial justice; they were most often complementary, and the same person might hold small offices from the king and the local lord.[19]

The Nation

Despite the diversity of language and legal regimes among the French provinces, the notion of French nationhood became strong, focusing on religion and on the sacred figure of the king. The cult of monarchy was emphasized in the French histories of the late Middle Ages, becoming a focal point of national sentiment; the royal myth, centring on Saints Louis and Denis, was largely confined to the Île-de-France until around 1415, but the exile of Charles VII's regime at Poitiers and Bourges helped to spread an essentially Parisian nationalism to southern France. The fact that France's kings had been involved on most crusades contributed to the myth of France as the 'most Christian nation', which had never known heresy, and its ruler as the 'most Christian king'. St Michael had been revered by all the Valois kings, but Charles VII (1422–61) chose him as his personal protector and in effect transformed him into a national saint. Joan of Arc saw visions of Michael. Louis XI instituted a perpetual thanksgiving festival to Michael on 23 December, and in 1469 created the first French national order of knighthood under Michael's patronage. The exaltation of Michael as the French patron saint corresponds to the case of St George, who became the official patron saint of England in 1415, from which time his cult almost disappeared in France.[20]

The sanctity of royal blood was also emphasized. By the fifteenth century the kings were linked to historical myths involving a common ancestor, most often Frankish. Bonds to Charlemagne were cultivated by the court scholars of the 'Charles' Valois kings after 1364. Clovis, the king who had led the Franks to Christianity, was revered as a saint in the late fourteenth century. Most French historiography tried to derive the nation from the Gauls in the sixteenth century, as the Trojan myth lost popularity.[21]

Given that the territory under royal control increased by almost a half in the century after 1461, a major work of assimilation and administration had to be undertaken. By the mid-sixteenth century the concept of the kingdom had changed from being the rights of the king or feudal overlordship over persons, to being a specific, unified territory in which the king ruled: he was transformed from 'king of the French' to 'king of France'. The concepts of sovereignty and plenitude of power also accompanied the spread of Roman law in northern France.

The parlements

In so far as any central institution could limit the king, it was the *parlements* rather than the Estates-General which did so. Sessions of the *parlement* were called *lits de justice* (beds of justice), after the couch on which the king sat while attending sessions. The only leverage that *parlement* possessed was its ancient right to register royal edicts after examining them, to make certain that they conformed to established law and privileges. Ultimately, however, the king could compel *parlement* by a *lettre de jussion* (command) to register the edict, and he and his council could also hear cases that had been appealed from *parlement*.[22]

In its judicial function, *parlement* heard anything concerning the king or his estate, and functioned as a court of peers for the nobility. It was a court of original instance for the royal domain, and a court of appeal for the rest that had no local *parlements*; but although cases could be appealed from the other *parlements* to the *Grand Conseil*, no appeal was possible from them to the *parlement* of Paris. By 1530 there were six additional *parlements*, their structures modelled on that of Paris, each of them sovereign in its province: Languedoc at Toulouse, Dauphiné at Grenoble, Gascony-Guyenne at Bordeaux, Burgundy at Dijon, Normandy at Rouen and Aix for Provence, in order of seniority. The *parlement* of Brittany at Nantes was added in 1554.

The major changes affecting *parlement* in the sixteenth century were a massive growth in its personnel and the practice of making positions in it available for sale and eventually inheritance. The basic organizational structure of the *parlements* did not change, however, and the *Grande-Chambre* (Chamber of Pleas) of the *parlement* of Paris had 34 councillors and four presidents in the early sixteenth century. From the time of Charles IX (1560–74) the first president sat on the *Conseil du Roi*, and there were two chambers of inquests, each with 15 councillors, while the chamber of requests had a president and five councillors. Criminal cases were heard by a delegation of the *Grande-Chambre*. The various branches had a total of about 100 councillors in Louis XII's time, but the royal courts grew tremendously in the sixteenth century. Ordinances of 1552–3 created judicial circuits staffed by officials who were masters of Requests of the *Hôtel*. In the seventeenth century the masters of Requests became permanently attached to a *generalité* and became the *intendants*. Councillors were originally chosen by the king from a slate of nominees presented to him by the *parlement*, but royal appointment without involving *parlement* became common in the sixteenth century. Although *parlement* was supposed to examine the credentials of the king's choices, this was done for the last time in 1584.[23]

Inefficiency and Venality

The French crown directly employed between 4000 and 8000 civil servants by 1515, with another 20,000 in the army; this had grown to 80,000 in bureaucracy and 50,000 in the army by the 1670s. The growth was not continuous; about half of the sixteenth-century increase came in the periods of Francis I and Henry II with the sale of offices and the creation of new posts in the *parlements*, Paris and provincial. But the royal government considered offices of state less from the perspective of enforcing policy than as sources of short-term income. Selling offices was forbidden by various statutes of the late fourteenth and fifteenth centuries, but by the sixteenth century the practice was common. The kings even created some offices for the purpose of selling them for profit. By 1550 most local offices and some in the central administration were for sale.

Even *parlement*, where education and skill were imperative, was not immune. In the late fifteenth century some members of *parlement* had in effect sold their offices by resigning them to others, and open sales began under Louis XII. The office of councillor became increasingly valuable, going from a sale price of 6000 *livres* in 1522 to 60,000 by 1600, by which time the first presidency sold for 200,000 *livres*. In 1554 Henry II tried to raise more money by doubling the number of masters in the *parlement*, each of them serving 6 months. Although this scheme was abandoned formally in 1558, the new personnel were simply transferred to a new 'Council'. By 1594 *parlement* had 188 officers, including seven presidents. In return for more money, the posts were made heritable in practice by the device of 'resigning in favour': the holder could alienate the office during his lifetime, usually to sons or other relatives, and only if the incumbent died in office did the king get to resell it. The sale of offices was an important aspect of the alliance of the middle nobility with the crown: members of the royal council turned their positions into networks of patronage. The situation became significantly worse in the seventeenth century, when the system of sales went into a second generation and more offices were created, many of purely honorific character, and established as fundraising devices for the crown and a means of gaining nobility for the buyers.

Although salaries were generally not large except at the top levels, princes usually gave gifts and various items of local as well as court patronage, so the offices were much more desirable than the bare salary might make them seem. The Spanish nobility became even more a courtier class than did the French. Furthermore, even before the inheritance of offices became normal, people in the central bureaucracies were often pluralists who could hire people to perform the offices that were less important but whose salaries they collected; and they could even sell these offices, which introduced a question of competence when something skilled like a judge's position was involved. As nobles were deriving an ever-decreasing proportion of their incomes from land, and as 'living nobly' (lavishly and conspicuously) became more expensive, the slack was taken up by the profits of officeholding. Patronage from the national courts was a source of immense wealth for all levels of the nobility.

The Estates-General

National meetings of the three Estates had been called in the fourteenth and early fifteenth centuries to approve taxes for the king, but their recommendations had to be implemented by provincial Estates to be binding. However, the Estates had surrendered effective power over so much income to the king by 1450 that their presence was needed infrequently thereafter. From 1484 the monarchs more often called the Estates-General to discuss policy problems with them than to get taxes approved, particularly during the wars of religion. Although the Estates-General could submit *cahiers* (dossiers) asking the king to redress grievances, they could not legislate, in contrast to the English parliament and the *Corts* of Aragon.

Royal Finances

The centuries after 1300 saw the birth of regular national taxation, and the rate of tax increase at least doubled during the sixteenth century, paralleling the mushrooming of the central bureaucracy. Finances were far more centralized than justice in France. There was no unitary state budget or administration, which was controlled by councils, although a new *trésorier de l'Epargne* (Treasurer of the Reserve) provided more coordination from 1523. Litigation concerning the collection of ordinary revenue (the domain) went to the *Cour du Trésor*, while extraordinary revenue (taxes) was handled at the *Cour des aides*. Cases could be appealed from both to the *Chambre des Comptes*, whose main seat was at Paris, with provincial chambres at Aix, Dijon and Grenoble. After a reorganization undertaken between 1436 and 1450, the royal domain was under four *trésoriers*, one for each *généralité*; and the number of *généralités* themselves was increased to 16 in 1542. The offices of treasurer and general were joined to become *trésoriers généraux* nine years later, and a varying number of them was placed at the head of each *généralité*, administering the combined receipts from ordinary and extraordinary incomes when the distinction between these two sources became effaced, as it was in England.

In England additions to the royal domain enriched the crown, at least until the lands could be sold; but this happened in France only through the annexation of entire provinces, which brought problems of administration along with the additional property. While under Philip IV (1285–1314) the domain had accounted for 39 per cent of the king's income, and was still at about one-third in 1400: this declined abruptly to a mere 2.17 per cent in 1483, rising to 7.25 per cent by 1514 with the annexations. But this meant that while high taxation only became a problem for England in the 1520s and to counter the Spanish threat in Elizabeth's late years, the growing expenses and inefficiency of the French monarchy could only be met by increasing a tax burden that even in 1500 was the highest in Europe.

The three major taxes had originated in the fourteenth century (see Part 1). What changed in the sixteenth century was an enormous increase in the sums required and a growing inequity of assessment that accompanied the territorial expansion of the royal domain. The *aides* amounted to a sales tax: their value rose from 400,000 livres in 1461 to 700,000 in 1547. The *gabelle* was both a sales monopoly and a tax: salt was brought to royal storehouses, then sold with a tax surcharged. Depending on whether the region in question produced salt or not, the tax ranged from the onerous to the negligible. The *gabelle*, however, was the most rapidly growing source of taxation, rising from a yield of 150,000 *livres* in 1489 to 720,000 in 1547.

But the notoriously inequitable *taille* provided perhaps three-quarters of the income of the French state in the late fifteenth century. The *taille* did not even mean the same thing everywhere: in Languedoc it was a land tax, while elsewhere both land and other property were liable. Since nobles and clergy were exempt from the *taille*, the burden was thrust onto the Third Estate, which consisted of citizens of settlements with charters and in general persons not demonstrably clergy or nobility. The Third Estate was dominated in the provincial Estates by townsmen, who tended to fix assessments for their own advantage. In addition, anyone who bought a title of nobility and any land purchased by a noble from a commoner became exempt from the *taille*, even while technically remaining in the Third Estate. Purchase of such land, in the overwhelming majority of cases by townsmen, was thus a double investment, in the rent and from the increasingly obtrusive tax burden. This, of course, increased the burdens on non-noble taxpayers, particularly the peasantry.

The *taille* had originated as a war tax in the early stages of the Hundred Years War: in 1439 the Estates-General had approved collecting a *taille* of 100,000 *livres* to maintain the new standing army. Although this was not intended to be permanent, Charles VII collected the *taille* for the rest of his reign without going back to the Estates-General. Thus the *taille* became a royal and annual tax, in a manner similar to that of the *aides* after 1360. The king's total income at the end of Louis XI's reign (1483) was about 4 million *livres* per year during peacetime, but much more during war. Resentment over this level of taxation forced Charles VIII's regents to call a new Estates-General in 1484, actually the first meeting of the national estates to be called 'general'. This was also the first time that the representatives of the clergy and nobility were chosen by election in their districts, rather than by royal appointment. The Estates approved personnel arrangements for the regency and, after tangled negotiations, got the new government to diminish the royal revenue by about half. This was followed by a slow and gradual rise to 1515, during which time the Estates did not meet.

The crown, however, devised other taxes that became superimposed on the *taille*. It raised about 3 million *livres* early in Francis I's reign, but to meet needs still unforeseen when the royal council set the amount for the year *crues* ('supplements') were levied that brought receipts to about 5.5 million *livres* in the 1520s. By the 1540s Francis was levying special taxes on 'propertied persons' and on walled cities. The wars in Italy had not cost much in the beginning, but when Charles V became the target they became very expensive; in addition the effort to have Francis I elected emperor cost about 1 million *livres*, and the French were paying regular subsidies to the Swiss and occasionally to the English as the result of treaties. The need for money became greater as Spanish silver entered the picture and made Spanish military action a greater threat; by 1557 the French standing army was more than double its size of 1450, and was more expensively equipped.

The wars of Henry II's period nearly doubled the royal tax burden; although the *taille* had stabilized at four million *livres* since the 1540s, there were ever-more-ingenious supplements. Henry II began taxing the clergy, in effect nullifying their exemption from the *taille*, and the total tax burden was more than doubled in 12 years. The kings also borrowed heavily. Before 1536 the crown's fiscal officers negotiated loans with the foreign banks that had offices in France, then increasingly from financiers at Lyon at a rate of 4 per cent per fair (16 per cent annualized). Beginning in 1522, they also borrowed by selling *rentes* at 8⅓ per cent interest guaranteed on the *hôtel de ville* of Paris, which amounted to creating a mechanism of public credit. By 1559 3 million *livres*' worth of these *rentes* were outstanding, and Henry II created a syndicate of his creditors, the Grand Parti of Lyon, with the intention of amortizing the debt. Henry II in 1557 suspended payment for one quarter – the Spanish crown at the same time defaulted on its entire debt – but the crown's debt in 1559 was 43 million *livres*, triple its normal annual receipt from all sources.

Taxation of church property continued, and in 1563 Charles IX's government went a step further by ordering the sale of property of the clergy, using the king's needs for funds to defend the church from heretics as the excuse. Most of the lands and rights were promptly repurchased or redeemed by the clergy who had held them previously. Other alienations between 1568 and 1586, when the clergy was less able to repurchase and thus lay purchasers were sought, brought the crown some 13.5 million *livres*. Income from the French church, in addition to the large sums that the kings controlled without involving the Estates-General, thus strengthened their financial position.

It has been argued that the great tax increases of the sixteenth century should be adjusted in real terms by the increase of population, the fact that taxes were suddenly lowered in 1484 before starting a new rise, and particularly inflation of the coin. Such a calculation makes the result appear far less catastrophic for the taxpayer than the raw figures for royal incomes would suggest. While it is undoubtedly true that the situation worsened considerably after 1600, this optimistic analysis ignores the continuing problems of civil war, agricultural depression and, above all, tax exemptions that render absurd any suggestion that population growth meant more taxpayers.

The inequities of tax assessment and distribution were based on social status – really amounting to classes in France – local institutions and geography. Provinces with their own Estates tended to have lower tax rates than those without them, whereas the royal *élus* simply took the taxes arbitrarily. Normandy, however, had Estates, but also one of the highest tax rates in France, because it also had *élus* as a result of its absorption by the crown in the mid-fifteenth century. Burgundy, which had Estates, and Picardy, which did not, had much lower tax burdens than Languedoc, the least economically developed part of France, which had Estates and paid about one-third of Normandy's rate. The Île-de-France was taxed above the national average, but much of the tax revenue collected elsewhere was spent there; while the *bonnes villes* had long had exemption from the *taille* to give them local authority to tax to maintain their walls. But in the sixteenth century the crown demanded supplementary levies from the towns, which in turn encouraged them to borrow, since for a city government to levy direct taxes on the citizenry was politically risky. The special war taxes of the 1550s were thus a major stage in limiting the independence of the French towns. Even with this, however, the Estates, which were dominated by townspeople, tended to shift most of their heavy burden to the rural areas, a problem exacerbated by the widespread purchase of rural property and acquisition of noble status by townspeople.[24]

The Institutions of the Spanish Monarchy

Spain had a diversity of legal traditions that led by 1600 to the most grossly inefficient bureaucratic state topped by the most theoretically absolute monarchy in Europe. For all his dreams of universal empire, Charles V and particularly Philip II established a stifling bureaucratic state in Spain, paying close personal attention to the minutiae of government, reading dispatches and signing letters. The personal leadership of armies, once absolutely necessary for a successful ruler, was now exceptional. Charles V was the last king before Gustavus Adolphus of Sweden in the seventeenth century to be a skilled military commander; Francis I commanded troops reasonably effectively in his youth, but became more prudent after he was captured at Pavia in 1525. Henry VIII's early military command at Tournai was amateurish, and age and obesity soon took him out of the field.

For the civil aspects of governance these kings and, even more, their successors relied on the advice of a chief minister, even as they reserved the final decisions for themselves. Almost all the chief ministers of monarchs of this period were considerably older than the princes they served and, at least in the case of the Spaniards, came from a social milieu rather different from that of other courtiers. The age element may be critical to the understanding of the psychology of Charles V: he was faced by Luther, 17 years older than he; his chief adviser at that time was the Italian Mercurio de Gattinara, 35 years his senior. All his councillors in the Netherlands had known him since his infancy. Even the chief minister in Spain of Charles' maturity, Francisco de los Cobos, was at least 20 years older.

No state had a regular budget in the sixteenth century. Except in France, where the king could set tax rates without consultation of any wider group than his council, only the ordinary income of the state could be anticipated, not the extraordinary. Thus all governments, but particularly the Spanish and imperial, had to rely on short-term borrowing in advance of a revenue grant, securing the loans on their domain or other incomes yet to be collected. In practice this often meant leasing crown lands and mines, which were particularly significant for the long-term success of the Spanish crown.

The marriage of Ferdinand and Isabella, each of whom became a ruling head of state by inheritance, created an unusual situation. The two kingdoms remained distinct, save with a right of survivorship for Ferdinand in Castile. The two seem to have agreed on most matters of policy, but it was sometimes possible to play them off against each other. As a practical matter each monarch handled the internal matters of his or her kingdom, while Ferdinand handled most foreign relations for both. Ferdinand and Isabella treated all their provinces separately, in terms of their own laws, making no effort to bridge the gaps, very differently from the attitudes of the north European monarchies.

Lay control of the churches was a common characteristic of all 'Renaissance' states, Protestant and Roman Catholic alike. In Spain this was combined with an insistence on religious orthodoxy even before the rise of Protestantism, which was the catalyst elsewhere. Accords with Pope Sixtus IV gave Ferdinand and Isabella *de facto* control over most bishoprics: as Leo X would do with the French in 1516, Sixtus agreed to choose bishops from a list furnished by the monarchs. Isabella and her ally Mendoza, archbishop of Toledo, were interested in personal if not institutional reform of the Spanish clergy. She tried to make the upper clergy as ethnically pure as possible, enforced celibacy and required bishops to reside in their dioceses, as well as holding national assemblies of clergy to bridge local customs. Between 1476 and 1523 the three military orders of Santiago, Calatrava and Alcántara fell to the crown when their last grand masters died. The orders had enormous rights of landholding, jurisdiction and rents: offices in them were prestigious and became a lucrative source of patronage for the crown. From the perspective of potential profit to the crown, this has a certain similarity to Henry VIII's seizure of the lands of the monasteries, but with the important difference that the Castilian crown, in contrast to the English, kept the lands, although it used them as collateral for loans.

Ferdinand and Isabella are best known for their treatment of religious minorities (see Chapter 5) and their patronage of overseas exploration (see Chapter 7); but they were also important in having built an institutional structure that would serve their interests, and were most successful in changing the customs of Castile. The principle of exemption from direct taxation by social order was established at the *Cortes* of Madrigal (1476), which levied a head tax on all but nobles and clergy. The *Cortes* of 1480 was the last in Isabella's reign that presented petitions. In 1484–5 the royal secretary, Alfonso Diaz de Montalvo, made a compilation of Castilian law, but what he in fact produced was less a compendium of existing practice than a royalist code based on imperial Roman law. All municipalities had to have a copy of this document; its existence both increased reliance on royal decree and meant that the *Cortes* had no need to legislate.

Decline of the Cortes in Castile

The *Cortes* of 1480 had also voted an enormous aid and approved ordinances that divided the royal council into five bodies. Separate councils were devoted to relations with the papacy, justice, and the treasury and accounting. A fourth council of knights and lawyers that handled policy for Aragon, Catalonia, Sicily and Valencia soon evolved into the Council of Aragon, while a fifth consisted of the representatives of the *hermandades* (brotherhoods) throughout the kingdom. The Inquisition soon became a sixth; and Isabella also had weekly meetings with a separate small council of close advisers. This arrangement deprived the ancient families that had enjoyed dignities that carried *ex officio* membership on the council of real power, for most military commands and offices that involved policy went to lower-born persons, including *conversos*. The signatures of three members of the royal council were required for anything to be legal, and it thus became the centre of a vast bureaucracy. Royal secretaries were the link between the monarch and the Council and prepared the council's agenda, so naturally they became important political figures.

The grant of separate privileges to nobility and clergy meant that they had no further financial interest in the *Cortes*; and since the assembly stopped presenting petitions after 1480, influence on statutes could not be gained that way. Thus the nobles and clergy were called only to two meetings of the *Cortes* in Charles V's reign, in 1527 and 1538. This left a single house *de facto*, rather than three estates. The absence of the nobles deprived the *Cortes* of the one group that could influence the ruler. More than 100 towns had sent delegates to the *Cortes* in the early fourteenth century, but this was fixed by 1500 at 18, each with two representatives. A group of 36 townsmen, however, was hardly in a position to defy the prince. To ensure their cooperation, Charles left most municipal oligarchies undisturbed. He also confirmed the right of officeholders, except judges (a significant difference with France), to sell their posts and resign them in favour of others, guaranteeing heredity in practice. The crown also paid the 36 a salary and expenses, and usually agreed to requests for favours to individuals that passed the *Cortes*. The Castilian *Cortes* had been thus deprived of real power by the sixteenth century.

Catalonia, Valencia and Aragon, by contrast, were able to preserve their long tradition of more public participation, at least in financial matters. Each had its individual *Corts*, although they sometimes met in joint sessions in the same town presided over by the king. They presented petitions, voted taxes, met regularly (every 3 years in Catalonia) and legislated: in Catalonia laws could be made and repealed only by king and *Corts* acting together.

They also had officers to handle business while the full *Corts* was not in session. This was the *Justicia* in Aragon and the *Generalitat* or *Diputació* in Catalonia and Valencia. The *Justicia* of Aragon was virtually hereditary in the Lanuza family by the late fifteenth century, but the *Generalitat* of Catalonia was a six-member standing committee of the *Cortes*, comprised of one *Diputat* and one *Oidor* (auditor) from each estate, holding office for 3 years and controlling the entire financial system of the country.These institutions were exported to the overseas territories. Sicily and Sardinia had their own parliaments that were similar to the Aragonese. Thus the Crown of Aragon was not ruled arbitrarily from Barcelona, but rather was a loose federation, each of whose members kept its own laws and institutions and voted money separately to the king. Each had a viceroy to handle business in the king's absence.

Royal Finances in Spain

Given nearly constant warfare and the scope of dynastic ambitions, no government of western Europe was solvent in the sixteenth century. The 'Renaissance monarchs' were not innovative financiers. Without exception, all of them used expedients to raise money for their dynastic and religious policies that were guaranteed to diminish rather than stabilize, let alone broaden the tax base. Charles V was not a bad manager of money, in contrast to Henry VIII and Francis I, but he had to pay for his religious and dynastic policies in Germany, which produced little revenue. Only from Philip II's early years did the American colonies contribute a major share of the monarchy's budget. The Netherlands was the richest area, and although taxation there had to be approved by the Estates of the individual provinces, it paid for much of Charles' imperial policy. Taxes were also heavy in Italy. Taxes on Spain increased particularly after 1540, but the Estates of Aragon were so powerful that Castile bore the brunt of them. Philip II called the Aragonese *Corts* only twice, in 1563 and 1585; the small sums that Aragon provided were not worth the bother of a *Corts*, since he got money from Castile without a *Cortes*. The paradox developed that within Spain Castile reaped most of the benefits of the overseas empire, since the royal government used mainly Castilians in the Americas, but the commoners of Castile also paid more than their share of taxes.

Castile was thus easier. The Crown's domain was more extensive than elsewhere, and the truncated Castilian *Cortes* became an agent of the monarchy. The sales tax, the *alcabala,* which had no equivalent in England but which was similar to the French *aides*, had accounted for some three-quarters of the ordinary revenue of the crown in the late Middle Ages. It was collected by tax farmers and did not require the consent of the *Cortes*. While the *alcabala* and clerical tithes together gave the crown between 80 and 90 per cent of its income early in Charles V's reign, they were down to

25 per cent by the end, for from 1525 it was customary to allow communities to commute the *alcabala* payment to the crown for a fixed sum although they continued to levy high rates locally. The *servicio*, a direct tax voted by the *Cortes*, from which the *hidalgos* (lesser nobles) were exempt, thus assumed increasing importance, and Charles had to call the *Cortes* frequently. At the *Cortes* of 1538 he attempted to introduce a *sisa*, a tax on food that would be paid by all. The nobles and clergy resisted, and he had to give it up. Thereafter the upper orders were not summoned to the *Cortes*, which simply voted taxes on the third Estate.

The 18 municipalities that were represented in the *Cortes* and amounted to administrative divisions of Castile administered the *encabezamiento*, which was introduced by Isabella in 1495. By this arrangement the *Cortes* guaranteed a fixed income to the crown, leaving the 18 'city-regions' free to apportion their share as they wished. Charles V added the *tercia*, a separate tax on the clergy. Rather than royal officials, the *Diputacion*, a standing committee of the *Cortes* corresponding to the *Generalitat* of Catalonia, oversaw the *encabezamiento*. The *Cortes* was also able to approve *servicios* (direct taxes), and from 1590 onwards *millones*, and they too were collected by the regimes of the 18 municipalities. Tax farmers still collected minor indirect taxes and tolls. Thus, while in England the tax burdens were distributed more equitably than on the Continent, the peasantry bore the brunt of taxation in France and the smaller towns did so in Castile.

Not surprisingly, the monarchy took over effective control of city governments. The towns had charters *(fueros)*, and most of them had been given jurisdiction extending far beyond their walls. Most *fueros* provided that a general assembly *(consejo)* composed of the heads of families would choose the major officers. Judges *(alcaldes)* handled both civil and criminal cases, but the real administration, corresponding to the councils of the north European cities, was in the hands of *regidores,* who were being appointed by the crown from the early fourteenth century onwards and who became a self-perpetuating oligarchy. King John II of Castile had begun to sell local municipal offices in defiance of the town *fueros*: thus local government became a battlefield for investment by rival families. Isabella reverted to fourteenth-century precedents: the *Cortes* revoked all hereditary grants of offices, and royal *corregidores* were appointed in all major cities to preside over the *regidores*. While the *corregidores* had important administrative duties, they were most intrusive in judicial matters, usurping much from the *alcaldes*, who had generally been limited to minor cases by the early sixteenth century. Given that the cities had jurisdiction over large districts outside their walls, the *corregidor* was similar to the English justice of the peace in function, but in contrast to him was not a resident of the place where he served. But the *corregidores* were chosen for patronage rather than skill, and unhappiness with them was one reason for the *comuneros* uprising.

Like all 'new' monarchs of the sixteenth century, the Spaniards averted bankruptcy – in their case only until 1557 – not only by increasing taxation but also by borrowing heavily. Charles V raised large sums by *asiento*, an arrangement with some similarities to the bill of exchange by which the lender paid a given sum outside Spain, then would be reimbursed later in Castile, often with the money assigned on the next treasure fleet or on future incomes of the Castilian crown. It could only be used by persons with access to funds both inside and outside Castile, and accordingly was used to pay for Spain's overseas commitments. The *asientos* were supposed to draw 12 per cent interest, but in practice the rate at times was as much as 30 per cent. They were mainly held by Spanish, German, *marrano* and especially Genoese financiers. The *asientos* were repaid preferably with American metal; but even at the height of exploitation of the mines in the 1580s and 1590s this was only a small part of what was owed to the holders. By the seventeenth century the debt owed on the *asientos* several times the annual yield of the mines. Thus much of the crown's income was committed in advance to cover its debts.

Juros were the equivalent of the French *rente*, amounting to state bonds, and Ferdinand and Isabella started selling them to finance the Granada war. Charles V extended the practice, paying interest of up to 7 per cent, a comfortable return as long as it was paid. But in 1557 the crown defaulted on its loans, and the church declared that it was not bound to pay the interest or even to repay the principal on grounds that the guaranteed rate of return was usurious and accordingly in violation of God's law. Just as the high rates of the *alcabala* meant that native Spanish goods were often undersold by imports, so further defaults in 1575 and 1596 ruined the credit of the monarchy as well as what was left of the native Spanish moneylenders.

The situation of Castile thus worsened under Philip II. Taxation trebled in Spain during the sixteenth century, but this was actually less than the rate of inflation. As Spain lost control of much of the Low Countries after 1566, the tax burden was shifted to Castile. While Germany was of no concern to Philip II, unlike his father, and Italy was generally quiet, he had foreign enterprises in France and England, and the Dutch war was being paid for by a Castile that was becoming exhausted. Philip II's wars were financed in large part with American silver, but supplies peaked after the 1580s. Silver had become so scarce in Spain by 1599 that a copper coinage was instituted.[25]

The Bureaucracy

The sale of offices and titles on a large scale came later to Spain than to France, with the problems of the monarchy in the seventeenth century. There were 124 titled nobles in 1597 and 241 by 1631. Between 1551 and 1575, 354 new members were admitted to the Order of Santiago and 2288 between 1621 and 1645.[26] Yet the Spanish kingdoms, particularly Castile, were even more stifled by bureaucracy than France in the sixteenth century. The individual realms kept separate governments, which entailed duplication of functions; and immense overseas expansion generated not only territories to be ruled, but also revenues for the crown that had to be administered. Most obviously, Charles V was a largely absentee king in Spain. Of 40 years as king, he spent 16 years there, mainly in the 1520s and 1530s, and was absent from Spain altogether after 1543 until his abdication, when he returned in retirement. He thus governed everywhere through regents. Until her early death in 1539, his main representative in Spain was his cousin-wife Isabella, daughter of King Emmanuel of Portugal. But the real power for two decades was the royal secretary Francisco de los Cobos, who kept things under strict enough control to permit Charles latitude in dealing with problems elsewhere.

The formal head of royal administration in Aragon, preparing matters for the prince's attention, was the chancellor, who was always a clergyman. He left real power to the Vice-Chancellor, who became the head of a strictly defined hierarchy of notaries and secretaries. In Castile, the closest equivalent of the Aragonese chancery was the *Consejo de Justicia* (*Consejo Real*), which prepared documents for the monarch's signature, which was less formally structured than the Aragonese chancery and thus was liable to abuse and conflicts of jurisdiction. The secretaries were intermediaries between members of the council and the monarch, but they often simply bypassed the councillors and went directly to the king or queen.

The royal secretaries became very powerful as the state became bureaucratized beyond the point where kings could keep direct control of it. The staff of Francisco de los Cobos was responsible for Castile, Portugal, the Indies and, after 1530, Italy. Despite his great power and influence, de los Cobos always handled correspondence personally for the king; his office routine can be reconstructed from the immense numbers of documents that he signed or prepared. De los Cobos opened letters himself, then gave them to clerks, who prepared summaries, particularly of long letters; then he assigned them either to an office or to the emperor himself. He also prepared a daily summary of what was going to the king, with recommendations for how the matter would be decided. The left margins of the documents were wide, and de los Cobos placed notes there on what the king said or how he wished the matter settled. The same procedure was used for the weekly meetings of the Council of Castile: de los Cobos conveyed the recommendations of the council, again noted on the left-hand margin, to the emperor for his final decision. Even a king as conscientious about business as Charles V thus read or was read copies that had already been edited: and when the ruler signed a paper, de los Cobos usually countersigned. As his power grew, requests were often sent to him personally rather than to the emperor, and he usually responded personally.[27]

There were central policy-making and advisory councils for Finances, State and War, which had members from the various parts of the Empire and which gave the king general advice. A council of the Indies was set up in 1524, and in 1555 Italian affairs were removed from the Council of Aragon and given to a separate Council of Italy. This remained the basic outline of the central government throughout the sixteenth century. Philip II used great nobles as viceroys, diplomats and military commanders, but, following his father's example, he did not use them in the offices of the central government. Thus local family network rivalries spilled over into the court; the Council of State was their battleground as they tried to get the royal ear. Although family ties were at the base of the bitter quarrels in Philip's Council that were perhaps at their worst in the 1570s and 1580s, policy issues were sometimes involved, particularly regarding the degree of harshness needed in the Netherlands. Charges brought before the Inquisition could also complicate a vendetta.

Most of the actual work of government was conducted through the Councils of the individual kingdoms through an increasingly oppressive bureaucracy, particularly under Philip II, who was unwilling to delegate responsibility and who tried to supervise the most minute detail. The Councils reported to viceroys appointed by the king, virtually all of them Castilian. By Philip II's time there were nine viceroyalties: Aragon, Catalonia, Valencia, Navarre, Sardinia, Sicily, Naples, New Spain and Peru; Castile did not have a viceroy, since in contrast to his father, Philip spent nearly all of his time there. The viceroys had enormous powers, but they had to keep in touch with headquarters. Any abuse would immediately come to the attention of the Council of the locality, which was always made up of local people who would react badly to violations of their traditional liberties and report them. The Councils usually met daily by the late sixteenth century. They discussed all public business, including the viceroy's dispatches, and minutes of these conclaves, called *consultas*, were sent to the king. His decision, often written in his own hand on the *consulta*, was then returned to the Council, whose secretary would prepare the proper documents to be sent to the viceroy for action. What this system gained in local autonomy it lost in stultifying centralization under an enormous bureaucracy which was unable to take any action. De los Cobos and his deputies were usually able to pass their offices on to their relatives, and this hindered change, or any abolition of unnecessary procedures or offices. The Council members, in the absence of a king who had personal knowledge of affairs, dispensed enormous patronage.

The Holy Roman Empire

Imperial institutions had little impact on the practicalities of government in the Empire during the sixteenth century. The religious divisions within it gave many princes yet another excuse to oppose the emperor, who was able to control only Austria effectively. The imperial Diet continued to meet

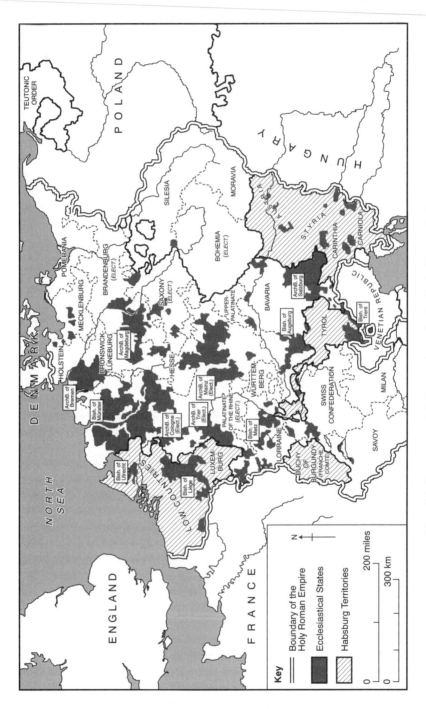

Map 6.2 Germany and Adjacent Areas in the Early Sixteenth Century

occasionally for debate and consultation, but meetings were infrequent after 1532, when Charles V returned to Spain. The Diet had three chambers: the house of electors, for the seven electoral princes; the house of princes, of whom between 50 and 60 usually attended; and the house of free cities. Although the cities financed the emperors and princes by forced loans and high taxes, including levies to finance campaigns against the Turks, only in 1648 did they get more than a consultative role in the Diet; while the knights were not represented at all.

Maximilian I (1493–1519) made important administrative changes to the Empire's structure. The Diet of Worms in 1495 proclaimed a perpetual public peace (*ewiger Landfrieden*). An imperial supreme court (the *Reichskammergericht*) was established, and a 'common penny' was established as an empire-wide tax on all inhabitants above the age of 15, while an imperial council (*Reichsregiment*) functioned as the emperor's advisory body for appointments and policy questions. At the Diet of Cologne in 1512 the territories that the emperor actually controlled were divided into districts (*Kreise*). In addition to these imperial institutions, Maximilian established a Privy Council (*Hofrat*) for the Habsburg lands alone. It took over most administrative functions in Austria, and in the emperor's homeland it thus defeated much of the purpose of the imperial institutions that he had fostered, being an agency of Austrian particularism. Thus in the next generation, with Charles V largely absentee, and concerned when he was in Germany with religion, and with his brother Ferdinand occupied in the Balkans against the Turks, the new imperial courts and revenues gradually came under the control of the territorial princes.

Provincial diets (*Landtage*) existed in most German states by 1500. Most had a three Estate structure, although the Habsburg lands, Bohemia and Prussia divided the noble Estate into lords and knights. In the principalities that became Protestant the clergy dropped out as a separate estate, and in some states of the south-west (Trier and Württemberg) the nobles became Imperial Knights (*Reichsritter*), a step that removed them from the jurisdiction of the local prince, and they thus left the *Landtage*. During the sixteenth century *Landtage* were occupied almost entirely by financial business. The ruler normally called the Estates only when he needed money. They in turn usually refused to vote taxes unless he at least confirmed or, if possible, extended their liberties. Most taxes were paid by the peasants, who had no representation in the *Landtage*. As in France and Spain, 'decisions on revenue matters were greatly facilitated by the circumstance that those who voted taxes rarely paid them'.[28] Since the princes did not have collecting and accounting bureaucracies before this time, some provincial Estates took over financial administration as well as tax voting.

Most *Landtage* did not develop a legislative competence in the sixteenth century. Although the princes often submitted matters of policy and major legislation, such as law codes, to the Estates for advice, they were not bound to take it. Some *Landtage* that had legislated in the Middle Ages simply lost the lawmaking function, which they could not exercise unless the prince submitted a statute to them for ratification. Internecine rivalries compromised the Estates' effectiveness, and the Roman legal tradition exalting the position of the ruler was very strong in Germany. Grievances were collected in local market courts, villages and towns, and sent to the central *Amt* (office) of the district: most were petitions to allow existing privileges to continue, such as access to common forests and streams. The Estates then would present dossiers to the prince, including their own complaints. Although some princes acted on these complaints in the early sixteenth century, after 1550 they were so routine, usually saying essentially the same thing, that little action was taken on them.

The right to present grievances was thus not translated into a power to legislate, and an immense number of *Landes-* and *Polizeiordnungen* (Territorial or Police Regulations) were simply issued by princes without consulting their Estates. By 1600 most states had a *Hofrat* (court or privy council), composed mainly of trained jurists who coordinated administration and served as an appeals court; and a *Geheimer Rat* (Secret Council) of intimate advisors. There were separate financial boards for ordinary finances, defence, ecclesiastical affairs and a chancery. Courts were established centrally and locally, but the offices were not for sale; the German princes knew the French problem and tried to avoid it, and the law did not make offices into property.

The spread of Protestantism and the consolidation of local institutions under the firm rule of the prince were symbiotic developments. The religious reform needed the princes in order to take root and survive, while controlling church affairs in this way also gave new opportunities to the princes, and once they had reformed religion they could use the precedent to expand their jurisdiction in other areas. In contrast to England, where mainly monastic land was seized and where the church had little governmental role except for the 'bawdy courts', the north German bishoprics had political power that was simply taken over by the secular state for the first time. Thus, while in England the benefits to secularization were mainly financial, in north Germany they were also jurisdictional.

When the official religion was established, a new Church Order was normally published either by the prince or the city government, which rarely involved Estates. The secular ruler punished violations of all religious matters, disciplinary or doctrinal. The level of social control that was possible at the local level in Germany and in England, which was by far the smallest monarchy of Europe, has since become possible elsewhere at the national level only in modern totalitarian states. The police power that is associated with establishing a new religious orthodoxy or returning to an older one gave new opportunities for intervention, including violating property rights in the interest of God's higher law. In a Bavarian case, the Rent Master of the duke reported on 'one Blaser, a burgher in Friedberg, who was reported to have eaten a piece of stewed liver on a Friday. When it became clear during interrogation that the said Blaser had taken only one bite of this liver and spat it out of his mouth as soon as he remembered what day of the week it was, a strong admonition was dealt him by the princely *Rentmeister* to be more careful in the future.' Virtually all German princes established Consistories. Faced with a problem of nobles appointing Protestants to church livings, the Catholic dukes of Bavaria established a *Geistliche Rat* (Spiritual Council) in 1570 to screen all church appointments in the duchy. Confiscation of church properties gave the ruler a freer financial hand; and his imposition of religion over the nobles strengthened his rights against them in other areas.[29]

The Dutch Republic

The institutions of the Dutch Republic changed considerably in the early years of its existence. A union was envisaged in 1579 of seven provinces that would remain sovereign in all respects except that defence, taxation for defence and foreign policy would be left to the States-General. The States-General were supposed to act only if there was unanimous consent among the provinces, each of which had one vote. Unanimity was soon a dead letter, and the States-General also intervened in the internal affairs of the provinces. In form the Netherlands was a confederacy similar to the Swiss; in practice it was more a federal state, with policy fixed by Holland, which led the rebellion against Spain and was the most economically developed of the provinces.

The States-General met infrequently until 1572, but they were in virtually continuous session from 1583 onwards, and were fixed at the Hague from 1587. It was the States-General, rather than the individual provinces, which appointed the stadholders until 1620, the most powerful being that of Holland and Zeeland. This title passed from William the Silent to his eldest Protestant son, Maurice. In principle the stadholders were administrators, overseers and judges, and the position also included a militia command: Maurice of Holland gained considerable prestige for the military exploits that kept the Spaniards at bay in the 1590s. The stadholder also selected town aldermen from slates presented by the outgoing regime. The relations of the States-General to the States and stadholder of the province of Holland thus were critical. The Holland States sat almost continuously after 1585, but the delegates could do nothing without referring back to their constituent governments. The knights, who represented the countryside, and Amsterdam were the most important delegations in the States of Holland, with the others then lining up behind one or the other. The other six provinces had similar organizations. Particularly in the seventeenth century, they tried to use the States-General to limit Holland, which often took unilateral action.

* * *

During the sixteenth century the European states were frequently at war and were always in a state of military preparedness. To this waste of resources was added the growth of bureaucracies whose efficiency decreased in proportion to their size. The institutions of royal government were not even responsive to the needs of the kings in the sixteenth century, let alone their taxpaying subjects, and their main beneficiaries were the tax-exempt groups that controlled most high offices of state. The Turks were an external threat to Europe in 1450, and their campaigns in the Balkans gave them a foothold on the Continent during the sixteenth century, and they were a naval threat throughout the century in the Mediterranean.

It is thus a strange paradox that during this century the Spaniards acquired an overseas empire in the Americas, while the Portuguese established trading ties and some territorial conquests in Africa and Asia, followed near century's end by the English, and then by the Dutch mainly after 1600. This expansion was the prologue to the later more general Europeanization through colonization of the Americas and parts of Asia.

|7|

The Besieged as Besieger: West European Expansion in Asia, Africa, the Americas and Slavic Europe

Between the mid-fifteenth and late sixteenth centuries Europeans expanded economically and, to a lesser extent, militarily and demographically at the expense of the indigenous peoples of Africa, Asia and the Americas. This growth involved a military advantage over Asian and Middle Eastern civilizations whose technological level had been superior to that of the Europeans.

Various explanations of the expansion have been given, most of which are undoubtedly part of the picture. One was a shifting balance in the sophistication of warfare. The Europeans had borrowed such techniques as the lateen (triangular) sail from the Muslims, but the Portuguese combined it with the traditional square sail on the caravel, a large but elongated and mobile ship that was developed during the fifteenth century. This craft was more stable than the Muslim boats had been, but also more mobile than other European ships. The Turks had armed their boats before the Europeans, but the Portuguese were apparently the first to install cannon on the decks of their ships, thus changing the nature of naval warfare. Turkish boats were also of flimsier construction than the Portuguese, due to their curious practice of lashing the planks together with ropes instead of using iron spikes or nails.

The Ottomans took over many of the western military innovations quickly, but with one important difference: they preferred big artillery pieces, while the westerners emphasized mobility and numbers. This in turn may reflect differing industrial capacities: the west could produce large numbers of manufactured items, even such heavy items as guns, while each gun in the east was a major undertaking. In addition, the westerners forti- fied their own siege camps when laying siege to a fort, while the Muslims

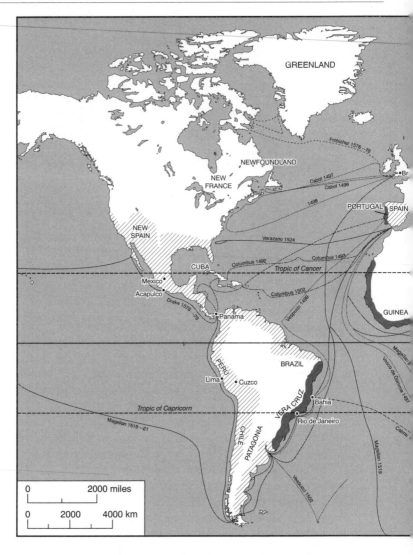

Map 7.1 The Expansion of Europe in the Fifteenth and Sixteenth Centuries

left their siege operations undefended. Islamic metallurgy was also less sophisticated. When the Venetians captured 225 bronze guns at Lepanto in 1571 they melted them down and recast them because the metal was so poor. Modern metallurgical analysis has shown that European iron and steel were also stronger.[1]

Although local communities in Europe controlled their interior market relations, sometimes quite minutely, there was significant competition both within and between larger political units. The growth of the modern state affected local trade scarcely at all, except by the high taxes that drained

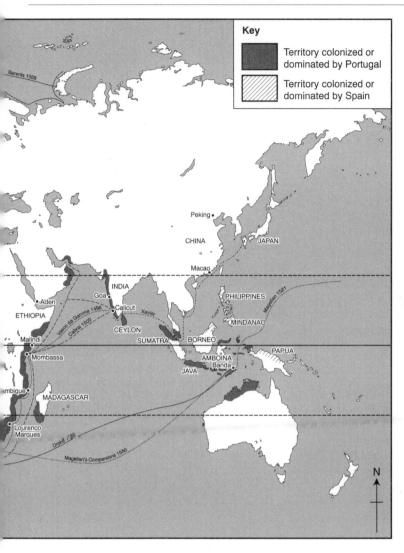

away the purchasing power of consumers; but this in turn gave the central states the resources to provide military backing to colonial ventures. The fact that capital was mobile also fostered competition and the ability to take risks. When conditions became bad in one place, as happened at Antwerp after 1577, the largely foreign-colonial infrastructure had no trouble moving elsewhere, in this case to Amsterdam.

The Castilian occupation of the Canary Islands and the Portuguese colonization of the Azores and explorations on the west coast of Africa were prologues to the more extended expansion of the period between 1450 and 1550. During this century European control was extended to Asia and the Indies, areas with which Europeans had traded but which they had never ruled politically. European influence in the extraction of raw materials and labour (gold, ivory and slaves) was extended in Africa, and the Americas and the Caribbean islands became sources of silver and gold. In the sixteenth century the Americas furnished other products, notably bullion, and became outposts of colonists who developed large sugar plantations, as happened also in the Canaries.

As sugar replaced grain as the main crop on the Atlantic islands, slave labour became valuable. The first big cargo of slaves arrived from Africa in 1443, and by the 1450s 1000 slaves every year were brought to Europe. After 1469 the Portuguese renewed their explorations down the African coast, reaching the Bight of Biafra in 1474, with more slaves, malaguette pepper (which was better than any other types except Indian), ivory and particularly gold as their reward. After an interruption during the war with Castile (1475–9) they built a fort at Elmina on the Gold Coast and began systematic exploitation. The Castilians agreed in 1479 that Africa was a Portuguese sphere of influence. Traders had to be licensed by the Portuguese crown, and the gold trade was a royal monopoly.

Columbus[2]

While the Portuguese moved south with the ultimate goal of reaching Asia, the early stages of the westward expansion were done under Castilian sponsorship. Christopher Columbus (1451–1506) was the son of a Genoese weaver. He went to sea in the early 1470s and by 1478 was an agent of the Centurione family of Genoa on a sugar-buying voyage to Madeira. In the early 1480s he sailed down Africa to the Gold Coast and to Ireland. Columbus was thus an experienced navigator who knew the Atlantic seas well.

During the 1480s he gave up navigation, becoming a cartographer and bookseller in Lisbon. Columbus was not original in understanding that the earth is round. All persons with mathematical and astronomical education, either academic or practical, knew it, as had the Greeks and Romans. It was only logical to think that the long and arduous voyage around Africa to Asia could be obviated by sailing west. Columbus became familiar with Ptolemy's *Geography,* but the book that he used most, Pierre d'Ailly's *Imago Mundi,* was also the least reliable. It had stories of miraculous and exotic peoples, plants and animals, and led Columbus into making some fundamental errors. Obviously, he had no idea that two continents separated Europe from Asia going that way. Yet a theory given wide currency by the appearance in print of an Italian translation of Strabo's *Geography* held that a second land mass, the Antipodes, existed in the Atlantic. It cannot be proved that Columbus read Strabo, but when word of his discovery got back, Italian geographers assumed that he had discovered the Antipodes. Second, Columbus relied on geographers of his own day who thought Asia extended farther eastward than it does: thus a voyage would not have to go as far before reaching land. Based on an erroneous equation of Arabic and Roman miles, he also thought that the earth was considerably smaller than it actually is. Exactly which of these ideas was uppermost in Columbus's mind is unclear: he was fundamentally an adventurer, who was voyaging for profit and social advance; thus any of these possibilities would have appealed to him.

Since the Portuguese had shown more interest than the Castilians in sailing to Asia, which, along with Africa, was the goal of all naval explorations to this time, including Columbus' own, he naturally went first to them. While in Portugal he became familiar with the work of the Nuremberger Martin Behaim, who had worked on secret maps for the Portuguese government to which details were added as new discoveries were made. The Portuguese became suspicious of Columbus, probably because he had an audience with Isabella of Castile in 1486, and forbade him access to their maps and other documents. But in 1488, the year when the Portuguese Bartolomeu Dias became the first European to round the Cape of Good Hope, making it only a matter of time before the Portuguese would reach Asia, Columbus and his brother managed to copy some Portuguese maps and smuggle them out to Castile. Their composite map showed more land that would have to be circumnavigated around southern Africa and in the Indian Ocean than was actually there, and a too-small Atlantic, which made the idea of sailing westward distinctly more attractive as an alternative to the Portuguese route. On this basis he sold the idea to Ferdinand and Isabella in 1492.

Columbus' plan also attracted the church, with its promise of converting countless infidels. After the fall of Granada in January 1492, Isabella agreed to Columbus' demand of ennoblement, the titles of admiral and hereditary viceroy and 10 per cent of the wealth of the countries that he conquered. The legend that she pawned her jewels to finance his first voyage is undocumented, but plausible; she had a vast amount of jewellery, and at other times had pawned a few items to raise small sums quickly. Sailing from Palos on 3 August 1492, Columbus stopped in the Canaries, then followed the westward currents. His three ships reached Santo Domingo on 12 October and Cuba soon thereafter. En route back to Spain, they landed on Hispaniola in early December. This was his most important discovery on any of his voyages, for the island had gold and a native culture that was wealthy enough to impress the Spaniards. Given that the Spaniards thought that they had reached some part of the Indies – now known as the West Indies – they did as the Portuguese would do when they got to the (East) Indies: they had planted a small colony on Santo Domingo by the end of 1493, then quickly exploited it by enslaving the natives in the interest of Spanish colonists.

Columbus was well received on his return, and in 1493 set sail again, this time with 17 ships. This time the crown sent judicial and financial officers as well as monks. During this second voyage Columbus's focus shifted from gold – he found little – to slaves, and he allowed his subordinates to punish and massacre the natives of Hispaniola because they would not accept Christianity, and coincidentally because they were an insufficiently tractable labour force. Although the monarchs had insisted that the natives be treated humanely and refused to countenance a slave trade, Columbus began exporting some 'Indian' slaves. Despite mounting evidence that this was new territory, Columbus insisted that Cuba was an extension of mainland China. He forced his men to swear to the accuracy of his calculation that Cuba was too large to be an island and thus had to be Asia. Yet by the time of his second voyage, several voyages had been made to and from the islands, for the navigational information from his first voyage had been accurate enough for others to follow him easily. Thus his attempt to falsify information to prove his contention that he had found the western route to Asia was easily discovered, and diminished his credibility, which was already suffering due to the lack of quick profits. Columbus was more interested in exploring than in administering, and rival factions at court got him recalled to Spain in the summer of 1494.

On his third voyage, in 1498, Columbus explored farther south, touching the Orinoco river delta in South America. He seems to have realized now that a previously undiscovered continent separated Europe from Asia, but then he refused to admit his evidence and insisted instead that it was the Asian site of the garden of Eden. Meanwhile there was trouble on Hispaniola. Columbus seems to have thought not of a large colony of tillers, but rather of a trading-post whose inhabitants would teach skills to the natives but would mainly export the riches of the place, while the Indians would provide all the labour. But the monarchs wanted a true colony, while the Indians were to be converted to Christianity.

While Columbus was on Hispaniola, news reached Europe that Vasco da Gama had rounded the Cape of Good Hope and proceeded to India. It was clear that the Portuguese had reached the Indies first and that Columbus had stumbled onto something else. The monarchs sent a new governor to Hispaniola, who imprisoned Columbus briefly. His credibility ruined, Columbus cultivated his own legend and returned to an earlier project of a crusade to Jerusalem. After raising money from Genoese bankers, he undertook his fourth and longest voyage, lasting 30 months from May 1502 until November 1504. It almost took him to the Mayan empire and the Pacific; he changed direction just before reaching each. He expanded geographical knowledge tremendously, but added nothing directly to the empire, and was eventually shipwrecked on Jamaica.

Columbus has been portrayed as a visionary, a genius, an incompetent navigator, and most recently as a racial and even biological imperialist. Seen in the context of his day, he was clearly an entrepreneur – the fact that he was Genoese is no accident in terms of explaining his outlook – whose persistence carried him far. Indeed, he often persisted in error in the face of demonstration to the contrary. The judicious conclusions of a recent scholarly evaluation must serve as our summary: quite apart from the land that Columbus discovered, he is notable for 'his decoding of the Atlantic wind system; his discovery of magnetic variation in the Western hemisphere; his contributions to the mapping of the Atlantic and the New World; his epic crossings of the Caribbean; his demonstration of the Continental nature of parts of South and Central America; his *aperçu* about the imperfect sphericity of the globe; his uncanny intuitive skill in navigation. Any of these would qualify an explorer for enduring fame; together they constitute an unequalled record of achievement.'[3]

The Portuguese in Africa and Asia

As the Spaniards moved west, the Portuguese intensified their eastward expansion. In 1488 Bartolomeu Dias became the first European to round the Cape of Good Hope. The Portuguese realized the implication for them of Columbus' voyages, although they quickly understood that he had not reached Asia. Trying to forestall future conflict, in 1494 Castile and Portugal made the treaty of Tordesillas, based on a papal mediation of the previous year. It divided the non-Christian world into a Spanish sphere of influence that included most of the New World, while Portugal got Africa and Asia and eventually a claim to Brazil, although the latter's existence was probably not known at the time. In 1501 Pedro Cabral, *en route* to India, strayed off course and landed on the coast of Brazil, which he claimed for Portugal. The Portuguese ambitions of sailing directly to Asia were realized in 1498, when Vasco da Gama reached Calcutta, having followed Dias' route, continued up the eastern coast of Africa, then struck out directly across the Indian Ocean.

The Portuguese were also using force to keep spices from coming from Asia to the sea routes toward the Mediterranean controlled by the Muslims. From 1505 onwards the Portuguese began to set up fortifications, naval bases and 'factories' along the coast of India, and in 1509 a small Portuguese fleet trapped a larger number of Muslim boats in the harbour of Diu. Although the Muslims were occasionally to attack the Portuguese again, the Portuguese dominated the sea lanes in the Indian Ocean for the rest of the century. The Portuguese blockade of the Red Sea routes to the Muslims was never totally effective, for the rulers of India were too strong for them to gain total control, but they did establish trading posts and made local agreements. Goa in 1510 was their first colony, followed by Malacca, Hormuz and Aden. Their stations at the Cape of Good Hope, Socotra at the entrance of the Red Sea, Bahrein and Hormuz on the Persian Gulf, and Malacca at the entrance to the South China Sea, their conquests of the islands of Madagascar and Mauritius and their protectorates over small Muslim states in East Africa gave them practical control of entrance to the Indian Ocean as well as a means to control navigation in it. Portugal had two captaincies, one each for the Red Sea and the Malabar Coast of India, with seven forts between them. The relations of the Portuguese with the natives whom they encountered were much more amicable than those of the Spaniards, English and Dutch, for they seem to have had some appreciation of the native cultures. They intermarried with the natives much more than the others did, which was perhaps easier for them since the Portuguese themselves were a mixture and had no strong ethnic consciousness.

Once they had established a monopoly of the Asian traffic, the Portuguese were as eager to trade with the Muslims as with Europeans. Hormuz became their staple, through which Asian goods that were being sent to territory controlled by the Ottomans had to pass. The customs revenues of the Hormuz staple were an important source of income for the Portuguese monarchy. Goods went overland by caravan from Hormuz to Aleppo and then to Anatolia and Istanbul, where the Venetians bought them for re-export to the west. The Asian voyages were long and dangerous. A voyage from Lisbon to Goa, some 10,000 miles, might require anywhere from 6 months to a year and a half, depending on wind and water currents. In the 3-year term of service that was normal for the Portuguese viceroy, he could only hope to get direct orders from home once or twice.

The Portuguese and Spaniards generally respected each other's spheres of influence, but the beginning of the Spanish conquest of the Philippines in 1565 caused the Portuguese to begin moving into East Asia, fearing that the Spaniards could cut their trade routes. From 1580, when Philip II of Spain became king of Portugal, the Portuguese were saddled with Castilian domination, and later the Dutch enemies of Castile transferred their enmity to Portugal. While the Portuguese had given up hostility to the Muslims, who were now their trading partners, the Castilians were still crusading against them. The result was Muslim hostility toward the Portuguese, leading to a revolt that started a long erosion of Portuguese power in the region. In reaction the Portuguese devoted more attention to Brazil, which was easier to reach from Europe than Asia and had only primitive tribes, not organized principalities.

The Americas after Columbus

The places visited by the Portuguese had been known by Europeans to exist, but Columbus, despite his protests, was exploring new territory. Even during his voyages others had followed his lead. Amerigo Vespucci, a Seville-based Florentine, discovered the mouth of the Amazon and explored the northern coast of South America in 1499. Returning in 1501 under

Portuguese sponsorship, he explored the southern coast and discovered the mouth of the Rio de la Plata. He developed a system for computing longitude, which Isabella had hoped that Columbus could do, and came within 80 kilometres of figuring the exact circumference of the earth. Vespucci did not claim to have been the first to realize that the new Continent was distinct from Eurasia or to have been the first European to land on it, but others made the claim on his behalf; and his description of the natives, a titillating account that gives details of their sexuality and gargantuan genitals, but also emphasizes their irreligion and lack of personal property, is so close to Thomas More's *Utopia* as perhaps to have inspired it. In 1507 the German Martin Waldseemüller gave the name *America* to South America in his *Cosmographiae introductio*. He realized soon that this was wrong, and in 1513 suggested using Columbus' name, but by this time the name 'America' was too general to be eradicated.

Most of the *conquistadores* (conquerors) were Castilian *hidalgos*, generally of poor but proud lineages who hoped to reconstitute their families' fortunes by finding the fabled riches of Asia. A substantial number of *caballeros*, knights who were not nobles, and miscellaneous adventurers also emigrated to Hispaniola, but few if any titled nobles did so, having no motive to leave Spain to seek their fortunes. The first European to see the Pacific ocean (in 1513) was Vasco de Balboa, an adventurer who had fled Hispaniola from his creditors in 1510, hid on a vessel to Panama and then overthrew the captain. He was executed when he fell from grace while preparing an expedition to Peru in 1519. More famous and considerably less scrupulous even than Balboa was Hernan Cortez, who conquered the Aztec civilization in Mexico. Also based on Hispaniola, he was commissioned to lead an expedition to Mexico in 1518, and was the first Spanish conqueror who bothered to get an interpreter for his dealings with the natives. Capitalizing on discord within the Aztec realm of Montezuma, and overawing the Indians by their display of firearms, the Spaniards played on the superstitions of Montezuma, who considered them descendants of gods. The Indians, who had no previous knowledge of the horse, thought that Cortez's horses might be immortal. To keep them in doubt, and knowing the value of symbolic gestures and punishments, Cortez buried horses that died at night. Despite the long-range disaster that his actions meant for the Aztecs, he seems to have admired them; he had more interest in the Indians as people than either Columbus or Vespucci did. The conquest was not easy, for Cortes was badly outnumbered, but it was accomplished by the fall of the capital of Tenochtitlán in 1521. As captain general, Cortez sent out expeditions that brought most of central America under Spanish control by 1526, when his enemies at court prevented him from becoming governor general. Although he was never formally disgraced, he had little influence thereafter.

The most ruthless of the *conquistadores* was Francisco Pizarro, the illegitimate son of a Castilian nobleman. He was in the Americas by 1510 and accompanied Balboa's expedition. Hearing stories of the wealth of the Incas, he got financial backing and church sanction for missions to Peru in 1524. In 1528 he obtained the authorization of Charles V, landed in Peru in 1532, and within months had seized the major cities and killed the Inca. Pizarro distributed land to his followers and founded new settlements, including Lima, which became the capital, subsequently sponsoring unsuccessful ventures in what are now Ecuador and Chile. His violence and treachery made enemies among the other Spaniards, and he was assassinated in 1541.

Spanish efforts were assisted immeasurably by the voyage of Ferdinand Magellan, the son of a Portuguese nobleman who failed to get financial backing from his native country for a venture to reach the Moluccas by a western route. Eventually he approached the Spaniards, using the Behaim globe of 1492; his plan was approved by Charles V in 1518 and was financed by the Fugger bank of Augsburg. He set sail for South America in September 1519, passed the straits that were later named for him, and then headed across the Pacific. Magellan was killed in the Philippines in 1521, but one of his vessels and 18 of his 265 men made it back to Spain in 1522, proving beyond doubt that the Americas were new territory to Europeans and providing other vital geographical information. The voyage was a diplomatic triumph for Charles V, but it did not break the Portuguese monopoly, for the new route to Asia was too long and dangerous.

The Administration of Spanish America

Castilian exploitation of the Atlantic islands had combined state enterprise and private investment, which depended on state authorization for its legal foundation. The monarchs had also made contracts with military leaders to fight the Moors that were similar to their *capitulaciónes* with the *conquistadores* in the Americas. These agreements always justified the conquests by stating that their purpose was to bring the unenlightened to the worship of the true God, and rights were guaranteed both to the Castilian crown and the entrepreneur.

The low technological level of the native populations facilitated the Spanish conquests. All the New World peoples were basically at the Stone Age level. They did not use iron, the wheel or domesticated animals except the dog. Most other metals were used chiefly for ornament. The Indians did have skilled artisans, a complex social and agricultural organization, and a wealthy nobility. The Spaniards introduced draught animals and sheep to their lands: the Indians had grown cotton, but now, with wool, used mainly for blankets, they had something exportable.

The Castilians thought of themselves as God's agents, called to Christianize and otherwise civilize the barbarians; and they were not subtle in dealing with those who declined to accept their ways. The Spanish crown tried to protect the natives, but was unable to save them from exploitation. The monarchs prohibited enslaving them unless they gave provocation, such as by cannibalism, assaulting a Spaniard or, most importantly, irreligion. In principle the Indians were supposed to keep all lands that they were cultivating when the Spaniards came, but all else fell to the conquerors, which meant in practice Castilians; even Aragonese and Navarrese Iberians were considered foreigners.

The crown thus distributed lands to reward the conquerors, using the *encomienda*, a form of tenure that was based on the example of the estates taken from the Moors and given to the military orders in Castile. Since the Spanish colonists refused to do agricultural work, the Indians were allocated as labourers to colonists from Spain. Technically these were grants of personal lordship over the Indians, not involving land and non-hereditary in law, whatever the case in fact many have been. The *encomendero* agreed in return to Christianize them. As fortune-hunters swarmed into central and south America and the Caribbean islands from Spain, towns were founded as centres of administration, and more buildings and roads were constructed. In combination with the establishment of mines and sugar plantations, this meant an enormous demand for labour, which evolved into *de facto* slavery. The result was hardship and high death rates among the natives. Word of Spanish atrocities in the Indies, some of it written by Spaniards, was common currency in Europe by the 1570s and raised consciousness of the Spaniards as beasts to be defeated: the *Apology* of William of Orange, written in 1581, mentions the slaughter of 20 million Indians as proof of the Spaniards' cruelty. In addition, the Spaniards did themselves a considerable disservice by their acts against civilian populations in the Netherlands.

Yet the *encomienda* system was weakened, from a practical perspective, by royal hostility to enslaving the Indians. Relatively few Spaniards lived in the New World in the mid-sixteenth century; the only large concentration of Spanish people was in Mexico City. Most were prosperous holders of *encomiendas* or state officials. The crown was aware of the dangers of exploiting the Indians and of creating a powerful group of grandees: the Indians had been forced to pay personal tribute, but some *encomenderos* had forcibly substituted forced labour in the mines for it. In 1542 Charles V abolished some types of *encomienda* and forbade any forcing of Indians to work against their wills. Although in Paraguay and Chile the government was unable to enforce this, the state gradually took over the mines from the *encomenderos* in Mexico and Peru and paid the Indians a wage. The *encomiendas* were not hereditary, and the crown bought some out, while others escheated to the crown when the holders died. Whether in practical terms this was very different from enslavement in the private sector is problematic, for crown officials could lease the services of Indians to private individuals for work in the mines or on estates.[4]

Slavery

Although the enslavement of Africans was to transform labour and social relations in the Americas, its main impact on Europe proper was economic. The most extensive use of African slaves post-dates our period and is linked to more extensive European colonization overseas. The justifications for black slavery were predictable enough. There was a tradition that the sons of Ham were made black and relegated to slavery; and the colour black was generally used for portraits of diabolical beings. Petrarch portrayed them as beasts. Missionaries, popes and canon lawyers argued that the African natives were bereft of true religion and accordingly of true sovereignty, which equated them with outlaws.

Black slavery had developed in the thirteenth century in the Mediterranean, but only on a small scale, with the slaves being used mainly as exotica in merchant households. Given the population density of southern Europe, there was no demand for slaves as farm labour, although it is striking that the use of them did not spread to northern Europe during periods of high farm wages. African slaves were used, however, as unskilled labour on the sugar plantations on the Canaries and above all in the New World, where in our period they mainly intermarried with the native 'Indians'.

Slavery was obviously profitable to merchant captains, particularly the Portuguese. The captains bought the slaves, most often from other Africans who had taken them as captives or for a bounty paid by the Europeans, then loaded them into boats under appalling conditions and transported them for sale to the overseas colonies, where black slaves were first used in 1503 and were present in large numbers from 1518. The slaves were cheap initially, but so many of them died *en route* to their destinations that there is some question of the profitability even to the slavers.

Rationalizing the Rationale

Having conquered, exploited for raw materials and, to a limited extent, colonized, the Castilians were faced with the need to justify what they had done in terms of larger imperatives. Although Europeans developed a superficial curiosity about the new worlds, their thought patterns remained Christian and classical. The first travellers' and explorers' accounts of Mexico and Peru showed amazement as they compared the riches of what they saw with the relative poverty of Europe; but during the sixteenth century this changed to a more aggressive sense of Europe's peculiar excellence and mission. Much of this was religious, the evangelizing of the American Indians and the work of St Francis Xavier in Asia. The religious motive was important for all colonists, although in the context this meant

Roman Catholicism, for no Protestant nationals except for the English and, on a much smaller scale, the Dutch, colonized anywhere, and then it was only later on. In the Americas, furthermore, it meant the rigid Roman Catholicism of Castile. Mendicant friars evangelized the Indians, particularly in the first 40 years after Columbus, and tried to stop their masters from enslaving them; but they lost patience with the Indians when they kept their native religions.

Although Christianity had originated in Asia Minor, it has historically been a European religion. Indeed, since Latin Christianity had once existed in areas outside Europe that by the sixteenth century were Turkish or Eastern Orthodox, Christianity was now a European religion in an even more restricted sense than earlier. But the sixteenth century was the first time since the Roman Empire when large numbers of missionaries worked outside Europe, for the crusaders had lived apart from the Muslims in Palestine and made little conscious effort to convert them. The sense of religious superiority quickly translated to racial pride. After the Spanish occupation, most commentators lauded the superiority of European civilization. They saw the discoveries as an opportunity to Europeanize and Christianize, and their attitude toward the colonies was to make them profitable for Europe, and as European as possible.

There was nothing new in this attitude. The central Middle Ages had witnessed an expansion of peoples from the core of what had been Carolingian Europe into Palestine, the Slavic East, Spain and the Celtic fringes of Britain. Beginning with military conquest, the newcomers then imposed their own institutions and religion. In eastern Europe newly founded villages and eventually cities became islands of German settlement, as in Ireland they became Norman nuclei. By 1300 the Christians had lost most of their ground in the east, and the Byzantine empire, which had deflected Asian attackers from the west, was so weakened by the Christian conquest after 1204 that it afforded little resistance. The military offensive continued in Iberia, and the English position was consolidated in Ireland as it was retreating in Scotland. In the Baltic East the Slavic military revival of the fifteenth century drove the Germans out of some areas that they had conquered, but they remained strong in Bohemia and the south-east.[5]

Wherever they went, the Europeans remained apart, using their own laws and vernacular languages and a common Latin and not assimilating or blending into the local populations. They thought of themselves implicitly as superior to the peoples among whom they moved, and this was translated into a zeal to spread the characteristically European religion, language and law. The Europe that was expanding beyond the European continent into the Americas, Africa and Asia in the fifteenth and sixteenth centuries was a Europe that was still conditioned, in polity and mental outlook, by earlier expansion on its own peripheries.

Given the domination of Spanish America by Castilians, whose religious zeal had become mingled with the policy of cleansing the areas under their control from the ethnic pollution of Muslims and Jews, it is hardly surprising that religious orthodoxy and the zeal to convert indigenous populations to Christianity would be a paramount motive of the conquests, in propaganda if not in fact. The Castilian kings had a passion to justify in theory everything they did, especially war; and anything involving a non-Christian population was given the rhetoric of a crusade. The myth of Reconquest became their justification for occupying the Canaries, as they claimed to be the heirs of the Gothic kings who had supposedly ruled the Canaries in the distant past. There is a striking similarity in the rhetoric used by the Castilians in dealing with the Canarian natives, the Moors and the American Indians.[6]

The neo-Roman legal notion of a Christian Empire as distinct from and superior to an ordinary kingdom was basic to Castilian claims in the New World. The emperor had a responsibility for defending and extending the faith. Even before the accident that the king of Castile was also the Holy Roman Emperor, the Castilians had used 'empire' to refer to their own activity against the Muslims. The Castilian claims in the New World rested on five bulls issued by Pope Alexander VI in 1493, in which he claimed the conquered lands for Christianity, then gave them to Castile, and they fictionalized a story that Montezuma had 'donated' his 'empire' to Charles V. Philip II considered taking the title 'Emperor of the Indies' to compensate for the passage of the imperial title to the Austrian branch of the Habsburg family in 1556, and in some publications of the seventeenth century the Castilian king was being called 'Emperor of America', but 'universal monarchy' was more often used than 'empire' in the language of the Spaniards by the seventeenth century. Various agencies of the church were intimately involved with the Spanish crown in taking and administering the Americas. Although Charles V had protested that he had no desire to make himself lord of the world, his entourage spoke different words, and the French and English, and later the Dutch, saw instead a threat of the imposition of aliens, bigotry and the Inquisition.

The Europeans generally treated Asians with respect, but had little direct dealing with them except along the coasts. They despised and demonized the Turks, a tendency that was inflamed by the publication of incendiary tractates, and tended to dismiss the Africans with contempt. But they realized that they were dealing with sophisticated if incomprehensible civilizations in the Americas, and accordingly spent much more intellectual energy trying to understand the American Indians. The work of Bartolomé de las Casas (1484–1566) is a landmark in European attitudes toward the American natives. He settled on Hispaniola as a planter, but after being impressed by the sermons of Dominican friars against brutality toward the native populations, de las Casas freed his Indians and eventually led an expedition without troops to colonize what is now Venezuela. He became a Dominican in 1523, and spent the next decade in intensive reading, then from 1535 returned to an active struggle for Indian rights both in the New World and in Spain. Yet while he wanted humane treatment of the Indians, he also wanted to Christianize them, justifying this in his own mind by minimizing the differences between Indians and Christians, and arguing that the Indians had voluntarily given lordship to the Castilian king. Much of his later reputation came from his public debate in 1550 with Juan Ginés de Sepulveda, who argued on grounds of Aristotelian doctrine that war against the Indians was justified because they were natural slaves. For the rest of the century there was debate in the faculties of canon and civil law at the Spanish universities about the right by which the barbarians were subjected to Spanish rule. Another important figure of assimilation is the Franciscan Bernardino de Sahagún (1499–1590), who went to Mexico in 1529 and remained there for the rest of his life, teaching Chrisitianity and Latin grammar to the children of Aztec dignitaries at the College of Tlatelulco in Mexico City. He learned Nahuatl, the Aztec language, and wrote his *General History of New Spain* in it, albeit providing a Spanish translation.[7]

There can be no doubt that American exploration was very profitable for Spain. Mexico was mainly agricultural and pastoral in the beginning, but still very profitable, given the large unfree labour force and the new animals and animal products that the Spaniards introduced. This changed in the second half of the sixteenth century with the discovery of silver in northern Mexico. Peru developed slowly, but the mines at Potosi were discovered in 1545 and were in full-scale operation by 1560, and thereafter formed the backbone of the silver export. The impact of American gold, and particularly silver, on Europe will be explored in Chapter 8. Contemporaries recognized the importance of American metal for the Spanish war machine, but their initial response was pirate raids on Spanish shipping rather than the founding of rival colonies.

As more Europeans settled in the Americas, there was increased demand after about 1550 in the Spanish colonies for European-manufactured items, particularly French, since Castilian goods were less good and more expensive even in Castile's own colonies. Foreign manufactures *en route* to the Americas were required to pass through Seville's *Casa de Contratación*, where tolls and brokerage fees enriched the government and the merchants of the city. But the trade was expensive, and a substantial part of the bullion that came to Europe had to be used to finance the next voyages for more bullion. Particularly from the 1570s onwards, the other European powers were promoting exploration with a view to finding easier routes to Asia and the north-west and north-east passages. Apart from the bullion supply, which the Spaniards controlled, this was a more lucrative trade than the Americas. The Baltic trade of Europe exceeded the Seville trade in volume; the difference in value came from the gold and silver involved in the Seville–America trade. The general economic contraction that started in the 1590s and reached its nadir in the 1620s in Europe also affected colonial markets, and a sharp decline in the Indian population in the late sixteenth and early seventeenth centuries diminished American demand for goods such as European cloth. The supplies of American silver also declined in the seventeenth century, probably in the wake of diminished demand in Europe, with catastrophic consequences for Spain's foreign and domestic positions.

The Asian and American Trades in Perspective

Asian spices had an impact on Europe earlier than did American products, and here the Portuguese were the leaders. Portugal largely controlled the African trade in gold, slaves, Sudanese ivory and *malagueta* pepper, and the arrival of the first cargoes of higher-quality pepper from Africa entrenched their position. When the Portuguese established their staple on pepper at Antwerp in 1501, they solidified the position of the Scheldt city as the successor to Bruges. The Portuguese trade was small quantitatively but had an enormous impact on the availability of spices on the exchange markets. In the sixteenth century they were sending an annual average of about seven ships to India, varying between 400 and 600 tons initially, although enormous carracks of 1500 to 2000 tons were common by 1600. The Spaniards moved a considerably larger quantity of merchandise to and from the Americas: as early as the 1520s they were sending nearly 100 ships across the Atlantic each year, having a total carrying capacity of about 9000 *toneladas* (1.42 cubic metres each). By 1600 the number of ships had nearly doubled, but the tonnage may have quadrupled, as the Spaniards were carrying not only gold and silver, but also hides, sugar and indigo. The volume of Atlantic trade was probably double that of Mediterranean trade in the late sixteenth century, and the predominance of bullion in the Spanish trade and of spices in the Portuguese convoys made the difference in cargo values amount even greater.[8]

Before the rise of the Atlantic trade of the Portuguese and Castilians, the Venetians had controlled most of the spice trade from the Mediterranean to the north, since all supplies that did not pass through Africa came overland from the Levant. Yet the Levantine trade continued to be important, particularly after the Portuguese spice trade with Antwerp began to decline in the 1530s. Mediterranean trade revived in the wake of the consolidation of Ottoman power in the Mediterranean, which led to an increased demand in the east for European goods that would come through Venice and, increasingly, Marseilles. Thus the growing prominence of Atlantic trade did not mean a decline in Mediterranean commerce. Both markets expanded during the sixteenth century, for they did not involve the same sorts of goods, and the result was a greater diversity of products to Europe even before many American agricultural products such as the potato and tomato were being grown in significant quantities there.

Private Capital and State Oversight in the European Expansion

Most explorers were entrepreneurs who were licensed to sail under the flag of the sponsoring state. Their capital was often provided by private interests, such as the Genoese investment in the Canaries. Once the enterprise had been successful, governments began to tap the wealth that had been generated for state purposes. All Europeans used force against native populations, directly in the case of the Spaniards and Portuguese. While the English East India Company and the Dutch United East India Company were autonomous trading companies, both were chartered by states that had no objection to the company using force on the natives and making open war against other European nationals as long as this did not impinge on the political aims of the home government. Economic policy overseas thus became an extension of the state.

Portugal had to trade to gain power, given its lack of internal resources, and trade thus became a virtual crown monopoly. After the Portuguese were established in India, the king established the *Casa da India* near Lisbon, through which all imports and exports had to pass and pay customs. By 1518 the spice trade, which along with precious metals had been a crown monopoly since 1506, produced 39 per cent of the crown's total income. The Portuguese government also sent patrols to the Indian Ocean to try to enforce its claim that all trading in the area had to be done in Portuguese vessels, practising what amounted to a protection racket on native Asian shipping.

Yet once the goods left the *Casa da India,* they often came under private control for transport to Antwerp, where Germans, Florentines and some Jews recently expelled from Portugal took the profits. At the other end of the trade, once goods left the Asian ports, Portuguese traded on an equal basis with natives for transmission into the interior and to Japan and China. In the long run this trade was more profitable than the state-regulated coast-to-coast trade, in which Portugal pursued a policy that was simply too ambitious for a small state, leading to widespread evasion of the regulations. Similarly, the crown gave out large territories in Brazil to private individuals, who established very profitable sugar plantations that were free of crown control.

Spanish commercial policy displays some similarities to Portuguese. Like Portugal's *Casa da India*, the Castilian *Casa de Contratación de las Indias* at Seville was an obligatory toll station through which colonial goods passed. But Spain, although larger, was more involved in expensive wars, and crown indebtedness was thus much worse than in Portugal. Most manufactured goods sent to the Americas came from outside Spain and were then funnelled through Spanish shipping to the colonies, and colonial goods in turn passed through Spain. While all the Portuguese colonies except Brazil were coastal, Spain had territories in the interior, and colonial administration was equally centralized, under the supervision of the *Casa de Contratación*. In contrast to the later Dutch and English companies, the Portuguese and Castilian *casas* were agencies of government regulation, not trading companies that were licensed by the government. The crown did not finance the colonies or the conquests; rather, it licensed those who did and who put up the money.[9]

Exploration and Colonization by North Europeans

The Europeans thus continued until the very end of our period to see the outer world as an extension of their homeland, to be Europeanized but not to be understood in terms of itself. The world was still Europe writ large. Although Europeans were taking some mental account of the Americas – Asia had already been in their consciousness for centuries – in the sixteenth century, only after 1650 did colonial trade become important in any domain except that of luxury spices from the Orient and gold and silver from the Americas.

Correspondingly, except for the Iberians there was no significant migration of Europeans to distant places as colonists until after 1550, and even then the involvement of others was in large part a reaction to the advantages that Asian and American wealth brought to the Spaniards and Portuguese. Given Spanish involvement in central and south America, the French and English made no serious efforts to settle there. Colonies were not planted to disrupt the Spanish trade, but rather were established far as possible from the Spanish colonies for security reasons.

Once it was recognized that a large land mass blocked Europe from a direct western route to the riches of Asia, considerable effort was expended to find a presumed 'north-west passage' through North America to Asia. Francis I sent Giovanni da Verrazzano in 1524 to find it, and then Jacques Cartier in 1534, who sailed around Newfoundland and got as far up the St Lawrence river as Montreal. However, an effort to found a colony in Canada by Cartier failed in 1541–2. Henry II tried to found a colony in Brazil, but it was destroyed in 1560 by the Portuguese. The next French attempt was an abortive effort by Coligny, with the cooperation of Catherine de' Medici, to found a colony as a haven for Protestants, first in what later became South Carolina and later in Florida. The first successful French venture in Canada began in 1604, when Henry IV chartered the New France Company.

Henry VII of England had sent John and, later, Sebastian Cabot to find the north-west passage, but thereafter English interest in exploration waned until the 1550s. In 1553 Richard Chancellor discovered a new route to Russia via the White Sea. Two years later, in the aftermath of the collapse of the Antwerp financial market, a group of investors based mainly on

London and the royal court got a charter for the Muscovy Company, the first English venture that was founded on the joint-stock principle. The crown's relations with the joint-stock companies were the same as with the earlier regulated companies: it licensed them, and intervened when necessary to protect their interests. The monopolies ended competition within England – to trade in the Baltic, for example, one had to be in the Eastland Company – and allowed the company to impose discipline on its members, such as requiring them to sail in convoy and at specific times; but it made no guarantees about action against non-English competition.

Interest in overseas developments became sharper as Spain became the national enemy in Elizabeth's period. Sir Francis Drake began planning his voyage to circumnavigate the world in 1577, ostensibly with the idea of going to South America, beyond the reach of the Spaniards, to get markets for English cloth and other goods. He also got influential backing at court; the queen owned one of the ships that he used on this voyage. Most of Drake's activity, however, was directed against Spanish shipping; he ambushed treasure ships *en route* to Europe from the West Indies.

Corresponding to the late entry of the English into colonial exploration, the first attempted English colony in the Americas was Ralegh's failed venture on Roanoke island in 1587, and the first one that survived was Jamestown in Virginia, established in 1607 and named after the king and the late Virgin Queen respectively. The Spaniards continued to be interested mainly in the Caribbean islands and central America, together with Peru as their major outpost in South America. The explorations of south-western North America by Coronado in the 1540s were undertaken from Mexico, and Ponce de Leon's discovery of Florida in 1513 was not followed by a permanent settlement until St Augustine was founded in 1565.

Europe and the Turks

Although the various Christian powers were outflanking the Muslims economically in the competition for overseas markets, they remained on the defensive militarily in the Mediterranean through most of the sixteenth century and in the Balkans until the Turkish siege of Vienna was lifted in 1683. The Muslim threat would have been considerably more serious had there not been dissension over the sultanate. The Muslims believed that since Allah had given power, it was illegitimate for one prince to arrange the succession before his death. This, combined with Mehmed II's ruling that a prince who was victorious could kill his rivals, meant that a succession quarrel was inevitable when he died in 1481. The victor was Bayezid II, but his brother Jem escaped to the west and was held captive by various western powers in succession as a threat to the sultan. Bayezid thus was initially less aggressive toward the west than his father had been, preferring to concentrate his attention on other frontiers. He also repaired some damage that his

Map 7.2 Eastern Europe and the Ottoman Empire

father's high-handedness had caused within the Turkish community. After Jem died in 1495, Bayezid renewed his war with Venice, quickly taking Venice's possessions on the eastern Adriatic and culminating in his seizure of Durazzo in 1501. In the next year he made peace with Venice, and in 1503 with Hungary.

The Venetian war showed that the Muslims now controlled the sea. In addition, Bayezid II, who preferred diplomacy to warfare, began cultivating relations with the western powers. He tried to divide them, for example when he allied with Milan and Naples against Venice. Bayezid's reign began a long process by which the Turks became what amounted to a fourth major power in the diplomatic configuration of Europe, although crusades continued to be preached against them for religious reasons. In 1512 Bayezid was forced to abdicate by his son Selim (1512–20), who wanted a more forceful policy. During his brief reign Selim conquered Syria in 1516 and ended the decadent Mamluk Sultanate in Egypt in 1517. The ending of a separate sultanate in Egypt gave ideological coherence to the Turkish empire, and gave the Turks control of much of the coast of north Africa.

The reign of Suleiman I 'the Magnificent' (1520–66) brought Turkish expansion both eastward against Persia and toward the west, where his major opponent was Charles V and his major ally Francis I, who provided naval help for him in the Mediterranean (Chapter 5). In 1521 Suleiman took Belgrade, and in 1522 he expelled the Hospitallers from Rhodes. The imperial Diets were reluctant to give Charles V much money without concessions on the religious issue; although they did give an aid in 1526, it was too late to prevent the defeat of King Louis II of Hungary at Mohács that year. Following Louis's death the Hungarian crown was disputed between the emperor's brother Ferdinand, who was married to Louis' sister, and John Zápolya, *voivode* of Transylvania, who accepted Turkish help to fight the Habsburgs. Hungary, which had led the resistance to the Turks for a century or more, thus deteriorated into a buffer state between the Habsburgs and the Turks. In 1529 Suleiman besieged Vienna to show support for Zápolya, but he had to withdraw after the German Protestant princes sent help to Ferdinand. Suleiman, however, continued to threaten Vienna, forcing Pope Clement VII to make his peace with Charles V. But Suleiman stopped his strikes against Hungary after 1532, evidently realizing that he was overextended. He made peace with Ferdinand in 1533 and turned his attention toward Persia. But he remained a danger on the Empire's eastern frontier, and Charles V and Ferdinand could not afford to antagonize the Protestant leaders, who for all their distaste for the Turks on religious grounds were also negotiating with them simply as a ploy against the Emperor.[10]

Ferdinand tried to make gains after Zápolya's death in 1540, but had to accept an unfavourable general Habsburg–Ottoman truce in 1545. The peace was broken in 1550 by Habsburg intervention in Transylvania, which was now ruled by Zápolya's son as a Muslim vassal state. But Suleiman had problems at home in the 1550s. A siege of Malta failed in 1565, and Suleiman died invading Hungary in 1566. His successor, Selim II (1566–74), invaded Venetian Cyprus in 1569. After the Turks seized Tunis, Philip II was able to constitute a Holy League of Spain, the papacy and other Italian states. The battle of Lepanto (7 October 1571) involved enormous fleets on both sides. Although the Christians lost perhaps one-quarter of their fighters, they destroyed the Turkish fleet. The battle restored Tunis to Christian control and made the military reputation of Don John of Austria, Philip's illegitimate half-brother and later governor-general in the Netherlands. But Lepanto did not stop the Turks from completing the conquest of Cyprus by 1573, and the Holy League collapsed. The Muslims quickly recovered their strength on the sea, recovering Tunis in 1574 and pushing on into the Maghreb. King Sebastian of Portugal tried in 1578 to counter Ottoman advances in Morocco, but he received no help from Philip II, and his death in the battle of Alcazar led to the Spanish occupation of Portugal in 1580 (see Chapter 5).

Selim's successor Murad III (1574–95) was considerably less effective in the west, although his forces continued to advance against Persia. As the English penetrated the Mediterranean after 1570, they took over markets from Catholic merchants who were barred from the trade. Between 1593 and 1606 the Habsburgs fought the 'Long War' with the Turks. It ended inconclusively with the Treaty of Zsitvatorok, which recognized the independence of Transylvania from the Turks. In an important symbolic gesture, the Sultan Ahmed I acknowledged for the first time in this treaty that the Emperor was his equal in rank. Instability at the Ottoman court thereafter gave the west a respite from the Turkish threat.

An important consequence of the Turkish military and naval threat to Europe was the growing vitriol of anti-Turkish propaganda in the sixteenth century. The Moors in Spain and even the Mamluks in Egypt had been much less threatening, but the Ottomans were an expansionist Muslim military presence. From the 1480s printed broadsides describing Turkish atrocities against Christian civilians and highlighted by gruesome woodcuts made such ideas more accessible, and brought the reality of the Turks more into the consciousness of 'ordinary' folk, more of whom could be reached by the pictures and a few words of printed commentary than by a thousand sermons or learned treatises. The Turkish practice of impaling was considered particularly barbaric, while western executions by evisceration and decapitation were simply passed over in silence.

During the Middle Ages European intellectuals had conceived of Latin Christendom as a common civilization, under the spiritual and moral leadership of the pope and in opposition to the Muslims and Mongols. The wars of the late Middle Ages and the Great Schism had weakened that sense of community, and the religious wars of the sixteenth century virtually finished it. Yet the word 'Christendom' was still used in diplomatic treaties and religious work directed against the Turks, and the second half of our period is important for the redevelopment of a stronger notion of common European identity, bridging superficial divisions of geography, culture and particularly language. The notion was not entirely consistent, for particularly as westerners became aware of other peoples, Christianity was associated everywhere with Europeans as their characteristic religion. There was also a shift away from a purely theological horror of Islam and toward an ethnic hostility toward the Turks, who brought the threat of heretical Islam to the gates of the Christian west. Islam became essentially the religion of the Turks for Europeans.[11]

The Northern and Eastern Peripheries of Europe

The Baltic had long been an important source of raw materials, particularly herring, forest products such as wax and furs, and grain for the west European regions. The Hanse, the league of north German cities, had controlled Baltic shipping during the late Middle Ages. Its military might had sufficed to defeat the Danish king in open war between 1367 and 1370, to inflict the same treatment on England between 1468 and 1474 and on two occasions to sustain long blockades of Flanders, which depended on the Germans for regular supplies of Baltic grain.

But in the fifteenth century the Hanse had trouble maintaining its unilateral privileges in the west against agitation by Dutch and English merchants, who paid higher export duties at home than did the Germans but who were not rewarded with reciprocal treatment in the cities of the German and Slavic East. By 1497, when the first Danish Sound Toll records survive, most of the boats passing it were Dutch. Lübeck, which had led most of the political battles of the German league, was still powerful, but it was losing its influence with the lesser Hanse towns; some in eastern Europe actually welcomed the Dutch as a break of Lübeck's monopoly. The westward shift of power and the decline of the German cities in the face of competition from merchants who were backed by the power of territorial states does not, however, alter the fact that the west remained cripplingly dependent on eastern Europe for raw materials. Sound toll records from the early sixteenth century show that exports from the Baltic were still roughly double the value of the salt, wine and cloth that westerners sold in German and Slavic Europe. Scandinavia had no natural deposits of salt and had to import it from the Baltic as a food preservative. Gustav Vasa stockpiled supplies during the Sweden's war with Denmark (1563–70); but when supplies ran low in 1566, the only thing that saved him was his navy capturing the entire Dutch fleet, with a cargo of 84,000 barrels of salt, or about a year's supply. The westerners evidently used pure silver to pay for their surplus imports.[12]

Denmark had played a role in the calculations of European powers during the Middle Ages, but its influence was restricted by the Hanse. The

Scandinavian kingdoms, however, were weaker institutionally and had less economic potential than Denmark, and foreigners still dominated most of Scandinavia's foreign trade. Stockholm, the largest town in Sweden, had between 6000 and 7000 inhabitants in 1500, against 20,000 for Lübeck and Gdańsk, and most of its merchants were German, while the region as a whole was culturally backward. While the print revolution was entailing so many changes in more southerly parts, there was never more than one printer at a time in all of Sweden in the sixteenth century, and often none at all. Although universities were founded at Uppsala and Stockholm, they had small and undistinguished faculties, and most northerners who sought higher education studied abroad. Given the expense, relatively few of them did so until the late sixteenth century, when a need for bureaucrats made state service a likely career venture for young noblemen.

Yet the Scandinavian kingdoms did begin to play a significant role in international politics in the sixteenth century, in part as a result of the religious strife. Denmark had dominated the Union of Kalmar of 1397, which had linked the Scandinavian powers and Denmark under a single elective monarchy, but in practice different persons often occupied the several thrones for brief periods until a Dane had imposed his rule by force. The king ruled through regents in Sweden and Norway, but in practice the monarchy was weak institutionally. The nobles had a hereditary right to seats on the royal council and ruled their extensive domains virtually without check. Sweden had a four-Estate (clergy, nobility, burghers, peasants) Diet. Denmark's Estates, on the other hand, did not achieve a genuinely consultative role; only the nobility had much impact on the monarchy.

Tensions heightened between Denmark and Sweden in the early sixteenth century. Much of the difficulty was due to Sten Sture, the regent in Sweden who clearly wanted to make himself king and was not above negotiating with the Muscovites against the Danes. The accession of King Christian II (1513–22) in Denmark meant a new push to isolate Sweden. Isabella, the sister of the future emperor Charles V, was betrothed in 1514 to Christian II, a personally unhappy marriage that would cause unexpected complications for the Habsburgs. Facing a noble insurrection in Sweden, Christian pressured the government in Brussels for help and the rest of Isabella's dowry; when it was not forthcoming, he got French aid. In 1520 Christian invaded Sweden and reunited the kingdoms; Sten Sture was killed, but the Sture family held out in Stockholm until November. At what was supposed to be a reconciliation assembly of the Estates, Christian, urged on by the archbishop of Uppsala, surrounded the meeting hall with troops and pronounced capital sentences the next day on 82 persons, who were executed immediately.

The subsequent outcry created an opportunity for Gustav Vasa, a relative of the Sture who had been in exile in Lübeck. Lübeck, fearful of Charles V, had not supported him initially; but after Gustav's troops seized Uppsala in the summer of 1521, and Christian II raised tolls at the Sound, the

Lübeckers supported his venture. In 1523 discontent in Denmark itself among the nobles led a counter-party to expel him and choose his uncle, duke Frederick of Holstein, as king. Vasa was elected king in Sweden by the council in 1523, and Christian II had to flee to the Netherlands. Even after Isabella died in 1525, leaving her three children to the care of her aunt Margaret in the Netherlands, Christian alternately pleaded for help from Charles V and embarrassed his hosts by flirting with Lutheranism.

The threat from Christian temporarily linked the policies of the two new kings, as did their desire to throw off the shackles of Lübeck, which had helped both of them gain their thrones. Both new kings faced rebellions in the first years. By this time any threat to a Habsburg kinsman had religious significance. The Reformation was more successful early in Denmark than in Sweden, where in 1527 the Estates, faced with a danger of return of Christian II, agreed in the face of Vasa's threat to abdicate to give him wide-ranging powers over the church, including appointments and collecting fines owed in church courts, although he did not embrace Protestantism as such. By the late 1530s all the northern kingdoms were Protestant, but they remained rivals among themselves. Only in 1544 did the Swedish Estates make the monarchy hereditary in Vasa's family. He was seen by contemporaries not only as a usurper, but also as unreliable and possessed of a violent temper; and he also faced internal dissension. His regime was made independent with the support of Lübeck, and initially he geared his foreign policy accordingly; but at various times he switched sides and supported the Dutch in their efforts to penetrate the Baltic over Lübeck's objections.

The efforts of Christian II of Denmark to regain his crown complicated relations among the northern powers, but the Swedes and Danes jointly reopened the Sound to Dutch shipping after he was captured in 1532. When Denmark refused to stop trading with the Dutch, Sweden and Lübeck went to war in 1533, and when King Frederick's death in 1533 prompted a succession crisis in Denmark, Lübeck supported a restoration of the imprisoned Christian II. Sweden joined the Danes, and in 1536 Lübeck had to sue for peace. The new king, Christian III, allied with the Protestant Schmalkaldic League, but also concluded a three-year truce with the regent of the Netherlands. In treaties between 1540 and 1542 the former enemies, Sweden and Denmark, were reconciled, and both joined Francis I against Charles V, although Charles had actively courted the Swedes.

Common threats from abroad tended to make Christian III and Gustav Vasa allies most of the time, but the deaths of Christian in 1559 and of Vasa in 1560 began a new period of hostility between their realms. The Russian invasion of Livonia in 1558 opened a new phase in the shifting power relationships of the north, and the seven-years' Northern War (1563–70) between Sweden and Denmark ended in Danish defeat, and ended Denmark's influence in Livonia. Another complication was the link of the Vasa family with Poland–Lithuania: the brother and rival of King Erik XIV of Sweden, Johan, duke of Finland, married Katarina Jagiellonica, daughter

Map 7.3 Trade Routes, 1300–1600

Key

———— Trade routes established prior to 1300

------- Trade routes established 1300-50

············ Trade routes established 1350-1500

N

0   300 miles

0   500 km

of the Polish king, and gained territory in Livonia in 1563 that his brother was besieging. Erik eventually went insane, and Johan succeeded him in Sweden in 1569. Meanwhile Ivan IV of Russia, who had personal grudges against Johan, was becoming hostile. In 1572 the Jagellion line in Poland ended, and an interregnum that included making the French crown prince Henry of Anjou king ended in 1576 with the crowning of the Transylvanian Stefan Batory. Although there was no formal alliance, in fact Poland and Sweden expelled the Russians from Livonia after 1578, culminating in the Swedish seizure of Narva in 1581. But then they split, and in 1587 the Polish Estates elected Johan III's son as king of Poland as Sigismund III. Poland and Sweden would vie for control of Livonia into the seventeenth century.

Johan III of Sweden died in 1592; his brother and rival, Charles, cooperated with the royal council which Johan had been fighting, to hinder the succession of the son who was now identified with Polish interests. An assembly at Uppsala declared Lutheranism the official state religion. Sigismund initially agreed to this, but he spent most of his time in Poland and left Sweden permanently in 1598. The Estates gave the crown to his uncle, who ruled as Charles IX (1604–11): Charles' son was Gustavus Adolphus, who would take Sweden to its pinnacle of military influence in the west.

The Rise of Russia

Russia expanded eastward in the sixteenth and seventeenth centuries. Ivan III (1462–1505), the grand duke of Moscow, extended his territory at the expense of neighbouring peoples and annexed several cities, notably Novgorod in 1478. He was the first duke who refused tribute to the Mongols who had ruled much of Russia since the thirteenth century, and in 1497 he married the niece of the last Byzantine emperor and began calling Moscow the 'third Rome', after Rome itself and Constantinople. Ivan IV 'the Terrible' (1533–84) had himself crowned 'Tsar' (Caesar) of Russia in 1547, not limiting himself to Muscovy. He consolidated his position at home by ruling in an increasingly despotic manner and by restricting the power of the great nobles, or boyars.

The expansion of Russia had economic implications for western traders who were trying to escape Hanse control of the trading lanes. Many of the Hanse's exports came from Russia, a trade through Novgorod that the Livonian Hanse towns wrested from Lübeck during the fifteenth century. The tremendous growth in shipping in western Europe was made possible by timber, particularly mast poles, from Russia, for the forest cover had been denuded in the west. Flax and hemp were also important nautical products, and skins and furs were also much in demand. The English controlled most Russian trade towards the west after Richard Chancellor's voyage and the foundation of the Muscovy Company, and the Russian capture of Narva on the Baltic in 1558 provided an accessible port that was beyond the reach of the restrictive Livonian towns, notably Reval.

The Russians also expanded eastward. Ivan 'the Terrible' seized the largest Tatar state, the Khanate of Kazan, in 1552 and by decade's end controlled the entire Volga, the route for all products of the north going to the Caspian Sea. After encouraging colonization east of the Urals from the early 1570s, Ivan began military campaigns in 1580–1. The process was long and arduous, made more difficult by the confusion following the death of Tsar Boris Gudonov in 1605, but before 1650 the Russians had brought Siberia under firm control.

Poland and Lithuania

The other big state in the east was the union of Poland and Lithuania. By 1500 the Jagiellon dynasty controlled a bloc of territory from the Danube to the Dnieper, Black Sea and Baltic. Poland and its kings dominated the federation, and the Lithuanians resented this; the two split at various times. The Poles in turn complained that the Lithuanians wanted military help against Russia but gave none for Poland's campaigns. Different members of the ruling house sometimes held Poland and Lithuania separately. When Grand Duke Casimir was elected king in 1447, the union was restored, but a new split came in 1492, when the Poles and Lithuanians chose different sons of Casimir as king. The Prussian duke Albrecht of Hohenzollern, who had been grand master of the Teutonic Order before secularizing his state as a duchy and making it a fief of the Polish crown in 1525, promoted Lutheranism in the region, but not without hindrance. He evidently hoped to use religion to stir up problems in Livonia that would give his overlord, the king of Poland, an opportunity to intervene there. The result, the treaty of Poswol of 1557, gave the Poles a *de facto* protectorate over Livonia, a step that involved them in frequent warfare with the Russians. In 1561 King Sigismund of Poland recognized the last Grand Master of the Livonian Order as duke of Kurland. Although most Livonians seem to have preferred Roman Catholicism, the Order had been tolerant of Protestants since 1530, and a new union of Lublin (1569) would last until the partitions of the eighteenth century.

Although Poland had a technically elective monarchy, the son of the previous king had generally been accepted by the magnates, as happened in Denmark after 1536. But from 1505 onwards the king had to obtain the assent of both chambers of the *sejm* (parliament) for all policy decisions. From 1572, when the Jagiellon dynasty died out, there was always a real election, and candidates for the throne had to make what amounted to campaign promises to the aristocrats who elected the king. In 1573, in a more specific concession, Henry of Anjou on becoming king agreed that the *sejm* would meet biannually and that its members would be consulted on foreign policy matters, notably before mobilization for war and before new taxes could be imposed. All subsequent kings had to confirm this arrangement, and nobles were guaranteed the right to renounce allegiance if the king behaved illegally, and in fact exercised that right in 1606 against Sigismund III. The king did not become a figurehead, but there was rarely continuity of policy between reigns.

The Polish–Lithuanian monarchy was internally divided along religious lines. After an initial flirtation with Protestantism, Poland remained mainly Roman Catholic. Most of the nobles who controlled the *sejm* were Protestant, but the monarchy was firmly Catholic and eventually isolated the Protestants. Northern Lithuania, which had only converted to Christianity in 1386, and then only superficially, embraced Protestantism, but this would be reversed in the seventeenth century. In places where the prince was indifferent and/or the gentry resisted efforts to change, such as Estonia, a nominal Roman Catholicism persisted, but in fact there was a reversion to pre-Christian practices.

* * *

During the sixteenth century the rulers of western Europe made themselves more powerful, and in some cases this was accompanied by a growth in state institutions. The bureaucracies of the French and Spanish monarchies, indeed, were so oppressively large that they impeded rather than furthered the efficiency of the kings in dealing with local populations. The ability of princes to make destructive war had never been greater. While conflict continued to be in large measure dynastic, Europe for the first time in its history was able to sustain, if not precisely afford, the 'luxury' of lay princes throughout Europe fighting one another and slaughtering civilian populations in defence of a religious orthodoxy that had now become a state ideology.

The political and military activity of the princes was predicated on a growth in the European economy that was steady during the century and a half after 1450 except during the 1550s and the 1590s. In discussing that growth in Chapter 8, we must remember that growth in Europe was fuelled by several artificial stimuli. Asian spices and east European raw materials were paid for by bullion, as in the late Middle Ages. It is at least arguable that the rising stocks of silver from the mines of eastern Europe might have paid for the domestic side of this expansion, but American gold and particularly silver were needed to slake the ambitions of the princes. When bullion stocks declined at the end of the sixteenth century, corrections became necessary.

If Europe had had a 'class'-based social structure, economic change should have been the major determinant of rise and fall in rank. Instead, social rank was based on status, which is less fluid than class and is usually dependent on such non-economic considerations as ancestry (which, in the case of inherited wealth, can apply to class as well) and above all on the position that one filled in the service and official hierarchy of the state. The fact that all west European princes, even those who faced theoretically strong parliaments, were able to act more or less as they pleased – the kings of Scandinavia, Denmark and Poland–Lithuania are obvious exceptions – meant that service to them was a quicker and more certain means of elevating or consolidating ancestral status than plumbing the uncertainties of an expanding, but at times dangerously fluctuating, economy.

8

The 'Long Sixteenth Century' in the Economic and Social Development of Europe

The Morphology of Demography

Notions of economic growth and recession are often linked, not entirely properly, to demography. Thus the population decline that accompanied the ecological crisis and the plagues and wars of the late Middle Ages is generalized into a general depression, despite qualitative improvements in business techniques and agrarian regimes and a rising standard of living. Correspondingly, the fact that population was growing everywhere after about 1450, and earlier in some regions, is seen as indicating economic expansion, despite the fact that, in a reversal of the late medieval situation, standards of living for most were declining in the wake of an inflation of food prices that outstripped wages and the growing dependence of Europe for a superficial prosperity on costly imports from elsewhere.

An increase in grain production contributed to the low grain prices of the early sixteenth century and made possible some population growth, but the change was due to returning to cultivation land that had been deserted or had gone to pasture during the plagues and wars of the late Middle Ages. Seed yields, which would indicate a qualitative change in agricultural technique, did not increase enough between the thirteenth and seventeenth centuries to explain the population growth of the period after 1450. Rather, as the population continued to grow, it outstripped the food supply, and real wages began to decline. Demographic growth was also not continuous, for it was interrupted by bad harvests in the mid-1550s and 1590s, and epidemics in the 1550s.

By 1600 the total population of Europe was about 75 to 80 million, the lower end of the estimates that are usually given for the early fourteenth century, but with the difference that a higher proportion lived in the cities than in 1300.[1] Population density is a more reliable indicator than total population per political unit: by 1600 northern Italy had about 44 inhabitants per square kilometre, the Low Countries 50, France 34, central

Germany from 18 to 22 and Castile 18. Local conditions, particularly the religious wars, affected population development. France probably reached its demographic nadir in the 1430s, when total population was about 10 million, a 50 per cent loss from the 20 million suggested by the tax returns of 1328; but rapid growth brought the total population to a new high of about 25 million by 1555. While population growth elsewhere intensified, with the lull in religious warfare after 1555 and the growth of overseas trade, the caesura of the 1550s was followed by three decades of civil war in France, which entailed a population decline of some 20 to 30 per cent by 1600 to approximately the level of 1300. As elsewhere, growth was most pronounced in the cities. Lyon grew from 20,000 in 1450 to 40,000 in 1500 and 70,000 by 1550. Rouen, which had had a population of about 40,000 before the plagues, expanded from 20,000 in 1450 to between 60,000 and 70,000 by 1560. Bordeaux and Toulouse were at about 20,000 in the late fifteenth century, and by 1550 had reached 50,000 and 40,000 respectively; while Paris rebounded to over 300,000 by 1560 and to perhaps 500,000 by 1600. There was considerable emigration from small towns to the large cities, yet demographic growth was so strong that apart from the small centres near Paris, which were stifled by the rapid growth of the capital, smaller towns grew in roughly the same proportion as the cities through about 1560; for, except in the under-developed south-east, the major cities of France had spheres of influence, attracted by the labour market and jobs.

There were also shifts among the cities. Some of the great centres of the late Middle Ages stagnated, but the expansion of overseas shipping and governments caused ports and political capitals to mushroom. The cities of the Empire during the late Middle Ages were smaller than those of Italy and the Low Countries. Cologne and Prague had about 40,000 inhabitants, making them comparable to London but much smaller even than Florence, Bruges and Ghent, which were declining from their medieval height. Nuremberg, Augsburg and Vienna grew in the late fourteenth and fifteenth centuries, but still numbered under 50,000 in the early sixteenth. Yet, although the Empire had no major metropolis, it had an unusually number of second-rank cities, such as Gdánsk, Metz and Lübeck, and this facilitated local trade.[2]

Seville, through which Castile's colonial trade passed, had a population of 150,000 by 1600. Antwerp, Lisbon, Messina, Milan, Palermo, Rome and Venice also had over 100,000, while Naples surpassed 200,000. London was the most rapidly growing; in 1500 it was still within its medieval wall, but the city's population was 200,000 by 1600, having doubled since 1570. In 1600 London thus contained about 5 per cent of the total population of England; all other places of over 5000 inhabitants accounted for only another 3 per cent.[3] English tax records suggest that the distribution of wealth, which of course is not the same thing as population, was at least double in urban areas in 1525 what it had been in 1334; but much of the explanation for this can be found in the economic growth of London at the expense of the provincial centres. London's share of England's woollen cloth export grew from 66 per cent in 1500 – already much higher than in 1400 – to 84 per cent in 1540.

The changing urban map of Europe also reflects broader modifications. There were 30 more cities in 1500 with a population of more than 10,000 than in 1300, showing that the cities had recovered through immigration the losses that they had sustained. Their geographical distribution, however, remained remarkably stable. Around 1500 Europe had 154 places of 10,000 or more and four of 100,000 or more. By 1600 the number had grown to 220 with over 10,000, eight over 100,000 and with most of the growth coming in the second half of the century. The expansion involved a gain in urban population from about 3.5 million to 6 million. Most of the newcomers to the list were smaller places that grew from under 10,000 inhabitants to much more, reflecting the strength of the local exchange economy rather than the international trading that produced most capital and which was associated with the shift of economic pre-eminence from Mediterranean to Atlantic. The greatest rate of growth was in the largest cities, which is an indicator of their domination of regional economies.

The growth of population during the sixteenth century was accomplished in the face of significant problems that hindered natural increase. Disease continued to depress population. Influenza was a killer; smallpox, typhoid fever carried through the polluted water supply, and, from the late fifteenth century, syphilis all caused severe mortality. Plague, although less serious than earlier, continued to be a threat. War and its related misfortunes, such as forced emigration, depressed populations intermittently in Germany in the 1540s and thereafter more seriously in France and the Netherlands. Most of the destruction was in the southern Low Countries, which had been the most economically and politically advanced part of the region before the 1560s. The 'Spanish Fury' that destroyed Antwerp in 1576 is particularly notorious, and in the 1570s and 1580s the Spaniards routinely sacked towns. Most villages of Brabant lost beetween 50 and 75 per cent of their population in the decade after 1576. Although conditions in the southern Netherlands stabilized after 1585, the region had barely recovered its population level of 1500 by 1600, a period when the population in the northern Netherlands grew by nearly 60 per cent, much of it from immigration from Flanders and Brabant.

Population growth was also hindered by structural considerations. The 'European marriage pattern' of northern Europe is associated with relatively advanced ages at first marriage and low rates of illegitimacy. Wives were generally some years younger than their husbands, as had been true in the Middle Ages, but the gap was still much greater in Italy. Women typically married later in the north to men slightly older than themselves, producing a more 'companionate' domestic situation. Although still higher than in Mediterranean Europe, however, the average age at first marriage in the north was declining somewhat in the fifteenth and sixteenth centuries. This meant a possibility of more children per marriage; and with the food supply stable, life expectancies rose, at least in areas unaffected by civil conflict. The average family size at century's end was six children, even where the woman had married more than once. Continental families were somewhat larger than English, probably because women married earlier; and both in England and on the Continent the early marriages of aristocratic women and generally better hygiene meant that they had more children than poorer families. Some dowagers lived to old age, with their marriage portions and dowers preventing the blood heirs, sometimes from their husbands' prior marriages, from getting the estate.

The birth rate was about 35 per 1000, amounting to less than 1 per cent per year, compared to between 40 and 45 per thousand in modern under-developed countries. The interval between births was rather long, probably because of prolonged nursing of up to three years. Although some have argued that there was an increase in fertility in the sixteenth century, the high infant mortality rates and a low life expectancy of about 30 to 35 years made sustained population increase difficult. This meant that the population was much younger than now; persons under the age of 15 made up between 35 and 45 per cent of the total inhabitants in most communities.[4]

The Growing Importance of the Atlantic Economies

The sixteenth century saw a slow shift of economic vitality from the Mediterranean, which had dominated long distance trade during the late Middle Ages, toward the Atlantic, a process which began with the 'commercial revolution' of the late thirteenth century. Where contacts between south and north had previously been overland, at the fairs of Champagne, the Italians were now making regular voyages through Gibraltar and up the Atlantic coast to Bruges and Southampton. As Italy furnished more Mediterranean and Levantine luxuries to the north after 1300, several of her cities developed substantial textile industries, which meant that they imported little from the north except raw wool. The Atlantic economies thus consumed more goods and used the services provided by Italian merchants. This process continued when Portuguese supplies of pepper were sold at Antwerp, whose port brought German and east European goods into easier contact with Atlantic markets.

From being essentially passive consumers in the early sixteenth century, the Atlantic powers were cutting into Italian and Baltic–German shipping in the north. Another stage was reached after 1570, when English boats first appeared in the Mediterranean, followed by the Dutch. By the 1590s northern manufacturers were finding markets in the Mediterranean by underselling the overpriced Italian products. With the increased use of Castilian wool in the Netherlands, and the continued importing of dyes and mordants from Italy, the Mediterranean was providing the raw materials for north European industries whose products were being sold in Italy, reversing the situation of the late Middle Ages. By the 1630s the economic ruin of Italy was complete.

Despite its long Atlantic coast, France did not become a major maritime or colonial power before 1650. There was some growth of French commerce in the Atlantic in the early sixteenth century, and the Norman and Gascon ports provided some competition to the Netherlands. Bordeaux and Rouen benefited not only from the Atlantic trade but particularly from the products of their hinterlands, dyes and linens, exports of which were growing in the early sixteenth century. Yet the French did not compete effectively with the Castilians except, paradoxically, in Castile itself. Yet territorial acquisitions after 1463 doubled the Mediterranean coast of France and gave it the port of Marseilles, which became France's major port for the growing Turkish trade. The major growth in France's trade in the sixteenth century, however, was overland rather than coastal.

Lyon became France's major port of entry for foreign goods after Louis XI granted four fairs to the city in 1464. The next year the Medici bank of Florence transferred its branch there from Geneva; by 1502 Florentines alone occupied 42 houses at Lyon. While the German bankers had surpassed the Italians in importance at Antwerp (below) by 1520, 143 of 169 banks at Lyon in the mid-sixteenth century were owned by Italians, and many of the rest by Castilians. Some foreigners intermarried with prominent Lyon families and stayed, although most marriages linked Italian to Italian; and the city government left trade largely unregulated. The Italians saw Lyon as a northern distribution centre for Levantine spices that could compete with the Portuguese-controlled spices that were being marketed at Antwerp. Since inflation struck France less severely than the Mediterranean, its products, when of good quality, could undersell foreign manufactures. Lyon thus became the export depot for French manufactures, notably linens from Bresse and cloth from Languedoc, both of which reached the Maghreb and the east. The city also became a manufacturing centre, mainly for books and silk.[5]

An important aspect of the shift toward the Atlantic was the quickening of Castilian trading ties with northern Europe. By the mid-sixteenth century the Netherlands trade, mainly in wool, colonial products and silver, accounted for almost half of Castile's exports, and Spain in turn bought substantial quantities of northern goods at Antwerp. Castilians also established themselves in the major French ports. The greatest Spanish contribution to economic growth in the Atlantic was the trade with its American colonies, which was conducted through Seville. The city derived some trade from the fairs of Medina del Campo and Burgos, where the crown established a monopoly on wool exports. Although Seville's port was poor, and most goods going out along the Guadalquivir also stopped at Cadiz, the crown's political decision to locate the *Casa de Contratación* there created the city's prosperity, and its population doubled in size in the sixteenth century. All goods to and from the colonies had to be diverted to Seville to pay toll. As demand from the roughly 175,000 to 200,000 Spanish colonists in the Americas changed, particularly from the 1560s, to include some luxury manufactures, Spanish production became insufficient, and imported goods, mainly from the Netherlands and France, went to Seville before being reconsigned to the New World.[6]

Apart from the Italians, the greatest carrier of goods to the demand markets of the north Atlantic was the Hanse of north German cities, which controlled the raw materials and grain exports of the Baltic. In the Middle Ages the Hansards had paid a lower customs rate on exporting cloth from England than native merchants did, but this privilege was much resented, since the Germans insisted on restricting the English from exporting directly from eastern Europe; and Elizabeth gradually restricted the Germans' privileges, ending them in 1598. The Hansards' monopolies were affected even more by the growing power of the south German cities, which used Antwerp rather than declining Bruges. Nuremberg was supplying Lübeck itself, the leading city of the Hanse, with goods from the south and also with cloth of Cologne and Flanders, and the Nurembergers used their high profile at the Frankfurt fairs to get control of markets in the east that the Hanse had previously dominated. Other German cities also received trading privileges in the Polish cities that had previously channelled their trade through the Prussian coastal cities of the Hanse.

Another important transition involves the very nature of the carrying trade. While previously the Italians had dominated the long-distance and overland trade within Europe, this had passed to the firms of the south German cities by 1500. Such places as Augsburg and Nuremberg combined a firm basis in their local economies, including manufacture, with substantial investment and control of overland and river routes. In contrast to the Hanse cities and, increasingly, the Italians, they not only transmitted the goods of others, but they also made items that others wanted to buy. The trade in Levantine spices from the Mediterranean was still important, even after the Portuguese gained access to Asia, and the south German cities conducted these goods to Antwerp, in effect bypassing the seaborne route that had been such an advance in the fourteenth century. The quickening of east European markets for western manufactures, accompanying the exploitation of Balkan copper and silver, gave new vitality to the Rhine and Danube routes.

Antwerp's market linked the diverse economic regions of Europe for most of the sixteenth century. It was dominated by the interaction of the English trading in cloth, the Italians in silk and spices, the Portuguese in spices, and the south Germans in metals and other raw materials from the east, and also benefited as the Baltic grain trade fell into the hands of north Netherlanders at the expense of Germans. Although primarily a commercial centre, Antwerp also had industry, most importantly the dyeing of English cloth, which was generally exported in undressed state until well into the seventeenth century; and its position on the Scheldt made it the natural market for the increasingly important tonnage coming down the Rhine from the south German cities.

Just as the guild master wanted tariffs to protect the captive local market for his product, so the great merchants relied on governmental privileges and charters that conferred special rights that others did not have. The commercial capitalism of the late medieval and early modern periods was not *laissez-faire* capitalism, in which the government regulates the free market only to the extent of protecting property and making fraud legally actionable. Traders naturally tried to drive out their competitors, but they preferred to do it by getting government concessions. England's cloth exports to Brabant and the eastern Low Countries had long been significant, and after Flanders in 1489 stopped trying to protect its textile industries and permitted the open sale of English cloth, the entire Low Country market and, through it, Germany was open to English cloth exports. In 1497 the crown chartered the Merchant Adventurers Company and gave its members a monopoly of English cloth sales through Antwerp, and the Adventurers acquired the right to take a fee from merchants not in their association who sold cloth at Antwerp, which in 1564 was extended to a monopoly on cloth exports throughout Europe. After Antwerp was burned in 1576 the Merchant Adventurers Company moved first to Emden and eventually to Hamburg.

Antwerp did substantial trade with Castile, but it was less spectacular initially than that with the Portuguese. After the Portuguese established their staple on pepper in Antwerp in 1501, Asian spices were the basis for Antwerp's prominence in international banking; but the large-scale import of American gold and silver through Spain was enabling the Portuguese to bypass the Antwerp capital market from the early 1540s. Venice at the same time became the staple for Portuguese and Levantine spices. Despite the losses, however, Antwerp was able to compensate by continuing to control that part of the south German market that did not go to Italy, particularly by exporting the manufactures of the southern Netherlands. While south European and south German merchants had dominated the first phase of the expansion, native Antwerpenaars did so from the 1540s: tax returns suggest that 76 per cent of the taxable wealth of the Burgundian and Spanish Netherlands was in Antwerp in 1545–6. The city's population grew from about 40,000 in 1496 to 104,000 in 1568, including some 14,000 transients and resident foreign merchants and soldiers.

With losses in the Mediterranean, Antwerp's money market went increasingly into state loans. The kings used their overseas assets as security: Charles V on cargoes of American silver, the Portuguese on spice cargoes, while the English and French kings in effect forced the colonies of their subjects living at Antwerp as merchants to guarantee their loans. The bankruptcies of Spain and France in 1557 and Portugal in 1560 damaged

Antwerp's financial security severely, and the city thus had lost much of its domination of the regional and inter-regional economies even before the religious warfare began in the 1560s. The outbreak of disturbances in 1566 caused many merchants to leave, and the loss of control of the Scheldt to the Holland and Zeeland rebels in 1572 was a major blow. In 1576 Antwerp was sacked in the 'Spanish fury', and several thousand of its inhabitants were massacred.

Continued disturbances in Germany, although less severe than earlier, affected cloth and metal production there; and competition from American silver at this time was driving out the east European mines that fed Nuremberg and, with it, Antwerp. When Antwerp fell in 1585, most of its trade was lost to the northern Low Countries; a substantial part of the upper bourgeoisie of Amsterdam in the seventeenth century had emigrated from Antwerp. The refugees also brought industrial talents north, for economic depression had accompanied the religious wars in the southern Netherlands: the woollen textile industry of Leiden and the linen-bleaching of Haarlem owed much to refugees from the decayed cities of Flanders and Brabant. Meanwhile, the population of Antwerp declined from its height of over 100,000 to 83,905 in 1582 and to 46,123 in 1591.[7]

The Urban Economy

The restriction of urban liberties by the incorporation of cities into nation-states is traditionally seen as a development of the early modern period, but a better contrast is with the period before 1300. In 1600 as in 1300, cities that were independent in fact existed only in Italy, the Swiss Confederation (which was partly rural), the Baltic coast of Germany and a few individual cases elsewhere in Germany. The Italian and north German cities had lost economic power by 1600, but although some of them had been incorporated into territorial principalities, as in the case of Florence in Tuscany, they were not institutionally parts of a nation. The cities of the Slavic East were arguably the most independent of Europe by 1600.

The expansion of the functions of the central states after 1300 resulted to some extent from the princes asserting the priority of their written law over unwritten custom, but it was most conspicuous when state power grew at the expense of cities that previously had enjoyed written privileges that guaranteed some measure of local autonomy but which the rulers now found inconvenient. Even regulation of prices, wages and industrial quality control, which had been most often left to local discretion in the late Middle Ages, passed to the territorial regimes in the sixteenth century.

In an age when the money supply was increasing, and money was increasingly needed to grease the machinery of the state, the cities were affected severely by the high taxes demanded by their princes. The great Flemish cities had a long tradition of independence, but this had been seriously restricted by the counts of Flanders even before the incorporation of Flanders into the Burgundian state after 1384. Everywhere except in Germany and Italy, which lacked national monarchies, princes who had enjoyed seigniorial control over their cities, as in England and the French royal domain, limited their rights. In the French case this was complicated by the fact that the *bonnes villes* received exemption from the *taille* on condition that they maintain their own defences, a situation that did not affect the mainly unwalled English centres. The kings negotiated with the towns for other subsidies. But the essential fact for France is the expansion of the royal domain into a territorial monarchy. Except in England, higher levels of taxation were accompanied by a shift of virtually the entire burden of direct taxation to the townspeople and peasants without a corresponding growth in the power of the Third Estate in statute-forming.

The rulers' officials in the cities became more intrusive in the sixteenth century. The Spanish *corregidor* was unusual in that he actually sat on the city council; he was rotated to a new post after a few years to keep him from becoming too close to the local élite. Elsewhere the ruler's officers operated independently of the city authorities, and in some places, notably Paris, there were two separate administrations. Some royal officers, such as the lord lieutenant or sheriff in England, were not permanently attached to the city. Princes interfered with municipal elections; even with the safeguards guaranteed by the cities' charters, they sometimes announced the results of elections to the city council in advance, quashed an election and appointed directly, or ordered the election of specific candidates. Bishops still had considerable influence in the cities of the Continent, although in some places their concerns were only for schools and charity, in addition to the obvious one of doctrine. Their 'immunity' districts were still outside the jurisdiction of the town and royal authorities, and some bishops were consulted about city policies in general.

Thus except for political capitals and the spectacular cases of growth that were tied to economic shifts, the appearance and functions that the European cities had assumed before 1450 would not change much until the nineteenth century. Except in England, the city walls continued to be the most obvious sign of demarcation from the countryside. Although their defensive function was being eroded by firearms, which made them more vulnerable to sieges, the walls were also for control as toll stations and generally to keep interlopers out, particularly vagrants and beggars. In addition to the comprehensive walls around the settlement, some of which were drastically over-extended and enclosed considerable vacant area after the depopulations of the late Middle Ages, the cities had internal walls. These had expanded during the central Middle Ages, although not concentrically, from their early medieval nucleus, and as this happened the successive walls were not torn down but became internal divisions, sometimes marking the boundaries of parishes or other administrative divisions.[8]

The medieval distinctions among categories of town (see Chapter 3) continued in a somewhat changed form, reflecting the legal bonds of the city with its lord more than functional distinctions. Although cities were always centres of trade and in most cases of some industry, most of them also sheltered agricultural labourers who had plots of ground outside the walls. But a firm distinction of city from countryside is also complicated by the practice of the city wealthy of investing in rural land; and throughout most of the sixteenth century the rural investments of city people were taxed with the cities. Citizens were expected to own property in the city, live there with their families for a year and a day, and pay taxes and do militia duty with their fellow-citizens. But many whose lands produced something marketable, such as vineyards, or who had bought patents of nobility, spent considerable time outside.

Particularly in France, the share of industry in the total economy of the cities was secondary to the service sector, in commerce and particularly in government. France had only a handful of cities whose economy was primarily geared toward manufacturing: Amiens for light cloth (*sayettes*), Tours and Lyon for silk. But all the large and medium-sized French cities were the seats of a *bailliage* or *senechaussée*; a few had a *parlement* or university; and the smaller ones had at least a *prévôté* and a bishopric. The élite in all French cities was either official or merchant or both, depending on the nature of local conditions: pastel merchants at Toulouse, wine merchants at Bordeaux, government at a *ville de parlement*. Rents on municipal loans were an important part of most merchant as well as officer financial portfolios from the second half of the sixteenth century.

The concentration of money in the cities without the creation of new jobs there, and the tendency of the guilds to try to preserve the industrial jobs for sons of incumbent masters, had created a volatile situation in which unrest was common in the cities of the late Middle Ages, but internecine conflicts had diminished in frequency and violence by the sixteenth century. As city governments became more effective, whatever the connection of this to royal influence in the city may have been, the conflicts became more channelled, sometimes involving issues such as religion that had rarely, if ever, been involved in the city rebellions of the Middle Ages. The victory of one religion over another was rarely accomplished peacefully in a city. The poor and vagrants were an element in petty crime but were hardly revolutionary.

The basic makeup of the city government, what groups had the right to seats on the council(s) and the format and incidence of local taxation had been incendiary topics in the late Middle Ages, but were rarely questioned in the sixteenth century. An important reason for this change is probably that although taxes were even higher than in the late Middle Ages, they were now assessed at the regional or national level. In only two major urban uprisings between 1450 and 1600 did the rebels replace, if only briefly, the basic institutions of the city, and both were tied to radical religious movements: Girolamo Savonarola's rebellion in Florence (1494–8) and the Anabaptist commune at Münster (1534–5). The incidence of urban rebellions became much higher in the seventeenth century. The cities suffered mainly from external violence, for they were important stragetic points in all wars. There were spectacular sacks of cities in the sixteenth century, notably the Spanish plunderings of Rome in 1527 and Antwerp in 1576, but disasters of this magnitude were unusual: in general the cities suffered more from quartering of troops, high taxes and the introduction of garrisons and sieges.[9]

The national capitals were growing with the proliferation of central bureaucracies in the sixteenth century. Although they are often taken as prototypes of consumer cities, however, their economic contributions were not negligible, particularly in the service sector. We have noted the growth of London. Merchants of Paris reconsigned goods from the south of France towards England, the Baltic and particularly Antwerp. Parisian manufactures were also growing in the early sixteenth century, particularly in the areas of woollen cloth and printing. When the king in 1565 tried to establish a national monopoly on the export of pastel, the Parisians protested on grounds that this would devastate their dyeing works; their protest shows a detailed knowledge of the agricultural process of growing pastel, which was produced in the Langeais, several hundred kilometres from Paris. Paris thus provided the focus of a national market. Parisians also provided investment capital for other places in France, and picked up some of the trade with the Turks that the Venetians were losing in the late sixteenth century.[10]

Urban Networks and the Interregionalizing of Goods and Services

Most townspeople did not live in a great city dominated by national government or international trade, but rather in places that were the trade and, to a lesser extent, manufacturing centres of their environs. Although these places could only survive by exporting and providing services, and their exports usually had a distinguishing characteristic that provided demand for this product as against some other, the business of most urban residents was in provisioning other city people and the peasants of the environs. Thus there is a remarkable continuity in their social structures and tax policies.

Urban taxation in the late Middle Ages and early modern period was 'progressive', striking the rich proportionally more severely than the poor. There was always a strong correlation between status and office-holding and wealth, particularly in France, and also between office-holding and long-distance trade. When a city developed a single major export, such as lacemaking at Frankfurt-am-Main, and had distribution facilities through its fairs like Frankfurt, the organization of industry was capitalized, with a putting-out structure: the merchants who imported the industrial raw materials 'put out' the various operations such as spinning, weaving and dyeing to individuals to whom they paid a wage, then used their inter-regional or international ties to market the finished product. Most artisans of Frankfurt paid little tax, while the merchants who sold their goods were much richer and paid correspondingly more in tax. Over half the male heads of household were artisans.

At Dijon, by contrast, although the city had a *parlement* and had been the capital of Burgundy, industry was less specialized and geared to export, and the percentage of male heads of households who were artisans was only one-third, most of them in the traditional food and drink and local market-ing occupations. All cities had a substantial percentage of inhabitants, most often 10 to 15, in the various construction trades, although this was higher in rapidly expanding cities. Clothmaking or clothing-making was also generally high, although the extent to which the local product was exported also conditioned this. Virtually all cities show that the level of occupational differentiation increases the bigger the town became.

The late medieval cities had been dominated by guilds that were nominally artisan, but which had in fact a small group of wealthy persons at their apices whose economic thrust was in wholesale trade and, increas-ingly, in moneylending and finance. The wealthiest and most status-bearing trades were not those that controlled the production of exportable goods, but rather those that monopolized importing and thus often conflicted with local persons who wanted to manufacture the goods themselves. The wealth of most large cities was created to some extent by manufactures that were consumed locally and in other cities, but even more by the trade in luxury items, some of them manufactured, that was directed toward princely courts and, increasingly, to the urban élites themselves. Such places as Venice, Seville and Antwerp became powerful because they controlled sources of supply of goods that were now considered indispensable as status symbols to the élites who controlled national governments and access to them through titles of nobility.

Thus the cities had a small group of persons who became wealthy in long-distance trade and finance, a larger group who manufactured but used the agencies of the wealthy within their guilds to export their goods, a still-larger group who made goods which were mainly consumed locally, and the service sector of persons in food provisioning, shipping and construction. Below them was an increasingly sizeable group of people who were frequently unemployed, and in some cases were unemployable, given the small and largely inelastic size of the manufacturing and service sectors.

The cities thus developed as economic centres of exchange networks that in their turn were linked through long-distance trade at the great fairs, notably Medina del Campo, Lyon and Frankfurt, and the great emporia such as Antwerp. The economic activity of cities was no more single-dimensional than that of individual merchants. Cologne's merchants bought woollens in England and Antwerp, but also bought finished English cloth at Antwerp, used the raw wool for textiles made at Cologne itself and transported English woollen products to east Germany, south Germany, the Frankfurt fairs, Italy and even the overseas colonies. Cologners bought copper at Antwerp, the major copper market of Europe by the late fifteenth century, through Nuremberg and even from Spain, finished it into implements and sold them throughout the world.[11]

The development of exchange networks also made the food supplies in the cities more secure and gave the urban wealthy a profitable source of investment. Since the twelfth century it had often been more profitable to import large quantities of grain by boat over a considerable distance to feed the major cities than to develop local exchange networks to their fullest potential, although the two were not mutually exclusive, as the case of London proves. The problem of low grain prices that drove many farmers off the land in the late Middle Ages was caused in some places by over-production for a market reduced by the plagues, but in others by their being undersold by grain brought from eastern Europe by the Hanse merchants, who in turn took it through customs, providing revenues to the state, then sold it to native brokers who saw to local distribution. Over-production was no longer a problem in the sixteenth century, but competition with cheaper imports was.

The grain trade far exceeded the more exotic trades in value, for the city markets provided enormous demand for it. Lyon's poor hinterland could only feed the city for two months of the year. At mid-century the grain consumed at Lyon was worth 1.5 times as much as the entirety of the Genoese velvet imported to France. Yet the grain trade was more vulnerable to interruption than the traffic in luxuries due to wars, bad harvests and change of climate. It was critically important to city authorities, who regulated it closely. Bread riots were dangerous and could be triggered by any fluctuation in grain prices: the worst in this period was the 'Grand Rebeyne' at Lyon in 1529 when, following a bad summer harvest, the rumour spread that Italian speculators had bought up the grain and exported it to Turin.

The volatility of urban populations, where poverty rates were high and much employment was intermittent, meant that the authorities regulated the labour and goods markets much more strictly than was ever done in the rural areas, although in many cases this was now simply a question of enforcing statutes issued by the central government. The extreme regulation is especially formidable where food supplies and prices are concerned. Grain had to be brought to a central location, often a hall, and could not be re-exported until local demand was satisfied. The grain market was on a fixed day or days, twice or more per week in the case of the large cities; the markets for other goods were on different days. Thus the farmers of the environs knew when to bring their produce to town. Particularly in times of crisis, the city governments might either buy their own supplies or make agreements with local merchants, guaranteeing them a certain price or financing their expeditions to get grain. Lyon in 1586 even created a municipal granary that was able to get the city over short-term crises. Whenever the king issued a regulation of the grain trade, it was generally prompted by some crisis on the urban markets, particularly that of Paris.

As had happened in the late Middle Ages, rulers tried to ensure tax revenues and supplies by issuing legislation requiring that exchange transactions above a given small amount be conducted in the cities. This had the salutary effect of covering scarcities in distant areas, as an urban network was developed; thus a brief scarcity in one region could be covered by buying grain at the chief place of another network, which was known also to have grain stores, with more regional interdependence as a result. But the city governments also tried to force the peasants of their environs to sell their goods on the urban markets, particularly perishable items such as vegetables that could not be imported easily and speciality items that might be sold on their markets and exported: Nuremberg developed a 'garlic land' north of the city by promoting irrigation channels and manuring. The same principle helps to explain the expansion of beer production, in which there was considerable inter-regional trade even as early as the fourteenth century. Bremen and Hamburg exported considerable quantities to the Netherlands, while Wismar and its neighbours supplied Scandinavia and Gdánsk was the market for the Baltic. The inland towns entered the inter-regional trade in beer in the mid-fourteenth century, some developing their own specialities, and at the end of the fifteenth century the Dutch began competing by exporting their own product into north-western Germany. The north Germans then began sending some of theirs to southern Europe, where beer began cutting significantly into wine sales in the early sixteenth century.[12]

The Great Inflation of the Sixteenth Century

The techniques of commercial capitalism were created during the demographic regression of the late Middle Ages (see Chapter 3) as a response to growing demand for goods and investment opportunities in the midst of a bullion shortage. But the movement of goods and services was facilitated in the sixteenth century not only by a great increase in supply of and demand for both luxuries and staple goods, but also by an increase in the money supply, which affected inter-regional trade within Europe at least as much as intercontinental trade in the sixteenth century.

Two indisputable developments had a profound impact on the European economy during the sixteenth century: the amount of silver in circulation increased, and prices at least quadrupled, rising much more rapidly than they ever had during the Middle Ages. The term 'price revolution' comes from the fact that this was thought to be unprecedented, a view that ignores the late medieval debasements of the coin. The most revolutionary thing about this 'revolution' was its duration, lasting from about 1470 until 1650, rather than its annual rate, which averaged 1.5 per cent in England between 1532 and 1580 and 2.6 per cent in France between 1510 and 1580. Interpretation of the figures is complicated by the usual problem of the 'lie of averages', for there was considerable seasonal variation in prices and some in wages, and seasonal employment in many trades. The relatively gentle annual and long-term rises thus obscure abrupt seasonal fluctuations that created hardship for the intermittently employed. Furthermore, the rise affected fewer commodities than are available now, when for example potatoes can substitute for bread as a carbohydrate source if grain is scarce.

The still unresolved question is whether the increase in the volume of money caused or contributed significantly to the inflation. Some contemporaries thought so: Jean Bodin and others attributed the price rise to the increase in the supply of metal from the Americas. The favourable balance of trade that Europe had enjoyed with the east in the thirteenth century had yielded by the fifteenth century to a balance-of-payments problem with three areas: the Baltic (East Prussia, Poland and Russia), the Levant and the Orient. The bullion famine of the fifteenth century was caused in large part by this and by heavy donations to the church. New silver mines were opening in eastern Europe in the mid-fifteenth century, reaching their maximum output in the 1520s, when they produced about 900,000 kilograms, a figure that American supplies would only equal from the 1560s onwards.

Although anticipated by the east European mines, American metal revolutionized the exchanges of Europe, for it continued to fuel the mints after the European mines declined. Not only was it used to finance wars in Europe, but it also enabled Europe to pay off its continuing debts for consumer goods in Asia and eastern Europe. Although Europeans took over much of the foreign carrying trade of the regions whose goods they imported, which generated some income, the fact remains that the rise of Europe to world domination in the sixteenth century would not have been possible without American gold and silver.

Gold initially dominated the metals trade. It was first plundered from the Aztecs and the natives of the Caribbean, and then mined. The silver mines at Potosi, in what is now Bolivia, discovered in 1545, produced so much that by the 1550s the value of American silver exceeded that of gold. Portuguese penetration in sub-Saharan Africa also increased the gold supply.

Arguments that American bullion was the basic cause of inflation, however, are more problematic. Since the increase in silver from European sources followed a bullion shortage, it had a greater relative impact than did the American silver. Prices rose more rapidly in the first half of the sixteenth century than in the second half, when most of the American silver reached Europe. Frequent debasement of the coin by princes, who hoped to retire some of their mounting obligations in cheap money, also contributed to inflationary pressures but was not tied to the bullion supply. Henry VIII debased the English coinage several times, and particularly severely between 1543 and 1551, while French money lost nearly half of its intrinsic value between 1521 and 1575. Devaluation was also severe in Spain under Charles V, although Philip II never debased.

In favour of the monetarist thesis is the fact that inflation was most severe in Spain, through which most of the bullion flowed, and least severe in England. Yet although Spain was the only significant beneficiary of American metal, inflation there was most severe in the 1520s, precisely when the European mines were producing most silver. There are problems with the monetarist explanation even for Castile, for bullion passed through Spain so quickly that there were temporary scarcities of coin there. When silver imports peaked in the early seventeenth century, another bullion shortage loomed. American silver and gold thus accelerated an inflationary process that had begun earlier.[13]

The most important problem with the bullionist explanation of the inflation of the sixteenth century is that the price rise everywhere was roughly twice as severe on food as on other items, which suggests a problem of supply and demand. Manufactured goods did not rise as rapidly, and cloth even fell in real terms. Most of the population increase of the sixteenth century came in the cities, whose inhabitants consumed food but produced little of it; and although the late Middle Ages had seen a general ameliora-tion of conditions of labourers, whose wages were rising while food prices, at least on grain, were declining, this was reversed in the late fifteenth century and throughout the sixteenth. Yet between 1500 and 1550 nominal wages (the face value of the money paid) and real wages (the nominal wage adjusted for inflation) were rather close, so that the decline in real wages was not enough to create a serious problem for the continuously employed wage-earner except in years when grain prices moved sharply upward, as happened in the 1550s and 1590s. Real and nominal wages diverged more sharply between 1550 and 1600, and especially after 1600. Furthermore, the figures that have been used to analyse the purchasing power of the household assume that only the male head of household had an income. *Family* incomes, however, were rising, due in large measure to the new industries, which provided part-time work for wives and children.[14]

Religion and Occupation

In 1904 the German sociologist Max Weber published an essay, 'The Protestant Ethic and the Spirit of Capitalism', in which he used the example of the English and Dutch economies to argue a causal link between Calvinist Protestantism and economic development. Weber's view was widely diffused in Britain and America by the English economic historian R. H. Tawney, in his *Religion and the Rise of Capitalism* (1926). Martin Luther believed that all persons have a 'calling', and that God gives the calling of the clergyman no higher dignity than the honourable lay occupa-tions. Calvin added the element of foreordination: all persons are saved (the 'elect') or damned by God from eternity, and the saved will be recognizable by their conduct in the temporal world. In the Weber and Tawney view, Luther legitimized secular occupations and gain, and Calvinists, if not Calvin himself, equated 'election' with material well-being as a sign of God's grace. Despite its inherent improbabilities – the fact that capitalism was developed in the Middle Ages by Roman Catholic Italians, who continued to dominate financial and, to a lesser extent, commodities markets in the sixteenth century, and the rule of pre-capitalist Scotland and East Prussia by Calvinists, for example – the Weber thesis has coloured much scholarly discussion of the economic changes of the sixteenth century.

The notion that most merchants had qualms of conscience about their gains until the 'Protestant ethic' emancipated them cannot be taken seriously. Most of the exceptions, such as the famous Francesco Datini (1348–1410) of Prato and Florence, reflect general disillusion or some other personal problem rather than a sense that acquiring wealth was sinful. The church in its turn was extremely wealthy, consumed conspicuously and actively raised money. The abstract positions of the theologians had even less impact on the activities of the professional merchants than they did on the clergy: the church became more infused with capitalism than the mer-chants became imbued with theology.[15] This is not to say that merchants were not religious. Most were actively involved in the piety, individual and collective, of their cities; many sons of merchants had church careers, and much of the artistic patronage provided by merchants went into church adornment. Most merchants were conventionally pious, but, then as now, few had the knowledge of theology to be bothered much by its subtleties, worrying more about the risk of loss than the damnation of gain.

Totally apart from the question of national churches, which owed much more to political and dynastic rivalries than to doctrinal questions, persons of the same economic, social and educational levels arrived at completely different religious views. Yet, while there can be no equation of receptivity to Protestantism with the development of commercial capitalism, efforts to link occupations or status to receptivity to particular religious doctrines have been more successful. Luther's message was influential only in the Empire and Scandinavia, where it was strongest among the cities and the princes and weakest among the peasantry. Calvin's doctrines attracted the nobility and upper bourgeoisie in France and the Netherlands, with Scotland, obviously, being a peculiar case. The total numbers of Calvinists even in these places (except Scotland) remained small, although they were disproportionately influential. And although some noble families turned to Protestantism, of the greatest French princes only the Bourbons did so for any length of time. Families were divided internally, and family feuds also contributed to the spread of Protestantism, notably the Montmorency against the Guise.

Attempts to correlate status or economic level and religious orientation within individual trades have been less successful. The wealthy persons who controlled the guilds usually followed the civic religion and were conservative, but the conservative view might be Protestant or Catholic. Merchants, particularly those with international interests, were more numerous among the early French Protestants than were bankers or financiers; notaries and lawyers also tended to turn Protestant, as well as many judges, although official pressure kept their number lower. The educational level of the Protestants in France was undoubtedly high, although this cannot be generalized to other parts of Europe.

There is more correlation between trades than for economic level within them: the Protestants were disproportionately strong in trades that had a new technology (such as printing) or high skills (painting, jewellery, goldsmithing, silkworking and armaments), but weak in the food-producing and -selling trades, such as grain merchants, vintners, butchers and bakers, and the construction trades. Except where a Protestant doctrine became the state religion, the urban proletariats remained firmly Catholic, which is partly explained by the continued strength of the older guilds, for their festivals accompanied the Catholic ritual year. The only textile workers who were attracted to Calvinism at Antwerp, for example, were those with unusual specialities, such as silks, satins, braids and trimmings, which were new at Antwerp and thus had a large immigrant population and either remained unorganized or formed separate guilds or brotherhoods.

Theology, Banking, Investment and Inter-regional Trade

The increased liquidity in the economy facilitated credit operations, investment and the movement of consumer goods, but religious considerations did not. The basis of the church's economic theory was the Mosaic law, which prohibited usury (the term then meant loaning money at interest *per se*, not impermissibly high interest, as now). Medieval canon lawyers had agreed that loans might be made at what amounted to interest as long as the profit was construed as reimbursement to the lender for the use of his money, and as long as the lender incurred some risk. This led to such devices as the bill of exchange, which concealed interest on investments in the fluctuating exchange rate. The church refused to countenance a guaranteed rate of interest, although this was widely ignored in practice, and its economic theory thus remained fundamentally pre-capitalist in an inflationary and capitalist age. It could be very useful to rulers who wanted to borrow without risk from their subjects (see Chapter 6), but it was a severe hindrance in the real world of the marketplace. The usury taboo was particularly burdensome for large scale transactions, such as long-distance commercial ventures and land purchases. Until the land market was flooded by the religious confiscations, most land changed hands by subdivision and inheritance, rather than sale, for there was a prejudice against selling inherited property. Most sellers, too, required the entire purchase price, and few buyers had that much cash on hand.

Facilities for the investment of capital were thus primitive, but not negligible. An interest rate of 10 per cent on loans was legalized in England between 1545 and 1552, and was allowed permanently from 1571. Money could be ploughed back into one's business to make more money, invested in rents or the money market through bills of exchange and the other devices, invested in status symbols such as land or titles or spent on luxurious consumer goods, which were also becoming status symbols. Hospitality was an important status-connected obligation for the aristocracy: this included not only entertaining one's peers, but also donations to the poor, which were considered a part of the social obligation of the wealthy. In each case except perhaps hospitality, the money was an investment that could make more money, although less rapidly than is often the case now. Consumer goods tend to appreciate over time, and purchase of an office in church, or particularly a state, or of a noble title would give exemption from direct state taxation on the Continent in a period when direct taxation was growing from the negligible in 1300 to the ruinous by 1600.

Modern banks, like their medieval ancestors, are storehouses of funds. They make money by accepting deposits on which they pay a low rate of interest, then lending to other persons at a higher rate of interest. The usury taboo made this impossible in late medieval and early modern banking. Instead, the banks made their profits by exchange transactions and by investing in profitable commercial ventures, of which there were many more in the early modern period than in the late Middle Ages. Such merchant houses as the Medici, and in Germany the Welsers, Hochstätters and Fuggers, were family businesses that took deposits which they then invested, initially from family members but soon from outsiders. The *Grosser Ravensburger Handelsgesellschaft* (Great Commercial Company of Ravensburg) dominated trade in Swabia for most of the period of its existence (1380–1530). It was constantly reformed by the inclusion and withdrawal of investors, but at its core were three families who owned about three-quarters of the capital in the early sixteenth century. As was true of medieval companies, these partnerships could be short-term, sometimes for a single venture. Each investor controlled his own capital, but he was liable for the entire debt of the firm in case of default. Even at Lyon, whose financial markets were dominated by Italians, most banks still had a strongly family character and lasted for anywhere from a few months to four years. But they were then reformed with new documents under essentially the same family management, which could lead to an actual persistence for a century or more.

The nature of investment mechanisms dictated a close connection between banking and merchant firms, particularly those specializing in spices, metal, grain and/or textiles. As in the late Middle Ages, the great merchant companies of early modern Europe had undifferentiated functions, mixing trade, retail sales, monetary exchange and banking, although the portfolio of techniques used by the Italians was essentially complete by 1500 and would not be altered significantly until the advent of modern industrialization. Partnerships in the north were much less sophisticated than the Italian ones. The partnership most widely used by the Hanse merchants was that of the 'Reciprocal Long-Distance Company', in which merchants in different places handled each other's business, sometimes for many years at a time, without accounts being rendered. The northerners' slowness in adopting Italian techniques is quite remarkable. Letters of exchange were unusual in the north until the last third of the sixteenth century, although letters obligatory were also generalized, with the result that fiduciary money was spreading just before the silver supply began to contract at the end of the sixteenth century, and cushioned its depressant impact.[16]

The transition to the seventeenth century is marked by the appearance of genuine joint-stock companies, in which the investors pool resources by purchasing shares in a permanent capital of the firm, then assume profits and losses in proportion to the scale of their investments in that capital. Earlier companies, including the Merchant Adventurers, had been 'regulated', operating under royal charter but with unlimited liability, and with each investor handling his own business within the larger firm. The Muscovy Company was the first English venture that was founded on the joint-stock principle, followed by several regulated companies and, in 1600, by the greatest of the English overseas commercial ventures, the joint-stock East India Company. The first charter to the East India Company was for only 15 years, but it then was extended.

Most potential investors had no reason or opportunity to invest in the great merchant banks. For them, credit mechanisms developed by the major cities since the late Middle Ages were more useful. The Italian cities pioneered the *monte*, the funded public debt, usually by consolidating various short-term loans that had been imposed on the wealthier citizens. Investment in shares of the debt became an important way to invest, particularly the '*monte* of the dowry', in which parents bought shares at a daughter's birth to accumulate interest until her marriage. In 1407 Genoa consolidated its debts into a municipal bank, the *Casa di San Giorgio*, which gradually took over the city's finances. The first bank in Germany that took both public and private deposits was the Exchange of Frankfurt (1402), while Basel and Strasbourg established state banks around 1504. These institutions accepted deposits from the local government, other towns and individual investors.

Some money-changers also took money on deposit during the Middle Ages, transferring funds among their clients, but by the fifteenth century their functions were being assumed by the city governments. In 1427 Nuremberg replaced four private changers with a single official, salaried and appointed by the city. The practice of city-operated banks taking deposits from the public spread to Italy only in the late sixteenth century, beginning with the Casa di San Giorgio of Genoa in 1586 and followed quickly by municipal banks at Venice, Milan and Rome. The municipal banks took deposits but seldom loaned to investors, since security of funds was their primary concern; and the Exchange Bank of Amsterdam, founded in 1609, revolutionized the money market, since it received money on deposit at interest, transferred it between accounts and credited and cleared bills of exchange.[17]

Given the extent of government manipulation of the money supply, and the necessity of gaining government licences to trade and to exploit such sources of income as mines, the greatest banks had to cultivate close relations with the state. Hans Fugger had come to Augsburg as a weaver in 1367; as late as 1468 Jacob Fugger was seventh among the merchants of Augsburg in the amount of tax paid. His youngest son, called Jacob the Rich (1459–1525), and a noble by the time he died, took the firm to its zenith at the turn of the new century. He entered the Tyrol silver trade, which involved him with the Habsburg rulers, then invested in Hungarian silver and copper. Copper and silver came from the same ore; and since copper was not subject to export tax from Hungary, the Fuggers set up factories in Thuringia and Carinthia to separate the rest of the silver from the copper ore. The silver was then expedited easily from Carinthia to Venice. The Habsburgs gave the Fuggers toll exemptions and other trading concessions, but in return relied on them for loans. They financed Charles V's election as Emperor in 1519, and were repaid with control of the revenues of the Spanish military orders. Although originally the Fuggers tried to bypass the Antwerp market, by 1504 they were selling Hungarian copper directly at Antwerp instead of through middlemen. They had offices throughout Germany in the late fifteenth century, one in Lisbon in 1505 and in the major Italian cities by the 1520s. Jacob the Rich expanded the firm's capital by 40 times.

Yet the Fugger firm kept an essentially late medieval organization. As Jacob's older brothers died, their partnerships with the firm had to be liquidated and their widows paid. Arrangements in 1512 gave Jacob firm control over his nephews; only in 1502 was a permanent capital of the firm established, on the Hungarian mines. The Fuggers' operations continued to grow until the 1540s under Jacob's nephew, Anton, but less rapidly, and they suffered reverses from 1546. Their fortunes were linked to the Habsburgs; they loaned them large sums in the 1550s and then were caught by the bankruptcy declaration in 1557. Anton's successors could not cope with the strains of financing Philip II, either; and the Spanish bankruptcy of 1575 and the increasing degree of Genoese control over Spanish credit also hurt. The Fugger firm was dissolved in the seventeenth century. Essentially, commitment to the Habsburgs, which had made the Fuggers' fortunes in Germany, sank them in Spain.[18]

Few merchants of late medieval or early modern Europe could operate at anything like the level of influence which the Fuggers had. They were even more at the mercy of government policy than are their modern descendants. Virtually all companies that traded with a more than purely local clientele had to send employees and factors and commission agents overseas, where they would represent the firm in such places as Antwerp, London, Lyon or Seville. This meant that they still had to obtain safe conducts and trading concessions from local princes that would enable them to compete favourably with the prince's own subjects, but they had to pay dearly for those privileges. The fact that money was more flexible than in the late Middle Ages stimulated economic growth, but this was more than balanced by the counterproductive economic policies of governments: excessive taxation that took money out of circulation, narrowing the tax base by making purchase of status that carried tax exemption one of the most profitable forms of investment, and imposing ruinous forced loans and bond sales and then defaulting on them. Repeated defaults on *juros* by the Spanish crown made investors unwilling to put money into Spain, while the French public debt, which paid 8 per cent interest, was 15 times the annual receipt of the French crown by 1600. The government, meanwhile, could raise more money only by increasing taxes and increasing the number of offices for sale, thus perpetuating the policies that had caused the problem.

Industry and Government Policy in Sixteenth-Century Europe

Long-distance commerce and finance, and the provision of luxuries to nobles and of material to governments continued to be the major generators of capital in the sixteenth century as before. But the improved infrastructure that turned yesterday's luxuries into today's perceived necessities also brought cheaper manufactured goods, many of them of European provenance, into regional and international markets. Alongside the manufacture of firearms and the development of printing and its auxiliary industries, a wider range of consumer goods now became available. Whether government policy promoted or hindered the development of viable industries whose products were desired by those civilians who, with the increased liquidity in the economy, had the money to buy them, was an important component of the fiscal integrity of national economies.

The princes of medieval and early modern Europe had some understanding of the economy, but with rare exceptions they subordinated the well-being of their subjects and, indeed, the financial health of their governments to dynastic and religious aims. Louis XI of France began the process of rebuilding after the catastrophes of the Hundred Years War, most of which

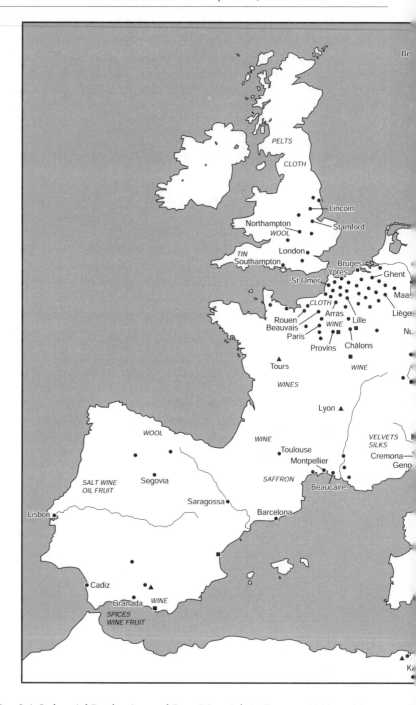

Map 8.1 Industrial Production and Raw Materials in Europe, 1300–1600

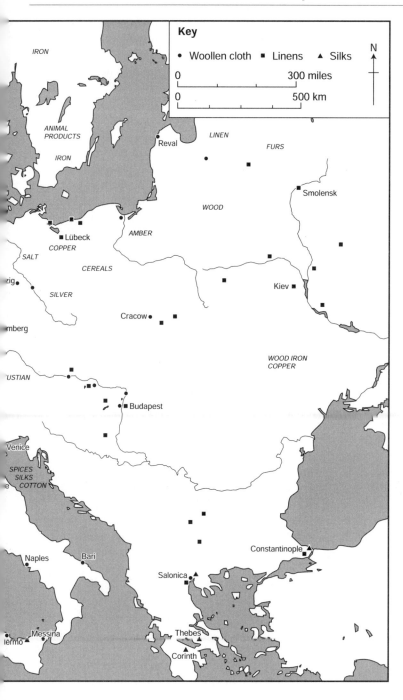

IRON

ANIMAL
PRODUCTS

IRON

LINEN

FURS

Reval

Smolensk

WOOD

Lübeck
COPPER

AMBER

SALT

CEREALS

zig

SILVER

WOOD

Kiev

Cracow

mberg

WOOD IRON
COPPER

USTIAN

Budapest

Venice

SPICES
SILKS
COTTON

Naples

Bari

Constantinople

Salonica

Thebes

Messina
ermo

Corinth

Key

● Woollen cloth   ■ Linens   ▲ Silks

N

0   300 miles

0   500 km

was fought on French soil, by trying to stimulate industrial production and make France economically independent. Although 'mercantilism' as a theory is associated with economic thought of the seventeenth century, its basic principles were of long standing and were applied by most north European governments in the sixteenth century.

All rulers wanted to remove hindrances to internal trade to prevent imported goods from underselling the domestic product. Although it was once thought that costs of interior transport of goods were significantly lowered in the sixteenth century, this seems much less true than for the seventeenth. There were 31 tolls on the Rhine between Basel and Cologne in the late sixteenth century, 35 on the Elbe, and 77 on the Danube in Lower Austria. The Loire and its tributaries in 1567 had 120 toll stations, at some of which more than one toll was collected. This meant that the undeniable increase in trade during the sixteenth century came largely in coastal and international trade, which were less subject to such hindrances. The French kings promoted and in some cases financed canal building and deepening existing channels. A royal edict in 1563 created a special court, the *tribunal des juges consuls*, to hear commercial cases; and similar courts were established in 33 other cities during Charles IX's reign.[19]

The English case is particularly instructive. England had enormous industrial potential. Iron production quintupled between 1540 and 1640, and coal production septupled in the sixteenth century, although it had to be used mainly as heating fuel rather than for industry until the technique for removing carbon from it was developed. Yet England had an enormous trade deficit, particularly with France, and mainly in manufactures.

The crown thus gave monopolies to producers of the new goods to encourage them to set up operations and give them a relatively risk-free introductory period. Monopolies were granted for goods made according to a specific technology; thus different forms of glass came under separate monopoly patents. The first cast-iron cannon in England was made in 1534 in Sussex, which remained the centre of the English weapons industry. The metals industry of Sussex also produced domestic items such as pots and pans, and English glassmaking expanded as well in the mid-sixteenth century. The unsettled religious conditions on the Continent also provoked the immigration of skilled craftsmen to England. Silkworkers came in the 1570s; Flemish immigrants to East Anglia introduced the lighter 'new draperies', which required more skill than the traditional English cloth; Netherlanders brought starch-making from wheat to England in the 1560s, when high starched collars became fashionable. By the 1580s, however, the monopolies of most original holders had expired, and they were given to persons, often courtiers, who simply speculated on the licenses and raised prices. The monopoly of the earl of Essex, Elizabeth's favourite, on the sale of sweet wines is a notorious example. In 1624 Parliament finally restricted monopoly grants to genuine inventors and for a single term of 14 years.[20]

The economic policies of the Spanish rulers, by contrast, are a case study in mismanagement. That the crowns were unable to capitalize on American gold and silver to build up the Spanish economy was principally due to the accidents of the Burgundian and German heritage of Isabella's successor and the religious fanaticism of Philip II, which in the terms of its day was no harsher than that of his great-grandparents. But more than this, the monarchs simply pursued policies that made no sense economically. The disruption of Castilian agriculture by the circuits of the Mesta's sheep since 1273 had created an exportable commodity, but meant that Castile had to import food. In 1492 Ferdinand and Isabella confirmed the Mesta's monopoly in return for high fees. The crown's control of much pastureland through its lordship over the military orders gave it a further interest. A law of 1501 reserved for pasture all land that had ever been used for that purpose, so that the owners could not shift to grain. The expulsion of Muslims and Jews and mistreatment of the *conversos* deprived Castile of many officials, weakened the moneylending urban middle class and made Castile dependent on foreign (mainly Genoese and to some extent French) capital, and in the case of the Muslims expropriated a farming group.

Ferdinand and Isabella restricted exports of grain, arms and iron, which kept prices in Spain lower, but they also sold export licenses. They promoted ironworking and the export of ironware, shipbuilding, and protected the silk industry of Granada. But Spanish manufacturing was unable to keep pace with demand either in the homeland or the overseas colonies. Castile's population grew strongly in the sixteenth century, particularly in the 1530s, and there is no doubt that Spanish textile-making also grew, but most of the products went to satisfy domestic demand and the Indies, and was not exported elsewhere in Europe, where the main Spanish products continued to be wool, wine and oil. Furthermore, there were complaints even from the domestic market about the poor quality of Spanish cloth, since untrained rural labourers were given the work. It was not only substandard, it was also expensive, which must have been due to the inflationary pressures caused by American bullion. By 1552 the crown had yielded to pressure from the *Cortes* to the extent of permitting foreign cloth in Spain and forbidding exports of the Castilian product except to the Indies. The result was that the market was swamped by cheaper and better foreign cloth, and in 1555 the ban on exporting Castilian cloth had to be rescinded. Protection of domestic industries against foreign imports was as common in the sixteenth century as in the late Middle Ages, but Castile has the dubious distinction of being the only country in Europe that attempted to guarantee that the domestic market be satisfied by forbidding the export of native products.

Corollary goals of government pre-mercantilist economic policy were to reduce imports by taxing them heavily and encouraging native production of the same goods, increase exports, develop overseas colonies to provide raw materials for and absorb the manufactures of the home country, and generally do whatever promoted the retaining of bullion at home. Although the home governments tried to force the colonists to buy products from the mother country only, until the seventeenth century the colonies produced little that the home country needed except bullion from the Americas. Spain even tried to hinder its colonists from producing goods that Spain could provide, and forbade them to acquire goods from any other than Spanish suppliers; but supplies from Spain were so irregular, and so expensive when they did come, that the colonists had to do both forbidden activities. French and Netherlandish exports thus went to the Spanish colonies, a process that the crown had to countenance as long as they went through the *Casa de Contratación* at Seville and paid toll.

While in the late Middle Ages the bullion shortage had meant that little coin actually changed hands, and north European merchants and their governments could hope at best to keep imports and exports in rough balance, now the vast increase in the money supply made keeping funds at home a more critical issue; the importance of limiting payment of church funds to Rome is particularly obvious in this context. The Spanish government was unable to prevent the transit through Spain of most American bullion, and it eventually found its way into the coffers of Spain's various enemies.

Yet industry remained a minor part of total economic production in 1600 as in 1300. Most goods were still made in the household and sold on a local market, while guild restrictions limiting the number of pieces that a single master's operation could produce hindered the development of large enterprises. The few exceptions, such as the alum mines in the papal states at Tolfa and the Venetian Arsenal, simply prove the rule. The guilds also resisted technological innovation on grounds that labour-saving machinery lowered quality.

Although new industrial products were made, the technological principles involved in their manufacture did not change fundamentally between the end of the Middle Ages and the Industrial Revolution, except in a few areas such as printing, gunpowder and shipbuilding; and of these, only gunpowder was based on some previously unavailable source of energy as opposed to human or animal muscle, water or wind. Technological improvements included some changes to the spinning wheel and improvements in bellows and furnaces, and especially the use of the blast furnace from the late fifteenth century, as well as in mechanical pumps used in the Dutch polders. Mining now required investment in heavy equipment, as better pumps and ventilation systems made it possible to dig deeper shafts.

The major changes, such as the manufacture of nails and pins, knitting and printing came in connection with new products, whose specific technology had developed since the guilds – which were as political as industrial in character – had become more or less fixed in number in the fourteenth century in most cities. The invention of the knitting frame by William Lee around 1590 turned knitting into a cottage industry in the East Midlands of

England and made possible the export of stockings. Production was increasing, but only because units of production were multiplying, not because they were becoming larger. The large number of artisans who emigrated for religious reasons during the Counter-Reformation period, many of them bringing techniques from their homelands that were not practised in their places of refuge, contributed to weakening the guilds' economic influence, although it did not affect their political role in controlling city councils, or their social prestige.

The guilds that still controlled the seats on most city councils were rarely composed purely of handworkers. Many had a strong merchant element, and the wealthy in all guilds sold wholesale as well as retail, branching into areas of endeavour not directly tied to the guild's formal reason for being. Guilds were complex and variable. Some smaller places had a single guild that included the masters of all crafts; others had several, which were composities of different occupations. Bristol, York and Norwich had over 100 crafts, and Nottingham, Northampton and Leicester over 60 each, but not all of them were organized formally into guilds. Seats on the town council, however, were generally apportioned among the chartered guilds.[21]

Merchants dominated all cities. In London the mercers and cloth-exporters were the wealthiest, but the grocers, who handled the spice trade and had investments in other areas, as well as the drapers, fishmongers and merchant-tailors, were also important. London in the sixteenth century had 12 incorporated 'liveried companies', descendants of the medieval guilds, and about 150 craft organizations. Membership in a company entitled one to the 'freedom', or citizenship, of the city of London, which meant only the 'city' proper, and not the suburbs; but since guilds claimed jurisdiction over the trade-related activities of their members, this gave them some opportunities in the suburbs, as their members increasingly lived outside the city. Membership in a company was normally inherited, and this entitled one to trade in the company's specialities; but it also left open the possibility that persons who were untrained could also practise it. This caused problems, particularly in the more industrial trades such as construction and weaving. Even the nominally industrial guilds were becoming more social. Despite the insistence of the craft leaders that entry fees had to be kept high in the interest of quality control of the product, minutes of meetings even of craft organizations show that less attention was paid to industrial regulations than to funerals and guild finances. The industrial element cannot, however, be discounted, for all guilds took seriously complaints of inferior workmanship as a threat to the markets of all.[22]

Admittedly, not all cities had strong guilds, or even guilds at all. Lyon, for example, and some cities in Languedoc, had a free labour market. Elsewhere, the lower orders were hurt by the closing of the guilds, most of which restricted the number of persons who could matriculate without being a kinsman of a guild master. The royal government saw the guilds as police agencies. From Francis I's time the French king assumed the right to name the 'master' or dean in every guild in France, and even before this the king was selling patents of mastership. A statute of 1581 fixed entry fees for mastership, varying between towns and depending also on the wealth and status of the trade, and gave masters' sons half the rate of others. There was thus little hope for journeymen (*compagnons*), since they would not have the money to rise to mastership.

Journeymen Brotherhoods and Vagabondage

As mastership in the sworn guilds became increasingly difficult to obtain in the late Middle Ages, journeymen formed their own fraternities: they had the requisite professional skills and worked for wages as needed, but were unable to own their own shops or participate in guild and hence civic affairs.[23] During the fifteenth century the fraternities became powerful in most parts of Europe except Italy and England, where they spread in the sixteenth. Some of them were charitable brotherhoods, but others were professional groups that tried to force the masters to respect their demands over wages and working conditions. In the Empire some journeyman associations were inter-urban, but this in turn presupposes that most of them had a principal place of residence. The authorities considered the brotherhoods revolutionary, with some justification; and given the need to migrate to find work, many journeymen were also transients, which also aroused rulers' suspicions.

As the journeymen became a more migratory group in the sixteenth century, the hostility of the civic authorities toward them as a potentially revolutionary element deepened. This caused the journeymen to go underground. Most of them travelled in groups of three or four, and they had their own rules and ceremonies. Contacts, often a 'mother' such as a tavernkeeper, would arrange lodging and sometimes work. These were thus secret fellowships, with signs, tokens, badges and handshakes. Since the city councils were so often formed by members of guilds, either an occupational guild or (particularly in some English cities) by members of a prestigious civic confraternity that included most prominent persons of the city, a conflict over labour necessarily involved the city fathers. The banquets of the civic confraternities, not only those of journeymen, sometimes became disorderly; a famous example occurred at the carnival at Romans in 1580. Some occupational guilds developed separate confraternities that took over the charitable functions that the guild had previously exercised. In 1539 a royal ordinance abolished the confraternities in France, but in 1541 the prestigious merchant drapers of Paris petitioned successfully for the restoration of their confraternity. In the following years the other 'merchant confraternities' were restored; but the Parisian authorities continued to ban the artisans' brotherhoods, which were reappearing in the other cities and were periodically forbidden.[24]

Concern over migrant labour was heightened during the wars of religion in France. A royal edict of 1565 required workers to present a written record of their previous employment to potential employers, while an ordinance of 1577 prohibited workers from leaving their masters without cause, and bound them to work for the same master for at least a year, a requirement that limited opportunities for journeymen still further. Some guilds that had previously had no requirement that a period as a journeyman should follow formal apprenticeship now instituted one. A royal edict of 1581 made this national policy, while simultaneously limiting the duration of apprenticeship to 3 years, which for most trades was actually a diminution; in practice this reduction of the term was a dead letter. Wage-control legislation tried to curtail demands for raises.[25]

The Symbiosis of Rural and Urban Industry

Disproportionate attention has been given in most economic histories to the role of clothmaking in the cities. It was important, not just for export but even more so because the population of the cities and their environs themselves had to be clothed. Other domestically bound occupations also involved a large portion of the workforce, notably construction and food preparation. The highest concentrations of wealth in most cities tended to be among importers and those who controlled the 'putting out' of exportable goods. While in the Middle Ages the skilled tasks had generally been put out to city-dwellers, while rural artisans did the spinning and combing, the proliferation of skilled rural artisans in the fifteenth and sixteenth centuries, and the declining profitability of arable farming, meant that the urban entrepreneurs gave out considerable work to rural artisans. Thus while most of the profit of English industry, particularly the exportable goods, came to a small group in the cities, this system meant that jobs were provided in both the rural and urban sectors. Except for London and Bristol, few English cities were substantially larger in 1600 than they had been in 1300, and the basic thrust of their economies was local trade and distribution both for the market within the cities (which was less protectionist than the continental cities had been in the Middle Ages) and also for the surrounding region.

While during the central Middle Ages most industrial activity – certainly the part of it intended for a distant market – was centred in the cities, from the late Middle Ages and particularly in the sixteenth century much actual manufacture was done in the rural areas, but for wages paid by the townspeople who sold the finished product. Much of the craftmanship done within the cities proper by this time was of utilitarian goods intended for a market within the city, and finishing goods that were largely made outside, such as turning iron into knives and undressed cloth into a finished textile. Putting-out was especially common in textiles, but it existed in other industries; for example, it dominated the metalworking and weapons industry at Nuremberg in the sixteenth century. But the putting-out arrangement involves a paradox: rural artisans, for most of whom cloth-working was a second occupation, often worked more cheaply than even the urban poor. The guilds generally resisted putting-out, but with mixed success.

Thus rural industry actually benefited the overseas trade of the cities that were nodal points of their economic regions. Important changes in the demand for cloth also fostered the rural–urban industrial symbiosis. Although the French towns, for example, were growing in the sixteenth century, they were mainly market centres. The growth of industry was largely rural; and thus the cloth became known by the name of the chief town of the region where it was produced. The demand for linen cloth in Europe peaked and declined in the fifteenth century, although it was still in demand overseas. France still produced considerable linen, but except for that of Paris and Reims it was often undersold even in France by Netherlandish or south German linen. Linens cushioned the decline of the heavy woollens of the Low Countries; in the Haarlem area they gave rise to a considerable industry, due to the excellence of the bleaching facilities. Fed by the easy access to Mediterranean cotton from Venice, production of fustian grew as linens declined in the same areas as those where linens had dominated, notably Lake Constance, Silesia and the cities of Swabia and the Rhineland.

Mining and metalworking too required urban capital to finance smelting, charcoal and hydraulic mills. There was a great increase in iron production in the sixteenth century with the use of hydraulic bellows and the stamping mill. Since the mills were powered by streams, iron, copper and brass were made most easily in the rural areas, while the implements were made in the towns. Thus the cities benefited by the expansion of mining both in terms of producing raw materials and manufactured goods. Businessmen of the large cities but also states invested in mining; in addition to the usual Nurembergers and Augsburgers, the dukes of Saxony realized much of their income from silver mines.[26]

The Peasantry

The economic changes of the sixteenth century generally worked to the disadvantage of the peasants. In the Slavic East and parts of Germany they regressed into a legal serfdom from which their medieval ancestors had escaped. Although prices on grain were high, the main beneficiaries were the lords. There was no reimposition of statutory serfdom in western Europe, but the peasants were often undersold by imported grain, and particularly in England and Castile the fact that sheep were more profitable than grain hurt them. While servile exactions cut into the peasants' purchasing power in the east, ruinous royal taxation did so in the west.

Old distinctions were breaking down. So many peasants worked part-time in the city and in their home villages for city merchants, and so many middle- and upper-class townspeople invested in land, that the contrast between rural and urban was often blurred. Serfdom was no more an invariable indication of poverty in the sixteenth century than it had been in the Middle Ages, for some serfs held considerable property. Rural rebellions occurred when prosperous peasants saw a threat to their independence, as happened in Germany in 1525; or in the face of specific grievances, as happened with Ket's rebellion in England in 1549; or when the less-prosperous peasants were pushed over the edge, as in the French peasant rebellions of the seventeenth century.

Ownership of land and the ability to keep property undivided were critical to the peasant's survival, but the population increase forced a division of family assets among more heirs than before. Daughters usually received a dowry in money, but sometimes in land; and in northern France the dowry was often returned when the parents died if the married couple wanted to share their parents' other assets with the other heirs. In the Germanic parts of the Low Countries inheritance was strictly partible, without regard to age or gender of the heirs, while the Walloon areas, and Picardy and Lorraine, had versions of the southern system. In southern France, where Roman law was stronger, the father could do more or less as he pleased, leaving different amounts to various heirs without the obligation to make an equal division. Means of hindering fractionalizing included excluding daughters (Normandy), favouring the eldest son (pays de Caux), excluding children with dowries (old recensions of Paris custom) or preferential legacy (Occitania). But none of these devices could prevent a strong tendency toward fractionalizing tenures in the sixteenth century. The northern regimes gave more weight to the nuclear family, the southern to the extended. In the customs written in the sixteenth century, the principle of equal treatment generally expanded at the expense of the optative arrangement in which the child's inheritance lay at the discretion of the father or both parents. Legal limitations on the discretion of the parents meant that there were few testaments in the north, but many in the south.

Except to some extent in Mediterranean Europe, the rights of the nuclear family took priority over those of the extended family. This meant that property could be alienated easily to raise money. The fragmentation of plots of land among nuclear families fostered exchange; since it was often difficult to make an income entirely by farming, there was a necessary diversification of talent and endeavour. Particularly in England, but also to a great extent on the Continent, most land transfers until about 1300 were between family members, but by 1400 the overwhelming majority were to non-family members within the same village. Much of this change is clearly due to the plagues of the fourteenth century, which wiped out entire families and brought land into the market. The sixteenth century thus saw a change only in that larger amounts of land entered the market due to the confiscations for religious reasons, but this seems to have benefited the gentry more than the peasants. The land law was not altered fundamentally.

In the mobile land market of the sixteenth century, the number of middle-sized peasant properties, which had been common in the fifteenth century, diminished in favour of many tiny plots that could not support a household, and a few large ones. The result was lower standards of living, despite high farm prices which benefited mainly the lords who had enough food to sell. Rural wages no more kept pace with costs than did urban. This situation was particularly true near the cities, which were more subject to penetration of urban capital and bourgeois landownership and where prices were high. In France many peasants were being bought out by merchants and the 'official' class, the two most rapidly growing social groups in sixteenth-century France, who saw land as a safe investment and as an entry route into the nobility. Peasant landholding persisted more successfully in areas without large cities.

While the division of resources among heirs, the fertility of the land and its accessibility to markets were constants, taxes and other public burdens were variables that could determine whether a farm family could survive without assistance. Given chronically low seed yields, one-fifth to one-third of one year's crop had to be held back as seed grain for the next. Direct taxation was severe and fell entirely on the Third Estate in France, absorbing a substantial part of the harvest, as did tithes and other payments to the church. The decline of servile duties to landlords, most of whom did not resume direct exploitation of their estates despite the rise of food prices, was accompanied by a growing burden of taxes to the state that probably increased rather than decreased most peasants' total obligation. Thus, as the value of the land's products rose, rents also climbed from the late fifteenth century, and the shift away from hereditary quitrents toward leases for a term of years that had dominated the land market after the late medieval plagues was accelerated. Thus most peasants were chronically in debt, particularly in the spring before new planting.

Eastern Europe was less economically developed, having exported grain and other raw materials to the west for centuries. High food prices in the west stimulated the lords of the east to extract all that they could from their peasants. Although the east exported increasing quantities of grain to the west in the sixteenth century, it was because population was less dense, and accordingly more land was farmed; yields on grain were about half what they were in the west. Direct exploitation of the demesne (the portion of the estate cultivated by tenant farmers as part of their rent) by lords thus persisted in eastern Europe and created a demand for cheap and available labour. The state helped: in Prussia five ordinances between 1526 and 1633 bound the peasant to the soil, required the return of runaway serfs to their masters and limited the bondsman's right to inherit property. In Poland from 1521 serfs could not appeal to the royal courts against their lords. The same trend is found in the Habsburg lands of the southeast. While in

Prussia, Pomerania and Austria the practice was to bind the peasant to his land, in Russia edicts of 1580, 1597 and 1607 bound him personally to his lord. The peasants of Denmark and Sweden were more independent than on those living on the south shore of the Baltic, although some serfdom remained in Denmark. The Scandinavian peasantry never saw the imposition of 'neo-serfdom' as happened in eastern Germany and Slavic Europe.

In the west, by contrast, high population density created a mobile labour force and a large rural population who could not support themselves on their plots of land and thus had to double as wage-earners. Demesne farming continued to decline in favour of cash rents and leases. While in western Europe labour services and payments in kind had been converted to cash for centuries, the reverse was occurring in the sixteenth century east of the Elbe. Lords also bought out peasant smallholders, converted the lands to demesne, and farmed the enlarged estates with tenant labour. Eastern Europe thus had a much larger proportion of large estates than did the west.[27]

England is a peculiar case. There the peasants were free under law, and they had customary rights on property that was not theirs, notably the village commons and meadows. In the Middle Ages most sheep that produced export-quality wool had been raised in northern England, but sheep-rearing now spread southwards, mainly to the east Midlands. This created a serious disruption in this area, the 'champion' country of the open fields, where villagers had traditionally ploughed everyone's strips in the fields jointly. But as the value of wool and cloth escalated it became profitable for individual farmers to enclose their own properties to facilitate the keeping of sheep. Enclosed land brought a much higher purchase price than unenclosed, since it could be used for more purposes than land still subject to common agricultural routines, notably 'convertible husbandry' (shifting from stock raising to agriculture from one year to the next, depending on market conditions).

Lords also converted meadows and village greens into sheep runs or parks. Exactly what the law was regarding property in such cases is not always clear. Changes in the legal standing of the peasant population also made it easier for lords and prosperous peasants to enclose and build up larger holdings. Although serfdom was rare by 1450, freeholders, who paid only a small rent and had complete security of tenure, were a small minority. Copyholders, who held land under varying conditions that had been 'copied' on manor court rolls, normally held their lands for lifetime at least, and some had heredity, but most heirs had to pay an 'entry fee' to assume the ancestor's tenement. There were also numerous tenants-at-will, who held land under terms that were totally at the lord's discretion. Lords often raised rents and entry fines on copyholders and tenants-at-will less with a view towards gaining additional income than to make it unprofitable for heirs to enter the tenement, which thus was more easily converted to sheep raising. The problem was so serious that Thomas More complained in a famous passage of his *Utopia* (1516) that sheep were devouring the land.

Parliament was passing statutes against enclosures from 1485, but these were enforced only intermittently. Part of the problem was the changing social composition of the House of Commons. Most members had been townsmen in the fifteenth century, but this shifted in the sixteenth century as increasing numbers of townsmen bought land in the wake of Henry VIII's confiscation and subsequent sales of the lands of the monasteries. Thus Parliament became a gentry-dominated body, and gradually lost interest in prohibiting enclosures. Yet the normal workings of the market-place were a palliative. Considerable land was enclosed between 1470 and 1520, but thereafter grain was profitable enough to take away much of the impetus to enclose, except during the 1540s when Henry VIII's devaluation of the coin provoked a brief boom in cloth exports. The resulting enclosures provoked Ket's rebellion in 1549 (see Chapter 5).[28]

The German Peasants' Rebellion of 1524–1525

One of the most discussed episodes of the social history of the sixteenth century is the 'German' 'peasant' rebellion of 1524–5.[29] In the fifteenth century most regions of southern Germany experienced serious disorders, and in uprisings in the Upper Rhine valley in 1517 a new element of these appeared: the demand that human relations be based on 'godly justice'. The revolt began in Swabia in 1524, then spread in more radical form through central and southern Germany in the spring of 1525 and eventually extended into parts of south-western France, Switzerland and Slavic Europe. The diverse rebel groups began by stating essentially legal grievances; but by early 1525, when leadership passed to Thomas Müntzer, who had been first a Franciscan and later a Lutheran before becoming disenchanted with both, the 'godly law' aspect became the dominant ideological motive. The rebellion was most radical in Tyrol. Led by Michael Gaismair, a former Habsburg official, the Tyrolese rebels produced a radically egalitarian 'Constitution' that called for the abolition of all privileges of rank.

The Swabian *Twelve Articles of the Peasantry* of 1525 provided a common programme for the rebels, known and cited in every region where the rebellion took hold. They suggest that the aims of the rebels were essentially traditional and tied to specific, recent abuses. Later manifestos were more radical. The rebels knew how to use printing for propaganda: 25 editions of the *Twelve Articles* appeared, involving perhaps 25,000 copies. Infringements on parish autonomy were to be ended, permitting parishioners to call and remove their own pastors. Tithes, which seem to have been relatively higher than in France and England, were to be restricted and restored by the lords to the local communities, and the incomes applied to village defence and poor relief. Serfdom was to be abolished, and villagers' rights to glean timber and firewood and to hunt and fish in the forests were to be restored unless the lords could document that the village in question had sold its rights. The same standard was to be applied to common meadows and fields. Village lords in the fifteenth century had been taking over many functions, such as regulation of communal agricultural routines that had previously been handled by village associations acting under their own bylaws. Labour services were to be reduced to their previous levels following recent elevations, and lease terms were to be respected. Rents and entry fees, which had been rising on term leaseholds but evidently not on heritable properties, were to be reassessed by 'honourable persons', but there was no call for their abolition. Finally, the word of God was to guide the conduct of all.

The question of whether lords were simply reasserting old rights that had not been used, as they claimed, or were inventing new ones, was immaterial from the peasants' perspective. The lords were also consolidating their authority as the sole powers within their states, while the peasants were their subjects. The peasants wanted a return to the 'old law', custom, which could limit the lords but also the peasants depending on how it was read. Roman law, used by the princes, was very effective against the essentially traditional and oral law to which the peasants had recourse. The peasants thus turned to the divine law, and this explains the eschatological overtones of the movement.

Like the English Peasant Rebellion of 1381, the German agitation soon developed an urban side. It was more through the imperial cities than the peasantry that Martin Luther's religious message (see Chapter 10) became conflated with the peasants' grievances. Upper Swabia, the Upper Rhine and Franconia had the strongest concentrations of imperial cities in Germany. Agitation was mainly urban in the Rhineland and Westphalia, which had little rural disturbance, but farther south-west townsmen often led what were basically peasant armies. The *Twelve Articles* were actually drafted by two townsmen from Memmingen and printed in Augsburg: Memmingen in early 1525 became the first Lutheran bastion in Swabia. The city had jurisdiction over several villages of the environs, into which Lutheranism then spread and became mixed with legal and social grievances. There were disturbances even at Augsburg, but the government kept the citizenry out of a formal alliance with the peasants. A common feature was sympathy for the peasants among the poorer urbanites, particularly weavers, and this was most open at Heilbronn. The leaders of the rebellion there, as indeed at Basel and Strasbourg, were not the poorest citizens, but rather those in a middle group, substantial but without political influence. Thus urban groups were using the disturbances to broaden the base of the local guild-based regimes. At Frankfurt-am-Main the revolt was turned against the city's patriciate. Most town governments were under severe pressure from both supporters and opponents of the peasants, and the ambiguity of their actions reflects this.

The rebellion was accompanied by widespread violence and pillage, particularly of church estates. The cities could not provide a strategic base for the rebellion, for most were too evenly divided between rebels and their opponents to be reliable. But the peasant armies were no match for the trained troops of the Swabian League and the nobles, and by the summer of 1525 the most serious disturbances were over. Despite the completeness of the nobles' victory, Charles V insisted that the rebels' grievances be discussed at the Diet of Speyer in 1526; but the final edict of the Diet simply asked the lords to be conciliatory.

The consequences of the rebellion varied. Conditions became worse for the peasants after 1525 in the smaller states, but even there most princes made some concessions that weakened serfdom, though without abolishing it. In the large states, where a more powerful territorial prince operated through Estates that gave some institutional basis for limiting him, there was more improvement, particularly on property rights and the limitation of labour services and rents. Having won on the battlefield, princes generally tried to limit abuses to prevent the same sort of agitation from happening again. Much of the lasting interest in the events of 1524–5 comes from the revolutionary ideologies of some of the leaders, although these were not shared by most of the participants. Michael Gaismair in Tyrol, Balthasar Hubmaier in the Upper Rhine, and Müntzer were absolutely certain of what the gospel meant about a godly society. Under torture after his capture, Müntzer said that all goods were to be held in common and that each should receive according to his need, and that lords who refused to honour this should be killed.

Peasant Agitation outside Germany

The German revolt of 1524–5 was by far the most serious rural rebellion of the sixteenth century, and even this had a substantial urban component. Castile, which probably had the poorest peasantry in Europe, had no purely rural rebellions after the *remençs* of the fifteenth century, although there was a rural dimension to the *comuneros* agitation (see Chapter 5). England had intermittent rural disorders, but the highest incidence of rural rebellion was in France, starting with 1548 in the south-west, where agitation erupted when Francis I introduced the *gabelle* there. The French disorders had numerous causes, depending on local circumstances: the *taille*, religious questions, activities of tax farmers, quartering of troops, and high bread prices were the most common. As a group the French rebellions were far less ideological than the German rebellions of 1524–5, but the vast majority did have an anti-fiscal component; and thus, except for the disturbances of the 1590s, they were usually aimed at the agents of the central government, particularly its fiscal officers, rather than the peasants' landlords. The Croquant uprisings of 1592–5 in the south-west were particularly serious, with both Roman Catholics and Huguenots being involved. They began with popular leadership, but soon gained aristocratic adherents. Henry IV was sympathetic at first, but when in 1594 the rebels formed separate armies along confessional lines, royal forces defeated them at Limoges. The rising ended in the famine of 1595, but 'Croquant' uprisings would continue to plague the authorities in the seventeenth century.

Poverty and Poor Relief

The population growth of the sixteenth century is all the more remarkable in that it was paralleled by a high incidence of poverty, particularly in the cities, a problem that had seemed to be ameliorating in the fifteenth century. Poverty now became associated more than before with vagabondage, whose incidence was undoubtedly increased by intermittent employment in the cities and the use of rural labour. Since the rural labour market was less stationary and less purely agricultural than in the late Middle Ages, the already heavy migration into the cities was intensified, compounding their problems of administration.

As during the late Middle Ages, a distinction must be maintained between the hard-core or structural poor, including widows, orphans and the physically incapacitated, who constituted between 5 and 10 per cent of most urban populations, and a larger number of persons (another 10 to 15 per cent) who took charity as needed but were able to work some of the time. But the incidence of poverty was higher than this in the larger cities, which attracted most migration. Statistics are suspect, for some cities classified as much as 40 or 50 per cent of their populations as 'poor', perhaps as a ploy to get tax relief from the central governments. But the figures cannot be ignored. In 18 towns in Lower Saxony nearly 30 per cent of the residents were poor, with women and children making up the bulk of those getting assistance. Norwich had about 2300 poor in 1570, of whom 1007 were children, 831 women and 504 adult men. Rural censuses in early sixteenth-century Normandy suggest about 15 or 20 per cent poverty in most places, and this was true also in the villages around Valladolid in the sixteenth century.

The growing problem of poverty is paralleled by changes in patterns of almsgiving and poor relief. Charity in the fourteenth century had often taken the form of donations to individuals and families with whom one was in personal contact, most often at the parish level, but from about 1450 most local governments were regulating poor relief. They issued tokens or scrip to 'deserving poor' which could be redeemed at local almshouses, but strict measures were taken against vagrants from outside the city, who were generally limited to a stay of only a few days unless someone gave them jobs or vouched for them. Vagrants were considered potentially dangerous as rioters. Thus the extent of poor relief dispensed by local governments and charitable organizations diminished in the late fifteenth century.

This practical response gave way in the late fifteenth and particularly sixteenth century to a more abstract form of charity. The humanists, whose ideas were being adopted by the city élites by this time, fostered large-scale philanthropy as a Christian obligation, but they were disgusted by many of the recipients of charity, notably beggars, and foundling hospitals and workhouses proliferated. None of the mainstream Protestant reformers favoured charity to the individual, arguing that it encouraged laziness. Christian charity became impersonal and directed toward 'durable' works like almshouses and schools, while fraternities stopped dispensing charity mainly to their own individual members, and began specializing in charity to acceptable categories of the needy, particularly the physically handicapped.[30]

The churches continued to dispense some charity, but most poor relief during the sixteenth century was provided by local secular regimes, often acting at the direction of national governments. Virtually all cities instituted a centralized system of poor relief. The Imperial Diet at Lindau in 1497 recommended that local governments provide for their own poor, a principle enshrined in an ordinance of Charles V in 1530. Although enforcement was usually local, the various previously existing funds were centralized into a 'common chest' in the sixteenth century. The German cities that did this earliest were Lutheran, starting with Nuremberg in 1522 and Strasbourg, Augsburg and a few smaller places in 1523. They funded the 'common chest' with incomes taken over from Roman Catholic hospitals and charitable foundations and from monasteries, as well as current church collections and private endowments. But cities that remained Roman Catholic were also establishing such funds, such as Lille, which established a *bourse commune* in 1506. Some cities set up collection boxes in the churches and gave the administration of the money to lay stewards. In Spain, although Charles V had encouraged localities to take over poor relief, not all did. Although the mendicant orders had objected unsuccessfully to ending begging in the Low Countries, they got a more receptive audience in Spain. Zamora took the lead with a new poor law of the early 1540s, resembling those of the Netherlandish cities, but it was not imitated, and attempts to consolidate the smaller hospitals into larger foundations foundered on opposition, including in the *Cortes*. There was considerable variation in Italy, where fraternities were generally more important in poor relief than in the north, and where there was some centralizing of hospital administration, although rarely as completely as in northern Europe.[31]

The French and English cities played a less direct role in poor relief during the sixteenth century than those of other regions that were more independent of royal control. In 1536 Francis I issued a general reform of poor relief: begging was prohibited, and the able-bodied poor were to be put to work, while those who were physically unable to work would be assisted by the parishes. This was altered by later edicts that made city governments responsible for the homeless poor, while the poor who had housing were to be cared for by the parishes. Local rulers were understandably reluctant to extend poor relief to recent immigrants. Edicts of Francis II and Charles IX made all citizens liable for contributions to poor relief, while limiting their responsibility to caring for poor persons who were established residents; others were to be returned to their former homes. This did not survive the religious wars, when royal authority was weak, and in the seventeenth century local churches rather than national policy controlled poor relief.

Attitudes were hardening even towards the poor who were willing to work. In 1473 *parlement* issued a statute for Paris that was adapted by other cities which distinguished between individual poor persons and organized bands, and which forbade giving charity to persons unwilling to work. Vagabonds were to be punished; there was general hostility to the idle poor, and most agreed that they should be put to work in exchange for support. As early as the thirteenth century some beggars were stigmatized by being forced to wear badges in France. Nuremberg in 1370 became the first imperial city to enforce this, but most of the others followed suit in the fifteenth century. The badges were worn on the clothing; after begging was forbidden, they were retained to show who was receiving public assistance. An English statute of 1547 required the branding of vagrants with a V on the chest.

Although numerous guild almshouses and private hospitals survived from the Middle Ages, and the towns had regulated grain prices for centuries and had generally cared for the indigent, before the Reformation most charity in England was associated with the churches. The dissolution of the monasteries and, even more, of the chantries, forced a complete revamping of the way the country handled poor relief. The almshouses generally survived the Reformation, but new establishments were also founded. As local governments complained that their resources were being strained by poor relief, the national government began issuing regulations that local communities were responsible for enforcing.

The truly impotent poor, who were thought physically or mentally unable to work, received what amounted to local begging licences, starting with Gloucester in 1504. A statute of 1531 required the justices of the peace to license beggars in the shires. By this time, however, most Tudor economic and welfare legislation assumed that the able-bodied could work if they wished to at some job, while others were simply trying to live at the expense of their more industrious neighbours. Until the late sixteenth century such a notion was not entirely unjustified, for labour was in short supply and only the totally unskilled could not find work. Thus the central government intervened increasingly in legislating poor relief, beginning with a proposal to use the able-bodied unemployed to work on public works, highways, fortresses and waterways.

The Poor Law of 1536 required all the parishes to maintain continuing funds for poor relief, assessed on local parishoners by the churchwardens, and it made statutory the distinction between those who were and were not physically capable of working. Parishes were made responsible for caring for the incompetent but for providing employment for the able-bodied in workhouses, usually in unskilled jobs at the beginning of the clothmaking process, and begging was made a punishable offence. These measures did not solve the problem, and other statutes tried to regulate poor relief, but matters reached critical proportions with the distress of the 1590s. Parliament codified the various regulations between 1597 and 1601, emphasizing the principle of responsibility of the parish to care for the poor.

The Poor Laws and the Statute of Artificers of 1563 are a logical culmination of the trend that began with the Statute of Labourers of 1349 for the central government to intervene in the local labour market. The Statute applied to the towns, but its main target was agricultural labourers. It was completely irrelevant for persons whose entire occupation was family-based and who neither worked for wages nor employed wage-earners, but it required all other unmarried persons under the age of 30 to work for any employer who needed him or her. The exceptions were class-based: 'a gentleman born, an heir to lands worth £10 a year or goods worth £40, already employed in a skilled craft or at sea, occupied in the supplying of London with grain, in mining, metal-working or glass-making, or attending a school or university'.[32] The Statute is best known for trying to extend apprenticeship, which was already the rule in urban occupations, into the countryside. Landowners had to take as an apprentice anyone between the ages of 10 and 18, without regard to ancestry or qualifications, keeping him until he was aged between 21 and 24. This was a radical change, for most rural labourers worked under short-term arrangements, rarely for more than a year, while the urban guilds were restrictive about enrolling apprentices. The provisions about apprenticeship proved impossible to enforce, although informants did a thriving business for a time. The Act also pegged wages at levels lower than their market value; although some employers gave more than the statutory wage, only in the 1590s did local magistrates start raising the rates.

London's measures for the able-bodied poor are indicative of public attitudes. In 1547 Edward VI's regents gave the empty palace of Bridewell to the city as a workhouse. The petition from the city did not say that there was no work for beggars, but rather that employers were reluctant to hire them, particularly former prisoners and those released as cured from the hospitals. Their work was therefore to be in areas that did not compete with domestic craftsmen, such as making nails and tick for beds, which were imported. Other cities established their own houses of correction, which were called 'bridewells'. The idea was to punish the poor because poverty was a sin, not to relieve them or train them; confinement in the bridewells generally came only after repeated orders to work were disregarded. Discipline there was strict. New inmates were whipped on admission, and they had to work from sunup to sunset. The intention was to pay for the costs of administration and support by the inmates' labour, but it rarely worked that way.[33] The idea behind Bridewell was later adopted by the Dutch too. Amsterdam established a 'house of discipline' for men in 1589 and a 'spinning house' for women in 1596. Other Dutch towns followed suit in the seventeenth century. Hospitals for beggars were also established in Italy in the late sixteenth century, but the point was charity, not putting them to work as in the north. The Spanish beggars' hospitals, like those of northern Europe, were quasi-penal.

While forcing the poor to work tends to be associated with Calvinism, there are plenty of examples of Catholic poor relief that included a work provision. The authorities realized the importance of training the poor for productive occupations. The *parlement* in 1535 permitted masters to employ children of the poor in addition to formal apprentices, and in 1545 it founded the Hospital of the Trinity at Paris, amounting to a workhouse, to provide job training for both boys and girls. The guild masters disliked the Hospital for undercutting their monopoly, and their apprentices saw it as competition for themselves. The monarchy eventually made it possible for trainees of the Hospital to become guild masters without going through the statutory term of apprenticeship.[34]

Lyon, faced with a permanently absentee bishop and a growing problem of indigence, established a General Almonry in 1534 by shifting funds from church to lay hands. Officers of the Almonry made house visits to the poor, who were provided free treatment for illnesses at the hospital. Lists of the poor were kept and revised continuously. Some got relief during temporary emergencies, but others were housed for more extended periods. The Almonry also assumed care of orphans. Two hospitals for orphans and foundlings were opened; the poor boys and some of the girls were taught to read and write, and the more intelligent orphan boys were sent to the municipal College of the Trinity, which was also attended by the well-to-do. The Almonry also paid the cost of apprenticing most of the boys, some of whom went into highly skilled trades. Girls were provided with dowries, but some were also put into service before marriage. The General Almonry was also involved in establishing the silk industry at Lyon, renting buildings where immigrant silkworkers could teach their skills, mainly to poor girls. In Lyon as elsewhere, begging was discouraged; the authorities could distinguish professional beggars from the genuinely needy, and forced them to work on public projects for wages, while the deserving poor might be removed from the relief rolls if they were caught begging.

By 1539 there was a 6-year residence requirement for weekly distributions of food, though not for medical care, the orphanage or emergency aid. Although transients were also cared for temporarily, guards at the city gates tried to exclude professional beggars. Other cities generally had residence requirements; at Paris it was 3 to 4 years. Between 1534 and 1561 just over 5 per cent of the population of Lyon got a weekly subsidy from the Almonry at some point, although not continuously. The children's hospitals accommodated 300 children, and the other hospitals were supervising still more as apprentices and servants. Given the willingness of the authorities to provide relief, these figures suggest a substantial but hardly catastrophic level of poverty.[35]

Women and the Family

Adult males are only a portion of any society, although they tend to have disproportionate influence through their control of offices of government and of industrial production. Even this may have been less true in the sixteenth century than in most times before the twentieth century: one thinks of the simultaneous rule of Mary and then Elizabeth in England, Mary Stuart in Scotland and the regency of Catherine de' Medici in France that evoked John Knox's *First Blast of the Trumpet Against this Monstrous Regiment of Women*. Yet the legal and, more generally, the economic situations of non-aristocratic women declined during the sixteenth century.

The independence of women had been receding in many places since about 1300, and in virtually all by 1400. One important reason, cutting across confessions and reinforcing patriarchy, was the spread of Roman law: Justinian's Code spoke of women's 'fragility, imbecility, irresponsibility and weakness'. Although Roman law had not initially required that adult women have male guardians, only that children should, early modern jurists began reinstating this requirement, which had been dying out in practice and often in law in the late Middle Ages. Roman law gave absolute authority to the father and his kin, including rights over children; thus widows who remarried were often deprived of guardianship of their children.

The limitations on women thus had little to do with religion, although women do appear to have been attracted in disproportionately large numbers in the beginning to the radical Protestant groups, particularly Anabaptism, where some assumed leadership roles. The cities had a high proportion of women, tending to cluster in the lower economic levels. Once polygamy was introduced at Münster (see Chapter 10), however, the women became disillusioned, and Anabaptist doctrine subordinated them to men as men to Christ.

There are significant differences between mainstream Protestant and Roman Catholic doctrines concerning the family and women, but in practice the similarities outweigh the distinctions. In the theologies of Calvin and Luther women and men were equal spiritually, but in every other respect women were inferior to men. The Protestants rejected the

Roman Catholic notion that celibacy was higher in God's estimation and accordingly the only proper life for His chosen servants, the priests. They agreed that marriage and the rearing of families was God's norm for both men and women, but in practice they applied it primarily to women, for whom marriage was considered to be the highest calling. Most of them argued that a believing woman could not even leave an unbelieving husband, although some radical reformers did not agree. Although Protestantism in theory fostered individualism within the marriage, in practice it also asserted parental control over the children, including over their marriages. The role of the husband and father as the economic and religious head of the family, for which Old Testament examples abounded, was thus strengthened across confessional frontiers, and in so far as women did economically productive work, this was secondary to the husband's within the household unit.

The medieval canonists had held that if both the man and the woman had reached their majority, their consent, exchange of words and consummation were all that were required for a valid marriage. This meant that couples could easily dispense with parental consent. Although a priest was not necessary, couples who were trying to avoid their parents' involvement often used them. However, in theory at least, the Protestants wanted to make marriage a more equitable partnership between the spouses: it therefore ceased to be a sacrament and became a civic institution, requiring the approval of the prince or the city. Zürich had a civic marriage court by 1525.[36] The Tridentine Decrees, however, restated the traditional Catholic position that marriage was a sacrament that was solely under church control.

The requirements became much stricter in the sixteenth century, however. Consent of two legally competent parties was still required, but now a clergyman and witnesses were also needed. As secular governments, using Roman law rather than their older customs, took over the solemnizing of marriages, parental consent was usually required for a valid union. Most Protestants also strongly encouraged the publication of banns. After some disagreement at the Council of Trent over the validity of marriages without parental consent, a compromise fixed the age (20 for men, 18 for women) below which marriages without parental consent were invalid. For older persons, marriages had to be solemnized in a church by a priest in the presence of witnesses, and only after three banns had been published. This made the Roman Catholic church directly involved in all valid marriages, but it was not much enforced before 1700.

The fact that marriage was a sacrament for the Roman Catholics meant that divorce was impossible, although the church continued to permit annulment on grounds that there had never been a valid marriage. Separation was also allowed, with the parties living apart, dividing property and unable to bind each other, but technically the marriage remained in effect. The Protestants allowed divorce for cause and remarriage, but the grounds for which these could be allowed varied. Martin Bucer called for divorce by mutual consent, but this was not taken up by any mainstream group. All permitted it for adultery; Luther added impotence and desertion. The attitude of the relatives played a role, for Protestant practice permitted only the innocent party to remarry. Thus, particularly if the woman was considered at fault, her relatives had to support her, since she could not contract another marriage. The city authorities divided conjugal assets at divorce. The 'guilty' party sometimes had to surrender all community assets to the innocent, but the courts usually allowed each to take out of the marriage whatever his/her family had put into it. In most places the evidence of city marriage courts suggest that divorce was so infrequent as to be a family scandal. A substantial number that were requested were denied.

The problems of women were exacerbated by developments in both broad confessional groups that were not tied specifically to doctrine. The Protestants ended religious processions that had included both men and women, such as Corpus Christi, and confraternities, some of which had contained only women, and others of which had admitted both sexes. In closing the nunneries and arguing for a married clergy the Protestants ended any opportunities for women to live religious lives, since in addition they could no more be ordained as pastors than as priests.The Roman Catholics in turn became more insistent than before that women religious be cloistered. Nearly one-fifth of Florentine women lived in convents in 1552, and the numbers were substantial in France and the Roman Catholic parts of Germany. The rationale was simple: putting girls into convents helped keep the family patrimony intact, and although the convent expected a financial settlement from the nuns' families, this was always much less than the cost of a dowry for an aristocratic marriage. This, of course, meant that many women became nuns who would have been more suited to a secular vocation, although it is hard to say how widespread this problem was.

Most Protestant groups emphasized the duty of the individual to read the Scriptures for him- or herself and reach informed conclusions. Yet efforts to discern higher levels of literacy among Protestant than among Roman Catholic women have been unsuccessful. Social status more than gender is involved in the attitudes of the authorities toward reading: in 1543 an Act of the English Parliament forbade all women except those of the gentry and nobility from reading the Bible, and the exempted groups were forbidden to read it aloud to others. Yet women's diaries and occasional heresy trials show that this restriction was rarely heeded. Some primary schools were segregated by sex, but others were coeducational, particularly in the rural areas; however, there were fewer schools everywhere for girls than for boys, and girls attended less long. Not surprisingly, urban women tended to be better educated than peasant women, and noblewomen were clearly a case apart. Several French noblewomen patronized humanists and eventually became Protestant and converted their families, most importantly

Marguerite of Angoulême and Marie de France. Calvin spent some time at both their courts before going to Geneva.

The point of education, for those who wanted women to have it at all, was self-improvement and to make the woman a better Christian. Women were allowed to hire tutors to educate them in the same subjects – classical languages, philosophy, theology and history – that men studied for professional reasons. Critics, however, recognizing the social-revolutionary implications of higher education for women, argued that they could get all the learning that they needed from their fathers and husbands. Humanist educational ideas (see Chapter 9) as they were applied to women are curious. Women as well as men of the élite were expected to be literate, but not in Latin, the language of law and power; they were expected to be 'accomplished', but not highly educated. They were meant to read and heed the examples of virtue in the classics; but the humanists also emphasized rhetoric and public life, which were not proper for a woman. Juan Luis Vives' *Instruction of a Christian Woman*, written in 1523 for Mary Tudor, the heir to the English throne, said that women who might have to have a public role, such as princesses, should have a humanist education, but he omitted rhetoric from it.

Although there are some exceptions, women tended to be somewhat less educated than their husbands regardless of religion. Among the urban élite most women were at least educated in the vernacular by tutors, although a Latin education was unusual. Literacy rates were rising in the sixteenth century, to the point where most artisans in the skilled trades could read; but their wives generally could not. Overall, the percentage of women who were literate probably remained about the same in the sixteenth century with the opening of new schools balancing out the closing of convent schools in Protestant areas; but the fact that most skilled urban male artisans could at least read helped close professional opportunities for women. Another important distinction is that while many women learned to read, at least at an elementary level, they were rarely taught to write. Nuns are an exception: much of the work written by women in the sixteenth century comes from the pens of nuns, virtually all of it in the vernacular rather than Latin.[37]

Middle- and lower-class women had little independent role in the economy. As in the late Middle Ages, disproportionately large numbers of women who worked outside the home went into domestic service, as the occupational opportunities open to women in the skilled trades declined. The role of women in manufacturing was confined mainly to food and beverage production, and even here they were excluded from the guilds, into which the more prestigious trades were organized. The fact that trades were becoming increasingly professionalized in the sixteenth century and that formal training was becoming necessary was detrimental to women, who rarely received formal training, however much they may have learned the practicalities from fathers and/or husbands. They were also excluded from some crafts because of their alleged lack of skill or natural incapacity, particularly from the newly developing ones, such as glass-cutting; yet they made lace and silk thread. Stocking-knitting was originally female, but the introduction of the knitting frame turned it into a male-dominated profession, for the men claimed that women could not use the machine. Similarly printing, involving the application of a heavy machine, was male-dominated. When the male head of household died, in most cases the family thus lost not only its only significant income but the only person who could carry on a trade, unless a teenage son could step in. Not surprisingly, women and young children dominated among the recipients of charity and the inmates of workhouses.

Although many persons still received part of the reward for their professional services or creations in kind rather than money, most received a wage that was quantifiable in some way. Women generally received about half the payment that men did even for the same unskilled work. Spinning, the only area apart from domestic service in which many women received wages, was badly paid. The capitalization of the labour market hurt women by de-emphasizing the value of their less tangible roles as nurturers and providers of food. In the rural areas the gender difference in wages made it more profitable for women to do most of the work on the family plot, while the men worked on other people's land for the higher wage, or took part-time industrial jobs. Since these were linked to the marketplace and required either training or demand for the man's labour, he was more highly regarded and better-rewarded.

Only in two areas did large numbers of women still work outside the home. While both men and women were frequently in domestic service in the late Middle Ages, by the sixteenth century it was an almost exclusively female occupation. Since the woman's wage was generally paid only at the end of the year or term of service, the employer was able in this way to keep her from leaving. City governments regulated servants' wages, a particularly sensitive point since demand for servants exceeded supply; they also restricted their freedom of movement, and tried to limit women to domestic service, even if they had other trades such as spinning. Apart from service, women were numerous only in retail trade. They could operate sale booths in the marketplaces, but they also kept small establishments where they sold the products that they or their husbands made, such as beverages, and some kept inns and taverns. In these cases they were really extending their domestic and household roles.

A salutary development of the sixteenth century was the gradual ending of public brothels, at least in northern Europe. Most large cities maintained these establishments in the late Middle Ages, licensing the madams for a fee. Municipal ordinances regulated the appearance of the buildings and the conduct and health of the prostitutes. Even in cases where the city government did not itself maintain an official brothel, the authorities tried to confine known prostitutes to certain streets, often just inside the city gates or in a side street. Prostitutes also had to wear special clothing. However, the restrictions were repeated so often that they clearly did not work.

Yet increasingly citizens were setting up endowments to cloister reformed prostitutes. 'Magdalene houses' in some cities were the equivalent of Beguinages, providing work for the women, who did not take vows but were expected to maintain chastity. During the sixteenth century the northern cities, both Protestant and Roman Catholic, rapidly did away with licensed prostitution, starting with Augsburg in 1532. The reasons given included public morality, but at Nuremberg the spread of syphilis was also mentioned. Municipal ordinances also became more restrictive on the activities and decorum of prostitutes outside the brothels. Some guild regulations denied entry to persons who could be proven to have had dealings with whores. In 1546 Frankfurt forbade the burial of prostitutes in consecrated ground, opening a new cemetery for them near the city gallows. France and England were somewhat slower, but in 1561 the French royal government banned brothels, and local authorities generally kept them closed; although casual prostitution was another matter, of course. Prostitution continued to thrive in Italy. Roger Ascham's influential treatise, *The Schoolmaster* (1570), recommended that English boys should not be exposed to Italians because of their immorality; and in 1570 a *Catalogue of all the Principal and Most Honored Courtesans of Venice* was published, evidently to advertise them as an attraction for foreign visitors.[38]

The Nobility

Nobility was the only legally recognized status that was based largely on descent. Ancestry was essential to the self-concept of the nobles. Although Philip II stood in awe of his father Charles V's achievements in contrast to his own failures, he said that he was a greater man than his father because he was the son of an emperor, while his father had been the son of a duke. To a greater extent than with the townspeople and the peasants, noble standing could be separated from levels of wealth. Yet in a technical sense Europe had an aristocracy rather than a nobility, for persons outside the group could enter it through marriage or purchase, or by occupying a state office that conferred nobility upon its holder. The nobility was not monolithic: there were different levels everywhere, with different criteria for membership to which different obligations attached.

The European nobility had originated as a warrior élite, but this function was seriously weakened during the Hundred Years War, and was true only of the command positions in the age of gunpowder. During the sixteenth century both the greater and lesser nobles were becoming a courtier, service group everywhere. The skills needed for this mode of life required a humanist education. The state was bureaucratic, but it was also based on patronage, both of the king and of the chief ministers, who promoted their own men. Baldessare Castiglione's *Book of the Courtier* (see Chapter 9), based on the court of the Este dukes of Mantua, shows this atmosphere. Most courtiers were not civil servants; rather, they simply lived in the duke's entourage, performing no discernible function of government. Mantua had a large and poor nobility who turned to careers at court, which was the only way to make money given the commercial backwardness of the place. Competition for places and the vicious backbiting of court life led to the courtiers cultivating an ethic of their own superiority over commoners.[39]

We have seen that the national monarchies and many territorial principalities were administrative states, in which offices had to have permanent occupants to keep the machinery of state moving. Some required professional skills, but by 1600 many and perhaps most offices in France and Spain were being sold to raise money for the government. Yet offices were also dynastic, and were often inherited in fact if the descendants paid the requisite fee. This is less true in England, where the problem did not become serious before the seventeenth century. Furthermore, county offices were never sold, and the gentry and nobles seem to have thought of them as a public obligation more than a perquisite. In France and Spain, however, the process began earlier and became more deeply entrenched. High office under the crown was an important mark of status. Since the office-holder or his ancestor had probably paid for his office and thought of it as an investment, it was unreasonable to think that he should not profit from it.

The English Nobility

The upper levels of the English nobility constituted the parliamentary peerage dominated by the earls and dukes, persons who had the hereditary right to a seat in the House of Lords. This group included members of the royal family, relative *nouveaux* who were given peerages by the king as a reward, and older lineages of many generations' standing. All possessed extensive lands, but the older the family, the more exclusively its assets were in lands and rents. The older houses, such as the Nevilles and Percies in the north, maintained armies of retainers that could and occasionally did defy the king. They were interested in affairs at court, but they were less likely to hold specific offices than the newer men, who still had to prove themselves and could not maintain their positions apart from the court. Yet all nobles depended to some degree on royal patronage, and the possibility of its withdrawal sparked most of the rebellions. Only the monarch could create a new peer. Henry VIII established some new peerages for his favourites, but Elizabeth kept the peerage stable at roughly 50 families, simply replacing those who were extinguished (such as Norfolk) with new appointments (such as Burghley).

The lesser nobility is often termed generically the 'gentry'. By 1450 'gentlemen' were the lowest rank among the gentry who were entitled to a coat of arms, while esquires were a middle group who could be dubbed knight. While during the fourteenth century virtually all persons who sat in Parliament as knights of the shire were actually dubbed knights, esquires and even gentlemen were often returned in the fifteenth. As the highest rank among the armigerous, knights became less numerous and more socially exclusive in the fifteenth century. Henry VIII and Mary granted knighthoods for patronage, but Elizabeth was more restrictive. There were about 500 knights in 1558, dropping to 250 by the 1570s, then rising to more than 300 by 1603. The status was usually given only at the conclusion of long and distinguished careers, initially in the military, but more often in the civil service by Elizabeth's time. It was a personal distinction, never inherited until James I created the rank of knight baronet in the early seventeenth century; even when son followed father as a knight, it was often after a long interval and required a separate dubbing.[40]

The French Nobility

The French nobility is customarily divided into the older nobles of blood, the 'nobles of the sword', who were the second Estate, and the 'nobles of the robe' (*robins*), who gained their status through office-holding and dominated the third Estate. In law the two had the same privileges, however great the social gap between them may have been; and the *robins* emulated the behaviour of the older lineages and intermarried with them whenever possible.

The notion that the old nobility concentrated on rural estates and the military, while the nobility of the robe concentrated on offices and was more urban, is basically true, but overdrawn. It does not always work even for northern France, from which the model is derived, and is even less true for the south, where there was less separation of rural and urban nobilities than in the north. The new nobles bought rural lands and the old ones bought offices. While the privileges of nobility in England were often intangible, both ranks of nobles in France enjoyed exemption from direct taxes, a right whose economic value increased considerably as taxes rose during the sixteenth century. Like the English nobles, they had the right to a coat of arms and enjoyed an unrestricted right to bear arms. Only nobles could normally transmit their property entirely to the eldest son. The crown also paid sizeable pensions to the nobles, particularly the most powerful of them, to the point where they constituted a significant portion of the income of the high aristocracy.

The nobility of the sword still provided much of the royal fighting force in 1500, but technological change and the growth in size of armies had ended this by 1600, by which time only a few hundred of the perhaps 200,000 nobles of France served in the royal force. The rationale that the nobles deserved tax exemption because they fought had become absurd: the power of the nobility of the sword was ultimately based on lineage and the possession of land. Nobility as a status cannot be equated with wealth, for there were some poor nobles, particularly in the south. The nobles' incomes from their lands were generally declining during the sixteenth century; for with their demesnes generally leased to tenants, the older lords were unable to capitalize on high grain prices. Even payments from households under their lordship, in the case of lords of entire villages, were usually fixed and, accordingly, diminished in real value during the inflationary sixteenth century. The most prosperous noble families were the newer ones, townspeople who had just entered the nobility, usually by purchasing patents of nobility and/or buying royal offices that conferred tax exemption, and they were more interested in exploiting estates for their products as well as for rent.[41]

Money and Status

Although most commentators professed to disdain commercial wealth, in practice it was the chief means of mobility between status, and of maintaining a status once achieved. During the sixteenth century for the first time large numbers of wealthy townspeople were moving into the lower nobility, gaining a significance to the state that corresponded to their riches. What determined status was how long one had enjoyed the wealth, and what one used money to buy. Patents of nobility were for sale; they conferred a change of status, and in the cases of Spain and France, where they also conferred exemption from direct taxes, they also included an economic return. Status considerations were the main reasons for buying noble titles; but while in the late Middle Ages a career in local government accompanied by the use of one's family's money to buy land might gain entry into the nobility, this was no longer true in the sixteenth century. First, social status was based less exclusively on landholding, and the role of money in achieving social status was correspondingly greater. Money could also be used to buy patents of nobility apart from land. Second, as town liberties were eroded by the expansion of the central state, local magistracies became the strongholds of old lineages whose ambitions were bounded by their home cities. To gain nobility, with the attendant benefits of political influence at the national level and tax exemption, service in the royal bureaucracy was needed, even if it was performed in one's home city or province.[42]

Thus the distinction between upper bourgeoisie and lower nobility, which was never rigid anywhere, was blurring in the sixteenth century, in England mainly by the availability of land for purchase after the confiscation of the monasteries' estates in the late 1540s, in France by the purchase of noble lands and offices. But in France, in contrast to England, nobility was a legal standing that one could lose through inappropriate behaviour.

Louis XI had encouraged nobles to engage in commerce, but the notion that nobles could lose their rank (suffer 'derogation of status') by engaging in trade was first expressed in the late fifteenth century and was the rule by 1600. Derogation meant that the former noble's name went onto the tax rolls; but it was not hereditary, and a noble could restore his status by ceasing the activity that had led to his derogation. Although petty commerce was disallowed, overseas or other large-scale operations were usually permitted. Particularly since industry often involved minerals or timber, the nobles as landowners could exploit these resources without losing standing. But nobles were not supposed to farm or buy municipal taxes or lower-level offices. The growing number of suits against nobles for derogation in the sixteenth century is not due to more noble involvement in commerce, but rather to the need of the crown and municipalities to get them subject to the *taille*. Merchants, as well as the royal government, were rigid about derogation, for if nobles were allowed to enter commerce their tax immunity would have given them an incalculable advantage over the others. Since the nobles were punished for entering trade, and wealthy town families were leaving trade to buy titles and offices that gave them prestige and tax exemption, a considerable pool of investment capital was diverted in France toward social rather than economic uses.[43]

Given the diverse ways in which nobility could be obtained, the French nobility was not a small portion of the population, amounting to roughly one per cent in both 1328 and around 1470, although under Louis XI the numbers grew rapidly. In 1471 he ennobled all fiefholders of Normandy in return for money, and generally issued individual letters patent conferring nobility. But the recipients had to 'live nobly' to continue to enjoy the rank. Nobility through office-holding only became significant in total numbers at the end of the fifteenth century. In the beginning most of these were by individual acts; but by 1515 councillors of the *parlements* were considered noble if their families had held their offices for three generations; and Francis I sold noble titles and attached them to particular offices. Nobility through office-holding was only permanent if it was maintained for three generations. This was the preferred avenue of access for lawyers, and as a non-military group who thus did not 'live nobly', they were especially resented by the older nobility of the sword. As in England, knighthood (*chevalerie*) became a much more restricted status, amounting to the middle range of the French nobility by the sixteenth century.[44]

The 'rise of the gentry' in the sixteenth century is sometimes considered a mainly English phenomenon, but it was European in scale. Many of the gentry families who gave the English monarchy such trouble in the seventeenth century originated with county families who used the availability of land after Henry VIII's confiscations from the monasteries to increase their estates. Although there are some exceptions, most of them were not town families, but rather county families on the rise. Of the lay purchasers of church lands seized in France in 1569, nobles accounted for

27 per cent, townspeople for 30 per cent and officials and jurists for 15 per cent, with the rest going to peasants. The parallel with England is striking, but with a major difference: the purchase of an office was the most direct route to nobility in France, granted that it often led to or accompanied land purchases, while in England the land route without offices – or in addition to a parliamentary career – sufficed.[45]

Nobility in Spain

Aragon's nobles never had much political influence. The greater Castilian nobility initially did, but lost it during the the sixteenth century; yet it was probably more socially cohesive and distinct than the French. Landownership in Castile was highly concentrated, with roughly half the land belonging to a few great families and most of the rest in the hands of lesser nobles. Most Castilian nobles did not become courtiers until the seventeenth century: instead they spent more time than their ancestors had done away from court, tending to their estates. Their social pre-eminence was enhanced when in 1520 Charles V fixed gradations of noble rank, with 25 'Grandees of Spain' at the top. The lesser Castilian nobility consisted of *caballeros* (knights) or *hidalgos* (nobles) – the terms by this time were interchangeable, designating who could have a coat of arms and add the prefix *Don* to his name – and it was a varied group in terms of both wealth and ancestry. The kings found this group more reliable than the grandees and thus used it in government. In addition to tax exemption, members of the lesser nobility could be tried in criminal cases only by special courts, and sentences against them had to be confirmed by the royal council. Although most lesser nobles were discreet about getting into commerce, that alone was not yet a cause for derogation of status in Spain. To prove that a family was entitled to its rank, genealogies were manufactured; but it was not strictly hereditary, for the crown granted patents of nobility, and from the 1520s the sales of titles were especially frequent as the crown needed money.[46]

Above all else, the nobles of Europe had a common culture. Conditioned by a classical education that inculcated ideals and responsibilities while perpetuating an ideology of wealth and consumption, they saw their privileges as the natural consequence of superiority. Education of the governing groups of Europe is an important aspect of the expansion and transformation of 'Renaissance' culture during the sixteenth century, the topic to which we now turn.

|9|

The Later Renaissance: From Classical Humanism to Vernacular Classicism

Literature and Art in Italy in the Late Fifteenth and Sixteenth Centuries

While 'Renaissance' can be associated with novel, if at times atavistic, cultural trends before 1450, the term becomes much more difficult to define thereafter. First, Italian humanism before 1450 had been largely although not exclusively Latin, but in Italy alone in the second half of the fifteenth century the impetus of scholarship shifted briefly to Greek. The diaspora of the Greeks after the fall of Constantinople in 1453 brought scholars to Italy and contributed to an interest in Plato's works that complemented the strength of Aristotle in the medieval schools.

Plato's work had been used by the early humanists (see Chapter 4), but the later Renaissance in Italy saw a strong shift of Platonism away from promoting active involvement and the civic life, and toward an emphasis on solitary contemplation. This may be one element in the passing of primacy to the north, where a modified Aristotelianism still reigned in the schools. On commission from Cosimo de' Medici, Marsiglio Ficino (1433–99) had translated Plato's works into Latin by 1469, also later translating the works of the Neoplatonists Plotinus and Proclus. Ficino anticipated the 'Christian humanists' of northern Europe in believing that theology should be purged of textual excrescences; but his study of the Neoplatonists also convinced him that there existed a universal religion that included pre-Christian elements and thus was enriched by the Greeks and the pre-Christian Romans. Their work could thus be understood as theology as well as philosophy in a continuing process of divine revelation. The famous Platonic Academy at Florence was not a formal academic foundation, but rather consisted of the humanist friends of Cosimo's grandson Lorenzo 'the Magnificent'. Pico della Mirandola (1463–94), who is most associated with the Academy, was not a disciple of Ficino, but carried his ideas of ascending hierarchies further, and unlike Pico was influenced by Arabic and Jewish as well as Greek thought. Philosophy became increasingly linked to philology, the study of word meanings through their origins.[1]

The new learning flourished earliest at Florence, but even before 1450 the courts of the popes and cardinals at Rome had provided considerable patronage for artists and literary humanists, and this intensified in the late fifteenth and sixteenth centuries. The greatest painters and sculptors, notably Raphael and Michelangelo, did their finest works for the popes. Humanism at Rome obviously assumed forms not found elsewhere. Cicero, both because he was pre-Christian and republican, could not be followed as closely at Rome as at Florence, but the numerous court scholars used his language to praise Christian virtues and those of their patrons, promoting the idea of the papacy as the heir to ancient Rome. The humanist Aeneas Sylvius Piccolomini as Pope Pius II (1458–64) began the restoration of St Peter's cathedral, and the popes' buildings were likened by humanist writers to the imperial buildings of antiquity. Sixtus IV (1471–84) insisted on a Christian context for humanist literary work and particularly for paintings, and patronized Botticelli and Perugino. His greatest project was the Sistine Chapel, and he also added substantially to the Vatican Library.

Pope Alexander VI (1492–1503) is best known for his efforts to advance his family's interests through his son Cesare and daughter Lucrezia, but he also commissioned paintings, including adornments for the famous 'Borgia Apartments' in the Vatican palace. Julius II (1503–13) is known for his military and diplomatic activity and also for his beautifying of Rome, notably his reconstruction of the basilica of St Peter and his other commissions for the architect Donato Bramante. In 1508 he employed Raphael, a native of Urbino who is best known for the Madonnas that he painted in Florence in his youth, to paint frescoes in the papal apartments, a commission that occupied Raphael until his death in 1520. Julius also admired sculpture; one of the great monuments of the Italian Renaissance is Michelangelo's tomb for him.

The lesser princely courts, such as Urbino, became centres of humanist patronage. Federigo da Montefeltro at Urbino amassed a library, undertook a programme of church- and fortification-building and commissioned paintings and sculptures for the interiors of the churches and convents, as well as remodelling his family palace in the centre of Urbino. His portrait, by Piero della Francesca, from Borgo Sansepolcro near Urbino, is a classic.

Venice was the slowest of the major centres in patronizing humanists, only embracing the new learning enthusiastically in the sixteenth century. The delay was important for the form that the Renaissance took in Venice, which was the most important centre of printing in Italy: thus the major works that are associated with the spread of humanism beyond court circles and toward a broader audience come from Venice. The roughly two hundred *scuole* (charitable guilds with civic obligations) of the city gave commissions to the greatest painters, Gentile and Giovanni Bellini and Carpaccio. Much patronage in Venice was done by the city government, and higher office-holders, particularly doges, were also expected to finance works out of their own pockets. Venice did not have the association with Roman antiquity that the other cities did; its history was Byzantine and Christian; thus, only from the 1490s was there much interest in classical topoi there. In the sixteenth century the owners of palaces on the Grand Canal were having them adorned with paintings in classical style; architecture was a major avenue of artistic patronage in Venice as it had been in Florence, although it was less classical. Paintings adorned the interiors of their palaces. Giorgione, who died at the age of 34 in 1510, is unusual among Italian Renaissance painters in favouring landscapes rather than human portraits. Titian (1477–1576), the last great painter of the Renaissance, flourished at Venice, as did Giorgio Vasari, a painter who is best known for his biographies of his predecessors, *The Lives of the Artists*.

The Roman and Venetian periods were the apogee of the Italian phase of the Renaissance. With the French invasion of 1494 primacy definitely passed from Florence, as the civic commitments of the humanists did not extend to staying in a place devoid of patronage. The great masters Leonardo, Michelangelo, Raphael, Donato Bramante, Giorgione and Titian were most active between 1495 and 1520, and all produced for authoritarian regimes, although Venice was nominally a republic. After 1520 Michelangelo's work assumed an increasingly grotesque, early mannerist style. Intellectual leadership had clearly passed to northern Europe by this time, in large part because religious agitation had replaced recovery of the classics as the major intellectual issue of the day. Titian was the only great painter in a 'Renaissance style' who was active in Italy after 1520.

Italian art of the late Renaissance thus changed significantly. The Netherlandish technique of oil painting was used for most portable works, including altarpieces, while church interiors and other mural paintings used other techniques, particularly the fresco, in which the paint is applied to wet plaster, as in Michelangelo's famous ceiling for the Sistine Chapel in the Vatican. As wealth increased among the upper classes there was an increasing market for scenes of actual occurrences, such as battles. Particularly outside Italy, taste was shifting away from the strictly classical and even religious, and toward realistic portraits of contemporary subjects. Portraiture, including family groups, was the most important new development in art in the sixteenth century. Houses were being furnished more elaborately, and works of art were adorning the homes of the middle and upper middle classes. The number of rooms in homes grew, even as the rooms themselves sometimes became smaller; and while earlier they had been furnished very sparely, some were positively cluttered in the sixteenth century. The price of art works remained behind the rate of inflation, but the most prized commodity of cultural display was still the book.[2]

Leonardo da Vinci and the Scientific Spirit (1452–1519)

Leonardo is a towering figure who is associated understandably in the public mind with the later Italian Renaissance. Essentially self-educated, the illegitimate son of a Florentine and a village girl of Vinci, he learned principles of mechanics and architecture from personal experience that gained him patronage from the secular princes of northern Italy and France. Although Leonardo is best known now for his unfinished paintings, including *The Last Supper* and the *Mona Lisa*, he was better known in his own time as an engineer. His achievements include observations in aerodynamics that foreshadowed modern air travel, and in anatomy, the result of his illicit observation of corpses in the morgue of Florence. Unfortunately, his originality landed him in trouble with the church authorities. He began as an apprentice painter at Florence, but moved to Milan in 1482, where he remained until the fall of the Sforza regime in 1498; he is the only major figure of the Renaissance who is associated principally with Milan. He designed churches there and developed an interest in town planning. Returning to Florence in 1500, he worked briefly as a military engineer for Cesare Borgia in the Romagna, developing an interest in and some machinery for swamp reclamation while in his service. He returned to Milan in 1506 to the service of the ruling French court there. He also worked for two years in Rome, but in 1516 took employment at Francis I's court, where he died. His notebooks are full of designs of projects never completed, and show an extremely fertile scientific imagination at work with a breadth of interest that has perhaps never been equalled. Widely regarded as a magician by his contemporaries, only in his painting did he train disciples.

Science in the Late Renaissance

Leonardo was the greatest applied scientist of the Renaissance. The period of this book is most notable for the progress of government, public administration, finance, the development of a world economy, and cultural and religious changes. It was not a period of great advance in sciences except for those related to mathematics, the most abstract of the sciences. Theoretical science was never a strong point of European culture, although the practical application of mechanical principles and the development of labour-saving devices was quite advanced. The argument has been made that advances in commercial techniques and quantification in the late Middle Ages, combined with the development of mathematical perspective in art and habits of criticism, were fostered by humanist textual analysis, but the void of demonstrable scientific achievement is overwhelming. From the perspective of the sciences as disciplines there is little to boast about until the ascendancy of inductive reasoning in the seventeenth century, for the humanism that had pervaded the schools, in both its pure and its 'Christian' or 'northern' form, was deductive.

The periodization of scientific advance is suggestive. We have seen that the half-century after 1275 saw the onset of numerous important cultural, social, economic and institutional developments that would culminate in the early seventeenth century. Alfred Crosby has recently noted that this period witnessed important practical applications of mathematical principles. The first mechanical clock was built by Richard of Wallingford, and by 1400 virtually all major cities sounded bells based on equal hours to begin, divide and end the work day. Cannon and eventually smaller guns revolutionized warfare, while the advances in navigation and commercial techniques that we have already discussed all required skill in quantification. Princes and some cities were keeping regular accounts before 1200 and virtually all did so by 1300, in much more detailed form than previously. Hindu or Arabic numerals had been known in the west since the twelfth century, but only came into general use in the fourteenth, even among merchants. The fact that late medieval Europe experienced a shortage of coin mean that its monetary system was more abstract than those of its neighbours who had more gold and silver. Thus quantification, value in the abstract, replaced coin to a considerable degree in the fourteenth and fifteenth centuries.[3]

The scientific advances of the sixteenth century were unconnected with humanism, and most of them resulted from practical experience rather than academic training. Leonardo is the most conspicuous case in point. The academic study of medicine in the Middle Ages was based on logical analysis of the ancient works of Galen and Hippocrates: a method of inquiry that was quite useful for law and theology was a disaster for one in which observation was crucial. The church prohibited dissection on grounds that the body must be left pristine for the corporeal resurrection. Not surprisingly, given this background, there were few significant advances in medical knowledge. Ambroise Paré (1517–90) began as a French army surgeon who applied poultices and bindings to wounds instead of cauterizing them with boiling oil. He also pioneered turning the foetus during childbirth for safer delivery, and invented several surgical instruments. Paracelsus (1493–1541) is more controversial, for he spared no effort in verbal abuse of his critics, and empirical science and alchemic quackery were disconcertingly mixed in his writings. The Netherlander Andreas Vesalius (1514–64) studied in Italy at the University of Padua and gained practical experience in hospitals. In 1543 he published *Seven Books on the Structure of the Human Body*, complete with original drawings, a work that laid the foundation for the modern study of anatomy.

The Egyptian Greek astronomer Ptolemy had deduced in the second century AD that celestial bodies revolve around the earth, a view that quickly became enshrined in astronomy and Christian theology. The Polish canon and astronomer Nicholas Copernicus (1473–1543), however, published *On the Revolutions of Celestial Bodies* shortly before his death. Copernicus demonstrated that the earth and the other planets revolve on their axes and move in orbit around the sun. Geography also made significant advances, not all of them connected to European contact with the Americas and Asia. The Fleming Gerard Mercator (1512–94) was the first who successfully drew a map of the round earth on a flat surface, and published detailed maps of the Low Countries as well as a world atlas. The English and French kings and individual German princes commissioned maps of their territories for military and economic purposes. By 1600 the internal geography and topography of Europe had been charted with remarkable accuracy.

Political Thought in the Late Italian Renaissance

While the early Renaissance is associated with a Latin literary humanism that includes a civic component, the sixteenth century is associated with changes in political thought that are based not on declamation of Ciceronian phraseology but rather on logical examination of the history of antiquity to derive relevant lessons from it. Although in fact the secular state exercised considerable control over the churches during the central Middle Ages, little political theory developed to justify this state of affairs. The quarrel between Philip IV of France and Pope Boniface VIII was a watershed (see Chapter 2): for the first time the pope's opponents gave at least as good as they got. The difference was the recovery of Aristotle and the use of his political writings in the schools. Secular thinkers argued from an Aristotelian perspective that 'politics', in the sense of civil society, was natural to man. The *Defender of the Peace* of Marsiglio of Padua (see Chapter 4) elicited horror and was banned until Henry VIII had it translated to use its anti-papal passages. But just as Machiavelli's justification of princely immorality in the interest of the prince's gaining state power was greeted with public reproach by the very princes who were putting his principles into practice, so Marsiglio's justification of civil society and the secular state in terms of themselves were reflected in actual conditions.

Niccolò Machiavelli (1469–1527) seems such a foreteller of the contemporary world that his significance for mainstream political thought of his own day has been exaggerated. No contemporary thinker quoted him approvingly. He was, however, an astute observer of politics, both of his own time and of antiquity. To call him a humanist may be an exaggeration, but he owed a great deal to the civic humanists of the previous generation. All of his writings were in Italian, but by his time – *The Prince*, his most famous if least profound work, was written in 1513 but only published in 1532 – this was not remarkable even among Italians. In contrast to the

Florentine Platonists, Machiavelli was deeply pessimistic about human nature, and concluded that that it could only be kept from self-destruction by authority. His most radical break from fifteenth-century Italian political thought was the role that he assigned to chance or fate. He did not deny that rational planning was needed, as in his exhortations to the prince to calculate carefully, but saw that things happen that ultimately no amount of planning can avoid. He saw religion purely as a tool of statecraft; whether the universe is governed by rational laws or God, fortune or fate can overturn all without warning.

Machiavelli's concern with fate came from personal experience. He witnessed the destruction of rural Italy and, more generally, of the old Italian state system, in the Italian and French invasions. He evidently knew Leonardo da Vinci from 1502, when Machiavelli was Second Chancellor of the Signoria of Florence and Leonardo was an architect and military engineer for Cesare Borgia. Machiavelli's understanding of the importance of public works projects and technology generally, as well as his admiration for Borgia, may have taken shape during this time.[4]

Machiavelli was a practising historian, the author of a *History of Florence* that was commissioned by the Florentine government in 1519. The *History* used original documents, breaking away from the Bruni tradition of using the phraseology of Roman historians. As his chief source for the 1420s, Machiavelli used Giovanni Cavalcanti, a Florentine historian who disliked the rulers of Florence in that decade, the same regime that Bruni had praised and that he served as chancellor. Machiavelli noted the neglect of Cavalcanti's position in the proem to his own work by saying that later generations had feared offending the descendants of the people whom Cavalcanti was criticizing. Machiavelli thus was aware of the bonds linking the early civic humanists, such as Bruni, to the patronage of the rulers of Florence.[5] More than is currently fashionable, he followed the humanist tradition by studying history for the lessons that it could give for human behaviour. Patterns could be deduced from history, he concluded, and Rome provided the best examples. He shared the humanist notion that humanity had declined progressively since antiquity, and he also introduced to western historiography the notion of patterns repeating in cycles.

The Prince is an early work, and the only one that is based largely on contemporary rather than Roman examples. Machiavelli uses the example of Cesare Borgia to argue that personal morality has no place in the statecraft of the prince, whose only function is to preserve his power at the least cost. Public relations are key: the ruler must give the appearance of being generous while in fact husbanding his resources. Dissimulation, covert manipulation and violence are the marks of the successful ruler. The prince is urged to be loved if possible, but to be feared if that cannot be combined with love. He should cultivate a reputation for generosity in the right places, but also know how to conserve resources. The personal morality of the prince has no connection with statecraft; the ruler is to be as deceitful and cunning as necessary in order to preserve the state and himself from their enemies.

As a Florentine, Machiavelli was less interested in the Roman Empire than in the Republic, which he studied in his most profound work, the *Discourses on the First Ten Books of Titus Livius*. Although his interest in Cesare Borgia is sometimes times attributed to Italian 'national' sentiment, he seems to have thought rather of nationalism in cultural terms, particularly after Italy was invaded in 1494 by persons whom he considered barbarians, different in language and culture from the Italians. Given that Machiavelli's political orientation was towards Italy and, to a lesser extent, the Germans who had figured so prominently in Italy's past, it is hardly surprising that 'nationalism' in the English or even French senses would not have occurred to him. His frame of reference was the Marsiglian city-state.

Machiavelli's significance was twofold: his argument that power was an end in itself and needed no external justification; and his purely mechanical analysis of the political process in terms of what past experience showed would work. While Marsiglio had justified the state against the church in terms of the fulfilment of man's basic nature, Machiavelli worked from the reality that the state was supreme, and concentrated on how it could work most effectively, especially how it could preserve the stability so sought by Marsiglio. Machiavelli shared with Marsiglio the Aristotelian notion of the origin of the state in a surrender of power by the human legislator to a ruler or rulers. His work thus is a stage in the development of the 'social contract' theory that would become so important in the seventeenth and eighteenth centuries. Morality is not absolute, he argued, but rather is conditioned by the norms that the ruler establishes to preserve order, the function transferred to him from the citizenry.

The Spread of Humanism to Northern Europe

Only after 1450 did Italian cultural trends spread to northern Europe. The Spanish and French campaigns in Italy wrecked the native culture, but also resulted in greater exposure to it by the north Europeans, whose political power was clearly ending the situation in which city-states could flourish disturbed only by one another. Thus some Italians, including Leonardo da Vinci, emigrated to the courts of the north in the wake of the disturbances, while others had to leave Italy as political refugees. A few went for religious reasons, mainly from the 1540s, while more went abroad to seek classical manuscripts. Several obtained teaching positions in the north, as such kings as Matthias Corvinus of Hungary, and particularly Francis I and to a lesser extent Henry VIII, financed chairs of rhetoric, Greek or Latin studies, or both. The better scholars stayed in Italy, but the very fact that the lesser figures were in demand shows the attraction of humanism for the northerners.

Art in Northern Europe in the Sixteenth Century

Humanism was spread mainly by northern intellectuals and artists, who came to Italy for training and returned to their homelands to spread the new learning. Although northerners were imitating Italian fashions in literature in the fifteenth century, the art market generally went in the other direction, with Italians buying Dutch paintings through Bruges. Then it changed, as Mediterranean perspective and portraiture gained the initiative from the Netherlanders. By the sixteenth century many northerners, including most Flemish and Dutch painters of note, went to Italy to study, and the art market also received a new impulse through printing woodcuts. Although colour paintings could not be printed, the Frankfurt fairs handled engravings and 'art woodcuts'. Yet the greatest northern artists, such as Pieter Brueghel and Albrecht Dürer, always returned home after their studies and painted on essentially native themes with some Italianate technical influence. Thus art with classical motifs remained mainly Italian, at least in the greatest works – northern imitations of them were less good – while northerners handled other topoi, particularly religious themes, in an essentially Gothic framework. German art dealt with essentially traditional and indigenous themes, mainly religious pictures and portraiture, through the 1530s. Then, as the old generation died out, they were replaced by imitators of the Italians.

Literary Humanism

Humanism itself underwent a profound change in the later Renaissance. An élitist literary movement in the early fifteenth century, by 1530 it was a broad scholarly and pedagogical current that reshaped educational institutions and aesthetic values throughout Europe. It always remained a fundamentally philological orientation, rather than a philosophical or artistic school; but in that form it hastened the demise of the older emphasis on logic and analysis of linguistic concepts. During the transition the humanist emphasis on establishment of the correct text was often applied to religious questions in the north, and thus it became associated with the Protestant movement.

Grammar

The Italian influence on the educational curriculum was felt first in the area of grammar. This subject, the initial one of the trivium, had been revolutionized in the academies of Italy during the fifteenth century by replacing the medieval grammars with classical. In the north, by contrast, grammar was normally taught in the universities. Replacing the old learning with the new caused considerable faculty debate, and was not accomplished in most places until the early sixteenth century. The same problem also occurred with theology: in Italy most of the earliest humanists except Greek emigrés had supported themselves with bureaucratic positions without holding academic appointments, and since theology was generally taught at religious houses rather than the universities, and the theologians were so weak at the Italian universities, there was not the level of academic conflict that existed in the north. The humanist curriculum was also resented in some quarters as an Italian intrusion.

It is no coincidence that Protestantism, with its emphasis on purity of ancient texts, was born in the Empire and in a university environment. Germany had only four universities before 1400 (Vienna, Erfurt, Cologne and Heidelberg), but there were 13 by 1500, most of them political creations, giving Germany the largest concentration of educational institutions in Europe, although most of them were small and they were certainly the most provincial, attracting a mainly middle-class clientele. But while most universities in Italy, Spain and France outside Paris emphasized law, with arts and theology of less significance, the less-developed German universities concentrated on the arts. Furthermore, although the universities of the central Middle Ages had international student bodies, all except Paris and Bologna attracted mainly their own nationals by 1500. Lectures were in Latin; after the victory of humanism the university curriculum was rather uniform throughout Europe. Thus one might get more famous or more exciting professors, or both, by studying abroad, but the period when universities were attended for subjects that were not taught elsewhere was long past.

Even before Italianate humanism became a serious issue the scholastic tradition had developed a deep fissure between the *via antiqua* and the *via moderna*. The ancients spent more time on the texts themselves, the moderns on theological questions based on the texts. The modern way was more concerned with linguistics and exact meanings of terms, and is associated with Ockhamite nominalism; while the ancient way associated with Thomist/Scotist realism was basic Aristotle pruned of the accretions of late Middle Ages. The first German universities were nominalist, but some, beginning with Cologne in 1415, began switching to the ancient-realist position in the fifteenth century. Louvain and Paris were also *via antiqua*, and the graduates of these three began having an impact in Germany after about 1450, often with the help of the local princes who were founding new universities. The university of Ingolstadt even divided arts into two faculties. At Tübingen, Mainz and, from 1499, Vienna, both versions were taught and had separate administrations. Wittenberg also had a separate chair in nominalist theology, which was held by Martin Luther from 1510.[6]

There were many routes by which the changes in grammatical instruction in Italy reached the north. The schools in the Netherlands of the Brethren of the Common Life are often associated with the northern Renaissance because Erasmus and other prominent humanists were taught the rudiments of Latin grammar in their school at Deventer, but the Brethren essentially helped spread it in their schools once others had introduced it. The classical tradition as such had always been alive and well in the north, however much the curriculum may have emphasized specialized readings and logic. As happened in Italy, humanism in the north first caught the imaginations of wandering scholars who had studied in Italy and then returned to the north, where they received university appointments that gave them much more influence on the future of the curriculum than they would have had otherwise.

While grammar had been linked to logic and linguistics during the scholastic period, the humanists tied it to literature. For them, moral and natural philosophy were needed to attain the ultimate goal of eloquence. For Conrad Celtis (1459–1508), as he explained in his famous inaugural lecture at Ingolstadt in 1492, Germany's problems, including foreign domination, came from its barbarism and the lack of eloquence of its supposedly educated men. In effect, he recommended teaching them poems and songs, which would instil love of fatherland, which would take care of all else! Celtis studied at several German universities, but his reputation was made when the emperor Frederick III invented the title of poet laureate for him in 1487. Only then did he go to Italy, returning in 1489 after a short stay. He brought back the idea of informal academies or 'sodalities', but he disliked the Italians' arrogance. He moved about from professorship to professorship: he was professor of poetry at the University of Vienna from 1497, and attracted the emperor Maximilian's attention. Maximilian saw the propaganda value of the humanists, who rewarded his patronage by fostering an image of him that has distorted perceptions of his actual power.[7]

The lecturers had their own favourite authors to use as models for Latin style, most often Horace, Terence or Cicero, but also such modern authors as Petrarch, Bruni or Filelfo. New grammars were written, starting with that of Bernard Perger, whose *Nova grammatica* of 1482 was largely lifted, as he admitted, from the *Rudimenta grammatices* of the Italian humanist Niccolò Perotti. Jakob Wimpheling was the most notable propagandizer of the need for eloquent grammar, and wrote extensively on pedagogy. He was not a strictly classical humanist, for his examples included church fathers, Italian humanists and contemporary writers. Most of the early humanists ignored logic, although Wimpfeling thought it useful: the very essence of German academic humanism consisted of replacing logic and system with rhetoric. The increasing emphasis on ethics found among the Italian humanists was much less pronounced in Germany.[8]

Except for Wimpheling, the early German humanists were essentially unsystematic literati, who could not have had much impact on pedagogical method. Their Italian ties were also superficial at best. The linkage of the northern and southern traditions seems to have been due to the vogue of

Italian literature combined with a tie, perhaps fabricated, to the new Italian grammars. After the German humanists achieved the grammar reform that they desired, the *De inventione dialectica* of Rudolf Agricola became the major work on argumentation, used in the universities of Protestant northern Europe from its first appearance in print in 1515 until the mid-seventeenth century, and replacing Perotti's grammar, which was preferred in Italy. Agricola, born near Groningen in 1444, studied at Ferrara under Battista, the son of Guarino of Verona; he taught Alexander Hegius, who taught Erasmus at Deventer. He died at Heidelberg, where he taught at the university, in 1485. But although he finished *De inventione dialectica* around 1479, it was only printed in 1515, in a form heavily edited by Erasmus, who inserted material that made it seem that Agricola was arguing in favour of substituting literary works for the traditional logic of the schools in the study of grammar. Erasmus in effect became the publicist for the new views on philology in the curriculum. Much the increased interest in Agricola came from references planted by Erasmus in successive editions of his *Adages* to Hegius, his own teacher, who was a link with his teacher Agricola, who in turn was a link with Guarino of Verona and Italy. He invented alleged personal memories of Agricola, whom he may have met once. Lisa Jardine has thus concluded that much of the linkage between northern and southern grammatical study was the result of Erasmus' imagination and skill at publicizing his own views.[9]

Much of the delay in receiving humanism in the north was due to personal hostility of the older professors to the unconventional living arrangements, including the large role played in them by alcohol and extra-marital sex, of the harbingers of the new learning. Peter Luder (1415–72), the earliest humanist to have much impact in Germany, studied at Heidelberg, went to Italy around 1434, studied under Guarino at Ferrara and returned to Germany in 1456. He then lectured at several German universities on the *studia humanitatis*, but he was forced out of each of them by a personal scandal. A faculty survey at Ingolstadt showed no one opposed to having a salaried poet on the faculty, but several objected personally to Celtis, who was frequently absent, drunk, and was known to have railed at his students as ignorant barbarians. Several recommended dismissing him and using his high salary to hire two replacements; one simply wrote, 'If he lectured, he'd be fine.'[10]

The fact that their reforms initially concentrated on grammar as the beginning of the liberal arts curriculum meant that it took considerable time for the humanists' curriculum to have much impact on the advanced courses. Yet the arts course even as revised by them included some theology. As the humanists became increasingly radical, they moved away from philo-logical concerns toward religious doctrine, which was taught in the higher faculty of theology. They also wanted to replace existing translations of Aristotle with new ones made in Italy during the fifteenth century. This was less innocuous than it might seem, for the old translations had been the basis of considerable logical work on Aristotle. The theologians claimed that discussing theology required a technical terminology that the humanists lacked, which is certainly understandable in view of the fact that the humanists insisted on using a Latin that was already archaic when Christians began writing in the language. The traditionalists in the arts faculties and the theologians resented the big salaries and positions being given to people who in many cases even lacked university training, but were setting themselves up as experts on poetry and other higher things.[11]

Given the common assumption that the classics were the only proper basis for education, what divided young from old was often not so much a restructuring of subjects as a willingness to use new and updated texts, along with more history and moral philosophy, in teaching subjects that remained standard. Most theologians admitted that grammar had become too theoretical and logic too lost in commentaries. Humanism came to dominate western education through the arts course, beginning with a revision of the texts used in grammar and rhetoric, downgrading logic and with it Aristotle, and replacing the required readings in medieval authors with more extensive, and more accurately edited, readings in the Greek and particularly Latin sources. Poetry, history and ethics became the thrust of the required readings in grammar and rhetoric, rather than theological material.

As the older generation died out and political conditions improved, curricular changes were made. The early humanists, who had matriculated only in the arts course, were younger than the professors who had gone through the entire curriculum and were teaching in one of the higher faculties. Over time, however, the young grew old and got into salaried positions through seniority; and since they were more receptive to humanism than the professors whom they had replaced, the humanist curriculum gradually became dominant from about 1515. By 1535 it was the basis of the arts course throughout Germany. Aristotle was still the basis for the logic course, but rather than commentaries his original works were used, and new translations replaced those of the scholastics. More stipends were provided for lectures on ancient authors, and lectureships in Greek and Hebrew were established. Beginning students studied grammar, rhetoric and poetry rather than logic. Emphasis in lectures was to be placed on the Bible, with commentary from the church fathers and, in the Protestant universities, from Luther's works. Princes founded more salaried professorships. Some statutes gave latitude as to which authorities might be used, and the required course was not exactly the same at any two universities. Not all German universities got rid of scholastic texts, but they did abolish the distinction in the arts course between the old (scholastic) and new (humanist) ways and assert that the way to truth was unitary and that the old schism between the two approaches had hindered progress. Degree candidates in arts generally had to study at least rhetoric and, in many cases, Greek.[12]

University Education in the West

Outside Germany, foundations of humanist bent included the College of Ildefonso at the new University of Alcalá, founded in 1508, with chairs in the three Biblical languages (Greek, Hebrew and Latin). The will of Jerome van Busleyden, who had studied law at Padua and evidently developed humanist interests there, established a trilingual college at the university of Louvain in 1517. Predictably, Latin attracted the most students, followed by Greek and, at some distance, Hebrew. Most men of letters of the sixteenth-century Netherlands studied at some time at Louvain, which thus became vitally important in the spread of the 'new learning' in the region.[13]

France had 13 universities by 1500, but most were still small; only Toulouse and Paris had more than 1000 students in the fifteenth century, and some of the new ones had fewer than 100. They provided competition for Paris, particularly since Paris did not teach civil law, which was a major route to nobility. Montpellier was the oldest school of Roman law in France, but it was less prestigious by the fifteenth century than Toulouse. Orléans and Angers provided further competition for Paris in the north. The university of Paris still had pride of place, but it was no longer supreme as before. It had lost credibility by supporting John the Fearless of Burgundy after the assassination of Louis of Orléans in 1407, by having supported the English in 1420 and having been involved in the trial of Joan of Arc.

Paris was the centre of considerable controversy in the sixteenth century. The Sorbonne, the theological faculty, which often arbitrated theological cases, was extremely conservative and lost ground to the colleges of Montaigu and Navarre. Although the university had been generally tolerant of humanism before 1515, the Reuchlin case (see Chapter 10), in which the Sorbonne arbitrated, sharpened antagonisms between the conservatives and proponents of the 'modern way'. Erasmus' satires of scholasticism, which he came to detest after being a student at the College of Montaigu for two years, had much to do with the disfavour into which scholasticism fell. After 1515, with the theological faculty led by Noel Beda, director of the College de Montaigu, the humanists and the theologians polarized into two antagonistic camps. Francis I was sympathetic to the humanists. Increasingly intrigued by Italian culture after his campaign there in 1515, as early as 1517 Francis projected a foundation at the Sorbonne on the Louvain model; but his military involvements and the unavailability of suitable candidates in Hebrew and Greek delayed the project until 1530, when it quickly became known as the College of the Three Languages. Part of the loss of prestige of the university of Paris was not only its conservatism, but also the fact that professors, like civil servants, sold and rented their offices to others, regardless of qualification, and sold degrees and attendance certificates, which conferred benefit of clergy. Given the value of a law degree, however, the problem was even worse elsewhere.

Although their curricula were somewhat antiquated in terms of the students' requirement of a profession after their studies, even with the growing vogue of humanism the universities remained a necessary prologue for careers in education, law, medicine and to a lesser extent government (birth counted for a great deal in the latter, but people outside the nobility could move upward through education). Spain had only six universities in 1450 but 33 in 1600, and much of the growth was due to royal patronage. While state offices in France were being sold without regard to qualifications, the Spanish crown insisted that the occupants of high offices have university training in law. Thus the *hidalgos* went to the universities, got law degrees and monopolized the bloated civil service. Given the link of the universities to state service, more overtly even than in England, the state increasingly oversaw appointments of university administrators and professors. For religious reasons the formerly flourishing universities of eastern Europe declined in the late sixteenth century, and except for Padua, most Italian universities also declined, although the large number of academies took up some of the demand for higher education.[14]

The humanist curriculum had little impact on England until the 1490s except for the foundation in 1458 of Magdalen College, Oxford, where the new curriculum in grammar and moral philosophy was taught. Few English scholars went to Italy before 1500, and the number was never as large as of Frenchmen and particularly Germans. Even more than on the Continent, where the classical heritage was always stronger and more visible than in England, humanist studies in England were usually an adjunct to careers in public administration, diplomacy and law. The actual practice of government in England anticipated much of the essence of humanist political thought, particularly the notion that political authority ascended from an informed and active citizenry to the prince. As a movement of political thought based on the notion of public participation by the informed citizen, civic humanism was already practised, if not preached in classical terms.[15]

The earliest notable humanists in England were William Grocyn (1446–1517), Thomas Linacre (1460–1524) and John Colet (1467–1519). All were interested in Greek, which by now was much more important in the Italian-humanistic programme of study than earlier. After travelling in Italy, accompanied by Linacre, for six years (1485–91), Grocyn became tutor to Prince Arthur. After establishing his reputation by translating Galen into English from the Greek, which in itself gives an idea of the backward state of English medicine at this time, Grocyn founded the Royal College of Physicians. Colet (1467–1519) came from a prominent mercer family of London – his father had been Lord Mayor – and became Dean of

St Paul's cathedral in London. His famous lectures at Oxford on St Paul's epistles in 1497 simply lectured on the text continuously, rather than glossing it with interpretations; this was a literary approach, and something quite revolutionary. With his family's wealth Colet established St Paul's school for teaching Latin and Greek and the works of Christian authors who wrote good (classical) Latin. The mercers' guild supervised the school.

English humanism is associated with theology and the universities, where new colleges with independent endowments trained humanists. Cambridge developed an even stronger humanist orientation in the sixteenth century than Oxford's. St John's College was founded in 1511 by John Fisher, Bishop of Rochester. Fisher was essentially traditional, and polemicized against Luther, but he supported the study of Greek and Hebrew. Even more than in France, humanists held important positions in the English government, most obviously in the case of Henry VIII's chancellor, Thomas More (1478–1535). Most of More's work was more theological than humanistic, but he did work with Erasmus on translations of Lucian, although his history of Richard III was a Tudor propaganda piece without historical value. More is best known for his *Utopia* (1516), which purports to be an ideal commonwealth founded entirely on rational principles. Initially it was more popular on the Continent than in England, where a vernacular translation of 1551 made its reputation. It is not a particularly profound social commentary, for the complaints of injustice that it contains were quite commonplace, often included as the justifications for parliamentary bills on such subjects as enclosure. There is a deep vein of irony in *Utopia*, and More may not have intended it as a serious reform programme.[16]

While earlier leaders had sought their servants from the church, Thomas Cromwell wanted university graduates. St John's graduates included Roger Ascham, the most notable educational theorist of sixteenth-century England and Princess Elizabeth's tutor for a time, and William Cecil, the chief minister of Queen Elizabeth. Corpus Christi College was established at Oxford in 1517. All the colleges required the ability to write and speak in Latin. In 1518 Cardinal Wolsey (see Chapter 5) projected a Cardinal's College at Oxford which would preserve the existing structure of faculties but would emphasize Greek and Latin studies within their curricula. His fall intervened, but Henry VIII at the end of his reign founded Christ Church College at Oxford along these lines, and also Trinity College Cambridge, which by 1564 housed nearly one-quarter of the undergraduates at Cambridge. The colleges, which were less aristocratic than the older halls, contributed to the rise of undergraduate commoners at the universities. Humanism thus became an important avenue of upward mobility. Extremely high numbers went to the university for a while but left without obtaining a degree. The House of Commons in 1563 had 67 members with some university training, and 145 in 1583.[17]

Northern Humanism and Religion: Desiderius Erasmus (1469–1536)

Humanism affected religious concerns in the early sixteenth century mainly through textual criticism and the primacy that it placed on the original and proper text of scriptures. While in Italy philological humanism, directed toward ethics, became increasingly focused on the scholar in his study, insulated from the material world, the northern humanists applied their philological insights to religion, which was a much more current topic, and certainly more influential among political leaders and the population at large than the Italians' aesthetic concerns. Although clearly adapted by the northerners from the Italians, humanism was preserved in its vernacular, religious northern form much longer than in the Italian version. It did not lack a secular side, for pagan authors were appreciated for their ethical lessons. Some northern scholarship turned toward the Ancient Near East as the culture that had given birth to Christ, rejecting as papist and pagan the traditional humanist emphasis on Rome.

The link of the humanist philological tradition of the south, and the northern concentration on correct texts in the interest of religion, is provided by the Dutchman Desiderius Erasmus (1469–1536). Erasmus is one of the earliest intellectuals who consciously cultivated his own career through the medium of print. He was undeniably a great scholar, but he also understood the need to cultivate an image to gain patronage. He culled his own papers and letters, destroying some and editing others, to enhance the vogue for his writings and remove things that might blemish his posthumous reputation.

Erasmus was educated at the school of the Brethren of the Common Life at 's Hertogenbosch. Although he is often portrayed as formed by the religious notions of the Brethren, in fact his 3-year stay there turned him against monasticism in all its forms. Yet in 1486 he entered the monastery of the canons regular at Steyn, near Gouda, where he discovered classical authors in the monastic library and learned to write and speak Latin. His correspondence from this time shows fervent classicism. He was ordained in 1492 and immediately left the monastery to become secretary in the household of the bishop of Cambrai, who had ties to the French/Burgundian court in Brussels. In 1494 he first read Augustine's *On Christian Doctrine*, and remained a fervent Augustinian for the rest of his life. The next year he began doctoral studies in theology at the Sorbonne. His early writings show tendencies that would mark his mature work: he criticized scholastism for inserting philosophy into theology and, indeed, showed little understanding of the great theologians of medieval Catholicism. He disliked the methodical Aristotle, preferring Plato's work.

As was common among advanced students, Erasmus took pupils at Paris. One was William Blount, the future Lord Mountjoy, with whom he spent

8 months in England between 1499 and 1500. He became acquainted with Thomas More in London, and met John Colet in Oxford. Colet had corresponded with Ficino, and gave Erasmus an introduction to Florentine Platonism. Erasmus had been a minor figure on the Continent, but he was so learned in comparison with what he found in England that he got an exaggerated reputation there. His first English visit turned Erasmus more toward the ancient church fathers and scriptures. He returned to Paris, where the first edition of the *Adages*, the work that established his reputation, was printed in 1500. His other early major work, published in 1504, was the *Handbook of the Christian Soldier*, a pacifist treatise emphasizing internal piety and asceticism. Devotion to the saints consisted of imitating their virtues, not praying to them or making bargains with them. This was a handbook for the Christian layman; it offended so many in the church establishment that it was put on the Index of Prohibited Books after Erasmus died. Erasmus next spent 3 years in Italy, where he met Aldus Manutius, the printer of Venice, who published the second edition of the *Adages*. He returned to England in 1509, remaining 6 years, and his criticism of non-Biblical church practices such as pilgrimages and relics intensified. It was under his influence that Thomas More's *Utopia* was published in 1516.

Erasmus published voluminously, always in Latin, in a vivid and always entertaining style. The work by which he is best known today, *The Praise of Folly*, was published in 1511 and dedicated to More. Folly is personified, accompanying the Christian everywhere, including in his encounters with popes, mendicants, bad preachers and other conspicuous churchmen. But after satirizing humans Folly makes a genuine conversion and confesses her error. *The Praise of Folly* was followed in 1515 by the third edition of the *Adages*, which was more critical of the clergy and church institutions than the earlier versions. The first edition of his *Colloquies* appeared in 1518. The *Colloquies* are in dialogue form, subtitled 'formulas of familiar conversation, useful to young people, not only for polishing their style but also for directing their lives'. Subsequent editions through 1533 doubled the size of the work, refined and added dialogues and directed it increasingly towards an adult audience rather than students.

Erasmus' scholarship is further shown in his critical editions of Latin authors and Latin translations of Greek authors. His letters, some of which he published himself, were intended for a wide audience. His Greek was largely self-taught, and he tried but failed to master Hebrew: he simply did not read modern vernacular authors. Thus, when the French and even some Italian humanists were getting away from the exclusive use of Latin, Erasmus tried to restore it. His pedagogical influence was thus retrograde and had little impact on the future. He was a grammarian, but he placed grammar at the service of theology, which conditioned his later critique of the Vulgate on the basis of comparison with the Greek New Testament. Much of the furore over his edition of the New Testament, published in

1516, was over its format. He printed a revised text, explaining his changes from the Vulgate in notes. By contrast, the Complutensian Polyglot Bible of 1521, sponsored by the Spanish cardinal Cisneros, printed parallel editions of the Vulgate with other texts, thus avoiding criticizing the older version directly. Much of the issue was a question of authority. Scholars admitted that the Vulgate was inaccurate in some respects, but they resisted the idea that a sacred text could be improved by mortals.

Erasmus's ambiguous relations with Luther and his movement were a turning-point in his career, so much so that in southern Europe he came to be identified as a heretic, although he remained in the church and was never excommunicated. Luther and Erasmus agreed that there existed many institutional abuses of the church, on the drawbacks of the scholastic method and the worthlessness of indulgences. The two corresponded, and Erasmus arranged to have Luther's views given a hearing at the university of Louvain, where he resided between 1517 and 1521. But Luther, although an educated theologian, was no humanist, and Erasmus was put off by his vitriolic language. Erasmus vacillated until 1524 when, seeing the need to take sides, he published *The Freedom of the Will*, which was anathema to Luther. Luther responded in 1525 with *The Bondage of the Will*, which among other things called Erasmus an atheist.

Erasmus was an alien spirit in the highly confrontational intellectual climate of the sixteenth century. He wrote against theologians who disparaged good literature, but also against the Italian humanists who exalted pagan literature against Christian. Although little known or understood in Italy, in the north he interested many who would later be attracted to Luther in scriptural texts and general moral reform; but when his work became known in Italy in the 1520s, the conservative theologians linked him to Luther. Erasmus published a work subordinating Cicero's work to Christianity, which got him into trouble with the Italian humanists, while his criticism of church abuses prompted condemnations of his work at the Sorbonne. What saved him from molestation or worse was probably his published critiques of Luther; he was simply too prominent an opponent of Luther for the Roman Catholics to risk going after him.[18]

The Fate of Latin

Educational theory and the curriculum were thus changed radically in both northern Europe and Italy, and by 1600 the Latin classics and classical grammars reigned supreme everywhere. But even in Italy the exclusive use of the classical Latin language by the early humanists was considered unrealistic by many, including persons who were both highly educated and appreciated the moral lessons to be gleaned from studying the ancients. Between 1450 and 1600 a classical education came to be required of all, certainly all who hoped to enter government service – the 'programme for the ruling classes' approach is probably more apropos for northern Europe by 1600 than it had been for Italy, apart from the princely courts, in 1450.

Medieval Latin was no longer acceptable, but since the classical Latin that all educated persons read well was a philological atavism, few wrote works in it or even used it for diplomatic correspondence. Despite Erasmus' near-20-year association with England, he spoke only Latin while there and never learned English; when he received a curacy in Kent it had to be filled by an absentee. Some of Luther's early works used Latin for his theological ideas, but he switched to German when discussing their practical implications, and virtually everything that he wrote after 1525 was in German. Beyond the school years, Latin was used by people whose language was not widely spoken outside their homelands to get an international audience.[19]

Most rulers spoke at least two vernacular languages; but although all of them read Latin, they did not speak it easily. Henry VIII of England received the title 'Defender of the Faith' for a Latin treatise against Luther, *The Vindication of the Seven Sacraments*, which was researched for him by a team of court scholars. Although Charles V understood spoken Latin, he never learned to speak it himself. Charles's native tongue was French; later he learned Spanish, and used it by preference in public pronouncements. He did not speak German or Dutch. The greatest diplomats were skilled Latinists; yet even ambassadors were prized most highly for their multilingualism in the vernacular tongues, which might dispense with the growing need for interpreters. None of the Germanic languages had international appeal; English, Dutch, and the Scandinavian languages got no farther than the border. German itself had significant differences between southern (High) and northern (Low) varieties. Of the Romance languages, which were easier to learn because of their Latin base, Italian was the most widely used in the mid-sixteenth century, perhaps because of the still-Europe-wide business networks of the Italians. Commercial Italian was taught at Antwerp, and scions of German business houses learned it in Italy. Italian literature was also popular in the sixteenth century, replacing the French chivalric romances, and Italian was written by French aristocrats. The fact that the northern powers were preoccupied with Italy militarily until 1530 and to a lesser degree until 1559 was also important. Thereafter, however, Italian declined in favour of French, which was 'the politician's second language' by the end of our period. As Latin declined as a language of politics, so its days as a legal language were numbered. Except for a brief experiment with English in the 1650s, it remained the language of the English courts until 1733, but the Austrian and French courts switched to German and French respectively in the sixteenth century.[20]

Knowledge of Latin did not 'decline' in the later Renaissance; rather, its restriction to the governing and educational élites became explicit. Thus although the sixteenth century has been called 'the first great age of translations',[21] this statement betrays an imprecise understanding of the use of the classics by medieval men of letters. Translations of philosophical works had been made from Greek into Latin since the central Middle Ages. Works such as the *lais* of Marie de France were also being translated between vernacular languages, and the Latin work of the French encyclopaedists was adapted for a Flemish readership by Jacob van Maerlant in the late thirteenth century. The travels of 'Sir John Mandeville' became popular in many languages. But in the earlier cases the translations were often unattributed and altered to fit local tastes, since it was assumed that anyone who read them would know their provenance. The sixteenth century saw two important changes in this. First, the intent became not to adapt and interpret, but rather to give a literal translation, which had not been common since the twelfth- and thirteenth-century translations of Greek into Latin. Second, the author was generally recognized, although he did not have copyright in the modern sense. Translations were made not only of modern authors, but also of classical authors into the modern vernaculars. The élite read the classics in the original languages, but by 1600 translations of the major Latin authors had been made into the five leading vernaculars except for German, which lagged behind in translations. Through the translations, humanist culture came to the lower classes.

Although the humanists outside Italy were competent in writing classical Latin, many of them wrote also, or by preference, in their native vernaculars. This would change to some extent after 1560, when considerable Roman Catholic theological writing was in Latin; the Protestants taught Latin in their schools but preferred to do their original writing in the vernacular. While before 1450 most translation was from Greek into Latin or occasionally from Latin into a vernacular language, thereafter works of theology, literature and scholarship were regularly written in the local vernacular and translated if there was sufficient interest elsewhere. Martin Luther was the first German whose works were rendered widely into other languages, mainly Latin, Dutch and Danish.[22]

Translations were also important in Iberia. The Italians considered the Iberians barbarians, a sentiment that was reinforced by the Spanish occupation of Italy in the sixteenth century. In turn, Spanish intellectuals felt a need to emancipate themselves from the Italians, even as they imitated them. Alfonso da Cartagena, a *converso* trained in law and theology at the university of Salamanca and a royal servant and bishop of Burgos, translated various works of Cicero into Castilian. In 1431, in reaction to Leonardo Bruni's attack on Aristotle unless he was presented in Ciceronian Latin, Cartagena argued that a knowledge of the context of Aristotle's philosophy was necessary in reconstructing what he was trying to say. He argued that the author's meaning was more important than the rhetoric in which it, or discussions of it, were couched. In the ensuing debate the Italians rejected this idea, claiming that Cartagena's admitted ignorance of Greek proved his barbarism.

A nationalist element is found in Cartagena, as with the French humanists. In his vernacular *Recapitulation of the Kings of Spain* Cartagena argued that the Castilian monarchy was descended from the Gothic kings of Hispania, making use of Seneca's birth in Cordoba and various other examples of the importance of Spain under the Romans. Rodrigo Sanchez de Arevalo, bishop of Palencia and a pupil of Cartagena, published a *Compendious Hispanic History* that went farther than Cartagena in arguing that Spanish civilization was actually older and more sophisticated than Roman. By century's end such notions were an article of faith in Castile. The tie of the monarchy with humanism became stronger under Ferdinand and Isabella. Patriotic poems imitating Latin epic style celebrated the fall of Granada, and triumphs were staged in the ancient manner. Antonio Martinez (1444–1522), who called himself Antonius Nebrissensis (Antonio of Nebrija), became one of Ferdinand's court historians in 1509. He was important in introducing humanist/classical Latin into the Spanish schools, but he also plagiarized and even invented sources shamelessly in the interest of glorifying ancient Spain.[23]

The 'Information Revolution' of Early Modern Europe

The development of printing sparked an information revolution comparable to that generated by the microcomputer in the late twentieth century. 'Printing' includes several inventions: movable metal type, oil-based ink and the wooden handpress.[24] Most printers used rag and pulp papers that were mass-produced and cheaper than vellum and parchment. Printing is sometimes associated with northern Europe rather than with Italy, on the grounds that a few Italian humanists and particularly their patrons objected to printing for artistic reasons; the point of a book for them was at least as much in its physical appearance as in its contents. Yet most humanists made full use of the new medium. The early printers did high-quality work, basing the shape of their letters on those of the manuscripts that they were printing. The earliest known printer in Europe was Johannes Gutenberg of Mainz, who flourished in the 1450s. Gutenberg printed in a Gothic type, but the Aldus Manutius firm of Venice devised the Italic or humanistic style, which is essentially an adaptation of Caroline minuscule. The two fonts are found in a roughly equal number of manuscripts during the first century of printing, but thereafter Gothic was generally preferred for fiction and religious work, and Italic for classical texts. Gothic was always stronger in Germany than in Italy and the west. Another shift that occurred from the mid-sixteenth century onwards was away from the book as a work of art. Printers emphasized speed and small-type fonts, getting out many editions quickly and cheaply. This was tied to a perceptible change in subject-matter: most printing before 1550 that was not religious pamphlet or broadsheet was old material, either the classics, humanist texts or chivalric literature, but modern original works were appearing more often in book form after 1550.

Printing thus became important in the second stage of the Renaissance. By the second generation after Gutenberg many of the leading printing houses were in Italy; they published the classics and texts written by contemporary humanists, and thus contributed to the rapid diffusion of the educational and ethical principles that had taken shape in their essentials by 1450. Few additional classical texts were recovered after the 1470s. The inventories of most of the early printers, even at Florence, consisted mainly not of humanist texts, but of Bibles, polemics, works in the chivalric tradition and didactic works. The printers of Strasbourg issued practical manuals on everything from anatomy and astronomy to mining and wine- and beer-making, and the authors included not only intellectuals but also businessmen, soldiers and housewives.

Even before printing, the number of technical manuscripts had been increasing on such topics as gynaecology, diet, recipes and remedies, drugs and even charms. The demand for such works obviously came from outside learned circles. Illustrations were also important for business in the non-scientific world. The spread of 'Spanish fashions' throughout the Habsburg Empire was aided by illustrated fashion books that gave patterns for dress-makers and tailors. Fifteenth-century medical manuscripts were often multilingual, with simultaneous versions in Latin and the local vernacular, and the early printers took over this format and capitalized on the strong demand for it.[25]

There was considerable hostility among Roman Catholics to the publication of religious works in the vernacular. Yet parallel-column editions such as the Spanish Polyglot Bible now became much easier to produce. Printing made possible the hardening of religious attitudes in fundamental texts other than the Bible, such as the Heidelberg Catechism of 1563, the English *Books of Common Prayer* (1549 and 1563) and the *Roman Ritual* of 1612. While religious doctrine and canon law had been largely centralized during the Middle Ages, local regions had remained free to use whatever patron saints, rituals and celebrations appealed. But variation was stamped out in the sixteenth century, with secular governments enforcing religious ortho-doxy and officially sponsored printed works defining permissible usage.[26]

At least before 1500, the presses of Florence produced fewer books than those of Venice, Rome and Milan, and they did not include many of the classics, even Cicero. Printers had to make money by catering to public taste, and accordingly published considerable material unconnected with the classics. Several north European printers studied in Italy or with northern humanists before becoming printers, and except for those who enjoyed government contracts, most of them concentrated on broadsheets. For complete volumes that had to be sold on the market, they published mainly old works of proven popularity, including vernacular literature. For such works a guaranteed sale market was at least foreseen, if only on the long term. Some authors were popular enough that publishers sought them out: in so far as publications were considered intellectual property, they belonged to the printer, not the author. Printers would buy copies of books on the market, then reset the type and publish new editions as their own. Some authors, including Erasmus, connived at pirated editions for financial reasons, undercutting the firm to which the original publication had been entrusted.

The master printers were businessmen, intellectuals and workers. They had to be educated, managers of shops, on good terms with officials, cultivators of writers, and salesmen. Many of the early ones were also scholars who translated and edited, such as William Caxton, who introduced printing to England. Aldus Manutius of Venice, who established the Aldine Press, was a humanist scholar who began as a tutor in several noble households, only becoming a printer when one of his pupils provided the capital. Manutius produced only Greek and Latin texts, including the first complete edition of Aristotle's works in Greek published in the west. But far from producing only for an aristocratic readership, the Aldine Press also produced cheap, competent editions for wider circulation, including modern works in Latin: the firm made considerable money by publishing Erasmus' works, and Manutius' son and grandson continued his tradition of exacting textual scholarship in publication. Most presses printed works of different viewpoints to make money from both markets. The printing-houses of the early sixteenth century as locales where authors, teachers and customers met to exchange ideas have been compared to the coffee-houses of the eighteenth century: the printers were generally in the same part of town, which facilitated the cohesion of an intellectual quarter.[27]

Printing thus became a significant industry in some cities. Although Antwerp lacked a university, it had a large and diverse population, with numerous foreigners, including religious refugees, Castilian *conversos* and Protestants from Germany and, at times, England. Most Protestant works written in English before 1540 were published at Antwerp: the 66 printers who are known to have been active between 1500 and 1540 published 2254 titles, and also sold and shipped elsewhere in the Low Countries numerous books written and/or printed abroad. The Low Countries had a large number of printers, comparable as a percentage of the population to Germany and Italy and far exceeding France and England. But while the other printing centres produced mainly single-sheet titles, such as ordinances, most of Antwerp's output was of books that were marketable internationally.[28]

Apart from Manutius, perhaps no early printer was as important as Christopher Plantin (1514–89) of Antwerp. When Charles V abdicated he was still a minor printer, but he made his fortune by dedicating a presentation volume to Philip II of poetry which he himself had composed, praising the new king and displaying his various type fonts and ornamental bindings. Plantin in 1558 was given a state subsidy to print the official account of Charles V's funeral, and became the official printer of the government in the Low Countries. In 1568 Philip gave Plantin the monopoly over printing and selling the devotional material that the Council of Trent had made obligatory for the parishes to have, and in 1571 this franchise was extended to Spain. Plantin was a scholar in his own right. His firm suggested to the crown and eventually published the Antwerp Polyglot Bible, which became an immense moneymaker, and his duties included supervising other printers throughout the Netherlands and checking their work for orthodoxy. In fact, however, Plantin was secretly heterodox, and in 1576 he became the official printer of the States General.[29]

Strasbourg was also a major centre of print culture in the sixteenth century. Although Latin continued to be used for scholarly work, most printing after 1520 was in German. Until 1499 most of the books were printed for the church, but much of even the religious material was for the laity in the sixteenth century, suggesting a strong growth of the lay market. In the 1520s religious work in the form of single-sheet broadsheets and pamphlets dominated overwhelmingly; thereafter, printers sought new markets in medical, technical and self-help books. The material in most of these was not original, and some had circulated in manuscript in the fifteenth century; but printing made it available to a wider readership. Printers at Strasbourg also produced more popular vernacular literature from about 1550, including new original works, some by citizens of Strasbourg; but prayer books, hymnals and catechisms for the laity dominated Strasbourg's publications in the last quarter of the sixteenth century, as confessional rigidity reheated.[30]

Printing's impact on intellectual change was thus in two directions: the spread of religious ideas and propaganda, and the shift of humanism from a Latin to an essentially vernacular literary movement in the late fifteenth and sixteenth centuries. The Protestants were the first to use printing effectively for religious goals. Luther's works, as well as papal denunciations of him, were short, and were made available quickly to a large readership through printing. Much of the printers' business was for governments, which used the new tool to publicize their enactments and influence public opinion. Yet printing also brought the works of the Italian humanists to a wide audience in northern Europe. Most of the copies of their works that were in university or private libraries in the north were printed editions; few were manuscripts. Printing also spread the humanist idea of the importance of textual criticism, and made it possible for multiple copies of a presumably correct text to be produced without the introduction of scribal error. Technical literature was particularly hard to copy by hand, since it included tables and diagrams, and the ability to reproduce drawings exactly, for example of anatomy or machinery, was crucial. Woodcuts and engravings, which were particularly important for technical literature, also had an application in religious propaganda that animalized or diabolicized the other side. Given the danger of a heresy accusation, when printers began publishing theological texts, they needed the best editions. Textual criticism was now a profession in itself; and since the theologians lacked the linguistic skills and often resisted the intrusion of persons not trained in theology in an area that they considered of divine inspiration as well as training, the printers turned to the humanists.

The printed 'national' Bibles helped fix the official vernacular languages, since they were read, if not owned, by virtually everyone who was literate. But printed volumes were much cheaper than manuscripts; and since people could own more books, it became possible to compare different sources and reach original conclusions. Much of what was printed in France before the 1530s, for example, was humanist material from Italy and devotional work from Germany and the Netherlands. In Paris these two currents were especially active in the 1520s, and the linkage meant more questioning of Christian doctrine and particularly texts by humanist standards than occurred in the more purely literary humanism of Italy.[31]

Primary and Secondary Education

The implementation of the classical curriculum as adapted to the imperatives of confessional religion, along with the easier availability of books, revolutionized primary and secondary education during these centuries. Education had always been the route to advancement in selected areas, particularly the learned professions and long-distance trade, but now it became important in most fields of endeavour.

Everywhere in Europe there was a great increase in the number of schools, the complexity of their facilities and the sophistication of their curricula. Far from being a development of humanism and the 'modern' period, schooling of this kind had begun in the early fourteenth century and then accelerated. Most English villages had at least one school by 1500, and another 400 had been established by 1650. Lay literacy was perhaps less widespread on the Continent in 1500, but the zeal of all religious groups to educate their young in the faith led to a proliferation of schools. The duchy of Württemberg in Germany had 50 schools in the fifteenth century, which had grown to 270 in 1581. These schools catered to the needs of laypeople and taught a classically based curriculum in the vernacular languages.

During the fourteenth and fifteenth centuries the number of vernacular schools that taught elementary literacy and calculating had been growing. Some were maintained by city governments, and all were under secular control. Some schools had a 'mistress of the girls' on the staff, teaching reading and writing, some arithmetic, and domestic skills such as sewing. Elementary schools for basic literacy had roughly equal numbers of boys and girls, but at the secondary level (the grammar schools) girls and most poorer students, except the few on stipends, were *de facto* excluded.

Latin was still taught mainly in church schools in the fifteenth century, but in the sixteenth century, under humanist influence, more secular institutions, particularly colleges founded by princes, taught Latin along with the vernacular. The churches, however, still claimed a monopoly over instruction and certification of masters, dating back to the time when Latin was the only kind of instruction available. Secular masters accused the churches of trying to control them as a matter of patronage, and surviving lawsuits suggest that the church schools were declining to such an extent that some city governments would no longer support their monopoly of Latin education.

The liberal arts (that is, the Latin curriculum) remained a church monopoly in France until 1489, when the government of Grenoble established a single Latin municipal college, which in practice meant ending the monopoly of the diocese. Although the cathedral kept the right to license masters nominated by the city, this was a formality. This practice had spread throughout France by 1530: the cities controlled schooling, and the church was virtually excluded from taking fees from masters. Given the general interest in good education, the cities did not have to pay for the new schools and masters entirely out of their operating budgets; many bequests and other gifts came from the laity and even some clergy. The principal masters' salaries were was high enough that they were expected to pay the subordinate personnel of the school, including teachers, and make certain that the best available teachers were hired. The masters were expected to be laypeople, and the principals married, so that they would give an example of domestic stability.

Different levels of qualification and salary were expected for masters who would teach the alphabet and elementary subjects to young children and those who taught more advanced subjects. The fact that masters were itinerant to a great degree, moving from a grade 3 in one city to a grade 2 in another, led to considerable standardization of the curriculum in France, so that the new masters and their employers would know what to expect. The most sought-after masters were those who had trained in Paris, where the humanist curriculum had become the standard. The Paris style became associated by the 1560s with a six-class system, beginning with the alphabet in Greek and Latin and ending with the great Roman rhetoricians.

The clergy led conservative resistance to the new colleges, which they considered hotbeds of heresy. Initially they subjected suspect masters to heresy trials, but this gave way during the period of the Counter-Reformation to attempting more subtly to replace suspect teachers with those who were orthodox, all within the municipal colleges, which most of the clergy by now realized that they could not eliminate. By the 1590s the city governments were much weaker relatively than early in the century, and the church became more militant. Depending on the local situation, the clergy demanded that suspect teachers or even suspect pupils be excluded. In the seventeenth century they began more openly to fight the whole idea of municipal schools, and to demand that the married clergy be replaced with priests or monks who knew the 'Parisian style' but were clergy of unquestioned orthodoxy. Thus French education in the seventeenth century fell increasingly under the control of the Jesuits and other new religious orders, who as a group were much better educated in the humanist curriculum than the traditional priests. In the beginning at least, the Jesuits were the only completely orthodox group to whom the church might point as examples of potential masters of strong enough humanist training to satisfy the city regimes' standards. The Jesuits had opened their own college in Paris in 1563, and over the years entered most others in the major cities; but their progress was much slower than in Spain and southern Germany, for they were regarded in France as Spanish agents, and were thus suspect to the crown and the municipalities. As the religious wars wore on, however, recruitment of lay masters was increasingly difficult, given the demands for religious orthodoxy.[32]

A similar development occurred in the Netherlands. At Antwerp, for example, there were numerous Dutch schools for elementary instruction, and five clerical schools for Latin instruction, of which that of the main cathedral was the oldest and most prestigious. The *scholaster*, a canon of the cathedral, had a right of inspection over both private and Latin schools throughout the city, and the deans of the two guilds of teachers had visitation rights over the private schools. From 1546 two city superintendents and the *scholaster* had to approve new admissions to the guilds. Yet private schools were providing increasing competition for the church schools even in Latin instruction. They offered a varied curriculum, but some included bookkeeping, arithmetic and foreign languages, which were not part of the standard course. Educational opportunities were expanding: Antwerp had 29 schoolmasters in 1530, 71 in 1562, and at least 88 masters and 70 schoolmistresses in 1576, the year of the Spanish fury, by which time the city's trade and population had been declining for a decade or more. The number of women is notable; only five schoolmistresses for 87 schoolmasters have been identified at Lyon between 1490 and 1570, and only one of 258 registered teachers in Venice in 1587 was a woman.[33]

While as late as the early fifteenth century municipal councils generally were filled by persons of wealth who sat because of guild affiliation and/or family influence, by the late fifteenth century, as written Roman law obtruded on customary law even in local practice, legal training became necessary. While the eldest son had priority for land inheritance, many English wills provided for younger sons to be educated. Much education was utilitarian; the notion of education as an end in itself, implicit in humanist education except as it relates to the public sphere through rhetoric, only became firmly established in the late sixteenth century.[34]

Given Protestantism's emphasis on laypeople reading the scriptures and forming their own conclusions, it has sometimes been assumed that the new schools were mainly in Protestant areas. Since the Protestants were abolishing so much of the physical environment that had accompanied traditional religion – images, chants, processions and the ritual accompanying the sacraments – it could not have had much appeal to persons who could not read or, indeed, who did not or could not think abstractly. Yet studies of individual localities have shown similar levels of literacy regardless of religious belief. Both Roman Catholics and Protestants wanted to promote literacy among their faithful, but stop the publication of heretical work. Erasmus, and in the late sixteenth century the Italian historian Guicciardini, said that the Netherlands had the highest literacy rates in Europe, extending even to many peasants; yet even in 1630 Amsterdam had a less than 50 per cent literacy rate.[35]

The only real test of mass literacy that has been used to date is the ability to sign one's name, which can be memorized and thus tends to exaggerate the extent of literacy. Protestant communities have achieved no higher scores than Roman Catholic, although literacy rates were much higher in areas where local or national governments paid the teachers' salaries than where the salaries came from student fees. After the early Protestant reformers saw that free reading of sacred texts could lead believers to positions that differed from theirs, they switched to urging a more controlled reading, which as the confessions hardened after 1550 often came to be little more than the ability to recite memorized catechisms. Schools were generally founded by lay princes and towns, and there were many more Roman Catholic of these than Protestant. Many more primary schools were founded in England in Mary's short reign than in Edward VI's time. The implementation of plans took time. John Knox and his followers began an educational campaign in 1560, but only in 1616 did the Scottish Parliament require all parishes to maintain schools and pay the teachers.

Secular Culture in Northern Europe during the Sixteenth Century

The term 'Renaissance' in the sense of 'rebirth' has little validity except for the addition of a classical Latin component to academic education. Although some Italian architects, artists and, less often, schoolmasters were hired by north European princes, lay culture owed more to modern Italian and even more to indigenous roots in the sixteenth century than to the classical revival.

French humanism was a cross between the active, civic-orientated humanism of Italy and the contemplative ethical/religious humanism of the Netherlands: many humanists who worked in France had been born in the Netherlands. French humanism had a historical sense that was second in development only to the Italians, and was certainly stronger than others in the north. The translator, philologist and jurist (he was a master of requests and a royal councillor) Guillaume Budé encouraged Francis I's intellectual interests. He was the leading French scholar of Greek and Greek civilization, and was largely responsible for introducing humanism into the law curriculum, rejecting the scholastic method of glosses and commentary in favour of a language-based historical interpretation. Budé's interests were chiefly in secular topics.[36]

In France, as elsewhere, poets and chroniclers wrote in both Latin and the vernacular. Like Petrarch, they thought their Latin work was their best, but most now consider their French work superior to it. The change now is that most of their own contemporaries agreed with the modern assessment. Little French painting or sculpture shows humanist influence before 1530, but thereafter the patronage of Francis I fostered a change. The monarch collected paintings, sculptures, and books. As well as this, Italian ideas of fortification and castle construction, emphasizing the castle as a comfortable residence, had been entering France since the campaigns after 1494. Francis I's favourite castle, Fontainebleau, was begun in 1528: the basic design was simple and gave rise to a 'Fontainebleau style' in France. Even though the structure took a century to finish, it shows an overall uniformity. Modern historians see it as more French than Italian, but the interior was definitely Italianate, designed by the Italian mannerists Gian Battista Rosso and Francesco Primaticcio. The royal library was moved from Blois to Fontainebleau in 1544, and the place became a haven for court scholars and men of letters. Work began in 1546 on rebuilding the Louvre, moving it away from fortification toward modern castle. Henry II continued his father's patronage. A group of poets who called themselves the Pleiades, after the constellation, were Greek and Latin scholars but wrote mainly in French: the best-known of them was Pierre Ronsard, a noble from the Orléanais. Henry II gave him a pension after his diplomatic career was ended by deafness. Ronsard wrote four books of Odes, using classical models, at times to the point of weakening his originality.[37]

François Rabelais (*c.*1490–1553) was the leading figure of French letters during the early sixteenth century. He was trained in orthodox fashion as a monk, and became proficient in Greek and Latin. His interest in science is unusual among humanists; he received a degree in medicine from the university at Montpellier in 1530. Moving to Lyon, Rabelais practised medicine, and in 1532 published what purported to be the life of the legendary giant *Pantagruel*, followed in 1533 by a similar work about Pantagruel's father *Gargantua*. The conglomerated work, which went through several editions and revisions, is one of the great monuments of world literature. The coarseness of the satire, the evident sympathy for church reform and the scatological puns obscured for many the seriousness of Rabelais' discussion. Although the other French humanists respected his knowledge, he had problems with the church, particularly after the Sorbonne declared *Gargantua and Pantagruel* heretical.

There is a decline in the quality of creative activity during the French wars of religion. Michel de Montaigne (1533–92) was the major literary figure of the period. His father's family were merchants of Bordeaux who bought the nearby estate of Montaigne. He received a rigorous humanist training from his father, and held a seat on the *parlement* at Bordeaux, but retired to Montaigne. He was troubled by the religious hostility, but like the *politiques* (see Chapter 5) he concluded that since human reason is such an uncertain guide, one must rely on the collective wisdom of the ages. Thus he remained Roman Catholic, but he also urged religious toleration, since he said that our knowledge could not be certain. Montaigne invented the essay ('attempt') as a literary form, and raised ideas for discussion in several published volumes of these short pieces. The *Essays* were widely read; Montaigne's undogmatic conclusion that scepticism leads, for lack of an acceptable alternative, to reliance on the church became a major point in Roman Catholic writing in the seventeenth century.

In England, although the humanist curriculum was pervasive, most of the early humanists were creatures of court and crown, and most of their original works were potboilers written in defence of Henry VIII's religious position. From the 1580s, however, England underwent a literary Renaissance that had little tie to a classical tradition or humanism, but perhaps for that reason was the more original and profound. Although the period is traditionally called the Elizabethan Age, the greatest writers actually owed more to the court patronage of the first two Stuart kings than to Elizabeth. She became a cult figure as a national heroine and personification of the nation, but she was notoriously parsimonious about display and personal expenses. She did enjoy plays, and patronized a company that included Shakespeare, but her great love was music. Her court composer was William Byrd, an unpersecuted Roman Catholic who wrote Latin masses and works for the English church and served as organist in the royal chapel.

Christopher Marlowe, who in his student days at Cambridge in the 1580s may have been a government agent who informed on Roman Catholic students, is a shadowy figure who was killed in a rooming-house in 1594. He vaunted his homosexuality, interest in the occult and atheism, and revolutionized the drama in his tragedies *Tamburlaine* and *The Tragical History of Dr. Faustus*, which build on medieval legends rather than classical antecedents. Marlowe was the first English dramatist to use blank verse; Shakespeare probably took the idea from him. Marlowe's plays are violent and brutal, usually concerning a hero with a tragic flaw. Edmund Spenser (1552–99), who spent time as a civil servant in Ireland, wrote long allegorical poems in which the poetry is associated with music, the best of which is his unfinished masterpiece *The Faerie Queene*, an allegory on the moral virtues, in which Elizabeth is eulogized as a symbolic figure. The work received no financial support from the queen, and late in his life Spenser wrote poems that show disillusion with court life. He was recognized by contemporaries as the finest poet of his age, and was a friend of other literary figures, including Sir Philip Sidney, a leading member of Elizabeth's court, who wrote poetry that is now highly regarded (most of it circulated only in manuscript during his lifetime), including some pastoral works in the style of Virgil.

The greatest literary figure of England during these years, and arguably of all time, was William Shakespeare (1564–1616). Shakespeare was born and educated in Stratford-upon-Avon, where his father was a member of the town council. The son never attended a university, although his family had the money to send him. Although much of the material for his plays came from independent reading, his formal education was limited to the local grammar school and is a considerable tribute to it. Between 1589 and shortly before his death, Shakespeare shuttled between London and his wife and children in Stratford.

Shakespeare's sonnets, which are the only works from his pen that suggest a homosexual inclination, were written in the 1590s when he was being patronized by the young earl of Southampton. Southampton probably bought him a share in the newly established Company of the Lord Chamberlain's Men, which became the King's Men after 1603. Shakespeare's plays were published under his own name, and even before 1603 he was well-known for his strongest comedies except *Measure for Measure* – his first play to be performed before James I – and for most of his histories. Shakespeare used his new wealth, from the sale of his published plays and fees for his performances as an actor, to purchase property in Stratford. *The Tempest*, written in 1609, is his last play and the only one in which the story is pure invention, although there are some suggestions of its themes in classical literature. His histories seem to be based on the stories in Holinshead's Chronicles, and various Italian works were the inspiration for several of the comedies, notably *The Taming of the Shrew* and *Romeo and Juliet*. The authorship of Shakespeare's plays has been contested in favour of various other figures, an argument that ignores their attribution to Shakespeare during his lifetime and the fact that, despite his obscure origins, he became prominent and wealthy.

Drama

Curiously, as the cases of Marlowe and Shakespeare demonstrate, drama was the last of the great literary forms to undergo a classical revival. With the decline of both passion and miracle plays in the sixteenth century a variety of other topics, including but not limited to classical subjects, were included, but the format of the drama remained essentially medieval, even in Italy. While earlier touring players had used whatever space was available for performances – streets, vacant buildings, courtyards – theatres were opening in London, beginning with the Red Lion in 1567; London's theatres had a total capacity of over 8000 by the early seventeenth century, and Paris's first theatre was opened in 1599. The formal theatres had doors that permitted charging admission instead of relying on voluntary donations, and the drama thus became professionalized in the late sixteenth and early seventeenth centuries. Patrons began investing in theatres, and commercial considerations played a considerable role in determining what was written and performed. Shakespeare was the first writer of serious dramas to become wealthy, but his wealth came from the shares that he controlled in the Globe and Blackfriars theatres and the acting company, not from publication royalties.

Historical Writing

The increasing interest in reading classical subjects in the vernacular languages gave rise to historical writing that was both more sophisticated and more popular, particularly after 1550. Cicero, Sallust and Livy had been honoured by the early humanists for their style and for the moral lessons that they could teach. Like them, and like the medieval chroniclers, the humanist historians wrote chronologically. Rulers consulted history, and they and their ambassadors cited history for precedent; but the humanists had been concerned only with classical antiquity. Particularly after 1500, most historical writing concerned more recent periods, for history was now a scholarly discipline, not simply a branch of ethics or rhetoric. The best historians, certainly those who wrote in the vernacular, used original documents to sustain their broader theses. As was true of most scholarly work except on religious themes, Latin was generally not used for historical writing after 1550 as presses capitalized on popular taste and abilities.

While the early humanist histories had been general, following the medieval tradition of universal history, and were more concerned with classical Latin form than with documentation, Italian works beginning with Machiavelli's *History of Florence* and Francesco Guicciardini's *History of Italy* were more limited, focusing on a single place or a specific event, often a war. There is a reversion to universal history with Paolo Giovio's influential, although Latin, *History of His Own Time* (1494–1547). Like Guicciardini, Giovio was basically a reporter rather than a historian in the sense of one who uses documents to investigate a past time. Every writer, however, interpreted history for its lessons, often those desired by the perceived readership and particularly court patrons. Guicciardini's *Ricordi (Maxims)*, observations that he made and constantly edited, were based on his experiences as a Florentine diplomat and the lessons that he drew from history. His conclusions were very different from Machiavelli's, and are closer to the Aristotelian ideal of a mixed constitution, with elements of aristocracy and democracy but showing a distrust of giving princes too much power.[38] Guicciardini and Giovio felt that historians should be teachers and active participants in the events of their own day, and like Machiavelli they had broken with the earlier humanists in using documentary evidence as well as the form of classical authors, particularly in the orations that they attributed to leading figures. The work of the Hellenistic Greek Polybius was first translated into Italian in 1545 and became very influential, in part because his work, from the period when the world was falling to Rome, seemed particularly applicable in an Italy that was coming under Spanish domination. Although Polybius provided a perceptive analysis of the Roman constitution, his work was used by historians who disliked the polemic use of history to teach moral lessons.

The Reaction Against Humanism

Traditional humanism, with its emphasis on the classical and rhetorical traditions, had always been a court culture. Even as broadened in the early sixteenth century, it was being rejected by many educated Italians by 1550. Perhaps the most widely read Italian (characteristically not Latin) work of the late Renaissance is *The Courtier*, by Baldessare Castiglione (1478–1529), which was essentially a book of manners. As the prince's function for Machiavelli was defined in terms of power and self-preservation, the courtier's was gaining and maintaining the prince's favour. The courtier did not necessarily have an office; he was simply 'there', to flatter and be flattered by his skill in social graces and the superficialities of fashion. Castiglione's work represented a shift in its emphasis on preparing youth for the court rather than for civic life in the classical sense. The courtier would be well-educated, having passed through the by now traditional humanities curriculum, supplemented by the best of the Tuscan vernacular authors, such as Dante and Boccaccio, and the verses and poetic treatises of Pietro Bembo (1470–1547), whose work conveyed more authority in his own day than later. But the courtier's education was to be broad rather than deep; he could not appear to be a pedantic nuisance to his prince and patron.

The superficialities of such attitudes were savaged by Pietro Aretino (1492–1566) in (among other works) a parody of *The Courtier* called *The Courtesan*. His work, essentially abusiveness for hire – he was a personal, vicious propagandist – was carried further by imitators who mocked the humanists and castigated their vaunted classical learning as useless intellectual ostentation. Although the vogue of classicism continued unabated, although without the slavish need to write everything in Latin, the Italians who had brought about the classical Renaissance became the stock themes of anti-court literature. Northerners associated them with neologisms and satirized them as empty-headed fops, flatterers and deceivers who were obsessed with meaningless ritual. Several English comedies of Shakespeare's period use a figure named 'Balthasar' or, more pointedly, 'Castellio' for the stupid courtier. The anti-Italian backlash was strongest in France, perhaps due to the large number of Italians at court under Catherine de' Medici.[39]

*   *   *

Even as the human mind expands its knowledge and horizons, it seems unerringly to search for first principles, an authority against which all else should be measured and according to which the newly acquired insights can be categorized and ultimately legitimized. The Italian humanists had a profound impact on educational attitudes and curricula into the twentieth century by propounding the thesis that ancient Rome represented the pinnacle of secular human achievement, but the reaction in favour of a more scientific or logical approach that is evident even in some literary work of the late sixteenth century was to culminate in the flowering of inductive reasoning in seventeenth-century thought. Even the humanists admitted, however, that the Christian revelation was an authority higher than imperial Rome, which indeed received much of its aura as the birthplace and time of Jesus and the church. We thus conclude this book by examining the violent and vitriolic disputes that developed as different ideas concerning the nature of that ultimate truth were expressed publicly during the sixteenth century.

10

Antiquity and Modernity: The Religious Division of Europe in the Sixteenth Century

The State of the Church and the Church of the State at the Turn of the Sixteenth Century

Abuses can never be totally absent from any institution controlled by human beings, but the church universal had particularly serious problems in the fifteenth century. It continued to garner large incomes from the laity, but in France and England more of this found its way to the royal treasuries than to Rome. The churches in Iberia were under stricter control of the crown than of the papacy. Even in Italy, which lacked a strong central government except for the papal state and the Aragon-dominated south, the city governments and their leaders patronized the local churches lavishly.

Although the popes were widely disliked, the connection of this to the development of Protestantism is not clear except in Germany. Their political involvements were a continuing scandal, from the Avignon papacy through the imperial-Spanish tilt of most sixteenth-century popes. Nowhere as much as in Italy were the political pretensions of the popes resented, and nowhere was their wealth and that of the cardinals more conspicuous; yet Italy remained firmly Catholic. For half a century after the restoration of the Roman line of popes in 1417 the pontiffs contented themselves with cultural patronage and with eradicating the threat of church councils to their position within the church. But from the time of Sixtus IV (1471–84) the political involvements of the popes in Italy multiplied; and after the French invasion of Italy in 1494, their dynastic ambitions for their children combined with their natural desire to keep potential north European enemies from their doorstep to bring the Holy See into repeated coalitions that involved military actions of Christian against Christian.

The opulence and power of the papal court, combined with its lax moral standards, also elicited negative comment. The wealth of the cardinals was legendary, and most used it to live extravagantly and advance their families' position. To reward Ludovico Gonzaga, the marquis of Mantua and a pupil of the humanist Vittorino da Feltre, for his help at the council of Mantua (1459), Pius II in 1461 named as a cardinal his younger son Francesco, then aged 17. The boy was so untrained that when he chanted the office on Christmas Day 1464 he forgot his lines and had to make something up, a story that greatly amused Pius's successor, Paul II (1464–71). Cardinal Gonzaga amassed such a magnificent collection of art works, jewels, tapestries, rare books and manuscripts (including some Greek and Arabic works that were purely for display, for Gonzaga read neither language) that his establishment was often used when the popes wanted to impress a foreign dignitary.[1]

The number of cardinals doubled during the sixteenth century, from 34 in 1510 to over 70 by the 1570s. Italians were always a substantial majority, most of them relatives of the popes or from prominent families. Pope Alexander VI (1492–1503) named 43 new cardinals, more than any previous pope, all for affection or cash. One was his son, Cesare Borgia, who resigned his cardinalate in 1498. Alessandro Farnese, the future Pope Paul III, was almost certainly made a cardinal because his sister Giulia was Alexander's mistress; wits called her the 'bride of Christ'. Although Farnese later acquired the appropriate intellectual credentials, he became cardinal at age 25 and fathered at least four sons. Pope Leo X (1513–21) was the nephew of Lorenzo dei Medici. He was made a cardinal at the age of 13 in 1489, and was pope at 37. He in turn made five relatives cardinals, including his cousin Giulio, the later Pope Clement VII (1523–34).

Clement VII's morals were unassailable, but he was also timid, and when Charles V's troops sacked Rome in 1527 he appointed imperial partisans as cardinals. Paul III (1534–49) appointed some cardinals for the usual reasons of nepotism and money, but some of them turned out to be church reformers, and his pontificate was long enough for a change of direction to occur. Gasparo Contarini was one of the most notable, a Venetian diplomat and a layman when he was made cardinal in 1535. While Contarini hoped to compromise with the Lutheran position on grace and justification by faith alone, Gian Pietro Carafa of Naples, who became cardinal in 1536, urged severe treatment of heretics and disobedience. As Pope Paul IV (1555–9) Carafa caused considerable turmoil in the church by his insistence that his political as well as theological views be accepted without question. Paul IV reluctantly agreed to recall the church Council to Trent, but the conservatism of its decrees is a tribute to the strength of his legacy.[2]

Although it is undeniable that there were conspicuous institutional abuses in the late medieval church, particularly at the upper levels, public distaste in areas that eventually developed significant Protestantism may have been more against the pope as a foreigner than against him as a church figure. Resentment against indulgences in Germany was directed against the use of the money in Italy. In Henry VIII's early years the pope was realizing less than one-third annually of what the English church was paying the king. The pope's power over English religious life in the years before the Reformation was mainly one of dispensation from provisions of canon law, particularly vows and regulations. Cardinal Wolsey was disliked for his great power and obvious secular use of high church office, and he incurred some odium as papal legate. But apart from hostility toward Wolsey, while there is no evidence of much affection for the pope in the years before the Reformation, there is also scarcely any record of disquiet. England does not seem to have had a serious problem of clerical immorality either, although a few spectacular cases of church abuse caused an uproar. The English bishops were undistinguished but, except for Wolsey, not glaringly immoral. Most had degrees in civil law, a few in canon law, and fewer still in theology, a fact that helps to explain why most of them followed Henry VIII so easily – they were already more civil servants than spiritual figures.

Although religious orientations were becoming less church-centred and more personal, mystical and Christ-centred than earlier, this did not translate into dissent on essential matters of belief, notably the theology of the essential mystery of the mass: many people were actively involved in their parish churches as members of confraternities dedicated to the cult of a saint. Most English parishes had lay churchwardens by the fourteenth century to oversee church property. Few doubted the efficacy of prayers by the living for the dead, and virtually all charitable donations included a requirement that prayers be offered by the beneficiaries for the souls of the donor and/or his deceased kin and friends. Particularly in England, many new churches were built in the late fifteenth century. But even as late medieval religion was becoming more private for those who bothered to think about theological topics, the vast majority were bound to the church through attachment to its rituals, notably the mass, festivals, fasts and celebrations. Prayers and donations came mainly from demand for them by the laity rather than oppression and preaching by the clergy; indeed, much of the polemical literature against priests in pre-Reformation Europe was written by other clerics. Thomas More also complained about the ignorance of the parish clergy, but his humanist view of what constituted lack of education can surely not be generalized.

The question of whether the resentment of Martin Luther and the other Protestant leaders over the institutional abuses of the late medieval church provoked them into doctrinal heresy thus remains unresolved. Luther claimed later that his was a purely doctrinal revolution, despite his outrage over the political involvements and great wealth of the popes, but this may be the faulty recollection of an elderly man. In England and particularly in France, where there was substantial secular control over the institutions of the church, and in Germany, where there was not, there was widespread anticlericalism and resentment over the financial preoccupations of the church leaders.

Although Italy remained firmly Roman Catholic in the sixteenth century, this did not mean that some of the sentiments that moved Protestants were not present in the south. The real ruler of Florence after the fall of the Medici regime in 1494 was the friar Girolamo Savonarola. He is famous for his campaigns against luxuries, including symbolic 'burnings of the vanities' in 1495 and 1497, in which public ceremonies were used to chastise secular literature, personal adornment and other sins. Savonarola struck a responsive chord among the poor by his preaching and by measures that he proposed, including restoration of the *monte di pietà*, low-interest credit banks patronized mainly by the poor. He used the carnival custom of allowing boys to demand money for food and drink from persons they met on the street by permitting it on condition that they used the money for poor relief. Parties formed; Savonarola's opponents controlled the government after the elections in 1497, and Alexander VI excommunicated him for preaching against the pope's personal vices. In 1498 the friar was seized by a mob, tried and burned for heresy.

Humanism and Protestantism

Just as there can be no clear answer to the question of whether theological Protestantism would have developed had personal and institutional abuses in the church not been so flagrant, so the links between northern philological humanism and the Protestant movement remain uncertain. The humanists objected to citing disjointed fragments of ancient authorities to prove a point that was foreign to their literary and historical context, and they preferred having direct recourse to the texts to using commentaries on them. They wanted to go back to the original texts of Cicero and other ancient authors, not what scholars had said about them, and also to understand the author in the context and situation in which he wrote. The primacy of the original text is thus important to both northern and southern humanism.

Humanism could also be put to the service of religious policies of the secular state. Henry VIII's court included prominent humanists such as Thomas More and Reginald Pole, who evidently expected church reform from him in 1529. Even when Parliament declared Henry Supreme Head of the Church in England in 1531, this did not bother the humanists overly, for in the context of the time – Francis I had done essentially the same – it was not incompatible with the universal church. Some of the humanists moved away from the king as Henry moved openly toward the annulment of his marriage, and more resigned in 1532 when Pole was safely in Rome. Others moved into the circles of the rising Thomas Cromwell and Thomas Cranmer, the new archbishop of Canterbury, and wrote court propaganda. The English humanists were acquainted with the classics and studied them in the original languages, but unlike the Italians they were translators, putting into English whatever devotional or classical work that would suit their purposes. William Marshal translated Marsiglio's *Defender of the Peace* in 1535 to buttress the notion of royal supremacy, and the next year Thomas Starkey published his Marsiglian *Exhortation to Unity and Obedience*.

Philosophy had been linked to religion during the Middle Ages, but this ceased to be so in the sixteenth century. While the humanists took a philological approach to the ancient thinkers, the Protestants objected to the idea that human reason could add to our understanding of a religious truth that was perceived only by faith. More positively, with the end of the religious tie philosophy became less metaphysical and more concerned with ethics, a development that is shown by the civic humanists and especially through the interest of such persons as Montaigne in the moral philosophers of antiquity, particularly the Stoics.

Basic to the problem too is the question of whether religious revelation continues or ended with the Bible. If revelation is continuous, as both Roman Catholicism and Judaism maintain, there was much of value in the commentaries on the ancient texts. Judaism uses the Old Testament, the Torah and the Talmud, while Roman Catholicism uses papal pronouncements, canon law and tradition more generally. Since both Luther and Calvin made the Bible the only source of authority, however, mainstream Protestantism in effect argues that revelation does not continue. The change simplifies religious belief in one sense by restricting authority to a single source, but complicates it by reliance on the believer's personal interpretation of that source.

Luther had an ambiguous relationship with contemporary humanists. Although he always subordinated textual scholarship to doctrine, he helped bring the humanist reform of grammar to the University at Wittenberg, and he together with other Protestant leaders was interested in using the new philological techniques to make a point about the Bible in its pure form. Luther used Erasmus' Greek New Testament in his teaching at Wittenberg. He also disliked the scholastic practice of subjecting religious topics to rational analysis, preferring the declamatory approach favoured by the humanists. Most German humanists, including those younger than Luther, welcomed him initially but turned away from him after 1520, as his movement breached the atmosphere of academic discourse and became attractive to the 'people' and to government leaders. But Luther had no sympathy for the central intellectual concerns of humanism or its views on the elevated nature of man. While the Italian humanists had been interested only in Greek and Latin, interest in Hebrew as the other Biblical language was strong among the Reformation intellectuals, although they backed away when they came too close to an appreciation of Judaism.

Yet a modified version of the humanist curriculum became standard in both the Protestant and Roman Catholic parts of Germany. The first professor of Greek at the University of Wittenberg was Philip Melanchthon, the nephew of the Hebrew scholar Johann Reuchlin (see below). Born Philip

Schwarzerd in 1497 (Melanchthon is Greek for 'black earth', the meaning of his German name), some considered him second only to Erasmus among the learned men of northern Europe. Melanchthon began as a moderate, not condemning dialectic; but in 1518 in his Greek grammar he rejected the scholastic approach to learning. More than most, however, he linked humanistic studies with church reform and claimed that the excesses of the old learning had led to a decline in piety that educational reform along his lines would restore. Melanchthon's *Loci Communes* ([*Theological*] *Commonplaces*) of 1521, initially a commentary through sermons on the book of Romans, was later expanded into a comprehensive theology, and he essentially wrote the Augsburg Confession of 1530, hoping for reconciliation with Rome long after Luther had given up the idea. In 1541 he met Cardinal Contarini at the Colloquy of Regensburg, and the two worked out a joint statement on justification by faith; but it was rejected by both Luther and the pope.[3]

The Reuchlin Case

Johann Reuchlin was a lawyer whose philosophical interests had been sparked by several trips to Italy, and was one of the few of his age who actually mastered all three ancient languages. Pico della Mirandola aroused his interest in the Hebrew Cabbala, with its mystical affinities to Pythagoras and Neoplatonism, and he also wrote two important works on Hebrew grammar.

Reuchlin's intellectual interests became a public controversy when the converted Jew Johann Pfefferkorn became obsessed with converting other Jews to Christianity and in 1507 began publishing anti-Semitic pamphlets. Emperor Maximilian initially countenanced Pfefferkorn seizing Jewish books, then changed his mind and asked for opinions from seven experts, one of whom was Reuchlin. Reuchlin was the only one who argued that Hebrew writings should not be suppressed, and a nasty conflict was carried through the print medium, led by Jacob von Hochstraten, the Dominican inquisitor for Germany. By 1511 the theologians of the university of Cologne weighed in, attacking Reuchlin's scholarship. The issue shifted from the suppression of Hebrew works to whether Reuchlin's work should be banned, and the conflict was still alive when he died in 1522.

There is little agreement even now about the real significance of the controversy. For most contemporary writers the Jewish aspect was the most important. Apart from the religious question, Reuchlin as a lawyer thought that the Jews were entitled to their property, although he made it plain, albeit under pressure, that he did not sympathize with their religion. Reuchlin was concerned that Christian Hebrew scholarship would be impaired by burning Jewish writings, since books could be lost, despite the emperor's mandate that they be copied first and put into Christian libraries. But he did not have universal support even among humanists: Erasmus admired him as a defender of 'academic freedom', but he thought the public controversy demeaning for a scholar. More importantly, the leading Christian humanist of the age had no use for Hebraic studies. Erasmus was interested only in the Greek New Testament and getting to the original meaning of the words of Christ, to which he considered the study of Hebrew and particularly the Cabbala irrelevant; and he thought that Reuchlin's Jewish contacts were corrupting him. Most of Reuchlin's German defenders were timid and their defences lukewarm: the only major exception was the strong support he was given in the *Letters of Obscure Men*. This collection of anonymous letters purported to be written by such of Reuchlin's opponents as Baldpate and Sausage, who sought advice on a variety of inconsequential topics. Many of the letters were written by the atypical humanist knight Ulrich von Hutten, whose student experiences at Leipzig and Frankfurt had made him bitterly anti-scholastic and anti-clerical, and the *Letters* go beyond the Reuchlin affair, satirizing the papal curia, scholasticism, indulgences and relics, among other problems.[4]

Conditions in the French and Spanish Churches before the Reformation

The French kings had taken advantage of the popes' need for their help in 1438 against the Council of Basel to impose the Pragmatic Sanction of Bourges, which had abolished some financial rights that the popes had exercised on benefices, and allowed them only to confirm elections of bishops and abbots, but not to appoint them. Appointments would be determined in France, and local councils called by the king as head of the Gallican church could legislate for it. The 'Pragmatic' also stopped payment of some papal fees and, most importantly, annates, the first year's income from a benefice. The general dislike of interference from Rome caused Gallican sentiment to grow. Although relations between crown and pope were generally good under Louis XII (1498–1515), after 1511 the French were fighting in Italy against the troops of Pope Julius II, who was just as grasping for money and intent on military conquest as Alexander VI had been, although he lacked his personal vices.

Of the major states of Europe, only England did not have a substantial Italian element in its upper clergy. By 1516 Leo X needed French help in Italy, and this led to new concessions. The Concordat of Bologna of 1516 thus gave the French king patronage of more than 600 benefices, while recognizing papal spiritual primacy. The king received the right to nominate candidates for vacant bishoprics and abbacies: the pope could reject the nomination, but the king could then nominate a second candidate; and in practice the pope never rejected the second nominee. But although generally favourable to the king, the Concordat allowed the pope to appoint the successors of bishops who died at Rome; and since there were numerous French cardinals and diplomats at Rome, this permitted the continuation of large numbers of Italian clergy in France, many of them absentee. The Concordat required that bishops be aged at least 27 and that they should hold a university degree in theology or canon law, but it made an exception for princes of the royal blood and members of great aristocratic families.

The upper clergy became increasingly secularized. Of 129 bishops appointed by Francis I, 102 were either members of the royal family or from lineages of the nobility of the sword; few met the theological requirements of the Concordat. The principle that the king could levy a tithe on clerical incomes for a just war, with papal approval, had been observed since the early fourteenth century, but the Concordat of Bologna permitted it without papal consent as a permanent right of the crown. Clerical assemblies approved the tithes, which were legally gifts although in fact none was ever refused, and Francis I set up a separate administration, the General Department of the Tithes, which by 1532 was collecting a nominal tithe every year. Essentially the French king controlled appointments and finances, the pope doctrine and discipline.[5]

Thus many of the personnel and financial problems that were vented in Luther's revolt in Germany also existed for the French church. The parish clergy was impoverished. An absentee priest could hire a curate to perform his duties, but some curates were also absentee and hired unbeneficed priests to conduct the services. Bishoprics were foci of patronage but also authority, and their structures were not the same everywhere. England had seventeen bishoprics and two archbishoprics, while France had more than 100 bishoprics and 14 archbishoprics. Granted that England was one-third the size of France, French bishops who were conscientious about their duties had a much smaller area of responsibility for the care of souls than their English colleagues. In Italy, too, virtually all substantial towns were seats of a bishopric. Flanders, by contrast, did not have its own bishopric until the sixteenth century. The difference in size and in the social composition and educational level of the bishops had much to do with how effective or inclined toward church reform they were.

The Spanish church, like the Italian and French, was enormously wealthy and politically powerful in the fifteenth century, although Ferdinand and Isabella ended most of its direct political power. The Italian bishops had more authority as local lords than all but the greatest Spanish bishops. Spain had seven archbishoprics and 40 bishoprics in Ferdinand and Isabella's time, and the wealth of the archbishop of Toledo alone was second only to that of the king. Both the crown and papacy were interested in limiting the autonomy of local churches. In 1486, to get Ferdinand's help in Italy, Pope Innocent VIII agreed that the monarchs appoint clergy to the churches that would be established in Granada, a principle that became the basis of the Castilian church settlement in the New World. In 1523 Pope Adrian IV conceded that the king could appoint all bishops in Spain, but the lower clergy were not affected, and most were appointed through local patronage networks. Ferdinand and Isabella prevented all appeals from their court to Rome. They did not get total control over the Spanish church or its resources, but with the assimilation of the assets of the military orders to the crown they got enough so that their successors never had the temptation for financial reasons to do as Henry VIII of England did in seizing the lands of the dissolved monasteries after 1536.

Before Luther's movement, only in Bohemia did a large group of persons get away for long with questioning a central theological doctrine, in that case gaining communion in both kinds for the laity. The French and English churches were essentially under lay domination, and perhaps for that reason they were quite conservative in theological terms. Only Henry VIII's divorce precipitated Thomas More's break with the crown, for the statute of Parliament that made the king supreme head of the church paralleled the language of the 1438 Pragmatic Sanction in France, which nobody was claiming was heretical. Although the legal position of the French and English kings over their national churches was strengthened after 1517, in the English case to the extent of excluding the pope, doctrinal revolution only came to England after 1547, and after 1555 and impermanently to France. The only other places where there was much doctrinal change were the Netherlands, which had no national monarchy, and Scotland and Scandinavia, where the monarchies were weak. Excommunication proves nothing regarding doctrinal heresy: Savonarola and many other completely orthodox persons were excommunicated by the popes for political reasons. But there is definitely a correlation between theological Protestantism and weak lay or state control over the institutions of the church.

The Birth of Theological Protestantism

The spark that ignited the Protestant rebellion was the question of indulgences. Since the twelfth century the popes had developed the notion of Purgatory as the place where salvageable souls went for purification before being admitted to Paradise. The length of time in Purgatory was diminished by one's own meritorious acts on earth, and also by worthy acts of other persons on behalf of the deceased's soul. Thus charitable donations were usually given to the church in the late Middle Ages on condition that prayers be offered for the repose of the souls of the donor and his late kinspeople. A 'treasury of merit' was established, where the deeds credited to each soul would be balanced against his or her sins. An 'indulgence' was simply a document that could be purchased to diminish the length of time to be spent in Purgatory. The sin was already forgiven; the issue was the penalty for it, and an indulgence was ineffective unless the purchaser had repented and confessed his sin. The theology behind indulgences rested on two fundamental premises: that good deeds could remit punishment, and that the actions of the living could affect the fate of the dead in the hereafter. But such theological subtleties were clearly lost on most who purchased indulgences in the hope of diminishing posthumous torments. Indulgences had been sold to raise money for church projects for many years before Luther became offended when he saw the Dominican Johann Tetzel hawking them to raise money for the rebuilding of St Peter's cathedral in Rome.

Luther's writings before 1517 show at least as much preoccupation with institutional abuses as with problems regarding free will and the other matters included in his Ninety-Five Theses. In posting the theses – in Latin, as befitted a theology professor – on the church door at Wittenberg on 31 October 1517, Luther was following established practice in the university faculties of stating theses as points of debate. He did not say until later that he believed that these propositions were true.

The Ninety-Five Theses quickly aroused the hostility of the authorities. They were brief enough to be spread by printed broadsheets, and a German translation was available by December 1517. They were sent to Pope Leo X, who after dismissing Luther initially as a 'drunken German', realized that he had to be forced to recant. After Luther refused the pope's order to come to Rome, he held an inconclusive debate at Leipzig in 1519 with the orthodox theologian Johann Eck, and after this the pope excommunicated him. In 1520 Luther issued the three short treatises by which his work became best known in the English-speaking world: *An Open Letter to the Christian Nobility of the German Nation*, in which he attacked the temporal power of the pope; *The Babylonian Captivity of the Church*, in which he attacked the seven sacraments on grounds that only two were mentioned in the Bible; and *The Liberty of a Christian Man*, which fixed his doctrines of the priesthood of all believers, the divine nature of honourable lay callings and solafideism (the doctrine that one is justified by faith alone and not by works). Printing gave Luther the chance of success that was denied Jan Hus (see Chapter 4): by the early 1520s some three million Lutheran pamphlets were in circulation.

The Leipzig Disputation had shown that Luther would not moderate his views. He had said initially that he disagreed with Hus's doctrines, but he evidently did not fully understand them. Thus he defended some of Hus's teachings at the Leipzig Disputation of 1519. Shortly afterward Luther, under safe-conduct, defended his views before the newly elected emperor Charles V at the imperial Diet at Worms. He refused an order to recant, and added that burning Hus had been an error. Outlawed by the Diet, Luther went into hiding, protected by Elector Frederick of Saxony; and during nearly a year out of sight he translated the New Testament into German.

The Spread of Lutheranism

The first and most notable success of Luther's movement outside Germany was in Scandinavia. Sweden and Denmark had been a single kingdom since the Union of Kalmar of 1397, but the union was never comfortable, and an independent kingdom of Sweden was established in 1521 by Gustav Vasa. The Swedes deposed Christian II of Denmark, husband of Charles V's sister Elizabeth, and the Danes followed suit in 1523. All the Scandinavian princes were sympathetic to the reformed religion, but their approaches differed. Even the exiled Christian II settled at Wittenberg and converted to Protestantism in 1523, his secretaries translating the New Testament into Danish in 1524. In Schleswig-Holstein Lutheranism was imposed by the prince on the bishops with little popular support.

In Denmark, however, the Reformation was more thorough. In 1526 a synod made the Danish church national, forbidding bishops to seek confirmation in Rome. All money that had previously gone to Rome became the income of the crown, and in 1527 King Frederick I allowed Lutheran preachers safe-conduct. Thus individual cities adopted the Lutheran reform, as was happening in south Germany, and in 1537 King Christian III promulgated a Danish Church Ordinance drafted by Johann Bugenhagen.[6] Protestantism took longer to take root in Sweden. Gustav Vasa (1521–60) kept control of the church, but took no position on most questions of doctrine. Although there were pockets of Protestantism in Stockholm and the coastal towns, Vasa did not make the church Lutheran until 1540, and a 'Protestant church order' was only introduced in 1571. Thus the Swedish church remained more independent of the crown than was usual in this part of Europe. Only in 1593 was Lutheranism declared the official doctrine of the Swedish church, although Calvinism was tolerated.

The Swiss Reformers and the Religion of the City

The German peasants were attracted to Luther's call for the secularization of church property and his arguments that all have equal worth in God's eyes through his grace. They interpreted Luther's doctrine of the priesthood of all believers as a call for ending social distinctions, and their leaders translated this into a social egalitarianism that was used in some of their propaganda during the rebellion of 1524–5. This was utterly foreign to Luther's intent, which was that of the godly, well-ordered territorial state. Clearly frightened by the violence that accompanied the rebellions, he issued a tract, *Against the Murderous and Thieving Hordes of Peasants*, in which he declared that the rebels had placed themselves in opposition to God, and in which he also called on the princes to slay them without mercy.

The intemperance of Luther's language, more than his support of the princes, cost him the widespread support that he had enjoyed in rural Germany. From 1525 on he became increasingly conservative and authoritarian, and Lutheranism became a religion that was imposed by princes and city governments on their subjects.

Luther's views were conditioned by his experience in Saxony, a well-run territorial state. His movement had some initial success among the north German princes, but not in the south; thus Lutheranism became a mainly urban movement in southern Germany, particularly after 1525. The Swiss and south German reformers were accustomed to independent cities and, in some cases, city-states. Most of the free imperial cities in Germany recognized Protestantism at some point in the sixteenth century, and more than half of them became permanently Protestant. Others gave tolerance to Protestants while remaining officially Roman Catholic. Cologne was the only large and free episcopal city that was always Roman Catholic, and some Protestant agitation found its way even there.

During Luther's time in hiding in 1521, other reformers became prominent, beginning with the Swiss Ulrich Zwingli (1484–1531), who had begun to differ publicly with established church doctrines slightly before Luther and who was the most vocal dissenter from Roman Catholicism in south Germany by 1524. Switzerland and Germany were the twin nuclei of theological Protestantism, but both were divided between Roman Catholics and Protestants in the second half of the sixteenth century. Although Maximilian had had to recognize the independence of the Swiss Confederation from the Empire in 1499, there was little cohesion or common interest among the cantons. The rural areas were suspicious of the ambitions of Zürich, which in the fifteenth century had subjugated the rural areas of eastern Switzerland. Many thus feared that there was more than religion behind Zwingli's reform, which was based in Zürich. As in England, the rural masses were strongly attached to their rituals, relics and patron saints, while the guild regimes that dominated the cities resented the separate powers that the church continued to enjoy.

Luther's message created a stir in Switzerland as throughout the southern German-speaking areas. The Swiss city fathers refused to accept the Edict of Worms in 1521 that outlawed Luther: they were prepared to allow the preaching of the purely Biblical gospel, but they were less entranced with Luther's other doctrines. Anticipating Calvin, Zwingli wanted a 'reformation' of all of civil society, led by the lay magistrates rather than the clergy. The Habsburg monarchs, against whom the Swiss had won their independence, were the most firmly Catholic princes of Europe, and were still a threat. Thus the Swiss sought allies among the imperial cities of southern Germany; but although Switzerland had experienced only minor disturbances in 1525, the Lutherans tried to inflame the princes against the Zwinglians by linking their beliefs to the rebellion. The divisions within the Protestant community were thus serious, and after Zwingli was killed in

1531 in a skirmish, the treaty of Kappel gave each canton the right to determine its own confession.

Although Zwingli and Luther disliked each other personally, their beliefs were different on only one important issue: that of the Eucharist. Luther believed that the elements underwent a symbolic transformation, while remaining bread and wine (the doctrine of consubstantiation, in contrast to the Roman Catholic transubstantiation, according to which the elements actually become the body and blood of Jesus). Zwingli believed that the ceremony was purely symbolic, and that the elements underwent no change. The two met at Marburg in 1529 but could not agree. From that point it was clear that the anti-Catholic movement would be split. John Calvin was Zwingli's spiritual heir more than Luther's, but his rigidity precluded unity among the Swiss Protestants. Bern remained Lutheran in the 1530s, refusing to follow Calvinism; Basel, however, was more cosmopolitan, open to German influences but also home to French religious refugees, and its printers published works from all sides of the conflicts. In 1536 officials of Basel moderated the meetings that produced the compromise First Helvetic Confession, which was mainly Zwinglian with some Lutheran elements.[7]

Elsewhere in Germany also, Protestantism was associated largely with the urban areas. It had little success among the peasants except when princes imposed it on them. Paralleling the associations of the civic humanists with ancient Rome, Lutheranism is linked to the development of a sort of civic religion in the early sixteenth century. Having made a careful study of the doctrines, the oligarchic city councils decided to adopt the new religion, then enforced it, in some cities allowing some measure of toleration to dissidents. Thus the church was added to the other elements of civic identity that characterized urban autonomy. The south German urban magistrates essentially took over the functions formerly reserved for the clergy, notably doctrine, ritual and marriage practice, which for the Protestants became a civil contract rather than a sacrament. Only in England did a Protestant region keep bishoprics. In Germany the bishop's functions passed to the city councils, which corresponded frequently and borrowed one another's ideas. In some cases religion became a point of contention and assertion of civic independence from the local prince. Calvinism, by contrast, is associated more in Germany with the élites, as in France, and with princely courts, although it became the civic religion at Emden and some other towns of northern Germany.

There was often vigorous debate on the councils before a decision was taken to change the civic religion, and the process might take several years. Pragmatic considerations were rarely if ever absent. The city council of Ulm in 1530 leaned toward the reformers, but only imposed Lutheranism after taking a poll of male heads of households that showed nearly 90 per cent support.[8] In Germany at least, the merchants, bankers and landholders and the wealthier guilds tended to be conservative in religious matters, but the conservative stance could be Protestantism or Catholicism, depending on local conditions. In France people of this economic level were often Calvinist Huguenots, at least at the beginning of the wars of religion. But in Germany, in contrast to France, Protestantism was sometimes imposed from above when the territorial prince was strong, as in Saxony; but it was never imposed from above by a radical city council against an unwilling populace.[9]

The term *protestantes* was first used in 1529 for those who signed a manifesto drafted by the chancellor of Saxony arguing that each should determine his own religion. The Protestants were divided, however, with the Saxons now wanting accommodation with the emperor. At the Diet of Augsburg in 1530 Philip Melanchthon formulated what came to be considered the authoritative Lutheran position on doctrinal matters, the Confession of Augsburg. The Lutherans who were present at Augsburg seem to have thought that this would bridge the gap with the Roman Catholics, particularly since they argued that church and state should be separated, and condemned the Anabaptists. Luther, however, saw the conflict as unbridgeable. When the Protestants refused Charles V's mediation at Augsburg he gave up on them, and both sides prepared for war. The League of Schmalkalden was formed by the leading Lutheran princes a month later, but they excluded the Zwinglians, whom Luther considered heretical.

Early Protestantism in Latin Europe

Such Protestant impact as Spain and Italy experienced in the sixteenth century was Lutheran, where attitudes toward the reformer were coloured by his personality and by the fact that Roman Catholic propaganda was always harsher on him than on his disciples, or even on Calvin. The state was effective enough to keep the number of open reformers small. Calvin's doctrines were never influential south of the Alps, perhaps because they came so late that the apparatus of control was already in place by the time they could have had much impact. Luther's works were known chiefly through imported books, which helps to explain the zeal to enforce the Index.

Italy

The religious climate in Italy is hard to generalize about, but except in the papal states it seems to have been less severe than in Spain. The papal Inquisition (below) was not monolithic, and any convincing liar could escape it if the secular authority supported him. Although the Counter-Reformation authorities tried to be repressive, they simply lacked the means to control all thought and expression. Although the pope was hardly beloved in Italy, the clergy as a whole was probably less unpopular among the laity than in the north. Lay confraternities, which were declining in the

north, remained strong in Italy, and the ill feeling about foreign upper
clergy that so marked northern Protestantism did not exist in Italy, so that
the anticlerical sentiment that preceded and fuelled doctrinal separatism
was more muted there. The use of printing for religious propaganda was
also less obtrusive than in the north. In Italy, where the reform as a movement of ideas arrived in the 1520s, they were spread in this essentially
private and oral form for almost two decades. It was unusual at this time
simply to read a book silently in the privacy of one's study. People read and
discussed, often in meetings; and a circle formed around the Venetian
nobleman and eventual cardinal, Gasparo Contarini, in the early 1520s,
who had associates in several cities of north Italy in the 1530s, including the
English exile, Reginald Pole. Most participants were interested in some
Protestant ideas as discussion points, but were unwilling to carry them to
the point of revolution. Even that degree of receptivity, however, was
enough to get some of them into serious trouble with the authorities, as
opinions hardened and enforcement mechanisms became more efficient
after 1540, and the works of German and Swiss reformers were censored.
To avoid the authorities, some heretical authors' works were published
anonymously or under someone else's name; some of Luther's works
circulated under Erasmus' name, which did not help Erasmus's reputation
in Italy.

Until the 1540s the Reformation in Italy lacked militant, committed
leaders; and after that the Pope was recovering the initiative. The Italian
reformers, some of whom were in positions of authority in the church
throughout the early 1540s, wanted a less dogmatic and more
Christocentric religion and less ritual, and in this sense were willing to make
superficial accommodations to Protestantism. By the 1540s the reformers
were becoming more open in many cities, but this in itself discredited those
in the papal Curia who had urged restraint and accommodation with the
Protestants. The failure of the Colloquy of Regensburg in 1541 hurt
Contarini's prestige. He died in 1542, and his movement was compromised
by the heresy trial of Bernardino Ochino, general of the Capuchin order,
who fled to Switzerland. The ensuing reaction allowed the Carafa faction
(above) in the papal court to establish the Holy Office (the Roman
Inquisition). Some Italian bishops with humanist training simply concealed
their beliefs and conformed outwardly to Roman Catholic ritual, or decided
that the threat of Protestantism was greater than the dangers of intolerance.
As in France and the Netherlands, 'Nicodemism' (concealing one's religious
beliefs and continuing Catholic observance) was widespread.[10]

Spain

Spain also had hints of religious change in the early sixteenth century that
came to nothing. Charles V's government was at its most effective here.

Erasmus was initially influential in humanist circles: his Greek New Testament of 1516 was given a four-year imperial monopoly in Spain, and only after that expired did the Polyglot Bible, prepared under Cardinal Cisneros' supervision, obtain a papal privilege in 1520. This remained the only authorized Spanish Bible. The Spanish *Index*, first published in 1551 and periodically revised, even forbade editions of some Bibles on grounds of doctrinally suspect translations. The Inquisition established by Ferdinand and Isabella became an instrument of terror in the 1530s, but its targets included *conversos* and Jews as well as persons suspected of Protestant leanings. Even Ignatius of Loyola, the eventual founder of the Society of Jesus, was interrogated. On the level of popular religion, the Illuminists began preaching in the early sixteenth century as a reform movement among the Franciscans, but their influence grew among the laity, particularly *conversos* and pious women known as *beatas*, who were associated with the Franciscan sister Isabel de la Cruz and who read the Bible and Thomas à Kempis's *Imitation of Christ*, being essentially passive mystics who taught submission to the divine will. It is uncertain what, if anything, the Illuminists owed to northern influences, for there is evidence of their movement existing before Luther. The more radically mystical of them were eventually condemned by the Inquisition.

France

Although France would remain Roman Catholic, conditions there were no more intrinsically unfavourable to religious revolt than in England. Although the numerical strength of the French Protestants peaked in the late 1560s, the French kings were political enemies of the pope for almost as much of the sixteenth century as the English kings were. The eventual king Henry IV (1589–1610) was a Protestant until 1593. Any French king except perhaps Henry II (1547–59) might have made a political break from Rome in the fashion of Henry VIII of England. There was strong sentiment in high places for some reform of the French church along Protestant lines, but without establishing a separate church, and certainly without foreign influence. The elderly humanist Jacques Lefèvre d'Étaples (1450–1536) anonymously published a French translation of the gospels in 1523 and, although in 1525 *parlement* ordered the suppression of vernacular translations of the scriptures, he published a translation of the entire Bible in 1530. These translations soon appeared on the first Index of prohibited books published by the Sorbonne in 1545.

Luther's doctrines were never widely received in France, but they probably stimulated more discussion there than in England, where Henry VIII's hostility was a damper. In 1521 the Sorbonne declared 104 of Luther's propositions heretical, and Lutheran books were being seized from private individuals and booksellers. But although France had no organized

Protestant movement until the 1540s, the idea that the Bible was the only word of God did gain some currency in the 1520s. The 'Meaux circle', led by Guillaume Farel, Michel d'Arande and Gérard Roussel, and including the local bishop Guillaume Briçonnet, owed more to Zwingli than to Luther. In 1525 the queen mother, Louise of Savoy, acting as regent for the captive Francis I, ordered the extirpation of Lutheranism from France and broke up the Meaux Circle. The more radical theologians at Meaux, including Farel, went abroad, in Farel's case to Geneva; but d'Arande and Roussel eventually became bishops in the French church. In early 1526 the *parlement* of Paris issued a list of heretical Lutheran doctrines. But the doctors were far from united; the debates showed that at least 15 of the 80 masters in theology sympathized with some Protestant doctrine. Francis I, who preferred to keep his options open and would hardly cavil at Protestants when he was willing to ally with the Turks against Charles V, stopped the persecutions when he returned from captivity; and most other 'Lutheran' heresy cases before 1534 came from incautious anticlerical comments rather than doctrine.[11]

In his early years Francis I was generally sympathetic to 'Evangelicals' and literary humanists, as long as they contented themselves with discussion, and was more liberal theologically than Henry VIII. Calvin obviously hoped to convert Francis, dedicating the first edition of his *Institutes* to him. The king had no sympathy for heresy as such, however, and he disliked Lutheranism. Francis I's humanist interests thus slowed the repression of Protestantism initially; but his attitude changed abruptly when on the night of 17 October 1534 a Protestant placard attacking the sacraments in abusive language was posted at many prominent places, including the door of the royal bedchamber at Amboise. The fact that the deed could come so close to the king suggested a link between danger to him personally and religious agitation. The placards had evidently been made in Switzerland and smuggled into France, the first sign that French Protestantism was leaning toward the Swiss and thus would be more radical than Lutheranism. None the less, the political need to conciliate the German Lutherans kept Francis from going too far, and in 1535 he even had discussions with Melanchthon. Although the government in 1542 made sale or possession of Calvin's *Institutes* a capital offence, there was a lull in physical persecutions while France was trying to gain the alliance of the German Protestants.

Anti-Protestant activity was intensified in Henry II's period. In 1547 Henry set up a chamber in the *parlement* of Paris to hear heresy cases. It became known as the *chambre ardente*, trying 323 cases before it was terminated in 1550. But the battle against heresy did not flag. The Edict of Châteaubriant (1551) gave the secular courts new powers of censorship. Printing, sale and possession of Protestant opinions was outlawed; bounties were given to informers; magistrates had the right to search private homes to find heretics. Protestants were forbidden public offices and teaching at any level, and between 5000 and 8000 cases of heresy were heard each year.

Yet the letter of the law was more severe than its application, and there was a higher proportion of acquittals in heresy cases than would be true of the witchcraft proceedings later. Secular courts were suspicious of the entire proceeding; when Henry suggested creating an Inquisition, it foundered on the opposition of the *parlements*. And as had been true of his father, Henry's need for German Protestant allies forced him to moderate his actions if not his opinions. The large number of humanist bishops whom Francis I had appointed refused to enforce the laws against Protestants, and some became Protestant themselves. The enthusiasm for suppression of the Protestants at this stage came from the royal government, which was losing control. Although the signs of a massive increase in the number of Protestants became unmistakable in the late 1550s (see Chapter 5), the Roman Catholic hierarchy did not remedy abuses such as pluralism and absenteeism. Both Francis I and Henry II were openly hostile to the council of Trent; they saw church reform as a problem whose solution would only help Charles V and would, if implemented, diminish royal control over the French church, and they forbade the French clergy to attend some of its sessions.[12]

Political conditions thus determined the success or failure of theological Protestantism. Luther in 1517 was opening a scholarly debate, and initially he seems to have thought of it purely in those terms. At this stage the questions that he raised struck a chord among thoughtful Christians such as Erasmus, who were not blind to the problems of the universal church. Luther's views evoked interest in places that for political reasons could not move to Protestantism. Sympathy with his position was probably lowest in England, which became Protestant but not Lutheran. Even in Italy there was interest in the early sixteenth century in reforming institutional abuses, emphasizing the Bible, creating higher moral and educational standards for the clergy and getting away from quarrels based on the views of theologians rather than the scriptural sources. There was some interest among even the Catholic orthodox in justification by faith, although in southern Europe it was never divorced from works, as in the case of the northern Protestants.

But carrying doubts about institutional problems to the point of breaking successfully with Rome required political acts, and these only happened in England, Scandinavia and some German principalities. For all the social and particularly political upheaval that it caused, Protestantism in the doctrinal sense was a minority movement everywhere in the first half of the sixteenth century except in parts of Germany, Bohemia, and perhaps Denmark. Both Italy and France in 1525 had more reform-leaning intellectuals than England, but they were unwilling to undertake the revolution against political and church authorities that going beyond discussion implied. After about 1560 the Inquisitions in Italy and Spain and the more openly secular arms of repression were strong enough nearly everywhere to enforce religious orthodoxy, which came with a political dimension, as the case of Elizabeth and the Spaniards demonstrates.

The Radical Reformation

The religious radicals are often associated with the Anabaptist movement, but the great variation among Anabaptist groups makes it hard to define their core beliefs. The Anabaptists (Re-Baptists, since they objected to infant baptism on grounds that the child cannot make a responsible decision) originated in Switzerland without reference to the question of adult baptism, but rather in a split with Zwingli over their demand for the immediate abolition of tithes and interest on loans. By 1530 they existed in large numbers in the Low Countries. The Swiss Brethren shared the belief of the other reformers that the Scriptures were the sole authority, but a radical fringe at the other extreme believed that as the vanguard of God they were not bound by Christian moral law. Some were pacifists, but Melchior Hoffman and the Anabaptists who established a radical regime in Münster in 1534–5 called for the annihilation of the godless. The Melchiorites, who evolved into the Mennonites, were made up mainly of urban marginals and migrants. Essentially mystics, they received inspiration from dreams and visions. While some were willing to obey Christian governments, and Hoffman wanted them to lead the reformation of the godly, the south German and Swiss Anabaptists were so disillusioned by the Peasants' Rebellion that they considered godliness incompatible with secular government.

The Anabaptist movement is often associated unfairly with the commune established at Münster in north-western Germany. Religious agitation had been intense in the city since 1531, and the city council adopted the new teaching in 1533. After the old Roman Catholic élite left the city, and a substantial number of Anabaptists came to Münster in the winter of 1533–4, mainly from elsewhere in Germany and the Netherlands, a radical city council was chosen in February 1534. The new leader of the populace was Jan Bockelszoon of Leiden. 'Jan of Leiden' was accepted as a prophet and established a regime that was supposedly based on the example of the early Christian communities recorded in Acts, including property held in common. This much was accepted without trouble, but the next step, the introduction of polygamy, provoked a rebellion. When it was crushed, Jan proclaimed himself king, allegedly recreating the days of King David. The revolutionary regime ended when the bishop's troops stormed the city on 24 June 1535 and restored the old Roman Catholic order.

With the fall of the Anabaptist kingdom in Münster, the movement split. A nucleus of radicals still believed that the New Jerusalem was at hand and that the ungodly should be put to the sword. More influential were the followers of the mystic David Joris, who also allowed his followers to attend church while maintaining Hoffmann's insistence on separation from the world. The most important strain of the radical Reformation is associated with Menno Simons (1496–1561), who worked in his homeland of

Friesland and along the lower Rhine, and who gradually became the leader of most remaining Melchiorites, publishing *the Foundation of Christian Doctrine* in 1539. The Anabaptists were understandably sensitive after the polygamy at Münster to charges of sexual licence. To keep their reputation for unblemished lives, the mainstream element had to establish authority under the elders; Simons even taught that the spouse of an excommunicated spouse had to shun him or her. Simons believed in separation from the world and the imminent second coming. Thus after 1535 the mainstream Anabaptists were essentially pacific, withdrawing from the world rather than trying actively to reform it.[13]

John Calvin (1509–1564)

Luther's movement was less theological in the beginning than that of Calvin, who came a generation later and knew his doctrines as a platform from which to build. By Calvin's time there was no realistic hope of reforming a universal church from within, and institutional abuses thus became secondary to establishing a coherent doctrine that was clearly distinct not only from the Roman Catholics but also from other 'Protestant' groups. Luther's message contained so many elements that preachers emphasized whichever of his views, or those of other reformers, they found most congenial. Solafideism, which became the theological centrepiece of Luther's doctrine, seems to have aroused less interest initially than his appeal to go back to the scriptures in their pure form. In Germany Luther was seen mainly as an institutional reformer, but outside Germany he was a theological innovator.

Jean Cauvin, who Latinized his name to Calvinus, studied the liberal arts at Paris before going to Bourges and Orléans between for legal studies. Although he gave up the law and returned to Paris soon after receiving his licentiate in 1533, his legal mind gave a systematic edge to his theology that was lacking in the other major Protestant reformers. By 1534 he was a Reformer, and he spoke later of a sudden conversion. Expelled from Paris in 1534, he went to Basel, where his *Institutes of the Christian Religion* (written in Latin) was published in 1536. The fact that French Protestantism would be Calvinist was determined by the success of the French translation of the *Institutes* in 1541. Calvin's later editions of the *Institutes* were genuine revisions; the final Latin edition of 1559 was almost twice the length of the first edition of 1536.

Calvin was the theologically dominant figure of the second half of the century, as Luther was of the first half. The Calvinists or 'Reformed' were the most theologically extreme of the 'mainstream' Protestant groups, if by 'mainstream' we mean those that gained enough converts to pose a political threat to Roman Catholic authorities or to control a government. Until Calvin, the only doctrinal deviations from Rome had been those of Luther and Zwingli and their disciples. Calvin's theology, bursting rather suddenly on the scene, galvanized a further stage and made it possible for English and French Protestants who disliked Luther and his doctrines to move toward a 'purification' of Roman Catholicism, which meant in practice abolishing its rituals and symbols.

The theological issues that separated Lutheran from Reformed were almost as great as those separating the Protestants generally from Roman Catholics, and accordingly the two hardened into warring confessions in the second half of the sixteenth century. While Luther saw only salvation as foreordained, Calvin taught that both salvation and damnation were predestined. While Reformed theology taught that all the sacraments were merely symbolic, Luther felt that baptism was necessary for salvation. Lutherans also believed that Christ's physical body was present in the Eucharist, but the Calvinists simply broke ordinary, unconsecrated and unleavened bread for the Lord's Supper. While the Reformers tried to end images and anything that was not clearly based on scripture, the Lutherans insisted on keeping music, vestments and pictures. Most artisans disliked Calvin's conservative social and political views, but they were precisely what made him attractive to the upper middle class and the nobility: Calvin's notion of predestination to both salvation and damnation hindered many who were less certain of their own intrinsic virtue from adopting the rest of his theology, including the purely symbolic nature of the sacraments. All Protestant groups believed in the ability of the layperson to read the Scriptures and interpret them for himself (herself was expected to take guidance from him) without guidance from church authorities or tradition. In practice, however, no one ever practised this. Luther's movement was split by rancorous divisions after 1547, until the threat from Calvin and the Counter-Reformation pulled them back together to some extent. Thus it is not surprising that the two camps were antagonistic, particularly as the Calvinists gained political influence in parts of Germany where the Lutherans were strong.

Calvin settled at Geneva in 1536. He was expelled for three years after 1538, but resided continuously at Geneva between 1541 and his death. Calvin's regime at Geneva is noted for its control of the city through an organization of lay elders or presbyters, chosen according to district of the city by the municipal government, with the power to excommunicate resting with the church rather than the city authorities. They were generally to oversee the moral and religious standards of the community, observe, and make weekly reports to the pastors. They met regularly as a consistory, which then recommended punishments to the civil arm, which alone had the power to impose them. Control of the church by presbtyters, rather than Calvin's theology, is the defining mark of 'Presbyterianism'. This scheme of church organization made it possible to organize local congregations easily in defiance of the authorities, and the rapid spread of Calvinism in France after 1555 was bolstered by missionaries sent from Geneva, although much of it was locally generated (see Chapter 5 for political Calvinism and the French wars of religion).[14]

The Calvinists extended the presbyterian system to France and Scotland. The consistories of each congregation were linked into presbyteries or (France) *colloquys*, and thence into provincial synods followed by national synods. Each lower body was subject to the discipline of the higher, and the churches enforced moral conduct and proper doctrine. Yet the 'lay control' element of Calvin's scheme must be understood in context. Calvin's attitude toward secular rulers was less pacific than Luther's. Luther became pessimistic about princes, and by the end felt that quiet piety was the answer. While in Lutheran areas the churches after 1555 became dependents of whatever secular government ruled, the Calvinist churches did not, for Calvin thought of a partnership with the secular arm in which the rulers would enforce right religion as determined by the church. Their discipline and hierarchy made the Calvinists better able than the Lutherans to resist when the authorities were unfriendly, and occasionally to take the offensive, as they did against Elizabeth in the last half of her reign.

The Strange Case of England

All princes of Europe had political problems with the papacy, but those of Henry VIII of England were less severe than most until he tried to have his marriage to Catherine of Aragon annulled. Henry's break with Rome was purely institutional: except briefly in the mid-1530s, when he was under Thomas Cromwell's influence, he persecuted theological Protestantism. Except for the resolutely Catholic Mary, his successors were more liberal.

The 'Reformation Parliament' of 1529 was the first one since 1523, and it had numerous items on its agenda; the king's annulment was not discussed until 1533. Various proposals for church reform were put to this Parliament, including limitation on pluralities and penalties for non-residence and against clergy engaged in commerce. The Act of Supremacy, which severed the ties of the English church with Rome, was passed by Parliament in 1534. Henry VIII's religious opinions were unfailingly conservative, but his views shifted depending on who had his ear and how he perceived the foreign scene. In 1536 he issued the Ten Articles, his most radical theological treatise, in which he reduced the number of sacraments to three (the Lutheran/Calvinist baptism and the Lord's Supper/Eucharist, and also penance). The Ten Articles distinguished between matters of belief that were necessary to salvation, and ceremonies that were permissible but not necessary. But the next year his *Institutions of a Christian Man* restored the seven Roman Catholic sacraments and revived tradition as an authority alongside the Bible. Henry's final statement of belief was the Six Articles of 1539, which reaffirmed most of Roman Catholic belief except the position of the pope.

Characteristically, the Reformation in England did not end the financial exactions of the church. Payments such as annates were simply retained, and paid to the crown instead of the pope. The structure of bishoprics and parishes was kept, and although they lost some revenues, Henry VIII was too concerned about having a loyal state church to deprive them of much. But the monasteries did not have this kind of political influence. In 1536 Henry dissolved the smaller monasteries, those with incomes of £200 per annum or less which thus had less political influence than the larger ones. In 1539 he dissolved the larger ones, accompanied by a ferocious propaganda campaign orchestrated by Cromwell, in which he attacked the credibility of the relics upon which much of the monasteries' devotions were based. The monasteries' lands and their plate, which was melted down for bullion, were forfeit to the crown.

The conventional wisdom that the English Reformation was essentially marital even more than political thus seems accurate. Henry VIII was a military posturer whose foreign adventures, but for windfall confiscations of Roman Catholic property, would have bankrupted the English monarchy, strong as it had become through the efforts of his father Henry VII and Edward IV. Henry had initially been concerned with silencing conservative opinion from the Roman Catholic side, but after 1534 he turned his attention more toward the theological Protestants. His instrument in this was Stephen Gardiner, bishop of Winchester. But Gardiner's influence declined after an ill-considered attack on Henry's last queen, Catherine Parr, whose circle included humanists. Most persecutions of 1543–4 are of rather humble persons, such as Anne Askew, a Yorkshire woman who renounced her marriage vows, moved to London, made no attempt to hide her radical views, and was tortured and burned in 1545.

The Six Articles of 1539 were a watershed. Many theologians went abroad, particularly to Zürich. Edward VI's regents imposed a theology whose strength was increasing but which was still mainly the province of an élite. The Protector, the earl of Somerset, had Lutheran sympathies, persuading Parliament to repeal Henry VIII's treason and heresy laws and withdraw the Six Articles. Parliament dissolved the religious guilds and the chantries in 1547, an act with immediately deleterious effects on local ceremonies and usages since some 90 colleges, many of which operated schools, and 100 hospitals were affiliated with chantries. Hoping to find a religious settlement which might accommodate everyone, in 1547 the duke of Somerset issued an intentionally vague Book of Common Prayer, but he simply offended the radicals on all sides, particularly after obedience to it was required by an Act of Uniformity in 1549. The Prayer Book ended most rituals and helped provoke the uprising of that year. Edward VI's regime sheltered Lutherans, particularly Martin Bucer, who left Germany after Charles V's victory in 1547. Bucer, who became Regius Professor at Cambridge, largely wrote the Second Book of Common Prayer of 1552 which, although theologically more radical than the first, restored the rituals. Such Calvinists as the Scot John Knox were also received in England. The Lutherans had no significant impact on English Protestantism after 1552. Given that Henry VIII made few doctrinal or ritual changes in Roman Catholicism, simply replacing the pope with the king as head of the church, the transitions were easy for most of his subjects.

Although Mary I (1553–8), known as 'Bloody Mary' for her burning of 286 Protestants, has become infamous, the fact that she found so few to burn suggests that as late as the 1550s Protestantism did not run deep, and that most people were willing to accommodate to whatever religion was favoured in Westminster. Yet Mary's reign was critical in shaping the character of English Protestantism. Some 800 people, most of them educated and prosperous, went overseas to escape the persecutions. They found a considerably warmer reception in areas controlled by Calvinists than in Lutheran regions. John Knox and his followers went to Geneva at this time, where the 'Marian exiles' became the theological backbone of the Elizabethan religious settlement.

Elizabeth's accession was greeted with cautious enthusiasm. She was known to be Protestant, but the degree of her commitment was uncertain. Elizabeth was willing to accept a much less overtly Protestant settlement than what was desired by the radicals returning from exile. The Parliament of 1559 repealed Mary's religious legislation and passed an Act of Supremacy and a slightly revised (in a Calvinist direction) version of the essentially Lutheran prayer book of 1552, using the latter document's form of quoting directly from Christ's words at the Last Supper rather than using an interpretation. This was risky, given that most of the population had been attending mass after 1554, and all bishops in the House of Lords voted against the Act of Uniformity that made it obligatory. Another provision ordered that the standard ornaments of the churches and the vestments of the clergy were to be those used during the second year of Edward VI, and any changes were reserved to the queen and the archbishop of Canterbury. The bishops took this to mean that there was no requirement to use them, but those who wished to could do so. But visitation teams were soon sent out, who seized the vestments in their zeal to purge the church from the 'idolatrous' associations of Roman Catholicism, and altars were replaced with communion tables.

Having achieved a Protestant religious settlement by 1563, Elizabeth spent the rest of her reign defending it, mainly from radical Calvinists who wanted to carry the Reformation farther. The Thirty-Nine Articles adopted by Convocation in 1563 were Calvinist in theology, but there was still a great deal of neo-Catholic ceremony in the Anglican service that offended those who were calling themselves 'Puritans' by the 1560s. Some clergy even in the Convocation of 1563 argued for stricter regulations against the Catholics and Protestant nonconformists, public penance for sinners, and 'further education' for the clergy. This amounted to a church independent of the state, the last thing Elizabeth wanted; she wanted no preaching clergy who would stir up trouble. When the Puritans in 1566 tried to have the Thirty-Nine Articles made statutory by Parliament, the queen, who considered religion her prerogative, ordered the bill halted as not originating with her, as was customary. She vigorously opposed 'prophesyings' (local colloquia of the clergy who would criticize one another's doctrines and personal conduct), and her attitude closed the church to Puritan reform from within. When the Puritans brought bills in the Parliaments of 1585 and 1586–7, in the latter case asking for the abolition of bishops and the Book of Common Prayer, Elizabeth refused to allow them read; and when Thomas Wentworth rose in the Commons to defend the right of Parliament to discuss these matters, she had him confined in the Tower of London. Preserving the settlement of 1559 and 1563 in its entirety thus became the cornerstone of her religious policy; and her longevity assured that a Protestant succession was passed to King James VI of Scotland in 1603.

Attending church and taking the sacraments were a civic duty for Elizabeth. She saw religion as an external matter of behaviour and politics, not an internal question of conscience. In contrast to her father, she did not normally meddle in doctrinal questions. As late as 1570 she was saying that she had no desire to 'inquire into men's consciences', but insisted that they attend church under Anglican approved ritual; in other words, she did not care what the Catholics really believed as long as they were Anglican communicants. Although the pope's bull of 1570 excommunicating her made this attitude harder to sustain, Elizabeth resisted Parliament's efforts to raise penalties against Catholics. She only required attendance at church; many in Parliament wanted to require taking communion. By 1603, 123 Catholic priests and 60 laypeople had been executed, but the persecutions of the Roman Catholics from the 1580s were aimed at priests and active lay leaders who helped them, not at the masses. On a personal level, the queen appeared more antagonistic towards Puritans than towards the Catholics. William Allen founded a Roman Catholic seminary at Douai, which sent missionaries on risky trips to England, not to convert Protestants but rather to encourage and strengthen the Roman Catholic community. They concentrated on the gentry of the south and east, and Roman Catholicism thus became a mainly upper-class religion in England. But the missionaries were successful in keeping the old religion alive in England.

The Roman Catholic Reformation

Some have found the term 'Counter-Reformation' objectionable because it suggests that only the Protestants were 'reforming' anything. If 'reform' means 'improvement', this view is understandable. But if it means 'change' or 'form again', 'Counter-Reformation' accurately describes what happened, for all significant changes in religious doctrine that were made in the sixteenth century were on the Protestant side. The Roman Catholic reaction was to improve standards and correct flagrant abuses without changing doctrine or even institutions.

The initial and to a great extent the eventual reaction of the papacy to the theologies of Luther and Calvin was simply to restate traditional belief. Yet other voices in the Catholic community as diverse as Erasmus and the emperor Charles V, for all their horror of heresy and personal distaste for Luther, were convinced that if the institutional abuses of which he had complained were remedied, the Lutherans would return to the fold.

The situation was complicated by the fact that the pontiff himself was widely perceived as a major institutional abuse. Charles wanted the pope to call a council, and at times was on the verge of calling one himself, to deal with the questions that the Protestants had raised. Pope Paul III (1534–49) appointed a commission in 1537 to make suggestions for changes in church government, and on its advice he made token reforms of the papal court. But the pope, understanding the limitations on the papacy imposed briefly by the councils of the fifteenth century, refused to call another until 1545. In that year he called a council at Trent, which was prorogued in 1547 and met again in 1551–2 and finally in 1562–3, when the Council issued decrees that have become the theological basis of modern Roman Catholicism.

Neither the pope nor the council ever wavered on doctrine or ritual, which by now was the major issue for Protestants outside Germany; for in contrast to Luther's, Calvin's message, now clearly the vanguard of the Protestant movement, was purely theological and had nothing to do with abuses, some of which were admittedly handled by the Council. The major concern of the church was a reform of institutions, not theology, which was of little concern to a largely illiterate population of believers; for the priests worked with the laity through church institutions and used traditional rituals to symbolize complex doctrines. Although the internal element was not completely missing, activity in the world, educating at a basic level and combating heresy at the local level where it counted, were the hallmarks of the Catholic Reformation. The church was concerned with reforming the morals and educational level of the local clergy and training them to minister among the laity, not introducing reforms in the papal curia, which the delegates at Trent had not been permitted to discuss. Although the private morality of the clergy undoubtedly improved after Trent, whose last session was presided over by a cardinal who had sired four children, the secular preoccupations of the sacred college did not. Even after Trent the cardinals were notorious pluralists, holding numerous bishoprics and abbacies simultaneously.

From the perspective of theology and ritual, the Council of Trent tightened the requirements for sainthood, evidently realizing that abuses had occurred; but Roman Catholic dogma never questioned the notion that saints could work miracles on earth. After 1523 there were no more canonizations until 1588; another 24 followed in the seventeenth century. Local saints continued to be venerated, sometimes before they were

Map 10.1 The Religious Divisions of Europe, 1550–1600

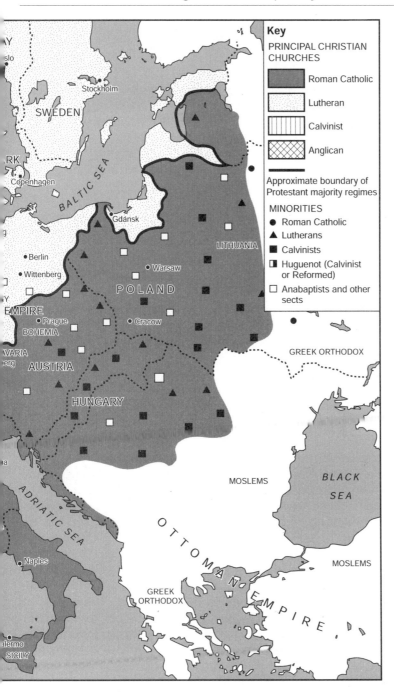

Key

PRINCIPAL CHRISTIAN CHURCHES

Roman Catholic

Lutheran

Calvinist

Anglican

Approximate boundary of Protestant majority regimes

MINORITIES

● Roman Catholic

▲ Lutherans

■ Calvinists

▯ Huguenot (Calvinist or Reformed)

□ Anabaptists and other sects

canonized officially, as happened with Carlo Borromeo of Milan. The Council reaffirmed the Vulgate as the authoritative Latin Bible rather than the more recent translations, as well as traditional beliefs concerning Purgatory, the treasury of merit and indulgences and the seven sacraments, including marriage. The equal weight given to tradition and scripture was also confirmed, and it restated the position that man's will through good works can effect his salvation. A revision was undertaken of Pope Paul IV's *Index of Prohibited Books*, which had appeared in 1559.

While the Council of Trent had an essentially institutional reaction to Protestantism, Counter-Reformation theology was an amalgam of the mystical and the authoritarian. St Ignatius of Loyola (*c.*1491–1556) was a Spanish knight who was severely wounded in battle in 1521. During a long and painful convalescence that left him crippled he turned to religious meditation. His *Spiritual Exercises* describe his struggle and his doubts, which he overcame by a sheer effort of will. The individual was to do whatever was necessary to cause his soul to submit, but submission to the church was the necessary prologue to the conquest of the soul. Prayer was the duty of each individual, clergy and lay. In 1534 Loyola founded the Society of Jesus (Jesuit Order), which was approved by Pope Paul III in 1540. He became a soldier of Christ and of the pope, to whom the Jesuits took an oath. The *Spiritual Exercises* were supplemented in 1550 by the *Constitutions*, which set strict educational standards for the Jesuits and instilled a military discipline in which every vestige of individuality was to be crushed by the superior in the order. The 'general' of the order was supreme below the pope.

Although the Jesuits did some poor relief, their major thrust was in missions and education. The *Spiritual Exercises* became the basis of a rigid system of primary and secondary education that served the church well in educating the young in what it meant to be Catholic. Although some Catholic princes distrusted their rigidity and unquestioned obedience to the pope, and saw a threat to themselves in the Jesuit doctrine that assassination of Protestant princes was a suitable service to God, the Jesuits became the major agents of the Counter-Reformation, in Spain and Portugal initially. In Germany Jesuit colleges were established at nine universities before 1570 under the leadership of Peter Canisius (1521–97). Canisius' catechisms were intended to counterbalance the impact of Luther's and provided short reference points that pupils could memorize easily. Just as Protestantism in the late sixteenth century is characterized by the catechism and devotional manuals emphasizing practice, so the French Jesuit Francis de Sales' *Introduction to the Devout Life*, originally written as letters to a lady to guide her spiritually, was in a sense the spiritual hallmark of the later Counter-Reformation, and was non-theological and directed toward laymen.

The concerns of some Catholics over private devotions and clerical morality sounded like early Protestantism, and some of the writing of both

Loyola and the Spanish mystic St Teresa of Avila caused them problems. The Roman Catholic clergy was split over reform between the newer, more Jesuit-inspired priests and those who defended the established ways. There was initial resistance to allowing the Jesuits into France, on grounds that they were variously too papal and a tool of the Spaniards; but by the 1570s they were influential, although not numerous. The Capuchins (a branch of the Franciscans, founded in the early sixteenth century, who emphasized urban preaching) were more favoured, spreading rapidly from the 1570s.

Lutheranism and Calvinism in Eastern Europe; Germany and the Empire

Charles V's defeat in 1555 was much more complete than it now appears, for most of Germany, including the Habsburg household lands, were dominated by Protestants. The next century, particularly from the 1590s, witnessed a process of re-Catholicizing, but until then the Habsburgs were often in a position analogous to Henry IV's in France before 1593. Just as the social position of the French Protestants gave them a disproportionate influence, so the strength of the German Catholics was greater because three of the seven electors and a majority of the nobles in the imperial Diet were Catholic. The greatest success of the Counter-Reformation was in the eastern parts of the Empire, which were firmly Protestant but not in each case Lutheran in 1555.

Ferdinand I (1556–64) had displayed less tolerance toward the Protestants in his youth than his brother Charles V had done, but he moderated considerably as emperor, respecting the creeds and property of his Protestant subjects. He disliked the pretensions of the popes, maintaining humanists at court who had little sympathy for the rigidity of the counter-Reformation papacy; and he actively promoted the activity of the Council of Trent, accordingly incurring the enmity of the popes, who gave the Council grudging acceptance at best. At Trent Ferdinand tried to have the marriage of priests permitted and the chalice given to the laity, and he and his successors concentrated on consolidating their control over the diverse Habsburg inheritance. The Habsburg homeland of Austria was a problem for them: it was so thoroughly Lutheran that Ferdinand had no practical choice but to tolerate the new doctrine.

Ferdinand's eldest son, Maximilian II (1564–76), the brother-in-law and eventual father-in-law of his cousin, Philip II – dynastic concern among the Habsburgs meant marriage among their kinsmen as well as linking them to other political families – was already king of Bohemia and Hungary when he became Holy Roman Emperor. His two younger brothers were given lands in the patrimony to administer. Maximilian was so tolerant that he was suspected of heresy, and may even have refused the Roman Catholic sacraments on his deathbed. He always permitted the Lutherans in his domain lands to worship publicly. Theological liberalism in his case, and concern over institutional abuses in the church in his father's, meant that they gave only lukewarm support to the religious movements of the Counter-Reformation, notably the Jesuits, who had little influence in Austria until the reign of Rudolf II (1576–1612). In most cities of southern Germany and some territorial states in the west, Catholics and Lutherans coexisted peacefully.

Bohemia was badly split along religious lines in the sixteenth century. The end of the civil war in 1433 left Hus's followers controlling most of Bohemia, but the traditional Roman Catholics were strong in the border areas, in Moravia, and were the majority in Silesia and Upper and Lower Lusatia. The Compactata of 1436 gave the two confessions legal standing; the monarchs were generally Catholic, but the majority of the country was 'Utraquist', taking both the bread and wine in the Lord's Supper. The settlement excluded some radical groups within Utraquism in the late fifteenth century, notably the Unity of Brethren, who were technically out-lawed until 1609 but in fact had wide support. In the sixteenth century the more radical Utraquists joined the Lutherans, while the conservatives became Catholics; the Brethren joined Luther initially, but later adhered to Calvinism. The Anabaptists and anti-Trinitarians also became strong in Bohemia and particularly Moravia, to the point where the vast majority of the population was non-Catholic. The situation was so confused that some measure of toleration was the only way out. The Bohemian Confession of 1575 was devised by theologians of various Protestant persuasions, and gave freedom to virtually all groups, although it was only accepted by the monarchy in 1609. This victory was ephemeral: after 1620 the victorious Habsburgs revoked toleration, and with surprising speed converted most of Bohemia to Roman Catholicism.[15]

Hungary had been ruled by western-based monarchs since the early fourteenth century, and by Habsburgs since the eventual emperor Sigismund became its king in 1387. There was an exceptional degree of ethnic diversity and foreign influence in Hungary, and the threat that the Turks would penetrate Europe through the Balkans gave it the same strategic significance for Europe that the Byzantine Empire had held earlier. Nobles were always powerful, and the rival claimants to the throne after 1526, including Ferdinand, had to try to buy their loyalty, which entrenched them even more. In this atmosphere Protestantism spread rapidly. Humanist and foreign influences were strong at the universities and among the upper clergy, who were notoriously rich. The large numbers of Germans in Hungary were receptive. Hungarian Protestantism was always largely German, but there was also a large Polish element – Polish Lutherans had helped evangelize Hungary, and Hungarians studied at the University of Kraków. The differences between confessions sharpened, as elsewhere, in the second half of the century. The spread of Lutheranism in Hungary, as in Bohemia, started among the numerous ethnic Germans, then spread to other elements in the population. The fact that large numbers of Germans had settled in the east and that they dominated the major cities gave access to Luther's essentially German message. But the fact that it was a foreign message also limited it, and made possible inroads on specific doctrines from various Swiss perspectives, leading eventually to a general strength of Calvinism, which was the major religion in Hungary by 1570. Ferdinand behaved carefully; only with Rudolf II did the Habsburgs try to impose Roman Catholicism, and Hungary still had a large number of Protestants until after the Turkish threat ended in the late seventeenth century.[16]

Calvinism in Germany

The main change in the religious situation after 1555, and accordingly in politics, was the spread of Reformed (Calvinist) Protestantism. Its nucleus was Heidelberg, home of the Elector Palatine, who converted in 1563. The early success of Lutheranism in Bohemia and Hungary, and accordingly the impotence even of Rudolf II to move against it, owes much to the fact that as a result of the movement of westerners into these areas during the central Middle Ages, the upper orders of the cities and much of the law that they used became predominantly German. But the fact that it was a foreign message also limited it: thus Calvinism was brought from Switzerland and replaced Lutheranism as the majority religion in Hungary by 1570. In Bohemia Calvinism remained a Protestant minority, albeit a significant one mainly from the turn of the seventeenth century. Calvinists and Lutherans were often as vitriolic toward each other as toward the Roman Catholics, and hostilities intensified from the 1580s. Eastern Europe also had a large number outside the traditional religious groups, mainly the various splinter Anabaptist groups and a large Unitarian or anti-trinitarian element, particularly in Transylvania.[17]

Lutheran versus Calvinist is also important in north-eastern Europe. In Prussia the major towns of Gdánsk, Elbing and Thorn were the centres of Protestantism. Royal privileges, beginning with Gdánsk's in 1557, guaranteed to the cities the right to choose communion in one or two kinds, but not the right to a city-based church. Thus the cities naturally became battlegrounds. The patricians leaned toward Calvinism, but the town councils were cautious, bringing in and hiring ministers from Lutheran and even Bohemian Brethren backgrounds. This in turn contributed to the break down of the consensus in the late 1570s, however, for the pastors of different backgrounds wanted to impose their own uniformity. Conflicting loyalties to external churches and states became an issue, since virtually all the clergy in these towns were from outside Prussia. The pastors also disliked the council's hegemony over the churches. The Lutherans successfully exploited the popular desire for images and ritual as a tool against the

Calvinist patricians and theologians, and each side abused the other, including imputations of the use of magic. From the mid-1590s the crown used the religious issue as a means of curtailing the autonomy of the towns by supporting Lutherans, who were often in the minority on town councils, and thus splitting the large cities from the Calvinist nobles; and from the early seventeenth century onwards this meant that Lutheranism in particular, and Protestantism in general, was identified with the German-speaking Prussian burghers. The Swedes, who invaded Prussia in 1626 and 1655, would use the Prussians' German and Lutheran identities as a rallying-cry.[18]

Religious Intolerance and Confessional Rigidity

After 1555 the theological orientations that had begun as revolutionary movements hardened into received doctrine that was enforced by states: there was little evolution of theological Lutheranism or Calvinism after the founders' deaths in 1546 and 1564, and the Tridentine Decrees of 1563 fixed Roman Catholic doctrine. Religion was even more defined by political regime than earlier.

The Peace of Augsburg of 1555 (see Chapter 5) worked reasonably well until about 1580, although when given the opportunity each confession tried to sabotage the other. Roman Catholics and Lutherans, the two creeds permitted by the peace, coexisted amicably in some south German communities. Even at Catholic Münster Lutherans and Anabaptists were tolerated, although their numbers were small. The example of the bloodshed in the Netherlands and France during these years contributed to maintaining peace in Germany.

But the younger generation, educated in the religious schools that were established during the interim of calm, thought that their elders had sold out. More conservative Lutherans came to dominate that confession, and in Bavaria and the church principalities, especially Würzburg, the Protestants were persecuted. The Calvinists, who were excluded from the Peace of Augsburg, were disliked by both the Lutherans and Roman Catholics; the conversion of the elector Palatine to the Reformed faith in 1563 was not followed by others until 1578. Most of the Calvinist gains were at Lutheran expense, and mainly among the élite, for Calvinism had little attraction for the lower orders except in Scotland. Calvinist clergy in Germany were not revolutionaries; they obeyed their princes. There was none of the anti-government rhetoric associated with Calvinism in Britain, the Netherlands, France and Switzerland.

Yet few, if any, seriously wanted religious toleration on principle. States rarely permitted all beliefs indiscriminately. Instead, specific named creeds were granted toleration, almost always the majority religion and one or, at most, two minorities that were seen as too numerous, and in some cases too well-organized into a formal church, to make it possible to extirpate them without provoking civil war. This was the case with the Peace of Augsburg.

Most tolerationists only wanted freedom of conscience, and in some cases limited freedom of public religious worship. But this was only a short-term solution, for absolute truth would eventually triumph. Thomas More told his son-in-law that he desired universal peace and uniformity in religion; he could not have had the one, and in fact he got neither. More had no objection in principle to persecution on religious grounds.[19] Calvin's famous burning of the Spaniard Michael Servetus at Geneva in 1553 is often taken as a milestone in the escalating intolerance. Servetus in his *Concerning the Errors of the Trinity* propounded a decidedly unorthodox view, seeing the Trinity as successive manifestations in time of a single God – creator, Christ and Holy Ghost. In his *Restitution of Christianity* he argued that God the Son was a link with a humankind that, through the individual will as expressed through partaking in the Lord's Supper, could be united spiritually with God the Father. Servetus was imprisoned by the Inquisition in Italy and escaped, but recklessly stopped in Geneva, where he was recognized at a service conducted by Calvin himself.

Basel, a centre of printing and for a time the home of Erasmus, was the main centre for the substantial minority of Protestants who wanted liberty of conscience and who objected to Calvin's burning of Servetus. In 1527 the council declared liberty of conscience, an attitude that has been linked to the strong humanist tradition at Basel, but which was probably more pragmatic; the council was dominated by businessmen who hoped to keep everybody happy and who wanted the conflicts to evaporate. In February 1529 Basel became Lutheran, ending the humanist phase of the city's history. Lutheran Basel was more receptive to religious diversity than other cities, even tolerating radical Protestants after persecuting some Anabaptists in the 1530s, but part of this attitude was the simple fact that the Lutherans who controlled Basel disliked Calvin and Geneva.[20]

Perhaps in reaction to the stifling religious climate in Italy, Italians who settled at Basel and elsewhere provided an intellectual foundation to the growing movement for toleration. Many Polish students came to the university at Basel, and their views were important in the Polish regime's decision to grant religious toleration in 1573. Bernardino Ochino (above) took refuge in Basel before moving on to Poland. The most famous defence of toleration as a positive good was the treatise *On Whether Heretics Should be Persecuted*, issued at Basel by the expatriate Savoyard Sebastian Castellio (1515–63) under a pseudonym in reaction to Servetus' execution. Castellio had come Geneva as a printer, but left after breaking with Calvin. He argued that while scripture was of divine inspiration and could be enforced, diversity of opinion and practice was permitted on matters not made explicit there. Castellio agreed that heretics who transgressed the moral law of the Bible could be punished by secular governments, but not those who misunderstood doctrinal points, for revelation continues and the scriptures are not always clear.

Roman law had defined heresy (incorrect religious belief) as sedition (incitement of rebellion) since 382. From 1539 in Languedoc, and by royal edict for the rest of the realm in 1541, the French royal courts took original jurisdiction over laypeople accused of heresy, while the church courts still handled clergy accused of heresy. Toleration only became a significant issue in France in the early stages of the religious wars. When the Reformed church began making significant conversions in the late 1550s, some hoped to end the schism with Roman Catholicism by a broad enough Gallican reform to satisfy the Huguenots. Others were willing to grant freedom of conscience, but not of public worship, which would lead to civil discord. On pragmatic grounds, by 1561 some at the royal court favoured giving freedom of worship to the Reformed church on the grounds that it was too strong to be extirpated.

Catherine de' Medici was inclined to accept toleration as a temporary expedient, if for no other reason than because she needed the support of the Bourbons. Hence the Edict of Saint-Germain of 1562 gave freedom of worship to the Reformed 'until such time as God by his grace reunites [our subjects] in one sheepfold'. There was a vast difference between something undesirable that circumstances forced the rulers to tolerate, and freedom of religion *per se*. The Edict of Saint-Germain punished disturbances and destruction of property, and left the question of permitting public religious services up to the king's local representative. But most of the country was unwilling to accept even this limited degree of toleration, and the *parlement* of Paris deprived the edict of legal force by refusing to register it.

Although even after 1565 the Huguenots were powerful enough to extract other edicts of toleration from the royal government, enforcement was impossible, because local magistrates of each confession persecuted the other whatever the royal government said. Few Protestants were willing to tolerate Roman Catholics whom they had a chance to persecute, seeing it instead as a duty of the French crown to adopt the one true faith. Ultimately toleration of Protestantism depended on the willingness of the staunchly Roman Catholic *parlements* to register the royal edicts, which would put them into effect locally. Eventually the monarchs realized that they were damaging themselves with their Roman Catholic subjects, who were a vast majority, by seeming to countenance the pollution of heresy.[21] The Edict of Nantes of 1598 (see Chapter 5) was enacted by an exhausted French government that had never intended it as more than a stopgap, with the ultimate end of restoring a united faith.

Not surprisingly, religion became more political and less theological as it passed into the hands of laymen who controlled a more sophisticated state apparatus that could guarantee conformity. Luther himself had seen what was coming. His early works, notably *On Secular Authority* (1523), had advocated toleration in the optimistic view that free access to the scriptures would cause all persons of good will to follow Christian (Lutheran) doctrines. He even said initially that lay authorities should not fight heresy with force, but he explicitly rejected this position after 1525. The early Luther was the classic 'outsider' who wanted toleration for himself; the later Luther was the leader of an established church who wanted the authorities to protect it, not only from Roman Catholics but also from Anabaptists. The deeply disillusioned monk felt that discipline was the chief need, requiring indoctrination in the modern sense: what mattered was who controlled the local government and, accordingly, the printing presses. This gave the ruler the capacity to indoctrinate the masses via literature against the godless opponents, particularly through easy catechisms that became exercises in recitation rather than understanding. Luther came to prefer to teach religion through the catechism than the Bible. His Shorter Catechism was drilled into children; parish records of the late sixteenth century show that most Lutheran children knew little and cared less of Evangelical theology. Rulers required outward conformity to their own religion and established a state apparatus to enforce it. Moral legislation against blasphemy, taverns and other forms of misbehaviour was included in the 'Church Ordinances' (see Chapter 6) in Germany, with fines for not attending catechism class and/or Sunday services. The Roman Catholics were doing the same thing in the areas that they controlled.[22]

Executions for Conscience

A sign of the growing confessional rigidity is that judicial executions of individuals for religious reasons, as opposed to warfare, were mainly a feature of the second half of the sixteenth century. The number who perished for their religious convictions cannot be calculated exactly, because of vague reports that 'many' people were executed. For cases where hard data survive, the annual average number of executions was quite low throughout the century. If such clearly atypical cases as 'Alva's terror' are excluded, the highest figures are for Germany, where 38 per year were executed in the 1520s (although this number declined to 13 between 1530 and 1554). The number of Protestants executed in Italy and Spain was insignificant. Although the Roman Inquisition was founded specifically to combat Protestants, it executed fewer than 50 Protestants before 1570, a fact that shows that the main force of the Inquisition was against other Roman Catholics. The totals for Europe as a whole suggest that roughly 50 people were executed per year between 1520 and 1554.

But this number more than doubled to 106 in the single decade from 1555 to 1564. In the Netherlands before Alva, 40 people per year were executed. Some figures are misleading. England at 30 per year is rather high, behind only the Netherlands, but virtually all of these executions took place within one period of a year and a half. Mary executed 286 Protestants, which is double the number of Lutherans executed in Spain between 1557 and 1565, in a vigorous campaign that succeeded in exterminating Lutheranism there. Only in France and the Netherlands were there significant heresy executions after 1565 of 'mainstream' Protestants; and the fires against the Anabaptists had largely cooled. More importantly, the executions were more often justified not on doctrinal grounds but because the confession or religious group was seditious: 'heresy executions became a form of state-building in Reformation Europe'. The church courts simply could not do the job; they could not even nail Luther. The fact that most deaths were now by hanging rather than burning shows that the crime was becoming secular. The number of executions drops sharply to eight in the last third of the century if the Netherlands are omitted. After 1575 there were few executions, except in Mediterranean Europe, and the numbers there paled beside those of the north earlier. The argument can be made that witch-burning made up for this; but the fact remains that doctrinal executions for heresy actually became less numerous during the 'Counter-Reformation' period than before, except in the politically explosive Netherlands. Omitting the unquantifiable, some 3,000 people were executed for religious reasons in the sixteenth century, two-thirds of them Anabaptists, and 80 per cent of these perished between 1527 and 1533.[23]

As princes enforced confessional orthodoxy much more rigidly than the supposedly monolithic medieval church had ever been able to do, the growth of zealotry that was reflected in mission work and witch persecutions was paralleled not by calls for religious toleration, but rather, by an increasing extent of indifference to religion as essentially a question of state and public order (the position of the French legal thinker Jean Bodin). There was even some intellectual agnosticism in the seventeenth century. Another compromise was Nicodemism, which permitted outward conformity while applying very basic or simple religious tests of religious orthodoxy, such as the ability to recite the Ten Commandments or the Lord's Prayer, and eventually in England to take communion in an Anglican church twice a year. Some French priests performed their functions for years before they eventually confessed that they did it to make a living, not because they believed in it.

These alternatives did not always translate to tolerance in practice. The political context of religion, particularly international Calvinism and Spanish Catholicism, meant that some rulers whose religious convictions would not have made them persecutors were forced to become so for political stability. Justus Lipsius of Leiden, a sceptic, also wanted religious persecution on grounds that religious pluralism fomented civil discord. His notions, published in 1589 (*Six Books of Politics*), were disputed in the 1590s by Dirck Coornhaert, secretary to the States of Holland, who felt that free access to the gospels and free expression would enhance, not diminish stability. Yet personal contact and the need to maintain relations with one's neighbours whom one did not wish to diabolicize also caused some growth of tolerance. Virtually all who wanted toleration, such as Coornhaert, Castellio and the Anabaptist David Joris, were non-dogmatic Christians; and except for Coornhaert, all of them published their works on toleration at Basel (where, in a classic irony, Calvin's *Institutes* were also published). Yet the doubts may have fuelled the intolerance of the hyper-orthodox. Religious mysticism could be translated in the practical sphere into a zeal to persecute.

The problems of reading and superficial understanding when the authorities were intolerant are illustrated by the famous case of Domenico (nick-named Menocchio) Scandella, the miller of the village of Montereale in Friuli (Italy). Menocchio had just enough theological knowledge to be confused, and he liked to talk, so word got around. He was subjected to two trials, 15 years apart, and was burned after the second one in 1599. A century later he probably would have been confined to a lunatic asylum, but in this early stage of the Counter-Reformation the authorities were more inclined to diabolicize incautious speech. Scandella was essentially self-taught. Six of the 11 books that he admitted in his trial to having read had been lent to him, which suggests a village network of readers, including women and priests. But Menocchio's ideas were personal interpretations that involved severe distortions of what he had read, and which applied theology to the practical needs of his material environment. In his trial Menocchio came down much harder on the church, which was still quite powerful as a landlord in his area and whose lands bordered his own, and on the clergy than on the lay authorities. He saw the sacraments and church laws as inventions to perpetuate the domination of the clergy. Scandella seems relatively unaffected by Lutheran doctrines, although he did use the name. He was more influenced by the Anabaptists, who were then quite active in northern Italy and whose theology of simplicity was closer to his own than Luther's was. Yet the fact that Menocchio still revered the mass means that he was not a closet Anabaptist. Like the Protestants, his theology took the gospels in their simplest form, and often in a social context, such as his stated belief that loving one's neighbour is greater than loving God. Much of what he believed, and his sceptical attitude toward the clergy, was perfectly acceptable among Protestants but impermissible in Italy. But he went much further than any mainstream Protestant group in denying the divinity of Christ and the immortality of the soul and rejecting the notion of original sin.[24]

Ritual, Symbol and Doctrine

Concern about proper rituals and the meaning behind their symbolism was a great constant underlying the messages of Luther and Calvin and, to a considerable extent, their ties with Hus. Given that religion was becoming simpler, often involving little more than reciting easily memorized material, it is not surprising that the ever-present gulf between theology and popular religion was widening in the sixteenth century. The concern with doctrine that was so evident early in Luther's movement gave way to a suspicion of anything emotional that involved ritual as 'magic'. Lutheran pastors were just as unhappy about the peasants and their carnal and untheological attitudes as Roman Catholic priests were. They went to church, recited the catechism and said prayers, but apart from that most only invoked the deity in time of stress. In Roman Catholic areas most people knew the local saint and sought his protection, but they knew little theology and cared little about the soul, the pope, the Turks and other distant problems or threats. Religion was practical, focused on the world, with spirits helping the believer to make a living. The theologians, both Protestant and Roman Catholic, as well as the Italian humanists, had a theoretical world-view derived from late antiquity, while the masses had more practical and contemporary concerns.[25]

'The religion of most people was more thaumaturgical than liturgical and more liturgical than theological.'[26] Much 'popular' religion was strongly ritualistic, consisting of a superficial grafting of Christian symbols and characters onto a belief structure that was mainly pre-Christian or even pagan. 'Christian belief' in the sense used now was almost exclusively a question for theologians during the Middle Ages, but the religious struggles of the sixteenth century brought more public understanding, at least to the point of believers being able to recite brief catechisms or confessions, as all sides tried to convert the masses to a specific belief system. Yet the refined theological controversies that occupied rulers and learned doctors and that generally bulk large in modern treatments of the Reformation period were simply beyond the knowledge, if not the understanding, of most. The result was a superficial understanding combined with dogmatic certainty that led to religious persecution and such excesses as the witchcraft hysteria.

Primitive man views anything extraordinary as the result of forces that are demonic or godly, depending on the consequences. Belief in supernatural intervention was virtually universal. Magic, benedictions, incantations and prayers outside the church were part of the individual's effort to invoke the cosmic order. Holy water was a cleanser and shelter; it protected plants over which it was sprinkled from worms, healed human sickness and repulsed evil spirits. People saw religion as an explanation and a cause of phenomena that appeared inexplicable through natural causation. But what bound believers who never experienced a miracle to their church was a combination of force of habit and attachment to familiar rituals, which in the Roman Catholic festival calendar emphasized the great transitions of birth, death, sowing and harvest.

There was a contractual attitude toward God. When he was pleased, he blessed the harvest; when not, he sent bad weather or plagues. Saints were treated similarly: when St Urban, the patron of vintners, was invoked in Germany for the wine harvest and the weather was good, he was honoured;

if it was bad, his image was desecrated. When weather bells were blessed in the name of God and the weather was bad, they were re-blessed in the name of the devil. Nothing showed the futility of the reformers' trying to do away with ceremonies as seriously as the Eucharist, which had been the great unifying symbol of Christendom before the Reformation, and could have been again had the Protestants agreed on its significance. But they did not, and their more abstract view of it, compared to the flesh-and-blood attitude of the Roman Catholics, was not easy to explain. Given the prevalence of such attitudes, the reformers were attempting the impossible in seeking to 'purify' religion; they were trying to change an entire world-view and/or mental outlook, which necessarily meant that they had to offer some other explanation for natural phenomena. Over time this occurred, with advances in science and general understanding of the world, but it did not always coincide with a change in doctrine or belief.[27]

The Protestants had a clearer idea than the Roman Catholics of the pre-Christian origin of many of the ceremonies and games that accompanied the liturgical year, such as Christmas, Shrovetide, May Day and the Midsummer festival of St John the Baptist on 24 June, which often corresponded to the feast of Corpus Christi and saw the most elaborate processions of the ritual year. The festivals were associated with fasting, candles and purifications, but also with feasting, drunkenness and general revelry. When Protestants gained power they generally tried to restrict or even abolish such observances, as they did with religious imagery. The iconoclastic fury in the Netherlands is a notorious example of how the religious zealotry of the Calvinists created a backlash against them among people who were not unsympathetic toward some of their doctrines. By the time Protestants gained control of governments, the ceremonies were already village routines that were older than living memory, and even in England the authorities were not able to abolish them completely. Elizabeth herself was more inclined toward ceremony than many Protestants, but she did not usually intervene when the more fervent evangelicals stopped them in their own localities. Her reign was so extended that by its end few could remember the old ways.[28]

The authorities had to be vigilant, for almost any type of religious exercise done in public could be linked to a disturbance somewhere. The worst violence was associated with the processions, particularly Shrovetide, Corpus Christi Day and the Roman Catholic carnivals that were often connected to Abbeys of Misrule, which were supplanting the Feasts of Fools in the popular imagination by the late fifteenth century. The Roman Catholic authorities realized more than the Protestants the importance of ritual and how much religious usages had worked their way into the secular work routines and thought patterns of the laity. The numerous festivals and rituals of late medieval Catholicism gave the laypeople a social and tangible fixture in this world that was a counterpoise to the sophisticated and ill-understood doctrines of the theologians. The Catholics' response to the fun was to keep it out of church buildings but not to care about it outside, seeing it as harmless, even when the celebrants mocked the authorities. In the late sixteenth century the Catholics even timed some of the festivities to coincide with church holidays that the Protestants had abolished. Protestantism was generally more successful in cities than in the rural areas, where the rituals and festivals were tied to the growing season; and in general this contributed to the success of the Roman Catholics in the late sixteenth century in winning back areas only superficially Protestantized.[29]

The Carnival

Carnivals marked the commencement of Lent, generally involving merry-making for several days preceding a culmination on Shrove Tuesday. People were expected to eat and drink to excess during carnival; Shrove Tuesday at Nantes was dedicated to 'St Dégobillard' (St Vomit). Carnivals were unusual in the late Middle Ages in the parts of Europe that became Protestant in the sixteenth century, when obviously, given their link to the Catholic liturgical year, they were associated with Italy and the Iberian peninsula, France, Switzerland and the Roman Catholic parts of Germany.[30]

Whatever their doctrinal reservations, the authorities had good reason to fear disorder at the carnivals. At Romans, a small city of about 8000 west of Grenoble in Dauphiné, carnival violence in 1579–80 became the catalyst of a regional revolt against taxes and the proliferation of bureaucracy, and against the nobles, whose exemption from the *taille* was extended to the lands that they owned. Resentment was especially strong against the newer 'nobles of the robe', who often behaved arrogantly. When they bought rural land, it became tax-exempt and thus increased the tax burden on the peasants. Most of the leaders of the revolt came from the crafts, while the mass strength came in large part from farm-workers, who worked in fields outside town while residing inside. Although a substantial part of the population was below the margin of subsistence, the totally indigent played little role in the revolt, which was mainly conducted by the lesser propertied groups.

Real power at Romans resided with the royal judge Antoine Guérin, the son of a country peddler who had married well, risen fast and had bought his office for life. Guérin blamed the violence on a Huguenot plot, but in fact the Reformed were scarcely involved. The disorders began with the carnival on 3 February 1579, the festival of St Blaise, the patron of the drapers. The chief of the carnival was a popular captain from a peasant background, Jean Serve or Paumier, called 'King of the Arquebus', who took control of the streets and town gates, at one point admitting several thousand peasants illegally. More serious disorders accompanied the next carnival in 1580. Kings of various factions took the names of beasts: hare, and the great rivalry between partridge and capon. The Partridge King was supposed to be the ruler of Romans during the festivities, and declared that the town was to turn itself into the legendary paradise, Cockaigne. He then issued a price ordinance that characteristically reversed the normal order of affairs, with normally cheap items made expensive and vice versa. Although toy weapons were used in the games, real arms were brought out of concealment after the festivities had lasted two weeks, and a massacre occurred in which the chief of the capon faction, who had fanned the discontent with Guérin, was killed.[31]

The Witch Craze

The zeal to detect and burn witches is clearly an aspect of the more general hostility to heretics that seems to have intensified after 1555. Even people who were inclined to grant toleration on doctrinal matters wanted witches exterminated. In an age when the body's natural tendency to heal itself was regarded as miraculous, practitioners of 'white' magic were considered beneficent, providing cures where medicine did not work. 'Black' magic, however, was diabolical, with intent to do harm, and was punishable. Few doubted that practitioners of both good and evil magic had the power to do the things they claimed or which were extracted from them under torture.

Persecution for witchcraft was rare before 1300. The early fourteenth century saw a few trials in France, England and Germany, most of them political, involving highly placed persons as victim or accused. Between 1330 and 1375 the political trials ended, and the focus shifted to sorcery, or more rarely diabolism, nearly all of them taking place in France and Germany. Between 1375 and 1435 there was a gradual increase both in total numbers and in the percentage of those involving diabolism. This may have been tied to the increasing use of inquisitorial procedure, which was state prosecution and facilitated accusations. Switzerland and Italy have increasing numbers, and the only cases of diabolism in this period came from Italy. Between 1435 and 1500 the number of trials increased, most of them in France, Germany and Switzerland, and more of it was in the form of mass outbreaks and involved diabolism.[32]

The publication of the *Malleus Maleficiarum* (*The Hammer of Malefactors*) in 1484 marks an important stage, but this seems clearer in retrospect than at the time. There was actually less witch-hunting in the first half of the sixteenth century than in the late fifteenth. But this period saw the publication, and above all the diffusion by printing, of witchcraft manuals and the elaboration of a theory of diabolism that prepared the way for the new onslaught in the 1560s. It had become a panic by century's end, and spread virtually everywhere, and the hysteria continued in the seventeenth century. During this time virtually all witchcraft allegations included heresy, aberrant religious belief and specifically diabolism.

Belief in the devil as a spirit who works in humankind became general.

But while good Christians avoided the devil, witches consorted with him (a male figure), often allegedly having intercourse with him. During physical contact with the devil, he left his mark on the witch, which cancelled the priest's baptism. Ordinary skin blemishes were minutely examined as signs of diabolical activity. Witchcraft was normally prosecuted in secular rather than church courts in northern Europe, but it was an exception to the general development of safeguards for the accused that characterized the evolution of court procedure at this time. Since the devil with his supernatural powers was at work to protect his faithful, torture to extract confessions was general, producing fantastic confessions, which undoubtedly contributed to the rumours of orgiastic activity with and by the devil, including the 'witches' Sabbath'. Most were accused of harming their antagonists' children or farm beasts, sending plagues or natural disasters on the crops. The peasants were interested mainly in *maleficium* and sorcery, the harm that witches were thought to cause to their neighbours, while the learned were more interested in the theological implications, such as the witches' meeting, night-flying, renunciation of baptism and demonolatry.[33]

Witchcraft was a largely north European phenomenon. There were many accusations in the Pyrenees, the Vaudois, and the mountains of Germany. Only in the Netherlands were witches associated with the cities rather than the rural areas. Except in Scotland, national governments had little to do with it; rather, the zeal of a local inquisitor would start the process. Although France had had more witch trials than other regions in the late Middle Ages, Germany accounted for about 50 per cent of all such executions in Europe in the sixteenth century. England witnessed between 500 and 1000 executions, most of them concentrated during Elizabeth's reign and proceeding from the activity of a single inquisitor, Matthew Hopkins, in 1645. Scotland, by contrast, had some 1300 executions in a much smaller population. While the trials in England were generally local, they were promoted in Scotland by the central government. The learned King James VI, later James I of England, introduced Continental ideas into Scotland in his treatise, *Daemonologie* (1597). Virtually all accused witches were lower-class, generally uneducated, often physically unattractive, sometimes deranged. Most were old women. Although some young persons and children were executed as witches, more cases involve them presenting evidence, sometimes against their parents.[34]

Concern with witchcraft was largely a Protestant phenomenon in the sixteenth century, and almost exclusively so thereafter. There appears to be a correlation between the decline of executions for doctrinal heresy and the rise of those for witchcraft after 1560. Probably no more than 3000 persons were executed for heresy between 1520 and 1570, including a rough estimate for the Netherlands, but there were at least 30,000 deaths for witchcraft in the century after 1560, with a notable growth after 1590. It is unclear whether there was an actual increase in the number of persons who practised or thought they were practising black magic, or whether the authorities were just becoming more aware of it and inclined to prosecute after 1550.[35]

There was little concern with witchcraft as such in Mediterranean Europe. The Inquisition in Spain reached the collective conclusion that the whole thing was a figment of the imagination. This did not, of course, mean that persecution for deviant belief or activity ceased, but only that the Inquisition was concerned with *conversos* and *marranos* rather than witches. Although Portugal had many 'cunning men' and 'wise women', there were few trials for witchcraft. The same holds true for Italy, where the Roman Inquisition was more concerned with different aberrations.

Some have seen the increasingly rigid patriarchy of the sixteenth century, reinforced by Roman law and more conservative interpretations of the socio-religious messages of the Bible, as responsible for a general hostility toward women in the male-dominated courts. Thus any woman who seemed to deviate from the pious, motherly norms of femininity was regarded with suspicion. Witchcraft prosecutions rose at the same time as other religious and sexual offences such as adultery, sodomy, infanticide and incest began coming in large numbers before the secular courts. While criminal prosecutions of women were rare before the sixteenth century, they were now being arraigned in large numbers. Although some males were accused, most of them were either related to female witches or were accused of some other crime in addition to witchcraft.[36]

Censorship

Censorship was closely linked to the growing religious intolerance. It had been relatively easy to censor unorthodox religious views in the Middle Ages, when all written communication was by hand, but printing opened new vistas for disseminating ideas and made censoring them much harder. The first censorship of printed books occurred in 1475, when the University of Cologne got the right from the pope to grant permission for works to be published, and the concomitant right to punish the unauthorized. The diocese of Mainz got this right in 1496, and in 1501 the pope extended it to all bishops in Germany. Inspired by the Lutheran agitation, by the 1520s most states were trying to censor works that could be printed or even imported. They were never completely successful, but censorship was a nuisance and led to the formation of secret societies.

Early efforts of the religious authorities to censor heretical books culminated in the establishment of the papal Index of Prohibited Books in 1559. The Index was not an unmixed success, causing problems for printers and for buyers who were powerful enough to ignore the Holy See. Enforcing the ban on Indexed books was the task of the Inquisition, whose efforts were sometimes ineffective, even in Italy. Part of the problem was that, in addition to books of unquestioned heterodoxy, the Index included non-heretical books by heretical authors, orthodox books issued by presses that had published heretical works, and still others which had to be banned simply because they had been printed in France or Germany, the former considered suspect because Pope Paul IV was an inveterate opponent of the French in international affairs, the latter because of Lutheranism. Inflammatory works were sometimes smuggled with false title pages.

Venice had the biggest printing establishment in Italy. When the Inquisition sent a list of prohibited books to Venice in 1555, the Venetian booksellers pointed out that *opera omnia* (all works) of some authors were condemned, including those not on religious topics, that there would be economic loss, and that some previously acceptable authors, like the Roman satirist Lucian, whom the church had tolerated for 1400 years, were on the list. When Paul IV issued the final Index in 1559, the Venetians initially refused their compliance, but they had to submit when Paul threatened to seize their bookshops in the papal state. Their inventories show that they gave up publishing Protestant books, but not some Italians who were on the Index, such as Machiavelli and Aretino.

Yet the Venetian booksellers had to stay in business, and this meant a subtle accommodation. They published more religious works in the 1560s than before, but most of them were vernacular devotional works for laypeople, not theological works. Business calculations likewise contributed to a growing Venetian reluctance to cooperate with the pope from the 1570s: the council of Trent had given the papacy the sole right to print the Roman Breviary, Missal, Tridentine Catechism and the Index, and the popes gave the monopoly to the press of Paolo Manuzio in Rome. Given that the Missal and Breviary were used in most religious worship, there was an enormous market, and the monopoly was resented. After 1590 the Venetian authorities stopped enforcing the Index's ban on imported heretical books.[37]

The Jews in Late Medieval and Early Modern Europe

The Reuchlin affair and the ferocious persecution of the Jews in Spain have given the impression that the Protestants were more tolerant toward the Jews than the Catholics were, but this is not the case; they cultivated Hebrew scholarship only in the interest of true faith. Reuchlin favoured reading Jewish books and insisted on the integrity of the Hebrew text, but this in turn led to the idea that the rabbis had perverted it. Luther initially considered the Jews part of God's plan, which meant that they would reject Jesus for a time but eventually convert. In contrast to Reuchlin, Luther did not defend the Talmud from the allegation that it contained blasphemy. He did write that it was impossible to mistreat the Jews and simultaneously expect them to convert. As he aged, Luther urged that the Jews be evangelized actively. He simply could not understand why the Jews did not convert when a palatable alternative to anti-Christian Roman Catholicism was presented to them. One of Luther's more vicious late diatribes is his *The Jews and their Lies* (1543), in which he urged persecuting them. Calvin was essentially traditional. He had less direct experience of Jews than Luther did and shared Luther's tendency to lump Jews and Roman Catholics together as enemies of true religion, and as polluting one another through contact. The Protestant reformers thus said little that was new about Judaism and/or the Jews; they were well within the medieval tradition. Although the Jews during this time were released from many of the old physical restrictions, they lived in their own walled communities virtually everywhere and had a separate status by virtue of their religion.

The popes until Paul III welcomed Jews who were being expelled from Spain and its dependencies into the papal states, but this quickly changed. The Counter-Reformation is associated with anti-Semitism. Julius III in 1553 declared the Talmud blasphemous and sacrilegious, and a papal bull of 1555 required that Jews should be segregated from Christians. Jewish writings and bodies were burned throughout Italy, and by 1600 there were few Jews left in the papal states. Jewish communities in northern Italy expanded in the last third of the sixteenth century; persecution in the papal states simply sent them elsewhere. Venice, where the word 'ghetto' originated, had the largest Jewish community in Italy. Giving way to Franciscan pressure to separate them, the authorities put the Jews into a 'Ghetto Nuovo', a walled area with a single entrance that could be policed easily. The argument was raised that the Jews were needed for Venice's poor, since the city, in contrast to most others in Italy, had no Monte di Pietà where they could obtain credit; and they stayed. Other national communities also banded together, but not under compulsion. Elsewhere in Italy, secular rulers were more inclined to protect the Jews, despite Spanish influence. Most gave them security of trading and contract, the right to lend money and freedom to worship and to control affairs inside the ghettos.

The Jews had been expelled from England and from areas controlled by the French kings at the turn of the fourteenth century, and did not begin to return to north-western Europe in large numbers until the late sixteenth. Although Charles V persecuted them through the Inquisition in the Netherlands, he and the Roman Catholic princes also protected them against the Protestants in the Empire. The Jews duly supported the Emperor against the Schmalkaldic League in 1546–7 through prayers and financial help. They were expelled from Saxony and other Lutheran territories, and there were riots against them in some towns. The Calvinists took a similar attitude; the Elector Palatine, the most conspicuous Calvinist prince, expelled the Jews in 1575.

The Jews tended to gravitate toward the peripheries of Europe. Bohemia also became a refuge for them, in part due to imperial patronage. In 1577

Rudolf gave the Bohemian Jews a charter that enabled them to practise crafts previously reserved to Christians, such as goldsmithing and jewellery. Maximilian II even brought his entire court to visit the Jewish quarter of Prague in 1571. During the late sixteenth century the Prague Jewry became the largest apart from Rome outside the Ottoman Empire, surpassing Amsterdam. The Jews may have constituted as much as 15 per cent of Frankfurt's population in the early seventeenth century, and Hamburg also developed a large Jewish community.

The Netherlands developed the largest Jewish population in the north-west, and it was of recent extraction. The Netherlands did not have a large Jewish population during the late Middle Ages, but the expulsion of 1492 sent many Iberian Jews to Antwerp. Although the Inquisition was established in the Netherlands in 1522, it was directed more at Lutherans than at Iberian Jews. With the coming of Calvinism, the religious situation was fluid. The Spaniards were in sufficiently firm control of the southern Netherlands by the 1580s that most Jews, like most Calvinists, simply migrated north. In addition, the Netherlands absorbed religious refugees of all persuasions from Germany. In the seventeenth century Amsterdam had replaced Antwerp as the site of the second largest Jewish community of northern Europe, and they played an even more significant role in banking there than they had in the Scheldt city.

Conditions throughout the west, however, were sufficiently difficult for Jews that increasing numbers went to Lithuania, the Balkans and particularly Poland, economically underdeveloped regions where Jewish capital was welcomed. The number of Jews in Poland and Lithuania grew from 20,000 or 30,000 in 1500 to between 100,000 and 150,000 by 1575, and numbers continued to grow in the seventeenth century.[38]

* * *

The 'modern' period is often taken to mark the onset of a more secular outlook, but the notion that people became less religious in the era of the Reformation is patently absurd. The priesthood and the monasteries were ended in Protestant areas, but state churches became entrenched in both Protestant and Catholic Europe and for the first time became national, in effect becoming the servants of their princes. While there were differences between German and French Catholicism in 1450, there was no national attachment to religion except to the extent that many Germans felt that the papacy was using the weakness of their monarchy to exploit Germany financially. But true religion was one of various incitements used by rulers in the sixteenth century to stir up opinion against both domestic and foreign heretics.

More laypeople were aware of religious issues in 1600 than in 1500 and felt deeply about them. The growing split within Protestantism among confessions, and the spiritual revival of Roman Catholicism from the 1560s onwards, meant that in becoming more certain of their own beliefs people had to understand at least what those beliefs were. To be a committed Calvinist and thus to despise Lutherans, you had to know enough about Calvinism to know what distinguised it from Lutheranism. Yet for most believers knowledge of other creeds was confined to what propagandists said through the print medium, and understanding of one's own was based on an easily recited catechism. Thus religious expression probably became less rational as a result of the Reformation. Certainly the growing vogue of mysticism and the interest in diabolical witchcraft would suggest this.

Conclusion: Retrospective, Prospective and Perspective

During the sixteenth century the theoretical foundations of absolute monarchy were created in France, Spain and the various German principalities. They were fleshed out by institutions of warfare, taxation with limited involvement of the governed, and regulations that were enforced by a mammoth bureaucracy. The Emperor had reduced the significance of the electoral college on a 'national' level as the imperial title became hereditary in fact, while the monarchies of Denmark and Sweden became much stronger. Probably no king of the seventeenth century was the intellectual or moral equal of his predecessors in the sixteenth. Yet the institutional apparatus that was already oppressive in the sixteenth century became self-perpetuating in less able hands. This led to a crisis of leadership, and it was this, rather than fundamental social or economic changes, which led to rebellions in the mid-seventeenth century. The only exceptions to the growing strength of absolute rulers in the seventeenth century were Poland, where the nobles dominated the kings, and England, where by 1688 the kings were clearly subordinated to Parliament.

No calculations are possible of the number of persons or percentage of total populations in central bureaucracies, but they grew significantly in the sixteenth century and probably more than doubled again in the first half of the seventeenth. Taxation may have risen no more in the sixteenth century than productive capacity, particularly when imported bullion is taken into account; but it rose considerably in the seventeenth century, as the changes that had begun in the sixteenth century, notably concerning the nobility, now became entrenched and hereditary. Warfare was nearly constant in the seventeenth century as in the sixteenth century, but armies were now much larger and more destructive, with the near-universal use of firearms. Louis XIV's army of 400,000 is famous, but even the Spanish armies probably had twice the troops in the mid-seventeenth century as Philip II had.

The mushrooming of bureaucracy – particularly the multiplication, sale and inheritance of offices – that had hindered governmental efficiency in France and Spain during the sixteenth century became even worse in the seventeenth. Tax burdens reached insupportable levels in both, made worse for the middle and lower social orders by the tax exemption enjoyed by nobles of all ranks. While in the sixteenth century the needs of an expanding state administration had created the offices, in the seventeenth the need of existing officers to create new ones to support their own clients, who were their power bases in the shifting winds of fortune at court, meant the invention of sinecures. While now, with government officials on salary, there is a limit beyond which bureaucracy cannot expand unless the financial resources of the state (including its credit) expand with it, many government operations were done privately (using the modern sense of that word) in the seventeenth century. Thus unnecessary offices multiplied, particularly in states where they were sold, which included most of them by 1615. And the bureaucratic growth of the seventeenth century occurred against a backdrop of the economic depression that succeeded the growth of the sixteenth.

In the sixteenth century and even more in the seventeenth, as now, the reaction of most of those in government to a need for money was to raise taxes, whatever the circumstances. It does not work, for taxation drains money from the private sector whose expansion through investment is necessary to build the tax base. When governments felt that they could raise taxes no more, they sold off part of their tax base, particularly by farming excises (which had been done before the sixteenth century) and the selling of offices and titles. The wars of the late sixteenth century, complicated in the case of France by civil warfare, had left all three western monarchies heavily in debt, but the fiscal problems became much worse in the seventeenth. Even more than in the sixteenth century, lending to the crown became a profitable investment, for usury prohibitions were no longer taken seriously. As more nobles relied on state bonds for a gentleman's income, money was diverted from trade and commerce and towards establishing and maintaining a noble style of life.

Even as the national governments were becoming less efficient, their desire to micromanage the economy became more obtrusive. 'Mercantilism' was formulated as a doctrine of economic nationalism only in the seventeenth century, although city-states had practised it for centuries on the local level without calling it that. Although the protectionism and bullionism that characterize mercantilist thought are at least defensible from an economic perspective, they require a large bureaucracy and a free play of market forces within the affected area. Yet at least until after 1650, the costs of government efforts to remove tolls and improve roads and canals were probably higher than the profits realized by them.

In addition to the institutional problems, the seventeenth century also witnessed an economic downturn. The 'long sixteenth century' had redressed the population decline that Europe had sustained after the early fourteenth century, but at the cost of severe dependence on bullion from the Americas that paid for warfare, and for the domestic expenses of spice imports from Asia and grain imports from eastern Europe. The climate had gradually worsened, and Europe entered a 'little ice age' in the seventeenth century, during which the population stabilized or declined virtually everywhere. Whether real wages rose or declined during the sixteenth century depends on how the figures are interpreted, but there can be no question that they declined catastrophically in the seventeenth in the wake of high food prices brought on by famine and war.

The most obvious economic change of the seventeenth century was the decline of the Mediterranean and a continued shift in pre-eminence towards the north Atlantic. By 1650 the Mediterranean and Baltic, each of which had had substantial inter-regional commerce in the late Middle Ages, had declined into more or less self-contained economic regions with internal exchange of products. Paralleling the decline of Spain, the Italians and south Germans lost control of the money markets in the late sixteenth century. Italy had been divided politically among the Aragonese in the Neapolitan south, the papal state in central Italy, and small dynastic states in Tuscany and Lombardy that had supplanted the city-states of the Renaissance. The city regimes had been inefficient and over-bureaucratized since the central Middle Ages, and their political rivalries drove costs up for all of them, but the problems had largely been concealed by Italian control over access to the costly eastern wares that were in such high demand in northern Europe. But the northerners were taking over the carrying trade even in the Mediterranean in the late sixteenth century, and by 1600 the Italians had definitely lost control of Asian markets to the Portuguese and Dutch and, to a lesser extent, the English. Italy still had substantial manufacturing, but the political power of the urban occupational guilds drove labour costs up. The Italians could not compete with cheaper English and Dutch wares, and a disastrous plague in the 1630s completed the economic ruin of Italy.

The Dutch and English were the new masters of the international economy. Long-distance and colonial trade thus became centred on the Atlantic, although even this was stagnating by 1620. The shift benefited chiefly the Dutch in the first half of the century and the English after 1660. The 'old capitalism' had been family-based; the new was based on the joint-stock company, at which the English and Dutch were adept. The development of the joint-stock company facilitated the participation in economic growth of more investors at less risk, and the institutional framework of a credit system was thus laid, even during a time of incipient and, from the 1620s, fully developed economic contraction.

The change was especially clear in colonial development. Spaniards continued to control large plantations, but the supply of bullion declined sharply and, with it, the profitability of overseas enterprise. England's first permanent colony in North America was established in 1607, when the chartered Virginia (named after the late Virgin Queen) Company under Sir Thomas Smith founded Jamestown (named after the king). This was followed quickly by settlement that gave the English priority on the eastern seaboard except for Florida. African slaves were introduced in 1619, and tobacco became a major export to Europe. The Company went bankrupt in 1623, and Virginia became a crown colony the next year. While Virginia was developed as an investment, the other English North American colonies of this period were havens for religious refugees: the French tried to prevent Protestants from contaminating their overseas colonies, but the English saw it as an opportunity to get them out of the way. Massachusetts (which started as Plymouth Plantation) began with a charter given for a colony north of Delaware Bay in 1620. In 1629 the Massachusetts Bay Company was chartered, led by John Winthrop. Most of the first settlers were Puritans, who established a religious tyranny that was even worse than Archbishop Laud's in England – the notion that the Puritans were seeking religious freedom is a myth. Rhode Island and Connecticut were founded by emigrants from Puritan Massachusetts, and in 1632 Charles I gave Lord Baltimore, a Roman Catholic, a charter decreeing religious toleration that was the origin of Maryland. Until after 1650 the colonies produced little that the mother country needed, but English entrepreneurs made considerable money through exports to the colonies, a trade that after 1651 they tried to monopolize by excluding the Dutch and others. The English East India Company also imported from Asia, but sold little there. Fundamentally, the east did not need western goods as much as the west needed those of the east. Even the Americas exported more than they imported. Only in the eighteenth century did the colonies provide much of a market for European manufactures, but in the seventeenth century, particularly after 1650, they were valued for exotic comestibles – foods, tea, coffee – and textiles such as calicoes, as their value for bullion declined.

The seventeenth century also saw a departure from established cultural patterns. Knowledge of some Greek, but particularly Latin, continued to be required in all schools above the primary level, but little writing was done in Latin after 1600 except in international law, natural science and Roman Catholic theology. Few technological changes had occurred after 1520, although there were advances in the theoretical sciences, medicine and astronomy. Outside the academy, new approaches in science began to emphasize empiricism and induction, rather than the essentially deductive reasoning that the earlier religious orientation of education had required. While the scholars of the Renaissance had revered the ancient authorities for their style and ethical content, the scientists of the seventeenth century subjected them to the same critical gaze that they applied to their own observed phenomena. Even in literature the ancients were revered more in terms of themselves and as adornments of an educated person than as practical guides, and they certainly had little impact on creative activity. Although the greatest achievements of the 'scientific revolution' would only come after 1650, the theoretical foundations were laid earlier by the work of Francis Bacon and René Descartes. Music remained essentially orientated toward church and court performance, but instrumentation became more varied and thematic development more elaborate. Except for Cervantes' *Don Quixote* and the German *Simplicius Simplissimus*, most original literature of the early seventeenth century was didactic and concerned with political or religious problems, and was not intended for entertainment; even *Don Quixote* had a serious undercurrent, satirizing the pretensions of the Spanish nobility. Both the scope and subject-matter of literature would change dramatically after 1660.

The new century opened with a king in France who had clear Protestant sympathies enforcing Roman Catholicism on his subjects in the interest of concord. Henry IV had never intended the Edict of Nantes of 1598 to be a permanent settlement, and began to withdraw the guarantees given to the Protestants as soon as the original eight-year term had expired. Even though he renewed the Huguenots' right to garrison 49 towns, he halved the subsidy given them by the crown to defer defence costs, and the subsidies were always in arrears. Magistrates and judges, overwhelmingly Roman Catholic, had balked at enforcing the concessions. Yet Henry's religious orthodoxy was doubted by the militant Roman Catholics, one of whom assassinated him in 1610. The government of Louis XIII (1610–43) took a much harder line against the Huguenots. In 1625 the remaining Protestant guarantees expired, and Protestant political assemblies were forbidden. Campaigns against La Rochelle, the principal Huguenot stronghold, were begun in 1621 and succeeded in 1628.

No Spanish ruler of the seventeenth century approached the competence or enjoyed the resources of Charles V or Philip II. Supplies of bullion from the Americas were still substantial in the seventeenth century, although they were much reduced from the levels of Philip II's time. Although the declining power of Spain was not completely apparent to the other courts of Europe until the 1620s, the governments of Philip III (1598–1621) and his successors were more occupied by keeping solvent than in foreign adventures. Philip was dominated by his chief minister, the Duke of Lerma, and Lerma's favourites. Castile continued to bear the brunt of heavy taxation, but it was no longer compensated, as earlier, by the profits of empire. Ethnic cleansing continued to be a major preoccupation of the monarchy. In 1609 the Moriscos were ordered to leave Spain, and most had done so by 1614. The economic impact of this expulsion was much less than with the exile of the Jews, but they were missed in low-level jobs, particularly in Seville. Moorish customs remained influential: Spanish women, including of the upper classes, were far less 'liberated' and public than those of northern Europe, and gaps between rich and poor in Spain were noted by contemporaries as more severe than elsewhere. The main sources of wealth, where careers were sought when possible, were the church and the royal government. Philip III reversed his predecessors' policy of keeping the great aristocrats out of central offices, and he also ran a much more lavish court than Philip II. The incomes that many grandee families enjoyed from rents had not kept pace with inflation, and court office and patronage now gave them a chance to recover. Philip III also named numerous new dukes and sold titles of nobility, which accentuated the gap between rich and poor and diminished the tax base. Nobles, in turn, spent lavishly and incurred debts.

Philip IV (1621–65) was more intelligent than his father, but just as lazy, and he continued to rely on favourites. His chief minister was the duke of Olivares, who was as energetic as Lerma had been indolent. Olivares seems genuinely to have wanted reform; at the least, he attended to state business. Yet he was also a traditional Spanish aristocrat, remaining committed to the imperial dreams of Philip II. Thus he rebuilt the navy, which Lerma had neglected, hoping eventually to recover the Netherlands, and Spanish troops fought in Germany on behalf of the Austrian Habsburgs.

Olivares' most radical proposal was a 'Union of Arms' of the Spanish kingdoms which would end Castile's privileges but also require the other states to assume some of the tax burden that had been borne by the Castilians. He tried to abolish the *millones* tax and replace it with a proportional obligation on local communities to support an army of 30,000 troops. But these proposals foundered on opposition from the *Cortes*, and the rate on the *millones* was actually increased, while the plan was killed by opposition outside Castile. Olivares needed to get taxes from Catalonia and Portugal, the two richest provinces, to ease the burdens on Castile; Catalonia had not paid an aid in 30 years in the 1630s, and when the Dutch seized much of Brazil in 1630, Castile paid for a relief expedition to which the Portuguese did not contribute. The loyalty of Catalonia to the Castilian crown was always dubious, and the Catalans took advantage of the new war with France after 1635 to rebel in 1640. When the Portuguese were ordered to send troops into Catalonia, they too revolted and put the duke of Braganza on the throne as John IV in 1640, thus ending the dynastic union of Castile and Portugal. Olivares was forced into retirement in 1643. Catalonia seceded and joined France, but Spanish troops reoccupied it in 1651 while the French were occupied with the Fronde.

The death of Elizabeth brought James I (1603–25) to the English throne, the son of Mary Stuart, who had been king of Scotland since 1567. Although James was conscientious, and on balance a more effective ruler than was once thought, his spendthrift habits, complicated by the mere fact that he was a foreigner and combined with problems over the debt, religion and the royal prerogative that had been festering in Elizabeth's last years inaugurated a period of instability in England. In the 'Great Contract' of 1610 James tried to regularize his financial relations with Parliament, offering to surrender most 'prerogative' taxation and fines (on items not needing Parliamentary consent, such as wardship and impositions) in return for a fixed annual income from Parliament. After the plan foundered on Parliamentary opposition the king's wastefulness became worse, and he began selling titles of nobility, inventing the rank of baronet, and eventually selling peerages.

The vocal Puritan element, which was a majority in his Parliaments after 1614, also disliked his plan to ally with Spain in the 1620s. When the king's effort to marry his heir to a Spanish princess fell through Parliament pressured James I into a war with Spain. Charles I (1625–49) then married Henrietta Maria, the sister of Louis XIII of France. But the duke of Buckingham, the chief adviser of both James and Charles, got England into a war with France in 1626 before the one with Spain was concluded, and the king saved him from impeachment only by taking personal responsibility for his actions – which, however honest and courageous, violated the maxim that the king could do no wrong. When the government failed initially to help the Huguenots who were defending La Rochelle, Charles and Buckingham seemed to be abetting Catholicism; they then reversed themselves and sent an expeditionary force that was defeated ignominiously and had to withdraw. The Huguenots in La Rochelle surrendered, feeling that they had no hope for help from England.

Charles I's entanglements also deepened in Germany. When in 1625 he heard of the defeat in battle of his uncle, Christian IV of Denmark, he began levying forced loans. While earlier forced loans had struck individuals, this one was assessed on all payers of the lay subsidy and thus required the consent of Parliament, which Charles refused to summon. The king also declared martial law and quartered troops in private homes. In 1628, however, he had to call a Parliament, his third in three years, to pay for the commitments that he had made to his Continental allies. Parliament forced him as a condition of payment to accept the Petition of Right, which forbade quartering troops on citizens, forced loans and non-parliamentary taxation generally, including tunnage and poundage (levies per tun of wine and pound of merchandise).

When Parliament returned the next year, however, the old quarrels resumed. The king maintained somewhat disingenuously that he had only given up the right to tunnage and poundage for a single occasion. The Puritans in the Commons were also pressing for religious changes. When Charles sent orders for the speaker to dissolve Parliament, several members held him in his chair until resolutions introduced by Sir John Eliot were passed. These resolutions, which had no legally binding force, criminalized fostering 'popery' and also the payment of taxation that had not been voted by Parliament. When the Speaker finally rose, he dissolved Parliament. It would not return for nearly 11 years.

Charles I's aborted foreign policy illustrates starkly the changes in the presuppositions of diplomacy since the age of Elizabeth and Philip II. Religion had then determined political alliances, and the leaders of the English Parliament, the strongest national representative assembly in Europe, still saw it that way. Desirous of a Europe-wide crusade against the diabolical Roman Catholics, the parliamentary Puritans pressured James I and Charles I into war with Spain, and then refused to vote enough money to finance it. Yet while religious hostility within nations sharpened in Germany and England, and certainly got no better in France – if less violently there, given the impotence of the Huguenots – religion played little role in international politics except in the decision by the Danes and Swedes to help the Protestants in Germany during the 1620s and 1630s. James I and, even more, Charles I, like Richelieu, saw larger policy objectives that would unite Protestant and Roman Catholic states.

Charles I's personal rule between 1629 and 1640 showed a certain ingenuity and economy, but he was levying taxes of dubious legality to pay for a minimal government and foreign policy. Yet religious orthodoxy and allegiance to a state church that many of Charles' subjects found uncongenial proved fatal. Charles fell under the domination of Archbishop of Canterbury William Laud, who saw absolute conformity to Anglican ritual as a precondition of effective monarchy. The misplaced English effort to force the Irish to accept Protestantism and, from the 1630s, to enforce the Anglican Book of Common Prayer on Presbyterian Scotland precipitated open warfare. Had Charles I not been diverted from his English troubles by disorders in his other two realms, his task in England would have been much more manageable; however, the 'Long Parliament' of 1640 began by forcing him to accept humiliating limitations on his power. The civil war that erupted in 1642 eventuated in the killing of the king and the establishment of the Commonwealth and Oliver Cromwell's Protectorate, followed by restoration of the Stuart kings in 1660.

These events are clearly a separate chapter. The English monarchy had survived the upheavals of the sixteenth century with its powers essentially intact. Although the powers of the crown had declined after 1377, Edward IV and the Tudors had restored them to something comparable to what Edward I had exercised in 1300. But the seventeenth century saw first the abolition of the English monarchy, then its restoration on a considerably limited basis after 1660 and particularly 1689.

The United Provinces of the Netherlands made a truce with Spain in 1609 that was renewed in 1621. Thereafter the two were generally at peace, although the independence of the Netherlands was only recognized formally in 1648. The Dutch made no further effort to take the southern provinces, which remained a Spanish possession. Holland's domination over the other six provinces was consolidated by its natural demographic and economic strength, which in the seventeenth century was growing through Dutch involvement in overseas markets. The Dutch dominated the carrying trade of Europe in the first half of the seventeenth century, when the *fluyt*, an unarmed and highly mobile cargo ship, entered the Mediterranean. With the foundation of the Dutch East India Company in 1601, the Dutch began to penetrate the Asian islands. Using the excuse that Portugal was under the Castilian crown, the Dutch seized Portugal's Asian possessions and Brazil (they were expelled from Brazil in 1654). The seventeenth century was thus the golden age of Dutch overseas commerce. At home, however, religious discords polarized the state. A serious rift developed within the Calvinist community between those who insisted rigidly on predestination and the Arminians, who felt that good works of the believer might have an impact on his or her posthumous fate. At the international synod of Dordrecht in 1619, the predestinarian position was victorious, and from that point on the local councils enforced Calvinism as a Dutch state church. None the less the stream of religious refugees, including Jews, into Amsterdam left it as a relative haven of toleration. The stadholder, a descendant of William the Silent, continued to provide direction of policy and to some extent to act as a counterweight to the preachers and to Holland.

The religious peace of 1555 had been unravelling in the Empire since the 1580s. The settlement of 1555 had not foreseen the rise of Calvinism, which was as distasteful to many Lutherans as Roman Catholicism was. Through most of the sixteenth century the Catholic Habsburgs had been ruling a largely Protestant Empire. When the Jesuit-educated Ferdinand II of Habsburg inherited the crown of Bohemia, the largely Protestant Bohemian nobles offered the crown to the Calvinist Elector Palatine, Frederick, the son-in-law of James I of England. After Ferdinand became emperor in 1619, a brief civil war ended the reign of the 'Winter King' in 1620. Ferdinand then expanded the war to the Palatinate (the Heidelberg area), conquering the region by 1623 before turning towards the north. The Danes under Christian IV resisted him on religious grounds, hoping to conquer some German territory in the process, but they were driven back by 1629. In that year Ferdinand, who had used his victory very effectively to restore Roman Catholicism in Bohemia, issued the Edict of Restitution, which ordered that all Roman Catholic lands taken since 1552 should be restored. This violated the Peace of Augsburg of 1555, which had allowed princes to determine the religions of their subjects, who would be expected to follow the ruler if he changed his beliefs.

The Edict of Restitution was enforced only in the parts of Germany that Ferdinand controlled, but it naturally aroused fears in the largely Lutheran north. King Gustavus Adolphus of Sweden invaded northern Germany in 1630 and, aided by the north German princes, defeated the imperial forces at several battles, including the one in 1632 in which he lost his life. Thereafter the troops raged out of control until 1635, when the north German Protestants, alarmed at the Swedish presence, joined Ferdinand in return for a modification of the Edict of Restitution. Faced with this considerable revival of imperial power, Cardinal Richelieu, the ministerial power behind Louis XIII's throne, joined the Swedes against the Habsburgs in 1635. At this point the Dutch and Spaniards entered the fray, which thus escalated into a war involving most of Europe except England. The French and their allies devastated Germany and were nearing Vienna when peace was finally made in 1648.

The Peace of Westphalia, actually a series of treaties involving the several participants, ended the 'Thirty Years War'. It withdrew the Austrian conquests and left the Habsburgs with the territorial status quo of 1620. The power of Sweden and the Protestant princes of northern Germany, particularly the Hohenzollerns of Prussia, meant that Roman Catholicism could never be restored there, and after 1648 the emperors had little influence in the north. The Habsburgs concentrated on Austria, although they continued to hold the imperial title, and the independence of the German princes was recognised. France and Sweden received territories in western and northern Germany, and the formal independence of the Netherlands and the Swiss Confederation was recognized also. Limited religious toleration was granted: Calvinism was recognized as a third permitted confession, and rulers were allowed to grant toleration if they chose. The tempo of religious exile diminished, and all persons were given the right to worship as their ancestors had done in 1624, regardless of the prince's attitude. The Thirty Years War was the last major international conflict in Europe that was fought even nominally over religious issues. Ferdinand II's domestic achievement, however, proved irreversible: he had restored southern Germany, Bohemia and much of German and Slavic Europe to Roman Catholicism.

Despite the French gains at Westphalia, the government of the regents of Louis XIV (1643–1715) in France was widely resented. The Fronde was a series of disconnected disturbances which began when a joint meeting of the central courts in July 1648 presented articles demanding administrative reforms and tax reductions. *Parlement* was supported by mobs in Paris, and the queen mother, Anne of Austria, had to yield. This agitation was directed against the king's advisers, but there was not a hint of popular sovereignty in the demands, nor was the claim raised that the child king should not rule. After 1650 the princes led the agitation but were unable to agree on a programme. Their leader, Louis II, prince of Condé, compromised himself by accepting Spanish help. With Condé's defeat in early 1653 – he commanded Spanish troops against the French until 1659 – the Fronde was over.

Some have spoken of a 'crisis of the seventeenth century' beginning in the 1620s. The timing of the great disturbances of the mid-seventeenth century – the Fronde, the Catalonian rebellion, the end of the Thirty Years War, the establishment of the English Commonwealth – is very suggestive. Although the causes and outcomes of the rebellions appear to have little in common except chronology, it is none the less clear that the weak economic underpinnings of the sixteenth-century expansion – bullion derived from conquests outside Europe rather than a favourable balance of trade, ruinous expenses for war and diplomacy and imports of both luxuries and necessities from outside Europe – were being undermined by the 1590s. When economic depression was combined with the inefficiency and waste of the institutional governments of France and Spain and the lack of institutional government in the Empire as a whole, however tightly individual principalities may have been operated, a general reaction was triggered. In the German and English cases this institutional overload became combined with religion, to force a pause, albeit a brief one, in the drift toward theoretical absolutism in an institutional framework untempered by constraints on the administrators.

This book opened with Europe on the verge of a demographic disaster and a century and a half of intermittent warfare. During that time, fundamental – if in many respects atavistic – changes in intellectual outlook were accomplished. Europeans gained a higher standard of living in the late Middle Ages, as per capita productivity rose and the pressure on resources that had precipitated the earlier population decline was ended. Yet the new prosperity for the survivors was predicated on the availability of imports from outside western Europe, luxuries from Africa and Asia and necessities from the Slavic east. The book closes with the intellectual changes of the Renaissance having run their course and become the property of an educational 'establishment'. The long recovery of the sixteenth century brought Europe's population back to its level of 1300, but it was now proportionally more urban. Despite the lack of qualitative improvements in agricultural techniques and technology, enough food was imported from outside Europe to bridge the gap. Even with a rise in population, standards of living did not decline. Of course, the incidence of fiscal poverty remained high in 1600, as it had been in 1350, for not all persons share in a general amelioration of the economy. But the bullion mined in Spanish America that had fuelled the economic revival and paid for the religious wars was diminishing. As religious war was resumed in the Empire in the seventeenth century, as France ended Protestantism while stifling all citizens with bureaucracy and taxes, and England experienced a revolution for essentially religious reasons, no state found itself with sufficient resources.

The transition from 'medieval' to 'modern' between 1300 and 1600 had left Europe with a formal educational system whose curriculum and pedagogy were even more antiquated – the classics of Greek and Roman antiquity, duly recited and imitated – than that of the Middle Ages. Primary education before the 'Renaissance' and the university curriculum through the arts course had been more flexible previously, and had emphasized interpretation of the classics and theology through logical exercise rather than declamation. But a much higher proportion of persons had university educations in 1600 than in 1300. The growth is most striking in theology and in law, which was increasingly becoming the public servant's career of choice. Yet there remained a divorce of higher education from creative life that was just as significant as it had been in the Middle Ages. In reality, humanism was a programme for the ruling classes.

The religious conflicts of the seventeenth century were more catastrophic for Germany than those of the sixteenth had been. While the changes of the sixteenth century had created a plurality of religious belief, in the seventeenth century specific creeds became national or entrenched in local principalities. Despite the reverse of 1648, the Habsburg Emperors were able to restore Roman Catholicism in the south and east, while Lutheranism remained the religion of most north Germans, and Zwingli's achievement divided Switzerland between Protestants and Catholics. In 1600 it was clear that the Huguenots had lost their battle to make France Calvinist. The only question was whether they would be tolerated by the victorious Catholics, and by 1620 the answer was clearly negative. Lutheranism consolidated its hold in national churches in Scandinavia, Calvinism in the Netherlands. Britain remained a battleground; but after more than half a century of intense Puritan agitation followed by civil war, after 1660 England reverted to the broad outline of the situation of 1603: a national Anglican church of Calvinist theology and neo-Catholic ritual. France under Louis XIV in wars against the Dutch and English and in the final push against the Huguenots took up the cudgel of religious orthodoxy that the Spaniards had dropped. But what ultimately brought Louis' ambitions to nothing was a national question, transcending religion. The more things change, the more they remain the same.

Europeans were better informed about one another and about the outside world in 1600 than earlier. Much of this was the natural consequence of printing with movable type, which meant that students now read more books and memorized fewer passages from them than in medieval education, and which also made possible the more rapid spread of ideas. It is most unlikely either that Protestantism would have spread with the vigour that it did, or that the Roman Catholics could have countered it as effectively as they did in Italy and Spain, without printing. The new medium had an incalculable impact on religious debate and on the spread of technical – including scientific – information. The availability of pithy and often abusive broadsheets probably contributed as much to the success of the humanist curriculum in the German universities as it did to that of Luther's revolt. But governments could also use printing to spread their versions of information, to publish statutes and to control expression. Europeans had more information about many more topics in 1600 than in 1300, but this was often superficial knowledge or misunderstanding.

Europe was divided into three main religious camps by 1600: Lutheran or Evangelical, Calvinist or Reformed and Roman Catholic – the Anglicans were a case apart. Each had the adherence of rulers who were willing to use the organs of the secular state to promote and enforce religious orthodoxy. Except for the Roman Catholic recovery in the Empire in the seventeenth century, confessional lines have not changed much since then. For all the warfare, Europeans became used to one other. The zeal to diabolize the ungodly was increasingly directed less at mainstream Protestants or Roman Catholics than at fringe groups such as the Anabaptists, and at marginals such as witches. The Turks, known only by reputation, because except in the Balkans none of them lived among the European Christians, became incarnations of evil. Their cultural and religious differences from those of Europeans were made glaringly known in monstrously distorted form to all who could read or even see pictures. A Europe divided was still a Christian entity that had a mission to resist the Turk and extend the benefits of European culture and civilization to the rest of the world, as the colonies became foci of settlement as well as units of economic exploitation. The fundamental political, religious and cultural patterns of modern Europe were created in the three centuries after 1300, and then consolidated in the seventeenth and early eighteenth centuries. In the long and tangled history of Europe and Europeans since the end of the Roman Empire in the west, only the two and a half centuries since 1750 have witnessed transformations that were as truly revolutionary as those that occurred in the three centuries after 1300.

Endnotes

2. Of Nations and States: The Institutions of Government

1 Quotations from English constitutional documents are taken from Carl Stephenson and F. G. Marcham, *Sources of English Constitutional History: A Selection of Documents from A. D. 600 to the Present* (New York: Harper and Row, 1937), 164, 160, 205.
2 Scott L. Waugh, *England in the Reign of Edward III* (Cambridge: Cambridge University Press, 1991), 181.
3 John A. F. Thompson, *The Transformation of Medieval England, 1370–1529* (London: Longman, 1983), 275.
4 Cited in Arthur Tilley, *Medieval France* (Cambridge: Cambridge University Press, 1922), 143.
5 Section based on Pierre Chaunu and Richard Gascon, *L'État et la Ville* (Paris: Presses Universitaires de France, 1970); Ferdinand Lot and Robert Fawtier (eds.), *Histoire des institutions françaises au moyen âge. II: Institutions royales* (Paris: Presses Universitaires de France, 1958); and Thomas Ertman, *The Birth of the Leviathan. Building States and Regimes in Medieval and Early Modern Europe* (Cambridge: Cambridge University Press, 1997).
6 David Nicholas, *Medieval Flanders* (London: Longman, 1992), 334–7, after W. Blockmans, *De Volksvertegenwoordiging in Vlaanderen in de overgang van Middeleeuwen naar Nieuwe Tijden (1384–1506)* (Brussels: Palais der Academien, 1978). Comparative analysis based on W. Blockmans, 'A Typology of Representative Institutions in Late Medieval Europe', *Journal of Medieval History*, 4 (1978): 189–215.
7 Discussion based on Lot and Fawtier, *Institutions royales*, and Frederick J. Baumgartner, *France in the Sixteenth Century* (London: Macmillan, 1995), 12–17.
8 Section based on Angus Mackay, *Spain in the Middle Ages: From Frontier to Empire* (London: Macmillan, 1977), 143–64.
9 Discussion based on Ertman, *Birth of the Leviathan*.
10 Argument of Robert C. Palmer, *English Law in the Age of the Black Death* (Chapel Hill: University of North Carolina Press, 1993).
11 For urban government in late medieval Europe, see David Nicholas, *The Later Medieval City, 1300–1500* (London: Addison Wesley Longman, 1997), 108–23, 156–79 and literature cited.

12 Brian M. Downing, *The Military Revolution and Political Change: Origins of Democracy and Autocracy in Early Modern Europe* (Princeton: Princeton University Press, 1993), 31.

13 Discussion based on Kenneth Pennington, *The Prince and the Law, 1200–1600. Sovereignty and Rights in the Western Legal Tradition* (Berkeley: University of California Press, 1993), esp. p.6; David Potter, *A History of France, 1460–1560: The Emergence of a Nation State* (London: Macmillan, 1993), 5–6; V. A. C. Gatrell, Bruce Lenman and Geoffrey Parker (eds.), *Crime and the Law: The Social History of Crime in Western Europe Since 1500* (London: Europa Publications, 1980); and Downing, *Military Revolution*.

3. Economic Integration and Social Change in Late Medieval Europe

1 Argument of David Hackett Fischer, *The Great Wave: Price Revolutions and the Rhythm of History* (Oxford: Oxford University Press, 1996).

2 David Herlihy, *The Black Death and the Transformation of the West* (Cambridge, Mass.: Harvard University Press, 1997), 19.

3 Christopher Dyer, *Standards of Living in the Later Middle Ages: Social Change in England, c.1200–1520* (Cambridge: Cambridge University Press, 1989); Walter Prevenier and Wim Blockmans, *The Burgundian Netherlands* (Cambridge: Cambridge University Press, 1985), 194–6.

4 General discussion based on Nicholas, *Later Medieval City*.

5 Cited by Herlihy, *Black Death*, 55.

6 Figures from Nicholas, *Later Medieval City*, 249 and literature cited.

7 Michel Mollat, *The Poor in the Middle Ages: An Essay in Social History* (New Haven: Yale University Press, 1979); Bronislaw Geremek, *The Margins of Society in Late Medieval Paris* (Cambridge: Cambridge University Press, 1987); and other studies cited by Nicholas, *Later Medieval City*, 248–57.

8 Nicholas, *Later Medieval City*, 123–41 and quotation 131–2; Michel Mollat and Philippe Wolff, *The Popular Revolutions of the Late Middle Ages* (London: George Allen and Unwin, 1973). For events in London, see Pamela Nightingale, *A Medieval Mercantile Community: The Grocers' Company and the Trade of London, 1000–1485* (New Haven: Yale University Press, 1995), 228–345. For the Ciompi, Gene A. Brucker, 'The Ciompi Revolution', in Nicolai Rubinstein (ed.), *Florentine Studies. Politics and Society in Renaissance Florence* (Evanston, Ill.: Northwestern University Press, 1968), 314–45.

9 Tom Scott and Bob Scribner, 'Urban Networks', in Bob Scribner (ed.), *Germany: A New Social and Economic History*, I: *1450–1630* (London: Edward Arnold, 1995), 129.

10 Lisa Jardine, *Worldly Goods: A New History of the Renaissance* (London: Doubleday, 1996), 111.

11 David Herlihy, 'City and countryside in Renaissance Tuscany', in Herlihy, *Women, Family and Society in Medieval Europe* (Providence, RI: Berghahn Books, 1995), 296–313; Nicholas, *Later Medieval City*, 87–103.

12 Peter Coss, *The Knight in Medieval England, 1000–1400* (Phoenix Mill: Alan Sutton, 1993); Waugh, *England in the Reign of Edward III*, 117–35, Chris Given-Wilson, *The English Nobility in the Late Middle Ages* (London: Routledge & Kegan Paul, 1987); percentages of nobles in total population are from Denys Hay, *Europe in the Fourteenth and Fifteenth Centuries*, 2nd edn. (London: Longman, 1989), 64–73.

13 Martha C. Howell, *Women, Production, and Patriarchy in Late Medieval Cities* (Chicago: University of Chicago Press, 1986); Barbara A. Hanawalt, *The Ties That Bound: Peasant Families in Medieval England* (Oxford: Oxford

University Press, 1986); David Herlihy, *Opera Muliebria: Women and Work in Medieval Europe* (Philadelphia: Temple University Press, 1990); Christiane Klapisch-Zuber, *Women, Family, and Ritual in Renaissance Italy* (Chicago: University of Chicago Press, 1985); Shulamith Shahar, *The Fourth Estate: A History of Women in the Middle Ages* (London: Methuen, 1983); David Nicholas, *The Domestic Life of a Medieval City: Women, Children, and the Family in Fourteenth-Century Ghent* (Lincoln: University of Nebraska Press, 1985); Erika Uitz, *Women in the Medieval Town* (London: Barrie and Jenkins, 1990); P. J. P. Goldberg, *Women, Work, and Life Cycle in a Medieval Economy: Women in York and Yorkshire, c.1300–1520* (Oxford: Clarendon Press, 1992).

14 Pierre Chaunu, *European Expansion in the Later Middle Ages* (Amsterdam: North Holland, 1979), 242–6; Urs Bitterli, *Cultures in Conflict: Encounters Between European and Non-European Cultures, 1492–1800* (Stanford: Stanford University Press, 1989), 57–60.

15 Suggestion of Felipe Fernández-Armesto, *Millennium. A History of the Last Thousand Years* (New York: Scribner, 1995), 2–3.

16 Section based on Felipe Fernández-Armesto, *Before Columbus: Exploration and Colonisation from the Mediterranean to the Atlantic, 1229–1492* (London: Macmillan, 1987), particularly 12–21, 33–41, 128–48, 174–9; see also Chaunu, *European Expansion*, 98–103.

4. Late Nominalism and Early Humanism: The Cultural Life of the Late Middle Ages

1 Walter Ullmann, *Medieval Foundations of Renaissance Humanism* (Ithaca, NY: Cornell University Press, 1977), 134, 119.

2 Discussion based on Brian Tierney (ed.), *The Crisis of Church and State, 1050–1300* (Englewood Cliffs, NJ: Prentice-Hall, 1964); Tierney, *Foundations of the Conciliar Theory* (Cambridge: Cambridge University Press, 1955), Walter Ullmann, *A History of Political Thought: The Middle Ages* (Harmondsworth: Penguin Books, 1965); and John B. Morrall, *Political Thought in Medieval Times* (repr. Toronto: University of Toronto Press, 1980).

3 Waugh, *England in the Reign of Edward III*, 145.

4 The classic statement of the political use of pageantry by the Burgundian princes remains Johan Huizinga, *The Autumn of the Middle Ages*, recently made available in a controversial new translation by Rodney J. Payton and Ulrich Mammitzsch (Chicago: University of Chicago Press, 1996); see also Prevenier and Blockmans, *The Burgundian Netherlands*, 214–40.

5 Christopher Allmand, *The Hundred Years War: England and France at War, c.1300–c.1450* (Cambridge: Cambridge University Press, 1994), 151–63.

6 Alexandra F. Johnston, 'Traders and Playmakers: English Guildsmen and the Low Countries', in Caroline Barron and Nigel Saul (eds.), *England and the Low Countries in the Late Middle Ages* (Stroud: Alan Sutton, 1995), 99–114.

7 Joseph Anthony Mazzeo, *Renaissance and Revolution: The Remaking of European Thought* (New York: Pantheon Books, 1965), p. 54 n. 13.

8 Charles G. Nauert, Jr., *Humanism and the Culture of Renaissance Europe* (Cambridge: Cambridge University Press, 1995), 31.

9 Argument from Nauert, *Humanism*, 42–9.

10 Alison Brown, *The Renaissance* (London: Longman, 1988), 64–5.

11 Mazzeo, *Renaissance and Revolution*, 19.

12 Nauert, *Humanism and the Culture of Renaissance Europe*, 69.

13 For this important point see Mazzeo, *Renaissance and Revolution*, 17–18.

14 Lauro Martines, *Power and Imagination: City-States in Renaissance Italy* (New York: Random House, 1979), 191.

15 Hans Baron, *The Crisis of the Early Italian Renaissance* (Princeton: Princeton University Press, 1966).

16 Important point made by Brown, *Renaissance*, 45.

17 Ronald Witt, 'The *Crisis* after Forty Years', *American Historical Review*, 101 (1996): 109–18.

18 Eugenio Garin, *Italian Humanism: Philosophy and the Civic Life in the Renaissance* (New York: Harper and Row, 1965), 31–4.

19 Leon Battista Alberti, *On the Art of Building in Ten Books*, translated by Joseph Rykwert, Neil Leach, and Robert Tavernor (Cambridge, Mass.: MIT Press, 1989); Richard Goldthwaite, *The Building of Renaissance Florence: A Social and Economic History* (Baltimore: Johns Hopkins University Press, 1980).

20 Important points made by Mazzeo, *Renaissance and Revolution*, 6–7, 18–19.

21 Example cited by John Hale, *The Civilization of Europe in the Renaissance* (New York: Atheneum, 1994), 232.

22 Brown, *Renaissance*, 55–60.

23 Argument of André Chastel, 'The Artist', in Garin, *Renaissance Characters* (Chicago: University of Chicago Press, 1991), 180–206, at 180, 184.

24 Section based on two extremely important recent works: Mary Hollingsworth, *Patronage in Renaissance Italy: From 1400 to the Early Sixteenth Century* (Baltimore: Johns Hopkins University Press, 1994); Lisa Jardine, *Worldly Goods. A New History of the Renaissance* (London: Doubleday, 1996), especially examples on pp. 12, 19, 27–8; see also Brown, *Renaissance*, 22–3.

25 Case cited by Garin, *Italian Humanism*, 24.

5. From the Politics of Religion to the Religion of Politics

1 Both the French *États* and Dutch *Staten* refer to assemblies arranged by social category, but the habit has crept into English usage of calling the French example 'Estates' and the Dutch 'States'.

2 Thomas J. Brady, Jr., *Turning Swiss. Cities and Empire, 1450–1550* (Cambridge: Cambridge University Press, 1985).

3 Section based on Mack P. Holt, *The French Wars of Religion, 1562–1629* (Cambridge: Cambridge University Press, 1996); M. Greengrass, *The French Reformation* (Oxford: Clarendon Press, 1987); and Frederick J. Baumgartner, *France in the Sixteenth Century* (London: Macmillan, 1995).

4 Example of the Griffarians from Natalie Zemon Davis, 'Strikes and salvation at Lyon', from Davis, *Society and Culture in Early Modern France* (Stanford: Stanford University Press, 1975).

5 Section on French political thought from Baumgartner, *France in the Sixteenth Century*, 300–8.

6 Interpretation of the Edict of Nantes follows Holt, *French Wars of Religion*, 164, and Baumgartner, *France in the Sixteenth Century*, 230–1.

7 Section on the Dutch revolt based on Herbert H. Rowan (ed.), *The Low Countries in Early Modern Times* (New York: Walker, 1972); Herbert H. Rowen, *The Princes of Orange: The Stadholders in the Dutch Republic* (Cambridge: Cambridge University Press, 1988); Jonathan Israel, *The Dutch Republic: Its Rise, Greatness, and Fall (1477–1806)* (Oxford: Clarendon Press, 1995); Geoffrey Parker, *The Dutch Revolt* (Ithaca, NY: Cornell University Press, 1977); and Guido Marnef, *Antwerp in the Age of Reformation: Underground Protestantism in a Commercial Metropolis, 1550–1577* (Baltimore: Johns Hopkins University Press, 1996).

8 Israel, *Dutch Republic*, 169, notes the similarity of the tenth penny to the Castilian *alcabala*.

9 J. H. Elliott, *Imperial Spain, 1469-1716* (New York: Mentor Books, 1966), 262–73; Henry Kamen, *The Iron Century: Social Change in Europe, 1550–1660* (New York: Praeger, 1972); Henry Kamen, *Philip of Spain* (New Haven: Yale University Press, 1997).

6. The 'Renaissance State'?

1 Garrett Mattingly, *Renaissance Diplomacy* (Boston: Houghton Mifflin, 1955), 170–78 and 211; Elliott, *Imperial Spain*, 130; Potter, *France*, 256–7; Donald E. Queller, *The Office of the Ambassador in the Middle Ages* (Princeton: Princeton University Press, 1967).

2 Nicholas, *Later Medieval City*, 35–6.

3 John A. Marino, 'The Italian States in the "Long Sixteenth Century"', in *Handbook of European History 1400–1600, Late Middle Ages, Renaissance, and Reformation*, 1 (Grand Rapids: William B. Eerdmans, 1994): 331–61; Gene A. Brucker, *Florence: The Golden Age, 1138–1737* (Berkeley: University of California Press, 1998), 184.

4 Argument follows Erdman, *Birth of the Leviathan*, and Downing, *Military Revolution and Political Change*.

5 Downing, *Military Revolution and Political Change* for this general argument on the military, esp. p. xi, 69; Thomas A. Brady, Jr., 'The Rise of Merchant Empire, 1400–1700: A European Counterpoint', in Tracy, *Political Economy*, 117–60.

6 Armesto, *Millennium*, 171.

7 Bruce Lenman and Geoffrey Parker, 'The State, the Community and the Criminal Law in Early Modern Europe', in Gatrell, Lenman and Parker, *Crime and the Law*, 11–48, at 28, 37–8.

8 This argument is from Lenman and Parker, *Crime and the Law*.

9 Gerald Strauss, *Law, Resistance, and the State: The Opposition to Roman Law in Reformation Germany* (Princeton: Princeton University Press, 1986), esp. 60–61, 153.

10 G. R. Elton, *The Tudor Revolution in Government* (Cambridge: Cambridge University Press, 1953).

11 David Starkey, *The English Court from the Wars of the Roses to the Civil War* (London: Longman, 1987), p. 82, upon which this line of argument is based.

12 D. M. Palliser, *The Age of Elizabeth: England Under the later Tudors, 1547–1603* (London: Longman, 1992), 371–7.

13 Wallace MacCaffrey, *Elizabeth I* (London: Edward Arnold, 1993), 381–90.

14 In contrast to the American system, in which a member of either house of Congress must reside in the district that elects him/her, there is no residence requirement in England.

15 Joyce Youings, *Sixteenth-Century England* (Harmondsworth: Penguin Books, 1984), 42–3.

16 Palliser's figures, *Age of Elizabeth*, 353.

17 Section on central government in France based on Baumgartner, *France*, 14–15, 126, and Potter, *France*, 58–65, 76–85, 92–7, 105–8.

18 Chaunu and Gascon, *L'État et la ville*, 75–7.

19 Baumgartner, *France*, 85-6; Potter, *France*, 110–23; Perez Zagorin, *Rebels and Rulers, 1500–1660. I. Society, States, and Early Modern Revolution* (Cambridge: Cambridge University Press, 1982), 113; Chaunu and Gascon, *L'État et la ville*, 62–3.

20 Colette Beaune, *The Birth of an Ideology: Myth and Symbols of Nation in Late-Medieval France* (Berkeley: University of California Press, 1991).
21 Potter, *France*, 17–22.
22 Baumgartner, *France in the Sixteenth Century*, 90; Potter, *France*, 30–7.
23 Chaunu and Gascon, *L'Etat et la ville*, 113–15.
24 Section on French royal finances based on Potter, *France*, 136–55; Baumgartner, *France in the Sixteenth Century*, 13–14, 128–9; Chaunu and Gascon, *L'État et la ville*, 46, 164; Emmanuel Le Roy Ladurie, *The French Peasantry, 1450–1660* (Berkeley: University of California Press, 1987), 239–52.
25 Discussion of Spanish finances based on Elliott, *Imperial Spain*, 91–4; Peggy K. Liss, *Isabel the Queen: Life and Times* (Oxford: Oxford University Press, 1992), 183–4; and Erdman, *Birth of the Leviathan*, particularly 114–17 for discussion of the *asientos*.
26 Kamen, *Iron Century*, 162–3.
27 Haywood Keniston, *Francisco de los Cobos: Secretary of the Emperor Charles V* (Pittsburgh: Pittsburgh University Press, 1959).
28 Strauss, *Law, Resistance, and the State*, 251.
29 Henry J. Cohn, 'Church Property in the German Protestant Principalities', in E. I. Kouri and Tom Scott (eds.), *Politics and Society in Reformation Europe: Essays for Sir Geoffrey Elton on His Sixty-Fifth Birthday* (London: Macmillan, 1987), 158–87; Erdman, *Birth of the Leviathan*, 240; Strauss, *Law, Resistance, and the State*, 250–1, 268-70, and p. 154 for the Blaser case quoted.

7. The Besieged as Besieger: West European Expansion in Asia, Africa, the Americas and Slavic Europe

1 Geoffrey Parker, 'Europe and the Wider World, 1500–1750: The Military Balance', in Tracy, *Political Economy*, 161-95, at 173–5.
2 Section on Columbus is based on Chaunu, *European Expansion*, 151–5, 171–3; Fernández-Armesto, *Before Columbus*, 245–52; and more generally on Felipe Fernández-Armesto, *Columbus* (Oxford: Oxford University Press, 1991).
3 Fernandez-Armesto, *Columbus*, 191.
4 Elliott, *Imperial Spain*, 57–74; J. H. Elliott, *The Old World and the New, 1492–1560* (Cambridge: Cambridge University Press, 1994).
5 Robert Bartlett, *The Making of Europe. Conquest, Colonization and Cultural Change, 950–1350* (Princeton: Princeton University Press, 1993).
6 Fernández-Armesto, *Before Columbus*, 213–15.
7 Anthony Pagden, *Lords of All the World: Ideologies of Empire in Spain, Britain and France, c.1500–c.1800* (New Haven: Yale University Press, 1995), 31–2, 51–2.
8 Herman Van der Wee, 'Structural changes in European long-distance trade, and particularly in the re-export trade from south to north, 1350–1750', in Tracy, *Rise of Merchant Empires*, especially 29–33, and Carla Rahn Phillips, 'The Growth and Composition of Trade in the Iberian Empires, 1450–1750', in Tracy, *Rise of Merchant Empires*, 34–101, esp. 42, 72.
9 M. N. Pearson, 'Merchants and States', in James D. Tracy (ed.), *The Political Economy of Merchant Empires: State Power and World Trade, 1350–1750* (Cambridge: Cambridge University Press, 1992), 41–116.
10 Section relies heavily on Norman Housley, *The Later Crusades, 1274–1580* (Oxford: Oxford University Press, 1992).
11 Hale, *Renaissance*, 41.
12 Section draws heavily on David Kirby, *Northern Europe in the Early Modern Period: The Baltic World, 1492–1772* (London: Longman, 1990).

8. The 'Long Sixteenth Century' in the Economic and Social Development of Europe

1 Except where otherwise noted, figures in this section are from Jan de Vries, *European Urbanization, 1500–1800* (Cambridge, Mass.: Harvard University Press, 1984), 29–42, 151; see also Carlo M. Cipolla, *Before the Industrial Revolution: European Society and Economy, 1000–1700*, 2nd edn. (New York: Norton, 1980), 4, 150–66.
2 Peter Moraw, 'Cities and Citizenry as Factors of State Formation in the Roman-German Empire of the Late Middle Ages', in Scribner, *Germany*, 100–27, at 105.
3 Figures from Palliser, *Age of Elizabeth*, 236.
4 Kamen, *Iron Century*, 15–16; Palliser, *Age of Elizabeth*, 50.
5 Chaunu and Gascon, *L'État et la ville*, 237–9; William J. Wright, 'The Nature of Early Capitalism', in Scribner, *Germany* 181–208, at 186; Ralph Davis, *The Rise of the Atlantic Economies* (Ithaca, NY: Cornell University Press, 1973), 27.
6 J. N. Ball, *Merchants and Merchandise: The Expansion of Trade in Europe, 1500–1630* (London: Croom Helm, 1977), 78–85; Elliott, *Imperial Spain*, 136.
7 Figures from Marnef, *Antwerp*, 5; Davis, *Atlantic Economies*, 35.
8 Christopher R. Friedrichs, *The Early Modern City, 1450–1750* (London: Longman, 1995), esp. 9–10, 22.
9 Friedrichs, *Early Modern City*, 293, 306.
10 Henry Heller, *Labour, Science and Technology in the Age of Valois and Bourbon 1500–1620* (Cambridge: Cambridge University Press, 1996), 8.
11 Cologne example given in William J. Wright, 'The Nature of Early Capitalism', in Scribner, *Germany*, 181–208.
12 Rolf Kießling, 'Markets and Marketing, Town and Country', in Scribner, *Germany*,145–79, at 155–6.
13 Ball, *Merchants*, 50–1.
14 Discussion based on Harry A. Miskimin, *The Economy of Later Renaissance Europe, 1460–1600* (Cambridge: Cambridge University Press, 1977), 28–46; Ward Barrett, 'World bullion flows, 1450–1800', in Tracy, *Rise of Merchant Empires*; Kamen, *Iron Century*, 59–70; Potter, *France*, 146; Joan Thirsk, *Economic Policy and Projects. The Development of a Consumer Society in Early Modern England* (Oxford: Clarendon Press, 1978), 173–4.
15 Alberto Tenenti, 'The Merchant and the Banker', in Garin, *Renaissance Characters*, 154–79, at 159.
16 Ball, *Merchants*, 24–7.
17 William J. Wright, 'The Nature of Early Capitalism', in Scribner, *Germany*, 181–208, at 185; Kamen, *Iron Century*, 105.
18 Convenient summary in Ball, *Merchants and Merchandise*, 106–11.
19 Figures from Kamen, *Iron Century*, 109–10 and Heller, *Labour, Science and Technology*, 94–5.
20 Joan Thirsk, *Economic Policy and Projects. The Development of a Consumer Society in Early Modern England* (Oxford: Clarendon Press, 1978).
21 Palliser, *Age of Elizabeth*, 281–5.
22 Summary of conclusions of Joseph P. Ward, *Metropolitan Communities: Trade, Guilds, Identity, and Change in Early Modern London* (Stanford: Stanford University Press, 1997).
23 Nicholas, *Later Medieval City*, 244–8.
24 George Huppert, *After the Black Death. A Social History of Early Modern Europe* (Bloomington, Ind.: Indiana University Press, 1986), 110–11.
25 Heller, *Labour, Science and Technology in France, 1500–1620*, 151.
26 Wright, 'The Nature of Early Capitalism', 190–1.
27 Discussion from Kamen, *Iron Century*, 212–21.

28 Joyce Youings, *Sixteenth-Century England* (Harmondsworth: Penguin, 1984), 50–60.

29 Factual summary but not interpretation based on Peter Blickle, *The Revolution of 1525: The German Peasants' War from a New Perspective* (Baltimore: Johns Hopkins University Press, 1985); and articles in Bob Scribner and Gerhard Benecke (eds.), *The German Peasant War of 1525 – New Perspectives* (London: George Allen and Unwin, 1979), particularly Horst Buszello, 'The Common Man's View of the State in the German Peasant War', 109–22.

30 Argument of John Bossy, *Christianity in the West, 1400–1700* (Oxford: Oxford University Press, 1985).

31 Discussion including statistics based on Robert Jütte, *Poverty and Deviance in Early Modern Europe* (Cambridge: Cambridge University Press, 1994), particularly 105–6, 117; Kamen, *Iron Century*, 388; Youings, *Sixteenth-Century England*, 254–303.

32 Youings, *Sixteenth-Century England*, 293.

33 Youings, *Sixteenth-Century England*, 284.

34 Heller, *Labour, Science and Technology in France*, 39–40.

35 N. Z. Davis, 'Poor Relief, Humanism, and Heresy', in her *Society and Culture*, 17–64; the calculation is on 48–9.

36 R. Po-Chia Hsia, 'The Structure of Belief: Confessionalism and Society, 1500–1600', in Scribner, *Germany*, 355–77, at 366.

37 Margaret L. King, 'The Woman of the Renaissance', in Garin, *Renaissance Characters*, 207–49, at 225; N. Z. Davis, 'City Women and Religious Change', in Davis, *Society and Culture*, 65–95.

38 Section on women based on Merry E. Wiesner, *Women and Gender in Early Modern Europe* (Cambridge: Cambridge University Press, 1993); Wiesner, 'Paternalism in Practice: The Control of Servants and Prostitutes in Early Modern German Cities', in Philip N. Bebb and Sherrin Marshall, *The Process of Change in Early Modern Europe: Festschrift for Miriam Usher Chrisman* (Athens, OH.: Ohio University Press, 1988), 179–200; Bossy, *Christianity*, 24–5; Margaret L. King, 'The Woman of the Renaissance', in Garin, *Renaissance Characters*, 207–49.

39 David Herlihy, 'Society, Court, and Culture in Sixteenth-Century Mantua', in Herlihy, *Women, Family and Society in Medieval Europe: Historical Essays, 1978–1991* (Providence, RI: Berghahn Books, 1995), 279–95.

40 Youings, *Sixteenth-Century England*, 328–9.

41 Huppert, *After the Black Death*, 56–65; Potter, *France*, 169.

42 Analysis based on Zagorin, *Rebels and Rulers*.

43 Gayle K. Brunelle, '"Narrowing Horizons": Commerce and Derogation in Normandy', in Mack P. Holt (ed.), *Society and Institutions in Early Modern France: Essays in Honor of J. Russell Major* (Athens: University of Georgia Press, 1991), 63–4.

44 Potter, *France*, 170–3.

45 Le Roy Ladurie, *The French Peasantry*, 243.

46 Elliott, *Imperial Spain*, 111–13.

9. The Later Renaissance: From Classical Humanism to Vernacular Classicism

1 George Holmes, 'Humanism in Italy', in Anthony Goodman and Angus Mackay (eds.), *The Impact of Humanism on Western Europe* (London: Longman, 1990), 118–36; Garin, *Italian Humanism*, 78.

2 See details in Hale, *Renaissance*, 264–6.

3 Alfred W. Crosby, *The Measure of Reality: Quantification and Western Society,*

1200–1600 (Cambridge: Cambridge University Press, 1996), particularly 18–19, 67.

4 Roger D. Masters, *Machiavelli, Leonardo, and the Science of Power* (Notre Dame, Ind.: University of Notre Dame Press, 1996).

5 John M. Najemy, 'Baron's Machiavelli and Renaissance Republicanism', *American Historical Review*, 101 (1996), 119–29.

6 Much of this discussion is based on James H. Overfield, *Humanism and Scholasticism in Late Medieval Germany* (Princeton: Princeton University Press, 1984).

7 Nauert, *Humanism*, 111.

8 Overfield, *Humanism and Scholasticism*.

9 Lisa Jardine, *Erasmus, Man of Letters: The Construction of Charisma in Print* (Princeton: Princeton University Press, 1993), ch. 3.

10 Nauert, *Humanism*, 102–3 for Luder example; Overfield, *Humanism*, 129 for quotation about Celtis.

11 Erika Rummel, *The Humanist-Scholastic Debate in the Renaissance and Reformation* (Cambridge, Mass.: Harvard University Press, 1995), 7.

12 Overfield, *Humanism*, ch. 8.

13 Peter Burke, 'The Spread of Italian Humanism', 1–22, from Goodman and MacKay, *The Impact of Humanism on Western Europe*.

14 Nauert, *Humanism*, 123.

15 Ullmann, *Medieval Foundations of Renaissance Humanism*, 186, based on Roberto Weiss, *Humanism in England during the Fifteenth Century* (Oxford, 1967).

16 Geoffrey Elton, 'Humanism in England', in Goodman and Mackay, *Humanism*, 259–78.

17 Kamen, *Iron Century*, 286–7.

18 Discussion from Halkin, *Erasmus. A Critical Biography* (Oxford: Blackwell, 1993), and Jardine, *Erasmus*.

19 Halkin, *Erasmus*, 41; Hale, *Renaissance*, 153.

20 Section on decline of Latin from Hale, *Renaissance*, 152–62, and quotation 163.

21 Hale, *Renaissance*, 292.

22 Bernd Moeller, 'Luther in Europe: His Works in Translation, 1517–46', in *Elton Festschrift*, 235–51.

23 Jeremy N. H. Lawrance, 'Humanism in the Iberian Peninsula', in Goodman and Mackay, *Humanism*, 220–58.

24 Except as noted otherwise, the section on printing is based on Elizabeth Eisenstein, *The Printing Press as an Agent of Change: Communications and Cultural Transformations in Early Modern Europe*, 2 vols. (Cambridge: Cambridge University Press, 1979), summarized in Eisenstein, *The Printing Revolution in Early Modern Europe* (Cambridge: Cambridge University Press, 1983).

25 Peter Murray Jones, 'Information and Science', in Rosemary Horrox (ed.), *Fifteenth-Century Attitudes: Perceptions of Society in Late Medieval England* (Cambridge: Cambridge University Press, 1994), 101–3.

26 Bossy, *Christianity*, 103.

27 Jean-Claude Margolin, 'Humanism in France', in Goodman and Mackay, *Humanism*, 164–201, at 170–1.

28 Marnef, *Antwerp*, 37–44.

29 Section on Plantin from Jardine, *Worldly Goods*, 218–20.

30 Miriam U. Chrisman, 'Printing and the Evolution of Lay Culture in Strasbourg 1480–1599', in Po-chia Hsia (ed.), *The German People and the Reformation* (Ithaca, NY: Cornell University Press, 1988), 74–100, a summary of Chrisman, *Strasbourg and the Reform: A Study in the Process of Change* (New Haven: Yale University Press, 1967).

31 Greengrass, *French Reformation*, 7.
32 Discussion based on George Huppert, *Public Schools in Renaissance France* (Urbana, Ill.: University of Illinois Press, 1984).
33 Marnef, *Antwerp*, 33–7.
34 Horrox, *Fifteenth-Century Attitudes*, 2.
35 Kamen, *Iron Century*, 273.
36 Jean-Claude Margolin, 'Humanism in France', in Goodman and Mackay, *Humanism*, 164–201, at 200.
37 Section on architecture, Fontainebleau, and patronage of Francis I and Henry II from Baumgartner, *France*, 188–205.
38 Francesco Guicciardini, *Maxims and Reflections of a Renaissance Statesman (Ricordi)*, translated by Mario Domandi (New York: Harper and Row, 1965).
39 Paul Grendler, 'The Rejection of Learning in Mid-*Cinquecento* Italy', *Studies in the Renaissance*, 13 (1966), at 243; Peter Burke, 'The Courtier', in Garin, *Renaissance Characters*, 120–1.

10. Antiquity and Modernity: The Religious Division of Europe in the Sixteenth Century

1 Jardine, *Worldly Goods*, 64.
2 Massimo Firpo, 'The Cardinal', in Garin, *Renaissance Characters*, 46–97.
3 Rummel, *Humanist-Scholastic Debate*, 140–1.
4 Overfield, *Humanism and Scholasticism*, ch. 7; Ulrich von Hutten *et al.*, *On the Eve of the Reformation: 'Letters of Obscure Men'* (New York: Harper and Row, 1964).
5 Baumgartner, *France in the Sixteenth Century*, 35; Potter, *France*, 220–30.
6 Ole Peter Grell, 'Scandinavia', in Andrew Pettegree (ed.), *The Early Reformation in Europe* (Cambridge: Cambridge University Press, 1992).
7 Thomas J. Brady, Jr., *Turning Swiss: Cities and Empire, 1450–1550* (Cambridge: Cambridge University Press, 1985); Bruce Gordon, 'Switzerland', in Pettegree, *Early Reformation*, 70–93.
8 Example from Friedrichs, *Early Modern City*, 74.
9 Thesis of Bernd Moeller, *Imperial Cities and the Reformation: Three Essays* (Philadelphia: Fortress Press, 1972).
10 Hudon, 'Religion and Society in Early Modern Italy', in Po-chia Hsia, *German People and the Reformation*.
11 Greengrass, *French Reformation*, 9; David Nicholls, 'France', in Pettegree, *Early Reformation*, 120–41.
12 Baumgartner, *France*, 138–48; Potter, *France*, 246–7; Holt, *Wars of Religion*, 29; Greengrass, *French Reformation*, 36–7.
13 Klaus Deppermann, 'The Anabaptists and the State Churches', in Greyerz, *Religion and Society*, 95–106; and R. Po-chia Hsia, 'Münster and the Anabaptists', in Greyerz, *Religion and Society*, 51–69. See in general George H. Williams, *The Radical Reformation* (Philadelphia: Westminster Press, 1962).
14 Holt, *French Wars of Religion*, 25–6; Greengrass, *French Reformation*, 30–40; Baumgartner, *France*, 138–46.
15 Jaroslav Pánek, 'The Question of Tolerance in Bohemia and Moravia in the Age of the Reformation', in Grell and Scribner, *Tolerance*, 231–48; Winfried Eberhard, 'Bohemia, Moravia and Austria', in Pettegree, *Early Reformation*, 23–48.
16 David P. Daniel, 'Hungary', in Pettegree, *Early Reformation*; Katalin Péter, 'Tolerance and Intolerance in Sixteenth-Century Hungary', in Grell and Scribner, *Tolerance*, 249–61.

17 Robert J. W. Evans, *The Making of the Habsburg Monarchy, 1550–1700: An Interpretation* (Oxford: Clarendon Press, 1979), 6–7.

18 Michael G. Müller, 'Protestant Confessionalisation in the Towns of Royal Prussia and the Practice of Religious Toleration in Poland-Lithuania', in Grell and Scribner, *Tolerance*, 262–81.

19 Hale, *Renaissance*, 130.

20 Kamen, *Iron Century*, 261; Hans R. Guggisberg, 'Tolerance and Intolerance in Sixteenth-Century Basle', in Grell and Scribner, *Tolerance*, 145–63.

21 Baumgartner, *France*, 180–183.

22 Gerald Strauss, 'The Reformation and Its Public in an Age of Orthodoxy', from Po-chia Hsia, *German People and the Reformation*, 194–214, and more generally from Gerald Strauss, *Luther's House of Learning* (Baltimore: Johns Hopkins University Press, 1978).

23 Discussion based on William Monter, 'Heresy Executions in Reformation Europe, 1520–1565', in Grell and Scribner, *Tolerance*, 48–64, with quotation p. 50.

24 Carlo Ginzburg, *The Cheese and the Worms: The Cosmos of a Sixteenth-Century Miller* (Baltimore: Johns Hopkins University Press, 1980), whose discussion is based on the record of Scandella's trial before the Inquisition in 1583.

25 Interpretation after Huppert, *After the Black Death*, 144–9.

26 David Nicholas, *The Evolution of the Medieval World: Society, Government and Thought in Europe 312–1500* (London: Longman, 1992), p. xiii.

27 Bob Scribner, 'Cosmic Order and Daily Life: Sacred and Secular in Pre-Industrial German Society', in Greyerz, *Religion*, 17–32.

28 Thesis of Ronald Hutton, *The Rise and Fall of Merry England: The Ritual Year, 1400–1700* (Oxford: Oxford University Press, 1996).

29 N. Z. Davis, 'The Reasons of Misrule', from Davis, *Society and Culture*, 97–123.

30 Bossy, *Christianity in the West 1400–1700*, 43–5.

31 Emanuel Le Roy Ladurie, *Carnival. A People's Rising in Romans, 1579–1580* (New York: Scolar Press, 1979). One sore point was removed when in 1583 the *parlement* of Grenoble ruled that city dwellers owning rural land would pay in the villages, even if they were noble.

32 Richard Kieckhefer, *Magic in the Middle Ages* (Cambridge: Cambridge University Press, 1989), 190–201.

33 Kamen, *Iron Century*, 248. Christina Larner, 'Crimen Exceptum? The Crime of Witchcraft in Europe', 49–75, in Gatrell, Lenman and Parker, *Crime and the Law*, 11–48; Larner, *Witchcraft and Religion: The Politics of Popular Belief* (Oxford: Blackwell, 1984).

34 Discussion and figures from Richard M. Golden, 'Satan in Europe: The Geography of Witch Hunts', in Michael Wolfe (ed.), *Changing Identities in Early Modern France* (Durham, NC: Duke University Press, 197), 216–47.

35 Monter, 'Heresy Executions', 63.

36 Larner, 'Crimen Exceptum?' 69–70.

37 Paul Grendler, 'The Roman Inquisition and the Venetian Press', *Journal of Modern History*, 47 (1975), 48–65.

38 Based on John Edwards, *The Jews in Christian Europe, 1400–1700* (London: Routledge, 1988).

The Rulers of Europe

France

Capetian dynasty

Philip IV 'the Fair'	(1285–1314)	Philip V	(1317–22)
Louis X	(1314–16)	Charles IV	(1322–28)
John I	(1316)		

Valois dynasty

Philip VI	(1328–50)	Louis XII	(1498–1515)
John II	(1350–64)	Francis I	(1515–47)
Charles V 'the Wise'	(1364–80)	Henry II	(1547–59)
Charles VI	(1380–1422)	Francis II	(1559–60)
Charles VII	(1422–61)	Charles IX	(1560–74)
Louis XI	(1461–83)	Henry III	(1574–89)
Charles IX	(1483–98)		

Bourbon dynasty

Henry IV	(1589–1610)

England

Angevin (Plantagenet) dynasty

Edward I	(1272–1307)	Edward III	(1327–77)
Edward II	(1307–27)	Richard II	(1377–99)

Lancastrian dynasty

Henry IV	(1399–1413)	Henry VI	(1422–61/71)
Henry V	(1413–22)		

Yorkist dynasty

Edward IV	(1461–83)	Richard III	(1483–85)
Edward V	(1483)		

Tudor dynasty

Henry VII	(1485–1509)	Mary I	(1553–8)
Henry VIII	(1509–47)	Elizabeth I	(1558–1603)
Edward VI	(1547–53)		

German Kings and Emperors

Rudolf I (Habsburg)	(1273–91)	Wenceslas (Luxembourg)	
Adolf of Nassau	(1292–8)		(1378–1400)
Albert I (Habsburg)	(1298–1308)	Rudolf of the Palatinate	
Henry VII (Luxembourg)		(Wittelsbach)	(1400–10)
	(1308–13)	Sigismund I (Luxembourg)	
Ludwig of Bavaria (Wittelsbach)			(1410–37)
	(1314–47)		
Charles IV (Luxembourg)			
	(1347–78)		

Habsburg dynasty

Albert II	(1438–9)	Ferdinand	(1556–64)
Frederick III	(1440–93)	Maximilian II	(1464–76)
Maximilian I	(1493–1519)	Rudolf II	(1576–1612)
Charles V	(1519–56)		

Castile

Ferdinand IV	(1295–1312)	Peter 'the Cruel'	(1350–69)
Alfonso XI	(1312–50)		

Trastamara dynasty

Henry II	(1369–79)	John II	(1406–54)
John I	(1379–90)	Henry IV	(1454–74)
Henry III	(1390–1406)	Isabella	(1474–1504)

Aragon

James II	(1291–1327)	Ferdinand I	(1412–16)
Alfonso IV	(1327–36)	Alfonso V	(1416–58)
Peter IV	(1336–87)	John II	(1458–79)
John I	(1387–95)	Ferdinand II	(1479–1516)
Martin I	(1395–1410)		

Neapolitan branch of Aragonese royal family

Ferrante	(1458–94)	Alfonso II of Naples	(1494–5)

Castile-Aragon

Charles I (Charles V of the Holy Roman Empire)	(1516–56)	Philip II	(1556–98)
		Philip III	(1598–1621)

Popes

Boniface VIII	(1294–1303)	Benedict XI	(1303–4)

Avignon

Clement V	(1305–14)	Innocent VI	(1352–62)
John XXII	(1316–34)	Urban V	(1362–70)
Benedict XII	(1334–42)	Gregory XI	(1370–8)
Clement VI	(1342–52)		

Rome (1378–1417)

Urban VI	(1378–89)	Innocent VII	(1404–6)
Boniface IX	(1389–1404)	Gregory XII	(1406–17)

Avignon (1378–1417)

Clement VII	(1378–94)	Benedict XIII	(1394–1417)

Rome after 1417

Martin V	(1417–31)	Leo X	(1513–21)
Eugenius IV	(1431–47)	Hadrian VI	(1522–3)
Nicholas V	(1447–55)	Clement VII	(1523–34)
Calixtus III	(1455–8)	Paul III	(1534–49)
Pius II	(1458–64)	Julius III	(1550–5)
Paul II	(1464–71)	Marcellus II	(1555)
Sixtus IV	(1471–84)	Paul IV	(1555–59)
Innocent VIII	(1484–92)	Pius IV	(1559–65)
Alexander VI	(1492–1503)	Pius V	(1566–72)
Pius III	(1503)	Gregory XIII	(1572–85)
Julius II	(1503–13)	Sixtus V	(1585–90)

Suggestions for Further Reading

1. Europe in the Era of the Hundred Years War

Allmand, Christopher. *The Hundred Years War: England and France at War, c.1300–c.1450* (Cambridge: Cambridge University Press, 1989).

Curry, Anne. *The Hundred Years War* (New York: St. Martin's Press, 1993).

Harvey, John. *The Black Prince and His Age* (Totowa, NJ: Rowman and Littlefield, 1976).

Housley, Norman. *The Later Crusades, 1274–1580* (Oxford: Oxford University Press, 1992).

Keen, Maurice. *Chivalry* (New Haven: Yale University Press, 1984).

Lewis, P. S. *The Recovery of France in the Fifteenth Century* (New York: Harper & Row, 1972).

Mackay, Angus. *Spain in the Middle Ages: From Frontier to Empire* (London: Macmillan, 1977).

O'Callaghan, Joseph F. *A History of Medieval Spain* (Ithaca, NY: Cornell University Press, 1975).

Palmer, J. J. N. *England, France and Christendom, 1377–99* (Chapel Hill: University of North Carolina Press, 1972).

Perroy, Edouard. *The Hundred Years War* (Bloomington, Ind.: Indiana University Press, 1962).

Sedlar, Jean W. *East Central Europe in the Middle Ages, 1000–1500* (Seattle: University of Washington Press, 1994).

Vaughan, Richard. *Valois Burgundy* (Hamden, Conn.: Archon Books, 1975).

Waugh, Scott L. *England in the Reign of Edward III* (Cambridge: Cambridge University Press, 1991).

2. Of Nations and States: The Institutions of Government

Ayton, Andrew and J. L. Price (eds.). *The Medieval Military Revolution: State, Society, and Military Change in Medieval and Early Modern Europe* (London: Taurus, 1995).

Beaune, Colette. *The Birth of an Ideology: Myth and Symbols of Nation in Late-Medieval France* Transl. by Susan Ross Huston, ed. Fredric L. Cheyette (Berkeley and Los Angeles: University of California Press, 1991).

Bellamy, John. *Crime and Public Order in England in the Later Middle Ages* (Toronto: University of Toronto Press, 1973).

Du Boulay, F. R. H. *Germany in the Later Middle Ages* (London: Athlone Press, 1983).

Goodman, Anthony. *A History of England from Edward II to James I* (London: Longman, 1977).

Leuschner, Joachim. *Germany in the Late Middle Ages* (Amsterdam: North Holland, 1980).

Lewis, P. S. *Later Medieval France: The Polity* (New York: Macmillan, 1968).

Pennington, Kenneth. *The Prince and the Law, 1200–1600: Sovereignty and Rights in the Western Legal Tradition* (Berkeley and Los Angeles: University of California Press, 1993).

Thomson, John A. F. *The Transformation of Medieval England, 1370–1529* (London: Longman, 1983).

3. Economic Integration and Social Change in Late Medieval Europe

Bartlett, Robert. *The Making of Europe: Conquest, Colonization and Cultural Change, 950–1350* (Princeton: Princeton University Press, 1993).

Bautier, Robert-Henri. *The Economic Development of Medieval Europe* (New York: Harcourt Brace Jovanovich, 1973).

Bowsky, William M. (ed.). *The Black Death: A Turning Point in History?* (New York: Holt, Rinehart and Winston, 1971).

Brucker, Gene A. *The Civic World of Early Renaissance Florence* (Princeton: Princeton University Press, 1977).

Brucker, Gene A. *Giovanni and Lusanna* (Berkeley: University of California Press, 1986).

Dyer, Christopher, *Standards of Living in the Later Middle Ages: Social Change in England, c.1200–1520* (Cambridge: Cambridge University Press, 1989).

Favier, Jean. *Gold and Spices. The Rise of Commerce in the Middle Ages* (London: Holmes 1998).

Fischer, David Hackett. *The Great Wave. Price Revolutions and the Rhythm of History* (Oxford: Oxford University Press, 1996).

Fourquin, Guy. *The Anatomy of Popular Rebellion in the Middle Ages* (Amsterdam: North Holland, 1978).

Geremek, Bronisław. *The Margins of Society in Late Medieval Paris* (Cambridge: Cambridge University Press, 1987).

Gies, Joseph and Frances. *Marriage and the Family in the Middle Ages* (New York: Harper & Row, 1987).

Gies, Joseph and Frances. *Women in the Middle Ages* (New York: Barnes and Noble, 178).

Given-Wilson, Chris. *The English Nobility in the Late Middle Ages* (London: Routledge, 1987).

Hanawalt, Barbara A. *The Ties That Bound: Peasant Families in Medieval England* (Oxford: Oxford University Press, 1986).

Herlihy, David. *The Black Death and the Transformation of the West.* Edited with an introduction by Samuel K. Cohn, Jr. (Cambridge, Mass.: Harvard University Press, 1997).

Herlihy, David. *Opera Muliebria. Women and Work in Medieval Europe* (Philadelphia: Temple University Press, 1990).

Howell, Martha C. *Women, Production, and Patriarchy in Late Medieval Cities* (Chicago: University of Chicago Press, 1986).

Huppert, George. *After the Black Death: A Social History of Early Modern Europe* (Bloomington, Ind.: Indiana University Press, 1986).

Larner, John. *Italy in the Age of Dante and Petrarch, 1216–1380* (London: Longman, 1980).

Miskimin, Harry A. *The Economy of Early Renaissance Europe, 1300–1460* (Cambridge: Cambridge University Press, 1975).

Mollat, Michel. *The Poor in the Middle Ages. An Essay in Social History* (New Haven: Yale University Press, 1979).

Mollat, Michel and Philippe Wolff. *The Popular Revolutions of the Late Middle Ages* (London: George Allen and Unwin, 1973).

Nicholas, David. *The Later Medieval City, 1300–1500* (London: Longman, 1997).

Nicholas, David. *Medieval Flanders* (London: Longman, 1992).

Nicholas, David. *The Metamorphosis of a Medieval City: Ghent in the Age of the Arteveldes, 1302–1390* (Lincoln: University of Nebraska Press, 1987).

Phillips, J. R. S. *The Medieval Expansion of Europe* (New York: Oxford University Press, 1988).

Platt, Colin, *King Death: The Black Death and its Aftermath in Late-Medieval England* (London: University College London Press, 1996).

Prevenier, Walter and Wim Blockmans. *The Burgundian Netherlands* (Cambridge: Cambridge University Press, 1985).

Shahar, Shulamith. *The Fourth Estate: A History of Women in the Middle Ages* (London: Methuen, 1983).

Thrupp, Sylvia L. *The Merchant Class of Medieval London* (Ann Arbor: University of Michigan Press, 1948).

Ziegler, Philip. *The Black Death* (Harmondsworth: Pelican, 1970).

4. Late Nominalism and Early Humanism: The Cultural Life of the Late Middle Ages

Baron, Hans. *The Crisis of the Early Italian Renaissance* (Princeton: Princeton University Press, 1955).

Brown, Alison. *The Renaissance* (London: Longman, 1988).

Garin, Eugenio. *Italian Humanism: Philosophy and the Civic Life in the Renaissance*. Transl. by Peter Munz (New York: Harper & Row, 1965).

Garin, Eugenio (ed.). *Renaissance Characters*. Trans. by Lydia G. Cochrane (Chicago: University of Chicago Press, 1991).

Goldthwaite, Richard A. *The Building of Renaissance Florence: A Social and Economic History* (Baltimore: Johns Hopkins University Press, 1980).

Goldthwaite, Richard A. *Wealth and the Demand for Art in Italy, 1300–1600* (Baltimore: Johns Hopkins University Press, 1993).

Hale, John. *The Civilization of Europe in the Renaissance* (New York: Atheneum, 1994).

Hay, Denys. *The Renaissance Debate* (New York: Holt, Rinehart and Winston, 1965).

Hay, Denis, and John Law, *Italy in the Age of the Renaissance, 1380–1530* (London: Longman, 1989).

Hollingsworth, Mary. *Patronage in Renaissance Italy: From 1400 to the Early Sixteenth Century* (Baltimore: Johns Hopkins University Press, 1994).

Holmes, George. *Florence, Rome and the Origins of the Renaissance* (Oxford: Clarendon Press, 1986).

Horrox, Rosemary. *Fifteenth-Century Attitudes: Perceptions of Society in Late Medieval England* (Cambridge: Cambridge University Press, 1994).

Huizinga, Johan. *The Autumn of the Middle Ages*. Transl. by Rodney J. Payton and Ulrich Mammitzsch (Chicago: University of Chicago Press, 1996).

Jardine, Lisa. *Worldly Goods. A New History of the Renaissance* (London: Doubleday, 1996).

Kieckhefer, Richard. *Magic in the Middle Ages* (Cambridge: Cambridge University Press, 1989).

Martines, Lauro. *Power and Imagination: City-States in Renaissance Italy* (New York: Random House, 1979).

Mazzeo, Joseph Anthony. *Renaissance and Revolution: The Remaking of European Thought* (New York: Pantheon Books, 1965).

Meiss, Millard. *Painting in Florence and Siena After the Black Death* (Princeton: Princeton University Press, 1951, 1964).

Morrall, John B. *Political Thought in Medieval Times* (Toronto: University of Toronto Press, 1980).

Nauert, Charles G., Jr. *Humanism and the Culture of Renaissance Europe* (Cambridge: Cambridge University Press, 1995).

Oakley, Francis. *The Western Church in the Later Middle Ages* (Ithaca, NY: Cornell University Press, 1982).

Pearsall, Derek. *The Life of Geoffrey Chaucer: A Critical Biography* (Oxford: Blackwell, 1995).

Swanson, R. N. *Religion and Devotion in Europe, c.1215–c.1515* (Cambridge: Cambridge University Press, 1995).

Ullmann, Walter. *Medieval Foundations of Renaissance Humanism* (Ithaca, NY: Cornell University Press, 1977).

5. From the Politics of Religion to the Religion of Politics

Aston, Trevor (ed.). *Crisis in Europe, 1560–1660* (New York: Basic Books, 1965).

Bonney, Richard. *The European Dynastic States, 1494–1660* (Oxford: Oxford University Press, 1991).

Brady, Thomas A., Jr., Heiko A. Oberman and James D. Tracy (eds.). *Handbook of European History, 1400–1600.* 2 vols. (Leiden: E. J. Brill, 1995).

Brandi, Karl. *The Emperor Charles V.* Transl. from the German by C. V. Wedgwood (London: Jonathan Cape, 1939, 1963).

Davies, R. Trevor. *The Golden Century of Spain, 1501–1621* (London: Macmillan, 1964).

Elliott, J. H. *Europe Divided, 1559–1598* (London: Collins, 1968).

Elliott, J. H. *Imperial Spain, 1469–1716* (New York: New American Library, 1966).

Evans, Robert J. W. *The Making of the Habsburg Monarchy, 1550–1700: An Interpretation* (Oxford: Clarendon Press, 1979).

Holt, Mack P. *The French Wars of Religion, 1562–1629* (Cambridge: Cambridge University Press, 1996).

Israel, Jonathan. *The Dutch Republic: Its Rise, Greatness, and Fall, 1477–1806* (Oxford: Clarendon Press, 1995).

Kamen, Henry. *Philip of Spain* (New Haven: Yale University Press, 1997).

Knecht, Robert. *The French Wars of Religion, 1559–1598* (London: Longman, 1989).

Koenigsberger, H. G., George L. Mosse and G. W. Bowler. *Europe in the Sixteenth Century.* 2nd edn. (London: Longman, 1989).

Liss, Peggy K. *Isabel the Queen. Life and Times* (Oxford: Oxford University Press, 1992).

Loades, D. M. *Politics and the Nation, 1450–1660: Obedience, Resistance and Public Order* (London: Collins, 1973).

Lockyer, Roger. *Habsburg and Bourbon Europe, 1470–1720* (London: Longman, 1974).

MacCaffrey, Wallace. *Elizabeth I* (London: Edward Arnold, 1993).

Parker, Geoffrey. *The Revolt of the Netherlands* (Ithaca, NY: Cornell University Press, 1977).

6. The 'Renaissance State'?

Baumgartner, Frederick J. *France in the Sixteenth Century* (New York: St. Martin's Press, 1995).

Bitton, Davis. *The French Nobility in Crisis: 1560–1640* (Stanford: Stanford University Press, 1969).

Downing, Brian M. *The Military Revolution and Political Change: Origins of Democracy and Autocracy in Early Modern Europe* (Princeton: Princeton University Press, 1992).

Eltis, David. *The Military Revolution in Sixteenth-Century Europe* (London: Tauris, 1995).

Elton, G. R. *The Tudor Revolution in Government* (Cambridge: Cambridge University Press, 1953).

Ertman. Thomas. *Birth of the Leviathan: Building States and Regimes in Medieval and Early Modern Europe* (Cambridge: Cambridge Uuniversity Press, 1997).

Gatrell, V. A. C., Bruce Lenman and Geoffrey Parker (eds.). *Crime and the Law: The Social History of Crime in Western Europe since 1500* (London: Europa Publications, 1980).

Hanley, Sarah. *The* Lit de Justice *of the Kings of France: Constitutional Ideology in Legend, Ritual, and Discourse* (Princeton: Princeton University Press, 1983).

Holt, Mack P. *Society and Institutions in Early Modern France: Essays in Honor of J. Russell Major* (Athens, Ga.: University of Georgia Press, 1991).

Kamen, Henry. *The Iron Century* (New York: 1972).

Keniston, Hayward. *Francisco de los Cobos, Secretary of the Emperor Charles V* (Pittsburgh: University of Pittsburgh Press, 1959).

Major, J. Russell. *From Renaissance Monarchy to Absolute Monarchy: French Kings, Nobles, and Estates* (Baltimore: Johns Hopkins University Press, 1994).

Major, J. Russell. *Representative Government in Early Modern France* (New Haven: Yale University Press, 1981).

Mattingly, Garrett. *Renaissance Diplomacy* (Boston: Houghton Mifflin, 1955).

Parker, Geoffrey. *The Military Revolution: Military Innovation and the Rise of the West, 1500–1800* (Cambridge, 1988).

Potter, David. *A History of France, 1460–1560: The Emergence of a Nation State* (London: Macmillan, 1995).

Rowen, Herbert H. *The Princes of Orange: The Stadholders in the Dutch Republic* (Cambridge: Cambridge University Press, 1988).

Starkey, David. *The English Court from the Wars of the Roses to the Civil War* (London: Longman, 1987).

Zagorin, Perez. *Rebels and Rulers, 1500–1660*. I: *Society, States, and Early Modern Revolution. Agrarian and Urban Rebellions*. II: *Provincial Rebellion. Revolutionary Civil Wars, 1560–1660* (Cambridge: Cambridge University Press, 1982).

7. The Besieged as Besieger: West European Expansion in Asia, Africa, the Americas and Slavic Europe

Bitterli, Urs. *Cultures in Conflict: Encounters Between European and Non-European Cultures, 1492–1800*. Transl. by Ritchie Robertson (Stanford: Stanford University Press, 1989).

Chaunu, Pierre. *European Expansion in the Later Middle Ages*. Transl. by Katharine Bertram (Amsterdam: North Holland, 1979).

Crummey, Robert O. *The Formation of Muscovy 1304–1613* (London: Longman, 1987).

Elliott, J. H. *The Old World and The New, 1492–1560* (Cambridge: Cambridge University Press, 1970).

Fernández-Armesto, Felipe. *Before Columbus: Exploration and Colonisation from the Mediterranean to the Atlantic, 1229–1492* (London: Macmillan, 1987).

Fernández-Armesto, Felipe. *Columbus* (Oxford: Oxford University Press, 1991).

Kirby, David. *Northern Europe in the Early Modern Period: The Baltic World 1492–1772* (London: Longman, 1990).

Martin, Janet. *Medieval Russia, 980–1584* (Cambridge: Oxford University Press, 1995).

McAlister, Lyle N. *Spain and Portugal in the New World, 1492–1700* (Minneapolis: University of Minnesota Press, 1984).

Pagden, Anthony. *European Encounters with the New World* (New Haven: Yale University Press, 1992).

Pagden, Anthony. *Lords of All the World: Ideologies of Empire in Spain, Britain and France c.1500–c.1800* (New Haven: Yale University Press, 1995).

Penrose, Boies. *Travel and Discovery in the Renaissance, 1420–1620* (Cambridge, Mass.: Harvard University Press, 1952).

Phillips, William D., Jr., and Carla Rahn Phillips, *The Worlds of Christopher Columbus* (Cambridge: Cambridge University Press, 1992).

8. The 'Long Sixteenth Century' in the Economic and Social Development of Europe

Baechler, Jean, John A. Hall and Michael Mann (eds.). *Europe and the Rise of Capitalism* (Oxford: Basil Blackwell, 1988).

Ball, J. N. *Merchants and Merchandise: The Expansion of Trade in Europe, 1500–1630* (London: Croom Helm, 1977).

Benedict, Philip (ed.). *Cities and Social Change in Early Modern France* (London: Unwin Hyman, 1989).

Benedict, Philip. *Rouen during the Wars of Religion* (Cambridge: Cambridge University Press, 1981).

Blickle, Peter. *The Revolution of 1525. The German Peasants' War from a New Perspective.* Transl. by Thomas A. Brady, Jr., and H. C. Erik Midelfort (Baltimore: Johns Hopkins University Press, 1985).

Braudel, Fernand. *Civilisation and Capitalism, 15th–18th Century.* 3 vols. (New York: Harper & Row, 1982).

Braudel, Fernand. *The Mediterranean and the Mediterranean World in the Age of Philip II* (New York: Harper & Row, 1976).

The Cambridge Economic History of Europe IV. *The Economy of Expanding Europe in the Sixteenth and Seventeenth Centuries* (Cambridge: Cambridge University Press, 1967).

Cipolla, Carlo M. *Before the Industrial Revolution: European Society and Economy, 1000–1700* (New York: W. W. Norton, 1980).

Clark, Peter (ed.). *The European Crisis of the 1590s: Essays in Comparative History* (London: George Allen & Unwin, 1985).

Davis, Ralph. *The Rise of the Atlantic Economies* (Ithaca, NY: Cornell University Press, 1973).

De Vries, Jan. *European Urbanization, 1500–1800* (Cambridge, Mass.: Harvard University Press, 1984).

Duplessis, Robert S. *Transitions to Capitalism in Early Modern Europe* (Cambridge: Cambridge University Press, 1997).

Flandrin, Jean Louis. *Families in Former Times* (Cambridge: Cambridge University Press, 1979).

Friedrichs, Christopher R. *The Early Modern City, 1450–1750* (London: Longman, 1995).

Heller, Henry. *Labour, Science, and Technology in the Age of Valois and Bourbon, 1500–1620* (Cambridge: Cambridge University Press, 1996).

Jütte, Robert. *Poverty and Deviance in Early Modern Europe* (Cambridge: Cambridge University Press, 1994).

Le Roy Ladurie, E. *The French Peasantry: 1450–1660* (Berkeley: University of California Press, 1987).

Miskimin, Harry A. *The Economy of Later Renaissance Europe, 1460–1600* (Cambridge: Cambridge University Press, 1977).

Ozment, Steven. *The Bürgermeister's Daughter: Scandal in a Sixteenth-Century German Town* (New York: St. Martin's Press, 1995).

Ozment, Steven. *Magdalena and Balthasar: An Intimate Portrait of Life in Sixteenth-Century Europe Revealed in the Letters of a Nuremberg Husband and Wife* (New Haven: Yale University Press, 1989).

Ozment, Steven. *The Reformation in the Cities: The Appeal of Protestantism to Sixteenth-Century Germany and Switzerland* (New Haven: Yale University Press, 1975).

Ozment, Steven. *When Fathers Ruled: Family Life in Reformation Europe* (Cambridge, Mass.: Harvard University Press, 1983).

Palliser, D. M. *The Age of Elizabeth: England under the later Tudors, 1547–1603*. 2nd edn. (London: Longman, 1992).

Pike, Ruth. *Aristocrats and Traders: Sevillian Society in the Sixteenth Century* (Ithaca, NY: Cornell University Press, 1972).

Scott, Tom (ed.). *The Peasantries of Europe from the Fourteenth to the Eighteenth Century* (London: Longman, 1996).

Scribner, Bob [Robert W.] (ed.). *Germany: A New Social and Economic History*. I: *1450–1630* (London: Edward Arnold, 1995).

Scribner, Bob, and Gerhard Benecke (eds.). *The German Peasant War of 1525 – New Viewpoints* (London: George Allen & Unwin, 1979).

Thirsk, Joan. *Economic Policy and Projects: The Development of a Consumer Society in Early Modern England* (Oxford: Clarendon Press, 1978).

Tracy, James D. (ed.). *The Political Economy of Merchant Empires: State Power and World Trade, 1350–1750* (Cambridge: Cambridge University Press, 1992).

Tracy, James D. (ed.). *The Rise of Merchant Empires: Long-Distance Trade in the Early Modern World, 1350–1750* (Cambridge: Cambridge University Press, 1990).

Wallerstein, Immanuel. *The Modern World System*. 2 vols (New York: Academic Press, 1980).

Wee, Herman Van der. *The Growth of the Antwerp Market and the European Economy*. 3 vols (The Hague: Nijhoff, 1963).

Wiesner, Merry. *Women and Gender in Early Modern Europe* (Cambridge: Cambridge University Press, 1993).

Youings, Joyce. *Sixteenth-Century England* (Harmondsworth: Penguin, 1984).

9. The Later Renaissance: From Classical Humanism to Vernacular Classicism

Brucker, Gene. *Florence: The Golden Age, 1138–1737* (Berkeley: University of California Press, 1998).

Chabod, Federico. *Machiavelli and the Renaissance* (Cambridge, Mass.: Harvard University Press, 1958).

Crosby, Alfred W. *The Measure of Reality: Quantification and Western Society, 1200–1600* (Cambridge University Press, 1996).

D'Amico, John F. *Renaissance Humanism in Papal Rome: Humanists and Churchmen on the Eve of the Reformation* (Baltimore: Johns Hopkins University Press, 1991).

Eisenstein, Elizabeth L. *The Printing Revolution in Early Modern Europe* (New York: Cambridge University Press, 1983).

Goodman, Anthony, and Angus MacKay (eds.). *The Impact of Humanism on Western Europe* (London: Longman, 1990).

Grafton, Anthony, and Ann Blair (eds.). *The Transmission of Culture in Early Modern Europe* (Philadelphia: University of Pennsylvania Press, 1990).

Grendler, Paul F. *Schooling in Renaissance Italy: Literacy and Learning, 1300–1600* (Baltimore: Johns Hopkins University Press, 1989).

Hale, John. *The Civilization of Europe in the Renaissance* (New York: Athenaeum, 1994).

Halkin, Léon E. *Erasmus: A Critical Biography*. Transl. by John Tonkin (Oxford: Blackwell, 1993).

Houston, R. A. *Literacy in Early Modern Europe: Culture and Education, 1500–1800* (London: Longman, 1988).

Huppert, George. *Public Schools in Renaissance France* (Urbana, Ill.: University of Illinois Press, 1984).

Jardine, Lisa. *Erasmus, Man of Letters: The Construction of Charisma in Print* (Princeton: Princeton University Press, 1993).

Laven, Peter. *Renaissance Italy, 1464–1534* (London: Methuen, 1966).

Masters, Roger D. *Machiavelli, Leonardo, and the Science of Power* (Notre Dame, Ind.: University of Notre Dame Press, 1996).

McConica, James J. *English Humanists and Reformation Politics* (Oxford: Clarendon Press, 1965).

Weiss, Roberto. *Humanism in England During the Fifteenth Century* (Oxford: Oxford University Press, 1967).

10. Antiquity and Modernity: The Religious Division of Europe in the Sixteenth Century

Bossy, John. *Christianity in the West, 1400–1700* (Oxford: Oxford University Press, 1985).

Bouwsma, William J. *John Calvin: A Sixteenth-Century Portrait* (Oxford: Oxford University Press, 1988).

Brady, Thomas. *Ruling Class, Régime and Reformation at Strasbourg, 1520–1555* (Leiden: Brill, 1978).

Brady, Thomas A., Jr. *Turning Swiss: Cities and Empire, 1450–1550* (Cambridge: Cambridge University Press, 1985).

Burke, Peter. *Popular Culture in Early Modern Europe* (New York: Harper & Row, 1978).

Davis, Natalie Zemon. *The Return of Martin Guerre* (Cambridge, Mass.: Harvard University Press, 1983).

Davis, Natalie Zemon. *Society and Culture in Early Modern France* (Stanford: Stanford University Press, 1975).

Dickens, A. G. *The English Reformation.* 2nd edn. (London: Collins, 1967).

Diefendorf, Barbara. *Beneath the Cross: Catholics and Huguenots in Sixteenth-Century Paris* (Oxford: Oxford University Press, 1991).

Edwards, John. *The Jews in Christian Europe, 1400–1700* (London: Routledge, 1988).

Ginzburg, Carlo. *The Cheese and the Worms: The Cosmos of a Sixteenth-Century Miller* (Baltimore: Johns Hopkins University Press, 1980).

Ginzburg, Carlo. *The Night Battles: Witchcraft and Agrarian Cults in the Sixteenth and Seventeenth Centuries* (Baltimore: Johns Hopkins University Press, 1992).

Greengrass, M. *The French Reformation* (Oxford: Oxford University Press, 1987).

Grell, Ole Peter, and Bob Scribner (eds.). *Tolerance and Intolerance in the European Reformation* (Cambridge: Cambridge University Press, 1996).

Greyerz, Kaspar von (ed.). *Religion and Society in Early Modern Europe* (London: George Allen & Unwin, 1984).

Haigh, Christopher. *English Reformations: Religion, Politics, and Society under the Tudors* (Oxford: Clarendon Press, 1993).

Harper-Bill, Christopher. *The Pre-Reformation Church in England 1400–1530.* Revised edn. (London: Longman, 1996).

Holborn, Hajo. *A History of Modern Germany: The Reformation* (New York: Alfred A. Knopf, 1964).

Hutton, Ronald. *The Rise and Fall of Merry England: The Ritual Year, 1400–1700* (Oxford: Oxford University Press, 1996).

Israel, Jonathan. *European Jewry in the Age of Mercantilism, 1550–1750* (Oxford: Clarendon Press, 1985).

Janelle, Pierre. *The Catholic Reformation* (Milwaukee: Bruce Publishing Company, 1963).

Kristeller, Paul Oskar. *Renaissance Thought: The Classic, Scholastic, and Humanistic Strains* (New York: Harper & Row, 1961).

Kristeller, Paul Oskar. *Renaissance Thought, II. Papers on Humanism and the Arts* (New York: Harper & Row, 1965).

Larner, Christina. *Witchcraft and Religion: The Politics of Popular Belief* (Oxford: Blackwell, 1984).

Le Roy Ladurie, Emmanuel. *Carnival: A People's Rising in Romans, 1579–1580* (New York: George Braziller, 1979).

Levack, Brian P. *The Witch-Hunt in Early Modern Europe.* 2nd edn. (London: Longman, 1994).

Marnef, Guido. *Antwerp in the Age of Reformation: Underground Protestantism in a Commercial Metropolis, 1550–1577* (Baltimore: Johns Hopkins University Press, 1996).

Moeller, Bernd. *Imperial Cities and the Reformation: Three Essays.* Ed. and trans. by H. C. Erik Midelfort and Mark U. Edwards, Jr. (Philadelphia: Fortress Press, 1972).

Muir, Edward. *Ritual in Early Modern Europe* (Cambridge: Cambridge University Press, 1993).

Mullett, Michael. *Popular Culture and Popular Protest in Late Medieval and Early Modern Europe* (London: Croom Helm, 1987).

Overfield, James H. *Humanism and Scholasticism in Late Medieval Germany* (Princeton: Princeton University Press, 1984).

Pettegree, Andrew (ed.). *The Early Reformation in Europe* (Cambridge: Cambridge University Press, 1992).

Po-chia Hsia, R. (ed.). *The German People and the Reformation* (Ithaca, NY, and London: Cornell University Press, 1988).

Po-chia Hsia, R. *The Myth of Ritual Murder: Jews and Magic in Reformation Germany* (New Haven: Yale University Press, 1988).

Roelker, Nancy Lyman. *One King, One Faith: The Parlement of Paris and the Religious Reformations of the Sixteenth Century* (Berkeley: University of California Press, 1996).

Rummel, Erika. *The Humanist–Scholastic Debate in the Renaissance and Reformation* (Cambridge, Mass.: Harvard University Press, 1995).

Strauss, Gerald. *Law, Resistance, and the State: The Opposition to Roman Law in Reformation Germany* (Princeton: Princeton University Press, 1986).

Strauss, Gerald. *Luther's House of Learning* (Baltimore: Johns Hopkins University Press, 1978).

Strauss, Gerald (ed.), *Manifestations of Discontent in Germany on the Eve of the Reformation* (Bloomington, Ind.: Indiana University Press, 1971).

Strauss, Gerald. *Nuremberg in the Sixteenth Century* (New York: John Wiley, 1966).

Strauss, Gerald (ed.). *Pre-Reformation Germany* (London: Macmillan, 1972).

Williams, George H. *The Radical Reformation* (Philadelphia: Westminster Press, 1962).

Wunderli, Richard, *Peasant Fires: The Drummer of Niklashausen* (Bloomington, Ind.: Indiana University Press, 1992).

Index

Acciaiuoli family, 111
accounting, 78, 79, 153, 255
Aden, 265
Adrian IV, pope, 183, 386
Adrianople, 48
Africa and Africans, 7, 84, 95, 108, 119–21,
    171–2, 174, 215, 258–9, 261–6, 270–2,
    279, 304, 430, 437
Agincourt, battle of, 29, 141, 144
Agricola, Rudolf, 354
agriculture, 91–8, 103, 107–8, 274, 315,
    320–7, 437
Ahmed I, sultan, 280
aides, see taxation
Ailly, Pierre d', 262
Aix-en-Provence, 135, 241, 243
Albania, 49
Albert Alcibiades, margrave of
    Brandenburg-Kulmbach, 189, 191
Albert of Brandenburg, 51
Albert of Habsburg, emperor, 41
Alberti, Leon Battista, 153, 155, 160–1
Albrecht of Hohenzollern, 287
Albret, Jeanne d', 237
alcabala, 67, 75, 249–251; see also taxation
Alcalá, 356
Alcantara, order of, 37
Alcazar, battle of, 280
Aldine Press, see Manutius, Aldus
Alençon, Francis, duke of, 198, 209
Aleppo, 266
Alexander III, king of Scotland, 17
Alexander VI, pope, 44, 173, 177, 272, 344,
    379, 381, 384
Alfonso V 'the Magnanimous', king of
    Aragon, 37, 44, 75, 97, 170
Alfonso X, king of Castile, 91; Alfonso XI,
    37, 67, 76, 187
Alfonso da Cartagena, 363–4
Allen, William, 402

Alpujarras, 215
Alsace, 173, 191
Alva, Fernando Alvarez de Toledo, duke of,
    196, 204–206, 413
ambassadors, see embassies
Amboise, 394
Americas, 7–8, 84, 108, 119, 204, 206, 215,
    217, 249, 251, 258–9, 262, 264, 266–8,
    271–2, 274–7, 288, 295–6, 304–5,
    315–16, 348, 386, 429–31, 437
Amiens, 299
Amsterdam, 109, 202, 205, 218, 257, 261,
    297, 310, 331, 371, 424, 435
Anabaptism, 191, 203–4, 300, 332, 391,
    396–7, 408, 410, 413–5, 438
Anatolia, 49, 266
Andalusia, 37, 120, 171
Angers, 239, 356
Anglican church, 414, 434, 438
Anjou, and dukes of, 22, 26, 29, 36, 47,
    125, 176, 196, 198–9, 209, 211
Ankara, 48
Anne, of Austria, 436; of Beaujeu, 176; of
    Bohemia, queen of England, 40, 132; of
    Brittany, 176, 237; of Cleves, queen of
    England, 188; of Hungary, 184
Antwerp, 109, 111, 189, 203–7, 261,
    274–6, 291–7, 300–2, 307, 310–11,
    362, 366–7, 370, 424
apanages, 25–6, 33, 61, 76, 239
apprenticeship, 87, 99, 330, 331
Aquitaine, 15–6, 18, 23
Arabic and Arabs, 120, 172, 215, 263, 344,
    379
Aragon, 2, 5–7, 36–7, 43, 66–8, 75, 82,
    115, 120–1, 169–70, 172–3, 176–7,
    181, 184, 215–16, 219–23, 243, 248–9,
    252–3, 263, 269, 344, 378–9, 429; see
    also Spain
Arande, Michel d', 394

architecture, 159–64, 237, 345, 345–6, 371–2
Aretino, Pietro, 376, 422
argenterie, 72, 236
aristocracy, *see* nobility
Aristotle, Aristotelianism, 5,126–7, 133, 155, 159, 273, 343, 348, 352, 354–5, 359, 363, 366, 375
Armada, Spanish, 211, 215
Armagnac, Bernard VII, count of, and faction, 28, 30
Arminians, 435
Arras, peace of (1435), 32; treaty of (1482), 176; Union of (1579), 207
art, *see* architecture, painting, sculpture
Artois, 19, 27, 176, 184, 188, 202
Ascham, Roger, 337, 358
Asia, 7, 8, 84, 108, 119–20, 258–9, 262–76, 288, 295, 304, 348, 429–30, 434, 437
Asia Minor, 47–8, 271
Askew, Anne, 400
assemblies, representative, *see* Cortes, Estates-General, Parliament
astrology, 123
astronomy, 347, 430
Athens, 45, 151
Atlantic, 7, 9, 36–7, 47, 108, 120–1, 172, 263, 265, 268, 274, 293–4, 429
Augsburg, 100, 146, 180, 185–6, 291, 295, 310, 320, 325, 328, 337, 391; Confession of, 188–9, 383, 391; Diet of, 391; Interim of, 190; Peace of (1555), 191, 216, 410–1, 435
Augustine, St, and Augustinianism, 126, 133, 157, 359
Austria, 2, 39–41, 181, 184–5, 206, 218, 227, 253, 255, 272, 314, 323, 362, 407–8, 432, 436
Auvergne, 237
Avignon, 25, 110, 113, 125–9, 150, 378
Avila, St Teresa of, 407
Avis dynasty, 23
Azores, 121, 261
Aztecs, 267, 273, 304

Bacon, Francis, 431
Bahrein, 265
Balboa, Vasco de, 267–8
Balkans, 8, 48–9, 186, 255, 258, 277, 295, 408, 424, 439
Balliol, Edward and John, 17, 19, 21
Baltic, 7–8, 47, 50, 109–11, 271, 273, 277, 281, 283, 287, 293, 295, 297, 300, 303–4, 323, 429
Baltimore, George Calvert, Lord, 430
banking, 46, 62, 112, 161, 180, 183, 209, 264, 294, 296, 307–11, 381, 390, 423
Bannockburn, battle of, 18
Barcelona, 36, 98, 110, 113, 249
Bardi, banking family of Florence, 111

Bari, 128
Barnet, battle of, 174
Baron, Hans, 158
Bartolus of Sassoferrato, 126
Barzizza, Gasparino, 153
Basel, 173, 309, 314, 325, 390, 397, 411, 415; Council of, 128–9, 384
Basil I and II, grand dukes of Moscow, 51
Batory, Stefan, 286
Battista of Verona, 354
Bavaria, 26, 32, 40, 223, 256, 277, 410
Bayezid I, sultan, 48; Bayezid II, 277, 279
Beaufort family, 33; Edmund, 174; John, 174; Margaret, 175
Beda, Noel, 56
Bedford, John duke of, 30, 32
Beguines, 131, 337
Behaim, Martin, 263, 268
Belgrade, 279
Bellini, Gentile, 164, 345, 347; Giovanni, 164
Bembo, Pietro, 376
Bergen (Norway), 109
Bergen-op-Zoom (Netherlands), 111
Bern, 41, 173, 390
Berry, 26, 139
Berwick, Treaty of, 21
Bessarion, 155
bill of exchange, 111–12, 251, 307–8, 310; *see also* commerce, techniques of
Biondo, Flavio, 148
bishoprics, 64, 67, 203, 227, 247, 256, 299
Black Death, *see* plagues
Black Prince, *see* Edward the Black Prince
Black Sea, 287
Blois, 199, 372
Boccaccio, Giovanni, 143, 150–1, 163, 376
Bodin, Jean, 198, 304, 414
Bohemia, 5, 40–1, 47–8, 68, 111, 128, 132–3, 180, 184, 220, 255, 271, 386–95, 407–9, 423, 435–6
Bojador, Cape, 121
Boleyn, Anne, 187, 193, 219
Bolivia, 304
Bologna, 184, 352; Concordat of, 177, 384–5
Boniface VIII, pope, 61, 90, 125–6, 129, 183, 348
Bordeaux, 15–6, 32, 73, 125, 135, 241, 291, 294, 299, 372
Borgia, Cesare, 344, 346, 349–50, 379; Lucrezia, 344
Borromeo, Carlo, 406
Bosworth, battle of, 175
Bothwell, James Hepburn, earl of 208
Botticelli, Sandro, 344
Boucher, Jean, 199
Boulogne, 189–90
Bourbon family, 176, 184, 195–6, 237, 306, 412; Antoine de, 195, 239; Charles, 184

Bourchier, Robert, 124
Bourges, 30, 135, 240, 397
Bouvat, Honoré de, 141
Brabant, 16–7, 19, 32, 68, 74, 139, 170, 173, 200, 206–7, 209–10, 292, 296, 297
Bracton, Henry, 55
Braganza, duke of, 432
Bramante, Donato, 344–5
Brandenburg, 39–40, 51, 189, 223, 227
Brazil, 265–6, 275–6, 432, 434
Bremen, 303
Brès, Guy de, 204
Bresse, 294
Brethren, Bohemian, 23, 46; of the Common Life, 352, 359
Brétigny, treaty of, 23, 46, 89
Briçonnet, Guillaume, 394
Bridewell, 330
Brill, 205
Bristol, 132, 317, 319
Brittany, 21, 29, 36, 145, 176, 239, 241
Broederlam, Melchior, 139
Bruce, Robert, 17–19; David, *see* David II, King of Scotland
Brueghel, Pieter, 351
Bruges, 16, 19, 68, 90, 99, 102, 107, 109–12, 120, 139, 142, 161, 274, 291, 293, 295, 351
Brunelleschi, Filippo, 161, 163
Bruni, Leonardo, 151–2, 158–9, 161, 349, 353, 363
Brunswick, 43
Brussels, 139, 191, 200, 202, 204, 207, 212, 219, 292, 359
Bucer, Martin, 192, 334, 400
Buckingham, George Villiers, duke of, 433
Buda, 135
Budé, Guillaume, 371–2
Bugenhagen, Johann, 388
bullion, 7–8, 85, 112, 172, 206, 215, 217, 244, 251, 273–4, 276–7, 281, 288, 294–7, 303–11, 315–16, 320, 347, 400, 427–31, 436–7; *see also* coinage
Buonsignori bank, 111
Burckhardt, Jacob, 162
bureaucracy, 3–4, 7, 9, 54, 76, 81, 84, 89, 124, 213–17, 251–7, 300, 418, 427–9, 437; *see also* government,
Burghley, William Cecil, baron, 207–8, 210, 228, 231, 237, 338, 358
Burgos, 294, 363
Burgundy, Burgundian state, 15, 26–30, 32, 36, 41, 44, 48, 60, 63, 68, 73–4, 81, 94, 122–3, 139–40, 144–5, 170, 173–84, 196, 200, 202–3, 216, 223, 230, 237, 239, 241, 245, 296, 298, 301, 315, 356, 359
Byrd, William, 213, 373
Byzantine Empire, 47–9, 51, 81, 120, 122, 135, 159–60, 271, 286, 345, 408

Cabbala, 383–4
Cabochien Ordinance, 77
Cabot, John and Sebastian, 276
Cabral, Pedro, 265
Cade, Jack, rebellion of, 32, 174
Cadiz, 120, 211, 294
Caen, 135
Calais, 21–2, 32, 90, 99, 180, 193
Calatrava, order of, 37
Calcutta, 265
Calvin, John, and Calvinism, 6, 11, 43, 191–9, 202–9, 212, 214, 224, 233, 305–7, 331–5, 382, 388–91, 394, 397–412, 414–15, 423–4, 435–8
Cambrai, 199, 359; League of, 177; Peace of, 184
Cambridge, 135, 358, 373, 400
Canary Islands, 121, 261–3, 270, 272, 275
Canisius, Peter, 406
Canterbury, 97, 193, 231, 381, 401, 434
Capetian dynasty, 18, 33, 60
capital and capitalism, 4–5, 9, 85–8, 92, 103, 109–10, 120, 122, 125, 161–2, 261, 275–6, 296, 299–322, 424, 429
capitals, 8, 218, 298, 300
Capuchins, 392, 407
Carafa, Gian Pietro, *see* Paul IV, Pope
cardinals, college of, 25, 128, 183, 193, 196, 200, 230, 344, 358, 361, 378–80, 385, 403, 435
Caribbean, 262, 269, 277, 304
Carinthia, 310
carnivals, 381, 417–19
Carranza, Bartolomé de, 211
Cartier, Jacques, 276
cartography, 262–8
Casa da India, 275
Casa de Contratación de las Indias, 273–6, 294, 316
Casa di San Giorgio, 309–10
Casas, Bartolomé de las, 272
Casimir III 'the Great', king of Poland, 50; Casimir IV, 50, 287
Caspe, Compromise of, 37
Caspian Sea, 287
Castellio, Sebastian, 411, 415
Castiglione, Baldassare, 154, 231, 338, 376
Castile, 2, 4, 6–8, 23–4, 26, 35–8, 66–8, 75–7, 80, 84, 91, 96, 114, 117, 120–2, 145, 169–72, 177, 180, 182–4, 206, 213–16, 218, 221–4, 226, 247–53, 261–3, 265–9, 271–5, 291, 293–4, 296, 305, 315, 320, 326, 342, 363–4, 366, 386, 431–2, 434; *see also* Spain
Catalonia, 36, 66, 75, 82, 97, 110, 120, 214, 248–9, 253, 432, 436
Cateau-Cambrésis, peace of, 193, 208
catechisms, 371, 406, 413, 416, 425
Catherine of Aragon, 177, 181, 187, 192, 219, 399

Catherine of Siena, St, 131
Catherine of Valois, 29–30
Catholic League, French, 198–9, 202, 210;
    German, 188
Cavalcanti, Giovanni, 349
Caxton, William, 366
Cecil, William, *see* Burghley
Celtis, Conrad, 353, 354
censorship, 214, 217, 221, 394, 421–2; *see
    also* Index
Centurione family, 262
Cerdagne, 170, 176
Cervantes, Miguel de, 431
Ceuta, 7, 121
Chamber, 71–2, 74, 230, 236
Chambre des Comptes (Chamber of
    Accounts), 72, 74–5, 236, 243
Chambre-aux-Deniers, 72, 236
Champagne, 16, 76, 108, 110, 189, 293
chancellor, 72, 75, 124, 227, 235–6, 252,
    349, 358, 391
Chancellor, Richard, 276, 286
chancery, 70–2, 141, 231, 252, 256
chantries, 329, 400
charity, *see* poverty
Charlemagne, 60, 140, 216, 240
Charles I, king of England, 230–1, 430,
    433–4
Charles IV, emperor, 18, 40, 135; Charles
    V, 7, 180–94, 200, 202–4, 215–16,
    219–20, 223, 225–6, 244, 246, 248–9,
    250–2, 255, 268–9, 272, 279, 282–3,
    296, 305, 310, 326, 328, 337, 342, 362,
    366, 379, 387–8, 391–2, 394–5, 400,
    403, 407, 423
Charles IV, king of France, 18; Charles V,
    21–6, 28, 33, 61, 65, 128, 138–9, 140,
    145; Charles VI, 25–6, 28–30, 63, 123,
    140; Charles VII, 30, 32, 35, 44, 65, 80,
    135, 173, 240, 244; Charles VIII, 44,
    175–7, 237, 244; Charles IX, 198, 208,
    241, 245, 286, 314, 329
Charles IX, king of Sweden, 286
Charles, duke of Anjou, 43, 47
Charles of Austria, Archduke, 208
Charles of Blois, 21
Charles the Bold, duke of Burgundy, 41, 44,
    145, 173, 176
Chartier, Jean, 145
Chartres, 30
Chastellain, Georges, 145–6
Châteaubriant, Edict of, 394
Chaucer, Geoffrey, 131, 140–143, 151
Chile, 268, 269
China, 33, 93, 119, 165, 264, 275
chivalry, 157, 362, 365
Christian II, king of Denmark, 181, 282–3,
    388; Christian III, 283, 388; Christian
    IV, 433, 435
Christine de Pisan, 139, 145

Chrysoloras, Manuel, 135, 154
Cicero, 6, 10, 127, 150, 152–3, 155, 157–9,
    161–2, 344, 348, 353, 361, 363, 365,
    375, 381
Cino of Pistoia, 126
Ciompi rebellion, 106–7
Cisneros, Francisco Jiménez de, 172, 180,
    361, 393
cities, 2, 4, 8, 11, 25, 33–7, 43–8, 50, 53,
    55, 57, 65–8, 75–7, 79–80, 82, 84,
    88–9, 91–3, 95, 97–110, 113–15, 117,
    127, 139–40, 142, 146, 153, 157–8,
    170, 173, 183, 185–6, 188, 190, 194–7,
    203, 205–6, 209, 219–20, 233, 244,
    246–8, 250, 255, 257, 268, 271, 281–2,
    286, 290–6, 306–7, 309–28, 334, 340,
    345, 347, 366, 370, 428–9
Clarence, George duke of, 174, 175; Lionel
    duke of, 28, 143
class, *see* status
Clement VII, pope, 181, 184, 187, 279,
    379; antipope, 27, 125, 128
climate, 91–2, 94, 429
Cobos, Francisco de los, 237, 246, 252–3
Cognac, League of, 184
coinage, 5, 7, 61, 85–90, 109–12, 122, 172,
    189, 232, 245, 304, 324, 347
Colet, John 357, 360
Coligny, Gaspard de, 190, 195–6, 276
colleges, 135, 356–8, 368–9, 400, 406; *see
    also* universities
Cologne, 40, 98, 110, 131, 135, 138, 146,
    291, 295, 302, 314, 352, 383, 389, 421;
    Diet of, 255
Colombe, Jean, 139
colonies, 7–8, 100, 119, 121, 185, 217–58,
    273, 294, 296, 302, 316, 429–30,
    439
Columbus, Christopher, 7, 262–7, 271
commerce, techniques of, 9, 107–13, 120,
    275–7, 290, 293, 346–7, 362; *see also*
    trade
Commines, Philippe de, 145
companies, organization of, 275–7, 308–10,
    317, 429
comuneros, 182–4, 250, 326
Condé, Louis prince of, 195–6; Henry of,
    197
confessions, *see* catechisms
confraternities, 105, 162, 318, 328, 380,
    391
conquistadores, 267–8
consistories, 212, 257, 398–9
constable, 75, 184, 190, 195, 235, 236
Constance, council of, 11, 128–9, 132
Constantinople, 47–9, 51, 154, 286, 343
Contarini, Gasparo, 379, 383, 392
conversos, 38, 171–2, 182, 214, 248, 315,
    363, 366, 393, 421
Coornhaert, Dirck, 414–15

Copernicus, Nicholas, 348
copper, trade in, 295, 302, 310
copyhold tenure, 97–8, 323
Cordoba, 364
Corfu, 186
Cornwall, 231
Coronado, Francisco Vásquez de, 277
corregidores, 183, 250, 298
Cortes, 66–8, 75–7, 115, 171, 182–3, 224, 226, 247–51, 315, 328, 432
Cortez, Hernan, 267
Corts, 66, 243, 249
Corvinus, Matthias, 350
cotton, 7, 102, 268, 320
Coucy, Enguerrand de, 27
Council of Troubles, 204
councils, church, 127–9, 132–4, 154, 186, 190–1, 378, 403, 406–7; city, 4, 8, 78, 99–100, 118, 188, 298–300, 317–18, 370, 390–1, 396, 410–11; royal, 53–4, 57, 64, 70–4, 80, 115, 124, 172, 195, 202–3, 208, 211–15, 229, 231, 234–7, 240–1, 246, 248, 252–3, 255, 282, 342
Counter-Reformation, 214, 317, 369, 391, 398, 402–8, 414–15, 423
courts, church, 124, 412, 414; royal, 2, 3, 29, 53–4, 65, 69–74, 97, 116, 124, 162, 173–4, 182, 191, 200, 224, 229, 231, 235–7, 243, 255–6, 436
Courtrai, battle of, 62
Coventry, 132
Cranmer, Thomas, 193, 381
Crécy, battle of, 21–2, 39, 63
credit, 67, 97, 110–11, 215, 301, 428, 429
Crépy, Peace of, 189
Crete, 120
Cromwell, Thomas, 188, 227, 230, 237, 358, 381, 399–400
Croquants, 200, 327
Crosby, Alfred, 347
crusades, 27, 47, 49, 55, 240, 272, 279
Cruz, Isabel de la, 393
Cuba, 263–4
custom, *see* law
Cyprus, 120, 280

Dante Alighieri, 126, 143, 149–51, 160, 163, 376
Darnley, Henry Stuart, lord, 208
Datini, Francesco, 113, 306
Dauphiné, 76, 241, 418
David II, king of Scotland, 19, 21
de la Pole family, 116; Michael, 24
Decembrio, Uberto, 158
Della Scala family, 44
demography, 4–5, 8, 84–5, 88, 91–8, 103, 107, 109, 117, 121–2, 194, 245, 274, 290–8, 301, 303, 307, 314, 318–19, 322–3, 327–32, 366, 384, 424, 428, 430, 434–5, 437

Denmark, 93, 110, 181, 223, 281–3, 287, 289, 323, 363, 388, 395, 427, 433–5
Descartes, René, 431
Deschamps, Eustache, 144
Deventer, 353–4
Devon, 231
Dias, Bartolomeu, 263, 265
Dijon, 73–4, 104, 139, 241, 243, 301
diplomacy, techniques of, 143, 218–20, 375
divorce, 117, 333
domain, royal, 3, 25, 33, 54–5, 60–1, 64, 71, 73–4, 76, 80, 89, 185, 228, 233, 237, 240–1, 243, 247, 249, 298
domestic service, 335–6
Dominican order, 38, 130–1, 154, 176, 199, 272, 383, 387
Donatello, 159
Donatus, 6, 153
Dordrecht, 205; synod of, 435
Doria, Andrea, 186
Douai, 16, 402
dowry, 18, 117–18, 130, 177, 309, 321, 334
Drake, Francis, 211, 277
drama, 141, 374–5
Dudley, Guilford, 192; John, 190; Robert, *see* Leicester
Duguesclin, Bertrand, 23
Duns Scotus, 133–4
Duplessis de Mornay, Philippe, 198
Dupplin Moor, battle of, 19
Duprat, Antoine, 235
Durazzo, 279
Dürer, Albrecht, 351
Dutch, Dutch Republic, *see* Netherlands

East Anglia, 314
East India Company, Dutch, 275, 434; English, 275, 309, 430
Eastern Orthodox church, 51, 271
Eastland Company, 277
Eck, Johann, 387
Eckhart, 131
economy, 4, 8–9, 15, 80, 85–122, 234, 275, 288, 290–342, 428, 436
Ecuador, 268
Edict of Restitution, 435
Edmund of Langley, 22
education, 6, 10, 77, 80, 134–8, 148–65, 219, 334–5, 342–8, 351–2, 355–8, 361, 368, 372–4, 430, 437–8
Edward I, king of England, 16–8, 34, 55–7, 90, 116, 125, 221, 228, 434; Edward II, 17–18, 58–9; Edward III, 15, 18–19, 21–4, 27–8, 32, 34, 57, 59, 67, 71, 90, 111, 116, 129, 138, 141, 143, 174, 229; Edward IV, 33, 60, 173–5, 228, 230–2, 400, 434; Edward V, 175; Edward VI, 189–90, 192, 228, 232, 330, 371, 400–1; Edward the 'Black Prince', 22–4, 35, 140; Edward, son of Henry VI, 174

Egypt, 120, 279, 347
Elbing, 409
Eleanor of Aquitaine, 15
Eleanore, sister of Charles V, 184
Eliot, John, 433
Elizabeth I, queen of England, 61, 124, 187, 190, 192–4, 198, 207–13, 222, 228–37, 243, 277, 295, 332, 338–9, 358, 373, 395, 399, 401–2, 417, 420, 432–3; Elizabeth, sister of Charles V, 181; Elizabeth of York, 175
Elton, Geoffrey, 227
élus, 80, 245
embassies and ambassadors, 218–20, 236, 319
Emden, 205, 296, 390
Empire, Holy Roman, and emperors, 5–7, 39–44, 67, 100, 124–8, 134–5, 140, 173, 175–7, 180–6, 188, 190–1, 193–4, 216, 218, 220, 223–4, 226, 252–7, 272, 279–80, 291, 306, 310, 318, 403, 407–10, 423, 427, 436–8
enclosures, 95, 165, 190, 323–4, 358
England, 1–9, 15, 18–19, 21–2, 25–30, 32–6, 38, 46, 50–1, 53–9, 61–71, 73–7, 80–4, 86–7, 90, 93–4, 96–9, 102, 104, 106, 108–10, 112, 114–17, 122, 124–6, 128–9, 134–5, 138, 140–8, 155, 165, 169, 173–7, 180–1, 184, 187–94, 198, 204, 207, 210, 214–21, 223–5, 227–37, 240, 243–4, 247, 249–51, 256, 258, 266, 271–2, 275–7, 280–1, 286, 291, 293, 295–6, 298, 300, 302, 304–5, 308–9, 314, 316, 318–21, 323–6, 328–9, 332, 334–5, 337–42, 348, 356–7, 360, 362, 365–6, 370–1, 373, 378, 380, 384–7, 389–90, 393, 395, 398–9, 413–14, 419–20, 423, 427, 429–30, 432, 434–8
Erasmus, Desiderius, 9, 155–7, 353–4, 356, 358–62, 366, 371, 384, 392, 395, 403, 411
Erfurt, 135, 352
Eric III, king of Norway, 17
Erik XIV, king of Sweden, 283
espionage, 219–21, 373, 394
Esplechin, truce of, 21
Essex, 231; earl of, 314
Estates, 50, 58, 66–8, 75–6, 114, 282–3, 286, 298, 328; Estates-General, 3, 44, 61–6, 68, 71, 75, 106, 176, 198, 199, 220, 224, 240, 242–5, 338
Este family, 44, 220, 338; Borso d', 44
Estonia, 47, 288
Eugenius IV, pope, 129
Evangelical, *see* Lutheranism
exchange, 111–12, 274, 304, 309–10, 321
Exchequer, English, 3, 70–1, 74, 174, 230; Norman, 73

exploration and colonization, 7–8, 119–22, 170–2, 217, 247, 259–89

fairs, 108, 110–12, 183, 293–5, 301, 302, 351
Falkirk, battle of, 17
families, 117–19, 293, 308, 321, 330, 332–9
famine, 92–4, 110, 327, 429
Farel, Guillaume, 394
Farnese, Alessandro, *see* Paul III, pope; Alexander, *see* Parma, duke of; Pier Luigi, 190
Feltre, Vittorino da, 153, 379
Ferdinand I, emperor, 171, 191, 255, 279–80, 407–9; Ferdinand II, 435–6,
Ferdinand II, king of Aragon, 2, 37, 44, 170–4, 176–7, 180, 183–4, 186, 191, 208, 215, 219, 247, 251, 263, 279, 315, 364, 385–6, 393
Ferrante, king of Naples, 170, 176
Ferrara, 43–4, 46, 129, 153–4, 354
Ferrer, St Vincente, 38
festivals, 60, 140, 142, 307, 416–17
feudal relations, 2, 15–8, 21–2, 34, 39, 46, 54–7, 61–2, 69–70, 82, 89, 228, 236–7, 240, 287, 341
Fibonacci, Leonardo, 153
Ficino, Marsiglio, 159, 343, 360
Filelfo, Francesco, 353
finance, 9, 61, 70–1, 74–7, 79, 90, 111, 170, 172, 174, 181, 185–6, 189, 222–3, 243, 245, 249, 251
Finland, 283
Fisher, John, 358
Flanders, 16–19, 21–2, 25, 27, 29, 32, 36, 62–3, 68, 74, 77, 79, 90–1, 102, 106, 109–12, 114, 124, 139, 142, 145, 170, 172, 182–4, 188, 193, 199, 202–4, 206–7, 209–12, 214, 223, 281, 292, 295–8, 314, 348, 351, 363, 385
Florence, 26, 45–6, 78–9, 98, 100, 104–7, 111–14, 129, 131, 135, 149–52, 154–5, 157–9, 161–3, 176, 181, 220, 266, 275, 291, 294, 297, 300, 306, 334, 343–6, 350, 360, 365, 375, 381
Florida, 276–7, 430
Flote, Pierre, 83
Flushing, 205
France, 1–9, 15–19, 23–6, 28–30, 33, 35–8, 40, 43, 45–6, 48, 50–1, 53–6, 59–69, 71–81, 84, 93–4, 96, 99, 106, 108–9, 112, 114–17, 121–6, 128–9, 134–5, 138–45, 148–50, 155, 170, 173–7, 180–4, 186–200, 202, 204, 207–14, 216–30, 232, 234–52, 255–6, 272–3, 276, 282, 288, 290, 292, 294–6, 298–300, 302, 304–7, 311, 314–22, 324, 326, 328–9, 334, 337–42, 345–50, 352, 356–60, 362–3, 366, 368–72, 376, 378, 380, 384–6, 390–5, 398–9, 406–7,

410, 412, 414, 418–20, 422–4, 427–8, 430–8

Francesca, Piero della, 344

Franche Comté, 176

Francis I, king of France, 177, 180, 182–91, 200, 202, 219, 223, 227, 235–7, 241, 244, 246, 249, 276, 279, 283, 317, 326, 328, 341, 346, 350, 356, 371–2, 381, 385, 394–5; Francis II, 190, 192, 194–5, 197, 208, 329

Franciscan order, 126, 130, 134, 273, 324, 393, 407, 423

Franconia, 325

Frankfurt-am-Main, 111, 295, 300–2, 309, 325, 337, 351, 384, 424

fraternities, see confraternities

Fraticelli, 130

Frederick II, emperor, 36, 38–9; Frederick III, 44, 173, 353; Frederick I, king of Denmark, 283, 388; Frederick, elector of Saxony, 387; Frederick, Elector Palatine, 435

Friedberg, 256

Friesland, 396

Friuli, 68, 415

Froissart, Jean, 35, 140, 144–6, 152

Fronde, 432, 436

Fugger family and bank, 180, 185, 308, 268, 310–11; Anton, 310; Hans, 310; Jacob, 100, 103; Jacob the Rich, 310

fustian, 102, 320

Gaismair, Michael, 324, 326

Galen, 347, 357

Gallican church, 129, 199, 384, 412

Gama, Vasco da, 264, 265

Gardiner, Stephen, 400

Garter, Order of the, 140

Gascony, 2, 15, 16, 18–19, 22, 24, 30, 32, 33, 63, 76, 174, 211, 241, 294

Gattinara, Mercurio de, 246

Gdánsk, 282, 291, 303, 409

Gelderland, 205

Generalitat of Catalonia, 75, 97, 249–50

Geneva, 195, 294, 335, 394, 398–9, 401, 411

Genghis Khan, 48

Genoa, 27, 36, 45, 93, 98, 110, 112–13, 120, 172, 177, 184, 186, 251, 262, 264, 275, 302, 309, 310, 315

gentry, 15, 77, 98, 233, 338, 341

Germanía, 183

Germany, 2–5, 26, 38–40, 43, 46, 49, 53, 63, 67–9, 77–9, 82, 90–1, 93–6, 99, 102–3, 108–10, 112, 116, 119, 122, 124–6, 135, 141, 146, 148, 155, 172, 180, 182–3, 185, 187–9, 191–2, 194, 202, 204, 216, 219–20, 223–7, 251, 255–6, 271, 275, 279, 281, 290, 293–8, 302–3, 308, 310, 315, 320–1, 323–8,

334, 348, 350–7, 362–4, 366–8, 370, 378–80, 382–3, 385, 387–92, 394–8, 403, 406–10, 413, 418–22, 424, 427, 429, 431–8

Gerson, Jean, 139

Ghent, 16, 19, 25, 68, 79, 98, 100, 107, 139, 173, 188, 207, 291; Pacification of, 206

ghetto, 423

Ghibellines, 43, 78

Gibraltar, 93, 110, 293

Giles of Rome, 126

Giorgione, 345

Giovio, Paolo, 375

Gloucester, 329; dukes of, 24, 30; Humphrey duke of, 32; Richard duke of, *see* Richard III

Goa, 265–6

Gold Coast, 262

Golden Bull, 40

Golden Fleece, Order of the, 140

Gonzaga, Francesco, cardinal, 379; Ludovico, marquis of Mantua, 158, 379

Good Hope, Cape of, 7, 263–5

Gothic style, 148, 160, 272, 364

Göttingen, 43

Gouda, 359

government, institutions of, 3–4, 53–84, 89, 99, 105, 107, 112, 115–16, 170–7, 181, 183, 188, 217–58, 268–9, 275–7, 298–9, 326–7, 368–9, 389, 412, 427

Gower, John, 140, 143

grain trade and prices, 8, 50, 85, 88, 93–6, 102–3, 107, 109–12, 121, 262, 281, 290, 295, 302, 305, 307, 309, 320, 330, 340, 429

Granada, 36–7, 98, 122, 170, 172, 215, 223, 251, 263, 315, 364, 385

Grand Ordinance, 64

Grand Parti of Lyon, 245

Grand Rebeyne of Lyon, 302

Granvelle, Antoine Perrenot de, 203

Great Schism, 25, 128–9, 280

Greece, 48

Greek, language and immigrants, 6, 9, 47, 49, 133, 135, 142, 148, 151–2, 154–6, 160, 163, 187, 262, 343–4, 347, 350, 352, 355–8, 360, 363, 366, 369, 371–2, 376, 379, 382–384, 393, 430, 437; Orthodox church, 47, 49

Gregory XI, pope, 26, 125, 128

Grenoble, 241, 243, 369, 418

Grey, Lady Jane, 192

Grocyn, William, 354, 357

Groningen, 354

Guarino of Verona, 153, 354

Gudonov, Boris, 287

Guelfs, 43, 78

Guérin, Antoine, 418–19

Guicciardini, Francesco, 371, 375

guilds, 77–8, 88, 91, 97, 99–100, 102, 105, 107, 118, 134, 142, 162–3, 188, 206, 226, 299, 301–3, 307, 316–19, 329, 331, 335, 337, 344, 358, 370, 389–90, 400, 429
Guines, 22
Guise family, 190, 195–6, 199, 236, 306; Charles of, 200; Charles of, cardinal of Lorraine, 196; Francis duke of, 196; Henry of, 199
Gustavus Adolphus, king of Sweden, 246, 286, 435
Gutenberg, Johannes, 364–5
Guy of Dampierre, count of Flanders, 16

Haarlem, 139, 206, 297, 320
Habsburg dynasty, 2, 7, 39–41, 47, 135, 170, 173, 176, 180, 184–186, 192, 202, 205, 209, 212, 216, 218–20, 223, 255, 272, 279–80, 282–3, 310–11, 322, 324, 365, 389, 407–9, 432, 435–6, 438; Archduke Albert of, 212
Hague, The, 218, 257
Hainault, 19, 21, 26, 32, 40, 145
Halidon Hill, battle of, 19
Hamburg, 296, 303, 424
Hanse, 47, 90, 95, 109–11, 281, 286, 295, 302, 309
Harfleur, 29
Hawkins, John, 211
Hebrew, 355–6, 358, 360, 382–4, 422
Hegius, Alexander, 354
Heidelberg, 135, 185, 352, 354, 409; Heidelberg Catechism, 365
Heilbronn, 325
Helvetic Confession, First, 390
Henrietta Maria, queen of England, 433
Henry I, king of England, 15; Henry II, 15, 54; Henry III, 15–6, 56; Henry IV, 24, 27–8, 60; Henry V, 28–9, 30, 32, 138, 141, 144, 174, 228; Henry VI, 30, 32, 60, 138, 144, 174, 228; Henry VII, 55, 60, 174–7, 180–2, 187–90, 192, 208, 228–32, 276, 400; Henry VIII, 6, 60, 175, 177, 180–2, 188–90, 192, 200, 211, 219, 221–2, 227–33, 235, 246–7, 249, 304, 324, 339, 348, 350, 358, 362, 373, 379–81, 386, 393–4, 399–401
Henry II, king of Castile, 23, 37; Henry III, 23; Henry IV, 170–1
Henry II, king of France, 181, 190–1, 193, 237, 241–2, 245, 276, 372, 393–5; Henry III, 8, 198–9, 210, 235, 237, 286–7; Henry IV, 196–200, 209, 211, 276, 327, 393, 407, 431
Henry of Anjou, king of Poland, *see* Henry III, king of France
Henry of Derby, *see* Henry IV, king of England
Henry of Nassau, 202

Henry of Navarre, *see* Henry IV of France
Henry of Trastamara, *see* Henry II of Castile
Henry the Navigator of Portugal, 121
heresy, 5, 127–32, 172, 192–3, 225, 367, 369, 380, 394, 400, 407, 412, 414, 422
hidalgos, 67, 114–5, 117, 214, 250, 267, 342, 357
Hippocrates, 347
Hispaniola, 263–4, 267, 272
history and historical writing, 9, 139–40, 144, 150–6, 240, 308, 348–9, 372, 375
Hochstätter bank, 308
Hochstraten, Jacob von, 383
Hoffman, Melchior, 396
Hohenstaufen dynasty, 39
Hohenzollern dynasty, 51, 287, 436
Holland, 17, 21, 26, 32, 39, 68, 170, 202–7, 209–12, 257, 297, 414, 434–5
Holstein, 283
Holy League, 177, 181–3
Holy Office, *see* Inquisition
Hôpital, Michel de l', 236
Hopkins, Matthew, 420
Horace, 353
Hormuz, 265–6
Hospitallers, 279
hospitals, 105, 328–9, 331
Hotman, François, 197–8
household, royal, 4, 69–77, 228–31, 234–7, 301
Hubmaier, Balthasar, 326
Huguenots, 194–200, 209–10, 214, 216, 225, 327, 391, 412, 418, 431, 433–4, 438; *see also* Calvinists
Hull, 116
humanism, humanists, 6, 9, 123, 127, 148–65, 214, 219, 225, 237, 328, 335, 337, 343, 348, 349–64, 367–8, 370–3, 375–7, 379, 381–4, 390, 392–5, 407–8, 411, 416, 437–8
Hundred Years War, 1, 2, 7, 18–19, 23, 29, 33–5, 50, 59, 63, 75–6, 79, 90, 93, 122, 140, 144, 152, 169, 181, 232, 244, 311, 337
Hungary, 8, 41, 43, 47–50, 111, 128, 181, 184, 186, 188, 191, 279–80, 310, 350, 407–9
Hunyadi, John, 49
Hus, Jan, 5, 11, 132–3, 180, 387, 408, 415
Hutten, Ulrich von, 384

Iberia, 3, 36, 52–3, 66, 75, 79, 81, 95, 120–2, 148, 185, 215, 269, 271, 363, 378, 418, 424; *see also* Aragon, Castile, Catalonia, Spain
iconoclasm, 197, 204, 205, 207, 216, 417
Illuminists, 393
immigration, 95, 98–9, 103, 212, 307, 314, 318–19, 323, 327–32, 366, 424, 430, 435

Incas, 268
Index of Prohibited Books, 214, 360, 391, 393, 421–2; French, 393; Spanish, 393
India, 264–6, 274–5
Indians, 264, 267, 269–74
Indian Ocean, 263, 265–6, 275
Indies, 262–3, 269, 272, 315
indulgences, 379, 384, 386–7, 406
industry, 4–5, 8, 77, 80, 85, 88–9, 98–9, 102, 108, 251, 259, 273, 294–5, 297, 299–301, 309, 311–20, 332, 335, 341, 429
Industrial Revolution, 316
inflation, 8, 86, 245, 251, 303–5, 307–11, 340–1, 432
'Information Revolution', 10, 364–8
Ingolstadt, 352–4
inheritance customs, 18, 25, 40, 117, 237, 242, 247, 308, 321, 323
Innocent VI, pope, 25; Innocent VIII, 385
Inns of Court, 83, 135, 213
Inquisition, Netherlands, 423–4; Roman (papal), 130, 172, 203–4, 383, 391–2, 395, 411, 413, 421–2; Spanish 38, 171–2, 213–15, 248, 253, 272, 393, 395, 421
institutions, *see* government
interest, *see* usury
Investiture Contest, 124
investment, 85, 100, 109, 114, 163, 250, 274–7, 299–311, 315, 317, 322, 341, 428–30
Ireland, 27, 213, 231, 233, 262, 271, 373, 434
ironworking, 89, 314–15, 319
Isabella, queen of Castile, 2, 7, 170–3, 176–7, 180, 183, 247–8, 250–1, 263, 267, 315, 364, 385–6, 393; her daughter 49; queen of Denmark, 283; sister of Charles V, 282; wife of Charles V, 252
Isabelle queen of England, 18; (Isabeau), queen of France, 26, 30
Istanbul, 164, 266
Italy, 1–2, 5–6, 9–10, 26–7, 36, 39–41, 43–6, 48, 61, 68, 77–9, 81, 90–1, 93, 95, 99, 102–4, 108–12, 114, 120–30, 135, 138, 141–3, 146–65, 170, 176, 181, 183–6, 190, 193, 198, 202, 204, 214, 216, 218–24, 230, 246, 249, 251–3, 262, 280, 290–8, 302, 306, 308–10, 318, 328, 331, 343–54, 357, 359–68, 371–2, 374, 376–82, 384–5, 391–2, 395, 411, 415–6, 418–19, 421–3, 429, 438
Ivan III, grand duke of Moscow, 51, 286; Ivan IV, tsar, 'the Terrible', 51, 286–7

Jacqueline of Bavaria, 32
Jacquerie, 64, 106
Jadwiga, queen of Poland, 50

Jagiellon dynasty, 287; Katarina, 283
Jamaica, 264
James IV, king of Scotland, 175; James V, 189, 192; James VI (James I of England), 175, 208, 211, 230–1, 339, 374, 402, 420, 432–5
James of Viterbo, 126
Jamestown, 277, 430
Jan [Bockelszoon] of Leiden, 396
Japan, 275
Jardine, Lisa, 354
Jean de Venette, 140
Jean le Bel, 145
Jerusalem, 264
Jesus, Society of (Jesuits), 370, 393, 406–408, 435
Jews, 37–8, 40, 62, 75, 120, 131, 170–3, 183, 214, 272, 275, 315, 344, 382–4, 422–4, 431, 435
Joan of Arc, 30, 146, 240, 356
Joanna the Mad, 173, 177, 180, 182
Joanna, queen of Naples, 26
Johan III, king of Sweden, 286
John, king of England, 15; John I, king of Portugal, 23, 121; John IV, 432; John II, king of Aragon, 37, 170; John II, king of Castile, 37, 170, 250; John II, king of France, 22, 25, 29, 64, 106; John III, duke of Brittany, 21,23; John IV, duke of Brabant, 32; John V, Byzantine emperor, 49; John VIII, Byzantine emperor, 49
John of Austria, Don, 206–7, 280
John of Gaunt, 23–4, 27–8, 33, 37, 60, 132, 139, 142, 143, 174
John of Montfort, 21
John of Nevers, 48
John of Paris, 126, 127
John the Blind, king of Bohemia, 21, 39
John the Fearless, duke of Burgundy, 27–30, 139, 356
John XXII, pope, 40, 125–6, 130–1, 134
Joris, David, 396, 415
journeymen, 99, 102, 105, 164, 197, 318–19
Juana, la Beltraneja, 171; of Portugal, 170
Julius II, pope, 177, 344, 384; Julius III, 190, 423
Justices of the Peace, 4, 69, 77, 221, 230, 234, 250, 329
Justinian, 81; Justinian's Code, 332
Juvenel des Ursins, Jean, 145

Kalmar, Union of, 282, 388
Kappel, treaty of, 390
Kazan, Khanate of, 287
Kent, 53, 362
Ket, Jack, rebellion of, 190, 321, 324
knighthood, 34, 40, 43, 47, 56–8, 62, 66, 116–17, 131, 140, 229, 231, 240, 255, 257, 339, 341–2, 384, 406

Knights Templar, 62, 121
Knox, John, 332, 371, 401
Königsberg, 50
Kosovo, 48–9
Krakow, 135, 408
Kurland, 287

La Rochelle, 431, 433
labour, 85–9, 94–5, 97, 99–100, 102,
    105–6, 118, 130, 161, 262, 264,
    269–70, 273, 299, 302, 305, 311–21,
    323, 325–7, 329–30, 336, 347, 366,
    429
Ladislas, king of Naples, 43–4, 158
Lancaster, dynasty of, 27–8, 33, 174–5, 228
land market, 9, 97–8, 114–15, 246, 307,
    321, 322, 324, 340, 341
Langland, William, 141–3
Languedoc, 62, 64, 66, 73, 76, 81, 239,
    241, 244–5, 294, 317, 412
Languedoi, 63
Latin, 6, 9–10, 131, 133, 138–42, 148–56,
    198, 219, 271, 273, 335, 343, 348, 350,
    352–3, 355–6, 358–70, 372–3, 375–6,
    382, 387, 397, 430
Laud, William, 231, 430, 434
law, 4, 18, 25, 34, 38–9, 49, 53, 60, 62, 67,
    69, 77, 81–4, 88, 94, 114, 150, 153,
    156, 159, 162, 171, 177, 180, 187–8,
    198, 203, 214, 224–7, 235–6, 240, 247,
    271, 297, 409, 437; civil, *see* law,
    Roman; customary, 4, 325, 370; canon,
    73, 117, 124, 127, 131, 134, 138, 270,
    273, 307, 333, 380, 382, 385, 415;
    common, 17, 73, 81–3, 135, 231;
    international, 430; Mosaic, 307; Roman,
    4, 17, 57, 70, 73, 81–3, 96, 116, 126–7,
    134, 159, 226–7, 240, 247, 256, 272–3,
    321, 325, 332–3, 352, 356, 363, 370–1,
    380, 412, 421; study of , 357, 397
lawyers, 16, 83, 229, 234, 307, 341
League of Venice, 177
Lee, William, 316
Lefèvre d'Etaples, Jacques, 393
Leicester, Robert Dudley, earl of, 208–10,
    237, 317
Leiden, 205, 297, 396, 414
Leipzig, 384; Leipzig Disputation, 387
Leo X, pope, 177, 183, 247, 379, 384, 387
Leonardo da Vinci, 161, 165, 345–7,
    349–50
Lepanto, battle of, 260, 280
Lerma, Francisco Gómez de Sandoval y
    Rojas, duke of, 431–2
Lewis of Bavaria, emperor, 19, 21, 39,
    125–6
liberal arts, 6, 133, 351–8, 369, 397
libraries, 155, 214, 344, 367, 372, 383
Liège, 145
Lille, 16, 74, 328

Lima, 268
Limbourg brothers, 139
Limoges, 23, 35, 140, 327
Linacre, Thomas, 357
Lincoln, 182
Lindau, 328
linens, 102, 297, 320
Lipsius, Justus, 414
Lisbon, 262, 266, 275, 291, 310
literacy, 11, 124, 195, 334–5, 368–71
Lithuania, 46–7, 50–1, 68, 287–8, 424
Livonia, 8, 47, 50, 283, 286–7
Livy, 152, 375
Lodi, peace of, 46, 176
Lollards, 28, 132
Lombardy, 43, 177, 183, 429
London, 24, 90–1, 97, 99, 102, 107,
    109–10, 116, 140–3, 174–5, 192,
    218–19, 231, 277, 291–2, 300, 302,
    311, 317, 319, 330, 357, 360, 374, 400
longbow, 17, 21–2, 34, 181
Lords Appellant, 24, 27
Lords Lieutenant, 234
Lords of the Congregation, 208
Lorraine, 173, 190–1, 193, 196, 321
Louis I the Great, King of Hungary, 41, 43,
    50; Louis II, 186, 279
Louis VII, king of France, 54; Louis VIII,
    25; Louis IX, 25, 47, 55, 83, 240; Louis
    XI, 44, 66, 145, 170, 173–6, 235, 240,
    294, 311, 341; Louis XII, 176–7, 237,
    241–2, 384; Louis XIII, 431, 433, 435;
    Louis XIV, 200, 218, 427, 436, 438
Louis of Anjou, 26; of Male, count of
    Flanders, 22; of Nevers, count of
    Flanders, 19, 21; Louis of Orléans, *see*
    Louis XII; *see also* Orléans
Louise of Savoy, 184, 394
Louvain, 135, 352, 356, 361
Low Countries, 7, 16–17, 19, 21, 27, 32, 39,
    41, 53, 60, 68, 77, 93, 103–5, 108, 122,
    131, 135, 145, 181, 194, 209–12, 216,
    223, 225–6, 251, 290–1, 296–7, 320–1,
    328, 348, 366, 396; *see also* Netherlands
Loyola, Ignatius of, 393, 406–7
Lübeck, 104, 111, 190, 281–3, 286, 291,
    295
Lublin, union of, 287
Lucerne, 41
Lucian, 358, 422
Luder, Peter, 354
Lusatia, 408
Luther, Martin, and Lutheranism, 5–6, 11,
    51, 132, 180, 186, 189–92, 194, 203–4,
    214, 246, 283, 286–7, 305–6, 324–5,
    328, 332, 334, 352, 355, 358, 361–3,
    367, 379–80, 382–99, 403, 406–16,
    421–5, 435, 438
Luxembourg, 26, 39–41, 44, 47–8; dynasty,
    39

Lyon, 196–7, 245, 291, 294, 299, 301–3, 308, 311, 317, 331–2, 370, 372

Macedonia, 47
Machaut, Guillaume de, 144
Machiavelli, Niccolò, 151–2, 159, 198, 207, 221, 348–50, 375–6, 422
Madagascar, 266
Madeira, 121, 262
Madrid, 218; Treaty of, 184
Magdeburg, 43, 190
Magellan, Ferdinand, 268
Maghreb, 121, 280, 294
Magna Carta, 56, 63
Maine, 22, 29, 32
Mainz, 40, 129, 352, 364, 421
Majorca, 75, 120–1
Malabar Coast, 266
Malacca, 265
Mali, 121
Malta, 280
Mamluks, 279
Manfred, 36
Manoel, king of Portugal, 177
Mantua, 153, 158, 338, 379; council of, 379
Manuel II, Byzantine emperor, 49
Manutius, Aldus, and Aldine Press, 10, 360, 364, 366
Manuzio, Paolo, 422
Marburg, colloquy of, 390
Marcel, Etienne, 106
March, earl of, 27
Margaret of Anjou, 32, 174; of Austria, 173, 202, 283; of Male, countess of Flanders, 22, 27; of Parma, 203–4; of Scotland, 17
Marguerite of Angoulême, 335; of Valois, 196
Marie de France, 335, 363
Marie of Guise, 190
Marignano, battle of, 177, 183
Marlowe, Christopher, 231, 373–4
marranos, 251, 421
marriage, 117, 189, 208, 231, 292–3, 321, 333–4, 390, 400
Marseilles, 274, 294
Marshal, William, 382
Marsiglio of Padua, 5, 126–7, 348, 350, 382
Martin I, king of Portugal, 37
Martin V, pope, 128–9
Martines, Lauro, 157
Mary I, queen of England, 181–2, 187, 192–4, 207–8, 232, 332, 335, 339, 371, 399, 401, 413; Mary I, queen of Scotland, 189, 190, 192; Mary of Burgundy, 41, 184, 173, 176, 188, 202; Mary of Guise, 208
Maryland, 430

Masaccio, 161
Massachusetts, 430
Maurice, duke of Saxony, 189, 191
Maurice of Nassau, stadholder of Netherlands, 189–90, 210, 212, 257
Mauritius, 266
Maximilian I, emperor, 41, 44, 173, 175–7, 180, 184–6, 220, 255, 353, 383, 389; Maximilian II, 407, 424
Mayas, 264
Meaux, 196, 394
Mechelen, 173, 205
Medici family and bank of Florence, 107, 161, 164, 183, 294, 308, 381; Catherine de', queen and queen-mother of France, 181, 195–6, 198–9, 218, 276, 332, 376, 412; Cosimo de', 45–6, 163–4, 176, 254, 343; Cosimo de' the younger, grand duke of Florence, 181, 220; Lorenzo de', 45, 176, 343, 379; Piero de', 45, 176
medicine, 134, 153, 156, 357, 372, 430
Medina del Campo, 183, 294, 301
Mediterranean, 8, 9, 292–7, 320, 351, 414, 429
Mehmed I, sultan, 49; Mehmed II, 49, 164, 277
Melanchthon, Philip, 382, 391, 394
Memmingen, 325
Mennonites, 396
mercantilism, 314–15, 428
Mercator, Gerard, 348
Merchant Adventurers, 296, 309
Messina, 291
Mesta, 91, 315
metalworking, 110, 119–22, 262–4, 269, 273; 297, 309, 320, 330; *see also* bullion
Metz, 191, 291
Mexico, 7, 267–70, 273, 277; Mexico City, 269, 273
Mézières, Philippe de, 35, 140
Michael VIII, Byzantine emperor, 48
Michelalgelo Buonarotti, 160, 344–5
Middelburg, 205
Milan, 26, 44–6, 78, 98, 158, 160, 163, 176–7, 181, 184, 188, 223, 279, 291, 310, 346, 365
military orders, 247, 251, 310, 315, 386
Military tactics and strategy, 9, 18, 21–2, 33–5, 41, 46, 51, 55, 62, 65, 115–16, 146, 171, 180–1, 183, 186, 202, 211–12, 222–3, 232, 244, 259, 267, 298, 300, 339, 347, 427, 432
mining, 89, 100, 110, 185, 247, 269, 304, 310, 316, 320, 330
Minorca, 120
Modena, 44
Mohács, battle of, 184, 186, 279
Moluccas, 268
monasteries, 50, 130, 233, 247, 256, 324, 340–1, 372, 386, 400, 413, 424

money, *see* coinage
money market, 112–13, 189, 203, 276, 296, 429
moneychangers, 38, 61, 112, 171, 309, 315
Mongols , 46–8, 51, 280, 286–7
monopolies, 89–90, 110, 112, 213, 231–3, 243, 262, 274, 277, 294–5, 300, 314–17, 331
Mons, 205
Monstrelet, Enguerrand de, 145
Montaigne, Michel de, 372–3, 382
Montalvo, Alfonso Diaz de, 247
Montefeltro, Federigo da, 344
Montereale, 415
Montezuma, 267, 272
Montferrand, 235
Montils-les-Tours, Ordinance of, 83
Montmorency faction, 195–6, 198, 306; Anne de, 190, 236
Montpellier, 83, 135, 356, 372
Montreal, 276
Moors, *see* Muslims
Moravia, 408
More, Thomas, 157, 227, 267, 324, 358, 360, 380–1, 386, 411
Morea, 49
Morgarten, battle of, 41
Moriscos, 215, 431
Morocco, 280
Moscow, 47, 51, 282, 286
Mudejars, 37
Mühlberg, battle of, 189–90
Munich, 185
Münster, 300, 332, 396, 397, 410
Müntzer, Thomas, 324, 326
Murad I, sultan, 41; Murad II, 49; Murad III, 280
Muscovy Company, 277, 287, 309
music, 213, 231, 373, 431
Muslims, 36–8, 47, 49, 51, 75, 119–22, 133, 170–3, 214–15, 223, 259, 265–6, 268–9, 272, 277, 279–81, 315
mysticism, 131, 396, 407, 415, 425

Naarden, 206
Nahuatl, 273
Namur, 206
Nancy, 173
Nantes, 241, 418; Edict of, 200, 412, 431
Naples, 37, 43, 46, 48, 75, 98, 135, 158, 170, 173, 176–7, 183–4, 218, 220, 223, 253, 279, 291, 379, 429
Narva, 286–7
Nassau, 202, 205, 210, 212
nation and nationalism, 2, 53, 63, 220–3, 239–40, 250
Navarre, 22, 36, 184, 195, 237, 253, 269; College of, 356
navigational techniques, 21, 119, 121, 165, 211, 215

Nebrissensis, Antonius (Antonio of Nebrija), 364
Neoplatonism, 131, 133, 157, 343, 383
Netherlands, 6, 7, 9, 46, 74, 82, 91, 94, 139, 141, 161, 170, 173–4, 180–1, 184–5, 188–9, 191–4, 196–9, 209, 211–13, 215–16, 218, 220–1, 223–4, 231–2, 246, 249, 257–8, 266, 269, 271–2, 275–6, 280–1, 283, 292–6, 303, 306, 314, 316, 320, 328, 345, 347, 352, 356, 367–8, 370–1, 386, 392, 396, 410, 413–14, 417, 420, 423–4, 432, 434–6, 438; revolt of, 200–7, 210–12
Neville family, 338; Anne and Cecily, 174
Newfoundland, 276
Niccoli, Niccolò, 154
Nice, Truce of, 188
Nicholas V, pope, 155
Nicodemism, 203, 392, 414
Nicopolis, 48; 'Nicopolis Crusade', 27
nobility, 3–4, 9, 37, 44–5, 50, 55, 57–8, 63, 66–7, 73, 77, 81, 83–4, 96, 98, 106, 109, 113–15, 117–18, 125, 138, 144–6, 172, 181–3, 194–7, 199, 208, 214, 217, 221–3, 231, 234–6, 239–40, 242, 244, 248, 250–1, 255, 267–8, 282–3, 286, 288, 301, 306, 308, 310, 322–3, 325–6, 330, 334, 337–42, 356, 362, 372, 385, 398, 408, 418, 427–8, 432–3, 435
Nogaret, Guillaume de, 83
nominalism, 5, 123, 133–4, 352–5
Nonsuch, Treaty of, 210
Norfolk, 190, 209, 338
Normandy, 15, 18, 22–3, 29–30, 32, 54, 63, 69, 73, 239, 241, 245–6, 271, 294, 321, 327, 341
Northampton, 317; treaty of, 1328, 18
Northern War, 283
Northumberland, 190, 192, 209
Norway, 223, 282
Norwich, 317, 327
notaries, 237
Nottingham, 317
Novara, 177
Novgorod, 51, 109, 286
nunneries, 130, 334–5
Nuremberg, 110, 185, 263, 291, 295, 297, 302–3, 310, 320, 328–9, 337

Occitania, 321
Ochino, Bernardino, 392, 411
offices, sale of, 4, 9, 76–7, 217, 241–2, 248, 250–1, 256, 308, 311, 322, 338–41, 356–7, 428, 432
Oldcastle, John, 28, 132
Oldenbarnevelt, Johan van, 212
Olivares, Gaspar de Guzmán, duke of, 432
Orange, William of, 202, 204–7, 209–10, 212, 257, 269, 435
Orchies, 16

Ordinances of 1311, 58, 71
Orléans, 15, 135, 176–7, 196, 237, 356, 397; faction, 29–30, 123, 176–7; Charles duke of, 27–9, 144, 176; Louis duke of 26, 28, 30, 144, 356; *see also* Armagnac
Osman, 48
Ottoman Turks, *see* Turks
Oxford, Provisions of, 56, 71, 221; university of, 131–2, 135, 175, 357, 358, 360

Pacioli, Luca, 161
Padua, 44, 347, 356–7
painting, 156, 159–60, 163–4, 344–6, 351, 372
Palatinate of the Rhine, 40, 191, 409, 423
Palencia, 364
Palermo, 98, 291
Palestine, 49, 271
Palmas, Cape, 122
Palos, 263
Panama, 267
Paracelsus, 347
Paraguay, 269
Paré, Ambroise, 347
Paris, 15–16, 22, 25, 27–30, 32, 61, 64, 73, 77, 80, 98–9, 105–6, 110, 116, 123, 131, 133, 135, 139–40, 144–5, 154, 173, 195–200, 218, 239, 241, 243, 245, 291, 298, 300, 303, 318, 320–1, 329, 331–2, 352, 356, 359–60, 369–70, 374, 394, 397, 412, 436; Paris, Matthew, 56
parlement, 3–4, 61, 72–3, 80, 173, 199–200, 235–6, 239–42, 299, 301, 329, 331, 341, 373, 393–5, 412, 436
Parliament, 3, 19, 24, 27–8, 56–62, 64–6, 69, 71, 73, 84, 94, 114–17, 141–2, 182, 192–3, 208–9, 211, 213, 218, 221–2, 224, 228–34, 243, 249, 289, 314, 324, 330, 334, 339, 358, 371, 381, 386, 399–402, 427, 432–4
Parma, Alessandro Farnese, duke of, 207, 209, 211
Parr, Catherine, queen of England, 190, 400
Passau, Peace of, 191
Paston family, 98
patronage, cultural, 5, 142–6, 151, 161–4, 213, 217, 221, 230, 236, 242, 247, 306, 338, 343–5, 357, 364, 372, 375, 378, 385–6, 428, 432
Paul II, pope, 379; Paul III, 190, 224, 379, 403, 423; Paul IV, 379, 406, 422
Paumgartner bank, 185
Pavia, 44, 184, 236, 246
Peace of Monsieur, 198, 200
peasantry, 4–5, 8, 87, 96–8, 113, 132, 200, 215, 255, 300, 302–3, 306, 320–7, 334, 371, 390, 418, 420; Peasants' Rebellion of 1381, 24, 59, 96, 142, 145, 186, 325; Peasants' Rebellion, German, of

1524–25, 324–6, 388, 396
Percy family, 338
Perger, Bernard, 353
Perotti, Niccolo, 353–4
Perrers, Alice, 24
Persia, 279–80; Persian Gulf, 265
Peru, 7, 253, 267–70, 273, 277
Perugino, 344
Peruzzi bank, 111
Peter I 'the Cruel', king of Castile, 23, 37; Peter III, king of Aragon, 36
Petit, Jean, 28
Petition of Right, 433
Petrarch, 126, 131, 143, 148, 150, 156, 159, 163–4, 270, 353, 372
Pfefferkorn, Johann, 383
Philip II Augustus, king of France, 15, 76; Philip IV 'the Fair', king of France, 16–18, 55, 61–3, 83, 90, 125–6, 129, 183, 235, 243, 348; Philip VI, 18–19, 21, 63; Philip II, king of Spain, 7, 181, 191–3, 195, 199–200, 204–8, 210–16, 218–19, 223, 225, 246, 249, 251, 253, 266, 272, 280, 305, 310, 315, 337, 366, 407, 427, 431–3; Philip III, 431–2; Philip IV, 432
Philip of Hesse, 189–91
Philip the Bold, duke of Burgundy, 22, 26–7, 74, 123, 139; Philip the Good, 30, 32, 74, 139, 173, 200; Philip the Handsome, 173, 177, 180, 202
Philippines, 266, 268
philology, 6, 152, 164, 344, 351, 354, 359, 362, 371, 381, 382
philosophy, 133–4, 155–9, 343–4, 351, 353, 359, 363, 382
Phocaea, 112
Piacenza, 190
Picardy, 245, 321
Piccolomini, Aeneas Sylvius, *see* Pius II, pope
Pico della Mirandola, 157, 343–4, 383
Picquigny, treaty of, 176
piracy, 36, 109, 205, 209, 211
Pisa, 45, 113, 128
Pistoia, 45
Pius II, pope, 129, 344, 379
Pizarro, Francisco, 267
placard affair, 187, 394
plagues, 4–5, 21, 81, 85, 91–6, 98, 104, 215, 290, 292, 302, 321, 322, 429
Plantagenet dynasty, 141, 216
Plantin, Christopher, 366–7
Platina, Bartolomeo, 158
Plato, 133, 155, 157–9, 343, 349, 359–60; Platonic Academy, 343
Pleiades, 372
Plotinus, 343
Poitiers, 22, 64, 106, 135, 140, 240
Poitou, 22

Poland, 8, 46–7, 49–50, 68, 111, 223, 283, 286–8, 295, 304, 322, 348, 408, 411, 424, 427
Pole, Reginald, 193, 381, 392
political theory, 5, 126, 130, 197–9, 205, 348–50
politiques, 198, 210, 373
Polybius, 376
Pomerania, 323
Pomerelia, 50
Ponce de Leon, 277
Ponthieu, 18, 21–3
Pontoise, peace of, 16
Poor Law of 1536, 330
poor relief, *see* poverty
Pope, Alexander, 11
popes, papacy, 5, 11, 25, 32, 39–40, 43, 46, 61–2, 123, 125–9, 131–2, 134, 150, 186–7, 189, 209, 214–15, 220, 224–5, 232, 235, 247–8, 280, 316, 344, 378–86, 392–3, 399, 402–3, 406–7, 416, 421–4, 429
Portinari, Tommaso, 161
Portugal, 7, 36–7, 119–21, 170–2, 177, 182, 215, 252, 258–9, 261–7, 270, 274–6, 280, 293–6, 304, 406, 421, 429, 432, 434
Poswol, treaty of, 287
Potosi, 273, 304
poverty and poor relief, 8, 77, 96–7, 103–7, 118, 231, 301–2, 308, 321, 325, 327–32, 336, 418, 423, 437
Praemunire, Statute of, 129
Pragmatic Sanction of Bourges, 129, 135, 384, 386
Prague, 132, 135, 218, 291, 424
Prato, 113, 306
prerogative, 211, 233, 432
presbyters, Presbyterianism, 208, 398–9, 434
Previsa, 187
prices, 4–5, 8, 86, 88, 92, 94–6, 103–4, 113, 190, 233, 290, 297, 302, 320, 322–3, 326, 419, 429; price revolution, 87, 303–5; price shear, 302
Primaticcio, Francesco, 372
printing, 10, 11, 113, 165, 197, 213–14, 224, 282, 307, 311, 316, 324, 336, 344, 364–8, 387, 390, 392, 394, 411, 413, 419, 421–2, 425, 438
processions, 334, 417
Proclus, 343
propaganda, 125, 140, 158, 205–6, 213, 272, 280, 324, 353–4, 358, 367, 388, 392
prostitution, 336–7
protectionism, industrial, 102, 319, 428
Protestant, Protestantism: *see* individual Protestant groups
Provence, 135, 188, 239, 241

Provisors, Statute of, 129
Prussia, 49–50, 255, 287, 295, 304, 306, 322, 409–10, 436
Ptolemy, 262, 347
Puritans, 210, 213, 233, 401–2, 430, 433, 438
Pythagoras, 383

Quintilian, 152–3

Rabelais, François, 372
Ralegh, Walter, 231, 277
Raphael, 161, 344–5
Ravensburg, 308
realism, 133, 352
reclamation, 85, 316
Red Sea, 265–6
Reformation, 329, 380–425
Reformed, *see* Calvinists
Regensburg, Colloquy of, 383, 392
Reggio, 44
Reims, 30, 145, 320
remenças, 97, 326
Renaissance, 1, 6, 9–11, 141, 146–65, 228, 231, 247, 249, 343–77, 430, 437
René de Chalon, 202
Rense, Declaration of, 40
rents, 78, 88–9, 91, 96–8, 104, 161, 322–3, 325–6, 432; annuity, 245, 251, 299, 311
representation, representative institutions, 56–69, 126, 231–4, 242–3, 248–50; *see also Cortes*, Estates-General, Parliament
Requesens, Luis de, 206–7
retainers, 70, 181, 223, 228, 338
Rethel, 27
Reuchlin, Johann, 356, 382–4, 422
Reval, 287
revolt of the earls, 209
Rhineland, 111, 131, 320, 325
Rhode Island, 430
Rhodes, 279
Richard II, king of England, 24, 26–7, 35, 40, 59–60, 71, 97, 132, 140–1, 228, 233; Richard III, 174–5, 229, 358
Richard duke of York, 28, 32
Richard of Wallingford, 347
Richelieu, Armand Jean du Plessis, cardinal, 434–5
Ridolfi plot, 209
rituals, 365, 370, 380, 389, 392, 409, 415–18
Rizzio, David, 208
Roanoke island, 277
Rochester, 358
Romagna, 26, 128, 177
Roman Catholicism, 11, 328, 331–4, 337, 363, 365, 371, 373, 378–425, 430–6, 438
Rome, Roman Empire, Roman Republic, 6,

10, 25, 39, 125, 128–9, 131–2, 135, 151, 158, 160, 163, 184, 187, 193, 219, 262, 271, 286, 291, 300, 310, 316, 318, 343–5, 349–50, 365, 369, 376–9, 383–4, 386–8, 393, 395, 399, 418–19, 422, 424, 437
Ronsard, Pierre, 372
Rosso, Gian Battista, 372
Rotterdam, 212
Rouen, 196, 241, 291, 294
Roussel, Gérard, 394
Roussillon, 170, 176
Rudolf I of Habsburg, emperor, 39; Rudolf II, emperor, 218, 408–9, 424; Rudolf IV of Habsburg, 135
Rupert, elector of the Palatinate, 40
Russia, 8, 47, 50–1, 109, 223, 276, 283, 286–7, 304, 323
Ruthenia, 50

sacraments, 117, 390, 399, 406, 410–1, 415, 417
Sahagún, Bernardino de, 273
Sahara desert, 121
Saint-André, sieur de, 195
Saint-Denis, abbey of, 144
Saint-Germain, Edict of, 196, 412
Saint-Quentin, 193
Salamanca, 363
Salerno, 135
Sales, Francis de, 406
Salic Law, 18
Sallust, 375
Salutati, Coluccio, 149, 154, 156, 158–9
Sanchez de Arevalo, Rodrigo, 364
Santo Domingo, 263
Sardinia, 36, 75, 249, 253
Savonarola, Girolamo, 176, 300, 381, 386
Savoy, 188, 411
Saxon League, 43
Saxony, 40, 189, 191, 227, 320, 327, 387, 391, 423
Scandella, Domenico, 415
Scanderbeg, George, 49
Scandinavia, 6, 93, 109, 194, 219, 281–2, 289, 303, 306, 323, 362, 386, 388, 395, 438
Schleswig-Holstein, 388
Schmalkaldic League, 180, 186, 188–9, 191, 283, 423
scholasticism, 156, 161, 352, 355–6, 359, 372, 382, 384, 391
Schwyz, 41
science, 148, 155–6, 164, 346–8, 372, 430, 438; scientific revolution, 430
Scotists, 134
Scotland, 2, 17–19, 21, 26, 28, 34, 55–6, 62, 175, 188, 190, 192, 194, 203, 208–10, 224, 232, 271, 306, 332, 371, 386, 399, 401–2, 410, 420, 432, 434

sculpture, 159–64, 372
Sea Beggars, 204–6
Sebastian of Portugal, 215, 280
secretaries, state, 188, 227–8, 230, 235, 237, 248, 252
Segovia, 76
sejm, 287–8
Selim I, sultan, 279; Selim II, 280
Sempach, battle of, 41
Seneca, 364
Senlis, Treaty of, 176
Sepulveda, Juan Ginés de, 273
serfdom, 24, 40, 54, 56, 59, 87–8, 94–8, 116, 320, 322–4, 325–6
Servetus, Michael, 411
Seville, 38, 98, 120, 171–2, 213, 266, 273, 275, 291, 294–5, 301, 311, 316, 431
Seymour, Edward, 190; Jane, queen of England, 190; Thomas, 346
Sforza family, 346; Giangaleazzo, 176; Francesco, 176; Ludovico the Moor, 176–7
'sHertogenbosch, 359
Shakespeare, William, 10, 142, 373–6
shipping, 110, 112, 205, 210, 274, 281, 434
Siberia, 287
Sicily, 43, 48, 75, 95, 170, 248–9, 253
Sidney, Philip, 231
Siena, 45, 98, 111
Sigismund, emperor, 30, 41, 43, 48, 51, 128, 132, 408; Sigismund I, king of Poland, 51; Sigismund III, 286–8
Silesia, 320, 408
silk, 294, 299, 307, 314–15, 331, 336
Simnel, Lambert, 175
Simons, Menno, 396–7
Sint-Baafs-Vijve, truce of, 24
Sixtus IV, pope, 171–2, 247, 344, 378
slavery, 119, 122, 262, 264, 269–71, 273–4, 430
Slavic Europe, 3, 7–8, 46–7, 49, 53–4, 93, 102, 271, 281, 297, 320, 322–4, 407–10, 436, 437
Sluis, 19, 35
Sluter, Claus, 139
Smith, Thomas, 430
Solway Moss, battle, 189
Somerset, 174, 190, 192, 400; earl of, 32
Somme, 175
Sorbonne, 135, 356, 359, 361, 372, 393
South Carolina, 276
South China Sea, 265
Southampton, 90, 293; earl of, 374
Spain, 2, 4, 6–9, 36–8, 41, 51, 54, 67, 75–7, 114–15, 119, 124, 135, 140, 169–73, 176–7, 180–2, 184–8, 190–5, 198–9, 200–25, 230, 237, 242–53, 255, 257–8, 263–77, 280, 288, 295–6, 298, 300, 302, 305, 310–11, 314–15, 328, 331, 338, 340, 342, 350, 352, 357, 362, 364–5,

Spain *cont.*
  367, 370, 376, 391, 392–3, 395, 406–7, 411, 414, 421–4, 427–9, 431–8
Spenser, Edmund, 213, 373
Speyer, Diet of, 326
spices, 7–8, 108, 110, 112, 119–22, 262, 265, 274–6, 288, 294–6, 309, 317, 429
Spinola, Ambrosio, 212
St Albans, 174
St Augustine, 277
St Bartholomew's Day massacre, 196–7, 209
stadholders, 202–7, 210–12, 218, 220, 257, 435
staples, 89–90, 110, 274, 296; Company of the, 90, 99
Star Chamber, 229, 231
Star, Order of the, 140
Starkey, David, 229; Thomas, 382
States General, 173, 200, 202–3, 205–7, 209–10, 212, 257, 367
status, 34, 162, 236, 245, 288, 300–1, 306, 308, 324–7, 330, 338–42
Statute in Favour of the Princes, 38
Statute of Artificers, 330
Statute of Labourers, 80, 94, 330
Statute of Rhuddlan, 17
Steyn, 359
Stockholm, 282, 388
Stoics, 382
Strabo, 262
Strasbourg, 173, 309, 325, 328, 365, 367
Stratford upon Avon, 374
Stuart dynasty of Scotland, 234, 373, 434; Henry, *see* Darnley, Mary, queen of Scots, 207–9, 211, 219, 332, 432
Sture, Sten, 282
Styria, 191
Sudan, 274
Suffolk, 32, 174
sugar, 262, 269–70, 274–5
Suleiman I, sultan, 279
sumptuary laws, 117
Surrey, 231
Sussex, 314
Swabia, 186, 308, 320, 324–5; Swabian League, 185, 326
Sweden, 51, 93, 223, 246, 281–3, 286, 323, 388, 410, 427, 434–6
Swiss Confederation, 6, 41, 46, 173, 177, 185–6, 194–5, 199, 202, 221, 223, 244, 257, 297, 324, 388–92, 396, 409–10, 418–19, 436, 438; Swiss Brethren, 396
Sydney, Philip, 373
syphilis, 292
Syria, 120, 279

Tacitus, 152
taille, 25, 64–5, 76, 80, 244, 246, 298, 326, 341, 418
Talavera, Hernando de, 172

Tallis, Thomas, 213
Talmud, 382
Tannenberg, 50
Tauler, Johannes, 131
Tawney, R, H,, 305
taxation, 3, 7, 9, 24–5, 45, 51, 53, 55–6, 59–67, 76–80, 84, 89–91, 96, 104–6, 109, 114–15, 117, 124–5, 129, 140, 171, 173, 182, 200, 202–3, 205, 211, 213, 215–17, 222–3, 228–9, 232–4, 243–4, 246–55, 260, 288, 291, 297–301, 303, 308, 310–11, 320, 322, 327, 339–42, 384–5, 400, 418, 427–8, 431–7
technology, 85, 94, 165, 268, 316–20, 322, 430
Terence, 353
Tetzel, Johann, 387
Teutonic Order, 8, 39, 47, 49–50, 51, 223, 287
Tewkesbury, battle of, 174
textile industry, 8, 16, 37, 88–91, 99, 100, 102, 106, 108, 112, 277, 292–3, 295–7, 299, 301–2, 305, 309, 314–15, 317, 319–20, 323–4, 430
theatres, 374
theology, 5, 11, 134, 138, 155, 157, 165, 225, 352, 354–61, 363, 368, 380, 385–7, 430
Thérouanne, 181
Thirty Years War, 194, 435–6
Thomas a Kempis, 393
Thomas Aquinas, 5, 127, 131, 133, 165, 352
Thorn, peace of, 50, 409
Thrace, 47–8
Thuringia, 131, 310
Timur 'the Lame' (Tamerlane), 48
Titian, 162, 345
Toledo, 171–2, 214, 218, 247, 385
toleration, 198, 200, 206, 209, 233, 236, 410–15, 419, 435, 436
Tolfa, 316
tolls, 89, 282, 314
Tordesillas, treaty of, 180, 265
Torquemada, 172
Toulouse, 73, 135, 195, 241, 291, 299, 356
Touraine, 29
Tournai, 19, 175, 181, 246
Tours, 30, 299; Truce of, 32
Tower of London, 174–5, 231
Towton Moor, battle, 174
trade and commerce, 9, 47, 78, 90, 102, 109, 170, 286, 299, 293–311, 320
translations, 362–4, 371, 393
transportation, 88, 91, 102–3
Transylvania, 49, 279–80, 286, 409
Trastamara dynasty, 23, 37–8, 75, 77
Trebizond, 49
Trent, council of, 11, 191, 199, 333, 367, 379, 395, 403, 406–7, 410, 422
Tridentine Decrees, *see* Trent, Council of

Trier, 40, 255
Troyes, Treaty of, 30
Tübingen, 352
Tudor dynasty, 33, 174–5, 221, 224, 227–9, 231, 233, 237, 329, 335, 358, 434; Edmund, 174
Tunis, 186, 280
Turin, 188, 302
Turks, 7–8, 46–9, 120, 122, 164, 173, 183–4, 186–190, 194, 225, 255, 258–9, 266, 271–2, 277–81, 294, 300, 394, 408–9, 416, 438–9
Tuscany, 43, 45, 141, 151, 220, 297, 376, 429
Tyler, Wat, 97
Tyrol, 227, 310, 324, 326

Ukraine, 51
Ulm, 390
Union of Arms, 432
United Provinces, *see* Netherlands
universities, 16, 28, 77, 83, 124, 129, 131, 133–8, 141–2, 148, 153–5, 234–5, 273, 282, 299, 330, 347, 351–8, 366–7, 372, 374, 382–3, 385, 397, 400, 406, 408, 411, 421, 437–8
Uppsala, 282, 286
Urban V, pope, 22, 26; Urban VI, 128; saint, 416
Urbino, 43, 344
usury, 87, 111, 163, 251, 307–11, 428
Utraquists, 132, 408
Utrecht, 124, 183, 202–3, 206; Union of, 207, 210, 257

vagabondage, 105, 299, 328–9, 318–19, 327
Valencia, 37, 113, 183, 248–9, 253
Valenciennes, 204
Valladolid, 76, 213, 327
Valois dynasty, 7, 18, 30, 60, 65, 145, 176, 192, 202, 216, 240
van Artevelde, Jacob; 19; Philip, 25, 145
van Busleyden, Jerome, 356
van der Goes, Hugo, 139, 161
van Eyck, Jan, 139
van Maerlant, Jacob, 363
Varna, 49
Vasa, Gustav, king of Sweden, 282–3, 388
Vasari, Giorgio, 160, 162, 345
Vassy, 195
Vatican, 155, 344–5
Vaudois, 420
vendetta, 106, 196, 306
Venezuela, 272
Venice, 10, 44, 46, 98, 102, 110, 120, 122, 145, 155, 163–4, 170, 177, 187, 219–20, 260, 266, 274, 279–80, 291, 296, 300–1, 310, 316, 320, 337, 344–5, 360, 364–6, 370, 379, 392, 422–3

Verde, Cape, 122
Vergerio, Pier Paolo, 153
Verona, 44–5
Verrazzano, Giovanni da, 276
Versailles, 218
Vervins, peace of, 200, 213
Vesalius, Andreas, 347
Vespucci, Amerigo, 266–7
Vicenza, 45
Vienna, 135, 218, 277, 279, 291, 352–3, 435
Villalar, 183
Villani, Giovanni, 104
Villon, François, 144
Virgil, 149, 160, 374
Virginia, 277, 430
Visconti family, 26, 43–4; Filippo Maria, 44, 46; Giangaleazzo, 44, 158; Valentina, duchess of Orléans, 26, 123, 177
Vives, Juan Luis, 335

wages, 8, 86–7, 91, 94–8, 100, 105, 290, 297, 305, 318–19, 322, 330, 336, 429
Wakefield, 174
Walcheren, 205
Waldseemüller, Martin, 267
Wales, 17, 28, 34, 55, 229; Prince of, 30
Wallace, William, 17
Wallachia, 49
Walter of Brienne, 45
War of the Eight Saints, 131
War of the Public Weal, 175
War of the Three Henries, 199
Warbeck, Perkin, 175
Wardrobe, 71–2, 236
Wars of the Roses, 32, 174–5
Warwick, Richard Neville, earl of, 174, 190
Weber, Max, 305–6
Welser bank, 308
Wenceslas (Wenzel), emperor, 40, 128, 132
West Indies, 7, 263, 277
Westminster, 16–17, 83, 135, 218, 230, 234, 401
Westmorland, 209
Westphalia, 325; peace of, 436
William IV, count of Holland, 40
William of Ockham, Ockhamists, 5, 11, 126–7, 130–1, 134, 352
William of Wykeham, 138
William the Silent, *see* Orange, William of
Wimpheling, Jakob, 353
Winchester, 138, 400
wine trade, 15, 64, 106, 299, 303, 307, 314–15, 416
Winthrop, John, 430
Wismar, 303
witch craze, 11, 123, 395, 414, 416, 419–21, 425
Wittelsbach dynasty, 26, 39–40, 185
Wittenberg, 352, 382, 387–8

Wladislaw, king of Poland, 50
Wolsey, Thomas, 181–2, 227, 230, 235, 358, 380
women, 89, 102–3, 105, 117–9, 145, 177, 195, 305, 321, 327, 331–7, 368, 370, 393, 420–1, 431
Woodville family, 175; Elizabeth, queen of England, 174–5
wool trade, 16, 19, 21, 59, 61, 67, 90–1, 96, 99–100, 102, 107, 110, 112, 268, 292–4, 297, 302, 315, 323
workhouses, 330, 336
Worms, Diet of, 1495, 255; Diet of, 1521, 186, 387; Edict of, 186, 255
Württemberg, 255, 368
Würzburg, 410
Wyatt, Thomas, 192, 231
Wycliffe, John, 5, 11, 127, 131–3, 139–40; *see also* Lollards

Xavier, St Francis, 270

York, 99, 142, 228, 317; dynasty of, 28, 33, 174–5, 193, 228; Statute of, 59
Yorkshire, 99, 400
Ypres, 16, 68, 139

Zamora, 328
Zapolya, John, 279
Zeeland, 21, 26, 32, 39, 202, 205–6, 210, 257, 297
Zierikzee, 206
Zizka, Jan, 132
Zsitvatorok, Treaty of , 280
Zürich, 41, 333, 389, 400
Zwingli, Ulrich, 6, 43, 186, 202, 214, 389–91, 394, 396, 398, 438